Meridians feminism, race, transnationalism

VOLUME 19 · SUPPLEMENT · 2020

20TH ANNIVERSARY READER

Ginetta E. B. Candelario

Speaking Our Peace
Celebrating Twenty Years of Women of Color Feminist
Transnational Knowledge Production in *Meridians*

> I hope that the contents of this issue . . . will encourage us each to plant
> new seeds—of hope, of rage, of insurrection, of peace—that might allow
> all of us to breathe more fully, to claim our ground even in the face of the
> most difficult challenges that inevitably color the contour of our lives.
> —Myriam Chancy

> Here I begin to provide a way of understanding the oppression of women
> who have been subalternized through the combined processes of racializa-
> tion, colonization, capitalist exploitation, and heterosexualism.
> —María Lugones

It strikes me as metaphorically appropriate that 2020 has brought anti-
Blackness, systemic racism, nativism, misogyny, sexism, health disparities, class violence, and quotidian police brutality into sharp focus for
typically myopic mainstream media and its consumers in the United
States. Yet, who could have anticipated the twists and turns that this year
would take? In January, we watched a theatrical presidential impeachment
trial in the Senate fail to hold a documented liar, racist, and misogynist
accountable for his actions. In February, we began hearing "rumors" of a
deadly virus spreading rapidly through China and Italy. In March, COVID-
19's arrival in the United States was unequivocally confirmed, and suddenly
our campuses, schools, workplaces, stores, restaurants, and in-person

MERIDIANS · feminism, race, transnationalism   Volume 19 Supplement 2020
DOI: 10.1215/15366936-8765096 © 2020 Smith College

social worlds began to shut down as "shelter in place" orders were issued and our lives moved online. Millions were furloughed, laid off, and fired, and thousands began to fall sick and die nonetheless. As of this writing, more than one hundred and ninety thousand people have died in the United States, disproportionately the people of color and immigrants who are now recognized (at least rhetorically) as "essential" laborers, live in overcrowded housing, and suffer from systemic health disparities. In April, presidential primaries, congressional, and state election dates and procedures began to be affected by the pandemic, and voting required inordinate courage and perseverance as polling places were closed, voting systems failed, and the threat of contagion was ever present (*Washington Post* 2020). In May, a White Minneapolis police officer named Derek Chauvin killed George Floyd—a Black man who had calmly acquiesced to all the officer's orders during the course of an unwarranted arrest. Chauvin kneeled on Mr. Floyd's neck for nearly ten minutes in broad daylight before dozens of witnesses, including three fellow police officers who failed to intervene and even assisted Chauvin in restraining his victim. Within days, the video of Mr. Floyd's death became the spark that lit the tinderbox that the president and his nationalist supporters have been fearing yet fueling. In June, massive national and international Black Lives Matter protests against police brutality erupted, campaigns to defund the police arose in communities large and small, and Confederate, Columbian, and imperialist monuments came crashing down. Confederate flags were removed from statehouses and NASCAR; Aunt Jemima and the Land O'Lakes Indian princess were forcibly retired; racist sports team mascots and names were finally acknowledged as such; and the stories of other Black people who have been recently murdered with impunity came to the fore.

We learned that twenty-three-year-old massage therapist Elijah McClain died of cardiac arrest in August 2019, after being subjected to a choke hold by Aurora, Colorado, police officers Nathan Woodyard, Jason Rosenblatt, and Randy Roedema. In October 2019, the story of Fort Worth, Texas, human resources professional, Atatiana Jefferson—who was playing video games with her eight-year-old nephew, whom she was babysitting at the time, when she heard a noise outside and looked out the window only to be shot dead by Officer Aaron Dean—garnered new media coverage. In June 2020, the Georgia vigilantes Travis McMichael and his father Gregory, who shot twenty-five-year-old jogger Ahmad Arbery in February, while their friend William "Roddie" Bryan filmed the murder, were finally charged as a result of protests. The Louisville, Kentucky, police who killed twenty-six-year-old EMT Breonna Taylor in her home when they rained bullets into her apartment after forcing their way as part of a "no-knock" warrant in the middle of a March night were fired, and protesters continue to pursue justice until they are charged. Nineteen-year-old Black Lives Matter activist Oluwatoyin Salau and seventy-five-year-old AARP volunteer Victoria Sims were found murdered in Florida, and their likely killer, Aaron Glee Jr., was apprehended and charged in June. In Atlanta, the killing of twenty-seven-year-old restaurant worker Rayshard Brooks by police at a Wendy's parking lot, where he had fallen asleep in the drive-through, triggered further protests and calls for justice in June as well. We add these to the long list of Black victims whose names we say in an incantation of hope and rage, and join the chorus of protests against police brutality, anti-Blackness, White supremacy, and the carceral state.

Between life and death there is the constant anti-Black racism and misogynoirism (Bailey 2010) of everyday life—whether microaggressions or overt harassment, verbal or physical assaults, or institutional and structural racism, the violence is pervasive and commonplace. In addition to the trauma of witnessing and documenting a slow death in broad daylight, Darnella Frazer, the seventeen-year-old Black girl who filmed George Floyd's murder has been subject to racist threats since then. Atlanta police officers violently assaulted twenty-year-old Spelman student Teniyah Pilgrim and twenty-two-year-old Morehouse student Messiah Young by tasing them and dragging them from their car as they were trying to return home after being caught in the protests over the Brooks killing (Green 2020). Likewise, Black people experience the weaponization of White womanhood in everyday life by women who threaten to or actually do call the police on them for the crime of going about their lives (Lang 2020). This pattern was perhaps best exemplified by Amy Cooper's threat to call the NYPD and tell them that Black birdwatcher Christian Cooper was "an African American man threatening [her] life" because his request that she leash her dog in accordance with Central Park rules enraged her. That this occurred on the same weekend that George Floyd was murdered illustrates the continuum of harm caused by the conjoined logics of anti-Blackness, White supremacy, settler-colonialism, imperialism, and patriarchal heteronormative gender norms.

Additionally, we have witnessed a dramatic increase in anti-Asian rhetoric and violence, thanks in large part to the president's racist insistence on attributing the deadly impact of COVID-19 to "the Chinese" rather than to the now undeniably evident inadequacy of our for-profit health-care system (Human Rights Watch 2020). Over fifteen hundred incidents of anti-Asian hate speech, discrimination, and physical attacks in the United States alone were documented by "Stop AAPI Hate" in an April 2020 report (Asian Pacific Policy and Planning Council 2020). Anti-Semitic violence in the United States likewise saw a dramatic increase, with the Anti-Defamation League documenting over two thousand assaults, vandalizations, and hate speech acts in 2019 (Schumacher 2020). At the same time, Islamophobia, another cornerstone of the revitalized White nationalist movements stoked by the president, has also increased apace. From the President's "Muslim bans" to mosque vandalizations to physical assaults and murder, persistent violence against Muslims and those mistaken for Muslims has increased exponentially since 2017 (Alsultany 2020; Klaas 2019). These hateful patterns are global, as anti-Asian, anti-Semitic, and anti-Muslim violence—state-sanctioned and otherwise—has increased everywhere.

In the Americas, Latin American migrants and asylum seekers are being denied their internationally recognized human rights through the current administration's new "Remain in Mexico" policy, which has essentially made Mexico a purgatory zone (Hinojosa 2020). For those who do make it across our increasingly militarized borders, the taking and jailing of their children—thousands of whom continue to languish in over two hundred "detention centers" and dozens of whom have died while in custody—has become normalized. In 2019 alone, eight-year-old Felipe Gómez Alonzo, sixteen-year-old Carlos Gregorio Hernández Vásquez, seven-year-old Jakelin Caal Maquín, two-year-old Wilmer Josué Ramírez Vásquez, and one-year-old Mariee Juarez survived the arduous journey from Guatemala to the United States, only to be taken from their mothers and fathers, fall ill, and die while in detention. The trauma of forcible separation from their parents, the abysmal conditions in the centers, and the sexual violence, illness, and death will haunt these children, their families, their people—and us, for we are accountable for our government's actions (Briggs 2020). That many of these migrants are also indigenous people of the Americas who have already survived centuries of Iberian/Ladino/mestizo settler-colonial violence *and* U.S. imperialist violence in their homelands—violence that triggers their exodus to el norte, where *they* are then presumptively criminalized—adds to the outrageousness of these detentions

(Asad and Hwang 2019; Davies 2019). Hate-mongering and scapegoating are intrinsically part and parcel of nationalism and settler-colonialism.

Yet simultaneously, voices decrying anti-Blackness have recently risen from many unexpected quarters—corporations, universities, the NFL, Facebook, Twitter, retailers, and sundry others—in support of the movement for Black Lives and, supposedly, to the work of dismantling systemic racism more generally. That these historically White-serving institutions are not just latecomers to the struggle but a root source of the problem perhaps goes without saying; one could reasonably respond to their "statements" with cynicism. Still, as with the Revolution of 1776, the War of 1812, Reconstruction, the Great Depression, and the late 1960s, it seems that we are once again at a critical juncture in the United States, a moment of reckoning with racism in which we can do the right thing once and for all. At *Meridians*, we hope that the multiracial, intergenerational, and cross-class protests that erupted this year indicate that we have reached a new tipping point toward accountability in the United States and globally.

Twenty years ago, the founding Smith-Wesleyan editorial group stated unequivocally in the introduction to the journal's first issue that "fundamental to our mission is the awareness that the production of knowledge is political" (Aggarwal et al. 2000: x). Critical optimism, radical hope, and faith in the power of knowledge production from the margins to change the world are central to our political project. We believe that lending our voices to the cacophonous conversations taking place about anti-Blackness and racism more generally has the potential to shift their tenor away from empty platitudes and toward empowering platforms. As Smith College President Ruth Simmons wrote in her foreword to volume 1, number 1, at *Meridians*, "we believe that issues affecting the lives of women of color must be given greater attention and support and that such support, both public and private, will result in increased economic prosperity, exciting scholarly innovation, and much societal good" (Simmons 2000: vii).

To that end, *Meridians* has made small but meaningful contributions to growing the pipeline of women of color faculty, to supporting the work of women of color artists and activists, and to expanding the reach of intersectionality into all our fields of labor. We have successfully addressed the conflict between the norms of historically White (male)–serving institutions and the innovative and contestatory nature of women of color feminist scholarship by undertaking a double-blind peer-review process in which, rather than the gatekeepers of old, our reviewers are truly *peers*—

other women of color feminist scholars with expertise in the fields, debates, and questions we engage with at *Meridians*. Our peer reviewers know what our authors are talking about, and typically offer constructively rigorous and generative responses. Although their labors are typically latent rather than manifest in the publications that result, we are as proud of our work growing a large community of thoughtful peer reviewers as we are of our authors. In order to preserve the double-blind promise of ano-nymity, we have not acknowledged our reviewers by name, but I take this opportunity to thank them collectively for their generous service.

Given the entrenched nature of the "publish or perish" tenure norm, in being a venue that recognizes and supports the expertise of both the reviewer and the author of works attending to feminism, race, and trans-nationalism, with the generous assistance of our peer reviewers *Meridians* has become a notable contributor to the project of changing the "face of the academy." Likewise, since volume 3, *Meridians* has solicited and published the work of women of color visual artists on our covers and as features, a practice that simultaneously materially supports independent artists and brings joy to our readers. Finally, regardless of the vehicle, *Meridians* pro-motes the understanding, development, and expansion of intersectional-ity as a paradigm and a practice (Crenshaw 1991).

I believe that these contributions are being made manifest in the upris-ings taking place all over the United States—on the streets, at the ballot box, in the classroom, on our screens, and at our kitchen tables. Protestors' trenchant refusals to accept subordination anymore is precisely what the contemporary White supremacist patriarchy of the United States has attempted to forestall ever since Reaganism initiated the attacks against the progressive policy initiatives won by the social justice movements of the late 1960s/early 1970s. In the world of higher education, right-wing attacks on academic freedom, faculty governance, and tenure have increased in tandem with the growing number of women, people of color, immigrants, and people of working-class origins who enter into the ranks of faculty and student bodies. We newcomers to the academy have developed and autho-rized new ways of knowing and being, demanded structural change, and are resourcefully transforming the ivory tower from a citadel of privilege into an accessible community resource. That is, rather than gratefully assimilate into the status quo, Black/Indigenous/people of color and pro-gressives are slowly but surely changing the America that had been so "great" for the White nationalist misogynists to whom the current presi-dent appeals to, most recently during his hateful speech at Mt. Rushmore on July 4, 2020 (Muller 2020). As editor emeritus Myriam Chancy put it in her first introduction for *Meridians*, it has always been our work "to plant new seeds—of hope, of rage, of insurrection, of peace—that might allow all of us to breathe more fully, to claim our ground" (Chancy 2003). This 20th Anniversary Reader is a sowing of those seeds.

Like seeds, some issues are perennial concerns for women of color feminisms. Nonetheless, deciding what to include in this anniversary reader required a set of principles by which to choose from the hundreds of essays, culture works, activist reports, memoirs, and poems that we have published over the past twenty years. I began the process by gathering impact data such as citation rates, downloads, and readings across multiple sites (Project Muse, e-Duke Journals, Academia, Research Gate, Google Scholar). Drawing from those combined sources, we identified the one hundred texts that appeared time and again on the various lists that result from this first phase.[1] Reading through those thousands of pages, I was struck by how rich and broad-ranging our authors' contributions have been, how cacophonous yet symphonic our voices, how steely-eyed yet generous our visions. I would have loved to publish all one hundred. Unfortunately, the reality of budgetary constraints set fixed spending limits and, by extension, a page limit.

Thus, I asked each Editorial Advisory and Creative Writing Advisory Board member to identify their top three favorites from among the one hundred texts in phase one. Although, not surprisingly, there were some idiosyncratic favorites, there was also a helpful degree of consensus about some of the pieces that facilitated developing the second-phase list of fifty texts. Once again, I was so moved by the quality and range of work on that shorter list that I struggled to narrow the list down further. Ultimately, I chose texts that represented all the feature areas we publish—In the Archives, Counterpoints, Culturework, Essays, In the Trenches, Memoirs, Media Matters, Pedagogy, and Poetry—and that, true to the *Meridians* project's mission, spanned disciplines, demographics, and geographies. Thus, the original 275 pages initially proposed to Duke University Press blossomed into the 559 pages you now hold in your hands. Even so, this represents but a sampling of the innovative and critical knowledge producers that *Meridians* has offered a platform from which to speak.

We consider this *Meridians* 20th Anniversary Reader a staple text for educators who undertake social justice pedagogy from kindergarten to graduate school. Beyond the classroom, we hope that this reader becomes a resource to activists laboring in the trenches of social justice globally and the realms of cultural work, from poetry to painting to photography to performance, because empowerment through education is our raison d'être. The authors include internationally renowned U.S.-based scholar activists such as Angela Davis and independent Global South scholars such as Sarah Ahmed; established poets such as Nikky Finney and younger poets such as Laurie Ann Guerrero, who after publishing in *Meridians*, would go on to become San Antonio's Poet Laureate a decade later; senior scholars such as the former president of the Latin American Studies Association, political scientist Sonia Álvarez, and younger scholars such as UC Berkeley lecturer in English Jennifer Cho. As a way of historicizing the journal's leadership, and also because they appeared in the lists generated in phases one and two, I also decided to include works by each of *Meridians'* editors—Kum-Kum Bhavnani (2001–2003), Myriam Chancy (2003–2004), Paula J. Giddings (2005–2017), and myself (2017–present).

Altogether, the texts in this reader are concerned with uncovering the gendered racialization of embodiment (Candelario 2000; Saraswati 2010); contesting the carceral state (Davis and Shaylor 2001; Palacios 2016); expanding archives and revising history (Giddings 2001; Basu et. al. 2002; May 2014); questioning the adequacy and accuracy of media representation (Bhavnani 2000; Brooks 2008; Deb 2016); memorializing resistance and organizing (Bachetta et. al. 2002; Majaj 2001; Torres 2009; Zook 2003); highlighting artivism (Calvo 2004; Mithlo 2009); documenting activism (Álvarez 2016; Barker 2006; Ferreira and Medeiros 2016; Thobani 2002); theorizing from the margins (Ahmed 2006; Cho 2011; Price 2010; Nash 2013); telling our stories in prose and poetry (Chancy 2011; Finney 2003; Guerrero 2009; Hammad 2002); and, to borrow a phrasing, teaching to transgress (May 2014; Palacios 2016; Rajgopal 2010; Wise Whitehead 2016).[2]

Meridians authors are largely—though not exclusively— women of color: Black diasporic, South Asian, Middle Eastern and North African, Asian American, Latin@/Latin American/Caribbean, Native American Indian/ Indigenous, and multiracial. They are typically feminist interdisciplinarians whose work has helped to transform the traditional borders and boundaries of disciplines in the humanities and social sciences, to decolonize ethnic and area studies, to globalize and transnationalize women/ gender/sexuality/feminist studies, and to center race as a critical intellectual project and political concern. Thus, I close by dedicating this reader to recently deceased María Lugones (1944–2020), whose life work was to both theorize and materialize resistance against modernity's oppressions.

Lugones's animating questions resonate with the spirit of this 20th Anniversary Reader: "How do we learn about each other? How do we do it without harming each other but with the courage to take up a weaving of the everyday that may reveal deep betrayals? How do we cross without taking over? With whom do we do this work? . . . How do we practice with each other engaging in dialogue at the colonial difference? How do we know we are doing it?" (Lugones 2010: 756). As our cover art by Samanta Tello, *Silenced Voices of Everyday Sheroes*, illustrates beautifully, *Meridians* believes that the answers lie in seeking—and speaking—our peace together. A *luta continua*.

Notes

1   Although our anniversary issue celebrates the past twenty years of knowledge production, I made the conscious decision not to include works published since I assumed the editorship in 2017. This choice does not imply that recent scholarship and creative work published in the journal is less meritorious; rather, it takes time and potential for impact to be ascertainable. It is my hope that we can publish a reader for our thirtieth anniversary that will include some of those recent pieces.
2   See hooks 1994.

Works Cited

Aggarwal, Ravina, Elizabeth Alexander, Ann Arnett Ferguson, Ann Rosalind Jones, Gayle Pemberton, Nancy Saporta Sternbach, and Susan Van Dyne. 2000. "Introduction." *Meridians: feminism, race, transnationalism* 1, no. 1: ix–xv.

Ahmed, Sara. 2006. "The Nonperformativity of Antiracism." *Meridians: feminism, race, transnationalism* 7, no. 1: 104–26.

Alsultany, Evelyn. 2020. "Islamophobia in the U.S. Did Not Start with Trump, but His Tweets Perpetuate a Long History of Equating Muslims with Terrorism." *University of Southern California Dornsife News*, January 29. dornsife.usc.edu/news /stories/3154/president-trump-perpetuate-long-history-of-islamophobia-in-usa/.

Alvarez, Sonia E. 2016. "'Vem Marchar com a Gente'/Come March with Us." *Meridians: feminism, race, transnationalism* 14, no. 1: 70–75.

Asad, L. Asad, and Jackelyne Hwang. 2019. "Migration to the United States from Indigenous Communities in Mexico." *ANNALS of the American Academy of Political and Social Science* 684, no. 1: 120–45.

Asian Pacific Policy and Planning Council. 2020. "In One Month, STOP AAPI HATE Receives Almost 1500 Incident Reports of Verbal Harassment, Shunning and Physical Assaults," April 24. www.asianpacificpolicyandplanningcouncil.org/wp -content/uploads/Press_Release_4_23_20.pdf.

Bacchetta, Paola, Tina Campt, Inderpal Grewal, Caren Kaplan, Minoo Moallem, and Jennifer Terry. 2002. "Transnational Feminist Practices against War." *Meridians: feminism, race, transnationalism* 2, no. 2: 302–8.

Bailey, Moya. 2010. "They Aren't Talking About Me . . . " *Crunk Feminist Collective*, March 14. www.crunkfeministcollective.com/2010/03/14/they-arent-talking -about-me/.

Barker, Joanne. 2006. "Gender, Sovereignty, and the Discourse of Rights in Native Women's Activism." *Meridians: feminism, race, transnationalism* 7, no. 1: 127–61.

Basu, Amrita, Paula Giddings, Inderpal Grewal, and Kamala Visweswaran. 2002. "September 11: A Feminist Archive." *Meridians: feminism, race, transnationalism* 2, no. 2: 251–53.

Bhavnani, Kum-Kum. 2000. "Organic Hybridity or Commodification of Hybridity? Comments on *Mississippi Masala*." *Meridians: feminism, race, transnationalism* 1, no. 1: 187–203.

Briggs, Laura. 2020. *Taking Children: A History of American Terror*. Oakland: University of California Press.

Brooks, Daphne A. 2008. "'All That You Can't Leave Behind': Black Female Soul Singing and the Politics of Surrogation in the Age of Catastrophe." *Meridians: feminism, race, transnationalism* 8, no. 1: 180–204.

Calvo, Luz. 2004. "Art Comes for the Archbishop: The Semiotics of Contemporary Chicana Feminism and the Work of Alma Lopez." *Meridians: feminism, race, transnationalism* 5, no. 1: 201–24.

Candelario, Ginetta. 2000. "Hair Race-ing: Dominican Beauty Culture and Identity Production." *Meridians: feminism, race, transnationalism* 1, no. 1: 128–56.

Chancy, Myriam J. A. 2003. "What Our Grandmothers Knew: A Few Words of Greeting from the Editor," *Meridians: feminism, race, transnationalism* 3, no. 2: v–x.

Chancy, Myriam J. A. 2011. "Under/Water: Memorial Day, May 31, 2010." *Meridians: feminism, race, transnationalism* 11, no. 1: 114–17.

Cho, Jennifer. 2011. "Mel-han-cholia as Political Practice in Theresa Hak Kyung Cha's *Dictée*." *Meridians: feminism, race, transnationalism* 11, no. 1: 36–61.

Crenshaw, Kimberle. 1991. "Mapping the Margins: Intersectionality, Identity Politics, and Violence against Women of Color." *Stanford Law Review* 43, no. 6: 1241–99.

Deb, Basuli. 2016. "Cutting across Imperial Feminisms toward Transnational Feminist Solidarities." *Meridians: feminism, race, transnationalism* 13, no. 2: 164–88.

Davies, James Giago. 2019. "Hispanic Immigrants Are Mostly Indians." *Native Sun News*, July 12. www.indianz.com/News/2019/07/12/native-sun-news-today-the -indigenous-imm.asp.

Davis, Angela Y., and Cassandra Shaylor. 2001. "Race, Gender, and the Prison Industrial Complex: California and Beyond." *Meridians: feminism, race, transnationalism* 2, no. 1: 1–25.

Ferreira, Claudia, and Adriana Medeiros. 2016. "March against Racism and Violence and in Favor of Living Well (*bem viver*), Brasilia 2015, National Black Women's March, November 18." *Meridians: feminism, race, transnationalism* 14, no. 1: 76–83.

Finney, Nikky. 2003. "The Making of Paper." *Meridians: feminism, race, transnationalism* 3, no. 2: 17–19.

Giddings, Paula. 2001. "Missing in Action: Ida B. Wells, the NAACP, and the Historical Record." *Meridians: feminism, race, transnationalism* 1, no. 2: 1–17.

Green, Emily. 2020. "Tasing of Two College Students in Atlanta Provokes More Out-rage Amid Protests." National Public Radio, June 3. www.npr.org/2020/06/03/869053425/tasing-of-two-college-students-in-atlanta-provokes-more-outrage-amid-protests.

Guerrero, Laurie Ann. 2009. "How I Put Myself through School." *Meridians: feminism, race, transnationalism* 9, no. 1: 30.

Hammad, Suheir. 2002. "First Writing Since." *Meridians: feminism, race, transnationalism* 2, no. 2: 254–58.

Hinojosa, María. 2020. "The Moving Border." Latino USA, National Public Radio, May 27. www.latinousa.org/2020/05/27/the-moving-border/.

hooks, bell. 1994. *Teaching to Transgress: Education as the Practice of Freedom.* New York: Routledge.

Human Rights Watch. 2020. "Covid-19 Fueling Anti-Asian Racism and Xenophobia Worldwide," May 12. www.hrw.org/news/2020/05/12/covid-19-fueling-anti-asian-racism-and-xenophobia-worldwide#.

Klass, Brian. 2019. "A Short History of President Trump's Anti-Muslim Bigotry." *Washington Post*, March 15. www.washingtonpost.com/opinions/2019/03/15/short-history-president-trumps-anti-muslim-bigotry/.

Lang, Cady. "How the 'Karen Meme' Confronts the Violent History of White Woman-hood." *Time*, July 6. time.com/5857023/karen-meme-history-meaning/.

Lugones, María. 2010. "Toward a Decolonial Feminism." *Hypatia* 25, no. 4: 742–59.

Majaj, Lisa Suhair. 2001. "On Writing and Return: Palestinian-American Reflec-tions." *Meridians: feminism, race, transnationalism* 2, no. 1: 113–26.

May, Vivian M. 2014. "Under-Theorized and Under-Taught: Re-examining Harriet Tubman's Place in Women's Studies." *Meridians: feminism, race, transnationalism* 12, no. 2: 28–49.

Mithlo, Nancy Marie. 2009. "'A Real Feminine Journey': Locating Indigenous Femi-nisms in the Arts." *Meridians: feminism, race, transnationalism* 9, no. 2: 1–30.

Muller, Jordan. "Trump Seeks to Claim the Mantle of History in Fiery Mount Rush-more Address." *Politico*, July 4. www.politico.com/news/2020/07/04/trump-mount-rushmore-speech-348618?fbclid=IwAR1IHg5zEL-rEgO9GmMAmxI1Phsvn99q8ed-oO492SjW4Ml6TcVsKuRhQwY.

Nash, Jennifer C. 2013. "Practicing Love: Black Feminism, Love-Politics, and Post-Intersectionality." *Meridians: feminism, race, transnationalism* 11, no. 2: 1–24.

Palacios, Lena. 2016. "Challenging Convictions: Indigenous and Black Race-Radical Feminists Theorizing the Carceral State and Abolitionist Praxis in the United States and Canada." *Meridians: feminism, race, transnationalism* 15, no. 1: 137–65.

Price, Kimala. 2010. "What is Reproductive Justice? How Women of Color Activists Are Redefining the Pro-Choice Paradigm." *Meridians: feminism, race, transnational-ism* 10, no. 2: 42–65.

Rajgopal, Shoba Sharad. 2010. "'The Daughter of Fu Manchu': The Pedagogy of Deconstructing the Representation of Asian Women in Film and Fiction." *Meridians: feminism, race, transnationalism* 10, no. 2: 141–62.

Saraswati, L. Ayu. 2010. "Cosmopolitan Whiteness: The Effects and Affects of Skin-Whitening Advertisements in a Transnational Women's Magazine in Indonesia." *Meridians: feminism, race, transnationalism* 10, no. 2: 15–41.

Schumacher, Elizabeth. 2020. "Anti-Semitism in the US Hits 4-Decade High." Deutsche Welle Akademie, May 12. p.dw.com/p/3c4PU.

Simmons, Ruth. 2000. "Foreword." *Meridians: feminism, race, transnationalism* 1, no. 1: vii–viii.

Thobani, Sunera. 2002. "War Frenzy." *Meridians: feminism, race, transnationalism* 2, no. 2: 289–97.

Torres, Lourdes. 2009. "Queering Puerto Rican Women's Narratives: Gaps and Silences in the Memoirs of Antonia Pantoja and Luisita López Torregrosa." *Meridians: feminism, race, transnationalism* 9, no. 1: 83–112.

Washington Post. 2020. "Election Calendar." www.washingtonpost.com/elections/calendar-2020/.

Wise Whitehead, Karsonya. 2016. "Rethinking *Meridians*: As a Critical Knowledge Project, a Pedagogical Offering, and a Black Feminist Quilted Narrative." *Meridians: feminism, race, transnationalism* 15, no. 1: vii–xvii.

Zook, Kristal Brent. 2003. "Dreaming in the Delta: A Memoir Essay." *Meridians: feminism, race, transnationalism* 3, no. 2: 278–88.

Passion, Generosity, and the Academy

Meridians Interview with Ruth J. Simmons

MERIDIANS: What made you want to help set up a journal like *Meridians* at Smith College?

RUTH J. SIMMONS: I spent some time at Spelman College (1989–91) and while there I was very interested in the work of *Sage*, a publication for and about African-American women. I was also aware of how difficult it was to produce *Sage*: difficult in the sense of bringing together scholars on the editorial board; of trying to persuade people institutionally to support it; of trying to convince people that the editorial time spent on the journal was worthwhile; of trying to identify stakeholders in the journal. I remember longing for a home for *Sage* like other scholarly journals had, where you didn't have to worry about resources or about the legitimacy of the work being contributed. At the same time I also was acutely aware, from my days as an Associate Dean of the Faculty at Princeton, how important the issue of venue was, especially for scholarly work by people who were interested in issues of race, identity, and gender. As early as my Princeton days I filed away in my mind that it would be wonderful to create a legitimate venue, thereby also creating support for scholarly work on race, gender, and identity.

When *Sage* came to an end some years ago, while I was President at Smith, I felt very strongly that in the bibliography of scholarly journals, there ought to be a place for one that really focused on women of color. I thought Smith College could be the home for such a venture.

MERIDIANS · feminism, race, transnationalism   Volume 19 Supplement 2020
DOI: 10.1215/15366936-8858119 © 2002 Wesleyan University Press, now published by
Duke University Press on behalf of Smith College

When we first started talking about *Meridians* in 1996 the response of people was "yes, but why would you have a journal that focuses on women of color? It's so specialized, there aren't many people who will be interested in that." And of course, when people say that, they're not thinking that women of color are the majority of women in the world.

So, both my experience in the tenure review process and my understanding of how difficult it was to find a home for publishing certain kinds of material meant that I knew how important it was to have the resources needed to develop a project such as *Meridians.*

And I think, frankly, down the road, I also anticipated that it would be wonderful if such a scholarly adventure would mature into a publishing enterprise for monographs on these subjects.

MERIDIANS: It is clear you like to think outside the mainstream.

SIMMONS: When I was a student, I knew that my tastes, my concerns, and my interests were not mainstream and, as importantly, that they were also not inferior. As a result, I have always wanted to find a place in the academy where very good ideas could be supported even though they fell outside the mainstream. When I was at Princeton (1983–1989; 1991–1995), I looked for the people who couldn't get their ideas through, for those gems of whom the academy was distrustful. I tried to look beyond what I thought was the appearance of quality to the underlying merit of ideas. I remember when I left Princeton where I was Associate Dean of the Faculty, some faculty described my role as a kind of ombudsperson. I thought that was a very odd way to describe it, but I suppose it isn't, because I aimed to be an honest broker for faculty who were innovative and had cutting-edge ideas.

From my youngest age in the academy I had the sense that the academy is extraordinarily rule-bound. By this I mean that it's easy to fall into patterns of endorsing the same kinds of work, vision, and scholarship that have been conducted before. Being so tightly rule-bound does not sit well for me in a place—the university—where creativity and a sense of adventure should be forever present. For example, the issues tackled by *Meridians* are the issues that rule-bound academic thinking does not encourage.

I think that what I fight for is the capacity of the academy to be true to its mission, which is to advance knowledge and to inspire new ideas. I fear that the academy has strong tendencies in the opposite direction. It rewards sameness, the embellishment of often discredited ideas, and it has a tendency to punish people for true innovation. The academy as an institution has a tendency to be frightened by that which is new and different, which is the exact opposite of what our mission is, to question and overturn the *status quo*.

MERIDIANS: How were you fortunate enough to realize that your ideas, despite being outside the mainstream, were not inferior?

SIMMONS: I don't know whether it was an evolution or whether it was something that arose within me at an early age.

My parents certainly understood well the world in which we were growing up: it was a dangerous world. My parents would stand up to people who derogated them, and seeing that as a child had an enduring effect. We lived in a southern town where if you didn't address white people as "Mr. Smith" or "Miss Smith" you could be summarily punished. In that context it is easy to see that my parents survived immense difficulties in an environment in which they had to constantly confront bigotry and disenfranchisement. Yet, they taught us that we were human beings who had a lot of potential. They set high expectations for my brothers and sisters and me, and they were very exacting in terms of our measuring up to those expectations, because they were in fact fighting for the right to live with dignity.

One of the results of our segregated world was that we were also surrounded by very brave people who were intent on preparing us for life. What they did for us was to teach us how people were going to tear us down, were going to laugh at us; how people were going to say that we were stupid and incompetent and they taught us how to cope with that. As a consequence, when I went to Harvard, or to Wellesley, and people behaved as if they thought I didn't belong, or that I didn't know very much, or that I couldn't do the work, I had a secret I had learned over nineteen or twenty years. And that is that I was very smart. I don't really know how I retained that secret, except there were a lot of people who worked with me as a young person and who said "Ruth, you are very smart and you should realize it; you can do anything you want to do."

But it was very hard at times to keep that sense of myself as capable and as having the potential to achieve whatever I wanted to achieve. At Wellesley I took a class in French. Although I had been a French major at Dillard University, I had never been in a class where French was spoken and I hadn't ever been to France. I knew the language and grammar but couldn't speak or understand spoken French. I sat in class for a while and, of course, all of these well-to-do, educated kids in my class were following the lessons and they were speaking French. I missed all the assignments, because they were delivered orally. In all, I felt pretty much like an idiot. After a week of this I said to my instructor "I'm very sorry but I'm going to have to drop your course." And he said "why?" "Because I'm completely lost. I don't understand anything that's going on in class, and I'm missing the assignments that were given orally in class. And I don't think I can ever get through this." And he said "Yes, you can. Just stay in class, continue to do the work, and one day you're going to understand it."

Well, I was furious at the time because I thought he was deeply insensitive not to understand my dilemma, but I had no choice except to go back to class and continue with the course. I had no money so could not even consider going home. Eventually, of course, I began to understand French, I did well, and even got a Ph.D. in it.

So once I understood that I could go from zero, that is, not understanding anything, to realizing there was a solution, and then solving the problem, I was never afraid again, ever. From that moment on, I've never been anywhere intellectually where I've been afraid and that is why I always regard every obstacle that I encounter as having a solution.

MERIDIANS: Experiencing and escaping such enormous political, social, and economic hardships can make people defensive, but that is not a quality that anyone associates with you.

SIMMONS: But I was defensive. As a young person, I was pretty angry: that was my response to ignorance and to bigotry. For example, when I was an undergraduate at Dillard University, a black college in New Orleans, I was a fiery activist. I took up the cause of all kinds of disenfranchised groups.

Dillard had a required chapel, which meant as a student you had to go to chapel, a Protestant service. My father was a Baptist minister and so this was a culture that I understood. But I had this notion that the requirement was unjust, because what if there were Jewish students, or Muslim students, or Hindu students and they had to go to a Christian religious service? Don't you see how horrible that would be? So I boycotted chapel. Well, the university was very severe about that because you couldn't graduate if you didn't go to chapel. In my senior year, the university sent a letter to my family saying that I would not be graduating because I had not gone to chapel.

MERIDIANS: Did you graduate from Dillard? How did that come about?

SIMMONS: I did graduate. In April of my graduation year I had been awarded a Fulbright and a Danforth Fellowship for graduate study, but it was unusual for students from Dillard to win these awards. The College had a dilemma. If I didn't graduate they couldn't announce that a Dillard student had won all these prizes, so they found a way to fix it—they found a solution. My family was so relieved.

That's the kind of person I was as a young person—very idealistic. I was perfectly awful in one sense because I was very self-righteous. However, something happened to me after I had been in the profession for about seven years, which was that I noticed that nobody was listening to me. I was predictable, arrogant, and self-righteous, and people dismissed me. So, I thought, "how can I fix this?" and decided that I might try listening instead, and that's what I started doing. I noticed that I got better results as a consequence of not talking all the time.

Gradually, I became less angry because I was having better results. And the better the results, the happier I was. Sometimes it's very hard to be generous when oppression is so great and when exclusion is so painful. Yet what I have learned is that it is essential to be your most generous when people are being their most awful.

MERIDIANS: It is clear you love education, and you have remained within formal education for that reason. Why?

SIMMONS: Although it is often a hackneyed rationale, I do think education offers the possibility of empowerment. My feeling is that if you can develop an intellect that has the capacity to understand the human condition and the history of what has transpired on the face of the earth, you have enormous potential for good.

It reminds me of the perspective of the astronauts when they went into space and looked back at the earth. "I'm just a speck tied to every other speck." But most of us don't get a chance to have that view. We dwell in closed realms. It's a frightening thing—how closed our worlds are. I grew up in a closed world because public policy forbade our leaving that world. But today, for the most part, certainly in the United States, if you dwell in a closed realm it is by choice because you can leave that realm and you can learn about others.

So I think education offers the greatest possibility for us to learn about the true scope of the life we live. And if we can learn that, I think we can solve a lot of the problems that we face. That doesn't mean that every person who is educated will be pure and just. Education doesn't make up for character deficiencies at all. But it can enlighten us and make us aware that we are deficient. So, I think I see that education—if we do it right, and I don't think we always do—can lead to empowerment and edification for the human psyche.

When I was a child, by all rights, I should have been willing to settle for little or nothing. But education empowered me to feel that with intelligence there were many things that could be done. I realized the development of the human intellect was a useful thing and it could be applied to conflict resolution, to overturning injustice, to healing, to being a caring person, and to passing on knowledge to the next generation. Everyone, every child, irrespective of their means, should have access to that kind of empowerment. That is why I stayed in education: it is a very powerful medium.

MERIDIANS: What can be done to improve formal education?

SIMMONS: I think the most important thing in our schools is to begin by setting appropriately high standards and goals for children. And that's one of the travesties in this country: many poor children are assigned to special education, which imposes low expectations for children who frankly shouldn't be in special education. It may impose such expectations because children can't sit in a chair long enough—such a ludicrous idea—or because children fight, or have a problem reading a particular text, or because they have difficulty with math. And the school system then decides that they are going to be relegated to some particular, limited area of the curriculum, and then that child never forgets that. We have to set our expectations appropriately high and broad for all children.

But second, I think the kind of stereotyping that goes on in society has no place in the schoolroom. If you're a girl, why would you want to do physics? Will a boy like you if you do physics? Or if you're a girl and you have all the answers in class—don't raise your hand so much because the boys won't like you if you're always the one who has the answers. Removing stereotypes is an ideal way to create the right environment in the classroom.

I do not in the end believe that children learn because of any one curriculum to which they are exposed. What you want most of all when children are young is to nourish curiosity, creativity, and self-confidence in learning. And if you can do those things, sooner or later, those children are going to flourish intellectually. I tend to focus less on the curriculum in the earliest grades and more on providing the right environment for learning.

MERIDIANS: Some people argue there is more space in private education to encourage this love of learning—what do you think?

SIMMONS: There are differences, certainly, between public education and private education. For example, if I wanted to get a journal like *Meridians* started in a public institution I think I might have had to confront a Board of Regents, for example. That is, people who would want to know why are we writing about sexuality with the taxpayers' money or ask questions such as "is this a communist publication?" At least in the private sphere you can do these things without being fearful that the board is going to cut off support. There's a high level of tolerance in private institutions for different kinds of ventures. That doesn't mean you don't have problems, but because of the wide range of funding sources, there is a greater variety in terms of what people will support. Yet there is not nearly enough innovation given the fact that private universities have such wide discretion.

MERIDIANS: What would you like to see done with that discretion?

SIMMONS: As I said recently, I'd like private universities to take more responsibility for the condition of K through 12 education in this country. That's number one. We could do that but we are still waiting on the sidelines. If private institutions played a larger role I think the rest of higher education would follow, with the result that schools across the country would be much improved.

The issue of access is an ongoing question, and that is something we have the capacity to solve in private education. We could eliminate some of the disparities of status between disciplines, we could elevate the pay of good teachers in the academy, and put research and teaching more in equilibrium than they currently are. There are so many different things that we could do but there's a lot of inertia in our profession.

Many excuses are given for that inertia. Most often in private institutions people claim that a powerful pool of donors might withdraw their support if you do something that's unpopular. I don't know if that's accurate. For example, at Smith, I was told that if we created an Engineering

Program the alumnae at Smith wouldn't support Smith to the same degree, yet the support for the College actually increased after we set up the Engineering Program.

MERIDIANS: Who and what are your own sources of inspiration?

SIMMONS: I've always felt very fortunate working in the academy because I just knew that it was some place I had to be—at a university with so many people thinking innovatively. When I was young, I thought there was something wrong with me because if my father said "yes," I said "no." And if my mother said, "do this," I did the opposite. I thought I was a very problematic child. But when I arrived at university and I saw so many people questioning the *status quo*, I knew I was in the right place. I have always wanted to be around people who were interesting interlocutors. The most exciting aspect of being in the academy is being alert to the possibility that things can be done differently and better and knowing that it is our task to make sure that we challenge society to question itself, to overturn things that are unjust. And there's no more exciting place to me for that reason.

I love what I do because every day I have a chance to be inspired by somebody. I don't often tell people, but it is the people who fight hardest, who are the most cantankerous, and the most different, and the most offbeat that I'm attracted to in the academy. Those are the people I always want to support first because to me they're closer to the soul of the academy and it doesn't matter to me that they might be wrong and it doesn't matter to me that they make my life uncomfortable—that's what I find thrilling. And, when I no longer find it thrilling to be in the presence of people who are at odds with the *status quo*, then it's time for me to retire.

I also enjoy immensely the variety of approaches to which we have access. Can you imagine working in a place where everybody is in the same discipline? It must be extraordinarily glum. But, on a daily basis, I can talk to a playwright and a physicist; to a philosopher and to a geneticist. And I do that everyday. Imagine that. What could be better?!

....

Ruth J. Simmons has served as President of Prairie View A&M University, located in her hometown of Houston, Texas, since 2017. A French professor before entering university administration, President Simmons held an appointment as a professor of comparative literature and Africana studies at Brown. After completing her PhD in romance languages and literatures at Harvard, she served in various faculty and administrative roles at the University of Southern California, Princeton University, and Spelman College before becoming president of Smith College, the largest women's college in the United States, from 1995 to 2001. At Smith, she launched a number of important academic initiatives, including an engineering program, the first at an American women's college, the Poetry Center, and the founding of the journal Meridians: feminism, race, transnationalism, which published its first issue in the fall of 2000. She left Smith to become President of Brown University from 2001 to 2012, which, under her leadership, made significant strides in improving its standing as one of the world's finest research universities. Simmons is the recipient of many honors, including a Fulbright Fellowship to France, the 2001 President's Award from the United Negro College Fund, the 2002 Fulbright Lifetime Achievement Medal, the 2004 Eleanor Roosevelt Val-Kill Medal, the Foreign Policy Association Medal, the Ellis Island Medal of Honor, and the Centennial Medal from Harvard University. Simmons is a member of the National Academy of Arts and Sciences, the American Philosophical Society, and the Council on Foreign Relations, and serves on the boards of the Houston Museum of Fine Arts, the Smithsonian National Museum of African American History and Culture, and the Holdsworth Center. She also serves on the Board of Directors of Square. Awarded numerous honorary degrees, she received the Brown Faculty's highest honor, the Susan Colver Rosenberger Medal, in 2011. In 2012, she was named a "chevalier" of the French Legion of Honor.

Note

Originally published in *Meridians* vol. 3, no. 1, 2002.

Ginetta E. B. Candelario

··

Hair Race-ing
Dominican Beauty Culture and Identity Production

Use to be
Ya could learn a whole lot of stuff
sitting in them
beauty shop chairs
Use to be
Ya could meet
a whole lot of other women
sittin' there
along with hair frying
spit flying
and babies crying
Use to be
you could learn a whole lot about
how to catch up
with yourself
and some other folks
in your household.
Lots more got taken care of
than hair . . . .
—Willi Coleman, "Among the Things
That Use to Be"

At the most banal level, a beauty shop is where women go for beauty. But as

MERIDIANS · feminism, race, transnationalism   Volume 19 Supplement 2020
DOI: 10.1215/15366936-8565825 © 2000 Wesleyan University Press, now published by
Duke University Press on behalf of Smith College

Willi Coleman evocatively notes, at beauty shops "lots more [gets] taken care of than hair." The degrees, types, and technologies of artifice and alteration required by beauty are mediated by racial, sexual, class, political, and geographic cultures and locations. Thus, beauty shops can be considered as sites of both cultural and identity production. Some have argued that if the female body generally has been subjected to "externalization of the gendered self" (Peiss 1994, 384), the explicitly racialized female body has been subjected to "exile from the self" (Shohat and Stam 1994, 322–33). With the rise of global colonialism, slavery, neocolonialism, and imperialism, African-origin bodies have been stigmatized as unsightly and ugly, yet, simultaneously and paradoxically as hypersexual (Hernton 1988). White female bodies are racialized as well, but this racialization is enacted via the assumption of de-racination, racial neutrality, and naturalized white invisibility (Frankenberg 1993). This White supremacist racial history interacts with masculinist imperatives of gender and sexual homogenization and normalization in particular ways (Young 1995). Moreover, bodily beautification requires material resources and aesthetic practices that are class bound. The beauty shop, then, can be analyzed as a site where hegemonic gender, class, sexuality, and race tropes simultaneously are produced and problematized.

In particular, hair—the subject and object of beauty shop work—epitomizes the mutual referentiality of race/sex/gender/class categories and identities. One can, as I found during a six-month participant observation at a Dominican beauty shop in New York City, "learn a whole lot of stuff sittin' in them beauty shop chairs." Here, the concern is to present both the representational and the production practices of hair culture as a window into the contextualized complexity of Dominican identity. The hair culture institutions, practices, and ideals of Dominican women in New York City during the late 1990s are presented as an instructive selection from a larger study (Candelario 2000).

Dominican Identity: Ethnicity and Race in Context

The importance of hair as a defining race marker highlights the centrality of beauty practices. Hair, after all, is an alterable sign. Hair that is racially compromising can be mitigated with care and styling. Skin color and facial features, conversely, are less pliant or not as easily altered. That Dominicans have equated whiteness both with *lo indio*, an ethno-racial identity based on identification with the decimated Taino natives of the island that now houses the Dominican Republic and "lo Hispano" or Hispanicity reflects the multiple semiotic systems of race they have historically negotiated. La/o india/o is invoked to erase the African past and Afrodiasporic present of Dominicans (Howard 1997). Hispanicity affirms the ethnoracial distance between Dominicans and Haitians, an organizing principle in Dominican national imaginaries since the rise of the state.

Operating in the context of both Latin American and United States' notions of race, transnational Dominicans engage in a sort of racial "code switching" in which both Latin American and United States race systems are engaged, subverted, and sustained in various historical, biographical, and spatial contexts and moments. For example, for a variety of reasons I explore at length elsewhere (Candelario 2000), Dominicans in Washington, D.C., identify as Black nearly twice as often as Dominicans in New York (see also Dore-Cabral and Itzigsohn 1997; Levitt and Gomez 1997; Duany 1994). Confronted in New York City with the U.S. model of pure whiteness that valorizes lank, light hair, white skin, light eyes, thin and narrow-hipped bodies, the Dominican staff and clients at Salon Lamadas continue to prefer a whiteness that indicates mixture. The identity category labeled "Hispanic" is deployed as the signifier of somatic, linguistic, and cultural alterity in relation to both Anglo whiteness and African American blackness. That Hispanic looks are preferred over both the Anglo and African American somatic norm images (Hoetink 1985) of the host society attests to resistance to acculturation and insistence on an alternative, or "other" space.

Dominicans, who might have been considered Black by European and U.S. observers were it not for their own colonial antipathy toward Haiti and later, toward Haitians, historically have been endowed with a sort of literary and political honorary whiteness in the service of both the domestic elite and the military and political-economic interests of the United States. It is an ethno-racial identity formulation predicated on the physical disappearance of Taino natives, coupled with their literary (Sommer 1983), iconographic, and bodily re-inscription, and a concomitant textual and ideological erasure of blackness (Torres-Saillant 1999). Rather than use the language of Negritude—negro, mulatto, and so forth—to describe themselves, Dominicans use language which limits their racial ancestry to Europeans and Taino "Indians"—indio, indio oscuro, indio claro, trigueño, moreno/a. The result is an ethno-racial Hispanicized Indian, or an Indo-Hispanic identity.

A series of regionally anomalous events in the political economic history of Santo Domingo accounts for this distinctive formulation of whiteness. Chief among those anomalies are the relatively short duration and limited importance of plantation slavery, the massive depopulations caused by White emigration, the impoverishment of the remaining White and Creole colonials during the seventeenth-century Devastation, and the concomitantly heavy reliance upon Blacks and Mulattos in the armed forces and religious infrastructure (Moya Pons 1995, Torres-Saillant 1996). At the same time, Spanish colonial norms of whiteness, what Hoetink (1967) has called the "Iberian variant" of a White "somatic norm image," were darker than the contemporary Anglo-European version.

French travel writers of the nineteenth century, when visiting the Spanish part of the island then called Saint Domingue, noted that people who seemed obviously of mixed African and Spanish descent considered themselves, not mulattos or colored, but *los blancos de la tierra*, literally, "the whites of the land." According to Moya Pons, "This meant that despite their color, [the Whites of the land] were different from the slaves whom they saw as the only blacks of the island" (1996, 16). In other words, in Dominican history, whiteness—whatever its bodily parameters—is an explicitly achieved (and achievable) status with connotations of social, political, and economic privilege. It is, moreover, understood to be a matter of context.

The Dominican Beauty Shop in New York City

The representation of Dominican women in the beauty shop occupations reflects both the importance of beauty culture to Dominican women, and the shifting opportunities available in the New York economy. When Dominican women first began to arrive in New York in the 1960s and 1970s, they generally frequented shops owned by other Latina/os, especially Cubans and Puerto Ricans, who were already established in Upper Manhattan (Masud-Piloto 1996, Rodriguez 1991, Sánchez-Korrol 1983). Although Dominicans had been migrating to New York City since the early nineteenth century, the Dominican community began to establish itself more permanently after the 1965 revolution and the 1965 U.S. Immigration Act (Martin 1966). The post–1980 flow of Dominican women into beauty shop occupations—whether as owners, hairdressers, manicurists, shampoo girls, estheticians, or masseurs—reflects simultaneously changes in the New York economy from manufacturing to service industries, changes in the demographics of the Washington Heights area, and changes in

Dominican beauty culture in the Dominican Republic as well (New York City Department of City Planning 1995). While Dominican women continue to be overrepresented in the nondurable goods manufacturing sector (Hernández 1989; Hernández et al. 1997), particularly in the apparel industry (Pessar 1987a, 1987b; Waldinger 1986), the volatility of that sector, together with the regimentation, occupational hazards, low pay, and low status of manufacturing and much service-sector employment, make beauty shop ownership and employment appealing by comparison.

In addition, in the Dominican Republic beauty culture has come to be seen as a respectable and professional field. Although commercial beauty shops have existed in the Dominican Republic since at least the 1930s, they generally serviced the elite. The majority of Dominican beauty culturalists operated out of their homes until the 1980s. Typically these shops were located in a converted front room, patio, or garage space and consisted of an owner-operator and a young neighborhood assistant. Shop owner-operators and assistants alike were considered nearly at par with domestic workers, and thus were of low socio-economic status. Additionally, beauty culturalists were reputed to be women of loose sexual morals. In the early 1980s, however, beauty culturalists began to professionalize, via the establishment of a professional organization, Asociación de Estilistas Dominicanas (Dominican Hair Stylists Association), the proliferation of beauty schools and certification programs, and a shift from the use of domestic and home-manufactured products to an increasing reliance upon hair-care products and technologies imported from the United States. Beauty shop work, in other words, has come to be viewed as a skilled profession one trains for and pursues.

Work in the New York Dominican beauty shop, while not entirely autonomous or especially well-paying, makes possible greater autonomy and flexibility and higher earnings and community status. Job quality and job satisfaction are often higher than in manufacturing or other service-sector employment. In addition, the Dominican beauty shop represents a female-dominated entrepreneurial sector, somewhat parallel to the male-dominated Dominican *bodega* (grocery store). In his study of Dominican entrepreneurs in New York City, Guarnizo (1993) found that entrepreneurial Dominican women frequently chose beauty shops as their niche. He reported, "One out of every five respondents is a woman. Unlike male [business] owners, however, women are clustered in a single sector: 60 percent of women own service firms (especially beauty salons and other personal service establishments) while only 25 and 15 percent of them own commercial or manufacturing firms, respectively" (121).

The appeal of this sector for Dominican women in New York City is manifold. In economic terms, beauty shop start-up costs are substantially lower than commercial or manufacturing firms, and therefore are more accessible to low-earning, poorly capitalized, or less-educated women. Further, barriers to entry are fewer, both in terms of fixed capital and human capital (Schroder 1978; Willet 1996). In cultural terms, beauty shop work is considered women's purview, while commercial or manufacturing ventures are generally considered male domains. *Bodegüeras* (female grocery shop owners), for example, while not uncommon, often have male kin *representandolas* (representing them) at the store counter. Similarly, while Dominican men do own beauty shops, they are less likely to be owner-operators, preferring instead to hire women managers.

Currently there is a thriving Dominican beauty culture industry in New York City, supported primarily by Dominican, and increasingly by African American women (Williams 2000). In Washington Heights/Inwood alone, that is, in the vicinity in northwestern Manhattan from 155th street to the 190s, from the Harlem River on the east to the Hudson River on the west, where 40 percent of the Dominican population in New York resides, there are 146 salons (1992 Economic Census, Service Industries, Firms Subject to Federal Income Tax, Zip Code Statistics, *Manhattan Yellow Pages*, April 1999–April 2000). On average, these salons are two-tenths of a mile (or one-and-one-half blocks) apart from one another. There is, in other words, a salon on nearly every single block in Washington Heights.[1]

By comparison, there are only 103 (or 40 percent fewer) beauty shops in the far wealthier Upper East Side, which is the district from East 61st to East 94th Streets, from Fifth Avenue to the East River. These salons are eight-tenths of a mile apart on average. In Harlem, where average per capita income is nearly identical to that in Washington Heights/Inwood, there are 112 shops. Shops in this district, which ranges from 114th to 138th Streets, and from Fifth Avenue to the Hudson River, are four-tenths of a mile apart on average. Washington Heights/Inwood is only slightly more densely populated than Harlem, but has 30 percent more shops. These numbers are all the more impressive given the exceedingly high poverty rate (36 percent) and low per-capita income level ($6,336) among Dominicans in New York City. It is quite clear that hair and beauty shops are important to Dominicans.

Today, the Dominican salon in New York City is a neighborhood institution that indicates community actualization. If, as the old sociological maxim holds, for most immigrant communities the establishment of ethnically specific funeral homes indicates community salience (e.g., Park et al. 1925; Gans 1962), for Dominicans, the beauty shop holds a similar role in the community. The Dominican beauty shop, with the physical space it plots out and the social relationships it contains, is a site that not only reflects transnational community development and cohesion, but helps sustain it.

Salon Lamadas

Salon Lamadas, where I spent six months as a participant-observer, is in many ways a typical Dominican salon.[2] It is located in the heart of Washington Heights, on St. Nicholas Avenue several blocks south of the 181st Street shopping district. Surrounding the salon are a telephone station, a pharmacy, a Pronto Envio (remittances center), and a family restaurant. This is a typically busy commercial and residential street, trafficked primarily by Dominicans, Puerto Ricans, Cubans, and, increasingly, Mexicans.

Founded in 1992 by an owner operator, Salon Lamadas is an average-sized shop with four stylists, including the owner, and a shampooer, a manicurist, and a facialist/ masseuse. Music is always playing at the salon, sometimes quite loudly. Generally it is merengue and salsa, although one or two ballads surface. Often in the afternoon the television is turned on, as well, and is usually tuned to *Cristina*, a popular Miami-based, Spanish-language talk show. In addition to the music and the television, the blow dryers are constantly going. Despite all this noise, the women hear each other quite well, and carry on conversations across the room. The atmosphere is one of conviviality and easy familiarity.

The salon is open seven days a week. Although many salons in the United States close on Mondays, Dominican salons do not. This is true for several reasons. First, Dominican women use salons for regular weekly hair care, not for intermittent haircuts and hair treatments. Therefore, there is steady demand throughout the week, although Fridays and Saturdays are still the busiest days. Second, the staff needs to work six days a week in order to earn enough money to survive in New York and to remit dollars to their families in the Dominican Republic (Hernández and Torres-Saillant 1998, Grasmuck and Pessar 1991). Third, because Dominican women are heavily represented in blue- and pink-collar work (Hernández 1989; Hernández, Rivera-Bátiz, and Agodini 1995), the salon must accommodate to their varied and long working hours.

Salon Lamadas, like most neighborhood salons, has a core of clients who frequent the shop regularly, usually once a week. Thirty of those "regulars" were approached for interviews. Fifteen agreed. Although this is not a statistically representative sample, neither in size nor in selection, they are a diverse group in terms of current age, age at migration, generation of migration, residency status, labor-force participation rates, professional status, educational attainment levels, Spanish- and English-language proficiency, marital status, household composition, and physical appearance.

The interviews consisted of two or three separate three-hour interviews. The first was a life-history interview, in which the respondent's migration, labor markets and educational experience, family life, and personal history were explored. The second interview inquired into the respondent's experience of Dominican beauty culture, both at Salon Lamadas and more generally. In addition, a third interview consisting of a photo elicitation component was conducted, following Furman (1997) and Kottak (in Harris 1964: 57). Using color photocopies of images copied from hairstyle books utilized at Salon Lamadas, respondents were asked to select and describe the women they found "most attractive" and "least attractive."

The explicit work of the salon, the transformation of a Dominican woman's hair into a culturally acceptable sign of beauty, hinges the customer's sense of self and beauty on certain racialized norms and models. The Dominican salon acts as a socializing agent. Hair care and salon use are rites of passage into Dominican women's community. At the salon, girls and women learn to transform their bodies—through hair care, waxing, manicuring, pedicuring, facials, and so forth—into socially valued, culturally specific, and race-determining displays of femininity.

Many of my respondents recalled visiting beauty shops as children with their mothers. Chastity, for example, said, "I used to always go with my mother to this shop in Flushing, where I grew up. She would go all the time and I'd go with her. I must have been real little because I remember being like 'Wow' and 'Ooo' about everything. They all looked glamorous to me. (Laughs) She still goes there, and it was the first shop I used myself. I still go there sometimes just to catch up on the neighborhood gossip."[3] As Chastity explains, for young girls with their mothers, the shop seems "glamorous" and adult, and therefore awe-inspiring.

These shops act as community centers; the exchange of information and women's insights is as much a part of their function as the production of beauty. Further, as in Chastity's case, it was often the mother's shop that young women first visited. Generally speaking, however, they themselves did not become beauty shop clients until they were about fifteen years old. That fifteen is the age when Latin American girls of means are introduced into society, and when Latin American girls generally are socially considered "women," is not coincidental (King 1998). Kathy recalled her first salon visit: "Aha, the first time I went to a shop I was already like fifteen years old. And it was to have my hair trimmed a little. But I already wanted to get out of the ponytails and buns already. And so I went to a neighbor who had a shop in her house and I had my hair washed, trimmed, and set. Oh, I looked so pretty." The repeated refrain of how "pretty" they looked after their first beauty shop visit also marks the transition from "innocent" childhood to "sexual" young womanhood. All of the respondents raised in the Dominican Republic, and several who were raised here, recalled that the transition from childhood to young womanhood was marked by the loosening of their hair from ponytails and moños (buns).

Others recalled first visiting a beauty shop in preparation for their migration to the United States, a moment which also might mark the transition from girlhood to adolescence. Nurka, for example, recalled that before migrating, when she was fourteen, her mother took her sisters and her to a beauty shop in town:

> Look, it was to come here. Exactly. Yes. (Chuckles) I had never gone to a salon. I always, I had two pony tails like this, and that was it. But I went. When we were coming here, mommy went to pick us up. And she took the three of us to the salon. I think my brother also had a haircut. And it was, we were in the country, and mommy took us to the east, to Baya-guana, the place was called. She took us there to have us all have our hair cut. They trimmed our hair, they washed our hair and it was, "Oh!" Everyone, "Oh! What pretty hair! Oh, how pretty!" (Laughs) And that was true, yes of course. I remember it as if it were today, yes.

For Nurka, the transition from childhood to adulthood was marked as much by the change from pigtails to hair done at the shop, as by the move to New York. Her transformation into young womanhood is socially recognized by people who acclaim her "pretty hair," now loose and womanish.

Like Nurka, Chastity remembers her grandmother styling her hair into pigtails and later moños for neatness and ease of care. So long as mother and grandmothers were responsible for their children's hair, these were the preferred styles. As Nana explained,

> Look, I hated those buns. It was three buns, one here, one here, and one here. My grandmother used to make them with a piece of string. And the other children used to make fun of them saying like "*Tin mari de dos pingó, cucara macara titire fué*" [a nonsensical children's rhyme]. I used to tear them [the buns] apart when I was walking to school. So then, when I became a little bigger, my grandmother told me that I was already old enough to take care of my hair myself. And that was such a joy for me! Oh! I started wearing curlers and styling my hair well.

The transition of hair care from one's caretaker's hands into one's own, thus, paralleled the increasing responsibility for one's own body and self.

Racialized Reproduction and Hair Culture

> *. . . Cause in our mutual obvious dislike*
> *for nappiness*
> *we came together*
> *under the hot comb*
> *to share*
> *and share*
> *and share*
> —"*Among the Things That Use to Be*"

A central aspect of Dominican hair culture has been the twin notions of *pelo malo* (bad hair) and *pelo bueno* (good hair). Bad hair is hair that is perceived to be tightly curled, coarse, and kinky. Good hair is hair that is soft and silky, straight, wavy, or loosely curled. There are clearly racial connotations to each category: the notion of bad hair implies an outright denigration of African-origin hair textures, while good hair exalts European, Asian, and indigenous-origin hair textures. Moreover, those with good hair are, by definition, not black, skin color notwithstanding. Thus, hair becomes an emblem of the everyday engagement of *blanqueamiento*, or whitening.

The Dominican salon, in being the preeminent site of Dominican hair culture practices and technologies, provides insight into the relative saliency of *blanqueamiento*, which is fundamentally about physical relations, sexual and otherwise, between people. This is not to say that *blanqueamiento* does not operate in nonmaterial culture realms as well, as Piedra's (1991) work on literary whiteness has aptly illustrated it does. However, there is an explicit physicality to *blanqueamiento*, particularly as it implicates racialized gender. It is there that beauty culture practices comes into play. *Blanqueamiento* is a long-term process of encoding whiteness bodily. Hair culture is a much more immediate, if more ephemeral, solution.

In the United States, non-African American women rarely have the opportunity to interact with African American women around beauty regimes. Consequently, they do not experience first-hand the variety of hair textures in the African diaspora through touching, washing, or styling "Black hair," through seeing media depictions of Black hair care, or through seeing African American women themselves caring for their hair. African American women, on the other hand, constantly are exposed to White women's hair care and hair textures through a variety of hegemonic media: dolls, television, cinematic and print media representations, and through observing first hand White women's hair ministrations throughout the day. Currently, women with non-African-diaspora hair textures spend a great deal of time throughout the day grooming their hair—brushing it, tying it up, loosening it, washing it, drying it, or otherwise fussing with it. By contrast, African-diaspora hair once styled retains its set and is typically washed every third or fourth day at home or in the salon. Thus, many non-African Americans simply do not know what "Black hair" feels like, how it is maintained, what products are used on it, and what beauty practices are employed.

The first time that many White women are exposed to Black women's hair in close quarters is when they are put into a communal living situation, such as a school dormitory or armed services barracks. A commonly cited experience of Black women is that of the White housemate who asks to touch her hair, thus exposing the White woman's segregated upbringing, the novelty (specifically, the racialized exoticism) of African-diaspora hair textures, and, ultimately, her own White aesthetic privilege. Black women often recount the strong impact and significance of these encounters, while White women seem surprised at the hostility with which their seemingly innocent desire to touch is met (Cary 1991; Frankenberg 1993).

Beauty shops in the United States originated as, and continue to be, socially segregated spaces, in practice if not by law (Willet 1996). Schroder, for example, relates the story of the disruptive effect of a new hire's "ethnic clientele" in the implicitly (if not explicitly) White racialized "atmosphere existing in the salon" (1978, 193). African Americans and Anglo Americans alike hesitate to frequent each other's shops, although from the mid-1980s a series of individual and legal challenges to those social norms have occurred (C. Coleman 1995, Goodnough 1995, Willet 1996).

Dominican women, conversely, do not experience this brand of racial segregation. Simply stated, Dominican families are comprised of people with a variety of hair textures, facial features, and skin tones. Girls and young women are allowed "hands-on" exposure to a range of hair textures throughout their lives. Fannie, for example, utilized one hair care regime at home suited to her mother's and her own fine, lank hair. As she came of age, however, and began to socialize with her cousins, whose hair care regimes included roller sets, relaxers and *doobies* (hair wraps), she became versed in those methods as well. Responding to the question of how she came to work in a beauty shop, she notes that her first experiences with Dominican beauty culture occurred in the context of her family, which is "very large" and very diverse. As she recalls:

> We would all go to the beach together, in Barahona, there are a lot of beaches. And when we would come back from the beach, I would return with my hair dry and straight, you know? And then, they would come with their hair, you know, curly. You know, bad hair that is relaxed? That when it comes into contact with sea waters it becomes, you know, Dominican hair, Black women's hair? And they would say to me, "Oh! You're all set to go dancing, but not me. Come on then, and get to work fixing my hair too." And so I, in order to hurry up and for us to all get ready at the same time, I wanted to help. And that's how I started practicing. "Let me set your hair." "Here, fix my hair." You know? Between ourselves, girls to the end, getting together.

Fannie's story highlights several themes that will be explored in this section. It was in participating in her cousin's hair care regimes that she learned and began to practice setting hair. Further, her cousins marshaled her assistance in caring for their hair, evidently undaunted by her personal unfamiliarity with their hair texture. In helping to care for each other's hair, a spirit of feminine intimacy across racial boundaries marked by hair care practices—"between ourselves, girls to the end"—was developed and sustained. Finally, although she herself is Dominican and has fine, lank hair, light eyes, and freckled white skin, Fannie equates "Dominican hair" with

"Black women's hair" and "bad hair that is relaxed." It is her cousins' beauty culture practices, in other words, that "typify" Dominican women's hair culture.

Similarly, Dominican mothers and daughters often have dissimilar hair textures, yet mothers have to care for and style their daughter's hair. Doris, for example, never used curlers herself, nor did her sisters, but she had to set her daughters' hair, which is thick and curly. "I myself haven't used them yet," she said. "It was out of necessity, out of necessity that I learned. I'd put them and they'd come out, more or less, with lots of pins and things like that. . . . I saw at the salon how they did it and I, more or less, in my mind I had an idea of how they were done, and I did them and they didn't come out too badly. Because you know, it's very difficult to get them to come out as nice as they do." This passage indicates that the salons Doris frequented catered to clients with hair like hers, as well as to clients who used roller sets. In other words, unlike U.S. shops, the typical Dominican beauty shop caters to women of various hair textures. Further, the work done in the shops, as Doris points out, is "very difficult" and requires a degree of skill. Finally, as with Fannie and her cousins at home, the beauty shop helped to socialize Doris, and later her children, into Dominican beauty culture.

"A Rice and Beans Face": Looking Dominican, Seeing Hispanic

For Dominicans, hair is the principal bodily signifier of race, followed by facial features, skin color, and, last, ancestry. Juan Antonio Alix's nineteenth-century *décima*, or ten-line poem, "El negro tras las orejas" ("Black Behind the Ears") illustrates this phenomenon well:

De la parienta Fulana	Such and such relative's
El pelo siempre se mienta;	Hair is always mentioned;
Pero nunca la pimienta	But never the black pepper
De la tía siña Sutana.	Of aunt so and so.
Por ser muy blanco se afana,	One strives to be very white,
Y del negro hasta se aljea	Even distances oneself from the black man
Nublando siempre una ceja	Always arching an eyebrow
Cuando aquél a hablarle viene	When he comes to speak with one
Porque se cree que no tiene	Because one thinks that one does not have
"El negro tras de la oreja."	"The black behind the ears."

[Alix 1996, 8, trans. by author]

Although Alix's *décima* was written in 1883, the role of hair as race-signifier among Dominicans dates back to at least the late eighteenth century (Moureau de Saint-Méry 1944, 95).

Given that Dominicans are endowed with many of the physical signs to which they attribute blackness, and that they draw a distinction between blackness and hispanicity, how do they discern who is "Hispanic" and who is not?[4] Hairstyle books offer an invaluable window into how Dominicans read bodies racially. I elicited formal responses to pictures in these books during interviews with salon clients. In addition, on several occasions when the shop was quiet and there were no clients, I opened the books and asked the staff, individually and collectively, for their opinions of the hairstyles and models depicted.

The core questions guiding the elicitation were: Who do Dominican women consider beautiful? Is the norm closer to, or further from, whiteness or blackness? How are "Hispanic looks" conceptualized? What is the relationship between aesthetic preferences and social status? While a sample of eighteen respondents is not a statistically valid one, the results resonate with larger, historical indications of Dominican notions of beauty and race, as well as with my ethnographic findings in the beauty shop.

At Lamadas, of the thirteen books customers use when selecting a hairstyle, ten are of White models and hairstyles. Three of the books feature African American women. One afternoon I approached owner-operator Chucha with one of the three African American hairstyle books and asked her about the styles it contained.

Chucha: I just bought that book. I bought it because my clients have to locate themselves in the hair they have.

Me: How so?

Chucha: Why, Dominican women don't want to see that book. They ask for the White women's book; they want their manes long and soft like yours.

Me: Why?

Chucha: It's because of racism. It's just that we don't even know what race we are. That if we're White, that if we're Black, indio, or what. . . . I don't want to know about Blacks, so I don't have to be fucking around with kinks. Look, I came out like one of my aunts, and that was suffering in my house in order to lower my kinks. The

Dominican woman wants her soft mane, long hair. I bought that book now so they can start to locate themselves well. They don't want to see that book. They ask for the White women's book, the one for good hair like yours. Look, I have a client who brings me a three-year-old girl so I can blow dry her hair. You know what that is? Three years old. And in the end, when she gets home and starts playing, her hair stands on end again. (Laughs.) The latest was that she wanted her to have her hair set. That little girl sat under the dryer better than some big ones, reading her magazine. Do you think that's right? That's suffering. It's not fair. I tell her, "Leave her with her curly hair, put a ribbon in it and leave it!" But no, they want their soft manes.

Chucha wants to help her clients "locate themselves," and the selves she is pointing Dominican women to are Black. But this is a self-image rejected by her clients, who "don't want to see that book." Instead, they "ask for the White women's book." Attributing the desire for long and soft hair to racism and to racial confusion, Chucha reiterates the equation of blackness with kinky, difficult hair, a result of failed *blanqueamiento*. As she indicates by tracing her own "*greñas*" (kinks) to her aunt, blackness is errant, and betrays. It leads to "suffering."

Interestingly, Chucha depersonalizes her own suffering, referring instead to "Dominican women," to her clients, or to her family's suffering. The ambivalence Chucha expresses, as a woman whose own hair was treated as a cause of sorrow in her childhood and as a stylist who actively participates in the very system she condemns, typifies the paradox of Dominican beauty culture. She is critical of her clients for choosing the White book, for subjecting their three-year-olds to suffering under the dryer, and for preferring "long manes." She relishes the resiliency and unruliness of a child's kinky hair that refuses to relax. Yet, she is an active agent of the very system she criticizes. Further, she is subjected to it herself, even as an adult.

The texture of Chucha's hair was variously presented as "*pelo macho*" (macho hair), "*pelo durito*" (slightly hard hair)" and "*pelo fuerte*" (strong hair) by her staff, and as "*greñas*" (kinks) and "*pasas que hay que bajarlas*" (these raisins that have to be tamed) by herself. Much like the customers who pretend not to notice the waiter's gaffe in order to support his role (Goffman 1959), Lamadas' staff politely overlook and accommodate Chucha's hair texture, both through their grooming of her hair and through their softened descriptions of it. Yet Chucha herself is ambivalent about her hair, as the following selection from my field notes indicates:

> Chucha and Leticia attended a Sebastian hair product seminar in New Jersey today. The topic was how to use a new color product. Chucha sat down and recounted the details of her experience to Maria: "They don't work on bad heads there. It's all for good hair, like hers (pointing to me) and yours (Maria)." I asked why not, and whether they had ever asked for a different kind of hair on the dummies. Again Chucha responded: "There it is! Our job is to adapt straight hair, good hair products, to ours. I was dying laughing, thinking about the surprise they'd experience if my hair got wet!" she laughed. "If my hair got wet!"

The "they" Chucha refers to are the Anglo-American producers, marketers, and beauty culturalists at Sebastian. Chucha's laughter and pleasure in relating the story indicate to me her awareness of her corporate host's reliance on superficial appearances. Water would return her hair to its natural, tightly curled state. Her looks, she recognizes with relish, are deceiving. So, it seems that on some level Chucha is well aware that she is transforming herself racially when she does her hair. The question is, what is she transforming into? I argue that it is not a desire for whiteness that guides Dominican hair culture. Instead, it is an ideal notion of what it means to "look Hispanic."

Again, situating Dominican identity in the appropriate spatial and political context is necessary. The use of the term Hispanic in Spanish by Dominicans in New York is an engagement with both the historic hispanophile identity institutionalized by the Dominican state and elite, and with the White supremacist foundations of the United States racial state (Omi and Winant 1994). For Dominicans, to say in Spanish that they are "Hispanic" is at once a connection to a European linguistic and cultural legacy and also a recognition of subordinate ethno-racial status in the United States (Oboler 1995). In this tense negotiation of multiple historical contexts and codes, the usual United States notions of both whiteness and blackness are subverted.

However, merely subverting whiteness and blackness is not liberating, for the concept of race as an organizing principle remains intact. The bounds of the categories are altered, but their hierarchical systematization is not. Blackness continues unabashedly to be equated with ugliness. When asked for their opinions of the appearance of women depicted in an

African American braiding book, Salon Lamadas' staff was vehemently derogatory in their commentary. At one point a debate ensued over whether the woman who Chucha had previously described as having "una cara de arroz con habichuelas" (a rice-and-beans face) was Latina or African American. Nilda, Maria, and Flor felt that she was Latina. Nené, Alma, and Leonora disagreed, particularly Nené, who felt that she was definitively black.

Nené: Her features are rough, ordinary—black muzzle, big mouth, fat nose.

Nilda: Blacks are dirty and they smell. Hispanics are easy to spot! (Turning to me.) You have something Hispanic.

Me: What?

Nilda: Your nose. Fannie is White, with good hair, but her features are rough Black ones.

Leonora: It's just that Black shows.

Hilda: Black is not the color of the skin. Really pretty, really fine. The White person has black behind the ears.

In this exchange, several things become apparent. First, those who "look" Latina/o could easily be African American, and vice versa. Second, "blackness" is discerned through a sometimes contradictory, but cohesive, system of bodily signs: hair, skin, nose, and mouth. When these features are "Black" they are perceived to be animalistic and crude, as the terms "rough" and "muzzle" and the attribution of filth and odor indicate. Yet, they are also common, if base, among Dominicans as the term "ordinary" implies. At the same time, an intermediate category, "Hispanic," is deployed to contain the fluid middle between Black and White. Ancestry, even if not discernible through skin color and facial features, is immutable. Thus, my nose indicates my African ancestry. But, as the repeated references to my "good" hair as signifier of whiteness indicate, ancestry does not determine current identity. Finally, the continuing currency of the one-hundred-year-old expression "black behind the ears" is striking.

"Black Women are Confusing, but The Hair Lets You Know"

But now we walk
heads high
naps full of pride

with not a backward glance
at some of the beauty which
use to be.
—*"Among the Things That Use to Be"*

Dominican women are lay anthropologists, employing the sort of reading of the racialized body utilized by, for example, Franz Boas. Boas was often called as an expert witness in legal cases in which the determination of a person's "race" was required. In one instance, he was asked to determine whether a "golden-haired blonde with beautiful gray eyes and regular features" married to a prominent Detroit doctor was passing for White. (Her husband was suing her for divorce based on his belief that she was.) Boas concluded that the woman was not Black, explaining, "If this woman has any of the characteristics of the Negro race it would be easy to find them. . . . One characteristic that is regarded as reliable is the hair. You can tell by a microscopic examination of a cross section of hair to what race that person belongs" (Boas, in Rooks 1996, 14). Microscopic examinations, it seems, can also be made without benefit of a microscope.

Bodies are racially coded in distinct, referential, and ultimately arbitrary ways in any given historical and cultural context (Gilman 1998; Gould 1996; Montague 1974). Race is a biological fiction that nonetheless has been institutionalized into a social fact through particular cultural practices. In a community that strives for *blanqueamiento*, race for Dominican women assumes immediate importance as a personal bodily, social, and cultural attribute.

Simply stated, Dominican women consider women they perceive to be Hispanic, and specifically Dominican, as most beautiful. *Hispanic* (or *Latina*) is often synonomous with *Dominican*. Both terms are taken to mean "a middle term," "a mixture of Black and White," an intermediate category. Latin looks, accordingly, are those that contain elements from each constitutive "race." As the illustrations below indicate women selected most often as looking Hispanic are also the ones most often selected as prettiest. The top three "prettiest" women were all thought to look Latina. The top eight of the nine women selected as prettiest were thought to look Latina by 20 percent of the respondents. Only the ninth woman of those selected as prettiest was a blonde-haired, white-skinned woman who was universally declared to "not look Latina." At the same time, there were no "White" women among the women perceived as "least pretty." Instead, as the Looks Hispanic Ratio indicates, the women considered "least pretty" were those

Prettiest

| Looks Latina Ratio | 13:13 | 7:13 | 6:13 |

Least Pretty

| Looks Latina Ratio | 4:13 | 4:13 | 1:13 |

Figure 1. Perceived Prettiness with "Looks Hispanic" Ratio
Note: The images in figures 1–4 are taken from these sources: *Before and After: American Beauté,* vol. 2 (Freehold, N.J.: Dennis Bernard); *Family Album III* (Auburn, Mass.: Worcester Reading Co.); *Family Images,* vol. 2 (Auburn, Mass.: Worcester Reading Co.); and *Ultra World of Hair Fashion* (Auburn, Mass.: Worcester Reading Co.).

African diaspora women furthest away from standard Hispanic-looking woman (fig. 1).

Since the Looks Hispanic category included women in nearly equal proportion from the White and Black hairstyle books, there does not seem to be a preference for "pure" or "European" whiteness. Rather, each of the women selected as looking Latina was selected because her face and/or hair were perceived to indicate some degree of both African and European ancestry (fig. 2). Those thought not to evidence any degree of mixed ancestry were also those thought to "Not look Hispanic." (fig. 3) It is the lack of "naturalness" in sculpted and obviously processed hairstyles that Dominican women point to as disconcerting, and as distinguishing African American hair culture from Dominican hair culture.

Dominican women place great emphasis on hair that appears "healthy,

Top Five	1st Choice	2nd Choice	3rd Choice	4th Choice	5th Choice

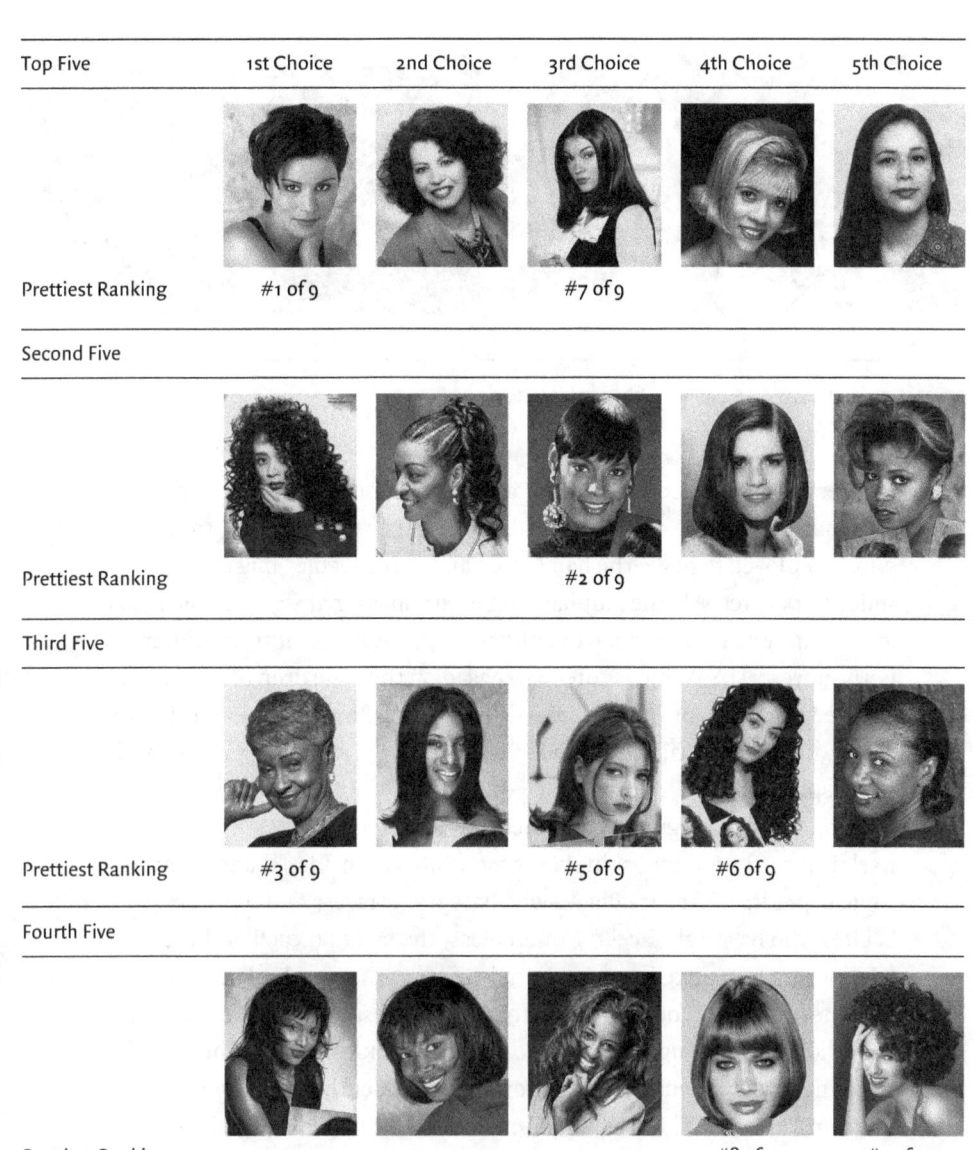

Prettiest Ranking	#1 of 9		#7 of 9		
Second Five					
Prettiest Ranking			#2 of 9		
Third Five					
Prettiest Ranking	#3 of 9		#5 of 9	#6 of 9	
Fourth Five					
Prettiest Ranking				#8 of 9	#4 of 9

Figure 2. "Looks Hispanic," in Order of Frequency Selected, and with Prettiness Ranking.

natural, and loose." As Nuris put it, "The difference between here and there, Black women here, they use a lot of grease, their hair looks, it doesn't look as loose as Dominican women's. Dominican women don't use it that way, they wear their hair processed, but the hair looks healthy, it stays well, very pretty, the hair, the hair always looks healthy. . . . I think the

9:9

Figure 3. "Does Not Look Hispanic," with Prettiness Ranking.

difference is like to look more natural. To look more, like, for the hair to look looser. That's it." In other words, the extensive technology, time, and effort employed to make the hair "loose and manageable" must not show. Indeed, it is precisely the emphasis on naturalness that signifies the racial iconography of Dominican hair culture. In this way, Dominican whiteness both subverts U.S. White supremacy based on the "one drop of blood rule" (where "one drop" of African "blood" makes one Black [Davis 1991; Harris 1964]) and sustains the blanqueamiento-based White supremacy of Dominican hispanicity.

Similarly, while light skin is generally valorized, White skin in and of itself is insufficient, and skin that is too white is considered unsightly. As Chucha put it: "There are Blacks who have pretty faces. And there are Whites who have ugly faces." Nonetheless, the fact that each of these possibilities is constructed as exceptional points to the standard equation of whiteness and blackness with beauty and ugliness, respectively. Consider the following exchange between Doris, a white-skinned, straight-haired Dominican woman married to a brown-skinned, curly-haired Dominican man, and me, a similarly white-skinned, straight-haired Dominican

Table 1 Binding of "Most Attractive" and "Least Attractive" Images

Descriptors	Number	Percent
"Most Attractive"	60	100
Selected from "White" hairstyle book	39	65
Selected from "Black" hairstyle book	21	35
"Least Attractive"	59	100
Selected from "White" hairstyle book	17	29
Selected from "Black" hairstyle book	42	71

woman. Recall that Doris is the woman who learned to set her daughters' hair by observing stylists at her salon.

> **Me:** Tell me something. You've just told me that we value hair a lot and color less, in the sense that if hair is "good" you are placed in the White category. What happens in the case of someone who is very light but has "bad hair"?
>
> **Doris:** No, that one is on the black side because it's just that the *jabao* in Santo Domingo is White with bad hair, really tight hair. Well, that one is on the Black side because I myself say, "If my daughters had turned out *jabá*, it's better that they would have turned out brown, with their hair like that, *trigueño*." Because I didn't want my daughters to come out White with tight hair. No. For me, better *trigueña*. They're prettier. I've always said that. All three of my children are *trigueños*.
>
> **Me:** Why? What makes them prettier?
>
> **Doris:** Well, their color. Because for me, someone White, an ugly, ordinary White person, looks worse than a brown one, a Black one who doesn't, who really is Black. If they're White like that, the way there are some white, those White people, white, white, fine, they look exaggeratedly White like that. They don't look good. To me, they're not attractive. I prefer someone of color.

Of color, but not black. The aesthetic model is the body that is a "middle term" as my respondents named it, neither too white nor too black. In other words, the mestiza/mulatta, the embodiment of the Taina/o icon displayed at the Dominican museum, in the Dominican beauty pageant, in the Dominican media, and in Dominican history books.

The question remains, however: How do contemporary Dominican women and girls look at pictures of African American women who look like them and yet distance themselves from this similarity? What is taking place when women at the salon identify with the women in the White hairstyles book, and distance themselves adamantly from those in the African American hairstyles book? Are they doing psychic violence to themselves? I argue that they are not, to the extent that Dominicans identify as "Hispanic" and consider those who evidence a degree of mixture to "look Hispanic." Thus, if one were to be guided simply by the fact that Dominican women at Salon Lamadas preferred to look at the White hairstyles book, it could easily be concluded that Dominican women prefer "White" looks. See table 1, which records the preference for images selected from the "White" book, and the concomitant rejection of images from the "Black" book.

Table 2 Perceived Ethnicity/Race and Perceived Prettiness

Attributes	Described as "Hispanic"		Described as Non-Hispanic "White"	Described as Non-Hispanic "Black"
	White Book	Black Book		
Prettiest	92%	100%	8%	—
Least Pretty	71%	83%	29%	17%

However, the symbolic and literal binding of the images into one of two choices—Black or White—reflects the U.S. dichotomization of race. There are no "Latina" or "Hispanic" hairstyle books. Once the images are considered outside of the context of their bindings, however, as they were by Salon Lamadas' clients during the photo elicitation interviews, it becomes clear once again that the preference is not for U.S. whiteness, but for "Hispanic" or mixed looks. In other words, it is neither the White book nor the Black book *per se* that Salon Lamadas' clients prefer or reject. It is the images contained in each book that they consider to approximate or not approximate a "Hispanic" ideal, an ideal dually defined as containing elements from both blackness and whiteness where Dominicans are concerned, and, more generally, as indicating *mestizaje* (see table 2). Thus, nearly all of the women selected as attractive from the "White" book, and 100 percent of the women selected as attractive from the "Black" book were also thought to look Hispanic. And while neither of the two women from the "Black" book who were considered to be unequivocally Black were considered among the prettiest, only one of the two White women considered unequivocally non-Hispanic was among the prettiest. None of the top three choices as the prettiest of the women was perceived to be a White Anglo (see fig. 1). The top choice was considered unequivocally Latina, while the second and third choices were "probably" Latina and "possibly Latina, possibly Black" respectively.

Again, although Anglo White women were not considered prettiest, they were also less likely to be categorized as "least pretty." The top three choices for "least pretty" all were perceived as closer to blackness and further from Latina-ness (fig. 2). What's more, those perceived to be whiter Latinas were more heavily represented among the top nine prettiest women. Most interesting, however, was the assessment of the appearance of the woman selected both as most Latina-looking and prettiest.

The top choice in both the "Looks Hispanic" and "Prettiest" categories

Figure 4. "Looks Dominican."

is almost stereotypically Latina. Clara Rodríguez has noted the media representation of "Latin looks" in the United States consists of skin that is "slightly tan, with dark hair and eyes" (1997, 1) a reasonable description of the top choice in this study. That said, it is important to note that half of the twenty women my respondents perceived to look Hispanic were drawn from the African American hairstyles book and had features that the respondents considered to connote a degree of ancestral blackness. Further, it was also those women that my respondents selected as looking "typically" Dominican (fig. 4). "Looking Dominican" as noted above, evidently means having visible African features. Thus, one discerns who is simply "black" and who is "Dominican" not only by signs of mixture—lighter skin, looser hair, thinner features—but by reference to hair culture, because, as Lamadas client Paulina explained, "Black women are confusing, but the hair lets you know."

Conclusion

> Cause with a natural
> there is no natural place
> for us to congregate
> to mull over
> our mutual discontent
> Beauty shops
> could have been
> a hell-of-a-place
> to ferment
> a . . . . revolution.
> —"Among the Things That Use to Be"

In stretching the bounds of whiteness in the United States to accommodate their own definition and understanding of it, Dominican women's hair culture stands in sharp contrast to African American hair culture. When Chucha notes that the job of the Dominican hair stylist is to "adopt White products to our hair," she is pointing to precisely that alternative understanding of whiteness. African Americans, by contrast, have developed their own unique system of hair care and hair care products—at times in opposition to, at times parallel to, and at times simply oblivious of the Anglo somatic norm image. For Hoetink (1967) it is "illogical" that African Americans "despite [their] adoption of the whole [White] preference pattern, nevertheless place [themselves] at the top of the [aesthetic] preferences list" as a study of African American's aesthetic preferences in St. Louis found (160). What Hoetink overlooks, and what therefore makes African American's self-valuation logical in the context of White supremacy, is that segregation forced African Americans to create their own social, economic, and aesthetic spaces. Straightening their hair, for example, is not necessarily a "White wish" on the part of African Americans. Rather, as Mercer (1994) points out, it is often a means to an explicitly "Black" hairstyle. Certain sculpted hairstyles require chemically processed hair for their construction. The explicit artificiality of hair sculpting stands in sharp contrast to naturalness in the European model, indicated not only by "hair that moves," but by "natural" styles such as Afros and dreadlocks.

In a recent video documentary featuring the African American millionaire and beauty products entrepreneur Madame C.J. Walker, several former Walker agents and customers emphasized that Black women cared for their hair with Walker products and methods, not in order to look White, but "to be beautiful" (Nelson 1987). They repeatedly stressed African American women's desire to be pretty in their own right, noting that Walker didn't sell "straighteners" or "relaxers," and that she emphatically disallowed the use of those words in her advertisements and sales pitches (Rooks 1996). The question for Dominican women is whether it is possible similarly to engage in beauty practice outside of the patriarchal imperatives of blanqueamiento.

Given that contemporary Dominican beauty practices require alteration, consumption, and production of ephemeral capitalist goods and services; expenditure of limited financial and temporal resources; and denigration of blackness, can beauty be empowering? Individual women do empower themselves through beauty. In the context of White supremacist and heteronormative patriarchy, beauty is a form of cultural capital that can be exchanged for symbolic and economic capital (Bourdieau 1984). But can Dominican women as a political group, as a social category, be empowered by beauty regimes? In a word, the answer is no. For beauty regimes require ugliness to reside somewhere, and that somewhere is in other women, usually women defined as Black. Who is Black in the Dominican context of New York City is mediated by the historic relationship between Haiti and the Dominican Republic, the current relationship between Dominicans and African Americans, and the continually mutual constituitiveness of beauty and race semiotic systems. Racial identity is enacted through racialized reproduction practices and beauty practices. Beauty is a scale, a continuum of some kind, whether hierarchical or linear. The absence of beauty, culminating in ugliness, carries the threat of derision, expulsion, and even violence.

And yet, while beauty regimes are not empowering, the community that is developed around beauty practices often is. Small revolutions ferment in the beauty shop daily when Dominican women confront oppressive conditions generated by government offices, hospitals, schools, employers, husbands, and lovers, with the support and assistance of their beauty shop community and kin. This is the paradox of Dominican women's beauty culture.

....

Ginetta E. B. Candelario is professor of sociology, Latin American and Latin@ studies, and the study of women and gender at Smith College. Since 2017, she has been the editor of *Meridians*. Her research interests include Dominican history and society, with a focus on national identity formation, feminism, and women's history; Blackness in the Americas; Latin American, Caribbean, and Latina feminisms; Latina/o communities (particularly Cuban, Dominican, and Puerto Rican); U.S. beauty culture; and museum studies.

Notes

Originally published in *Meridians* vol. 1, no. 1, 2000.
The research for this article was funded by a Rockefeller Fellowship at the Dominican Studies Institute of the City College of New York and by a Latino Studies Predoctoral Fellowship at the Smithsonian Institute.

1   Dominican population data are taken from Duany 1994. Information on number of salons is taken from the 1992 Economic Census, and geographic dispersal of salons is derived from the yahoo.maps website.

2   Proper names of businesses and of individuals interviewed have been changed
     in the interests of confidentiality.
3   All interview excerpts have been translated from Spanish by the author.
4   The term *hispano* (Hispanic) almost universally was used interchangeably with
     Latino. It was the more prevalent term, however, and will be used here when
     paraphrasing or quoting others. *Latina/o* will be used as the author's
     descriptive.

Works Cited

Alix, Juan Antonio. 1966. *Décimas inéditas*. With a prologue by Emilio Rodríguez
    Demorizi. Santo Domingo: Impresora Moreno.
Bourdieu, Pierre. 1984. *Distinction: A Social Critique of the Judgement of Taste*. Cambridge,
    Mass.: Harvard University Press.
Candelario, Ginetta E.B. 2000. "Situating Ambiguity: Dominican Identity Forma-
    tions." Ph.D. Diss., City University of New York Graduate Center.
Cary, Lorene. 1991. *Black Ice*. New York: Alfred A. Knopf.
Coleman, Calmetta Y. 1995. "Style Over Substance: Power of a Good Perm Brings Us
    Together." *Wall Street Journal*, 22 September.
Coleman, Willi. 1983. "Among the Things That Use to Be." In *Home Girls: A Black Femi-
    nist Anthology*. Edited by Barbara Smith. New York: Kitchen Table: Women of
    Color Press.
Davis, F. James. 1991. *Who Is Black? One Nation's Definition*. University Park, Pa.: Pennsyl-
    vania University Press.
Dore-Cabral, Carlos and José Itzigsohn. 1997. "La formacion de la identidad hispana
    entre los immigrantes dominicanos en Nueva York." Paper presented at Con-
    greso Internacional: La Republica Dominicana en el Umbral del Siglo 21. 24–26
    July. Pontífica Universidad Católica Madre y Maestra, Santo Domingo, Domini-
    can Republic.
Duany, Jorge. 1994. "Quisqueya on the Hudson: The Transnational Identity of
    Dominicans in Washington Heights." New York: Dominican Studies Institute,
    City College, City University of New York.
Frankenberg, Ruth. 1993. *White Women, Race Matters: The Social Construction of Whiteness*.
    Minneapolis: University of Minnesota Press.
Furman, Frida Kerner. 1997. *Facing the Mirror: Older Women and Beauty Shop Culture*. New
    York: Routledge.
Georges, Eugenia. 1987. "New Immigrants and Political Process: Dominicans in New
    York." Occasional Papers. New York University.
———. 1992. *The Making of a Transnational Community: Migration, Development and Cul-
    tural Change in the Dominican Republic*. New York: Columbia University Press.
Gilman, Sander L. 1998. *Creating Beauty to Cure the Soul: Race and Psychology in the Shaping
    of Aesthetic Surgery*. Durham, N.C.: Duke University Press.
Goffman, Erving. 1959. *The Presentation of Self in Everyday Life*. Garden City, N.Y.:
    Doubleday.
Goodnough, Abby. 1995. "Refused a Haircut, an Official in Stamford Closes a Salon."
    New York Times. 20 March.

Gould, Stephen J. 1996. *The Mismeasure of Man.* New York: Norton.

Grasmuck, Sherri, and Patricia Pessar. 1991. *Between Two Islands: Dominican International Migration.* Berkeley: University of California Press.

Guarnizo, Luís. 1993. "One Country in Two: Dominican-Owned Firms in New York and in the Dominican Republic." Ph.D. diss. Johns Hopkins University.

Harris, Marvin. 1964. *Patterns of Race in the Americas.* New York: Walker.

Hernández, Ramona. 1989. "Notes on the Incorporation of Dominican Workers into the Labor Market of New York." *Punto 7 Review* 2, no. 1.

Hernández, Ramona, Francisco Rivera-Bátiz, and Roberto Agodini. 1995. *Dominican New Yorkers: A Socioeconomic Profile, 1990.* New York: Dominican Studies Institute, City College, City University of New York.

Hernández, Ramona, and Silvio Torres-Saillant. 1998. *The Dominican Americans.* Westport, Conn.: Greenwood Press.

Hernton, Calvin C. 1988 [1965]. *Sex and Racism in America.* New York: Grove.

Hoetink, Harry. 1985. "'Race' and Color in the Caribbean." In *Caribbean Contours.* Edited by Sidney Mintz and Sally Price. Baltimore: Johns Hopkins University Press.

———. 1967. *The Variants in Caribbean Race Relations: A Contribution to the Sociology of Segmented Societies.* London: Oxford University Press.

Howard, David. 1997. "Colouring the Nation: Race and Ethnicity in the Dominican Republic." Ph.D. diss. Jesus College, Oxford University.

King, Elizabeth. 1998. *Quinceañera : Celebrating Fifteen.* New York: Dutton.

Levitt, Peggy, and Christina Gomez. 1997. "The Intersection of Race and Gender among Dominicans in the U.S." Paper presented at the ASA Conference, Toronto, Canada, 8–13 August.

Martin, John Bartlow. 1966. *Overtaken by Events.* New York: Doubleday.

Masud-Piloto, Félix. 1996. *From Welcomed Exiles to Illegal Immigrants: Cuban Migration to the United States, 1959–1995,* Lanham, Md.: Rowman and Littlefield.

Meisenheimer, Joseph R. II. 1998. "The services industry in the 'good' versus 'bad' jobs debate." *Monthly Labor Review* (February).

Mercer, Kobena. 1994. *Welcome to the Jungle: New Positions in Black Cultural Studies,* New York: Routledge.

Montague, Ashley. 1974. *Man's Most Dangerous Myth: The Fallacy of Race.* New York: Oxford University Press.

Moreau de Saint-Méry, M.L. 1944. *A Topographical and Political Description of the Spanish Part of Santo Domingo.* Translated by C. Armando Rodríguez. Ciudad Trujillo: Editora Montalvo.

Moya Pons, Frank. 1995. *The Dominican Republic: A National History.* New York: Hispaniola.

———. 1996. "Dominican National Identity: A Historical Perspective." *Punto 7 Review.* 3, no. 1.

Nelson, Stanley, director. 1987. *Two Dollars and A Dream.* New York: Filmakers Library.

New York City Department of City Planning, 1995. *The Newest New Yorkers, 1990–1994.* New York: New York City Department of City Planning.

Oboler, Suzanne. 1995. *Ethnic Labels, Latino Lives: Identity and the Politics of (Re)Presentation in the United States.* Minneapolis: University of Minnesota Press.

Omi, Michael, and Howard Winant. 1994. *Racial Formation in the United States: From the 1960s to the 1980s*. New York: Routledge.

Pessar, Patricia. 1987a. "The Dominicans: Women in the Household and the Garment Industry." In *New Immigrants in New York*. Edited by Nancy Foner. New York: Columbia University Press.

———. 1987b. "The Constraints Upon and Release of Female Labor Power: The Case of Dominican Migration to the United States." In *Women, Income, and Poverty*. Edited by D. Dwyer and J. Bruce. Stanford: Stanford University Press.

Piedra, Jose. 1991. "Literary Whiteness and the Afro-Hispanic Difference." In *The Bounds of Race: Perspectives in Hegemony and Resistance*. Edited by Dominick LaCapra. Ithaca: Cornell University Press.

Peiss, Kathy. 1994. "Making Faces: The Cosmetics Industry and the Cultural Construction of Gender, 1890–1930." In *Unequal Sisters: A Multicultural Reader in U.S. Women's History*, 2nd ed. Edited by Vicki Ruiz and Ellen Carol DuBois. New York: Routledge.

Rodríguez, Clara E. 1991. *Puerto Ricans: Born in the U.S.A.* Boulder, Colo.: Westview.

———, ed. 1997. *Latin Looks: Images of Latinas and Latinos in the U.S. Media*. Boulder, Colo.: Westview.

Rooks, Noliwe M. 1996. *Hair Raising: Beauty, Culture, and African American Women*. New Brunswick, N.J.: Rutgers University Press.

Sánchez Korrol, Virginia. 1983. *From Colonia to Community: The History of Puerto Ricans in New York City, 1917–1948*. Westport, Conn.: Greenwood.

Schroder, David. 1978. *Engagement in the Mirror: Hairdressers and Their Work*. San Francisco: R & E Research Associates.

Shohat, Ella, and Robert Stam. 1994. *Unthinking Eurocentrisim: Multiculturalism and the Media*. New York: Routledge.

Sommer, Doris. 1983. *One Master for Another: Populism and Patriarchial Rhetoric in Dominican Novels*. Lanham, Md.: University Press of America.

Torres-Saillant, Silvio. 1989. "Dominicans as a New York Community: A Social Appraisal." *Punto 7 Review* 2, no. 1.

———. 1996. "The Tribulations of Blackness: Stages in Dominican Racial Identity." Unpublished manuscript.

———. 1999. "Introduction to Dominican Blackness." Dominican Studies Working Paper Series 1. Dominican Studies Institute, City College of New York.

Waldinger, Roger. 1986. *Through the Eye of the Needle*. New York: New York University Press.

Willet, Julie A. 1996. "Making Waves: Race, Gender, and the Hairdressing Industry in the Twentieth Century." Ph.D. diss., University of Missouri–Columbia.

Williams, Monte. 1999. "Flak in the Great Hair War; African-Americans vs. Dominicans, Rollers at the Ready." *New York Times*, 13 October.

Young, Robert J.C. 1995. *Colonial Desire: Hybridity in Theory, Culture and Race*. New York: Routledge.

Kum-Kum Bhavnani

....

Organic Hybridity or Commodification of Hybridity?
Comments on *Mississippi Masala*

I am an Indian woman who immigrated to London, England, with her family at the age of seven and eventually exchanged her Indian passport for a British one. In September 1991 I moved from England to Santa Barbara, California, in the United States. I am now in a relationship with John Foran—we are lifetime sexual companions—and have two children, a daughter (Cerina), who is four years old, and a son (Amal), who is two years old. I did not give birth to either of our children, and John, Cerina, Amal, and I look very different from one another in terms of hair texture and skin color, as well as in sex and height. I have my green card ("Resident Alien Status") and luxuriate in the explicitly hybrid nature of my life.

In the late 1960s and throughout the 1970s most of us involved in left political struggles in Britain behaved as if identities organized around "race," gender, nation, and sexuality were static.[1] Yet, somehow, of course, we knew they were not. I would go from my women's group, where all the women were White, and they didn't even notice I was not, to the antiracist group, where most people were also White, but where my identification as a Black woman had a particular currency, to the trades union work I was involved with, where White working-class men explicitly ran the show and would refer to me as "petal" or "flower" as well as "our colored sister." I would go from there to the Black group, where we would try to make connections across British racism, the prison system in Britain and the United

MERIDIANS · feminism, race, transnationalism   Volume 19 Supplement 2020
DOI: 10.1215/15366936-8565836 © 2000 Wesleyan University Press, now published by
Duke University Press on behalf of Smith College

States, the war in the North of Ireland, the South African struggles, and how trades unionists could support the boycott of South African goods. And there were many comrades who went from one meeting to another in this way.

I fought and fought against the racism and anti-immigrant sentiments in some arenas, the sexism in others, the anti-lesbian and anti-gay feelings in some, the nationalism and Eurocentrism in others—and all of us were continuously arguing about "class": were we born into it? could we ever remove ourselves from our class origins? how did patriarchy and capitalism work together? how did migration affect class? what would the classless society look like? Yet in doing that, and despite our experiential insistence that we were not just women, or heterosexual, or trades union members, we still organized our politics along those separate, yet seemingly equal, axes. Not because we wanted to have that separation, but because we could see no other way to "do politics." We were wrong—we did not understand that hybridity was, in fact, a binding notion for our lives.

This brief inventory shows how my personal biography and political history is one that has always prevented me from being easily placed into tidy categories: all the elements of my identity are not neatly related to each other, but, instead, act to irritate and collide with each other. My trades union sympathies were, at times, in conflict with my feminist ones, which, in turn, were in conflict with what I designated as White feminism. When I now read uni-dimensional analyses, I become uncomfortable, for these analyses seem not to be able to capture the complexity and unpredictability of the lived experiences of most people I know; often it seems that the analysts have not drawn upon their own critical imagination, or life experiences, or both.

The biography above has followed a certain logic: I mention experience and identity (as an immigrant, mother, heterosexual lifetime companion, being of South Asian Indian origin, political activist), and link that to culture and its representation, as well as to migration and power. While these are not mutually exclusive—experience and identity are inextricably linked with culture, which, in turn cannot be grasped without comprehending representation, politics and power—each provides a different lens through which to view our biographies.

In "The Study of Philosophy," Gramsci discusses the role of identity in the development of a world view. He argues that "in acquiring one's conception of the world, one always belongs to a particular grouping . . .

of . . . social elements which share the same mode of thinking and acting"
(Gramsci 1929–35, 324). He later continues: "To criticise one's own conception of the world . . . means criticism of all previous philosophy. . . .
The starting point of critical elaboration is the consciousness of what one
really is . . . as a product of the historical process to date which has depos-
ited in you an infinity of traces, without leaving an inventory" (324).
Edward Said points out that Gramsci then finished that thought by stating,
"therefore it is imperative at the outset to compile such an inventory" (Said
1979, 25). In saying this, Gramsci argues that, in order to develop resistances to undermine capitalism, the nation-state, and the bourgeois family, among others one first needs to develop lucid insights ("critical elaboration") into one's own personal commitment to those institutions. My
starting point for the description of myself was an attempt at critical elaboration and inventory, in order to examine how identity and hybridity
might provide a place from which to analyze racism and cultural politics.
No longer is it necessary to belabor the point that analyses of "race" and
racism—be they within or outside the academy—often ignore the relationship between racialized inequalities, as well as other axes of resistance
and domination including sex, gender, class, sexuality, and age. The various contributors to *All the Women Are White, All the Blacks Are Men, But Some of
Us Are Brave* (Hull et al. 1981), made that point very powerfully, as have many
other writers since then, including those in the collection *Charting the Journey* (Grewal et al. 1988), published in the United Kingdom. Many writings
which address these issues are by women and feminists, of color and not,
living all over the world.[2]

The main critique is that many of the most frequently cited writings on
"race" and ethnicity are written as if there is no differentiation between
women and men. Of course, when challenged, many cultural critics/
scholars concede the point. Yet such a concession is not adequate, for the
question has to be asked, "Why does this lack of attention to gender and
sexualized difference keep recurring?" Why is masculine heterosexuality
that is White still treated as transparent? Why are women still invisible in
some discussions and hypervisible in others? One defense to this set of
questions is to respond that, because men and women have different experiences, men who write on race matters, for example, should not presume
to speak of women's experiences in such matters. This reply is an evasion,
however, for what is being asked for is not a speaking *for* women's experiences, but an analysis of the ways in which "difference"—along lines of

class, sexuality, gender and age—has material, political, cultural, and ideological consequences for all. In addition, a response such as the above implies that some critiques are authentic, because they are presented by those who experience certain oppressions most directly. Consequently, other critiques come to be called inauthentic, because the analyst has not experienced that oppression or violation at first hand. That is, lack of experience with a particular axis of inequality may be used as a response to the question of why interconnections are not addressed. However, this type of discussion not only assumes that some analyses *are* authentic and others not, but, in addition, it misses out on identifying key elements, such as the political implications of who conducts the analysis (at times, experience is key, but at others experience is not key), why it is being conducted, and the implications of the politics of the analysis.

Another more plausible response to the question is to explain that specification of the interconnections among axes of inequality is almost impossible, given shifts in region, nation, and class. For example, it is now almost a truism to assert that racisms affect different peoples differently, in terms of ethnicity, gender, class, sexuality, and age. For example, young lesbians of African origin, when subject to racialized, sexualized, age-based, and gendered discrimination in the United States will experience that discrimination differently from the way in which young gay men of East Asian origin in the United Kingdom will experience it. And these young gay men, will, in turn, experience the discrimination differently from the way in which older White gay men in both the United States and Europe experience it. This differential racism has been nicely analyzed (Brah 1997; Hall 1978), enabling us to look more closely at the ways in which racisms, identities, and cultures interconnect.

There also appears to be a theoretical difficulty in specifying the interconnections among axes of inequality, such as gender, sexuality, "race," nation, ethnicity, and class. As Werbner and Modood (1997, 3) ask, "How are we to make sense of claims [for cultural difference] when the very concept of culture disintegrates at first touch into multiple positionings according to gender, age, class, ethnicity, and so forth?" As a consequence of this question, their edited collection focuses on cultural hybridity. To make the point explicit, I, along with many others, argue that any attempt to theorize interconnections among axes of inequalities inevitably leads to discussions of cultural hybridity.[3] (See, for example, Lowe 1996 and Perez-Torres 1998 for discussions of cultural hybridity in relation to the United

States, and also see Lipstiz 1998 for a discussion of whiteness that is very helpful.)

Situational and Organic Hybridity

Robert Young discusses the many meanings of hybridity in the historical context of British and English cultures.[4] In analyzing Bakhtin's distinction between organic and intentional hybridity in relation to linguistic developments, he quotes from Bakhtin: "It must be pointed out that . . . that while it is true the mixture of linguistic world views in organic hybrids remains mute and opaque, such unconscious hybrids have been at the same time profoundly productive historically" (Young 1995, 21).

For Bakhtin, Young argues, intentional hybridity "sets different points of view against each other in a conflictual structure," while in organic hybridity, which draws upon the unconscious as a core aspect, "the mixture merges and is fused into a new language" (22, 21). Although Bakhtin discusses hybridity specifically in relation to linguistic development, I draw on his work to reflect on cultural hybridity, or hybrid identities. Thus, I suggest that hybridity be analysed as either *situational* or *organic* rather than as intentional or organic. In so doing, I deliberately shift the focus away from an opposition between intentionality and the unconscious, for all hybrid identities are always and already composed of both.

Situational hybridity occurs when elements of identity and culture are present such that each element remains as a discrete and distinct unit, although the elements are not necessarily oppositional or in a conflictual relationship with each other. That is, the elements/axes of identity simply cut across each other and seem not to be dramatically changed or challenged by the presence of other elements. Examples of situational hybridity are often based on consumption: of clothing, jewelery, foods, and music, similar to the "saris, steel bands and samosas" approach to multiculturalism which was to be found in Britain in the 1970s (see, e.g., Bhavnani and Bhavnani 1985). Situational hybridity usually sidesteps and masks political discourses. Thus, when it is argued that cultural hybridity is merely a commodification and essentialization of identity, I see that argument as referring to a particular type of situational hybridity. The qualification "particular type" is key, because neither commodification nor appropriation adequately captures some of the nuances within situational hybridity. That is, situational hybridity is not always an intrinsically conservative move.

Situational hybridity is not simply to be despised—for practices that may be categorized as examples of situational hybridity are an important means by which we, for example, enjoy foods, clothes, and music otherwise unavailable to us. Yet the limitation of situational hybridity is that it often implies essentialist understandings of culture—namely, that cultures are static and self-contained—and such practices rarely question the cultural categories on which they are based. For example, if I say, "This is Indian food, which I serve at an installation of African art, installed in a European museum, and which is loved by the lesbian community," I imply that each of these elements is discrete and distinct the others, that each is internally homogeneous and always will be so. This form of situational hybridity can also suggest that, in the last instance, there is an "authentic" culture which is expressed through food, representation, institutions, and communities.[5]

When discussing culture, the notion of organic hybridity implies merged and fused identities which create a mixture in which it is difficult to specify the significance of any one individual axis of inequality. Organic hybridity can, therefore, explicitly play with genders, cultures, sexualities, nationalities, and racisms to suggest new prospects for relationships and politics. Thus, any discussion of organic hybridity demands a look at how identity, experience, and culture articulate with one another and, simultaneously, with representation, politics, and power.

Films are one means through which it is possible to discuss cultural forms and practices without the limitations of citing individual experiences which others have not shared and which often, therefore, cannot be debated. As with written texts, one can discuss the ideas within a film as well as the reception of those ideas. Finally, films arouse strong passions because "films are [often] how we talk about politics and [they] make certain things clear to us, or, if not clear, urgently discussable" (Meridians reviewer's comments). To exemplify my use of the term *organic hybridity*, I therefore shall draw upon an a feature-length film, Mississippi Masala.

Mississippi Masala
This film, released in the United States in 1992, was made on a comparatively modest budget of $7 million and was directed by Mira Nair and Sooni Taraporevala. The two have worked together on previous projects, notably *Salaam Bombay* (1988), a quasi-documentary film about young children who survive on the streets of Bombay. *Salaam Bombay* was nominated for an

Academy Award in the Foreign Films category. *Mississippi Masala,* although occasionally relying on documentary techniques to represent exile, is a fictional film that depends on excitement and energy to portray themes of "love, home [and] displacement" (Orenstein 1992, 61). A central element in the film's narrative is the exile of a South Asian Indian family from Uganda in 1972, following Idi Amin's edict to expel all "Asians" from the country. Jay Loha, a barrister who has a reputation for defending progressive Black dissidents in the law courts in Uganda, has to leave his country with his wife, Kinnu, and their five-year-old daughter, Mina, as a result of the edict. He also has to leave his best friend, Okelo, a "Black African." After Jay gives an interview to the BBC, during the course of which he says that Amin is "mad," Okelo tells Jay that he should leave the country. Jay responds:

> [Jay] "I was born here! I have always been Ugandan first, Indian sec-
>   ond . . . My countrymen have called me a traitor [because of this] . . .
>   What should I have done [in that interview?] Been a coward?"
> [Okelo] "Don't talk to me of cowards, you're scared of leaving Uganda."
> [Jay] "Where should I go? This is my *home."*
> (And Okelo replies, affectionately but firmly:)
> "Not anymore. Africa is for Africans. *Black* Africans."

implying that Jay can no longer think of himself as being African. In other words, Okelo suggests that no longer is it possible for an African identity to be a hybrid identity, although, previously, the possibility of such a hybridity was a real one. This exchange, which is referred to throughout the film, also lets the viewer know that there are unlikely to be any easy ways to read off experiences directly from identities, from cultures, or from representations.

We next see the Loha family eighteen years later. They are living in the United States, in Greenwood, Mississippi, after an initial (unseen) period of exile in Britain. Jay manages a motel in Greenwood, his wife runs a liquor store in a Black neighborhood, and a number of cousins, brothers, aunts, and uncles live nearby. Mina works at the motel—she is shown both working behind the reception desk and cleaning bathrooms—and she has African American friends.

Early in the film, Mina goes to a disco with an eligible young Indian man, after attending a cousin's wedding. She leaves, however, having become romantically interested in another man, Demetrius, whom she had met earlier through a traffic accident. Demetrius is a Black American whose family also lives in Greenwood: his father works at a small local restaurant owned by White people, his younger brother is unemployed and friendly with other young Black men in the same situation, and his aunt and grandfather also live nearby. An amorous and sexual relationship develops between Demetrius and Mina.

The affair between Mina and Demetrius is a key means through which the filmmaker explores not only love, but also her other two main themes, home and displacement: The film, says Mina Nair, "explores the notion of home for both African Americans who have a mythic notion of Africa as home, and for the Indians who lived in Africa . . . and felt Indian even though they had never lived there" (Orenstein, 1992, 61). The film success-fully shows humor, affection, irritation, and suspense in rhythmic combi-nations, as the emotions generated by this love—the interracial love between Mina and Demetrius, as well as the love within their families. There is no central White character, so racism from White people toward Demetrius and Mina is not a major issue in the film until the very end.

On Mina's twenty-fourth birthday, her relationship with Demetrius becomes a physically sexual one. They are discovered in a Biloxi motel room, where they had spent the night together, by Mina's relatives and family friends. This discovery leads to a number of discussions about the nature of interracial love and friendships in the American South, as well as about the ways in which racism and self-hatred can be expressed by one minority group toward another. At the end of the film, Jay has returned to Uganda to seek out Okelo, and Mina and Demetrius escape the suffocating parochialism of Greenwood to make a happy life together, we presume, somewhere else.

This was Mira Nair's first full-length feature film, and, as a result, a number of cultural critics and scholars have discussed the possible impact of the film on discussions about the Indian diaspora, as well as about rac-ism in the United States. Most commentators have been critical of the film, arguing that it reproduces stereotypical notions about Indians in the United States, as well as about Black people and families in the South.

There seem to be three types of reservations about the film. The first is that the central characters of the film do not engage with the political imperatives that shape, and determine at times, histories of migration, exile, and racism. Whilst I usually have sympathy with a critique that a film is refusing to engage with political issues, I suggest that this film does engage with politics by drawing on organic hybridity to hint at how individuals can negotiate different ways of living and of identification to subvert the rigid political realities of their lives. Thus, although the British (Sandhurst)-trained dictator Amin insists that South Asians cannot be Ugandan, or, indeed, African, because of their relationship to British colonialism, the fictional character Jay Loha challenges essentialist conceptions of Ugandan identity. He is a South Asian/Indian/Ugandan barrister who defends those who speak out against the Amin dictatorship. He insists that he is Ugandan and that Uganda is his only home. The organic hybridity of Jay Loha's identity, despite the pressure of politically and culturally essentialist understandings of who he is and who he can be, is a consistent theme throughout the film.

The second type of criticism of *Mississippi Masala* is of the love relationship between Demetrius and Mina. For example, bell hooks and Anuradha Dingwaney argue that Mira Nair's message is "that romantic love represents that interaction which most powerfully enables individuals to move beyond systems of domination (like nationalism, imperialism, racism, sexism) to bond despite differences (race, class, religion)" (hooks and Dingwaney 1992, 41). Similarly, Radhakrishnan suggests that the film "[revels] uncritically in the commodification of hybridity. The two young lovers walk away into the rain in a Hollywood resolution of the agonies of history" (1994, 225). Later he continues, "My point here is that individualized escapes . . . may serve an emotional need but they do not provide an understanding of the histories of India, Uganda, or the racialised South" (226).

Although many films made in the United States do refuse to question the imperatives of late capitalism, which bank on cultural hybridity to ensure a continuation of commodification and consumption, I read the film differently and consider the issues it raises to be more ambiguous than is suggested by Radhakrishnan and other critics.[6] While the commodification of ethnic hybridity in the United States is apparent through even a cursory examination of (usually women's) clothing, jewelery, and food, the strictures against racial miscegenation—including its representation on the big screen—ensure that a heterosexually explicit "hybrid" romance along the lines of Mina's and Demetrius's is not socially sanctioned. This is true despite a (limited) social rhetoric about the desirability of "rainbow relationships." To argue that the relationship between Demetrius and Mina is merely a commodification and, therefore, a co-optation of hybridity, is to ignore the valorization of cultural purity in the United States, especially as expressed in relation to ethnicity, racialization, and sexual relationships. Such an argument also ignores the politics inherent in such relationships, given that the participants constantly have to tackle issues of "race" and ethnicity with each other as well as with almost everyone else they encounter.

Radhakrishnan's assertion that a focus on the individualized escape ignores the histories of Uganda, India, and the racialized American South points to a trap which I consider the film to have avoided. Mira Nair has created individualized escapes in this context to tell about the ways in which possibility, desire, and fantasy conspire to sustain Mina and Demetrius' relationship, *in spite of* their histories of difference and distance. For me, the way in which the film ends does suggest something about the histories that Radhakrishnan mentions: it shows us that it is possible to imagine circumstances under which people are able to make history, even when those circumstances are not of our choosing.

The third type of criticism of this film focuses on the gender roles illustrated by Mina and her mother. For example, hooks and Dingwaney's reading is that Mina "is no civil-rights activist in the making" (1992, 43). They add, "She chooses a path not unlike the one her mother has chosen (i.e. the woman who stands behind her man)." This view is echoed by Sonia Shah, who argues that Mina, in particular, "is a standard Western defined beauty. . . . Although a refugee from Uganda living in Mississippi with Indian parents, she was phenomenally unconcerned with issues of race, history, culture and gender" (Shah 1994, 157).

These comments about gender roles in the film do not take into account the vast variety of ways in which gender and ethnic roles can be challenged. To argue that Mina is "no civil-rights activist in the making" or that she is "phenomenally unconcerned with issues of race, history, culture and gender" ignores the way in which Mina lives her life. That is, she goes beyond the narrow confines of the Gujarati community in Greenwood by being close to many Black people in the town, by refusing the route of arranged marriage, and by relating to her relatives and parents with both love and critique. In addition, to criticize her for "standing behind her man," ignores the enormous step she has taken to remain in an explicitly heterosexual relationship with an African American man despite the anger and racism of her family and the Gujarati community of Greenwood.

I, however, see the film as displaying a deeper set of insights, which have organic hybridity at their core. Whiteness is not at the center of this film, and the nature of the relationship between Mina and Demetrius demonstrates the intertwining of their personal and political histories. For example, Demetrius makes the following introduction to his family: "This is Mina. She's from England, India, Africa—anywhere else?" Demetrius's father asks Mina, "How come they got Indians in Africa?" leading to this exchange:

> **Mina:** "The British brought them there to build the railways."
> **Father:** "Like slaves?"
> **Mina:** "Yes, that's how my grandfather came . . . "

The attempt to establish historical links between enslavement and indentured labor, despite the different consequences of these forms of domination, could be seen as an overly simplistic way by which to move from historical particularities to cultural commonalities. That is, both Demetrius's father and Mina know that enslavement and indentured labor are not the same, but they make an experiential connection between the two. However, given the apparent cultural and class differences between the two families, such a move is not simplistic, but, rather, is a way of negotiating cultural differences into mutually comprehensible experiences and representations: they manage to link Uganda and the United States, two extremely different locations with very distinct histories and politics. In the above exchange, there is no suggestion of either group's cultural specificity being appropriated by the other. Rather, the exchange is an attempt to show how such negotiations are desired and, therefore, made possible. East is not East, West is not West, and cultural *difference*—which implies hybridity—is the means through which Demetrius's father and Mina establish links with each other. It is this active and enthusiastic engagement with difference (without always valorizing difference) that forms one facet of organic hybridity.

The film also plays with hybridity in other ways. For example, it is clear that Mina is a "free-thinking" woman, not a mere stereotype of Indian women. In the same way that the film portrays complex and contradictory identities based on racialized ethnicities, it does so as well with gender. The important thing to note here is that these organically hybrid identities are formed through the simultaneous interplay of gender with culture, migration, and nation. Vron Ware, among others, has argued that "the construction of White femininity—that is, the different ideas about what it means to be a White female—can play a pivotal role in negotiating and maintaining concepts of racial and cultural difference" (Ware 1992, 4). Just as cultural constructions of femininity, both Black and White, can maintain racial and cultural difference, however, so can it also challenge a difference which is presented as unbridgeable. So Mina is not overdetermined by her gender, her culture, her history, or her migrations, and it is this lack of overdetermination which allows for gendered/cultural exchanges such as the following, which takes place as Mina and Demetrius are driving to meet Demetrius's family:

> **Demetrius:** How long have you been in Mississippi?
> **Mina:** Three years.
> **Demetrius:** And before that?
> **Mina:** England, and before that, I was in Africa.
> **Demetrius:** Oh yeah? (with intrigued interest).
> **Mina:** Yeah. I've never been to India.
> **Demetrius:** You've never been to India? (with disbelief)
> **Mina:** (She laughs.) I'm a kind of a mixed masala.
> **Demetrius:** What's that? Kind of a religious thing?
> **Mina:** (Laughs again.) It's a bunch of hot spices.
> **Demetrius:** Hot spices?

This exchange could be read as self-exoticization ("I'm a kind of a mixed masala") on her part, and cultural ignorance and stereotyping ("What's that? Kind of a religious thing?") on his. In other words, merely as an example of situational hybridity. However, something else is going on here. For example, Demetrius laughs at himself for his assumption that religion is the defining feature of her Indian-ness, and thus lightens a possibly tense moment. They also establish a mutual concord, for, despite his initial disbelief that she had never been to India, he was able to understand that she could still be "Indian," just as he is "African," without ever having been to Africa.

In other words, the relationship between the two shows how cultural information can be exchanged and questioned without feelings of racism, intrusion, or patronization. It shows that asking for information about cultural difference need not always be racist. This is another aspect of organic hybridity, namely, that cultural exchange is a necessary part of coming to know someone else and that such exchange need not necessarily be racist in its discourse. The above dialogue is possible because the relationship between Demetrius and Mina has been developed along interconnected axes of culture, gender, race, politics, and nation. Simultaneously, their relationship is not inscribed into predictable hierarchies of race, ethnicity, gender, and class. Thus, he is a Black small-business-man who is not socially conservative; she is an Indian woman who cleans toilets, despite her father's background as a barrister and motel manager. These facets in *Mississippi Masala* represent organic hybridities; for the identities we see are deeply intertwined and often exist in unpredictable combinations.

It is an unusual film that places non-White hybridity at its center and that creates a hybridity which is organic, not situational. *Mississippi Masala* plays with identity, "race," culture, experience, and history in ways that create the possibilities of new subjectivities. Thus, even though there are moments when it seems as if the film is about to reproduce racialized, gendered, or ethnicized stereotypes, the narrative subverts such reproduction in an easy and nondidactic manner.

Along with an active engagement with difference and an ability to uncouple culture from racism, organic hybridity also has love as an essential aspect. By this, I do not mean only heterosexual love, such as between Mina and Demetrius, or, indeed, same-sex physical love, but, rather, the idea that love is a means through which people shift their identities and consciously become hybrid subjects.[7] For example, when Mina and Demetrius's romance has been "discovered" by her family, and Mina is fighting with her parents about her love for Demetrius, her mother says, "Who is he? What do you know about this family?" Mina replies, in exasperation and righteous anger, "This is America, Ma—no one *cares*."

What Mina is asserting here is that she knows what having an American identity means and that her mother does not comprehend this at all. Mina's identification of tradition, motherhood, and family as Indian, and her setting up of these elements up in opposition to the supposedly American characteristics of modernity, individualism, and independence does grate on me and has done so every time I have watched the film. Yet, at the same time, the frustration, exasperation, and irritation expressed by both mother and daughter toward the other at particular moments in the film do speak to many people about the multiple identities and negotiations that enforced migration serves to create, especially in relation to family members. It is also evident in the exchange above that Mina and her mother have a fine love between them.

Throughout the film, it is evident that the relationship between Mina and her mother is not always about "culture clash" or "intergenerational conflict." For example, early on in the film, just before they go to a wedding, Mina's mother asks Mina to change her shoes for more appropriate ones for the occasion. This situation is loaded with possibilities of generational clashing but instead depicts affection: Mina says indulgently to her mother, as she goes to change her shoes, "The things I do for you, Ma." Tensions between mothers and daughters, as well as the love between them, have, of course, been written about extensively. This film is remarkable in showing the deep love between a mother and daughter, informed by forced migration and downward class movement, but never at risk. My reading is open to the charge of romanticism, but I would ask, when, in the very few Hollywood mainstream films about the South Asian diaspora, has a relationship between mother and daughter been portrayed as warm and loving, albeit fraught, rather than as sentimentally sugary or as oppositional and immovable?

The love between Jay and Okelo is also a theme throughout the film. It is rarely explicitly commented upon, yet, it clearly contains seeds of optimism and possibility. There is a powerful bond between the two men, whose friendship, begun in childhood, seems to have developed against all odds, including their racialized ethnicities in Uganda. In the early part of the film, Jay's determined refusal to see the conflict behind Okelo's urging that Jay leave the country because he is concerned for Jay's safety means that Okelo's statement "Africa is for Africans. Black Africans" reads as signaling his agreement with the Amin edict. The viewer does not know Okelo's true sentiments, but it is possible to imagine that, out of love for his frightened and bewildered friend, Okelo says the unsayable. Asking Jay to leave Uganda does destroy their friendship, for Jay interprets it as Okelo's agreement with Amin's edict. Yet, Okelo's insistence that Jay is not African leads to Jay's eventual realization that he has to leave Uganda. This, we are led to understand, probably saves Jay's own life and that of his family. In other words, Okelo's love for Jay was such that he sacrificed their friendship in order to save Jay's life. Jay's stubbornness in refusing to say goodbye to Okelo on the point of his departure from Uganda is later seen to be misguided, and he is loaded with regret when he finally does return to Uganda in 1991. This incident underlines the fact that in a relationship built on organic hybridity, such as the one between Jay and Okelo, love must be present.

Another especially fascinating element in the film is the contrast between Jay's friendship and love for Okelo and his outrage at his daughter's love for Demetrius. This is the standard racist outrage with which we are, sadly, all too familiar—"People stick to their own kind, Mina," Jay says. But his adding, "I know that now" also implies that there was a time when he had thought there were other possibilities. It is Jay's experience of being exiled that has driven him to perceiving ethnicity and "race" (along with their associated histories of colonization and migration) as transhistorical essences, not as terms constituted temporally and spatially. The viewer also understands that the very opposite could have happened. *Mississippi Masala* is a film about people whose biographies, subjectivities, and politics are complex and three-dimensional. This implies an unpredictability in their response to their shifting histories.

Mississippi Masala suggests ways in which people can develop relationships across lines of ethnicity, "race," class, gender, and nationality. The key aspect of such relationships is that they engage forms of organic hybridity. Organic hybridity permits identities to be challenged and to shift, for it is a form of hybridity that engages with difference, that permits an uncoupling of culture from "race" and that treats love with respect, as a complex phenomenon. It is organic hybridity that permits us to imagine new subjectivities—such as those represented in *Mississippi Masala*—and it is these new subjectivities that are eventually so crucial in countering racisms.

....

Kum-Kum Bhavnani is Distinguished Professor of Sociology, Feminist Studies, and Global and International Studies at the University of California, Santa Barbara. Her scholarly interests include globalization, women and international development, cultural studies, and critical social psychology. In addition to several books and articles, she has completed several feature documentary films on environmental justice, leisure pastimes, and science learning among Buddhist monastics.

Notes

Originally published in *Meridians* vol. 1, no. 1, 2000.
Early versions of this paper were presented at Columbia University in 1994 as an Opening Keynote at the 1997 Vienna *Countering Racism* conference, and published as a chapter "Rassismen Entgegnen: Quervebindungen und Hubridität" in Brigitte Kossek 1999 (ed.) *Rassismen. Konstruktionen. Interventionen.* Argumentverlag: Hamburg. The arguments were developed further at the University of Waikato

and Smith College in May and September 1999. I am grateful to the anonymous reviewers from the Smith-Wesleyan Editorial Group for their reading of that earlier chapter and for their help in reworking this essay.

1   I use quotation marks to denote that, while "race" is a crucially central category in understanding social formations, it simultaneously has no validity as a biological concept: "Racism is a system of domination and subordination based on spurious biological notions that human beings can be fixed into racially discrete groups. Racism is identified as a 'natural' process, and is seen to be a logical consequence of the differentiation of human beings into 'races'. Given that there is no sound evidence from the natural and biological sciences to justify the assumption that the human species can be divided up into separate 'races', both 'race' and racism come to be economic, political, ideological and social expressions; in other words, 'race' . . . is created, reproduced and challenged through economic, political and ideological institutions" (Bhavnani 1997, 28).

2   I shall use the phrase "of color," although it is a phrase with which I feel uncomfortable, for it implies that others have no color.

3   Some have suggested to me that the use of *hybridity* resonates with a biologistic approach to culture, given that the term has its origins in botany and plant husbandry. I have been struck by that comment and am still struggling to find another word to capture adequately the many meanings that *hybridity* currently connotes.

4   I am grateful to Rafael Perez-Torres for directing me to this source.

5   I am, of course, aware that the above description does also convey some cultural information which is comprehensible to many. Hence my argument that situational hybridity is not merely to be rejected. I also suggest that situational and organic hybridity have roots that intertwine them with each other; that is, that they are also interconnected, an argument I cannot develop in this paper.

6   There are examples of situational hybridity, but I suggest that they are questioned and shown as being untrue for the Loha family. For example, early in the film, as the family is leaving Uganda, the airport bus on which they travel is stopped by soldiers, and Kinnu Loha is ordered out. The soldiers kick open her suitcase, laugh at the photograph of Jay in his barrister's robes that she clutches, and ask her to turn on the tape recorder she holds. The tune it plays has the following words:

Mayra joota hai Japaani,	(My shoes are Japanese)
Yai patloon, Inglistani,	(These trousers are English)
Mayra lal topi Rooski,	(My red hat is Russian)
Phir mai dil hai Hindustani.	(Yet my heart is Hindu).

Clearly, the song is included in the film to demonstrate the workings of what I have termed situational hybridity. However, the context in which this song is played—the displacement and forced exile of South Asians from Uganda—indicates to the viewer that South Asians were seen as a group with a cosmopolitan lifestyle, but that, their claims to be international, or hybrid, never truly shifted the heart of their Hindu identity. I do not know if this generalization about South Asians in Uganda is accurate, yet it is clear in the film that such a distancing between lifestyle and identity is not wholly true for the Loha family, who do claim a Ugandan identity.

7 I am aware that in saying this I am in danger of being read as advancing a romantic, liberal framework to resolve grand political questions. However, in order to discuss why and how identities and practices shift at an interpersonal level, I consider it necessary to discuss love, although not in the sense of the bourgeois romantic emotion that organizes most Hollywood films.

Works Cited

Bhavnani, Kum-Kum. 1997. "Women's Studies and Its Interconnection with 'race,' ethnicity, and sexuality." In *Introducing Women's Studies*, 2d ed. Edited by Diane Richardson and Victoria Robinson. London: Macmillan.

Bhavnani, Kum-Kum, and Reena Bhavnani. 1985. "Racism and Resistance in Britain." In *A Socialist Anatomy of Britain*. Edited by David Coates, Gordon Johnstone and Ray Bush. Cambridge: Polity.

Brah, Avtar. 1992. "Difference, Diversity and Differentiation." In *"Race": Culture and Difference*. Edited by James Donald and Ali Rattansi. London: Sage.

Gramsci, Antonio. 1929–35. "The Study of Philosophy." In *Selections From Prison Notebooks* by Antonio Gramsci. Edited by Q. Hoare and G. Nowell Smith. London: Lawrence and Wishart.

Grewal, Shabnum, Jackie Kay, Liliane Landor, Gail Lewis, and Pratibha Parmar, eds. 1988. *Charting the Journey Writings by Black and Third World Women*. London: Sheba Feminist Publishers.

Hall, Stuart. 1978. "Racism and Reaction," a talk given on the BBC. In *Five Views of Multiracial Britain*. London: British Broadcasting Corporation and the Commission for Racial Equality.

hooks, bell, and Anuradha Dingwaney. 1992. "Sisters of the Yam: *Mississippi Masala*," Z 5 (July/August).

Hull, Gloria T., Patricia B. Scott, and Barbara Smith, eds. 1982. *All the Women Are White, All the Blacks Are Men, But Some of Us Are Brave: Black Women's Studies*. Old Westbury, N.Y.: The Feminist Press.

Lipsitz, George. 1998. *The Possessive Investment in Whiteness: How White People Profit From Identity Politics*. Philadelphia: Temple University Press.

Lowe, Lisa. 1996. *Immigrant Acts: On Asian American Cultural Politics*. Durham, N.C.: Duke University Press.

Orenstein, Peggy. 1992. "Salaam America: An Interview with Director Mira Nair" in *Mother Jones* 17 (Jan./Feb.).

Perez-Torres, Rafael. 1998. "Chicano Ethnicity, Cultural Hybridity, the Mestizo Voice." *American Literature* 70, no. 1.

Radhakrishnan, R. 1994. "Is the Ethnic 'Authentic' in the Diaspora?" In *The State of Asian America: Activism and Resistance in the 1990s*. Edited by Karin Aguilar-San Juan. Boston: South End.

Said, Edward. 1979. *Orientalism*. New York: Vintage.

Shah, Sonia. 1994. "Presenting the Blue Goddess: Towards a National, Pan-Asian Feminist Agenda." In *The State of Asian America: Activism and Resistance in the 1990s*. Edited by Karin Aguilar-San Juan. Boston: South End.

Ware, Vron 1992. *Beyond the Pale: White Women, Racism and History*. London: Verso.

Werbner, Pnina, and Tariq Modood, eds. 1997. *Debating Cultural Hybridity: Multi-Cultural Identities and the Politics of Anti-Racism*. London: Zed.

Young, Robert. 1995. *Colonial Desire*. London: Routledge.

Paula J. Giddings

....

Missing in Action
Ida B. Wells, the NAACP, and the Historical Record

Abstract: In 1930, Ida B. Wells-Barnett was surprised and disappointed to find that, despite her pioneering role as an anti-lynching activist and a founder of the NAACP, her name was not included in a contemporary Black history text by Carter G. Woodson, the "Father of Negro History." This essay inter-rogates the social and political forces, beyond conventional racism and sex-ism, that marginalized Wells-Barnett's place in history.

When Ida B. Wells-Barnett (1862–1931)[1] sat down at her long dining room table in 1928, three years before her death, to begin writing her autobiog-raphy, her place in history was hardly assured. In addition to leading the nation's first anti-lynching campaign, Wells-Barnett co-founded the National Association for the Advancement of Colored People (NAACP) and organized a Black settlement house in Chicago, the Negro Fellowship League. She established the only Black women's suffrage club extant in Illinois when women became partially enfranchised there in 1913, and subsequently ran for a senate seat in the state. Wells-Barnett was also the instrumental force behind the first national Black women's movement in the United States.

Although in recent years there has been growing attention paid to her achievements, Wells-Barnett has yet to be fully acknowledged in the canonical literature. Racism and/or sexism, in part, explain this oversight, as does the fact that scholars have only recently recognized the ways in which "difference," and the intersections of race, class, and gender

MERIDIANS · feminism, race, transnationalism   Volume 19 Supplement 2020
DOI: 10.1215/15366936-8565847 © 2001 Wesleyan University Press, now published by
Duke University Press on behalf of Smith College

informed Wells-Barnett's analysis of racial violence. Wells-Barnett was the first activist to link lynching to cultural attitudes about women—Black and White—and to sexuality. There remains however another unstudied factor that has affected Wells-Barnett's place in history: she was marginalized by the civil rights establishment—including those who thought her too militant and yet incorporated her insights into their own strategies without crediting her.

In January of 1930, when Wells-Barnett and her oldest daughter, Ida B. Jr., attended a Negro History Week meeting in Chicago, her worst suspicions were confirmed. The group discussed a book by Carter G. Woodson—who had inaugurated Negro History Week and was known as the "Father of Negro History"—a book in which her own anti-lynching efforts were not mentioned (Wells-Barnett 1930). Compounding this oversight was the fact that Woodson had met Wells-Barnett when he spoke before the Negro Fellowship League in 1915, the year he organized the Association for Study of Negro Life and History in Chicago (*Chicago Defender* 7 August 1915). Another founder of the Association, a Chicagoan named George Cleveland Hall, had been Wells-Barnett's physician and had delivered at least one of her four children. Wells-Barnett quickly realized that if she was going to establish her place in history, she had better chronicle her own life. Thus, Wells-Barnett became the first Black woman political activist to write a full-length autobiography.

One of the most significant reasons why the full breadth of Ida B. Wells-Barnett's impact on history has never been documented was her vexed relationship with the NAACP, the leading civil rights organization of the twentieth century. Most chroniclers have focused on Wells-Barnett's difficult personality, her "need to dominate," and her disputatious ways in explaining her tensions with the civil rights organization specifically, and with nearly every liberal leader regardless of race, sex, or place on the political spectrum (see, e.g., Thompson 1990 and McMurray 1998). The personal observation about her is accurate but should not obscure the very real ideological differences that this uncompromising activist had with many individuals and groups. Her differences with the NAACP in particular, which kept Wells-Barnett on the margins of mainstream African-American and women's history, were evident from the earliest years of that organization. Ironically, the formation of both the Negro Fellowship League, Wells-Barnett's primary base of operations, and the NAACP had the same catalyst: the 1908 riot in Springfield, Illinois.

In the summer of 1908, the city of Springfield, Illinois, was preparing for the centennial celebration of its native son, Abraham Lincoln, born just a short distance away. But in the sweltering heat of the season, the largely rural White population of Kentucky- and southern Illinois-born migrants had something other than the Great Emancipator on their minds. The city had grown taut with fear. Whites and unskilled laborers, many of them foreign-born, felt that their jobs were being threatened by the growing number of Black migrants from the South. At the same time, Whites in general had lost confidence in city officials to protect their interests. In their eyes, Springfield had grown lax with corruption. As one newspaper noted, the city had begun to rival Chicago and San Francisco in the "wickedness of its saloons, brothels and narcotics dens" (quoted in Crouthamel 1960, 164). Legislators were widely seen as tainted by the disease of urbanization in general, and by an increasing proclivity to pander to the Black vote in particular.

In a ritual only unfamiliar because of its northern location, Springfield melted down in a paroxysm of violence in mid-August. An accusation by Nellie Hallam, a twenty-one-year-old married White woman, set off the action. Hallam said that a Black man had grabbed her by the throat in her own kitchen, and then dragged her out of the house into the garden, where he assaulted and raped her. The assailant was finally scared away, she said, by her screams and the assistance of her in-laws. An African-American by the name of George Richardson was arrested for the crime. At first Richardson was criminalized in the press, but later he was acknowledged to have never before been in trouble with the law. Although Richardson and his wife insisted that he had been at home on the day of the crime, Hallam's identification of Richardson's voice alone got him indicted, then jailed. Both Richardson and James were spirited out of town when there were signs that a mob was forming outside of the jail.

The murderous resolve of the mob that formed on August 14 was strengthened by the arrest, five weeks earlier, of Joe James, a Black vagrant from Birmingham, Alabama. James allegedly had been caught outraging a sixteen-year-old girl in her bedroom by the girl's father and James slashed him with a razor. A mob snatched James from the police and beat him to a bloody pulp before he was again taken into custody.

Egged on by a middle-aged White woman, Kate Howard, who challenged the men to protect their women, the mob of angry White men went to the jail only to find out that the prisoners were no longer there. Not to be denied, they took their frustration out first on the restaurant and car of the man who had purportedly taken James and Richardson away, then set their sights on unsuspecting Blacks throughout the city. Before the violence subsided, at least five porters were beaten at the railroad depots, other Blacks were dragged off streetcars, Black-owned businesses were looted and destroyed, and the predominantly Black eastern end of the city was burned virtually beyond recognition. Finally, the crowd routed the shop of an elderly Black barber, Scott Burton, shot him, and dragged him through the town at the end of a rope. This was followed by the lynching of an eighty-four-year-old Black man named William Donegan, targeted because of his thirty-four-year marriage to a White woman. Donegan was taken from his own yard, where he was sleeping, and hanged from a tree right across from the State House. While he was still alive, the mob cut his throat and hacked his body with knives. Although thousands of Blacks fled the city, encouraged not to return by Whites who refused to sell them food and other staples, only the presence of nearly four thousand militia, called in by the governor, prevented further violence. In the end, two more Blacks and four Whites were killed, all of them bystanders, and $150,000 to $200,000 worth of property was destroyed (Crouthamel 1960, 173).

One hundred-fifty suspected mob leaders were arrested, including Kate Howard, one of three rioters thought to be directly connected to the lynching. The other two were a Russian Jew, Abe Raymer, and an unemployed Irishman, Ernest "Slim" Sullivan. She alone, however, was found guilty but avoided her sentence by ingesting poison on the way to her prison cell. George Richardson, the purported attacker of Hallam, was eventually exonerated. Two weeks after the riot, Hallam signed a statement that said that neither Richardson, nor any other Black man, was responsible for her injuries. The assailant, she admitted, was a White man whose identity she would not disclose. Nevertheless, Springfield Whites, who were also involved in the mayhem, including its "best citizens," remained unrepentant about the city's actions.

Several daily papers had called Wells-Barnett to ask what she was going to do in response to the lynching of Black men "under the shadow of Abraham Lincoln's tomb," as she put it (Wells-Barnett 1970). But after sixteen years of activism she had made enough enemies among the Black leadership—in Chicago as well as outside, including the powerful accommodationist Booker T. Washington—to be obstructed from the usual venues for large protests. In this period, the large Chicago churches like

Bethel, Quinn, and Institutional were loathe to permit protest meetings held by insurgents, and especially Wells-Barnett.

In the end, she did write an article about the mob action that elicited praise from the Black Chicago newspaper, the *Broad Ax*, for the consistency of her and her husband's "agitation" over the years (Wells-Barnett 1908). Still, her inability to mobilize a broader response through an effective organization gave Wells-Barnett a "feeling of impotency," as she wrote years later (Wells-Barnett 1970, 229). When she expressed her frustrations before her Sunday school class at Grace Presbyterian Church, several of the young men asked what could be done about the situation. Three out of the thirty present accepted her invitation to come to her house to discuss it further. That meeting was the beginning of what became known as the Negro Fellowsip League.

The riot in the Illinois capital also had alerted a group of White liberals, many of them socialists, whose ties to traditions of progressive reform had earned them the moniker of neo-abolitionist. Among them was William English Walling, born of a wealthy former slaveholding family in Kentucky, who wrote about Springfield in a popular national publication called the *Independent*. In an article entitled "Race War in the North," he challenged liberals to act decisively. "Either the spirit of the abolitionists must be revived and we must come to treat the negro on a plane of absolute political and social equality, or Southern senators Vardaman and Tillman will soon have transferred the race war to the North" (Walling 1908, 442–43). The statement was also a signal that the accommodationist policies of Tuskegee Institute head Booker T. Washington were no longer viable.

One of the article's earliest respondents was another socialist, Mary White Ovington, a Unitarian and social worker who, for the past four years, had been researching Black life for a study of Negroes in New York City (Ovington 1914). In January 1909, she, Walling, and Dr. Henry Moskovitz, a Jewish social worker in New York City, determined to launch an organization that reflected Walling's vision and invited Oswald Garrison Villard, grandson of the great abolitionist William Lloyd Garrison and publisher of the New York *Evening Post*, to join them. In an article coinciding with Lincoln's birthday in February, Villard published what became known as "The Call" for a conference in New York City for all the "believers in democracy to join in a national conference for the discussion of present evils, the voicing of protests, and the renewal of the struggle for civil and political liberty." This was the beginning of the NAACP.

Two Black women responded to the petition: Wells-Barnett and a rival of hers, Mary Church Terrell, who had been elected the first president of the National Association of Colored Women in 1896, an organization whose founding owed much to Wells-Barnett's anti-lynching campaign. Wells-Barnett was the only Black person among the six Chicagoans responding to the first summons (see Reed 1997 for information on the Chicago branch of the NAACP).

The first meeting of what became known as the National Association for the Advancement of Colored People, took place in New York City's Charity Hall on May 31 and June 1, 1909. The opening meeting was the harbinger for the new face of reform. The anthropologists, political economists, and philosophers who spoke to a mixed audience of three hundred men and women, Blacks and Whites, engaged a debate about not only civil rights but also the economic issues and scientific racism that shaped the struggle. In the afternoon, Celia Parker Woolley, a settlement house worker and Unitarian minister who had co-founded the interracial Frederick Douglass Center with Wells-Barnett in Chicago, delineated the relationship between the issues of race, women's rights, and labor—a linkage that White Progressives largely had ignored. The prominent scholar, W.E.B. Du Bois dwelled on the myriad implications, both social and political, of Black disenfranchisement and the correlation between cheap labor and racial practices and policies (Kellogg 1967, 20). The socialists, Walling and Ovington, also talked about race from economic points of view.

Wells-Barnett, whose talk was entitled, "Lynching, Our National Crime," distilled her experience of nearly two decades of activism on the issue. Although she would receive little credit for it in the NAACP, she laid out, succinctly and in deceptively simple terms, the approach that the organization would adopt years later. There were three salient facts about lynching, Wells-Barnett exhorted her audience: "First: lynching is color line murder; Second: Crimes against women is the excuse, not the cause; and Third: It is a national crime and requires a national remedy" (Wells-Barnett [1908] 1990, 261). Focusing on the example of Springfield, she examined the circumstances of 258 lynchings, including 100 in 1908, an increase of 63 from the year before. She underlined the need to address the falsity of the rape charge that provided the motive for lynching, as well as employing a strategy that acknowledged it was not a regional issue but a national one that required federal legislation. And, perhaps thinking about the role she would begin to carve out for herself as one of the nation's earliest investigative journalists, Wells-Barnett suggested that the organization "establish a bureau for the investigation and publication" of the details of lynching to arouse public opinion. Finally, as she had done since 1892, she backed up her convictions with statistical methodology that reflected the modern techniques of the newly emerging social sciences. In the past quarter of a century, Wells-Barnett pronounced, 3,284 men, women, and children had been put to death; and from 1899 to 1908, 102 Whites and 857 Blacks had been lynched (Wells-Barnett [1908] 1990, 261–62).

Before the last day of the conference ended, however, the cool, academic flavor of the previous session evaporated into a cacophony of resolution-making and the winnowing of the delegates to form an interim governing body called the Committee of Forty. The militants, like Boston editor Monroe Trotter, Wells-Barnett, and others, were particularly vigilant to keep the spirit of Tuskegee out of the deliberations. Villard and Booker T. Washington had cordial personal relations, they knew, and, although Washington had declined an invitation to come, his spies were everywhere. Wells-Barnett, acting as the liaison of the militant group, was confident that she would be named to the committee and would represent that faction. The night before she had had dinner with Du Bois and others, and presumed the deal had been made. She was wrong. On June 1, when Du Bois, the only Black on the selection subcommittee, read the names of what became known as the Founding Forty, she was not among the twelve Blacks in the group. The omission caused a commotion—Wells-Barnett described it as "bedlam" breaking out—as she huffily stormed out of the room. On the way, she passed Mary White Ovington, who had an "air of triumph and a very pleased look on her face," Wells-Barnett wrote (Wells-Barnett 1970, 325).

In a familiar, if not necessarily inaccurate, self-depiction device, Wells-Barnett described what happened next in the most self-complimentary terms. She said that John Milholland, another leader in the Association, told her that it was "unthinkable" that she, who had fought alone for twenty years while "the rest of us were following our own selfish pursuits," had been left out. Taking a frequent pose of the hurt but gracious martyr, Wells-Barnett said that evidently someone didn't want her on the list and that she was just glad that "there was going to be a committee which would try to do something in a united and systematic way, because the work was far too large for any one person" (Wells-Barnett 1970, 325). Before Wells-Barnett could leave the premises, however, the secretary of the group was dispatched to bring her back. When she returned, Du Bois came up to her to explain that he had taken her off the list because he assumed that she and her husband would be represented by Woolley, through the Frederick Douglass Center. In Wells-Barnett's place, Du Bois had put his friend, Charles E. Bentley, a Chicago activist and dentist, to represent the Niagara Movement, an organization that Du Bois had founded in 1905 and that opposed Booker Washington's policies. Wells-Barnett reported that after she reminded Du Bois that Bentley had not even "thought enough" of the occasion to attend, he was willing to put her back on the list. Wells-Barnett, whose anger "outweighed her judgement," as she later admitted, refused the offer. Subsequently, however, Milholland—who offered to resign to put Wells-Barnett in his place—and Woolley persuaded a reluctant Villard to add Wells-Barnett's name. "I came away from New York steadfast in my refusal to permit any change," Ida wrote, "but somehow before the committee sent out its letterhead they added my name to the list" (Wells-Barnett 1970, 326).

Unfortunately, there appears to be no further direct documentation that reveals what was behind this curious episode. Why would Du Bois take Wells-Barnett off of the list in favor of, of all people, Celia Woolley, a White woman who was sympathetic to Booker Washington and who had a reputation for patronizing Black women?[2] There are a number of possibilities, including Du Bois's genuine desire to get a member of the Niagara Movement on the list, and his fear that Wells-Barnett's militancy and outspokenness would offend moderates. Indeed, writing about the meeting in the June issue of *Survey Magazine*, Du Bois described an unnamed woman, undoubtedly Wells-Barnett, who "leapt to her feet and cried in passionate, almost tearful earnestness—an earnestness born of bitter experience—'They are betraying us again—these white friends of ours'" (Wells-Barnett 1909). Villard, who was in more direct control of the selection, though he never mentioned Wells-Barnett by name, had expressed his impatience with Trotter and other vociferous militants in the meeting (see, e.g., Villard 1909).

But there is also the issue, demonstrated in Du Bois's general correspondence, that the Black scholar from Great Barrington, Massachusetts had few close ties with Black women activists, save for the wives of his friends. On the other hand, as in the case of Ovington, he was closer to many of the White women reformers—a number of whom worked on his sociological studies with him. Du Bois may well have taken their advice on matters concerning women, Black and White. Perhaps Ovington's "look of triumph" could be explained in part by her satisfaction that Woolley was also a social worker and both Woolley and Bentley were fellow Unitarians. Nevertheless, although Ovington wrote that Wells-Barnett was "wisely," if illegally, reinstated, she believed that neither Wells-Barnett nor Trotter belonged in an organization like the NAACP. "They were powerful personalities," Ovington wrote, "who had gone their own ways, fitted for courageous work, but perhaps not fitted to accept the restraint of organization" (Ovington 1947).

Of course, the observation was largely accurate. Trotter and, especially, Wells-Barnett were single agents who always seemed to stir up clouds of dust when they ventured beyond their own doorsteps. But there were other issues at play than personality alone. Trotter and Wells-Barnett also were activists who believed in mobilizing people to act through pride and passion, not just through abstract theories of law or social science. Wells-Barnett, in particular, measured success by putting her ear to the ground, where she could hear the thunder of the masses. But the times were changing. The emergence of the new interracial organizations reflected the influence of a certain class of reformers who did not want to rely on grassroots activists. They considered them unpredictable and too unsophisticated to take the moderate sensibilities of the establishment into account. Wells-Barnett, who had had the wherewithal to start an anti-lynching campaign in the South virtually alone nearly two decades before—when Du Bois still was a student in Europe—certainly was not going to sit still to be lectured by wealthy White liberals, or anyone else, about the needs of the race. Her attitude could not help but marginalize her.

However, the issue was more complicated than attitude. This nascent organization promised not only a new political configuration, but a social one as well: it was the first organization where Whites and Blacks, men and women, worked side by side on such a broad-based and public level. Sexual tension under these circumstances was natural, especially in a period when even many liberals believed that the rape of White women was indeed driving the lynchings. After all, Black migrants, largely uneducated, often threatening, were a disturbing phenomenon to Blacks and Whites alike, especially the middle classes. Even Jane Addams, the famous Hull House founder, who was far ahead of many of her peers in the field of race relations, assumed that the articulated fears of southern Whites were real. In 1901 Wells-Barnett wrote an article challenging Jane Addams's views that did not question the "new crime of rape," only that lynching was not the way to deter it (Addams 1901; Wells-Barnett 1901).

That the Whites in the NAACP tended to be elites made Wells-Barnett—who, in economic terms was doing "well" but still below the "well-to-do" or "rich" categories—stick out like a sore thumb in style, if not substance. Additionally, as difficult as it might have been for some men to deal with Wells-Barnett's strident personality in all-Black settings, the very last thing they could have wanted was to be challenged by her in front of White women, particularly upper-class, educated White women, with whom they were working as colleagues for the first time. More acceptable would be the two other Black women named to the list, Maria Baldwin, an unassuming, if accomplished, school principal from Cambridge, and Mary Church Terrell, who, though independent, was a confirmed member of the elite and whose husband, Robert, was a beneficiary of Booker T. Washington's patronage. In any case she was a "backroom" negotiator, rather than a militant challenger.

The founding of the NAACP also coincided with a development in the social reform field that impacted on the perception, if not the role, of Black women. A younger generation of White reformers was working to distinguish social work from casework, to emphasize scientific inquiry, with its need for training, and to raise social work to the level of a bona fide profession.[3] By 1911 Black women were an important category of analysis in their research. In that year Ovington published *Half A Man: The Status of the Negro in New York*, in which she specifically wrote on "The Black Woman as Breadwinner." And Jane Addams, who became the first president of the Chicago Branch of the NAACP shortly thereafter, authored "Social Control," which pondered "the lack of social restraint" on the part of Black women (Addams 1901).

The good news was that these reformers criticized both attitudinal and institutional racism and focused on environmental factors as influencing behavior, not on an inherent racially-based "nature." But there was also bad news. Blacks were expected to be grateful for the attention of reformers, and often there was an odor of cultural inferiority, if not a biological one. Addams's article, for example, intimated that slavery had made Black families too dysfunctional to restrain their daughters, as immigrants did. The article was published in the NAACP organ *The Crisis*. Another publication from a member of the Chicago NAACP branch, *The Colored People of Chicago* by Louise de Koven Bowen, delineated the rise of prostitution and criminality among Blacks and advocated that Chicago grant them every opportunity *except* social equality.[4] Both women were against racism, but they were not advocates of integration. As for Ovington, she may not have objected to social equality, but she certainly had no record of practicing it with her Black female peers. That she could take on the mantle of expertise about their experience, and have her findings published more frequently in the *Crisis* than Wells-Barnett's ever would be, was a lot to bear. Wells-Barnett wrote about Ovington that, "basking in the adoration of a few college-bred Negroes," she had "made little effort to know the soul of the Black woman; and to that extent has fallen far short of helping a race which has suffered as no white woman has ever been called upon to suffer or to understand" (Wells-Barnett 1970, 328).

Wells-Barnett published an essay in the *Original Rights Magazine* in April 1910 entitled "The Northern Negro Woman's Social and Moral Condition" that made several counterpoints to the portraits drawn by White reformers. She argued that moral laxity among Black women was the exception, not the rule, and went on to extol the sacrifices many hardworking Black women made to provide for their families. It seemed strange to ask, Wells-Barnett wrote, if Black women had the "same love for husbands and children, the same ambitions for well-ordered families that white women have" (Wells-Barnett 1910, 33). Expressing this view was important because, as Wells-Barnett saw first-hand, stereotypes about Black female immorality were adversely affecting the growing numbers of Black women who were coming to the northern cities, particularly Chicago. Wells-Barnett noted, "Even the Model Lodging House announces that it will give all women accommodations except drunkards, immoral women and negro women" (quoted in Phillpott 1978, 300–01). She also indirectly criticized the tendency to compare Black women with all Whites, instead of with those of the same social class.

Wells-Barnett, however, was also making a different point from the familiar protestation of difference made by many elite Blacks regarding their poorer, often Southern-born, brothers and sisters. In the Black community, social status and, certainly, cleanliness of living, was not particular to one class. As Wells-Barnett insisted, "Many of the best men and women of the race make their living in menial service." Another aspect of the "social condition" of Black women that she wrote about was the isolation that Black women felt. She wrote, "The social as well as the industrial edict is: Only as a menial—and not always that—will you be tolerated." Often met by "the frozen stare or chilly word," the Black woman concluded that it was evident that "she was not wanted." She must be "deaf, dumb and blind to gibe, insult or hostility almost invariably displayed when she accepts public invitations" (Wells-Barnett 1910, 33). This would include, for Wells-Barnett, invitations to the NAACP councils.

Wells-Barnett missed the December 1909 meeting of the Committee of Forty, instead going to Cairo, Illinois, to deal with lynching and race on her own terms. In early November, Cairo had been the scene of the brutal lynching of William James, a Black man accused of killing a twenty-six-year-old white shopgirl whose nude body had been found. The lynching was witnessed by 10,000 citizens, including, noted the *Chicago Tribune*, 500 women who actually pulled the rope over a steel arch with electric lights from which the poor man was hung (*Chicago Tribune* 13 November 1990).

Wells-Barnett traveled there with the object of ensuring that a 1904 Illinois statute was enacted despite the reluctance of the governor. The statute dictated the removal of any sheriff whose prisoner was lynched and further required the law officer to petition for reinstatement. After negotiating through a tangle of politics—the sheriff's support was important to the upcoming gubernatorial race, and local Black leaders were apprehensive—Wells-Barnett was able to provide enough effective testimony against the sheriff to prevent his reinstatement (Wells-Barnett 1970, 309–20).

Wells-Barnett was seen as a hero in the affair, but in such a way as to make her acceptance in an organization with the dynamics of the NAACP no easier. "Ida Wells-Barnett is to be highly lauded for her courage and magnanimity, bugled the *Springfield Forum*, a Black newspaper. "She towers high above all of her male contemporaries and has more of the aggressive qualities than the average man. It belittles the men to some extent, to have a woman come forward and do the work that is naturally presumed to be that of the men, but Mrs. Barnett never shrinks nor evades, she is a heroine of her age and the nation is better off for her having lived in it—long live Mrs. Ida B. Wells-Barnett" (*Springfield Forum* 11 December 1909). The same point was reiterated by the five-year-old *Chicago Defender*, just beginning to make a real mark in the city. "If we only had men with the backbone of Mrs. Barnett, lynching would soon come to a halt," said the *Defender* in a report on Wells-Barnett's appearance before three hundred people at the Bethel Literary and Historical Club (*Chicago Defender* 1 January 1910).

One of Wells-Barnett's White male allies in the NAACP, John Milholland, told Wells-Barnett that her accomplishments in Cairo were the "most outstanding thing that had been done for the race" that year. Would she please attend the May 1910 meeting? Wells-Barnett quickly responded that she was sorry, but she had no funds to make such a trip. To this Milholland replied that the organization would pay for her expenses—quite an offer, as the organization had very few funds at the time and had hired their first paid staff member only that past January. The gesture, wrote Wells-Barnett, left her "no choice" but to attend (Wells-Barnett 1970, 327). However, Frances Blascoer, the staff member, characterized Ida's capitulation a little differently. She wrote to Isabel Eaton, a sociologist who had aided Du Bois in his Philadelphia study, "Ida Wells-Barnett has finally calmed down, and has practically accepted an invitation to come on again and speak—we to pay her expenses" (Blascoer 1910).

This was not the last triumph that Wells-Barnett would put under her belt, and such triumphs would be increasingly harder to come by. Three months after she returned from the May meeting, she heard about the case of Steve Green, an Arkansas tenant farmer, who had escaped to Chicago, after shooting, in self-defense, the owner of the land he worked on. Betrayed by an alleged friend, Green was caught by Chicago police, whose attempts to extradite him made the farmer so desperate that he tried to kill himself by ingesting matches (*Crisis* 1910; Kellogg 1967, 62; Wells-Barnett 1970, 355–56).

Wells-Barnett immediately got a lawyer to file habeas corpus proceedings, but before the petition reached the court, Green was handed over to Arkansas authorities. By the time she heard the news, the Black man was on the Illinois Central Railroad headed south. Not to be denied, Wells-Barnett had the lawyer obtain permission from the State's Attorney's office to offer a $100 reward for Green's return. In the interim, the lawyer hastily raised the reward money from "various colored men in town" and telegraphed every station along the route. Ironically, it was the new sheriff in Cairo who recaptured Green as the train stopped to prepare for ferrying across the Mississippi River. By the time the farmer was returned to Chicago, lawyers had found a flaw in the extradition papers and the judge was forced to release him, but he was still not out of danger. Learning that Chicago authorities were determined to amend the extradition papers unfavorably to Green, Wells-Barnett hid the man away in the Negro Fellowship League office, until they were able to spirit him to Canada (Wells-Barnett 1970, 337).

It was the publicity about Green that moved Joel E. Spingarn, an independently wealthy professor at Columbia University and future president of the NAACP, to first become interested in the nascent civil rights organization (Ross 1972, 21; Kellogg 1967, 62–71). Not lost on the NAACP, or on Wells-Barnett and her Fellowship League, was the fact that this was the kind of case which drew the attention and support of such people. Spingarn immediately sent the NAACP $100 toward Green's defense fund, and subsequently wrote to Villard asking if Green needed more money. Villard wrote Wells-Barnett for an update on the case and later reported her words to Spingarn. "I have received the following from Mrs. Ida Wells-Barnett, the reliable representative of the Association in Chicago of whom I spoke to you over the telephone the other day," Villard wrote (Villard 1910). He relayed the news that Green had already started for Canada but couldn't be contacted immediately because he did not know how to read or write, and the Chicagoans were afraid to inquire about him. The farmer did make it to Canada, where he was able to stay until the authorities gave up their active pursuit of the case. Subsequently, Green returned to Chicago and stayed out of sight by working at night and sleeping days at the Fellowship League. He was one Negro, Wells-Barnett concluded with an air of satisfaction, "who lives to tell the tale that he was not burned alive according to the program" (Wells-Barnett 1970, 337).

"Steve Green's Story" was the prominent headline in the inaugural issue in November of the NAACP's official organ, the *Crisis*, edited by W.E.B. Du Bois. Although the short article mentioned the fact that Green had "lawyers" who helped him, there was no indication of the role that the Black community of Chicago—particularly one of the NAACP's own, Wells-Barnett—played in saving his life (*Crisis* 1910). That the *Chicago Defender*, characterizing her as "that watchdog of human life and liberty," credited her with being the one who had brought the attention of the case to the lawyers, didn't seem to count for much for Du Bois (*Chicago Defender* 27 August 1910). But then, Wells-Barnett did not mention the NAACP, or any of the other participants, in her own two-page account of the Green case in her autobiography. Nevertheless, the pattern of what must have been conscious exclusion did not end with the Green case. The attitude even extended to the "What to Read" list printed in that same November 1910 issue of the *Crisis*. Although Wells-Barnett recently had published her article on Northern Black women in a mainstream publication, it was not listed among the other articles selected. However, several of Du Bois's articles, as well as three by Mary White Ovington, found their way onto the list.

When a NAACP meeting was held in Chicago subsequent to the Green affair, Wells-Barnett wrote despairingly to Joel Spingarn that she had been excluded from it. She even had trouble finding out what had occurred. "Both Mr. Villard and Prof. Du Bois gave me the impression that they rather feared some interference from me in the Chicago arrangements," she wrote Spingarn (Wells-Barnett 1911). "They also gave me very clearly to understand at the executive meeting there in New York that I was not expected to do anything save to be a member," she continued. "Unfortunately, a few of our 'exclusives' have the same idea that Mr. Villard has, that the organization should be kept in the hands of the exclusive academic few. This same academic few," she wrote, "are perfectly willing to be identified with a movement that has Miss Jane Addams as its head in order that they may bask in the light of her reflected glory and at the same time get credit for representing the race that they ignore and withdraw themselves from on every occasion of real need. Of course I am not very popular with the academic few," Wells-Barnett concluded, "and I can not say that I look with equanimity upon their patronizing assumptions."

Despite her protest to Spingarn, Wells-Barnett did not abruptly end her relations with the NAACP organization. She gave a report in April 1911 to the Negro Fellowship League about NAACP conferences she had attended in New York and Boston. And both Barnetts were on the planning committee of the April 1912 meeting in Chicago. Although it must have rankled her to read Ovington's "expert" views on lynching in the *Defender* (30 March 1912), Wells-Barnett invited the NAACP officers and delegates to the second anniversary dinner of the Negro Fellowship League, where virtually all of the leaders of the Chicago branch, including Jane Addams, were given platforms to speak (*Chicago Defender* 27 January 1912). But her direct association with the NAACP would, no doubt to the satisfaction of the "academic few," begin noticeably to diminish after the Chicago meeting. Ironically, if not purposely on the part of the association, her attenuated affiliation came at the precise time that the NAACP—urged on by a number of particularly gruesome cases in 1911—began to focus on lynching. Once anti-lynching was in the middle of their plate, the NAACP, sans Wells-Barnett, replicated her earlier strategies. In the immediate wake of a lynching in Kentucky where a Black man was tied up on an opera house stage and tickets were sold for the right to riddle him with bullets, Washington D.C. NAACP members urged President William Howard Taft to intervene. In response to subsequent lynchings, Ovington, Villard and others stressed on-site investigations, efforts to get evidence against those committing the murders, fundraising, protest meetings, and attempts to pass appropriate legislation. In 1912, an anti-lynching rally held by the NAACP in New York City attracted four hundred persons, and the association published a sixteen-page pamphlet, *Notes on Lynchings in the United States*.

Twelve years later, Mary White Ovington wrote about the early years of the NAACP for Carter G. Woodson's *Journal of Negro History*. In describing the beginning of the organization's campaign against lynching in 1911 she noted that mob violence was erroneously "represented as the action of an irate but just mob against a rapist." Ovington praised the NAACP, which, by "its publications and by its continuous propaganda on the platform and in the press has shown the falsity of this excuse." In the early part of the campaign, Ovington continued, "the best work was done by women" (Ovington 1924, 112–13). Three were mentioned for special commendation. Ida Wells-Barnett's name was found nowhere in the piece.

....

Paula J. Giddings is a former book editor and journalist, and is the author of several African American women's history texts, including *Ida: A Sword Among Lions* (2009), winner of the Los Angeles Times Book Prize for Biography. She is the Elizabeth A. Woodson 1922 Professor Emerita of Africana Studies at Smith College and served as editor of *Meridians* from 2001 to 2017. She is a member of the American Academy of Arts and Sciences.

Notes

Originally published in *Meridians* vol. 1, no. 2, 2001.

1 After June of 1895, when Ida B. Wells married Ferdinand L. Barnett, she used her full name: Ida B. Wells-Barnett. Since this article refers to a period after that date, her full name is used.

2 See *Broad Ax*, 7 July 1906, which said that Woolley believed that "colored women lack executive ability."

3 See Muncy 1991, especially chapter 3, for the discussion about the development of social work.

4 See Lasch-Quinn 1993, 16; and Phillpott 1978, 299, for the discussion of race attitudes of the White settlement house reformers.

Works Cited

Addams, Jane. 1901. "Respect for Law." *The Independent* LIII (3 January).

———. 1911. "Social Control." *The Crisis* (January).

Blascoer, Frances. 1910. Letter to Isabel Eaton, 26 March. Special Collections, Amherst College, Amherst, Massachusetts.

Crouthamel, James L. 1960. "The Springfield Race Riot of 1908." *The Journal of Negro History* 45 (July 1960): 164–81.

Chicago Defender. 1910. 1 January.

———. 1910. 27 August.

———. 1915. 7 August.

Chicago Tribune. 1909. 13 November.

Crisis. 1910. November.

de Koven Bowen, Louise. 1913. *The Colored People of Chicago. The Survey* 31, 5 (November 1): 117–20.

Du Bois, W.E.B. 1909. "Du Bois on the National Conference." *The Survey* (June 12). Quoted in Herbert Aptheker, *Documentary History of the Negro People of the United States,* Vol. 2. New York: Citadel Press.

Kellogg, Charles Flint. 1967. *The NAACP: A History of the National Association for the Advancement of Colored People.* Vol. I, 1909–1920. Baltimore: Johns Hopkins Press.

Lasch-Quinn, Elizabeth. 1993. *Black Neighbors: Race and the Limits of Reform in the American Settlement House Movement, 1890–1945.* Chapel Hill: University of North Carolina Press.

McMurry, Linda O. 1998. *To Keep the Waters Troubled: The Life of Ida B. Wells.* New York: Oxford University Press.

Muncy, Robert. 1991. *Creating a Female Dominian in American Reform, 1890–1935.* New York: Oxford University Press.

Ovington, Mary White. 1911. *Half a Man: The Status of the Negro in New York.* New York: Longmans Green.

———. 1914. "How the National Association for the Advancement of Colored People Began." New York: NAACP. Pamphlet.

———. 1924. "The National Association for the Advancement of Colored People." *Journal of Negro History* IX (April): 107–116.

———. 1947. *The Walls Came Tumbling Down.* New York: Harcourt, Brace and Co.

Phillpott, Thomas Lee. 1978. *The Slum and the Ghetto: Neighborhood Deterioration and Middle Class Reform, Chicago, 1880–1930.* New York: Oxford University Press.

Reed, Christopher Robert. 1997. *The NAACP and the Rise of Black Professional Leadership 1910–1966.* Bloomington, IN: Indiana University Press.

Ross, Joyce. 1972. *J. E. Spingarn and the Rise of the NAACP.* New York: Atheneum.

Springfield (Illinois) Forum. 1909. 11 December.

Thompson Mildred. I. 1990. *Ida B. Wells-Barnett: An Exploratory Study of an American Black Woman, 1893–1930.* Brooklyn, NY: Carlson Publishers.

Villard, Oswald Garrison. 1909. Oswald Garrison Villard to Frances Garrison, June 4. The Oswald Garrison Villard Papers. Houghton Library, Harvard University.

———. 1910. Villard to Spingarn, 19 October. Villard papers. The Oswald Garrison Villard Papers. Houghton Library, Harvard University.

Walling, William English. 1908. "Race War in the North." *The Independent* LXV (August 20).

Wells-Barnett, Ida B. 1901. "Lynching and the Excuse for It." *The Independent* LIII (May 16).

———. 1908. "Crusader Tells the Story." The Schomburg Center for Research on Black Culture; *The Broad Ax*, 22 August.

———. 1910. "The Northern Negro Woman's Social and Moral Condition." *Original Rights Magazine* (April): 35.

———. 1911. Wells to J. E. Spingarn, 21 April. Moorland Spingarn Collection, Howard University.

———. 1930. Diary of Ida B. Wells, 13 January. Ida B. Wells Papers, University of Chicago Library.

———. 1970. *Crusade for Justice: The Autobiography of Ida B. Wells.* Alfreda M. Duster, ed. Chicago: University of Chicago Press.

———. 1990. "Lynching, Our National Crime." In Mildred I. Thompson, *Ida B. Wells-Barnett: An Exploratory Study of an American Black Woman, 1893–1930.* Brooklyn, NY: Carlson Publishers.

Angela Y. Davis and Cassandra Shaylor

Race, Gender, and the Prison Industrial Complex
California and Beyond

Abstract: Despite the transnational growth of the prison industrial complex and the rapid expansion of the carceral state in the United States and beyond, violence against women in prisons has remained largely invisible. Reports from people inside prisons, amplified by activists on the outside and international human rights organizations documenting prison conditions, highlight rampant violations of human rights behind walls. The gendered nature of racism, which fuels the growth of the prison industrial complex, results in experiences of violence, including medical neglect, sexual abuse, lack of reproductive control, loss of parental rights, and the devastating effects of isolation, that manifest in particular ways in women's prisons. Advocates who are challenging conditions inside increasingly are connecting with activists across the globe and organizing their efforts to resist this violence in concert with a broader resistance to carcerality overall.

Women's Rights as Human Rights

A central achievement of the 1995 United Nations Fourth World Conference on Women in Beijing was the emphatic articulation of women's rights as human rights. In specifically identifying violence against women in both public and private life as an assault against women's human rights, the Beijing Conference helped to deepen awareness of violence against women on a global scale. Yet, even with this increasing attention, the violence linked to women's prisons remains obscured by the social invisibility of the

MERIDIANS · feminism, race, transnationalism   Volume 19 Supplement 2020
DOI: 10.1215/15366936-8565858 © 2001 Wesleyan University Press, now published by
Duke University Press on behalf of Smith College

prison. There, violence takes the form of medical neglect, sexual abuse, lack of reproductive control, loss of parental rights, denial of legal rights and remedies, the devastating effects of isolation, and, of course, arbitrary discipline.

Recent reports by international human rights organizations have begun to address the invisibility of women prisoners and to highlight the severity of the violence they experience. For example, Human Rights Watch and Amnesty International have specifically focused on the widespread problem of sexual abuse in United States' prisons. In 1999 the United Nations Special Rapporteur on Violence Against Women issued a report on her findings—which were even more disturbing than prison activists had predicted—from visits to eight women's prisons in the U.S. In general, although international human rights standards rarely have been applied within the context of the U.S., particularly in the legal arena, UN documents (such as the *International Covenant on Civil and Political Rights and the Standard Minimum Rules for the Treatment of Prisoners*) have been used productively by activists to underscore the gravity of human rights violations in women's prisons.

The Prison Industrial Complex

As prison populations have soared in the United States, the conventional assumption that increased levels of crime are the cause has been widely contested. Activists and scholars who have tried to develop more nuanced understandings of the punishment process—and especially racism's role—have deployed the concept of the "prison industrial complex" to point out that the proliferation of prisons and prisoners is more clearly linked to larger economic and political structures and ideologies than to individual criminal conduct and efforts to curb "crime." Indeed, vast numbers of corporations with global markets rely on prisons as an important source of profit and thus have acquired clandestine stakes in the continued expansion of the prison system. Because the overwhelming majority of U.S. prisoners are from racially marginalized communities, corporate stakes in an expanding apparatus of punishment necessarily rely on and promote old as well as new structures of racism.

Women especially have been hurt by these developments. Although women comprise a relatively small percentage of the entire prison population, they constitute, nevertheless, the fastest growing segment of prisoners. There are now more women in prison in the State of California alone than there were in the United States as a whole in 1970 (Currie 1998). Because race is a major factor in determining who goes to prison and who does not, the groups most rapidly increasing in number are Black, Latina, Asian-American, and indigenous women.

Globalization of capitalism has precipitated the decline of the welfare state in industrialized countries, such as the U.S. and Britain, and has brought about structural adjustment in the countries of the southern region. As social programs in the U.S. have been drastically curtailed, imprisonment has simultaneously become the most self-evident response to many of the social problems previously addressed by institutions such as Aid to Families with Dependent Children (AFDC). In other words, in the era of the disestablishment of social programs that have historically served poor communities, and at a time when affirmative action programs are being dismantled and resources for education and health are declining, imprisonment functions as the default solution. Especially for women of color, who are hardest hit by the withdrawing of social resources and their replacement with imprisonment, these draconian strategies—ever longer prison sentences for offenses that are often petty—tend to reproduce and, indeed, exacerbate the very problems they purport to solve.

There is an ironic but telling similarity between the economic impact of the prison industrial complex and that of the military industrial complex, with which it shares important structural features. Both systems simultaneously produce vast profits and social destruction. What is beneficial to the corporations, politicians, and state entities involved in these systems brings blight and death to poor and racially marginalized communities throughout the world. In the case of the prison industrial complex, the transformation of imprisoned bodies of color into consumers and/or producers of an immense range of commodities effectively transforms public funds into profit, leaving little in the way of social assistance to bolster the efforts of women and men who want to overcome barriers erected by poverty and racism. For example, when women who spend many years in prison are released, instead of jobs, housing, health care, and education, they are offered a small amount of release money, which covers little more than a bus ride and two nights in an inexpensive hotel. In the "free world," they are haunted by the stigma of imprisonment, which renders it extremely difficult for a "felon" to find a job. Thus they are inevitably tracked back into a prison system that in this era of the prison industrial complex has entirely dispensed with even a semblance of rehabilitation.

The emergence of a prison industrial complex means that whatever rehabilitative potential the prison may have previously possessed (as implied by the bizarre persistence of the term "corrections") is negated. Instead, the contemporary economics of imprisonment privilege the profitability of punishment at the expense of human education and transformation. State budgets increasingly are consumed by the costs of building and maintaining prisons, while monies dedicated to sustaining and improving communities are slashed. A glaring example of the misplaced financial investment in punishment is the decreasing state support for public education; for example, in California in 1995 the budget for prisons exceeded that for higher education.

Corporations are intimately linked to prison systems in both the public and the private sector. The trend toward privatization is only one manifestation of a growing involvement of corporations in the punishment process. While a myopic focus on private prisons in activist campaigns may tend to legitimate public prisons by default, placing this development within the context of a far-reaching prison industrial complex can enhance our understanding of the contemporary punishment industry. In the U.S., there are currently twenty-six for-profit prison corporations that operate approximately 150 facilities in twenty-eight states (Dyer 2000). The largest of these companies, Corrections Corporations of America (CCA) and Wackenhut, control 76.4% of the private prison market globally. While CCA is headquartered in Nashville, Tennessee, its largest shareholder is Sodexho Marriott, the multi-national headquartered in Paris, which provides catering services at many U.S. colleges and universities. Currently, CCA, Wackenhut and the other smaller private prison companies together bring in $1.5 to 2 billion a year (Dyer 2000).

Though private prisons represent a fairly small proportion of prisons in the U.S., the privatization model is quickly becoming the primary mode of organizing punishment in many other countries (Sudbury 2000).[1] These companies have tried to take advantage of the expanding population of women prisoners, both in the U.S. and globally. In 1996, the first private women's prison was established by CCA in Melbourne, Australia. The government of Victoria

adopted the U.S. model of privatization in which financing, design, construction, and ownership of the prison are awarded to one contractor and the government pays them back for construction over twenty years. This means that it is virtually impossible to remove the contractor because that contractor owns the prison. (George 1999, 190)

However, to understand the reach of the prison industrial complex, it is not enough to evoke the looming power of the private prison business. Of course, by definition, those companies court the state inside and outside the U.S. for the purpose of obtaining prison contracts. They thus bring punishment and profit into a menacing embrace. Still, this is only the most visible dimension of the prison industrial complex, and it should not lead us to ignore the more comprehensive corporatization that is a feature of contemporary punishment. As compared to earlier historical eras, the prison economy is no longer a small, identifiable, and containable set of markets. Many corporations, whose names are highly recognizable by "free-world" consumers, have discovered new possibilities for expansion by selling their products to correctional facilities.

In the 1990s, the variety of corporations making money from prisons is truly dizzying, ranging from Dial Soap to Famous Amos cookies, from AT&T to health-care providers. . . . In 1995 Dial Soap sold $100,000 worth of its product to the New York City jail system alone. . . . When VitaPro Foods of Montreal, Canada, contracted to supply inmates in the State of Texas with its soy-based meat substitute, the contract was worth $34 million a year. (Dyer 2000, 14)

The point here is that even if private prison companies were prohibited —an unlikely prospect, indeed—the prison industrial complex and its many strategies for profit would remain intact.

Moreover, it is not only the private prison—CCA and Wackenhut in particular—that gets reproduced along the circuits of global capital and insinuates itself into the lives of poor people in various parts of the world. Connections between corporations and public prisons, similar to those in the U.S., are currently emerging throughout the world and are being rein-forced by the contemporary idea, widely promoted by the U.S., that imprisonment is a social panacea. The most obvious effects of these ideas and practices on women can be seen in the extraordinary numbers of women arrested and imprisoned on drug charges throughout the world. The U.S.-instigated "war on drugs" has disproportionately claimed women as its victims inside the U.S., but also elsewhere in Europe, South America, the Caribbean, Asia, and Africa (Stern 1998). In what can be seen as the penal equivalent of ambulance chasing, architectural firms, construction companies, and other corporations are helping to create new women's prisons throughout the world.

Race, Gender, and the Prison Industrial Complex

Activist opposition to the prison industrial complex has insisted on an understanding of the ways racist structures and assumptions facilitate the expansion of an extremely profitable prison system, in turn helping to reinforce racist social stratification. This racism is always gendered, and imprisonment practices that are conventionally considered to be "neutral"—such as sentencing, punishment regimes, and health care—differ in relation to the ways race, gender, and sexuality intersect.[2]

The women most likely to be found in U.S. prisons are Black, Latina, Asian American, and Native American women. In 1998, one out of every 109 women in the U.S. was under the control of the criminal justice system (Greenfeld and Snell 1999). But where these women are located within the system differs according to their race: while about two thirds of women on probation are White, two thirds of women in prison are women of color. An African-American woman is eight times more likely to go to prison than a White woman; a Latina woman is four times more likely. African-American women make up the largest percentage of women in state prisons (48%) and federal detention centers (35%), even though they are only approximately 13% of the general population (Greenfeld and Snell 1999). As the population of Latinas in the U.S. grows, so does their number in prisons. In California, for example, though Latinas comprise 13% of the general population, they make up around 25% of women in prison (*Characteristics of Population in California State Prisons* 2000). Though there is no official data maintained on the numbers of Native American women in prison, numerous studies document that they are arrested at a higher rate than Whites and face discrimination at all levels of the criminal justice system (Ross 1998).

Given the way in which U.S. government statistics fail to specify racial categories other than "White," "Black," and "Hispanic" (figures regarding women who self-identify as Native American, Vietnamese, Filipina, Pacific Islander, or as from any other racially marginalized community, are consolidated into a category of "other"), it is difficult to provide precise numbers of women from these groups in prison (Greenfeld and Snell 2000). However, advocates for women prisoners report that the numbers of Asian women, including Vietnamese, Filipinas, and Pacific Islanders, are growing in women's prisons.[3]

The vast increase in the numbers of women of color in U.S. prisons has everything to do with the "war on drugs." Two African-American women serving long federal sentences on questionable drug charges—Kemba Smith and Dorothy Gaines—were pardoned by President Bill Clinton during his last days in office. In the cases of both Smith, who received a twenty-four-and-a-half year sentence, and Gaines, whose sentence was nineteen years and seven months, their sole link to drug trafficking was their involvement with men who were accused traffickers (Newsome 2000).

Considering only the federal system, between 1990 and 1996, 84% of the increase in imprisoned women (2,057) was drug-related. In the entire complex of U.S. prisons and jails, drug-related convictions are largely to blame for the fact that Black women are imprisoned at rates that are twice as high as their male counterparts and three times the rate of White women (Bush-Baskette 1999, 220). Harsh sentencing laws, such as mandatory minimums attached to drug convictions and "three strikes" laws, which can result in a life sentence for a relatively minor drug offense, have created a trap door through which too many women of color have fallen into the ranks of disposable populations.

Violence Against Women in Prison

Dorothy Gaines and Kemba Smith were fortunate, but they are only two of the women incarcerated during the Clinton years, during which more women than ever were sentenced to prison. What happens to the vast numbers of women behind walls? In the first place, contrary to international human rights standards, imprisonment means much more than just a loss of freedom. Women's prisons are located on a continuum of violence that extends from the official practices of the state to the spaces of intimate relationships. Both public and private incarnations of this violence are largely hidden from public view. But while domestic violence increasingly is an issue of concern in public life, the violence of imprisonment rarely is discussed. Prisons are places within which violence occurs on a routine and constant basis; the functioning of the prison depends upon it. The threat of violence emanating from prison hierarchies is so ubiquitous and unpredictable that some women have pointed out the striking structural similarities between the experiences of imprisonment and battering relationships (Chevigny 1999).

Though many women prisoners have indeed experienced intimate violence, the profile of "the woman prisoner" tends to imply that this victimization in the "free world" is the cause of imprisonment. Such a simplistic
causal link fails to recognize the complex set of factors related to the social
and political legitimation of violence against women, emphasizing *domestic*
violence at the expense of an understanding of *state* violence—both in the
"free world" and in the world of prison.

Violence in prison is directed at the psyche as well as the body. Increasingly, prisons in the U.S. are becoming a primary response to mental illness among poor people. The institutionalization of mentally ill people,
historically, has been used more often against women than against men.
However, for women who do not enter prison with mental problems,
extended imprisonment is sure to create them. According to Penal Reform
International,

> [l]ong term prisoners may develop mental and psychic disturbances by
> imprisonment itself and by being cut off from their families. Mental
> problems also arise and may become chronic in big prisons, where there
> is much overcrowding; where there are few activities; where prisoners
> have to stay a long time in their cells in daytime. . . . (*Making Standards
> Work* 1995, 95–96)

Thus, this organization interprets the *Standard Minimum Rules for the
Treatment of Prisoners* (SMR) as not only proscribing the incarceration of
mentally ill persons in prisons, but as also calling for compassionate care
by medical, psychological, and custodial staff of those who suffer mental
and emotional problems as a consequence of imprisonment.

Most women in prison experience some degree of depression or post-
traumatic stress disorder. Very often they are neither diagnosed nor
treated, with injurious consequences for their mental health in and out of
prison. Many women report that if they ask for counseling they are offered
psychotropic medications instead. Despite legal challenges, prison
regimes construct prisoners who suffer the effects of institutionalization
as "sick" and in need of treatment with psychotropic drugs (Kupers 2000).
Historically, this "medicalization model" has been most widely used
against women (Dobash 1986).

As technologies of imprisonment become increasingly repressive and
practices of isolation become increasingly routine, mentally ill women
often are placed in solitary confinement, which can only exacerbate their

condition. Moreover, women prisoners with significant mental illnesses frequently do not seek treatment because they fear harsh procedures (such as being placed in a "strip cell" if they say they are suicidal) and/ or over-medication with psychotropic drugs. While women who have mental health concerns are mistreated, women with serious physical conditions often are labeled mentally ill in order to preempt their complaints—sometimes with grave consequences.[4]

Medical Neglect

At the historic legislative hearings recently conducted inside California women's prisons,[5] prisoner Gloria Broxton declared: "They don't have the right to take my life because they thought I was worthless. I didn't come here to do my death sentence. I did a stupid thing, but I should not have to pay for it with my life" (*Truth to Power* 2000).[6] As Broxton's words indicate, she would probably not be dying of endometrial cancer today had she been granted earlier treatment. Violence is promoted by prison regimes, which also divest prisoners of the agency to contest them. The most salient example of this habitual violence is the lack of access to decent health care—in prison, medical neglect can result in death. Widely accepted interpretations of UN documents, such as the *Convention Against Torture, and Other Cruel, Inhuman or Degrading Treatment or Punishment,* and the *International Covenant on Civil and Political Rights* (Articles 6.1 and 7), and the *Standard Minimum Rules for the Treatment of Prisoners,* emphasize the importance of health care in prisons. "The level of health care in prison and medication should be at least equivalent to that in the outside community. It is a consequence of the government's responsibility for people deprived of their liberty and thus fully dependent on state authority" (*Making Standards Work* 1995, 71).

Women in California prisons overwhelmingly have identified lack of access to medical information and treatment as their primary concern. At the hearings on conditions in women's prisons in California, witnesses reported that they often waited months to see a doctor and weeks for pre-scriptions to be refilled. For women with heart disease, diabetes, asthma, cancer, seizures, and HIV/AIDS, such delays in medication can cause serious medical complications or premature death. For example, Sherrie Chapman, an African-American woman imprisoned at the California Institution for Women, testified about extreme delays in treatment that led to the development of a terminal condition. Chapman sought diagnosis of breast lumps for ten years and was denied access to medical care. By the time she received treatment, she was subjected to a double mastectomy, and ten months later a hysterectomy. Despite the fact that at the time of the hearings her cancer had metastasized to her head and neck, she consistently was denied adequate pain management. As she testified: "I can't just go to the doctor and ask for help without being looked at and thought of as a manipulator, a drug seeker" (Truth to Power 2000). Her requests for a compassionate release—in order to live with her mother until she dies—have been denied, and she will likely die in prison.

Tragically, all too often medical neglect in prison results in premature death. As Beverly Henry, a prisoner peer educator, testified:

> I have seen women die on my yard, women that I was very close to and women that I knew. If I could see that the whites of their eyes were as yellow as a caution sign, why couldn't somebody else? I watched a woman's waist grow from approximately 27 inches to 67 inches because her liver was cirrhoted [a sign of advanced liver failure]. She could not wear shoes, she looked nine months pregnant, and every day she asked me: "Am I gonna die here? Am I gonna die here? Do you think this is what is gonna happen to me?" And she died. And there was nothing we could do about it. And I know that something could have been done. (Truth to Power 2000)

During an eight-week period at the end of 2000, nine women did, in fact, die in the Central California Women's Facility (CCWF) in Chowchilla, California. Though these women died of a variety of illnesses, all of their deaths were in some way attributable to severe medical neglect on the part of the prison.[7] One of these women was Pamela Coffey, a forty-six-year-old African-American woman who complained of a mass on her side and swelling in her abdomen for several months but was denied medical treatment. On the night she died, she complained of extreme abdominal pain, swelling in her face and mouth, and numbness in her legs. Her roommates called for medical help, but for three hours no one came. She collapsed on the bathroom floor in her cell, and when a Medical Technical Assistant (MTA)—a guard with minimal medical training—finally arrived, he failed to examine her or to call for medical help. He left the cell, and Coffey's condition deteriorated. Her cellmates again called for help, but by the time the MTA arrived thirty minutes later, Coffey was dead. Prison staff then left her body in the cell for over an hour, further traumatizing her cellmates. Pamela Coffey's death exemplifies the severe medical neglect many women prisoners face, as well as the punishment all women are subjected to in an environment in which medical neglect is rampant. Many women are forced to watch other women deteriorate and sometimes die, and as a result must live in fear that they or someone they care about will be next.

Following the deaths, prison officials attempted to further criminalize the women who died by claiming that their deaths were attributable to illicit drug use in prison, despite the fact that there was no evidence to support such a claim. Prison administrators thus easily relied on widely circulating stereotypes of women prisoners as drug addicts—stereotypes fueled by the "war on drugs"—to demonize women who died as a result of medical neglect. Prison staff also instituted a new practice of treating the cell of a woman who called for medical help after hours as a "crime scene," which meant searching all of the women, upending the cell, and seizing property. Such a practice serves to make women fearful of calling for help because they or their cellmates will be punished. All of the women who died at CCWF were determined to have died of "natural" causes. Given that these premature deaths were preventable, they cannot be considered to be "natural." On the other hand, given that women prisoners are systematically denied appropriate health care leading to the development of serious illnesses and premature death, medical neglect and death in prison have become, sadly, all too "natural."

Women prisoners are consistently accused of malingering, and medical staff often use intimidation to dissuade them from seeking treatment. In order to complain about inadequate medical care, women must first file written grievances with the staff person with whom they have a problem. In other words, the recipient of the complaint is the only person who ostensibly can provide them with the care they need. Because there is only one doctor on each prison yard, women prisoners have told outside advocates that they rarely complain in order to avoid retaliation and the denial of treatment altogether. This process clearly violates the spirit of Rule thirty-six of the SMR, which encourages prison authorities to make confidential channels available to prisoners who decide to make complaints.[8]

Beyond the ongoing epidemic of medical neglect of individual women prisoners, prisons also operate to create and exacerbate public health crises such as Hepatitis C Virus (HCV) and HIV. Lack of treatment and callous disregard for individual women's lives is even more frightening within the context of such massive infectious epidemics. HIV rates are at least ten times higher among prisoners than among people outside of prison, and the rate is higher among women prisoners than men (DeGroot, Hammett, and Scheib 1996). HCV has reached epidemic levels in California prisons—the California Department of Corrections estimates that 40% of the prison population is infected (Steinberg 2000). Because the Department of Corrections regularly fails to test women for HCV or to provide information about prevention, advocates for women prisoners believe the numbers to be considerably higher. Not only is there a dearth of access to treatment but also to information about prevention. Women report that when they request to be tested for communicable diseases, they often do not get the results, even if they test positive. By virtue of this medical neglect, the prison promotes the spread of these diseases both inside prison and in the communities outside of prison to which women go when they are released.

Medical neglect in prison reflects and extends the lower value society places on the provision of preventative care and treatment to poor women of color outside of the prison. The abuse of women prisoners through medical neglect recapitulates a long history of inadequate healthcare for women, particularly women of color, which is often explicitly justified by sexist and racist ideologies.

Reproductive Rights

Reproductive health care in prisons is equally informed by these ideologies and often equally abysmal. Pregnant women are provided limited pre-natal care, and in several U.S. jurisdictions, women are shackled during labor (Amnesty International 2001). Women prisoners wait months, and sometimes years, to receive routine gynecological examinations that protect against the development of serious health conditions.[9] For some women, these delays, combined with a consistent failure of prison medical staff to address treatable conditions early, result in the development of serious reproductive health problems. Theresa Lopez, a young Latina in her twenties, developed and died of cervical cancer, a condition that is easily treatable in its early stages, because prison medical staff failed to provide her with basic medical treatment.[10]

In an interview with community activists recording women prisoners' oral histories, Davara Campbell described the politics of reproductive health in prisons:

> In the 1970s I was suffering severe menstrual cramps and a tilted uterus. As a young woman in the criminal justice system serving a life sentence complicated by medical female "disorders" and subject to misdiagnoses

by questionable, unprofessional, unethical medical personnel, it was recommended I have a hysterectomy. I was maybe twenty-years-old. Having
some enlightenment about genocide, I felt that the prospect of my being
able to have a family was being threatened, so I escaped from prison to
have a child. I had a son. He is now 28 years old, and I have four grandchildren who I would not have if I had given up my rights. Any imposition
upon reproductive rights is an injustice against the well-being of family
units—the rights of women, children, and grandchildren, or the promise
of the future. (Campbell 1999)

As this account highlights, gynecological and reproductive health services in prisons are inadequate at best, dangerous and life-threatening at
worst. Inside prisons, women are subject to substandard gynecological
care that sometimes results in loss of reproductive capacity or leads to premature death. Often this inadequate care amounts to practices of sterilization, as Campbell's analysis highlights. The use of sterilization as a
"solution" to women's gynecological problems resonates with racist practices that women of color in the U.S. have experienced historically.

In the contemporary efforts to justify the abolition of welfare, continu-
ing accusations of over-reproduction directed at African-American and
Latina single mothers legitimize differential claims to reproductive rights.
Racist ideologies circulating outside prisons then enable the kinds of
assaults on women's reproductive capacities inside prisons that are remi-
niscent of earlier historical eras, such as the forced sterilization of Puerto
Rican and Native American women and forced reproduction of enslaved
Black women. Thus prisons operate as sites where those reproductive
rights putatively guaranteed to women in the "free world" are often systematically ignored, especially where women of color are concerned.

Gynecology is one of the most problematic areas in prison health care.
Historical connections with racist gynecological practices continue to live
on within the prison environment. More generally, to say that imprisonment deleteriously affects the health of women is clearly a criticism of
health care in women's prisons, conditions that have been abundantly
documented by legal and human rights organizations. But it is also to raise
questions about the inertia that appears to prevent significant change in
health care conditions, even when there is acknowledgment that such
change is necessary. Why, for example, do accusations of sexual abuse
continue to hover around medical regimes in women's prisons? Why have

women prisoners complained for many decades about the difficulty of gaining access to skilled medical personnel? One of the ways to answer these questions is to look at the prison as a receptacle for obsolete practices—a site where certain practices, even when discredited in the larger society, acquire a second life.

There are children and families left behind in the "free world" on whom the imprisonment of women undoubtedly has a devastating impact. Almost 80% of women in prison have children for whom they were the primary caretakers before their imprisonment (Belknap 1996). The removal of a significant number of women of color, coupled with the alarming rates of incarceration for their male counterparts, has a disabling effect on the ability of poor communities to support families, whatever their constellation. When mothers are arrested, children are often placed in foster care and, in line with new laws, such as the Adoption and Safe Families Act of 1997, many are streamlined into adoption. All ties with birth mothers and extended families are thus systematically severed. In many instances, this process tracks children into juvenile detention centers and from there into adult prisons. For women who are reunited with their children upon release, the challenges for them are amplified by new welfare reform guidelines that prevent a former prisoner from receiving public benefits, including housing assistance. When previously imprisoned women are divested of their rights to social services—a move related to the political disenfranchisement of former prisoners in many states—they are effectively tracked back into the prison system. This is one of the modes of reproduction of the prison industrial complex.

Sexual Harassment and Abuse

The development of putatively "feminist" campaigns by prison administrators has had deleterious consequences for women in prison. The assumption that formal gender equality inevitably leads to better conditions for women is contradicted by the recent pattern of modeling the architecture, regimes and staff of women's prisons after the men's counterparts. The current tendency, for example, is to place gun towers in women's maximum-security units in order to render them equal to similar men's units. The hiring of male custodial staff, who have visual access at all times to women's cells—even when they are changing clothes—and to the showers, creates a climate that invites sexual abuse. In U.S. women's prisons, the ratio of male to female corrections staff is often two to one and sometimes three to one. Though this disproportion alone does not inevitably lead to abuse, the administration and culture of the prison creates an environment in which sexual abuse thrives.

Partly as a result of these increasingly repressive models, and partly because of the rampant sexist and racist ideologies that support and sustain women's prisons, routine sexual abuse and harassment amount to a veritable climate of terror. Among the many abuses women prisoners have identified are inappropriate pat searches (male guards pat searching and groping women), illegal strip searches (male guards observing strip searches of women), constant lewd comments and gestures, violations of their right to privacy (male guards watching women in showers and toilets), and in some instances, sexual assault and rape (UN Special Rapporteur on Violence Against Women 1999, 12–14).

According to international human rights standards, the rape of a woman in custody is an act of torture. Furthermore, violations of rights to privacy and preservation of human dignity are protected by the *International Covenant on Civil and Political Rights*. Recent studies by human rights organizations have confirmed that these international standards are routinely violated in U.S. prisons. Human Rights Watch, for example, found that sexual abuse is often related to perceived sexual orientations of prisoners (Human Rights Watch 1996, 2). Sexual abuse is also frequently linked to medical practices. Many women in California prisons have indicated that they avoid much-needed medical treatment because male doctors can force them to submit to inappropriate pelvic examinations regardless of their symptoms (Nightline 1999). However, only a small proportion of sexually harassed women report these incidents to prison authorities, not only because staff perpetrators are rarely disciplined, but also because they themselves may suffer retaliation.

Sexual harassment and abuse are also linked to the new technologies of imprisonment. For example, the rapidly proliferating "supermax units," which isolate prisoners in individual cells for twenty-three out of twenty-four hours a day, render women even more vulnerable to sexual assault and harassment. In a legal interview, Regina Johnson, a thirty-six-year-old African-American woman in the Security Housing Unit at Valley State Prison for Women in Chowchilla, California, reported being required to expose her breasts to a male guard in order to obtain necessary hygiene supplies (Johnson 1998).

"Cell extractions," a practice linked to the "supermax," involve subduing a prisoner, usually by means of restraints, and performing a strip-search before removing her from her cell. The involvement of male guards—although female guards also participate—especially imbues cell extractions with a very real potential for sexual abuse.

In the State of Arizona, the sheriff in Maricopa County has installed video cameras in the women's holding and search cells in the county jail; he broadcasts live footage of women in these cells on the internet at <www .crime.com>. Though such prurient monitoring is unacceptable in any detention setting, it is particularly disturbing in the jail setting because many of these women are pre-trial detainees who have not been found guilty of any crime and, therefore, presumably are not yet to be subjected to any form of punishment.

Policing Sexuality

Such sexual harassment of women, in the guise of being "tough on crime," illustrates the myriad ways in which prisons attempt to control women and their sexuality through sexual violence. In the sexualized environment of the prison, prison guards and staff learn not to fear sanctions for being sexually abusive to women. At the same time, women's sexuality, both inside and outside of prison, is policed and punished. A significant number of women enter the prison system as a direct result of the criminalization of sexual practices. Laws against sex work in most United States' jurisdictions result in the arrest and conviction of thousands of poor women. Sex workers most often arrested work the streets, as opposed to working in organized environments such as brothels, parlors, or escort services. Street workers, who are disproportionately women of color, are most likely to land in jail. In several states, there is now a charge of "felony prostitution" for sex workers with a known HIV-positive status, carrying a mandatory minimum sentence of four years. The criminalization of sex work creates a cycle of imprisonment: women are arrested, sentenced to jail time and often charged heavy fines and court fees, which then force them back onto the streets only to be arrested again.

Such criminalization of women's sexuality begins at a young age; girls are now the fastest growing population in the juvenile justice system. Most often these girls are arrested for "status offenses," which include truancy, underage drinking, breaking curfew, running away, and prostitution. Boys are less likely to be arrested for similar behavior, reflecting an obvious gender bias, but race determines which girls will actually end up in juvenile hall. As in the prison system, communities of color are represented disproportionately in juvenile justice systems. Almost half of girls in juvenile detention in the United States are African American and 13% are Latina. While seven out of ten cases involving White girls are dropped, only three out of ten cases involving African-American girls are dismissed (American Bar Association and National Bar Association 2001). This increasing imprisonment of girls occurs despite the fact that the juvenile crime rate, particularly violent crime, has continued to decline since 1994 (American Bar Association and National Bar Association 2001). The targeting of girls of color for imprisonment in juvenile detention is a precursor to their later entrapment in women's prisons, because a majority of women in prison first entered the prison system as girls.

The anxieties about women's sexualities that circulate outside of the prison, and often lead to women's criminalization, are exacerbated and foregrounded within the prison. Guards and staff sexualize the space of the prison through their abuse of women, and in so doing not only cast women prisoners as criminal but also as sexually available.

At least since the publication of Rose Giallombardo's *Society of Women: A Study of a Women's Prison* (1966), the most salient characteristic of women's prisons is assumed to be women's intimate and sexual involvement with each other. Yet the ideological presumption of heterosexuality is policed more systematically than in the free world. Women's prisons have rules against "homosecting"—a term used within prisons to refer to same-sex sexual practices among prisoners. The racism and sexism associated with prison regimes intersect in the construction of women of color as hyper-deviant, and the addition of hetereosexism means that lesbians of color face a triple jeopardy. A Latina lesbian couple at Valley State Prison for Women reported in a legal interview that masculine-identified prisoners are targeted for verbal harassment and sometime physical assault by male guards, while their feminine-identified partners are sexually harassed by those same guards (Mendoza and Garcia 1998). This gendered form of harassment exemplifies the ways in which gender identity is rigidly policed inside prisons.

Women's Prisons and Anti-Immigrant Campaigns

Women immigrants to the United States are policed and punished in myriad ways. Racist and xenophobic campaigns against immigrant communities, which particularly target people from Mexico and Central America (and increasingly people from Asian countries), have contributed to the criminalization of immigrants, the militarization of the U.S.-Mexico border, and the build-up of the Immigration and Naturalization Service (INS) as an arm of the prison system.

The INS has shifted its focus from providing services to immigrants seeking refuge in the U.S. to enforcement and detention of individuals labeled "illegal aliens," thus establishing itself as a significant component of the prison industrial complex. In many cases, immigrants choose to travel to the United States in order to escape economic dislocation produced by global corporations (often U.S.-headquartered) in their own countries. The profit potential of INS detention centers mirrors that of state and federal prisons both for corporations and for state institutions. For example, the INS rents space in public and private prisons, as well as county jails, often paying twice what the state government would pay for the same beds (Welch 2000).

Immigrant rights and human rights organizations have documented conditions in INS detention facilities that violate basic human rights: detention of immigrants for inordinately long periods, sometimes years; denial of basic medical treatment; and forcing immigrants to sleep on cell floors. (American Civil Liberties Union 1993; Human Rights Watch 2000). Furthermore, the INS practice of purchasing space for detainees in state systems often means that detainees are placed in state prisons and jails that already face lawsuits over poor conditions. In New Orleans Parish Prison in Louisiana, for example, women detainees are housed in a jail that is being sued for sexual abuse of women prisoners (Welch 2000).

Beyond warehousing immigrants for the INS, state and federal prisons in the U.S. independently play a significant role in criminalizing and punishing women from other countries. In federal prisons, for example, approximately 30% of prisoners are foreign nationals (Federal Bureau of Prisons 2001), many of whom are in prison for extremely long sentences as a result of the "war on drugs." Many of these women face deportation upon conclusion of their prison sentence.

As a consequence of the Illegal Immigration Reform and Immigrant Responsibility Act of 1996, immigrants who have criminal convictions have been deported systematically. This law added offenses that are considered misdemeanors in many states to the list of "Aggravated Felonies," for which immigrants face mandatory deportation. Further, the law enabled the INS to use convictions from years before to justify deportation, and it eliminated the ability of judges to review the actions of the INS. As a result of this law, many women are separated permanently from their families in the U.S. and effectively are exiled to a country of origin to which they have no ties.

In states with larger immigrant populations, prisoners in the state system often confront dilemmas produced by the intersection of xenophobia and criminalization. In California, for example, Sylvia Rodriguez was dying in prison of metastasized cancer, but if legal advocates were able to secure a compassionate release for her, she would face deportation.[11] She was sixty-seven years old and had moved to the U.S. from the Philippines when she was nine years old. She knew no one in her country of origin and was suffering from a terminal illness, but the INS would not guarantee that they would allow her to go home to be with her family before she died. In the process of fighting for her release, she died in state custody.

Legal Challenges to Women's Imprisonment

Over the past thirty years, prisoners have faced the steady erosion of laws that ostensibly protect them against the abuses of the punishment system. The Supreme Court of the United States has systematically dismantled civil rights protections for prisoners, making it virtually impossible for prisoners to demonstrate that their mistreatment violates the Eighth Amendment to the U.S. Constitution, a provision that is supposed to protect against "cruel and unusual punishment." In addition to court decisions that detrimentally impact prisoners' access to justice, the U.S. Congress has also undermined legal protections for prisoners. In 1996, with little opposition, the legislature passed the Prison Litigation Reform Act (PLRA), which creates almost insurmountable legal barriers to prisoners and their advocates seeking remedies in court.

One of the most difficult provisions of the PLRA requires a prisoner to "exhaust available administrative remedies" before seeking assistance from a court. This requirement fails to acknowledge how systematically the prison denies prisoners agency and basic human rights. Indeed, it establishes a double-bind for the women who must fulfill it. The PLRA states that if there is any procedure in place, however flawed, a prisoner must prove that she has fulfilled the requirements of that procedure. In California, for example, a woman must first file a grievance form with the person with whom she has a complaint (e.g., the guard who sexually assaulted her or the doctor on whom she relies for treatment) and then pursue the complaint up several levels of review. Many women report that they never see the complaint again after they submit it at the first level. Others have described guards tearing up the complaints in their faces. But regardless of how fruitless the process may be, and considering that it ultimately most often fails, the fact remains that a woman cannot take a complaint to court without completing the procedure.

This process encapsulates and perpetuates the abuse of women inside. As the space of the prison becomes increasingly repressive, prison litigation "reform" only acts to obscure human and legal rights violations in prison, exacerbate the suffering of women inside, and facilitate the expansion of the prison industrial complex. As a result, women in prison in the U.S., the so-called "free" world, are neither free nor able to pursue legal remedies deemed basic and necessary human rights by international standards.

Organizing for Change

Despite the significant obstacles encountered by those who want to challenge conditions of their confinement, especially through traditional legal methods, women prisoners find many ways to meaningfully organize and contest the injustices of imprisonment. In many states, women prisoners organize formal or informal peer networks that provide information and support on a wide range of issues, including health care prevention and treatment, child custody, labor conditions, and legal rights. In New York, women at Bedford Hills Correctional Facility organized a program called AIDS Counseling and Education (ACE), which provides prevention and treatment education and support to women in prison about HIV and AIDS. In California, peer educators have organized against the spread of HIV and HCV in prison and have provided health care information about a variety of medical conditions. Women prisoners have also filed individual and class action lawsuits demanding protection of their legal and human rights. In Washington, D.C., Massachusetts, and Michigan, for example, women successfully organized lawsuits challenging systemic sexual abuses in state prisons. The Legislative Hearings in October 2000 marked the first time in the history of California that proceedings were conducted inside women's prisons with prisoners serving as the primary witnesses. Approximately twenty women testified at two institutions on medical neglect, sexual assault, battered women's issues, and separation from their children and families. As a result of this testimony, two bills were introduced in the California legislature that will potentially have a far-reaching impact on health care in California prisons.

Advocates for women in prison are increasingly locating their efforts to ameliorate conditions of confinement within the frame of a broader resistance to the prison industrial complex. Human rights instruments are deployed to emphasize the systematic denial of human rights further exacerbated by the contemporary corporatization of punishment. However, the strategic goal of this work is not to create better prisons but rather to abolish prisons insofar as they function as a default solution for a vast range of social problems that need to be addressed by other institutions. It is within this context that the most far-reaching challenges are emerging to the racism that has been bolstered by the expansion of prisons. In California, for example, a number of groups work collaboratively to develop more radical approaches of working with and for women in prison. Justice Now is an organization that actively contests violence against women in prison and its connections to the prison industrial complex by training students, family members, and community members to provide direct services to women prisoners in California in conjunction with community-based education, media, and policy campaigns. The California Coalition for Women Prisoners organizes activist campaigns with and for women prisoners to raise awareness about inhumane conditions and advocate for positive changes. Legal Services for Prisoners with Children provides civil legal services to women prisoners, support to prisoner family members, and it also organizes in the communities from which prisoners come. California Prison Focus investigates and exposes human rights violations in California prisons, in particular those in Security Housing Units and supermax prisons. Critical Resistance (CR) builds national campaigns framed by analyses of the prison industrial complex that foreground the intersections of race, gender, and class. In the course of these campaigns, CR encourages people to envision social landscapes where ubiquitous state punishment will have been replaced by free education, health care, and drug rehabilitation, as well as affordable housing and jobs.

While national campaigns are rapidly advancing in the U.S., the World Conference Against Racism, Racial Discrimination, Xenophobia, and Related Intolerance provides a major opportunity to learn from and share experiences with organizations in other parts of the world. Greater emphasis must be placed on the global reach of the prison industrial complex and the further proliferation of the gendered racism it encourages. It is especially important that the punishment industry be seen as a significant component of the developing global political economy. An overarching recommendation for action thus calls for international networking among organizations that acknowledge the link between prisons and racism and that locate the important work of providing services to imprisoned women within a strong anti-corporate and anti-racist framework.

Further recommendations for action include the decriminalization of drug use and the establishment of free drug rehabilitation programs that are not tied to criminal justice agencies and procedures. This would drastically decrease the number of women in prison. In conjunction with these decarceration strategies, local and transnational campaigns to prevent the construction of new public and private prisons are also necessary. Legislation is needed that makes state and federal governments, as well as individual perpetrators, responsible for sexual abuse and harassment of women prisoners. In line with human rights standards, women's reproductive and family rights must be guaranteed. This means that civilian boards with enforcement powers should be established to review and act upon the grievances of women prisoners, especially those involving medical neglect, arbitrary discipline, and sexual abuse. In general, more widespread education and media campaigns are needed to expand and deepen awareness of the central role women's prisons play throughout the world in perpetuating misogyny, poverty, and racism.

....

Angela Y. Davis is a scholar, activist, writer, and Distinguished Professor Emerita of History of Consciousness and Feminist Studies at the University of California, Santa Cruz. Her work as an educator—both at the university level and in the larger public sphere—has always emphasized the importance of building communities of struggle for economic, racial, and gender justice. She is the author of ten books, including *Women, Race, and Class* (1981); *Are Prisons Obsolete?* (2003); *The Meaning of Freedom: And Other Difficult Dialogues* (2012); and *Freedom Is a Constant Struggle: Ferguson, Palestine, and the Foundations of a Movement* (2015). Having helped popularize the notion of a "prison industrial complex," she now urges her audiences to think seriously about the possibility of a world without prisons and to help forge a twenty-first-century abolitionist movement.

Cassandra Shaylor is an activist and attorney based in Oakland, California. She is a cofounder of both Critical Resistance and Justice Now—abolitionist organizations focused on dismantling the prison industrial complex and building safe and healthy communities. Her academic and written work has focused on the intersections of race, sexuality, gender, and punishment. Over the past ten years she has worked in development for community-based organizations and served as a fundraising and communications consultant for a range of social justice and environmental justice groups.

Notes

Originally published in *Meridians* vol. 2, no. 1, 2001.

This essay was prepared as a contribution to the report presented by the Women of Color Resource Center, Berkeley, Calif., U.S.A. to the United Nations World Conference Against Racism, Racial Discrimination, Xenophobia, and Related Intolerance, held on 31 August–7 September 2001, in Durban, South Africa.

1   Julia Sudbury offers an analysis of the growing trend toward privatization of prisons in England in particular.

2   For a discussion of intersectional analysis, see Kimberlé Crenshaw, "Mapping the Margins: Intersectionality, Identity Politics, and Violence Against Women of Color."

3   Interview with Cynthia Chander, Co-Director, Justice Now, May 25, 2001; Interview with Heidi Strupp, Legal Assistant, Legal Services for Prisoners with Children, June 1, 2001.

4   For example, Jody Fitzgerald recently died at the Central California Women's Facility. In legal interviews with staff of Legal Services for Prisoners with Children, several women prisoners testified that prison staff ignored Ms. Fitzgerald's serious physical symptoms—claiming they were "all in her head"—and sent her to a psychiatric unit where she subsequently died.

5   Legislative hearings were conducted at Valley State Prison for Women on October 11, 2000, and at California Institution for Women on October 12, 2000. Twenty women provided testimony about medical neglect, sexual abuse and harassment, separation from their children and communities, and criminalization of battered women.

6   The contributions of women prisoners to this report were drawn from a number of sources: public testimony at legislative hearings; legal interviews with attorneys at Justice Now and Legal Services for Prisoners with Children; and oral histories recorded by community activists Cynthia Chandler and Carol Kingery. Names of women prisoners are used only when they offered public testimony or when they gave explicit permission for their names to be used. Otherwise the authors have assigned pseudonyms to protect their privacy.

7   Based on extensive interviews with women prisoners, reviews of medical records, and reports of outside doctors, legal advocates at Justice Now and Legal Services for Prisoners with Children concluded that all of the deaths of women at CCWF were attributable to medical neglect in one form or another.

8   See the discussion of prisoners' complaints machinery in *Making Standards Work* 1995, 37–40.

9   Legal interviews conducted by lawyers at Justice Now and Legal Services for Prisoners with Children with hundreds of women at Valley State Prison for Women, Central California Women's Facility and California Institution for Women reveal a pattern and practice of extreme neglect of women's reproductive health in prisons.

10 Theresa Lopez was a client of Justice Now who was granted compassionate release a few days before she died.

11 Ms. Rodriquez was a client of Justice Now.

Works Cited

ABC News. 1999. *Crime & Punishment: Women in Prison: Medical Care*. Nightline. 2 November.

ACE Program. 1998. *Breaking the Walls of Silence: AIDS and Women in a New York State Maximum Security Prison*. Woodstock, NY: The Overlook Press.

American Bar Association (ABA) and National Bar Association (NBA). 2001. *Justice by Gender: The Lack of Appropriate Prevention, Diversion and Treatment Alternatives for Girls in the Juvenile Justice System*. Washington, D.C.: ABA and NBA.

American Civil Liberties Union Immigrant Rights Project (ACLU). 1993. *Justice Detained: Conditions at the Varick Street Immigration Detention Center*. New York: ACLU.

Amnesty International. 1999. *"Not Part of My Sentence": Violations of the Human Rights of Women in Custody*. New York: Amnesty International.

Belknap, Joanne. 1996. *The Invisible Woman: Gender, Crime, and Justice*. Belmont, CA: Wadsworth Publishing Company.

Bush-Baskette, Stephanie R. 1999. "The 'War on Drugs': A War Against Women?" In *Harsh Punishment: International Experiences of Women's Imprisonment*, edited by Sandy Cook and Susanne Davies. Boston: Northeastern University Press.

California Department of Corrections. 2000. *Monthly Ethnicity Population Report*. November. www.cdc.state.ca.us/reports/montheth.htm.

Campbell, Davara. 1999. Unpublished interview on file with Justice Now. Central California Women's Facility. 16 July.

Chevigny, Bell. 1999. *Doing Time: Twenty-Five Years of Prison Writing*. New York: Arcade Publishing.

Cook, Sandy and Susanne Davies, eds. 1999. *Harsh Punishment: International Experiences of Women's Imprisonment*. Boston: Northeastern University Press.

Crenshaw, Kimberlé. 1995. "Mapping the Margins: Intersectionality, Identity Politics, and Violence Against Women of Color." In *Critical Race Theory: The Key Writings that Formed the Movement*, edited by Kimberlé Crenshaw, Neil Gotanda, Gary Peller, and Kendall Thomas. New York: The New Press.

Currie, Elliot. 1998. *Crime and Punishment in America*. New York: Metropolitan Books, Henry Holt and Company.

De Groot, A., T. Hammett, and R. Scheib. 1996. "Barriers to Care of HIV-Infected Inmates: A Public Health Concern." *The AIDS Reader*, May/June.

Department of Corrections Services Division. 2000. *Characteristics of Population in California State Prisons By Institution*. Offender Information Services Branch. Estimates and Statistical Analysis Section, Data Analysis Unit, 30 June. Sacramento, CA.

Dobash, Russel P., R. Emerson Dobash, and Sue Gutteridge. 1986. *The Imprisonment of Women*. Oxford: Basil Blackwell.

Dyer, Joel. 2000. *The Perpetual Prisoner Machine: How America Profits from Crime*. Boulder, CO: Westview Press.

Federal Bureau of Prisons. 2001. *Quick Facts: April 2001.* 1 June. http://www.bop.gov
/facto598.html#Citizenship.

Garcia, Maria and Gina Mendoza. 1998. Legal Interview. Valley State Prison for
Women. 20 October.

George, Amanda. 1999. "The New Prison Culture: Making Millions from Misery." In
Harsh Punishment: International Experiences of Women's Imprisonment, edited by Sandy
Cook and Susanne Davies, 211–29. Boston: Northeastern University Press.

Giallombardo, Rose. 1966. *Society of Women: A Study of a Women's Prison.* New York:
John Wiley.

Greenfeld, L.A. and T. Snell. 1999. "Women Offenders." *Bureau of Justice Statistics Special Report.* Washington, D.C.: U.S. Department of Justice.

Human Rights Watch. 1996. *All Too Familiar: Sexual Abuse of Women in U.S. State Prisons.*
New York: Human Rights Watch.

Human Rights Watch. 1998. *Locked Away: Immigration Detainees in Jails in the United States.*
New York: Human Rights Watch.

Human Rights Watch. 2000. *Letter to* INS *Commissioner Doris Meissner.* New York:
Human Rights Watch.

Johnson, Regina. 1998. Legal Interview. Valley State Prison for Women. 3 March.

Kupers, Terry. 2000. *Prison Madness: The Mental Health Crisis Behind Bars and What We
Must Do About It.* San Francisco: Jossey-Bass.

Live Jail-Cam. 2001. 23 May. http://www.crime.com.

Newsome, Melba. 2000. "Hard Time." *Essence Magazine* 31, no. 5:146–50, 210–14.

Nightline. 1999. "Crime and Punishment: Women in Prison: Medical Care." ABC
News, 2 November.

Penal Reform International. 1995. *Making Standards Work: An International Handbook on
Good Prison Practice.* The Hague: P.R.I.

Ross, Luana. 1998. *Inventing the Savage: The Social Construction of Native American Criminality.* Austin: University of Texas Press.

Steinberg, Susann. Deputy Director of Health Care Services Division, California
Department of Corrections. 2000. Meeting with prisoner advocates. California
Department of Corrections, Sacramento, CA. 10 October.

Stern, Vivien. 1998. *A Sin Against the Future: Imprisonment in the World.* Boston: Northeastern University Press.

Sudbury, Julia. 2000. "Transatlantic Visions: Resisting the Globalization of Mass
Incarceration." *Social Justice* 27, no. 3:133–49.

Truth to Power: Women Testify at Legislative Hearings. 2000. Excerpts from Legislative
Hearings on Women in Prison at Valley State Prison for Women, 11 October, and
California Institution for Women, 12 October. Produced by Women in Prison
Emergency Network. 40 min. Videocassette.

UN Special Rapporteur on Violence Against Women. 1999. *Report of the Mission to the
United States of America on the Issue of Violence Against Women in State and Federal Prisons.*
New York: United Nations Economic and Social Council.

Welch, Michael. 2000. "The Role of Immigration and Naturalization Service in the
Prison-Industrial Complex." *Social Justice* 27, no. 3: 73–88.

Lisa Suhair Majaj

....

On Writing and Return
Palestinian-American Reflections

Abstract: This article situates the Palestinian right of return within the context
of Palestinian-American literary reflections and the intersection of wom-
en's and human rights. Providing a brief history of Palestinian dispossession and the struggle for return, it explores the multiple dimensions of
"return" in the context of physical displacement, loss, cultural erasure, and
diaspora negotiations of belonging and exile. Identifying return as both a
right and as a metaphor, it looks at gendered realities of Palestinian and
Palestinian-American experience, critiques the dichotomy of nationalism
and feminism, and explores how Palestinian-American literature, emerging
from personal and political displacement, narrates a literary claim to both
reclamation and transformation, in which to return is to claim what was
lost and to construct Palestinian reality anew. Drawing on the words of several Palestinian-American authors and the author's own experiences, the
article voices "return" as a claim to the past and a foundation for the
future.

I have learned the world's histories,
and mine are among them.
My hands are open and empty:
the weapon you place in them is your own.
                    —from "Claims"

Return—to what was lost when the state of Israel was first created on the
geographic area of historic Palestine, and to what continues to be lost to
land confiscation, home demolitions, settlement expansion, military
assault, appropriation of resources, cultural and economic strangulation,

MERIDIANS · feminism, race, transnationalism   Volume 19 Supplement 2020
DOI: 10.1215/15366936-8565869 © 2001 Wesleyan University Press, now published by
Duke University Press on behalf of Smith College

and the attempted erasure of Palestinian national history—is a compelling issue confronting Palestinians today. Amid the current Intifada in the West Bank and Gaza, Israeli military reprisals, and the cultural, economic and military siege of Palestinian communities, the fundamental failure of the 1993 Oslo Accords to fulfill international law and Palestinian human rights has become starkly evident. In this context, the issue of return—always the dominating theme of Palestinian existence, but for decades rendered almost invisible on the international scene—arises with new potency.

The following essay situates discussion of Palestinian return within several contexts: the struggle for women's human rights (a struggle that is feminist even if "gender oppression" is not its sole focus); writing by Palestinian-American women, whose literary responses to displacement offer new perspectives on exile and homecoming; and personal reflections. Within these intersecting contexts, "return" emerges not only as a pragmatic response to historical injustice, but as an issue that has multiple layers of resonance for feminists, activists, writers, and all those concerned with issues of home and exile, justice and injustice, women's rights and human rights.

During the creation of the state of Israel in 1947–48, over 750,000 Palestinians were forced out of their homes and villages in Palestine, amid planned Zionist assaults on Palestinian communities and forced marches that became, for many, death marches. Hundreds of emptied Palestinian villages were razed to the ground in an attempt to eradicate the memory of prior Palestinian existence—although the cactus plants that rimmed the original villages often remain, in a ghostly echo of what were once living communities. In other areas Palestinian homes were taken over by Israeli Jews, despite the fact that their refugee owners, denied reentry, possessed (and still possess) title deeds and front door keys. Now numbering over four million, Palestinian refugees live in often desperate conditions in camps in Lebanon, Jordan, and the West Bank and Gaza, and individually in other countries. Although fifty-three years have intervened since their original dispossession, neither their desire to return nor the legal and moral potency of their right to return have diminished. This is true not only in the Diaspora, but also in the West Bank and Gaza, where massive bypass roads,[1] land confiscations, and Israeli settlements accentuate the stark realities of ongoing displacement. And it is true despite the systematic thwarting by Israel and other countries, particularly the U.S., of the international laws, universal human rights charters, and elemental human justice that mandate the return of Palestinians to their homes.

In the United States in particular, the Palestinian right of return, and the legal and moral basis for this right, has historically been rendered almost invisible. Media presentation of the 1993 Oslo Accords, much celebrated at the time, left virtually unmentioned the fact that these accords ignored (and in fact sought to render inapplicable) international law, in particular the repeatedly renewed United Nations resolutions calling for occupied territories to be relinquished and for Palestinian refugees to be allowed to return to their homes and lands. Instead, the Oslo Accords appear to have been predicated upon the assumption that Palestinian right of return would disappear from the international lexicon altogether, to be replaced by limited negotiations over "disputed" (rather than "occupied") territories.[2] But as the conclusive breakdown of the framework set in place by those Accords has made clear, Palestinian rights, including the right of return, cannot be so easily erased. Nor can memories of home and homeland, grief and dispossession be easily dispelled.

Palestinian-American literature emerges from the context of personal and political displacement that has characterized Palestinian experience over the last half century. A relatively recent body of literature, offering an unprecedented charting of Palestinian experience in a language and diction accessible to U.S. readers, Palestinian-American writing is informed by the longing to return to the original Palestinian homeland, and by the historical, political, and military events that have made such return impossible. It is also informed by other layers of displacement and exile, whether cultural, personal, or gendered. Because Palestinian-Americans, like other Palestinians, are forbidden to return (except, at best, as tourists) to their historical homeland, and hence to their own history, their literature in many ways charts an attempt to "return," as it were, through writing. The homeland to which they seek return is one rooted in history and in memory. At the same time it is, of necessity, a homeland of the imagination, grounded not just in the past, but also in the future. This is particularly true for Palestinian-American women, who, like all women, must negotiate the constraints of gender along with other historical, cultural, and personal exigencies. For those negotiating multiple identities and experiences (as perhaps all exiles must), the return to Palestine becomes on some level a metaphor for the return to the self—a return that for writers

most often occurs through language. As Palestinian-American poet
Nathalie Handal puts it, poetry becomes homeland (1999b).

As Palestinian-American women writers make evident, to write as a
Palestinian woman is to write not only from an understanding of the personal as political (that tried-and-true dictum of feminism) but also from an
understanding of the political as personal. It is to write out of a recognition
of the ways in which the multiple layers of history and politics, exile and
displacement situate and shape individual lives. And it is to write from an
awareness of the ways in which personal and gendered issues are integrally
related to, rather than separate from, the struggles for freedom, justice,
and peace. The struggle for women's rights is embedded within the struggle for human rights: one struggle does not occlude the other.

This assertion of the relevance of human rights to feminism may seem
unnecessary. But there has been an all-too-frequent slippage between, on
the one hand, recognition of Arab women's multifaceted struggles on
political, economic, social fronts, and, on the other hand, the perception
of an irredeemably static gender oppression embedded in Arab culture.
Arab women's feminist struggles have too often been located against this
constructed backdrop of an unchangeably misogynistic Arab culture, a
stereotype that encourages the assumption that Arab women must reject
their own culture to improve their lot, instead taking succor in a flight to
western feminism. Palestinian women have been particularly caught
within this dichotomy of nationalism and feminism. But as any assessment of contemporary Palestinian women's issues makes clear, issues of
nationalism and feminism cannot be so easily opposed to each other. Virginia Woolf's famous claim notwithstanding (that as a woman she had no
country), Palestinian women can no more be expected to "choose" between
their national and gender identities than U.S. women can be expected to
"choose" between being American and being feminist. Moreover, Palestinian women are hardly likely to endorse flight from their own culture as any
kind of a solution: after fifty-three years of exile and displacement, they
have had enough of flight. Indeed, it is flight's opposite—return—that
today looms as the overriding issue, in both political and human terms, for
Palestinian women and men alike.

Of course, "return" is a term that may have different connotations
depending on its context. Palestinian refugees in camps, struggling to
survive under atrociously difficult conditions, may view return to their

original homes with more pragmatic urgency than do Palestinians in more privileged circumstances: when exile is mediated by homes, travel documents, and monetary resources, the need to return to a long-denied historical and familial legacy may be experienced largely on an emotional level. Moreover, "return" may take on a multitude of meanings for writers and artists whose works interweave multiple layers of exile and displacement, expressing the human longing to return both to a homeland and to a sense of self. But return, whether literal or metaphorical, lies at the heart of Palestinian identity and existence. And like most realities that challenge the status quo, the issue of return has been persistently pushed to the border, where it lingers: unheard, but not unvoiced.

To return, it should be made clear, is not simply to go back: it is also to go forward; to create a new future from the fragments of a reclaimed past. This dual nature of return is made clear in some recent Palestinian-American literature, especially by women. Consider, for instance, the work of poet Suheir Hammad, a young Palestinian-American writer whose poetry collection, *Born Palestinian, Born Black* (1996a),[3] memoir, *Drops of This Story* (1996b), and inspired oral performances have gained her a following among a variety of audiences. In a poem titled "broken and beirut" (1996a) Hammad pleads for a new future for Palestinians, one that will not simply repeat but make possible a re-envisioning of the past. Invoking painful scenes of searching through rubble for body parts, the repeated cycles of massacre and war to which Palestinians have been subjected, Hammad writes of being "tired of taking fear and calling it life" (1996a, 96). Instead, she cries out "to remember what i've never lived/a home within me within us/where honey is offered from my belly . . . to return to the belly of my honey/and feed myself earth . . . [to] return to what we've forgotten . . . never forgetting/where we come from/where we've been/and how sweet honey/on the lips of survivors" (96–97).

These and other lines of Hammad's make clear the extent to which return—to history, to an imagined future, and ultimately, to the self, whether personal or communal—lies at the heart of both memory and transformation. In her work, return to Palestine is not return to patriarchal structures, but to a homeland created anew. The journey may be difficult, even impossible: the past lies irretrievably behind us; homelands lie unreachable beyond borders marked by barbed wire and guns. But it is through return, Hammad suggests—to the past, to memory, to the homelands that exist in reality and the ones we create—that we ground the self and hence provide the means to move forward into the future.

Return is of a particularly crucial importance for Palestinians because the denial of their return is enacted both on the physical and on the cultural level. Not only are Palestinians forbidden the right to physically go home (prevented from returning through a variety of means, including military force, political collusion, confiscation of identity papers, imprisonment, and worse), they have also been denied the right to a cultural and historical return: in particular, the right to preserve, express, document, and transmit their history. For instance, Palestinians in Israel and in the Occupied Territories were long forbidden to teach their own history in schools, and were forced to use textbooks that eradicated any mention of "nationalist" Palestinian history. Palestinians have been routinely subjected to a censorship so severe that even children's centers displaying drawings in red, white, green, and black (the colors of the Palestinian flag) risked closure for "seditious activity," and simple mention of "the beloved" in a poem could lead to a writer being summoned by the military authority. During the invasion of Lebanon in 1982, one of the most pointed actions of the Israeli military was the ransacking of the Palestinian archives in Beirut, as a result of which countless books, documents and artifacts documenting Palestinian experience and the Palestinian struggle were either destroyed or carried off to Israel. This looting represents but one of the ways in which Israel has sought to render Palestinian history and experience invisible, undocumented, and therefore (it must have been hoped) "untrue."[4] Such suppression of cultural expression and transmission has significant ramifications; indeed, it is a form of cultural genocide that goes hand in hand with the physical destruction of Palestine that has been enacted since 1948.

This history of censorship and cultural suppression makes clear the deep Israeli investment in countering Palestinian narratives of origin in the land of Israel/Palestine. But these narratives of origin are not fantasies; nor are they dispensable. As Hammad reminds us, our sense of self, both on an individual and a communal level, our vision of our place in the world, is based on a sense of origins. We seek to return to our starting point, in person or in memory, in order to reconstitute ourselves, for it is through memory that we understand who we are and that we lay a foundation for who we hope to become. We return in order to remember, and remember in order to return. But one of the lessons taught by Palestinian history is that both memory and identity are rooted in contested ground. And so personal return cannot be separated from political return, because whether we wish it or not, Palestinian memory, like Palestinian history, is always already political.

On some level, Palestinian return is always literal. Particularly for refugees in camps, living without passports or officially recognized nationalities, unable either to travel to another place or to build a future where they are, struggling merely to stay alive under devastating economic and political conditions, subjected to physical and social oppression and to military assault, "return" most often connotes just that: a physical return to the homes and lands from which they were forced over fifty years ago. This return is a right at once affirmed and denied over decades of suffering. Palestinian repatriation has been legally and morally mandated by a plethora of universal human rights charters and United Nations resolutions, and by the most elemental principles of justice. Indeed, the return of Palestinians displaced before and during Israel's creation was an original precondition for Israel's acceptance into the United Nations. But fifty-three years later, the refugees are still waiting to return. The usual arguments against Palestinian repatriation—that there is not enough room in Israel, or that return of the refugees would unsettle Israeli demographics—are on the one hand inaccurate (recent geographical studies indicate that there is ample unpopulated refugee land in Israel to which Palestinians could be repatriated) and on the other hand indicative of the underlying racism of a "democracy" predicated upon keeping the land's indigenous population in the minority.

Those of us in more privileged circumstances, whether Palestinian or not, should not doubt that the refugees' plight is intricately connected to our own struggles as feminists and as human beings. Consider, for instance, a Palestinian refugee woman living in a densely populated refugee camp without basic facilities such as water and sewage lines, struggling under severe economic deprivation, subjected to bombings and military assault by one of the most powerful armies on earth, trying to feed and educate her family and herself, to live her life, plan her future, take stock of her past. Such a woman is, on some level, like any one of us: a person with dreams and aspirations, struggling against life's difficulties. Perhaps she has the genius of a doctor, an engineer, an architect; perhaps she writes poetry late at night. As a woman whose goals are thwarted by forces beyond her control, she invokes the solidarity and co-struggle of feminists the world round. But her situation as a Palestinian refugee forces us to recognize the extent to which feminist struggles against gender oppression alone do not adequately account for all the ways in which women suffer. As a Palestinian, this refugee woman's life is defined and foreclosed not simply by the limitations that any woman might face—of resources, opportunities, patriarchal structures, social conventions—but also by political agendas, by brutal military force, and by nationalist ideologies that construe her as a non-person. Like so many other Palestinians, this woman may still hold the deed to her family house, the key to a long-lost front door. Certainly she remembers what was lost half a century before; very likely she dreams of return. The house itself from which her forbears fled may or may not have been destroyed amid the concerted attempt to eradicate the memory of Palestinian existence in what is now Israel. Absolute return to a particular home may no longer be possible. But return in a broader sense to the village or locale of origin is physically possible, humanly necessary, and mandated by international law. And the pragmatic condition of such refugees (stateless, homeless, and suffering under a level of oppression perhaps difficult to imagine from a comfortable American academic perspective) accentuates the need for a return that is not just metaphorical, but actual.

For Palestinians in places such as the U.S., living under less tenuous circumstances, free from military assault and from the indignities and oppressions wrought under occupation, the longing for return may be played out largely on the level of cultural memory. Palestinians in the U.S. are circumscribed by the pressures of American immigrant life, silenced by the ideologies (American as well as Israeli) that construe the Palestinian dream of return to pre-1948 areas as not just impossible but also somehow "immoral," and constrained by the political realities preventing Palestinians from both Israel and the Occupied Territories, including East Jerusalem, from going home.[5] Perhaps in response, some displace the dream of repatriation with the attempt to recreate Palestinian culture in the diaspora. Preserving traditions of food, cultural practices, social behaviors, family roles and the like, they seek to preserve the homeland in the only space available to them—the home. But as is so often the case in immigrant contexts, memory thus sustained becomes gendered, with the labor of cultural reproduction falling largely on women's shoulders, and often leading to the replication of patriarchal structures. Meanwhile, location in the American context may hinder some Palestinian women's claims to independence and to self-transformation, denying them the options that would have been theirs in the old world, where familiar social structures often allow greater freedom of movement. Indeed, Palestinian women in the U.S., charged with maintaining through their labor and through their very being a Palestinian home-in-exile, may be at once empowered and disempowered by the politicization of domestic space. While the reification of memory implicit in the recreation of Palestinian culture in the Diaspora makes possible a bridging of past and present, it also leaves little space for women to define their own futures.[6]

It is to such complex realities that contemporary Palestinian-American writers such as Hammad, Handal, and others speak.[7] When, for instance, Hammad writes of longing to return to a past she has only imagined, she brings together the potency of memory (historical, familial, and personal) with a transformative vision of the future, one in which women's bodies and women's words occupy liberatory spaces. Underlying her invocation of return is not just the need to return to what was lost, but also the need to imagine Palestinian reality anew, to transform the oppressions of the past, gendered as well as political. For instance, Hammad writes fiercely of what Arab women have been subjected to in the name of gender: "they beat you blue/ripped each hair out your head/each one by one in the name/of god and land spit on you and/cursed the evil that is/woman" (Handal 2000, 116). Yet forced to leave her own family in order to find space for herself, she writes of "missing my family/who couldn't understand/we struggling to understand/we were where we needed to be/we are who we have to be" (Handal 2000, 112). Multifaceted and multivoiced, her work arises out of a deep homesickness not just for the past but also for a transformed future.

Such Palestinian-American writers are in many ways split at the root, distanced by political events, culture, and geography from both their Palestinian origin point and from their American context, and haunted by many layers of exile. In their work, "return" invokes actual return to the homeland, gives voice to an historical and familial legacy, and suggests the responsibility brought to bear by familial and communal history, something poet Naomi Shihab Nye once termed being "doomed by our blood to care" (see Orfalea 1991, 56). Writing thereby becomes a repatriation of marginalized memory. But "return" in this literature is at the same time a step forward, toward the creation of a new future. Informed by multiple modes of displacement, giving voice to a return that is both metaphorical and actual, these authors acknowledge the possibility of transforming exile. Handal, for instance, writes of the dream of return as at once family memory, personal quest, and literary focus, a search that shapes both her writing and her sense of self. "I did not lose my way," she writes, describing her family's displacement from Palestine and her own dream of return, "but didn't know when I would be back. I was present in my absence, an absence which was in itself absent . . . my way back was always for me a matter of time" (1999, 140). The longing to return becomes, in her work, a search for the self, in the course of which homelessness is transformed. "In our journey to finding this identity that we think can be settled," she continues, "we confuse ourselves, for I have come to believe that we will forever travel in margins. But margins of our own" (141).

This is not to say that the loss of homes and land do not press in the U.S. diaspora as well. Ask any Palestinian-American, and you will learn of family inheritances decimated, homes lost, not just to a fifty-three-year-old history, but also to present-day outrages: Jewish-only bypass roads carved out of the Palestinian hillsides, houses demolished without notice, leaving entire families without shelter, land confiscated for yet more illegal settlements. The taste of loss lingers and will not be dispelled. But for Palestinians with roofs over our heads and passports in our hands, the need for return may be, in many ways, more emotional and existential than pragmatic, based on a quest for human justice rather than on personal need. Yet it still exerts a constant pressure. This is partly true because what we have lost is not just personal property but family legacies: the land, homes, and history that should have been our children's birthright. What has been lost is not just our past but also their future. And how do we teach new generations about their heritage, show them where their roots lie buried when Palestine does not even appear on the map? As writers and as human beings, we seek to give voice to our histories, to speak of what the world refuses to know. But even as we are denied the physical right to return, so too are we denied what Edward Said calls the simple "permission to narrate" (see Said 2000). And so our memory languishes, held hostage at the border by politics.

The title of the conference panel on which this essay was originally presented, "Memory and Politics at the Border," offers a strikingly apt description of Palestinian experience. Our lives are constituted at the intersection of memory and politics, delineated by border crossings and border exclusions. Our memories, communal and personal, are foreclosed by the politics that set Palestinians adrift in the world in the first place, leaving us stateless in a world of nations. Our histories are shaped by the agendas that continue to view Palestinians as a dispensable population, invisible on the world's radar screen except as "terrorists" and "obstacles to peace."

In 1998 I traveled from Cambridge, Massachusetts, to Jerusalem to introduce my ten year-old daughter to an elderly, ailing relative whom I knew would not live long. At the port of Haifa, where I entered, the border official, an American woman from Brookline, Massachusetts (in other worlds, my neighbor) was friendly enough until she saw my father's name on my entry form. At that, she brusquely stamped my passport before I could protest (although Israeli border officials are in theory supposed to get permission before stamping passports, since the Israeli stamp prevents entry to some countries) and sent me to another room for interrogation. There, the security guard, another woman, questioned me aggressively about whom I was planning to see, where I was planning to go, why I had come there in the first place. As I tried to answer her repeated questions, to soothe my wailing child, to stay calm despite the surge of fear and anger gripping me, I was struck, not for the first time, by the extent to which merely being Palestinian is, to an Israeli, a threat. My own reasons for the journey—personal memory, family ties, the desire to transmit to my young daughter some element of her Palestinian heritage—were, in my interrogator's eyes, wholly political. Had she intuited the other memories at the back of my mind, her suspicion of me would have been far greater. These memories included: the family land lost to a bypass road; the Israeli refusal to allow my father's body to be brought to Palestine for burial; the aunt killed by a Zionist bomb, leaving two small children behind; the experiences of my grandmother's family forced into impoverished exile in Jordan. When I asked her (of course knowing the answer in advance) why I, apart from other travelers, was being subjected to this interrogation, she looked at me as if I were mentally impaired. "What do you expect?" she asked me. "You're Palestinian." "I'm an American," I pointed out, holding up my passport. The guard was not impressed. "Your father was Palestinian," she retorted. "That's enough."

What this Israeli guard made clear (and what all Palestinians know) is that the most personal of experiences and desires are, if Palestinian, inevitably political. The smallest detail of landscape held in memory—a fragrant lemon tree, a dun-colored stretch of hillside, a crumbling, hand-laid stone fence—becomes, in the eyes of our interrogators, a political declaration. For they know too well that to remember is to long to return, and return is a threat. Palestinian return, whether in person or in memory, is therefore inescapably fraught with political tension. Our journeys are hindered by interrogations or foreclosed altogether by the lack of the necessary permits and by the politics that render refugees stateless. When we seek a point of connection between our past and our present, we find ourselves treated as usurpers of our own history, silenced by the official narratives that deny our existence and challenge our memories. Languishing at the borders of political, national, historical, geographical, and cultural discourses, we are forever relegated to the margins of our own past.

In response to such marginalization, we write. The act of literary production has been described in countless discussions of modernist and feminist literature as a way to counter a sense of exile, to build a home in language, to find a grounding for the self amid the multiple permutations of modern life. Whether the sense of exile derives from political uprooting, or from a more existential sense of homelessness rooted in gender, race, sexuality, class, ethnic origin, or religion, writing offers a counterweight: the possibility, however provisional, of home. Feminists have long written about the sense of exile experienced by women, relegated by gender to the economic, political, cultural, social, and discursive margins of life. This awareness of displacement as an existential condition, shared by marginalized groups of all kinds, intrinsically links (or should link) feminists to the Palestinian struggle in much the same way that the sense of shared exile has historically linked women to the struggles of other oppressed groups. For Palestinians, as for women, displacement is experienced on both a literal and a metaphorical level, pervading every aspect of life. And for both, literature becomes a mode of resistance to displacement.[8]

For Palestinian authors in general, writing offers a means of "going home," of asserting a claim to the Palestinian past and the Palestinian future. This is evident throughout Palestinian literature, most famously in the work of poet Mohammed Darwish. For Palestinian-American authors, the act of writing charts a multilayered search, a longing for return to Palestine, to the legacy of the past, but also to that space between "Palestinian" and "American" where "home" is as much created as found. As Hammad puts it, "Home is within me. I carry everyone and everything I am with me wherever I go. Use my history as the road in front of me. . . . Why do I write? 'Cause I have to. Cause my voice, in all its dialects, has been silenced too long'" (1996a, ix). Writing becomes a way of confronting and interweaving the splintered memories that constitute our legacy. Haunted by the flight of families, by a generation's dream of return, by our own unsettled longing for a sense of home, we travel back to our parents' homeland, in person or through memory, seeking touchstones to bring back with us into exile, back home. Detained at borders, our luggage searched, our motives questioned, we return to memory, personal and historical, in search of futures we can call our own.

And so our work rises from return, from the impress of loss and the insistence of memory, from the stories we seek to transform, the historical narratives we refuse to forget. Weaving together shards of memory and history with our own visions of the future, we seek to give voice to what was lost and what is yet to be created. And from these origins we shape our futures. In the absence of political repatriation, we create homelands of language, lyrical spaces in which we return, at last, to ourselves. For as Handal writes, "Being Palestinian is always living in between skylines. It is 'wandering one's whole life among foreign tribes . . . ' Except in our land of poetry, poetry as homeland" (1996, 143).

....

Lisa Suhair Majaj, a Palestinian-American, was born in Iowa and raised in Jordan. She earned her BA from the American University of Beirut and two MAs and a PhD from the University of Michigan. She coedited three volumes on international women writers, and her own poetry and essays have been widely published. Her books include the prize-winning poetry volume *Geographies of Light* (2009), and a children's book, *Naila Shares a Story*. She resides in Cyprus.

Notes

Originally published in *Meridians* vol. 2, no. 1, 2001.

This essay is based on a talk presented at the *Meridians'* inaugural conference at Smith College, March 8–11, 2001, as part of the panel "Memory and Politics at the Border." I am grateful to anonymous *Meridians* reviewers for their insightful comments. Unfortunately, time constraints and lack of access to resources as I converted the conference presentation into a written piece, amidst the tumult of an overseas move, made it impossible to elaborate more fully on the themes raised here. This essay therefore represents work in progress.

1 Palestinian territories are crisscrossed by an extensive network of "bypass roads" that link illegal Jewish settlements with each other and with Israel while bypassing Palestinian communities in the same areas. These roads ensure continued Israeli control over Palestinian land and people even in the case of territorial "concessions," and thus serve as a mechanism for implementing Israeli strategies of expansion and apartheid.

2 Immediately after the signing of the Oslo Accords, Israel sought to replace the term "Occupied Territories," which accurately describes the territories seized by Israel during the 1967 war, with the inaccurate "disputed territories," a term that seeks to legitimate continued Israeli occupation, settlements, and annexation of Palestinian land.

3   The title of Hammad's book demonstrates her deep commitment to establish-
    ing points of intersection between different racial and ethnic communities,
    and to making common cause on issues of justice across the boundaries of
    "identity." It also invokes, and stands as a tribute to, the words of African-
    American poet June Jordan, who wrote in a poem mourning the massacre of
    Palestinians at Sabra and Shatila refugee camps in Beirut in 1982, "I was born a
    black woman/and now/I am become a Palestinian."

4   It should be noted that a number of revisionist historians in Israel, working
    from newly declassified material from Israeli archives, have begun to document
    Palestinian historical claims, belying the official Israeli narrative of the origins
    of the state of Israel.

5   Palestinians from occupied East Jerusalem have been subjected to a focused
    program of "ethnic cleansing," in an attempt to decrease the number of Pales-
    tinians in East Jerusalem and increase the number of Israeli Jews, and thereby
    consolidate Israeli claims to Jerusalem. Palestinians with Jerusalem residency
    have been stripped of their residency permits for reasons including marriage,
    location of work, study abroad, and violation of various Israeli regulations; resi-
    dency cards are also confiscated for purely arbitrary reasons. In contrast, a
    recent decision in the Knesset provided special monetary incentives to encour-
    age Israeli Jews to reside in East Jerusalem.

6   On the roles of Palestinian and Palestinian-American women in the U.S., and
    the dynamics of Palestinian cultural reproduction in this context, see Cainkar
    1988 and 1990.

7   See, for instance, Hammad 1996a and 1996b; Nye 1994a, 1994b, 1995, 1996, 1997
    and 1998; Handal 1999a and 1999b. See also the selections by Palestinian-
    American authors in Kadi 1994, Mattawa and Akash 1999, and Handal 2000.

8   The connections between the modes of exile experienced by women and by Pal-
    estinians, and hence the linkage between feminist and Palestinian struggles,
    deserve more extended discussion than I can offer at the present time.

Works Cited

Cainkar, Louise. 1988. "Coping with Tradition, Change and Alienation: The Life
    Experiences of Palestinian Women in the United States." Ph.D. dissertation,
    Northwestern University.
———. 1990. "Palestinian Women in the United States: Who Are They and What
    Kind of Lives Do They Lead?" In *Images and Reality: Palestinian Women under Occupa-
    tion and in the Diaspora*, edited by Suha Sabbagh and Ghada Talhami, 55–66. Wash-
    ington, D.C.: Institute for Arab Women Studies.
Hammad, Suheir. 1996a. *Born Palestinian, Born Black*. New York: Writers and Readers.
———. 1996b. *Drops of This Story*. New York: Writers and Readers.
Handal, Nathalie. 1999a. *The Neverfield Poem*. Sausalito, CA: Post Apollo Press.
———. 1999b. "Poetry as Homeland." In *Post-Gibran: Anthology of New Arab-American
    Writing*, edited by Khaled Mattawa and Munir Akash, 139–43. A special issue of
    Jusoor 11/12. Distributed by Syracuse University Press.

———. 2000. *The Poetry of Arab Women: A Contemporary Anthology*. New York and North-ampton: Interlink Press.

Kadi, Joanna. 1994. *Food For Our Grandmothers: Writings by Arab-American and Arab-Canadian Feminists*. Boston: South End Press.

Majaj, Lisa Suhair. 1994. "Claims." In *Food for Our Grandmothers: Writings by Arab-American and Arab-Canadian Feminists*, 84–6. Boston: South End Press.

Mattawa, Khaled and Munir Akash, eds. 1999. *Post-Gibran: Anthology of New Arab-American Writing*. A special issue of *Jusoor* 11/12. Distributed by Syracuse University Press.

Nye, Naomi Shihab. 1994a. *Red Suitcase: Poems*. Brockport, NY: BOA Editions, Ltd.

———. 1994b. *Sitti's Secrets* [children's picture book]. New York: Four Winds Press.

———. 1995. *Words Under the Words: Selected Poems*. Portland, OR: Eighth Mountain Press.

———. 1996. *Never in a Hurry: Essays on People and Places*. Columbia: University of South Carolina Press.

———. 1997. *Habibi*. New York: Simon & Schuster Books for Young Readers.

———. 1998. *Fuel*. Rochester, NY: Boa Editions.

Orfalea, Gregory. 1991. "Doomed by Our Blood to Care: The Poetry of Naomi Shihab Nye." *Paintbrush* 18, no. 3 (Spring): 56–66.

Said, Edward. 2000. "Permission to Narrate." In *The Edward Said Reader*, edited by Moustafa Bayoumi and Andrew Rubin, 243–66. New York: Vintage.

Edited by Amrita Basu, Paula Giddings,
Inderpal Grewal, and Kamala Visweswaran

....

September 11
A Feminist Archive

Abstract: The links among feminism, race, and transnationalism, which are key
to the *Meridians* project, are also crucial to understanding the events of 9/11
and the war on Afghanistan. Some pieces in this archive provide feminist
perspectives on the impact of war and fundamentalism on women's lives in
Afghanistan and Pakistan. Other pieces analyze the ways in which racist
representations of Muslim women and of Islam have come to play a key
part in colonial and neocolonial "great games" being played in South,
West, and Central Asia. Yet others link the U.S.-sponsored war in Afghanistan to the repression of the media and the attacks on civil liberties within
the U.S. itself. In constructing an archive of these courageous testimonies,
Meridians honors the courage and integrity of women in the United States
and around the world who aspire to a better, more just world.

As this issue goes to press, the United States is engaged in a sustained
military intervention in Afghanistan. By the time this issue is actually
printed, however, we may already have enough hindsight to understand the
particular forms of devastation this war has had for the Afghan people—
apart from the damage already wrought by more than thirty years of civil
war, unrest, and violence. As feminists, the questions, "Who speaks?" and
"Who speaks for Afghanistan?" have weighed heavily upon our efforts as
scholars and educators to make available to a larger public the many compelling voices of dissent that circulate on the margins of what opinion polls
are calling a "popular" war. These forms of dissent take the form of poetry

MERIDIANS · feminism, race, transnationalism   Volume 19 Supplement 2020
DOI: 10.1215/15366936-8565880 © 2002 Wesleyan University Press, now published by
Duke University Press on behalf of Smith College

(as in Suheir Hammad's piece, "first writing since"), of life testimony (Ayesha Khan's interview with an Afghan woman refugee), statements of denunciation (by RAWA, WLUML), statements of support (Medica Mondiale, Rigoberta Menchu), as well as speeches directed against U.S. foreign Policy. We are particularly pleased to reprint Barbara Lee's speech to Congress in which she spoke against authorizing President Bush to have increased wartime powers, not only because Lee was the lone dissenting voice in Congress, but because she articulates the thoughts of many who oppose the war and the extraordinary measures undertaken by the U.S. government in order to pursue it. The same is true of Sunera Thobani, a professor of Women's Studies at the University of British Columbia, Canada, whose speech critical of U.S. foreign policy led the Canadian government to bring her up on hate speech charges. As a letter to the San Francisco Chronicle makes clear, the FBI investigation of Women in Black, a transnational women's peace group dedicated to nonviolent resolutions of conflict in the Middle East and elsewhere, is yet another example of the attempt to suppress unpopular speech and opinion. Among the many things this war has taught us is the need to stand for the academic freedom to voice dissenting opinion at the university. It is no accident that women of color have been on the front lines of such free thought, or sadly, that they number among the first to be singled out and punished for it.

Our goal for this collection was to highlight opinions and voices that were considered unimportant to foreign policy debates by the popular media in the U.S. (or in most parts of the world) but which seemed to us to provide important and progressive insights and opinions. Although there were many other pieces that we could have included, such as Arundhati Roy's statement in the Guardian, or Barbara Kingsolver's piece in the San Francisco Chronicle, we believed that these had already had plenty of exposure and were easily available. We felt that it was important to include opinions of Afghan women and women's groups, critiques of fundamentalist regimes by Muslim women and groups who have been struggling against them for many years, as well as statements by other feminists who opposed militarism, imperialism, and state oppression.

The statements and commentaries that are collected here provide important links among the three terms—feminism, race, and transnationalism—which are key to the Meridians project. These links seemed to us to be crucial for understanding the events of 9-11, as well as the war on Afghanistan. Thus while some pieces address the issue of geopolitics in relation to Afghanistan and Pakistan, they do so with reference to feminist concerns of women in those regions and the impact of war and fundamentalism on women's lives. Other pieces refer to the ways in which racist representations of Muslim women and of Islam have come to play a key part in colonial and neocolonial "great games" being played in South, West, and Central Asia. Yet others link the U.S.-sponsored war in Afghanistan to the repression of the media and the attacks on civil liberties within the U.S. itself. Such repression of civil liberties goes along with the harassment and killings of people of Middle Eastern and South Asian descent as well as those who look "Middle Eastern." Highlighted here are understandings of masculinity, militarism, fundamentalism, and of gendered and racialized patriotisms and nationalisms.

No doubt there are important pieces and voices that we have not included here. In the effort to provide a timely intervention, we have had to work fast in order to make publication deadlines. We also realize that some pieces might appear to be somewhat rough and unpolished, but that is to be expected of statements that were written in urgent response to a rapidly changing situation. Despite these concerns, we offer this collection of writings as a testimony to the nuanced, thoughtful, and important analyses that women and feminists offered in response to the events of September 11, 2001. In constructing an archive of these varied forms of dissent, *Meridians* honors the courage and integrity of women in the United States and around the world who aspire to a better, more just world.

....

Amrita Basu is the Domenic J. Paino Professor of Political Science and Sexuality, Women's and Gender Studies at Amherst College. She has published extensively on religious nationalism, global feminism and women's activism. She is the author of *Violent Conjunctures in Democratic India* (2015) and the editor of *Women's Movements in the Global Era: The Power of Local Feminisms* (2010). She teaches courses on populism, social movements, and postcolonial nationalism.

Paula J. Giddings is a former book editor and journalist, and is the author of several African American women's history texts, including *Ida: A Sword Among Lions* (2009), winner of the Los Angeles Times Book Prize for Biography. She is the Elizabeth A. Woodson 1922 Professor Emerita of Africana Studies at Smith College and served as editor of *Meridians* from 2004 to 2017. She is a member of the American Academy of Arts and Sciences.

Inderpal Grewal is professor emerita in women's, gender, and sexuality studies at Yale University. She is the author of *Home and Harem: Nation, Gender, Empire, and the Cultures of Travel* (1996), *Transnational America: Feminisms, Diasporas, Neoliberalisms* (2005), and *Saving the Security State: Exceptional Citizens in Twenty-First-Century America*

(2017). She has coedited *An Introduction to Women's Studies: Gender in a Transnational World* (2002), *Scattered Hegemonies* (1994), and *Theorizing NGOs: States, Feminisms, and Neoliberalism* (2014). Her current projects examine security regimes, patriarchal authoritarianism, and bureaucracy.

Kamala Viswesaran is T. T. & W. F. Chao Professor of Asian Studies at Rice University. Viswesaran writes in the fields of feminist theory and ethnography, South Asian social movements, ethnic and political conflict, human rights, colonial law, postcolonial theory, South Asian literatures, transnational and diaspora studies, and comparative South Asia and Middle East studies. She has taught in Nepal and Sri Lanka and worked in Tamil Nadu and Gujarat, India, and has received Fulbright and American Institute of Indian Studies awards for her research, as well as fellowships at the University of Chicago Humanities Institute, the Radcliffe Institute of Advanced Study at Harvard, the Stanford Center for Advanced Study in the Behavioral Sciences, and the Princeton Institute of International and Regional Studies. She is an editor of the journal *Feminist Studies*, and was the North American editor of *Cultural Dynamics* from 1998 to 2005.

Note

Originally published in *Meridians* vol. 2, no. 2, 2002.

A Statement by Paola Bacchetta, Tina Campt,
Inderpal Grewal, Caren Kaplan,
Minoo Moallem, and Jennifer Terry

....

Transnational Feminist
Practices against War

Abstract: This piece was written collaboratively as a response to the bombing of sites in Afghanistan in September 2001 as the United States began to retaliate for Al-Queda attacks on U.S. targets. Anticipating the invasion and occupation of Iraq and a broader, globalized "War on Terror," the authors wanted to offer an antiracist, antinationalist feminist analysis that insisted recognizing the importance of histories of colonialism and empire in the structuring of state and interstate violence.

October 2001

As feminist theorists of transnational and postmodern cultural formations, we believe that it is crucial to seek non-violent solutions to conflicts
at every level of society, from the global, regional, and national arenas to
the ordinary locales of everyday life. We offer the following response to the
events of September 11 (9-11) and its aftermath:

First and foremost, we need to analyze the thoroughly gendered and
racialized effects of nationalism, and to identify what kinds of inclusions
and exclusions are being enacted in the name of patriotism. Recalling the
histories of various nationalisms helps us to identify tacit assumptions
about gender, race, nation, and class that once again play a central role
in mobilization for war. We see that instead of a necessary historical,

MERIDIANS · feminism, race, transnationalism   Volume 19 Supplement 2020
DOI: 10.1215/15366936-8565891 © 2002 Wesleyan University Press, now published by
Duke University Press on behalf of Smith College

material, and geopolitical analysis of 9-11, the emerging nationalist discourses consist of misleading and highly sentimentalized narratives that, among other things, reinscribe compulsory heterosexuality and the rigidly dichotomized gender roles upon which it is based. A number of icons constitute the ideal types in the drama of nationalist domesticity that we see displayed in the mainstream media. These include the masculine citizen-soldier, the patriotic wife and mother, the breadwinning father who is head of household, and the properly reproductive family. We also observe how this drama is racialized. Most media representations in the U.S. have focused exclusively on losses suffered by White, middle-class, heterosexual families even though those who died or were injured include many people of different races, classes, sexualities, and religions, and of at least ninety different nationalities. Thus, an analysis that elucidates the repressive effects of nationalist discourses is necessary for building a world that fosters peace as well as social and economic justice.

Second, a transnational feminist response views the impact of war and internal repression in a larger context of global histories of displacement, forced migrations, and expulsions. We oppose the U.S. and European sponsorship of regimes responsible for coerced displacements, and we note how patterns of immigration, exile, and forced flight are closely linked to gender oppression, and to the legacies of colonialism and structured economic dependency. Indeed, history shows us that women, as primary caretakers of families, suffer enormously under circumstances of colonization, civil unrest, and coerced migration. Taking this history into account, we critique solutions to the contemporary crisis that rely on a colonial, Manichean model whereby "advanced capitalist freedom and liberty" is venerated over "backward extremist Islamic barbarism." Furthermore, we draw upon insights from post-colonial studies and critical political economy to trace the dynamics of European and U.S. neocolonialism during the Cold War and post-Cold War periods. Thus questions about the gendered distribution of wealth and resources are key to our analytical approach. Neo-liberal economic development schemes create problems that impact women in profound and devastating ways in both the "developing regions" as well as the "developed world." So while middle-class Euro-American women in the United States are held up as the most liberated on earth, even while they are being encouraged to stand dutifully by their husbands, fathers, and children, women in developing regions of the world are depicted as abject, backward, and oppressed by their men. One of the important elements missing from this picture is the fact that many women in Afghanistan are starving and faced with violence and harm on a daily basis not only due to the Taliban regime but due also in large part to a long history of European colonialism and conflict in the region. The Bush administration's decision to drop bombs at one moment and, in the next, care packages of food that are in every way inadequate to the needs of the population offers a grim image of how pathetic this discourse of "civilization" and "rescue" is within the violence of war. We see here a token and uncaring response to a situation to which the U.S. has contributed for at least twenty years, a situation that is about the strategic influence in the region and about the extraction of natural resources, not the least of which is oil.

Third, we want to comment on the extent to which domestic civil repression is intrinsically linked to the violence of war. Thus the effects of the current conflict will be played out in the U.S. and its border zones through the augmentation of border patrolling and policing, as well as in the use of military and defense technologies and other practices that will further subordinate communities (especially non-White groups) in the U.S. Such state violence has many gendered implications. These include the emergence of patriarchal/masculinist cultural nationalisms whereby women's perspectives are degraded or wholly excluded to create new version of cultural "traditions." And, for many immigrant women, other devastating effects of state repression include increased incidents of unreported domestic violence, public hostility, and social isolation. In practical terms, policing authorities charged with guaranteeing national security are likely to have little sympathy for the undocumented immigrant woman who is fleeing a violent intimate relationship, unless her assailant fits the profile of an "Islamic fundamentalist." Thus we need an analysis and strategy against the "domestication" of the violence of war that has emerged in these last few weeks and whose effects will be felt in disparate and dispersed ways.

Fourth, we call for an analysis of the stereotypes and tropes that are being mobilized in the current crisis. These tropes support, sustain, and are enabled by a modernist logic of warfare that seeks to consolidate the sovereign (and often unilateral) power of the First World nation-state. When President Bush proclaims that "terrorist" networks must be destroyed, we ask what this term means to people and how it is being used to legitimate a large-scale military offensive. The term is being used to demonize practices that go against U.S. national interests and it permits a kind of "dragnet" effect at home and abroad which legitimates the suppression of dissent. We also want to inquire into constructions of "terrorism" that continue to target non-native or "foreign" opposition movements while cloaking its own practices of terror in euphemisms such as "foreign aid." Deconstructing the trope of "terrorism" must include a sustained critique of the immense resources spent by the U.S. in training "counter-terrorists" and "anti-Communist" forces who then, under other historical circumstances, become enemies rather than allies, as in the now famous case of Osama bin Laden. We are concerned about the ways in which the "war against terrorism" can be used to silence and repress insurgent movements across the globe. We also emphasize how racism operates in the naming of "terrorism." When the "terrorists" are people of color, all other people of color are vulnerable to a scapegoat backlash. Yet when White supremacist Timothy McVeigh bombed the Murrah federal building in Oklahoma City, killing 168 men, women, and children, no one declared open season to hunt down White men, or even White militia members. The production of a new racial category, "anyone who looks like a Muslim" in which targets of racism include Muslims, Arabs, Sikhs, and any other people with olive or brown skin, exposes the arbitrary and politically constructed character of new and old racial categories in the U.S. It also reveals the inadequacy of U.S. multiculturalism to resist the hegemonic relationship between being "White" and "American." Finally, the short memory of the media suppresses any mention of the Euro-American anti-capitalist and anti-imperialist "terrorist" groups of the 1970s and 1980s. A critical attention to the idioms of the present war mobilization compels us to deconstruct other politically loaded tropes, including security, liberty, freedom, truth, civil rights, Islamic fundamentalism, women under the Taliban, the flag, and "America."

Fifth, we recognize the gendered and ethnocentric history of sentimentality, grief, and melancholy that have been mobilized in the new war effort. We do not intend to disparage or dismiss the sadness and deep emotions raised by the events of 9-11 and its aftermath. But we do think it is important to point out that there has been a massive deployment of therapeutic discourses that ask people to understand the impact of the events of September 11 and their aftermath solely as "trauma." Such discourses leave other analytical, historical, and critical frameworks unexplored. Focusing only on the personal or narrowly defined psychological dimension of the attacks and the ensuing war obscures the complex nexus of history and geopolitics that has brought about these events. We are not suggesting that specific forms of therapy are not useful. But the culture industry of "trauma" leads to a mystification of history, politics, and cultural critique. Furthermore, therapeutic discourse tends to reinforce individualist interpretations of globally significant events and it does so in an ethnocentric manner. Seeking relief through a psychotherapeutic apparatus may be a common practice among Euro-American upper- and middle-class people in the United States, but it should not be assumed to be a universally appealing or effective way to counter experiences of civil repression and war among people of other classes, ethnicities, and cultural backgrounds. Signs of the current trauma discourse's ethnocentricity come through in media depictions staged within the therapeutic framework that tend to afford great meaning, significance, and sympathy to those who lost friends and family members in the attacks on the World Trade Center and the Pentagon. By contrast, people who have lost loved ones as a consequence of U.S. foreign policy elsewhere are not depicted as sufferers of trauma or injustice. In fact, they are seldom seen on camera at all. Similarly, makeshift centers in universities around the U.S. were set up in the immediate wake of 9-11 to help college students cope with the psychological effects of the attacks. They tended to assume that 9-11 marked the first time Americans experienced vulnerability, overlooking not only the recent events of the Oklahoma City federal building bombing, but moreover erasing the personal experiences of many immigrants and U.S. people of color for whom "America" has been a site of potential or realized violence for all of their lives.

Sixth, our transnational feminist response involves a detailed critical analysis of the role of the media especially in depictions that include colonial tropes and binary oppositions in which the Islam/Muslim/non-West is represented as "uncivilized" or "barbaric." We note the absence or co-optation of Muslim women as "victims" of violence or of "Islamic barbarism." We note as well the use of those groups of women seen as "White" or "Western" both as "rescuers" of non-Western women but also as evidence of the so-called "civilizing" efforts of Europe and North America. We see these discursive formations as a result not only of colonialism's discursive and knowledge-producing legacies, but also of the technologies and industrial practices that produce contemporary global media, and transnational financing of culture industries. We seek especially to analyze the participation of women in these industries as well as the co-optation of feminist approaches and interests in the attack on a broad range of Islamic cultural and religious institutions, not just "Islamicist/extremist" groups. Thus we point out as a caution that any counter or resistance media would need to have a firm grasp of these histories and repertoires of practice or risk reproducing them anew.

Seventh, we call for a deeper understanding of the nature of capitalism and globalization as it generates transnational movements of all kinds. Thus, we seek to counter oppressive transnational movements, from both the "West" as well as the "non-West," with alternative movements that counter war and the continued production of global inequalities. We note in particular that religious and ethnic fundamentalisms have emerged across the world within which the repression of women and establishment of rigidly dichotomized gender roles are used both as a form of power and to establish a collectivity. Such fundamentalisms have been a cause of concern for feminist groups not only in the Islamic world but also in the U.S. Feminist and other scholars have noted that these movements have become transnational, through the work of nation-state and non-governmental organizations, with dire consequences for all those who question rigid gender dichotomies. Since these movements are transnational, we question the notion of isolated and autonomous nation-states in the face of numerous examples of transnational and global practices and formations. The recent displays of national coherence and international solidarity (based on nineteenth- and twentieth-century constructions of international relations) cannot mask the strains and contradictions that give rise to the current crisis. Thus, we need an analysis of the numerous ways in which transnational networks and entities both limit and at the same time enable resistance and oppression. That is, the complex political terrain traversed by transnational networks as diverse as al-Qaida and the Red Cross must be understood as productive of new identities and practices as well as of new kinds of political repression. Transnational media has roots in pernicious corporate practices yet it also enables diverse and contradictory modes of information, entertainment, and communication. Feminist analysis of these complex and often contradictory transnational phenomena is called for.

In closing, we want to make it very clear that we oppose the U.S. and British military mobilization and bombing that is underway in Afghanistan and that may very well expand further into the West, Central, and South Asian regions. We are responding to a crisis in which war, as described by the George W. Bush administration, will be a covert, diversified, and protracted process. At this moment we call for a resistance to nationalist terms and we argue against the further intensification of U.S. military intervention abroad. We refuse to utilize the binaries of civilization vs. barbarism, modernity vs. tradition, and West vs. East. We also call for an end to the racist scapegoating and "profiling" that accompanies the stepped up violations of civil liberties within the territorial boundaries of the U.S. We urge feminists to refuse the call to war in the name of vanquishing a so-called "traditional patriarchal fundamentalism," since we understand that such fundamentalisms are supported by many nation-states. We are also aware of the failures of nation-states and the global economic powers such as the IMF and the World Bank to address the poverty and misery across the world and the role of such failures in the emergence of fundamentalisms everywhere. Nationalist and international mobilization for war cannot go forward in our name or under the sign of "concern for women." In fact, terror roams the world in many guises and is perpetrated under the sign of many different nations and agents. It is our contention that violence and terror are ubiquitous and need to be addressed through multiple strategies as much within the "domestic" politics of the U.S. as elsewhere. It is only through developing new strategies and approaches based on some of these suggestions that we can bring an end to the violence of the current moment.

....

Paola Bacchetta is professor of gender and women's studies at the University of California, Berkeley. She has written or cowritten six books and over sixty articles on political conflict, transnational feminist and queer of color theory, decolonial and postcolonial theory, multiplicities (intersectionality, assemblages, articulation theorizations, coformations, coproductions), political conflict, and space. Her most recent books are *Co-Motion: On Feminist and Queer Alliances* (forthcoming) and *Global Racialities* (coedited with Sunaina Maira and Howard Winant, 2019).

Tina Campt is Owen F. Walker Professor of Humanities and Modern Culture and Media at Brown University and a research associate at the Visual Identities in Art and Design Research Centre (VIAD) at the University of Johannesburg, South Africa. She is the author of four books: *Other Germans* (2004), *Image Matters* (2012), *Listening to Images* (2017), and *The Black Gaze* (forthcoming 2021).

Inderpal Grewal is professor emerita in women's, gender, and sexuality studies at Yale University. She is the author of *Home and Harem: Nation, Gender, Empire, and the Cultures of Travel* (1996), *Transnational America: Feminisms, Diasporas, Neoliberalisms* (2005), and *Saving the Security State: Exceptional Citizens in Twenty-First-Century America* (2017). She has coedited *An Introduction to Women's Studies: Gender in a Transnational World* (2002), *Scattered Hegemonies* (1994), and *Theorizing NGOs: States, Feminisms, and Neoliberalism* (2014). Her current projects examine security regimes, patriarchal authoritarianism, and bureaucracy.

Caren Kaplan is professor emerita of American studies at the University of California, Davis. Her research draws on cultural geography, landscape art, and military history to explore the ways in which undeclared as well as declared wars produce representational practices of atmospheric politics. Her recent publications include *Aerial Aftermaths: Wartime from Above* (2018) and *Life in the Age of Drone Warfare* (2017).

Minoo Moallem is a professor of gender and women's studies and director of media studies at the University of California, Berkeley. Trained as a sociologist, she writes on postcolonial feminist studies, transnational cultural studies, nationalism and consumerism, immigration and diaspora studies, Middle Eastern studies, and Iranian visual cultures and diasporas. She is author of several research monographs, edited collections, and articles, and she recently completed a digital media project, "Nation-on-the Move."

Jennifer Terry is professor and chair of the Department of Gender and Sexuality Studies at the University of California, Irvine. Her books include *Attachments to War: Biomedical Logics and Violence in Twenty-First-Century America* (2017), *An American Obsession: Science, Medicine, and Homosexuality in Modern Society* (1999); and two coedited anthologies, *Deviant Bodies: Critical Perspectives on Difference in Science and Popular Culture* (1995) and *Processed Lives: Gender and Technology in Everyday Life* (1997). She has written on reproductive politics, the history of sexual science, contemporary scientific approaches to the sex lives of animals, love of objects, signature injuries of war, and the relationship between war-making practices and entertainment.

Note

Originally published in *Meridians* vol. 2, no. 2, 2002.

Sunera Thobani

....

War Frenzy

Abstract: Following a speech against the war on terror the author presented at a conference on Violence Against Women, she was publicly attacked and threatened for "hate-mongering." This paper was written in the aftermath of the controversy that followed. The author's speech highlighted the history of U.S. foreign policy and sought to mobilize feminist opposition to the invasion of Afghanistan. The war, she argued, was reviving the colonial/imperial global divide and would be catastrophic. The author explores here how a number of carefully considered words used in the speech were treated in the public controversy that followed as too "incendiary" and used to shut down political opposition to the invasion of Afghanistan. By publicly branding her an ungrateful and hate-filled immigrant woman, and an apologist for terrorism, the media provided a platform to shut down political opposition and advance the racist and Islamophobic political ideology of the war.

October 12, 2001

My recent speech at a women's conference on violence against women has generated much controversy. In the aftermath of the terrible attacks of September 11, I argued that the U.S. response of launching "America's new war" would increase violence against women. I situated the current crisis within the continuity of North/South relations, rooted in colonialism and imperialism. I criticized American foreign policy, as well as President Bush's racialized construction of the American nation. Finally, I spoke of

MERIDIANS · feminism, race, transnationalism   Volume 19 Supplement 2020
DOI: 10.1215/15366936-8565902 © 2002 Wesleyan University Press, now published by
Duke University Press on behalf of Smith College

the need for solidarity with Afghan women's organizations as well as the urgent necessity for the women's movement in Canada to oppose the war.

Decontextualized and distorted media reports of my address have led to accusations of me being an academic impostor and morally bankrupt, and of engaging in hate-mongering. It has been fascinating to observe how my comments regarding American foreign policy, a record well documented by numerous sources whose accuracy or credentials cannot be faulted, have been dubbed "hate-speech." To speak about the indisputable record of U.S.-backed coups, death squads, bombings, and killings ironically makes me a "hate-monger." I was even made the subject of a "hate-crime" complaint to the Royal Canadian Mounted Police (RCMP), alleging that my speech was a "hate-crime." Despite the virulence of these responses, I welcome the public discussion my speech has generated as an opportunity to further the public debate about Canada's support of America's new war. When I made the speech, I believed it was imperative to have this debate before any attacks were launched on any country. Events have overtaken us with the bombing of Afghanistan underway and military rule having again been declared in Pakistan in the recent past. The need for this discussion has now assumed greater urgency as reports of casualties are making their way into the news. My speech at the women's conference was aimed at mobilizing the women's movement against this war. I am now glad for this opportunity to address wider constituencies and in different forums.

First, however, a few words about my location: I place my work within the tradition of radical, politically engaged scholarship. I have always rejected the politics of academic elitism which insist that academics should remain above the fray of political activism and use only disembodied, objectified language and a "properly" dispassionate professorial demeanor to establish our intellectual credentials. My work is grounded in the politics, practices, and languages of the various communities I come from, and the social justice movements to which I am committed.

On American Foreign Policy

In the aftermath of the terrible September 11 attacks on the World Trade Center and the Pentagon, the Bush administration launched "America's War on Terrorism." Eschewing any role for the United Nations and the need to abide by international law, the U.S. administration initiated an international alliance to justify its unilateral military action against Afghanistan. One of its early coalition partners was the Canadian government which committed its unequivocal support for whatever forms of assistance the United States might request. In this circumstance, it is entirely reasonable that people in Canada examine carefully the record of American foreign policy.

As I observed in my speech, this record is alarming and does not inspire confidence. In Chile, the CIA-backed coup against the democratically elected Allende government led to the deaths of over 30,000 people. In El Salvador, the U.S.-backed regime used death squads to kill about 75,000 people. In Nicaragua, the U.S.-sponsored terrorist Contra war led to the deaths of over 30,000 people. The initial bombing of Iraq left over 200,000 dead, and the bombings have continued for the last ten years. UNICEF estimates that over one million Iraqis have died, and that 5,000 more die every month as a result of the UN-imposed sanctions, enforced in their harshest form by U.S. power. The list does not stop here. 150,000 were killed and 50,000 disappeared in Guatemala after the 1954 CIA-sponsored coup; over two million were killed in Vietnam; and 200,000 before that in the Hiroshima and Nagasaki nuclear attacks. Numerous authoritarian regimes have been backed by the United States including Saudi Arabia, Egypt, the apartheid regime in South Africa, Suharto's dictatorship in Indonesia, Marcos in the Philippines, and Israel's various occupations of Lebanon, the Golan Heights, and the Palestinian territories. The U.S. pattern of foreign intervention has been to overthrow leftist governments and to impose right-wing regimes, which in turn support U.S. interests, even if this means training and using death squads and assassinating leftist politicians and activists. To this end, it has a record of treating civilians as entirely expendable.

It is in this context that I made my comment that the United States is the largest and most dangerous global force, unleashing horrific levels of violence around the world, and that the path of U.S. foreign policy is soaked in blood. The controversy generated by this comment has surprisingly not addressed the veracity of this assessment of the U.S. record. Instead, it has focused on my tone and choice of words (inflammatory, excessive, inelegant, un-academic, angry, etc.).

Now I have to admit that my use of the words "horrific violence" and "soaked in blood" is very deliberate and carefully considered. I do not use these words lightly. To successive United States administrations the deaths resulting from its policies have been just so many statistics, just so much "collateral damage." Rendering invisible the humanity of the peoples targeted for attack is a strategy well used to hide the impact of colonialist and imperialist interventions. Perhaps there is no more potent a strategy of dehumanization than to proudly proclaim the accuracy and efficiency of "smart" weapons systems, and of surgical and technological precision, while rendering invisible the suffering bodies of these peoples as disembodied statistics and mere "collateral damage." The use of embodied language, grounded in the recognition of the actual blood running through these bodies, is an attempt to humanize these peoples in profoundly graphic terms. It compels us to recognize the sheer corporeality of the terrain upon which bombs rain and mass terror is waged. This language calls on "us" to recognize that "they" bleed just like "we" do, that "they" hurt and suffer just like "us." We are complicit in this bloodletting when we support American wars. Witness the power of this embodiment in the shocked and horrified responses to my voice and my words, rather than to the actual horror of these events. I will be the first to admit that it is extremely unnerving to "see" blood in the place of abstract, general categories and statistics. Yet this is what we need to be able to see if we are to understand the terrible human costs of empire-building. We have all felt the shock and pain of repeatedly witnessing the searing images of violence unleashed upon those who died in New York and Washington. The stories we have heard from their loved ones have made us feel their terrible human loss. Yet where do we witness the pain of the victims of U.S. aggression? How do we begin to grasp the extent of their loss? Whose humanity do we choose to recognize and empathize with, and who becomes just so much "collateral damage" to us? Anti-colonial and anti-imperialist movements and theorists have long insisted on placing the bodies and experiences of marginalized Others at the center of our analysis of the social world. To fail to do so at this moment in history would be unconscionable. In the aftermath of the responses to my speech, I am more convinced than ever of the need to engage in the language and politics of embodied thinking and speaking. After all, it is the lives, and deaths, of millions of human beings we are discussing. This is neither a controversial nor a recent demand. Feminists (such as Mahasweta Devi, Toni Morrison, Gayatri Spivak, and Patricia Williams) have forcefully drawn our attention to what is actually done to women's bodies in the course of mapping out racist colonial relations. Frantz Fanon, one of the foremost theorists of decolonization, studied and wrote about the role of violence in colonial social organization and about the psychology of oppression; but he described just as readily the bloodied, violated Black bodies and the "searing bullets" and "blood-stained knives" which were the order of the day in the colonial world. Eduardo Galeano entitled one of his books *The Open Veins of Latin America* and the post-colonial theorist Achille Mbembe talks of the "mortification of the flesh," of the "mutilation" and "decapitation" of oppressed bodies. Aime Cesaire's poetry pulses with the physicality of blood, pain, fury, and rage in his out-cry against the domination of African bodies. Even Karl Marx, recognized as one of the founding fathers of the modern social sciences, wrote tren-chant critiques of capital, exploitation, and classical political economy, and did not flinch from naming the economic system he was studying "vampire capitalism." In attempting to draw attention to the violent effects of abstract and impersonal policies, I claim a proud intellectual pedigree.

Invoking the American Nation

In my speech I argued that in order to legitimize the imperialist aggression which the Bush administration is undertaking, the President is invoking an American nation and people as being vengeful and bloodthirsty. It is *de rigueur* in the social sciences to acknowledge that the notion of a "nation" or a "people" is socially constructed. The American nation is no exception.

If we consider the language used by Bush and his administration to mobilize this nation for the war, we encounter the following: launching a crusade; operation infinite justice; fighting the forces of evil and darkness; fighting the barbarians; hunting down the evil-doers; draining the swamps of the Middle East, etc., etc. This language is very familiar to peo-ples who have been colonized by Europe. Its use at this moment in time reveals the nature of a fundamentalist and racialized Western ideology which is being mobilized to rally the troops and to build a national and international consensus in defense of "civilization." It suggests that any-one who hesitates to join in is also "evil" and "uncivilized." In this vein, I have repeatedly been accused of supporting extremist Islamist regimes merely for criticizing U.S. foreign policy and Western colonialism.

Another tactic to mobilize support for the war has been the manipula-tion of public opinion. Polls conducted in the immediate aftermath of the September 11 attacks were used to repeatedly inform us that the over-whelming majority of Americans allegedly supported a strong military retaliation. They did not know against whom, but they purportedly sup-ported this strategy anyway. In both the use of language and these polls, we are witnessing what Noam Chomsky has called the "manufacture of consent." Richard Lowry, editor of the *National Review* opined, "If we flatten part of Damascus or Tehran or whatever it takes, this is part of the solution." President Bush stated, "We will bear no distinction between those who commit the terrorist attacks and those who harbor them." Even as the bombing began, he declared that the war is "broader" than against just Afghanistan, that other nations have to decide if they side with his administration or if they are "murderers and outlaws themselves." We have been asked by most public commentators to accept these calls for military aggression against "evil-doers" as natural, understandable, and even reasonable, given the attacks on the United States. I reject this position. It would be just as understandable a response to re-examine American foreign policy, to address the root causes of the violent attacks on the United States, and to make a commitment to abide by international law. In my speech, I urged women to break through this discourse of "naturalizing" the military aggression, and recognize it for what it is, vengeful retribution and an opportunity for a crude display of American military might. We are entitled to ask: Who will make the decision regarding which "nations" are to be labeled "murderers" and "outlaws"? Which notions of "justice" are to be upheld? Will the Bush administration set the standard, even as it is overtly institutionalizing racial profiling across the United States?

I make very clear distinctions between people in America and their government's call for war. Many people in America are seeking to contest the "national" consensus being manufactured by speaking out and by organizing rallies and peace marches in major cities, about which there has been very little coverage in Canada. Irresponsible media reporting of my comments which referred to Bush's invocation of the American nation as a vengeful one deliberately took my words out of this context, repeating them in one television broadcast after another in a grossly distorted fashion.

My choice of language was, again, deliberate. I wanted to bring attention to Bush's right-wing, fundamentalist leanings and to the neo-colonialist/imperialist practices of his administration. The words "bloodthirsty" and "vengeful" are designations most people are quite comfortable attributing to "savages" and to the "uncivilized," while the United States is represented as the beacon of democracy and civilization. The words "bloodthirsty" and "vengeful" make us confront the nature of the ideological justification for this war, as well as its historical roots, unsettling and discomfiting as that might be.

The Politics of Liberating Women

I have been taken to task for stating that there will be no emancipation for women anywhere until Western domination of the planet is ended. In my speech I pointed to the importance of Afghanistan for its strategic location near central Asia's vast resources of oil and natural gas. I think there is very little argument that the West continues to dominate and consume a vast share of the world's resources. This is not a controversial statement. Many prominent intellectuals, journalists and activists alike, have pointed out that this domination is rooted in the history of colonialism and rests on the ongoing maintenance of the North/South divide, and that it will continue to provoke violence and resistance across the planet. I argued that in the current climate of escalating militarism, there will be precious little emancipation for women, either in the countries of the North or the South.

In the specific case of Afghanistan, it was the American administration's economic and political interests which led to its initial support for and arming of Hekmatyar's Hezb i Islami and its support for Pakistan's collaboration in and organization of the Taliban regime in the mid 1990s. According to the Pakistani journalist Ahmed Rashid, the United States and Unocal conducted negotiations for years with the Taliban for an oil pipeline through Afghanistan in the mid-1990s. We have seen the horrendous consequences this has had for women in Afghanistan. When Afghan women's groups were calling attention to this U.S. support as a major factor in the Taliban regime's coming to power, we did not heed them. We did not recognize that Afghan women's groups were in the front line resisting the Taliban and its Islamist predecessors, including the present militias of the Northern Alliance. Instead, we chose to see them only as "victims" of "Islamic culture," to be pitied and "saved" by the West. Time and time again, Third World feminists have pointed out to us the pitfalls of rendering invisible the agency and resistance of women of the South, and of reducing women's oppression to various Third World "cultures." Many continue to ignore these insights. Now, the U.S. administration has thrown its support behind the Northern Alliance, even as Afghan women's groups oppose the U.S. military attacks on Afghanistan, and raise serious concerns about the record of the Northern Alliance in perpetrating human rights abuses and violence against women in the country. If we listen to the voices of these women, we will very quickly be disabused of the notion that U.S. military intervention is going to lead to the emancipation of women in Afghanistan. Even before the bombings began, hundreds of thousands of Afghan women were compelled to flee their homes and communities, and to become refugees. The bombings of Kabul, Kandahar, Jalalabad, and other cities in the country will result in further loss of life, including the lives of women and children. Over three million Afghan refugees are now on the move in the wake of the U.S. attacks. How on earth can we justify these bombings in the name of furthering women's emancipation?

My second point was that imperialism and militarism do not further women's liberation in Western countries either. Women have to be brought into line to support racist imperialist goals and practices, and they have to live with the men who have been brutalized in the waging of war when these men come back. Men who kill women and children abroad are hardly likely to come back cured of the effects of this brutalization. Again, this is not a very controversial point of view. Women are taught to support military aggressions, which is then presented as being in their "national" interest. These are hardly the conditions in which women's freedoms can be furthered. As a very small illustration, just witness the very public vilification I have been subjected to for speaking out in opposition to this war.

I have been asked by my detractors that if I, as a woman, am so critical of Western domination, why do I live here? It could just as readily be asked of them that if they are so contemptuous of the non-Western world, why do they so fervently desire the oil, trade, cheap labor, and other resources of that world? Challenges to our presence in the West have long been answered by people of color who say, We are here because you were (are?) there! Migrants find ourselves in multiple locations for a myriad of reasons, personal, historical, and political. Wherever we reside, however, we claim the right to speak and participate in public life.

Closing Words

My speech was made to rally the women's movement in Canada to oppose the war. Journalists and editors across the country have called me idiotic, foolish, stupid, and just plain nutty. While a few journalists and columnists have attempted balanced coverage of my speech, too many sectors of the media have resorted to vicious personal attacks. Like others, I must express a concern that this passes for intelligent commentary in the mainstream media.

The manner in which I have been vilified is difficult to understand, unless one sees it as a visceral response to an "ungrateful immigrant" or an uppity woman of color who dares to speak out. Vituperation and ridicule are two of the most common forms of silencing dissent. The subsequent harassment and intimidation which I have experienced, as have some of my colleagues, confirms that the suppression of debate is more important to many supporters of the current frenzied war rhetoric than is the open discussion of policy and its effects. Fortunately, I have also received strong messages of support. Day by day the opposition to this unconscionable war is growing in Canada and all over the world.

I would like to thank all of my family, friends, colleagues, and allies who have supported and encouraged me.

I have since learned from my lawyer that the Ottawa police have dismissed the complaint against me. While I am glad that the police have decided not to proceed with the case, I believe we cannot discount the effect this incident has had on creating a chilly and fearful climate for anti-racist, feminist, and anti-war organizing in the country. Nor can we discount the serious personal and financial consequences to activists who stand up against this form of harassment.

....

Sunera Thobani is professor in the Department of Asian Studies at the University of British Columbia. She works on critical race, postcolonial, transnational, and feminist theory; intersectionality, social movements, and critical social theory; colonialism, indigeneity, and racial violence; globalization, citizenship, and migration; South Asian women's, gender, and sexuality studies; representations of Islam and Muslims in South Asian and Western media; and Muslim Women, Islamophobia, and the war on terror. Her research ranges across Canada, the United States, South Asia, and the South Asian diaspora.

Note
Originally published in *Meridians* vol. 2, no. 2, 2002.

Works Cited
Cesaire, A. 1983. *The Collected Poetry*. Translated by C. Eshleman and A. Smith. Berkeley: University of California Press.
Chomsky, N. 1985. *Turning the Tide: U.S. Intervention in Central America and the Struggle for Peace*. Boston: South End Press.
Devi, M. 1997. *Rudali: From Fact to Performance*. Translated by A. Katyal. Calcutta: Seagull Books.

Fanon, F. 1963. *The Wretched of the Earth*. New York: Grove Press, Inc.

———. 1986. *Black Skin, White Masks*. London: Pluto Press.

Galeano, D. 1974. *Open Veins of Latin America*. New York: Monthy Review Press.

Herman, E. and N. Chomsky. 1988. *Manufacturing Consent: The Political Economy of the Mass Media*. New York: Pantheon Books.

Mbembe, A. 2001. *On the Postcolony*. Berkeley: University of California Press.

Morrison, T. 1994. *Beloved*. New York: Alfred A. Knopf.

Rashid, A. 2000. *Taliban: Militant Islam, Oil & Fundamentalism in Central Asia*. New Haven: Yale University Press.

Spivak, G. C. *The Post-Colonial Critic: Interviews, Strategies, Dialogues*, edited by S. Harasym. New York: Routledge.

Williams, P. J. 1991. *The Alchemy of Race and Rights*. Cambridge: Harvard University Press.

Suheir Hammad

First Writing Since

September 2001

1. there have been no words.
i have not written one word.
no poetry in the ashes south of canal street.
no prose in the refrigerated trucks driving debris and dna.
not one word.

today is a week, and seven is of heavens, gods, science.
evident out my kitchen window is an abstract reality.
sky where once was steel.
smoke where once was flesh.

fire in the city air and i feared for my sister's life in a way never before.
and then, and now, i fear for the rest of us.

first, please god, let it be a mistake, the pilot's heart failed, the plane's
    engine died.
then please god, let it be a nightmare, wake me now.
please god, after the second plane, please, don't let it be anyone who
looks like my brothers.

i do not know how bad a life has to break in order to kill.
i have never been so hungry that i willed hunger

MERIDIANS · feminism, race, transnationalism   Volume 19 Supplement 2020
DOI: 10.1215/15366936-8565913 © 2002 Wesleyan University Press, now published by
Duke University Press on behalf of Smith College

i have never been so angry as to want to control a gun over a pen.
not really.
even as a woman, as a palestinian, as a broken human being.
never this broken.

more than ever, i believe there is no difference.
the most privileged nation, most americans do not know the
    difference
between indians, afghans, syrians, muslims, sikhs, hindus.
more than ever, there is no difference.

2. thank you korea for kimchi and bibim bob, and corn tea and the
genteel smiles of the wait staff at wonjo—smiles never revealing the
heat of the food or how tired they must be working long midtown
shifts. thank you korea, for the belly craving that brought me into the
city late the night before and diverted my daily train ride into the world
trade center.

there are plenty of thank yous in ny right now. thank you for my lazy
procrastinating late ass. thank you to the germs that had me call in
sick. thank you, my attitude, you had me fired the week before. thank
you for the train that never came, the rude nyer who stole my cab going
downtown. thank you for the sense my mama gave me to run. thank
you for my legs, my eyes, my life.

3. the dead are called lost and their families hold up shaky printouts in
front of us through screens smoked up.

we are looking for iris, mother of three. please call with any
information. we are searching for priti, last seen on the 103rd floor.
    she
was talking to her husband on the phone and the line went. please
    help
us find george, also known as adel. his family is waiting for him with
his favorite meal. i am looking for my son, who was delivering coffee.
i am looking for my sister girl, she started her job on monday.

i am looking for peace. i am looking for mercy. i am looking for
evidence of compassion. any evidence of life. i am looking for life.

4. ricardo on the radio said in his accent thick as yuca, "i will feel so much better when the first bombs drop over there. and my friends feel the same way."

on my block, a woman was crying in a car parked and stranded in hurt. i offered comfort, extended a hand she did not see before she said, "we're gonna burn them so bad, i swear, so bad." my hand went to my head and my head went to the numbers within it of the dead iraqi children, the dead in nicaragua. the dead in rwanda who had to vie
    with
fake sport wrestling for america's attention.

yet when people sent emails saying, this was bound to happen, lets not forget u.s. transgressions, for half a second i felt resentful. hold up with that, cause i live here, these are my friends and fam, and it could have been me in those buildings, and we're not bad people, do not support america's bullying. can i just have a half second to feel bad?

if i can find through this exhaust people who were left behind to mourn and to resist mass murder, i might be alright.

thank you to the woman who saw me brinking my cool and blinking back tears. she opened her arms before she asked "do you want a hug?" a big white woman, and her embrace was the kind only people with the warmth of flesh can offer. i wasn't about to say no to any comfort. "my brother's in the navy," i said. "and we're arabs." "wow, you got double trouble." word.

5. one more person ask me if i knew the hijackers.
one more motherfucker ask me what navy my brother is in.
one more person assume no arabs or muslims were killed.
one more person assume they know me, or that i represent a people. or that a people represent an evil. or that evil is as simple as a flag and words on a page.

we did not vilify all white men when mcveigh bombed oklahoma. america did not give out his family's addresses or where he went to church. or blame the bible or pat robertson.

and when the networks air footage of palestinians dancing in the
    street,
there is no apology that hungry children are bribed with sweets that
turn their teeth brown. that correspondents edit images. that archives
are there to facilitate lazy and inaccurate journalism.

and when we talk about holy books and hooded men and death,
    why do
we never mention the kkk?

if there are any people on earth who understand how new york is
feeling right now, they are in the west bank and the gaza strip.

6. today it is ten days. last night bush waged war on a man once openly
funded by the cia. i do not know who is responsible. read too many
books, know too many people to believe what i am told. i don't give a
fuck about bin laden. his vision of the world does not include me or
those i love. and petitions have been going around for years trying to
get the u.s. sponsored taliban out of power. shit is complicated, and i
don't know what to think.

but i know for sure who will pay.

in the world, it will be women, mostly colored and poor. women will
have to bury children, and support themselves through grief. "either
you are with us, or with the terrorists"—meaning keep your people
under control and your resistance censored. meaning we got the loot
and the nukes.

in america, it will be those amongst us who refuse blanket attacks on
the shivering. those of us who work toward social justice, in support of
civil liberties, in opposition to hateful foreign policies.

i have never felt less american and more new yorker—particularly
brooklyn, than these past days. the stars and stripes on all these cars
and apartment windows represent the dead as citizens first—not
    family
members, not lovers.

i feel like my skin is real thin, and that my eyes are only going to get
darker. the future holds little light.

my baby brother is a man now, and on alert, and praying five times a
day that the orders he will take in a few days time are righteous and
    will
not weigh his soul down from the afterlife he deserves.

both my brothers—my heart stops when i try to pray—not a beat to
disturb my fear. one a rock god, the other a sergeant, and both
palestinian, practicing muslims, gentle men. both born in brooklyn
and their faces are of the archetypal arab man, all eyelashes and nose
and beautiful color and stubborn hair.

what will their lives be like now?

over there is over here.

7. all day, across the river, the smell of burning rubber and limbs floats
through. the sirens have stopped now. the advertisers are back on the
air. the rescue workers are traumatized. the skyline is brought back to
human size. no longer taunting the gods with its height.

i have not cried at all while writing this. i cried when i saw those
buildings collapse on themselves like a broken heart. i have never
owned pain that needs to spread like that. and i cry daily that my
brothers return to our mother safe and whole.

there is no poetry in this. there are causes and effects. there are
    symbols
and ideologies. mad conspiracy here, and information we will never
know. there is death here, and there are promises of more.

there is life here. anyone reading this is breathing, maybe hurting, but
breathing for sure. and if there is any light to come, it will shine from
the eyes of those who look for peace and justice after the rubble and
rhetoric are cleared and the phoenix has risen.

affirm life.

affirm life.

we got to carry each other now.

you are either with life, or against it.

affirm life.

....

Suheir Hammad is an American poet, author, and political activist. She was born in Amman, Jordan. Her parents were Palestinian refugees who immigrated along with their daughter to Brooklyn, New York when she was five years old. Her parents later moved to Staten Island. When hip-hop entrepreneur Russell Simmons came across the poem included in this issue, he signed Hammad to a deal with HBO's Def Poetry Jam. In 2008, she was cast in her first fiction role in cinema, the Palestinian film *Salt of this Sea* by Annemarie Jacir, which premiered as an official selection of the Cannes International Film Festival.

Note

Originally published in *Meridians* vol. 2, no. 2, 2002.

Kristal Brent Zook

···

Dreaming in the Delta

A Memoir Essay

Abstract: In 1990, in Indianola, Mississippi, there was a catfish-processing plant owned by 178 White male farmers. The workforce inside the plant was ninety percent Black and female. Led by an ordinary working mother turned union organizer named Sarah White, the women at Delta Pride led the largest strike of Black laborers ever to take place in that state, and won. Kristal Brent Zook, an award-winning journalist, traveled to Indianola to meet with White and others in an effort to understand the plight of working class women in the modern-day South. What she found there taught her as much about herself, as it did about human rights and dignity in America today.

"Does your mama know you're in Mississippi?"

The person asking was Geri Taylor, an organizer with the United Food and Commercial Workers Union. We were seated around a conference table at Local 1529 in Indianola, Mississippi. Four other women were there, bags of fast-food chicken splayed out between us. Carolyn Bradford was a Tennessee-based organizer, while Margaret Hollins and Mary Sibley were local UFCW reps, as was Sarah White, the woman I had come to see.

This was the work of 1529: strategizing around conference tables, color coding charts. Setting up in dusty hotels for months at a time, their mission was to convince workers to stand together, one by one, and be counted. In this way, the women had organized poultry and catfish plants, nursing homes and grocery stores. They had brought modest health benefits, wage increases, paid holidays, and even a modicum of job security.

MERIDIANS · feminism, race, transnationalism   Volume 19 Supplement 2020
DOI: 10.1215/15366936-8565935 © 2003 Wesleyan University Press, now published by Duke University Press on behalf of Smith College

More importantly, they brought something that had been missing for far too long from the lives of working women: dignity.

At Delta Pride, restroom breaks were considered a privilege, not a right. Such everyday indignities had made the women tough—but not in an urban, fast way. Tough like the south. A place that was utterly foreign to me.

We were in the heart of Sunflower County. I knew that Fannie Lou Hamer had been jailed and beaten less than thirty years ago in nearby Humphries County just for registering poor Black farmers to vote. And I knew that in 1955, Lamar Smith, a sixty-three-year-old farmer and World War II veteran, was shot dead before dozens of witnesses on the city courthouse lawn for the same offense. Nor had the brutality ended with the civil rights era. During the 1990s more than twenty Black men were found hung "under suspicious circumstances" in local Mississippi prisons. Now here I was, a high-yella gal cruising along backwoods Southern roads in a zippy rental, as though my life could not be taken in the blink of an eye for asking too many questions. Hence the query: "Does your mama know where you are?"

Before traveling to Mississippi in the early 1990s, I had never heard of Sarah White, never read her name in any newspaper, or seen her face on any television. I had no idea that in 1990 she had led the largest strike of Black workers in Mississippi history. I did not know that she and nearly 1,000 workers—most of them Black women—had taken on Delta Pride, the largest catfish plant in the country. Their strike was "one of the most significant labor and civil rights victories of the decade," according to the 1991 documentary, *This Far by Faith*, narrated by Alfre Woodard. So why hadn't any of us heard the good news: that Black women in the 1990s were leading movements as grand as anything the 1960s ever saw?

Delta Pride first came to Indianola in 1981. Sarah White was twenty-two. She had been employed at the nearby Con Agra catfish plant, but was finding it difficult to work the night shift and take care of her family. In 1983 she was hired at Delta Pride, working days and earning $3.40 an hour. "We felt it was a new beginning," she recalls. "A chance to get off the welfare lines and make a better life for our kids." But Sarah soon discovered that conditions at Delta Pride were no different from those of hundreds of poultry, catfish, tobacco, and steel plants across the south. Other than Christmas Day, no holidays were honored, no sick days allowed, and no health care provided. If you or your child became ill, you risked being fired. If you dared use the bathroom outside of your allotted break time, get to packin'. Carpal-tunnel syndrome, a repetitive motion injury of the hands and arms, was a serious health risk at the plant. But afflicted workers were given aspirin by company nurses and ordered to continue working. Scalding hot "fish water" could cause serious burning and there were countless eye injuries from splashing bleach and ammonia.

The women at Delta Pride were also subjected to sexual harassment by White male supervisors. "They would come up behind you," explains Sarah, speaking with a slow southern drawl and revealing a gold-capped front tooth. "They'd feel on you, and ask where you live. And say that if they could come by and see you, they'd put you on an easier job."

"They were right behind you all the time," recalls another Delta employee, "pressuring you to go faster. 'Why did you even leave home today?' they'd say. 'You should have stayed there.'" At the B.C. Rogers chicken plant in McComb, Mississippi, women worked "cone lines," where they were responsible for skinning chickens, hanging them, pulling breasts off, and digging out tenders, at an inconceivable rate of *thirty-two birds per minute*.

Lunch hour at Delta Pride takes place on wooden, indoor picnic benches, where workers sit, still wearing blood-splattered work jackets and blue hairnets. Even outside, there is no escape from the stench. A few go out for fast food. Others have brought plastic containers from home filled with beef, sweet potatoes, chicken. No one here eats catfish; they know too much about it. Some play cards, or rest their heads. One woman studies a copy of a book called, *A Woman's Guide to Spiritual Warfare*.

"Lawd ha' mercy," someone exclaims, passing a photo of a Greenville firefighter-slash-stripper around the table. When the snapshot makes it into to my hands I understand why. "Mandingo," as he calls himself, boasts a huge erection in his sheer, red bikini briefs. "Oh it's real," adds the photographer. "I guarantee you. It's *real*."

There is laughter here. In fact, the blasé, everydayness of the moment makes me dizzy. I need to walk away, splash water on my face. I need to know that I haven't imagined the horror of this place. When I emerge from a gray bathroom stall—now equipped with doors thanks to the union—a scrap of notebook paper on the floor catches my eye. It says simply: "He shall direct your path: Proverbs 3–6." Now I remember why I came.

"Working at these factories is like being on a plantation," says Charlie Braxton, a Mississippi-based journalist and poet. "You walk in boots because your feet are covered in entrails and blood. It's the worst kind of work you could possibly do." Braxton recounts a story about a young man who lasted exactly eight hours at the B.C. Rogers poultry plant in McComb. "He came out and his hands were all bloody and raw, and he said, 'Man, I can't do this. They treat you like animals in there. They won't even let you go to the bathroom.' The kid ended up selling crack," says Braxton. "That life was more appealing to him than working in the chicken plantations. The younger generation is totally different," he adds. "Young people are saying they'd rather go to jail, or to the army and risk getting killed. And their anger is coming out in hip hop."

In 1986, Sarah White was the mother of a four-year-old son. Going into the army, selling crack, or rapping were not options for her. What was an option was signing the union card that her co-worker, Mary Young, had received in the mail. "Things began to move real quick from there," recalls Sarah, in conversations we had in her car, at the office, and in her home over the course of two visits. "I was scared when we started," she told me, "because I knew I had a baby to take care of." Bobby Moses, of the legendary Algebra Project, was a UFCW representative from Atlanta at the time. He advised the women not to go out alone at night. "We'd known," says Sarah, "since the days of Dr. King, that people had been shot and hurt doing this kind of work. As far as being afraid for our lives, that was a sense we all had too."

"The people who run the catfish farms are related to the same people who ran the plantations," offers Braxton. "They're on the same family land." Plantation families did not disappear after slavery, agrees historian Clyde Woods. They simply expanded their monopolies—over agriculture, land, water, and banking. Humiliation was a time-honored tradition used to insure that workers remembered "their place." Perhaps the most perverse evidence of an ongoing "plantation mentality" was Delta's bathroom policy, whereby workers were forced to ask for permission, like children, to relieve themselves. Often, they were refused. Tales of grown women and men urinating on the processing line and having to continue working were legion. When permission was granted, supervisors followed close behind with a timer. Outside normal breaks, workers were allowed a total of five minutes per week for bathroom "privileges." Management even removed stall doors to prevent them from dawdling.

What was I doing here?

In 1995, I spoke on the CNN talk show, "Both Sides With Jesse Jackson."

Many women of my generation often do not feel connected to social movements or to women's issues, I said. Later, Reverend Jackson urged me to visit the workers in Mississippi. "These are women who eat lunch standing up," he explained, "a sandwich in one hand and a cigarette in the other. Women who work all day and night and still live below the poverty line." Indeed, nearly forty percent of Sunflower County residents live below the poverty line. One in six work in catfish.

I went to the Delta because someone I respected told me that I should. I went because there was no front porch outside my house where I could sit and hear stories about what was happening to the folk down south or up north. Because there were no Pullman porters to drop clandestine copies of the Black press along the road so that I could find out where I should be and what I should be doing in the struggle. Because my grandmother worked the night shift in a plastics factory in Chicago in the 1940s, while cleaning White folks homes and caring for three young babies. Because I could not create a conversation out of nothingness and distance. I went to Mississippi because my heart said go. I trusted it, to tell me why.

Mary Young and Sarah White spent the winter of 1986 in Young's unheated old "jalopy," going door-to-door and collecting signatures from co-workers. They stood outside the local Wal-Mart for long hours trying to convince terrified friends and associates to stand with them. Most of the women were understandably afraid of losing their jobs. But Sarah White spoke to them with the oratorical force of a natural preacher: "I know throughout this South . . . of plants with inhumane treatment of women. Because they feel we can't fight, and we have no other choices. But you *do* got other choices," she bellows. "You don't have to just bend down and let the man ride your back! And then, once you break that barrier," she continues, "it's a relief that lifts up off of you. . . . " She shakes her head, overcome with emotion. "Like you could never imagine! I want every woman to feel that feeling of joy that I have. That I'm proud, Black, beautiful, and free. Got a voice of my *own*."

Within two months, Sarah and Mary had built an organizing committee of fifty workers. Enough to call for a union vote. "Ya'll know anything about a union coming here?" asked their supervisors, suspicious of secret activity during the quiet winter months. "No, ma'am," they replied. "You'll be fired," continued the supervisors, "if you're involved with any union." "Yes, ma'am."

It was a vicious campaign. Delta owners hired Mayor Charles Evers, the brother of assassinated civil rights leader Medgar Evers, to campaign against the workers. Nevertheless in 1986, workers voted overwhelmingly to join the UFCW. "We were excited that first year," recalls White. "We got three-year contracts saying we had job security. And we got the right to use the bathroom six times a week, five minutes each time."

Ironically however, harassment became worse after the victory. "We was good to you before," threatened management, according to one worker. "We gave you catfish for the holidays, but that's all over now." Hazardous work conditions also remained unchanged. Sarah suffered second- and third-degree burns when scalding hot water crept through her work boots. In 1989, Delta was fined $32,800 by the United States Occupational Safety and Health Administration (OSHA) for failing both to prevent and treat carpal-tunnel syndrome among its workers (an amount Delta has yet to pay in full). In 1990, a year the company generated some $144 million in sales, workers were still receiving a starting wage of $3.80 per hour. "It seemed like they had control of our minds," wrote White. "Nobody really understood that there was an avenue we could go down to break through to a better place."

In response to a list of grievances presented by the union, which included an immediate pay increase of $7.50 per hour for workers with eighteen months seniority on the job, Delta's owners countered with an offer of a $5.00 per hour increase over the next two years—a slap in the face, as it coincided with a federal minimum wage increase anyway. At an impasse, management once again threatened to take away bathroom rights. "So the people voted to go ahead and strike," recalls Sarah.

In fact, they agreed (410–5) to walk out on jobs they desperately needed. "There was a lot of animosity on both sides," says Sarah. "Supervisors would come out shooting at night." One worker, Mary Green, was approached by an officer while walking the picket line and told that she was under arrest. When Green asked why, she was answered with a blow to the stomach. "Nigger bitch," replied the officer, as he beat her across her arms and legs.

Sarah White traveled to Washington, D.C. along with Mary Green and Margaret Hollins, to testify before members of the Congressional Black Caucus. With the support of legislators, the women garnered publicity and support for a nationwide consumer boycott. As major grocers in St. Louis, Chicago, Atlanta, and Detroit refused to stock Delta Pride fish, the two-pronged strategy of boycott and strike worked. By December, three months after they had walked out on the job, Local 1529 was victorious. In a new contract, they were guaranteed ten paid holidays per year, time and a half after eight hours of work, a pension plan, and the right to a harassment-free work environment. They also won the right to use the bathrooms as *needed*. I am stunned by the thought that dignity is really defined in such simple terms. "That strike," says Sarah, "was really about the bathrooms."

There are many things that I learn about her during my visits to Indianola: That she was one of eleven children and painfully withdrawn. That she was ashamed of the simple, homemade dresses her mother forced her to wear to school. Ashamed that her family couldn't afford a pair of blue jeans like the other kids had. That her father deserted the family after a car accident that left her mother in a coma. Sarah tells me that union organizing ended her shyness about public speaking, but not her insecurity about being overweight. And she tells me about a steel worker named Sam, a man she lived with for eleven years. "Sam was . . . sorta mean," she says, euphemistically. "He was always proud of me and what I stood for. But it was like . . . it didn't apply to him. Not as a woman."

"You know," she confides one day in the car, on our way back to the office. "I don't speak about it. But strong as I may appear, I've had abuse as far as a relationship with a man. And I had to really find my way back. It just had me feeling like I wasn't important, like I wasn't nobody." Today she is wearing a black leatherette vest over a flowing white blouse, blue jeans and low-heeled black sandals. Working for the union has given her a financial leg up, relatively speaking. She has the money to pay the note on a Ford Taurus. She is doing well, by regional standards.

"Because . . . that man," she continues, "was like, my inspiration that I could be successful. Sometimes in our minds, we have that, you know? Where we think that *he's* what makes us special. And I had to really find my way back, with the help of close friends and other people talking to me. A lot of the women here in the factories, they don't feel good about themselves. Because that's what's been crushed in us. And I try to tell them that you can. It's your choice to have that. You've just gotta stand up for yourself."

There are other things that Sarah does not share with me. She does not tell me that her sister came to visit from Memphis, and was shot to death by her boyfriend in White's own living room. Nor does she mention that she received a four-year degree from Mississippi Valley State University at age twenty-two. Or that she took the test for a teaching credential, twice, failing by just a few points both times. Or that she has always wanted, really, to be a nurse. When I ask why she didn't pursue her dreams, her response tears at a place deep inside of me. "I guess I just didn't have the smarts," she says. "I lost interest after a while."

Last year, the State of Mississippi agreed to spend $500 million to improve its historically Black colleges—including Jackson, Alcorn, and Mississippi Valley State—which were found to be "vastly inferior to the colleges that whites attended" according to the federal courts. Perhaps this landmark civil rights case, initiated in 1975 by Jake Ayers, a Black share-cropper, on behalf of his son might have made for an entirely different future for Sarah White, had it not taken twenty-six years to win. Instead, twenty-two-year-old Sarah took a much-needed job at Delta Pride, where she would remain for the next two decades.

"You're a Libra?" I ask her one day, filling the silence at 1529.

"Yep."

"So am I. Librans believe in justice, you know."

"Yeah, they do," she says, flashing a gold-toothed smile.

"I don't know why women are at the forefront," says Sylvester Fields, an organizer in the Jackson office of the UFCW, "but they are. A good base of strong women will usually bring the men along. The worst thing owners can have in a plant is some mad women." "Where are the men?" answers Sarah, in response to my question. "In jail. On drugs. Or pursuing careers and don't care about us. But there's women everywhere," she continues, her voice rising to rhythmic preaching levels. "Women in the chicken plants, women in the catfish plants, women in the grocery stores, and women in the nursing homes. Women are everywhere."

Working for the union, White is still employed by Delta, but as a liaison, which means that she negotiates complaints, mediating between workers and management. During my visit, we travel to Belzoni, another Delta Pride plant, to discuss the three-day suspension of a young Black worker named Milton. Once inside, the three of us (Milton, Sarah, and myself) take seats on stiff wooden chairs, facing a blue-jean wearing supervisor with dirty blond hair, who sits behind a sturdy wooden desk. Milton was suspended for refusing to work a double shift without advance notice. Before that, he had been fired and rehired, shuffling that cost him a signif-icant pay cut. This was, as Sarah explained to me, common practice at Delta; a loophole whereby high-paid workers could be dismissed and later brought back at minimum wage.

As I watch her, I'm struck by the way Sarah maneuvers within a hostile situation. The room is silent except for the click-click of a ballpoint pen the supervisor holds in her hand. She claims to have lost the "grievance" forms filed by Milton. Opening and closing desk drawers in a show, she eventually sighs, tossing a stack of yellow sheets across the desk toward Sarah. "These here is all I got," she says finally, click-clicking away.

"Milton wrote two &%#$@ pages on that grievance!" screams UFCW representative Rose Turner a couple of days later. Turner was the rep who first filed the paperwork. "He sat down under a tree and wrote it out, and then in the morning he say, 'I had some more to put to it, so I went on back and put that in.' And I told Milton!" she adds, at the top of her lungs, "to keep it short, because if you put too much $#@% in there, they just turn it around and use it against you!" Today Rose is at a doctor's appointment (not surprisingly) and Sarah is filling in for her as mediator.

Turning her attention to a nearby window, she fixes her gaze somewhere outside and pauses. Then, turning to address Milton, she says calmly: "We got a grievance procedure here. That means that you say what you need to say. As far as if somebody not treating you with respect, or if they harassing you, or not treating you like a man, you have a voice through this union. So, now, Milton. You got the floor."

"Well," he begins, still wearing his white overcoat and hair net, "I basically feel like I'm doing the job of two men. I starts at 9 o'clock and I stays sometime until 11 o'clock at night. There's a man who supposed to be helping me," he continues, "but he got a different job. I don't know what he do. They call him the 'ice man.' But he don't wear no gloves or coat. He just walk around."

White listens, pauses, and then speaks. "As far as with Lisa," she explains, "she supposed to have a open-door policy where you can come and file your grievance. But if she don't hear you, or won't hear you, you can come to us. You know, Milton," she continues, "you doin' your job, you got a family to feed. Lisa doin' her job, she got a family to feed. And you gotta be careful with that strain, Milton, working them hours. Cuz then, if you have a problem and need medical treatment. . . . " She says these last words without ever removing her gaze from Milton's, but the words are intended for Delta Pride alone: "You know, they might need to think about if things need to be redone in that area. Delta."

Plantation diplomacy in the contemporary South: a coup of the spirit.

And yet, it is hard for me to predict, from day to day, whether Sarah

White will be feeling upbeat or defeated. "We just be losin' elections lately," she confides one evening around midnight, a cherry Coke in one hand, Benson and Hedges in the other. We're sitting across from one another at her dining room table: me taking notes, and she smacking flies with a plastic swatter. Outside, her Taurus is parked in the dirt road beside a faded, steel mailbox. Beyond that, a low wall of thick weeds separates Sarah's home from railroad tracks. A chorus of crickets reaches a powerful crescendo. "It be close fights," she continues, becoming agitated, "but somewhere at the end, the man give 'em ten cents more. And it frustrates the hell out of me. They just don't wanna get up off them minimum wages."

When asked again about her dreams, Sarah takes a few contemplative drags from her cigarette before responding. "[Activist] Jeruba Hill down in Greenville got this thing called the Worker's Rights Center," she says. "If I had the money I would build the biggest center that could hold people! With different sections like, welfare, and worker's rights, a section for education, workshops set up for women, and for children. It would be a facility with computers and stuff they can use. And I would have like a tunnel, where you could see Fannie Lou on this side, Martin Luther King on this side. Because I know we need that education here in the Delta more than anything else. Girl, if we only had that. The barriers it would break down. I could go out on those [gambling] boats right now and win a million dollars. But I couldn't sleep at night if I didn't buy some books for the school."

My time with Sarah White changes me. I begin to feel powerful again. Connected. Returning to Los Angeles feels lonely. "Where are you?" exclaims Geri Taylor into the phone when I call a few days later, alone again at my computer. Hanging up, I replay Sarah's words from a microcassette recorder: "I truly believe that when God gives to you, it's for you to put it back. Because when you get a taste of what prejudice feels like, it hurts. And then when you get a taste of freedom, you never forget it. It makes you feel good about yourself. It gives you peace."

Already, I missed the gentle breezes of the Delta, and the six-foot-tall sunflowers, growing in ordinary yards, behind ordinary houses. Already, I missed the women of Local 1529. And I missed Sarah most of all, who had opened the door and invited me in. This is why I went to Mississippi. To be counted. And invited in.

Kristal Brent Zook is an award-winning journalist and the author of three books, including *Black Women's Lives: Stories of Power and Pain* (2006) and *Color by Fox: The Fox Network and the Revolution in Black Television* (1999; featured on CNN's *The Nineties*). A former contributor to *Essence* and the *Washington Post*, she writes about social justice issues, culture, gender, multiracial identity, and blackness. Dr. Zook is currently a professor of journalism at Hofstra University. To read her work, please go to kristalbrentzook.com.

Note

Originally published in *Meridians* vol. 3, no. 2, 2003.

Nikky Finney

....

The Making of Paper

For Toni Cade Bambara (1939–1995)
In the early 80s, I spent two years in a writing workshop that Toni Cade
Bambara held in her Atlanta home. Anybody in the community who was
writing was welcome. I adored the opportunity to sit at this great writer's
feet who knew so much about so much. In 1990, she moved to Philadelphia
and was later diagnosed with cancer. We talked on the long-distance line
when we could. I would always ask if there was anything she needed that I
could send. She usually answered no. But in our last conversation, which
took place one week before she crossed over, she held the phone a little
longer. "Maybe," she said, "maybe you could send some paper and what
about one of those fat juicy pens?"

Imagine that,
you asking me for paper.

For the record let me state
I would hunt a tree down for you,
stalk it until it fell
all loud and out of breath
in the forest.

Much as I love a tree,
fat, tall and free.

MERIDIANS · feminism, race, transnationalism   Volume 19 Supplement 2020
DOI: 10.1215/15366936-8565924 © 2003 Wesleyan University Press, now published by
Duke University Press on behalf of Smith College

As anti-violent and pro-vegetarian
as I am.
Never been much
for strapping a gun
to any of my many hips,
for any reason whatsoever,
but on the copper penny eyes
of my grandmother, I tell you
this: I would hunt a tree down for you.

And when found
I would pull it all the way down the road
through congested city streets all by myself
and deliver it straight away
to your hospital bed,
one single extra-large floral arrangement,
something loud and free,
with red and purple bow.

Or better yet,
this tree-loving
gun-hating Geechee girl
would strap a wild west
gun belt machete
around her hips
enter the worst part of the woods alone
and go trunk to trunk
until the right one appeared
growing peaceful in its thousand-year-old
natal plot.

Look it
right in its
round rough ancient eyes
and confess away,
tell it straight to its woody face,
my about-to-do deed.

I've even touch it
on its limbs
fingers begging forgiveness,
give as much comfort to it
as I could, while trying to
explain the necessaryness
of its impending death;
me standing there,
my *Gorilla My Love* eyes
spilling all over everything,
sending up papyrus prayers
that all begin with,
"I'm so sorry but Toni Cade needs paper."

Only then would I slash its lovely body
into one million thin black cotton rag sheets
just your uncompromising size.

Send you some paper?
Oh yes,
paper is coming Toni Cade
wagonloads
in the name
of you sweet Black writing life,
from Black writers everywhere
refusing to leave
the arena
to the fools.

Paper is on the way.

· ·

Nikky Finney was born by the sea in South Carolina and raised during the Civil Rights, Black Power, and Black Arts Movements. She is the author of *On Wings Made of Gauze* (1985), *Rice* (1995), *The World Is Round* (2003), and *Head Off & Split* (2011), which won the National Book Award for Poetry in 2011. Her new collection of poems, *Love Child's Hotbed of Occasional Poetry* was published in 2020.

Note

Originally published in *Meridians* vol. 3, no. 2, 2003.

Luz Calvo

· ·

Art Comes for the Archbishop
The Semiotics of Contemporary Chicana Feminism
and the Work of Alma López

Abstract: Inspired by the Chicana feminist artist Alma López's *Our Lady* (1999), this essay explores Chicana cultural and psychic investments in representations of the Virgin of Guadalupe. As an image of the suffering mother, the Virgin of Guadalupe is omnipresent in Mexican-American visual culture. Her image has been refigured by several generations of Chicana feminist artists, including Alma López. Chicana feminist reclaiming of the Virgin, however, has been fraught with controversy. Chicana feminist cultural work—such as the art of Alma López, performances by Selena Quintanilla, and writings by Sandra Cisneros and John Rechy—expand the queer and Chicana identifications and desires, and contest narrow, patriarchal nationalisms. By deploying critical race psychoanalysis and semiotics, we can unpack the libidinal investments in the brown female body, as seen in both in popular investments in protecting the Catholic version of the Virgin of Guadalupe and Chicana feminist reinterpretations.

The Virgin of Guadalupe is omnipresent in Chicano/a visual space. She is painted on car windows, tattooed on shoulders or backs, emblazoned on neighborhood walls, and silk-screened on t-shirts sold at local flea markets. Periodically, her presence is manifested in miraculous apparitions: on a tree near Watsonville, California; on a water tank, a car bumper, or a freshly made tortilla.[1] She is the sorrowful mother, a figure who embodies the suffering of Chicano/a and Mexican populations in the context of colonization, racism, and economic disenfranchisement.

MERIDIANS · feminism, race, transnationalism   Volume 19 Supplement 2020
DOI: 10.1215/15366936-8565946 © 2004 Smith College

The Virgin of Guadalupe is a polyvalent sign, able to convey multiple and divergent meanings and deployed by different groups for contradictory political ends. For example, the Catholic Church deploys the image of the Virgin of Guadalupe in service of its regressive sexual politics. However, progressive movements have also carried the image of the Virgin of Guadalupe to signify resistance to colonization and economic exploitation, as in the War of Mexican Independence and in the United Farm Workers' struggle for economic justice. Chicano/a cultural workers—from graffiti artists to novelists—use the Virgin of Guadalupe as a sign of racial solidarity, for she is imagined to have brown skin,[2] or as a sign of transnational solidarity, for she is the patron saint of Mexico. Chicano/a artists have reproduced and reinterpreted the Virgin of Guadalupe in their *retablos*, paintings, murals, posters, films, performance, and literature. Almost without exception, Chicano/a films include the image of Guadalupe in their sets, nodding to her importance in Chicano/a visual space. And merchants in Chicano/a neighborhoods use the Virgin of Guadalupe to sell their product: it is commonplace to see a mural devoted to the Virgin on the outside of a neighborhood liquor store or to find Virgin of Guadalupe auto "air fresheners" at the car wash.

Because of her ubiquity and her polyvalence, the image of the Virgin of Guadalupe is a sign that is especially available for semiotic re-signification and cultural transformation. Alma López, a Chicana lesbian artist, has seized this semiotic possibility, creating a series of digital images that break open and transfigure previous interpretations and uses of the Virgin. Lopez's images make manifest the sexuality and desire that are embedded in Chicano/a attachments to the image of the Virgin of Guadalupe. As might be expected, Lopez's work has been quite controversial. Her 1999 digital collage *Our Lady* (fig. 1) incited demonstrations, community meetings, and letters to the editor when it was displayed at the Museum of International Folk Art in Santa Fe, New Mexico.[3] Angered by López's image, a vocal group of Chicano and Catholic activists called for its removal from the museum. Rhetorically reducing the image to the language of fashion, these activists repeatedly described López's piece as a depiction of "the Virgin of Guadalupe in a bikini." The demonstrators gained the support of Santa Fe Archbishop Michael J. Sheehan, who called the piece "insulting and sacrilegious," asserting that in López's image the Virgin is "shown as a tart or a street woman" (Office of Communications, Archdiocese of Santa Fe, 2001). Chicano nationalists tried to maintain control over the meaning

Figure 1. Alma López, *Our Lady* (1999). Courtesy of artist.

of the Virgin of Guadalupe and contain her within the semiotic structure of the Catholic Church.

The protests that surrounded *Our Lady* caused considerable consternation and debate within Chicano/a communities in New Mexico and beyond.[4] Ultimately, however, López's defenders successfully deployed First Amendment arguments and the New Mexico museum's Committee on Sensitive Materials decided that the work would remain on display. Undoubtedly, free speech arguments have strategic value—that is, they protect a space for the public articulation of queer desire and the display of images that contest fixed and static ideas about cultural identity. However, First Amendment arguments cannot begin to account for the kind of cultural work achieved by queer and feminist Chicano/a art. Speaking from the position of a queer Chicana cultural critic, I argue that rights-based arguments assume that we (artists and critics of color, queers, and other disenfranchised people) already have what we seek to defend: namely, equal footing with the imagined subject of Western liberal democracy. In my view, López's art poses a critique and challenge that is about more than free speech or even equal rights.

López's art breaks open a public, cultural space for the articulation of queer Chicana desire. This desire is at once sexual and political. Her images seduce the spectator into new desiring positions by exposing Chicano/a libidinal investments—conscious and unconscious—in the Virgin of Guadalupe. Her images mobilize and disturb these investments, channeling Chicano/a desire in queer directions. Significantly, *Our Lady* refuses to indulge in the disavowal of the body that informs conventional, religious representations of the Virgin. Instead, *Our Lady* represents the interlinkage of racial identities and sexual and political desires, while, at the same time, pointing to the constitutive ambivalence of the heart of Chicano/a—and other—identity formations.

Working in digital collage, as well as other in media, López—a relatively young artist—has already produced a sizable oeuvre, much of which is displayed on her Web site, at www.almalopez.net. López is a public artist and the Internet allows her work to circulate beyond the confines of the museum or art gallery. When López's work appears in art exhibits and galleries, most of her prints are relatively small, and the three images I discuss in this essay are all 11" × 17." López's images are more commonly viewed on computer screens, as individual users visit her Web site. The scale of López's work is most important in her large digital murals, which have been installed on the outside walls of buildings in East Los Angeles and at San Francisco's Galleria de la Raza. In these works, López locates herself within the Mexican and Chicano/a mural tradition, which changes community space by producing art on the walls of housing projects, public buildings, local businesses, and so forth. As another way of circulating her art, López has produced art for the cover of a number of important books in Chicano/a cultural studies and for a number of important Chicano/a conferences. The book covers and posters circulate her art in bookstores, universities, living rooms, and dormitories.[5] Through her diverse artistic interventions, López is having a significant impact on Chicano/a visual space.

In *Our Lady*, Lopez reconfigures the Virgin of Guadalupe, opening up her feminist and queer potential. *Our Lady* makes reference to the "original" image of *La Virgen de Guadalupe* (fig. 2), which hangs in the basilica in Mexico City.[6] In the original image, the *Virgen* is posed with hands in prayer and eyes cast down. She wears a long-sleeved gown, which covers her from neck to toe. Over her gown, a blue mantle drapes her head and the back of her body. The mantle is adorned with gold stars. She stands upon a dark crescent moon, held aloft by a little angel. López's *Our Lady* presents significant changes to the original version: in her image, López draws attention to the brown female body by exposing more of it. López's image features a photograph of Latina performance artist Raquel Salinas, her legs, arms, and midriff bare. Salinas is clothed only in roses, a symbol of the "proof" of the Virgin's 1531 apparition in Mexico. López modifies some other characteristics of the traditional image: The patterned rose-colored gown, which usually obscures the Virgin's body, is here rendered as background. The Virgin's traditional starry blue shawl is now draped and folded on a platform at the bottom of the frame. A modified blue-gray cloak covers the model's shoulders—this one filled in with the image of the Aztec goddess Coyolxauhqui, the rebellious daughter. The angel who holds up the moon in the traditional image has been replaced with a bare-breasted (and pierced) Latina (Raquel Gutiérrez) superimposed over a butterfly. Finally, and importantly, López changes the stance of the Virgin of Guadalupe, who traditionally stands demurely with eyes cast downward and her hands together in prayer. In López's image, the model has her hands on her hips and her gaze cast forward defiantly, toward the spectator.[7]

López draws from earlier Chicana feminist artistic engagements with the Virgin of Guadalupe by artists such as Ester Hernández and Yolanda López. Hernández's *La Virgen de Guadalupe Defendiendo los Derechos de los Xicanos* (1975) and Yolanda López's *Guadalupe Triptych* (1978) also refigure the pose of the *Virgen*. These images represent the Virgin of Guadalupe in active stances and with contemporary Chicana identities: practicing karate or running a marathon, as a seamstress or an *abuelita* (grandmother). In other images, these two artists explore the sexual potential of the Virgin: Hernández's *La Ofrenda* (1988) depicts a tattoo of the Virgin on the back of a Chicana lesbian; while Yolanda López's *Guadalupe Walking* (1978) portrays

Figure 2. The Virgin of Guadalupe.

the Virgin walking in a dress and open-toed heels. Like Alma López's *Our Lady*, these two images were received with threats and, in some cases, violence.[8]

The level of controversy that attends to feminist and queer revisions of the Virgin of Guadalupe reveals the high stakes of Chicano/a cultural identity—and its constitutive ambivalence. Images—such as the Virgin of Guadalupe—that purport to represent identity are inevitably locked in a paradoxical position, in that they can never fully achieve their goal: This is the gap between the signifer and the signified and the ambivalence at the heart of representation and identity. To use an example, the declarative utterance "I am Chicana" can never capture the complexity of the subject, who both exceeds the declaration (is more than that) and inevitably falls short (can never be Chicana enough). As in this example, there is always a disjuncture between representation and the subject. Attempts to disavow this gap anchor the meaning of ethnic identity in static, fixed, and often retrograde ways, resulting in what Emma Pérez—drawing on Michel Foucault—names a "fascist militancy" (1999, 124). Pérez productively considers Foucault's provocation: "How does one keep from being a fascist, even (especially) when one believes oneself to be a revolutionary militant?" (qtd. in E. Pérez, 123). Emma Pérez is correct in warning us of the potential political danger posed by those who try to control, police, and anchor the meaning of Chicano/a identity—or, by extension, the meaning of the Virgin of Guadalupe.

Reading contemporary Chicano/a politics as a space where "power polices desire," Emma Pérez argues: "We are threatened once again by a reemergence of uncompromising nationalist movements in which feminisms are dismissed as bourgeois, in which queer voices are scoffed at as a White thing, in which anyone who does not sustain the 'family values' of modernist, patriarchal nationalism is not tolerated and is often silenced" (1999, 124). In the case of the controversy surrounding Alma López's *Our Lady*, Emma Pérez is exactly on point, for it has been precisely those elements of the Chicano community that remain invested in "patriarchal nationalism" (namely, the church and male nationalist activists) who have been most vigorous in their attempts to silence the Chicana lesbian artist.[9]

The controversy surrounding López's art exposes the danger of fascism that arises from attempts to erase ambivalence. The Virgin of Guadalupe has the potential to be the sign of this fascist impulse. In a psychoanalytic reading, Emma Pérez argues, "The nationalist imperative is to move back in time, a regression, a return to the mother, but the mother cannot be Malinche. She must be La Virgen de Guadalupe; she cannot be sexual" (1999, 122). Nationalists mobilize Oedipus to structure Chicano/a identity in a heterosexual direction, embedding it in relations of patriarchal power and the incest taboo. However, as lesbian scholars such as Teresa de Lauretis have argued, the meaning of Oedipal structures is never as static—or heterosexual—as it might first appear (1994).

In Alma López's art, the Virgin of Guadalupe is claimed by Chicana lesbians, troubling the heterosexual matrix of Chicano/a nationalism. The nationalists root their politics in a mythic past and an image of totality that insists on the mother's heterosexual desire. However, Chicana feminism also mobilizes a notion of totality, although differently inscribed. In Chicana feminist art, the image of the Virgin signifies plentitude and omniscience: she is *nuestra madre* (our mother) who watches over us in the context of racism, sexual violence, economic injustice, and, even, homophobia.

Postcolonial critic Homi K. Bhabha, explaining the working of identification, argues that "identity is never an a priori, nor a finished product; it is only ever the problematic process of access to an image of totality" (1994, 51). In Chicano/a contexts, the Virgin is the sign of such totality, hence her significance to the production of Chicano/a identifications. While Chicano nationalists assume that identity is unified, fixed, and needs to be guarded from outside influence (such as queer sexualities), postcolonial critics such as Bhabha and Emma Pérez understand identity as something produced by always ambivalent and never stable psychic processes. What Bhabha means when he writes of "access to an image of totality" is a plentitude and fulfillment that can never be fully achieved: it is the desire for an impossible object, whether it be the mother or complete freedom.

The psychoanalytic concept of identification provides a tool for understanding identity as an open-ended process, never complete and always fraught with ambivalent desires. Identification is the process by which a subject introjects an object from the outside. Introjection takes an object from outside (another subject or an image) and incorporates it into one's own ego. The relationship between young Chicana fans and late pop star Selena is an excellent example of the way that identification works in Chicana contexts. This identification is the subject of *Corpus: A Home Movie for Selena*, a 1999 documentary by Lourdes Portillo. Her film opens with a scene of young Chicana fans lip-synching the songs of the recently deceased Selena. The young women emulate Selena's style, body gestures, and dance moves. In this identification with Selena, the girls introject Selena into their own egos, or sense of self. The young girls are able to deal with the loss of their idol (in Freudian terms, their "ego-ideal") by keeping her alive inside themselves. Sigmund Freud provides a more trivial example of this process of introjection: "A child who was unhappy over the loss of a kitten declared straight out that now he himself was the kitten, and accordingly crawled about on all fours, would not eat at the table, etc." (Freud 1921, 109). This example of the lost kitten illustrates the relationship between identification and loss. The child's pain over the loss of the kitten leads the child to incorporate the pet into his own ego (his sense of self): the child, in order to keep the kitten alive, becomes the kitten. In psychoanalytic terms, the "ego" (a psychoanalytic term for identity) is comprised entirely of identifications with objects that have been lost.

When Chicana girls (and, not incidentally, Chicano drag queens) impersonate Selena, it is a melancholic identification that constitutes the ego/identity along the axis of loss (Selena's death) and plentitude (Selena's Chicana body). Chicano/a identification with Selena is—like all identifications—ambivalent and aggressive: her death, while experienced as an intense loss, is also an opportunity to replace Selena, that is, the opportunity to be the next pop star, to be adored and to be loved. In a footnote to her discussion of Selena's death, Emma Pérez reports a conversation she had with Teresa de Lauretis (E. Pérez 1999, 158). The two scholars watched a 1995 Univisión interview with Yolanda Saldívar, Selena's murderer and the president of her fan club. They speculate that Saldívar was less likely to be motivated by lesbian desire (this rumor circulated widely) than by the desire to be Selena: "a psychological condition experienced by obsessed fans who want to become the star" (E. Pérez 1999, 158). Like the infamous Aimee discussed by Jacques Lacan, Saldívar's aggression, notes Emma Pérez, "has linked herself in memory, in history, to Selena" (E. Pérez 1999, 158). As is often the case in psychological phenomena, this extreme form of fandom shares a similar psychical structure to the more benign forms of fan desire: in both cases, identification with the star masks an aggressive component.

For her fans, Selena's brown female body signifies a plentitude in the context of a racial imaginary that devalues, degrades, and disparages female and brown bodies. In hegemonic U.S. cultural texts, brown female bodies are simultaneously sexualized and repudiated, desired and found disgusting. The brown female body is invested with particular social meanings resulting from her position at the intersection of racial and sexual categories; her body becomes the repository for U.S. cultural anxieties about both sexual and racial difference. In the case of Selena—as with the Virgin of Guadalupe—the brown female body is the cultural sign that encourages Chicana identification, even though, on the surface, these two figures appear to be very different. Selena's body is exposed, celebrated, and commodified, while the Virgin's body is hidden and disavowed. Politically, however, identification with Selena and the Virgin both allow for a certain recuperation of the brown female body, a possibility that can occur with public figures, either religious or pop.

Sandra Cisneros, in her essay "Guadalupe the Sex Goddess," directly addresses the issue of Chicana investment in the representation of brown female bodies. Cisneros's essay powerfully engages the slippery, mutually embedded categories of racial and sexual difference. Writing of her relationship to the Virgin of Guadalupe, Cisneros reveals a desire to lift the Virgin's dress, to see her underwear and her sex:

> When I see *La Virgen de Guadalupe* I want to lift her dress as I did my dolls' and look to see if she comes with *chones*, and does her *panocha* look like mine, and does she have dark nipples too? Yes, I am certain she does. (1996, 51)

Cisneros's desire to see the Virgin's body underscores the complexity of the nexus of racial and sexual difference in the formation of Chicana subjectivity. Within a cultural context where brown bodies and female bodies are undervalued, Cisneros wants to see her own image of her body (her "body-ego," in Freud's terms) reflected in a sacred icon. Perhaps paradoxically, she also constructs her self of body-ego in relation to a pornographic film featuring a White woman.

Cisneros writes, "Once, watching a porn film, I saw a sight that terrified me. It was the film star's *panocha*—a tidy, elliptical opening, pink and shiny like a rabbit's ear. To make matters worse, it was shaved" (Cisneros 1996, 50–51). If the sight of the Anglo porn star's genitals evoked in Cisneros feelings of horror, it was because of a difference that was at once racially and sexually coded. Here, the Lacanian concept of lack has application not (only) to the lack of the phallus but to the lack of the "white slit" that Cisneros witnessed in the pornography film. Cisneros interprets the porn star's genitals in relation to her own self-image: "I think what startled me most was the realization that my own sex has no resemblance to this woman's. My sex, dark as an orchid, rubbery and blue purple as a *pulpo*, an octopus, does not look nice and tidy, but otherworldly" (1996, 51). Cisneros uses figurative language to describe her genitals ("an orchid," "an octopus"). The image of her Chicana body is constructed through language, including the language of pornography, religious iconography, and poetic metaphor. In short, her brown, Chicana body is not an essential characteristic but rather a position within a grid that figures racial and sexual difference *inside* particular social symbolic structures.

Cisneros's description of her horror at the sight of the porn star's genitals recalls a scenario imagined by Freud: the scene of castration anxiety. In Freud's scenario, a young boy is surprised to learn that his mother does not have a penis. The scene of castration constitutes the boy as threatened: his penis could be taken away. At the same time, the scene reveals to the boy that he is "endowed," that is, he realizes that he has something his mother does not. A few notes of caution for those who would reject Freud's account outright: First, this is an allegory of sexual difference and should not be read literally. Second, this account of the constitution of male subjectivity is firmly entrenched in historically situated, patriarchal social relations: it is not ahistorical. Finally, the male subjectivity that is constituted in this scenario is thoroughly ambivalent. In her Lacanian reading of this scenario, Judith Butler argues that being endowed with the penis (or, in other terms, "phallus") is "a symbolic position . . . which is only partially and vainly approximated by those marked masculine beings who vainly and partially occupy that position within language" (1993, 63). The scene of castration constructs a masculinity that is in perpetual crisis.

David L. Eng makes productive use of Freud's allegory of castration in his book *Racial Castration*. He argues that feminist and queer theories that deploy "psychoanalytic theory to deconstruct naturalizing discourses of sexual, and in particular heterosexual, difference must be rethought to include viable accounts of race as well" (2001, 5). Eng thoughtfully undertakes this project by reading race back into psychoanalysis, finding in the case of castration that "castration is always racial castration" (2001, 5). Drawing on Eng's theoretical intervention (which I can only gloss here), I read Cisneros's essay in terms of racial castration anxiety.

For, in some sense, Cisneros's fantasy of lifting the Virgin's dress is also a search for the penis—that is, for a symbol of cultural power denied to Chicana subjects. Here, "the" penis would figure both sexual and racial difference. Cisneros's claim that she is searching for a "*panocha* like hers" hides another desire: that is, to find the Chicana mother's penis. This claim, of course, takes Freud's scenario in a different direction. However, if we read castration to be about the binary of presence/absence, then, perhaps, it is productive to consider "race" (imagined as manifested on or through the body) in these terms. The enigma of the meaning of "race" for racialized subjects produces a number of questions, captured in Cisneros's allegory of lifting the Virgin's dress—which can only be interpreted as a scenario to find the social symbolic meaning of her sexed and raced body. What she finds is an ambivalent position: while she claims to find her body under the Virgin of Guadalupe's gown, Cisneros's rhetorical consideration of pornography demonstrates that the Chicana body is overdetermined by the cultural binary of virgin/whore and presence/absence.

López's *Our Lady* provides yet another response to the binary of virgin/whore, presenting the materiality of the brown female body as a site of desire. While Cisneros explores Chicana identification (implicitly, heterosexual, because of the author's explicitly heterosexual—though queer-friendly—public identity) with the Virgin's brown body, López presents the brown body of the Virgin as desirable, perhaps, even as seductress, thus encouraging and inciting a queer reading. The queer potential of the Virgin of Guadalupe is made explicit in *Encuentro* (fig. 3), which depicts the celestial meeting of *la sirena* and *La Virgen de Guadalupe*, and in *Lupe & Sirena in Love* (fig. 4), which depicts the two in a sexual embrace.

Encuentro introduces three iconic elements that recur throughout López's work: *la Virgen*, *la sirena* (the mermaid), and *la mariposa* (the butterfly). The viceroy butterfly—an orange butterfly with black markings—is a recurring motif in López's images. In an artist statement, López discusses her choice of the viceroy butterfly, which resembles, and indeed mimics, the better known monarch butterfly. The monarch butterfly, unlike the viceroy, is poisonous to its predators. López explains:

> The Viceroy pretends to be something it is not just to be able to exist. For me, the *Viceroy* mirrors parallel and intersecting histories of being different or "other" even within our own communities. Racist attitudes see us Latinos as criminals and an economic burden, and families may see us as perverted or deviant. So from outside and inside our communities, we are perceived as something we are not. When in essence we are very vulnerable Viceroy butterflies, just trying to live and survive. (López 1999)

There is a play of recognition and misrecognition suggested by the metaphor of the viceroy butterfly. Ultimately, this butterfly (the queer Chicano/a subject) must forego the possibility of recognition; in order to survive, she must mimic the monarch (someone less vulnerable than herself). *In Our*

Figure 3. Alma López, *Encuentro* (1999). Courtesy of the artist.

Lady, the placement of the bare-breasted, pierced Chicana superimposed on the viceroy butterfly sustains the metaphor equating the butterfly with the queer Chicano/a subject. Like Cisneros, López uses figurative language and images to represent Chicana subjectivity and bodies.

To represent the Virgin of Guadalupe's love interest, López chooses the mermaid from the popular Mexican game *lotería*. In *lotería*, as in bingo, players hold a card with a grid. In the Mexican version, the grid is filled not with numbers but with images that map a Mexican national imaginary and construct Mexican identity.[10] In this way, the game figures identity in much the same way as I have discussed it in this essay, as a grid in which one finds one's (albeit ambivalent) place. The categories of people depicted on the

Figure 4. Alma López, *Lupe & Sirena in Love* (1999). Courtesy of the artist.

lotería cards reflect (often problematic) national, class, racial, and gendered categories. Perhaps, the most problematic cards are those that figure race: there is a card picturing a Black dandy entitled *El Negrito*[11] (fig. 5) and another picturing an Indian wearing a feather headdress and carrying a bow and arrow, entitled *El Apache* (fig. 6). Similarly, racialized gender is reproduced in a conventional fashion. In a card entitled *La Dama* (fig. 7), a slender, light-skinned woman wears a ladies suit and carries a matching handbag. Masculinity is portrayed on a card entitled *El Valiente* (fig. 8),

Figure 5. El *Negrito*, lotería card.

Figure 6. El *Apache*, lotería card.

Figure 7. *La Dama*, lotería card.

Figure 8. El *Valiente*, lotería card.

portraying a mestizo working-class man wielding a machete, and on another even less flattering card entitled El Borracho, which portrays a drunk mestizo man with a bottle stumbling on a sidewalk. El Catrín, in contrast, shows a light-skinned, upper-class effete man dressed in a tuxedo. Within the grid of mexicanidad mapped by lotería, la sirena stands out as a hybrid subject: she is part woman, part fish. This sirena appears to be of mestiza heritage, because instead of the usual blonde hair this mermaid has long wavy black hair. She is yet another figural representation of Chicana subjectivity.

As we have seen, Encuentro is structured by the combination of three elements—lotería's mermaid, the traditional Virgin of Guadalupe, and a butterfly. Semiotics holds that meaning is derived from two axes: selection (the paradigmatic axis) and combination (the syntagmatic axis). Meaning is constructed from the manner in which elements are selected and combined. The string of symbols on the lotería card is an excellent example of what semioticians call a "paradigmatic axis." Out of a set of possible lotería characters, the artist selects one, la sirena. Just as the artist selects la sirena instead of, say, el apache, she chooses the viceroy butterfly instead of the monarch butterfly and La Virgen de Guadalupe instead of an image of Tonantzín (a pre-Columbian goddess). And yet, because these other— unchosen—elements exist in what Victor Burgin calls the "popular pre-conscious," these elements linger in the field of meaning evoked by López's image, the "pre-text" (Burgin 1996, 60). The popular preconscious is defined by Burgin as "those ever-shifting contents which we may reasonably suppose can be called to mind by the majority of individuals in a given society at a particular moment in history; that which is 'common knowledge'" (1996, 58). Burgin, however, does not account for the different knowledges of those not in "the majority." In the case of the elements in López's work, the pre-text is not common knowledge for hegemonic U.S. subjects, while it most likely is recognized by Chicanos/as. Of course, this does not mean that the image is unreadable to non-Chicanos/as, but simply that the pre-text will yield a different set of images along the paradigmatic chain. For example, the composition of López's Encuentro recalls Michelangelo's portrayal of the creation of Adam on the Sistine Chapel ceiling, a scene that is in the preconscious of many, but not all, educated in Western cultural traditions. Thus, it should be clear that chains of association are open-ended, which means that a "meaning" of any particular image is never fixed or sealed. Rather, there are multiple meanings and the same image will register differently (produce another set of associations) with each spectator, depending in large part on their cultural location.

Subaltern artistic practice makes use of a postcolonial preconscious, which is distinct from the "common knowledge" of the society at large. The subaltern's specialized knowledge produces a particular kind of viewing pleasure for those who "get it." For example, a chain of linguistic associations along the paradigmatic axis suggests queerness: *mariposa* (butterfly) is connected to the words "*marimacha*" (dyke) and "*maricón*" (fag) through the prefix "mari" (and the prefix is etymologically linked back to María, the Virgin Mary). Moreover, queer meaning is also constructed along the syntagmatic axis; that is, by the combination of two female forms in a sexual relationship.

In *Lupe & Sirena in Love*, the three iconic elements of *Encuentro*—the mermaid, the Virgin of Guadalupe, and the viceroy butterfly—are combined with more images: the cityscape of Los Angeles; the wall at the Mexico-U.S. border replete with a mural of the traditional image of *la Virgen*, superimposed with "1848," the year of the signing of the treaty of Guadalupe-Hidalgo; and a photograph of a man being chased by an agent of the *migra* (U.S. Immigration and Naturalization "Service"). Three blond cherubs holding a gold ribbon and bouquets of roses frame this scene. In this image, there is a depth of field and layering of images, which contrasts with the relative flatness of *Encuentro*.

Finally, both *Encuentro* and *Lupe & Sirena in Love* suggest a Chicana lesbian primal scene: the fantasy of *nuestra madre* (our mother) in a sexual embrace with another woman.[12] This imagined scene stages the conception of queer desire in explicitly Chicano/a terms. In *Lupe & Sirena in Love*, queer desire is inseparable from its racial and cultural context and from its geographic location in the Mexico-U.S. borderlands. Moreover, the sense of place mapped in Lopez's images reflects geography more akin to psychic space than physical space.[13] By placing the Los Angeles cityscape and the fence at the Mexico-U.S. border in one frame, Lopez begins to map Chicana psychic geography as a transnational formation. Moreover, its geography is not that of the rational, imperialist cartographer but rather the layered space of the unconscious, where past and present, here and there, can exist in one image.

Collage, by self-consciously recycling images, enacts the postmodern notion that one cannot begin from outside of existing image regimes. Instead, cultural workers intervene by reworking preexisting images and remapping existing fantasies. Collage as an art form takes existing images and through a process of selection and combination shifts the terms of their meaning. Collage is not unlike the process of the constitution of the postmodern subject, who must piece together a self, however fragmented and shifting, by sampling bits and pieces from different histories, iconographies, and relationships. López uses the digital format to make transparent the process of assembly and juxtaposition. Digital collage differs from traditional collage because digital images are endlessly available and cut-and-paste technology allows artists to resize, blend, and create images that appear "seamless." López's images, however, are not seamless; instead, they call attention to the cut-and-paste technique used by the artist to piece together her statement.

Ironically, one of López's most vociferous detractors, New Mexican artist Pedro Romero Sedeño, astutely reads her work as "a hodge-podge of ideas digitally mixed." He compares López's art to Mary Shelley's Dr. Frankenstein, who, "in his lab, assembled human body parts, and was able to fabricate or interpret his own kind of being" (Romero Sedeño, 2002). While Romero Sedeño intended this interpretation pejoratively, I think that his analogy is evocative, suggesting both Chicano/a and postmodern aesthetic practices, and the possibility of assembling new subject positions from a "hodge-podge." The form of López's work draws attention to the process of fabrication and thus to the hybridity of Chicana identity. Her work challenges Chicano/a nationalist ideologies that disavow mixedness in favor of a fantasy of "pure" Chicano/a identity.

There is, I think, a further similarity among collage, post-colonial hybridity, and the Chicano/a aesthetic stance called "*rasquachismo.*"[14] Tomás Ybarra Frausto has described *rasquachismo* as a "stance rooted in resourcefulness and adaptability, yet ever mindful of aesthetics" (1996, 171). Poverty fuels the practice of *rasquachismo*, for it is a "making do," a piecing together, selecting from bits and pieces recovered from other uses or cheaply acquired. Ybarra Frausto finds that such "utilization of available resources makes for syncretism, juxtaposition, and integration" (1996, 171). However, reliance on things at hand does not mean that a highly developed code does not exist, nor that items are selected at random. Rather, *rasquache* aesthetics provide an apt example of a language structured by rules of selection and combination. In *rasquachismo*, the rules of selection run counter to bourgeois sensibilities and, indeed, this is part of their pleasure.

Like *rasquachismo*, digital art uses selection and combination to create new meanings. López does not attempt to create a queer Chicana viewing pleasure from scratch; instead, she culls from existing images of Mexican and Chicana women. She chooses from popular art forms, rather than from so-called high art; she selects her "bits and pieces" from the existing repertoire of working-class Chicano/a visual culture. While López, as an artist working in digital media, has access to high technology, she uses that technology to develop a digital rasquachismo. Like many Chicano/a artists, López does not reject the popular cultural practices; instead, she deploys rasquachismo as an aesthetic stance. She selects and combines images from popular and available sources, she uses layering and bright colors, and she juxtaposes religious iconography to photographs of her friends.

In both its popular practice and its academic production, rasquachismo exhibits a particularly non-normative—indeed queer—pleasure, as in the following definition proffered by Ybarra Frausto:

> In the realm of taste, to be rasquache is to be unfettered and unrestrained, to favor the elaborate over the simple, the flamboyant over the severe. Bright colors are preferred to sombre, high intensity to low, the shimmering and pattern filling all available space with bold display.
> (1996, 172)

In this vivid account, a queer camp aesthetic is embedded in a distinctly Chicano/a artistic practice through the "unrestrained," "the flamboyant," and "the shimmering." Rasquachismo is not an essential characteristic of either gay or Chicano/a communities, but rather, an aesthetic stance that is historically and culturally produced.

In its rejection of bourgeois sensibility, rasquachismo is a cultural practice that doesn't care what the neighbors think, wears too-bright colors and a flower in its hair. An example of Chicano/a rasquache aesthetics is depicted in the novel The Miraculous Day of Amalia Gómez, by gay Chicano author John Rechy. In his introduction to the second edition, Rechy describes his encounter with a woman who becomes Amalia, the protagonist of his novel:

> [At Thrifty's Drugstore] I . . . encountered one of the most resplendent women I've ever seen, a gorgeous Mexican-American woman in her upper thirties, a bit heavier than she might like to think, but quite lush and sexy. She wore high-heeled sling shoes—and a tight red dress, to show off proud breasts, but she had added a ruffle there to avoid any hint

of vulgarity, a fashion that defied all fashion except her own. She had a
luxuriance of black shiny hair, and into its natural waves she had
inserted . . . a real red rose. (2001, vii–viii)

Throughout this novel, Amalia is constructed as an icon of Latina suffering
and working-class beauty, by an author most widely known for his portrayals of gay hustlers. Amalia's style is staunchly *rasquache*, produced by a
gay author in admiration for such women. This novel stages an extradie-
getic identification of the gay Chicano author with the working-class, *rasquache*, Chicana protagonist. Rechy's brilliant staging of this identification
reveals an intersection of queer and Chicano/a working-class desire.

Mobilizing a similar *rasquache* aesthetic—with its embedded queer
potential—López has revised and recontextualized Chicana fascination
with the Virgin of Guadalupe. In *Encuentro* and *Lupe & Sirena in Love*, López
stages a primal fantasy: that is, a fantasy that constitutes a desiring subject. As in other primal fantasies that produce cultural locations and incite
all kinds of desires (sexual, political, and racial), López's art focuses attention on Chicana feminist and queer Chicana subject formation. López
depicts a scene of lesbian seduction as a founding moment of Chicana
subjectivity. In so doing, she places a queer Chicana love story on the same
symbolic terrain as the apparition of the Virgin of Guadalupe and thus
transfigures the Virgin of Guadalupe. Making productive use of the visual
image of everyday Chicano/a life, López's images begin to create a Chicana
feminist and queer iconography. Far from starting from something completely "new," López's art reworks (and reveals) the political-sexual desire
that is latent in the omnipresent image of the suffering Virgin. By mobilizing the semiotic processes of selection and combination and occupying the
Chicano/a aesthetic stance of *rasquachismo*, López's images successfully
invite and sustain queer interpretations of the Virgin of Guadalupe
and open polymorphous and perverse spaces for sexuality and desire in
Chicano/a imaginaries.

In conclusion, reading López's artistic reimaginings of the Virgin of
Guadalupe through Sandra Cisneros's desire to see the Virgin's brown body
has revealed the constitutive lack that fuels all Chicano/a identifications
with the Virgin of Guadalupe. It becomes clear that the imagined brownness of the Virgin has always structured Chicano/a allegiance to her. Chi-
cano/a desire for a brown-skinned Guadalupe is formed in and through the
social and historical institutionalization of racial hierarchies, a direct

result of the colonization of the Americas and its enduring racial legacies. However, the imagined collective allegiance to a sexless brown mother has come at considerable cost: women's active sexuality. The cultural work of Cisneros and López stretches Chicano/a collective imaginaries, shifting the terms by which Chicano/a subjects understand themselves, desire others, and act on the social world.

. . . .

Luz Calvo received their PhD from the history of consciousness program at the University of California, Santa Cruz. They are currently chair of the Department of Ethnic Studies at California State University, East Bay, where they teach courses in Chicanx/Latinx studies, gender and sexuality studies, and food justice. They are coauthor of *Decolonize Your Diet: Mexican-American Plant-Based Recipes for Health and Healing* (2015) and have written numerous articles in the fields of critical psychoanalysis and queer cultural studies.

Notes

Originally published in *Meridians* vol. 5, no. 1, 2004.

I would like to thank Catrióna Rueda Esquibel, Thuy Linh Nguyen Tu, Tomás Ybarra Frausto, and the anonymous readers at *Meridians* for their productive and generous critiques of my essay.

1   The 1993 discovery of an image of the Virgin of Guadalupe on a tree near Watsonville is referenced by Cherríe Moraga in her poem "Our Lady of the Cannery Workers" (1996) and her play *Watsonville: Some Place Not Here* (2002).

2   In this essay, I use the term "brown skin" to signal a collective cultural belief about Chicano/a bodies and not to reify some bodies or skin colors as more or less authentic. Indeed, "brown" Chicano/a bodies come in all shades. Brownness is a position within a social symbolic structure and is, I argue, constructed through language and fantasy, and it is not, as some might assume, an essential or biological characteristic.

3   *Our Lady* was part of Cyber Arte: Tradition Meets Technology, an exhibit that ran from 25 February to 28 October 2001.

4   López has documented this debate, collecting e-mails from detractors and supporters, newspaper articles from around the world, and letters to the editor on her Web site at http://www.almalopez.net/html. This site is an invaluable resource for researchers.

5   For example, López has designed the covers of *Puro Teatro: A Latina Anthology*, ed. Alberto Sandoval-Sanchez and Nancy Saporta Sternbach (University of Arizona, 1999); *Chicano/a Renaissance*, ed. David R. Maciel, Isidro D. Ortiz, and María Herrera-Sobek (University of Arizona, 2000); and *Velvet Barrios*, ed. Alicia Gaspar de Alba (Palgrave, 2003). She also designed posters for the "Otro Corazón: Queering the Art of Aztlan" (10 February 2001, University of California,

Los Angeles) and for the National Association of Chicana and Chicano Studies Conference (2–6 April 2003, Los Angeles, CA).

6   The "original" image of the Virgin of Guadalupe is thought to reference a statue of the Virgin Mary in Estremadura, Spain, which was also known as the Virgin of Guadalupe. Others understand the Virgin of Guadalupe to be a refiguration of a pre-Columbian goddess. As in all representation, the notion of an "original" referent is complicated.

7   López always names and thanks her models in public descriptions of her work. This gesture draws attention to the fact that her photographs depict particular subjects, with names, histories, and a relationship to the artist.

8   These images and their reception have been widely discussed by Chicana visual theorists, such as Angie Chabram-Dernersesian (1992), Yvonne Yarbro-Bejarano (1995), Alicia Gaspar de Alba (1998), Laura Elisa Pérez (1999), and Deena González (2003).

9   While the men were the most vocal detractors of López's art, some Chicana and *nuevomejicana* women also joined in the public critique. Such women present a challenge to my argument, and I hope that future research might be done— perhaps an ethnographic study—to explore their political and cultural formation.

10 The signifying system of *lotería* is further complicated by a series of verbal descriptions of each card. In many versions of the game, instead of the caller simply yelling out "*la sirena*," she will instead provide a popular saying. For example, for the mermaid card, the saying is "*Con los cantos de sirena no te vayas a marear*" (Don't get dizzy with the songs of the mermaid). Thus, the meaning of *lotería* images is anchored not only to the descriptive title of each card but also to the popular saying that accompanies them.

11 ALLGO, a queer Latino/a organization in Austin, Texas, has created a queer version of *lotería*. In a smart rhetorical move, they recast "*El Negrito*" as San Martin de Porres, a popular Black saint from Peru and renamed the card "*El Santo*" (the saint) (ALLGO, 2002).

12 See de Lauretis (1994, 81–142) for her recasting of the primal scene as a site of lesbian desire, and Emma Pérez (1999, 110–14) and Calvo (2001, 74) for discussions of the primal scene of colonialism and the formation of Mexican and Chicano/a subjectivities.

13 Anzaldúa (1987) also maps this psychic space in her theorization of "the borderlands."

14 Thanks to Tomás Ybarra Frausto for his helpful suggestions regarding *rasquachismo*.

Works Cited

ALLGO Austin Latino/Latina Lesbian, Gay, Bisexual, & Transgender Organization. 2002. "Lotería Jotería." Organization Web site. 30 November 2002. http://www.allgo.org/Viva_Cultura/Loteria_Joteria/loteria_joteria.html.

Anzaldúa, Gloria. 1987. *Borderlands/La Frontera: The New Mestiza*. San Francisco: Aunt Lute Books.

Bhabha, Homi. K. 1994. *The Location of Culture*. London: Routledge.

Burgin, Victor. 1996. *In/Different Spaces: Place and Memory in Visual Culture*. Berkeley: University of California Press.

Butler, Judith. 1993. *Bodies That Matter: On the Discursive Limits of "Sex."* New York and London: Routledge.

Calvo, Luz. 2001. "Lemme Stay, I Want to Watch: Ambivalence in Borderlands' Cinema." In *Latino/a Popular Culture*, ed. Mary Romero and Michelle Habell-Pallán, 73–81. New York: New York University Press.

Chabram-Dernersesian, Angie. 1992. "I Throw Punches for My Race, but I Don't Want to Be a Man: Writing Us—Chica-nos (Girls, Us)? Chicanas—in the Movement Script." In *Cultural Studies*, ed. Lawrence Grossberg, Cary Nelson, and Paula A. Treichler, 81–95. New York: Routledge.

Cisneros, Sandra. 1996. "Guadalupe the Sex Goddess." In *Goddess of the Americas: Writings on the Virgin of Guadalupe*, ed. by Ana Castillo, 46–51. New York: Riverhead Books.

de Lauretis, Teresa. 1994. *The Practice of Love: Lesbian Sexuality and Perverse Desire*. Bloomington: Indiana University Press.

Eng, David L. 2001. *Racial Castration: Managing Masculinity in Asian America*. Durham, N.C.: Duke University Press.

Freud, Sigmund. 1921. "Group Psychology and the Analysis of the Ego." In *The Standard Edition of the Complete Psychological Works of Sigmund Freud*. Volume 18, 67–134. London: Hogarth Press.

Gaspar de Alba, Alicia. 1998. *Chicano Art Inside/Outside the Master's House: Cultural Politics and the CARA Exhibition*. Austin: University of Texas Press.

González, Deena. 2003. "'Lupe's Song': On the Origins of Mexican-Woman-Hating in the United States." In *Velvet Barrios: Popular Culture and Chicana/O Sexualities*, ed. Alicia Gaspar de Alba, 251–64. New York: Palgrave.

López, Alma. 1999. "Mermaids, Butterflies, and Princesses." Artist statement online. 25 November 2002. http://home.earthlink.net/~almalopez/digital/lupesire/encuentro.html.

———. 2001. "Artist Statement, April 2001." Artist Web site. 25 November 2002. http://www.almalopez.net/other/artist.html.

Moraga, Cherríe. 1996. "Our Lady of the Cannery Workers." In *Goddess of the Americas: Writings on the Virgin of Guadalupe*. ed. Ana Castillo, 124–27. New York: Riverhead Books.

———. 2002. "Watsonville: Some Place Not Here." In *Latino Plays from the South Coast Repertory*, ed. H. P. Project, 339–425. New York: Broadway Play Publishing.

Office of Communications, Archdiocese of Santa Fe. 2001. "Archbishop Michael J. Sheehan on Our Lady of Guadalupe Portrayal." Archdiocese of Santa Fe. 25 November 2002. http://www.archdiocesesantafe.org/Offices/Communications/PressReleases/Archived%20Press%20Releases/01.5.22.OLGuadalupe.html.

Pérez, Emma. 1999. *The Decolonial Imaginary: Writing Chicanas into History*. Bloomington and Indianapolis: Indiana University Press.

Pérez, Laura Elisa. 1999. "El desorden, Nationalism, and Chicana/o Aesthetics." In *Between Woman and Nation: Nationalisms, Transnational Feminisms, and the State*, ed. Caren Kaplan, Norma Alarcón, and Minoo Moallem, 19–46. Durham, N.C.: Duke University Press.

Rechy, John. 1991. *The Miraculous Day of Amalia Gomez*. New York: Arcade Books.

———. 2001. *The Miraculous Day of Amalia Gomez*. 2nd ed. New York: Grove Press.

Romero Sedeño, Pedro. 2002. "Frankenstein Guadalupe." E-mail posted to Alma López's Web site. 23 February 2002. 25 November 2002. http://www.almalopez .net/email/020223.html.

Yarbro-Bejarano, Yvonne. 1995. "The Lesbian Body in Latina Cultural Production." In *¿Entiendes? Queer Readings, Hispanic Writings*, ed. Emilie L. Bergman and Paul Julian Smith, 181–97. Durham, N.C.: Duke University Press.

Ybarra Frausto, Tomás. 1996. "The Chicano Movement/The Movement of Chicano Art." In *Beyond the Fantastic: Contemporary Art Criticism from Latin America*, ed. Gerardo Mosquera, 165–82. Cambridge, Mass.: MIT Press.

Sara Ahmed

···

The Nonperformativity of Antiracism

In this paper, I reflect on institutional speech acts: those that make claims "about" or "on behalf' of an institution. Such speech acts involve acts of naming: the institution is named, and in being "given" a name, the institution is also "given" attributes, qualities, and even a character. By "speech acts" I include not just spoken words but writing and visual images—all the materials that give an institution interiority, as if it has a face, as well as feelings, thoughts, or judgments. They might say, for example, "the university regrets," or just simply, "we regret." More specifically, in this paper, I examine documents that are authorized by institutions (such as race-equality policies, which are often signed by, say, the vice-chancellor on behalf of an institution), make claims about the institution (for instance, by describing the institution as having certain qualities, such as being diverse), or point toward future action (by committing an institution to a course of action, such as diversity or equality, which in turn might involve the commitment of resources).

Such speech acts do not do what they say: they do not, as it were, commit a person, organization, or state to an action. Instead, they are nonperformatives. They are speech acts that read as if they are performatives, and this "reading" generates its own effects. For John Langshaw Austin a performative refers to a particular class of speech. An utterance is performative when it does what it says: "the issuing of the utterance is the performing of an action" (1975, 6). For Austin, conditions have to be in place to allow such words to act, or in his terms, to allow performatives to be "happy." The

MERIDIANS · feminism, race, transnationalism   Volume 19 Supplement 2020
DOI: 10.1215/15366936-8565957 © 2006 Smith College

"action" of the performative is not in the "words," or if it is "in" the words, it is "in" them only in so far as the words are "in the right place" to secure the effect that they name. Performatives succeed when they are uttered by the right person, to the right people, and in a way that takes the right form. As Judith Butler argues, "performativity must be understood not as a singular or deliberate 'act', but, rather as the reiterative and citational practice by which discourse *produces the effects that it names*" (1993, 2, emphasis added).

The speech acts that commit the university to equality, I suggest, are non-performatives.[1] They "work" precisely by not bringing about the effects that they name. For Austin, failed performatives are "unhappy": they do not act because the conditions are not in place that are required for the action to succeed (for example, if the person who apologizes is insincere then the apology would be unhappy). In my model of the "nonperformative," the failure of the speech act to do what it says is not a failure of intent or even circumstance, but it is actually what the speech act is doing. In other words, the nonperformative does not "fail to act" because of conditions that are external to the speech act: rather, it "works" *because* it fails to bring about what it names. My paper will be structured by taking up four specific forms of institutional speech acts: admissions, commitments, performances, and descriptions.

Second, in this paper, I want to suggest that the nonperformativity of antiracist speech acts requires a new approach to the relation between texts and social action, which I will be calling "an ethnography of texts." Such an approach still considers texts as actions, which "do things," but it also suggests that "texts" are not "finished" as forms of action, as what they "do" depends on how they are "taken up." To track what texts do, we need to follow them around. If texts circulate as documents or objects within public culture, then our task is to follow them, to see how they move as well as how they get stuck. So rather than just looking at university documentation on diversity for what it says, although I do this, as close readings are important and necessary, I also ask what they do, in part by talking to practitioners who use these documents to support their actions. This paper hence draws on interviews with diversity and equal opportunities officers or staff from personnel units with responsibility for diversity at ten universities in the United Kingdom, an analysis of policy documents and my own participation in discussions within universities and policy conferences.

The academic and political background to this research is provided by scholarship in critical race studies that has analyzed institutional racism in higher education in the United Kingdom, in all of its complexity (Modood and Acland 1998; Shiner and Madood 2002; Law, Phillips, and Turney 2004). My argument extends this work by pointing to a relationship between the new discourses of racial equality and the extension of institutional racism. In other words, rather than considering the turn to promoting racial equality as a sign of overcoming institutional racism, my argument will explore the "terms" on which this promotion is happening within higher education.

Admissions

In order to reflect on the politics of institutional speech acts, I want to think first about a politics of admission. I begin by analyzing the concept of institutional racism and the paradoxes that follow when institutional racism becomes part of institutional language. This has happened in the United Kingdom, where institutions (in particular, the police) have either recognized themselves as being institutionally racist or have adopted a definition of institutional racism within their race-equality policies. The Macpherson Report (1999) on the police handling of the murder of a young Black man, Stephen Lawrence, has been the key in this public turn. The Macpherson Report is an important document insofar as it recognizes the police force as "institutionally racist." According to the report, institutional racism amounts to "the collective failure of an organisation to provide an appropriate and professional service to people because of their colour, culture, or ethnic origin. It can be seen or detected in processes, attitudes, and behaviour which amount to discrimination through unwitting prejudice, ignorance, thoughtlessness, and racist stereotyping which disadvantage minority ethnic people" (1).

The language of institutional racism was not, of course, invented by the report, but it draws on a long history of Black activism and scholarship. How is this language used here? Defining an institution as racist involves recognition of the collective rather than individual nature of racism. Moreover, it forecloses what is meant by collective and institutional by seeing evidence of that collectivity only in what institutions fail to do. In other words, the report defines institutional racism in such a way that racism is not seen as an ongoing series of actions that shape institutions or the norms that get reproduced or posited over time. We might wish to see racism as a form of doing or even a field of positive action, rather than as a form of inaction. For instance, we might wish to examine how institutions become White through the positing of some bodies rather than others as the subjects of the institution (querying, for example, who the institution is shaped for and who it is shaped by). Racism would not be evident in what we fail to do, but what we have already done, whereby the "we" is an effect of the doing. The recognition of institutional racism within the Macpherson Report reproduces the whiteness of institutions by seeing racism simply as the failure to provide for non-White others because of a difference that is somehow theirs.

It is worth noting that psychological language that creeps into the definition: "processes, attitudes, and behaviour which amount to discrimination through unwitting prejudice, ignorance, thoughtlessness, and racist stereotyping" (Macpherson Report 1999, 1). In a way, the institution becomes recognized as racist only through being posited as an individual, as someone who suffers from prejudice but who could be treated so that they would act better toward racialized others. To say "we are racist" is here translated into the statement it seeks to replace, "I am racist," where "our racism" is described as a bad practice that can be changed through learning more tolerant attitudes and behavior. Indeed, if the institution becomes like the individual, then one suspects that the institution also takes the place of individuals: it is the institution that is the bad person rather than this person or that person. In other words, the transformation of the collective into an individual (a collective without individuals) might allow individual actors to deny or refuse responsibility for collective forms of racism.

But there is more to understanding how institutional racism becomes an institutional admission. What does it mean for a subject or institution to posit itself as being racist? If racism is shaped by actions that do not get seen by those who are its beneficiaries, what does it mean for those beneficiaries to see it? I would suggest that such admissions might work both by claiming to see racism (in what the institution fails to do) and by maintaining the definition of racism as unseeing. If racism is defined as unwitting and collective prejudice, then the claim to be racist by being able to see racism in this or that form of practice is also a claim not to be racist in the same way.

The paradoxes of admitting to one's own racism are clear: saying "we are racist" becomes a claim to have overcome the conditions (unseen racism) that require the speech act in the first place. The logic is, first, we say, "we are racist," and insofar as we can admit to being racist (and racists are unwitting), then we show that "we are not racist," or at least that we are not racist in the same way. What is important here is that the admission converts swiftly into a declarative mode: the speech act, in its performance, is taken up as having shown that the institution has overcome what it is that the speech act admits to. Simply put, admissions of racism become readable as declarations of commitment to antiracism. What does this conversion of admissions into commitments do?

In the United Kingdom, there has been a proliferation of documents on race equality; we might even say that race equality is increasingly being documented or turned into documents. The circulation of race-equality documents in the public sector is a direct result of the 2000 Race Relations Amendment Act, which requires all public bodies to have and enforce a race-equality and action plan. This is an important piece of legislation insofar as race equality now becomes a positive duty; something that organizations must do. The first specific duty under the act for higher and further education organizations is that they must write a race-equality policy. The RRAA has fascinated me partly as it has generated a huge amount of documentation: the documentation is, as it were, one of the objects of the act, what it points toward.

My own experience of writing such a document as part of a race-equality team was instructive. We adopted the Macpherson definition of "institutional racism" in the document, although we fell short of naming our institution itself as "being institutionally racist." In working on this policy, we tried to bring a critical language of antiracism into the wording of the document. This meant that in the document we identified inequalities and racism as the history behind the document: in other words, we took up "diversity" and "equality" as terms within the document given that they do not describe the institution.

I was taught a good lesson, which of course means a hard lesson: the language we think of as critical can easily lend itself to the very techniques of governance we critique. So we wrote the document, and the university was praised for its policy by the Equality Challenge Unit (ECU), and the vice chancellor was able to congratulate the university on its performance: we did well. At a meeting with staff, the vice chancellor praised staff for their excellent work, referring to the letter from the ECU. It was a feel good moment, but those of us who wrote the document did not feel so good. A document that documented the racism of the university became usable as a measure of good performance. Here, having a good race-equality policy quickly got translated into being good at race equality. Such a translation works to conceal the very inequalities that the documents were written to reveal. The document becomes a fetishized object, something that has value by being cut off from the process of documentation. In other words, its very existence is taken as evidence that the institutional environment documented by the document (racism, inequality, injustice) has been overcome; as if by saying that we "do it" means that's no longer what we do.

Commitments

Such documents function as statements of commitment to race equality: indeed, such commitments are often made in the first sentences of the policies. Having a race-equality policy, especially having a "good race-equality policy," is about making an institutional commitment public. The documents are read as signs of commitment and in turn seem to commit the institution to doing something. Or do they?

Let me quote from the opening paragraphs of two race-equality policies:

The Race Relations (Amendment) Act 2000 (RRAA 2000) places a requirement on a wide range of public authorities, including all Further and Higher Education institutions, to promote race equality in a proactive way through all their functions and to publish a Race Equality Policy. This Race Equality Policy has been published to inform all [xxx] staff and students and all other partners of our institutional commitment under the requirements of the RRAA 2000. [xxx] recognises that by embracing diversity it can achieve its ultimate goal to become a 'world class University' and pursue excellence in research, teaching and clinical service.
. . .
[xxx] values its diverse community and is opposed to racism in all its forms. The [xxx] is committed to the fair and equal treatment of all individuals and aims to ensure that no-one in the [xxx] community is disadvantaged on the grounds of race, cultural background, ethnic or national origin or religious belief.

These documents show the different ways in which the university is imagined as a subject with a commitment to race equality. In the first one, the policy begins with law: it frames the institutional commitment in terms of compliance with law. In a way, then, the document names its commitment by framing that commitment as a requirement: we commit insofar as we are required to do so. Commitment here is literally under the law. We might note that while this institutional commitment is named, it is not named as a commitment to something; we are simply committed to whatever the law commits us to do.

The second quote seems to take us further, insofar as it names racism and declares the organization as being opposed to racism. At the same time, the statement also functions to bring the organization into the policy as being antiracist, a self-declaration that ironically can participate in the concealment of racism within the university. Declaring a commitment to opposing racism might function as a form of organizational pride: antiracism as a speech act might then accumulate value for the organization, as a sign of its own commitment. A university that commits to antiracism might also be one that does not recognize racism as an ongoing reality, or if it did recognize such racism, then it would be more likely to see that racism as coming from "strangers" outside of the institution rather than "natives" inside it. It is as if the university now says, if we are committed to antiracism (and we have said we are), then how can we be racists? Declarations of commitment can block recognition of racism. Paradoxically, the recognition of racism can be taken up as a sign of commitment, which in turn blocks the recognition of racism. The work of such speech acts seems to be precisely how they function to hinder rather than enable action. In other words, the failure, or the nonperformativity, of antiracist speech acts is a mechanism for the reproduction of institutional authority, which conceals the ongoing reality of racism.

In one 2005 newspaper article about racism experienced by international students at Royal Holloway, we can see exactly this mechanism at work. Students from Korea complained about racism experienced on campus and about the failure of the college to respond adequately: "Students, particularly east Asian students, feel fearful of these attacks and are deeply concerned that something should be done. But, they have no proper channels of complaint and are worried that too much noise would have a negative effect on their status at college" (Pai 2005, 3). The article highlights the multiples ways that racism can affect the experiences of Black and Asian students: it can involve direct violence, and it also affects how students respond to such violence, fearing that reporting racism would lead to further marginalization. But the response of the college to this report was to deny the students' charges: "Royal Holloway's spokeswoman said: 'This could not be further from the truth. *The college prides itself on its levels of pastoral care*'" (Pai 2005, 3, emphasis added). In other words, organizational pride and the self-perception of being good block the recognition of racism. Organizational pride in being good at hearing messages prevents the message getting through. Such a speech act does exactly what it says that it does not do: it refuses to hear complaint in the very moment it says that it does hear complaint. If colleges have pride in their policies of pastoral care and antiracism, then they also fail to hear about racism. Being committed to antiracism can function as a perverse performance of racism: "you" are wrong to describe us as uncaring and racist because "we" are committed to being antiracist. Antiracism functions here as a discourse of organizational pride.

As I have suggested, many of the race-equality documents function as statements of commitment and take a simple form: "we are committed to. . . ." Such statements of commitment might work to limit rather than enable action, insofar as they block recognition of the ongoing nature of what it is the organization is committed to opposing. However, we can still ask the question, what do statements of commitment commit institutions to do?

When asking practitioners about this process of writing race-equality policies, I ask specifically about statements of commitment. What do they (or do they?) commit the university to do? In the following exchange between me and three interviewees from the personnel department of a university, we can see the hesitation that follows such a question.

Question: It's a statement of commitment clearly as many of them are, do you feel that the statement itself commits the university to something?

Responses:
   I would say yes but don't say why.
   Yes it does, but my angle, I suppose, is that you have to have reminders, examples, arguments all the time.
   And I think it's a good working document that people can take with them.
   But people don't like being told to read it.
   Yes they don't like it.
   We don't like being told we have to tick these boxes.
   It is true, but it exists, and I think it's a reference document and people will go back and read it if they wanted to find out something. But people don't want to be told to read it.

If we took statements of commitment as performatives, we would say that they commit a person to something. But such performativity is not assumed by practitioners. The first response is that the statement of commitment does "commit," but for unknown reasons. This uncertainty is itself telling, for it suggests that commitment is in some way mysterious and would need to be explained. In other words, the commitment does not simply follow the letter of the document. The word "commitment" does not do what it says. The second response also is a "yes" but a qualified one: the statement of commitment does commit, but it has to be supplemented by other forms of institutional pressure (reminders, examples, and so on). In other words, the commitment is not given by the document but depends on the work generated around the document. It is interesting that the next intervention begins with further qualification: "but people don't like to be told to read it." If the statement of commitment does not necessarily commit the university to doing anything, then practitioners have to keep up the pressure; it is this pressure that can mean that documents do not work. This is a telling pressure for diversity workers: we have to put pressure on the document because it does not work, and the pressure on documents is what makes them not work. The compulsion to read the document means that it loses rather than gains currency. If people are required to read it, then they "don't like it." Indeed, the following utterance moves from "they don't like it" to "we don't like being told to tick these boxes." The commitment itself becomes a "tick" in the box. Now "commitment" is usually described in opposition to the "tick box"; a tick box approach to diversity would be where institutions go along with the process, but are not "behind" the action. For commitment to become a tick in the box is to suggest that "being behind" can itself be a matter of institutional performance. We create the illusion of being behind an action, even at the moment the action is not performed.

The final utterance describes the statement of commitment as a "reference document" that people can use. This document then exists insofar as people refer back to it, as something that can help them to do things. Such documents by implication can only work if they are not obligatory: if people do not have to use them, then they might work. What this sequences of utterance shows is not only how documents of commitment are perceived as non-commitments in and of themselves but also how this lack of commitment in the document—which implies that we have to be committed to them to make them work—is what makes them less likely to generate commitment in others.

The question then becomes where commitment is located, if it is not in the statements of commitment or in the people who generate such statements. Why does commitment matter so much to diversity and equality work, if it seems always not to be where it should be? I asked why statements of commitment matter to another practitioner:

> Oh that's hard. I think you cannot not have them, if you don't have them, well to me as a practitioner it's a starting point, again it's whether that gets fitted into practice. Commitments can't come without other actions. So the commitment to me is about what the institution believes in and what it intends to do—it can't stand alone, it has to come with how you're actually going to do it. I think if they weren't there then, well I refer to them quite a lot as you well know, if you're trying to, let's say there's an issue that's come up and somebody is not, maybe there's an issue and perhaps they're racist in what they bring up in their practice or something like that, and it's good to refer back to these documents, but actually you're an employee of the university and the university has made a statement about this. So in terms of watching the other members of staff and in my own experience, I've used it for that.

The sentence "commitments can't come without other actions" is instructive because it suggests that commitment is an action, but it is one that does not act on its own. Instead, it depends on other actions, or on what is done with it. Commitment might be, in other words, a technology that can be used or deployed within specific settings. The work of commitment is how you act on the action: it is about what the action allows the practitioner to do. The statement of commitment is also described as a reference point, something you can use, when challenging how people act within the institution. In other words, the statement of commitment does not commit the institution to anything, but it allows the practitioner to support their claims for or against specific action. The statement functions as a supporting device.

So although a statement of commitment can block action by constructing the university or organization as already committed to race equality, these statements also can support other actions precisely by giving this *illusion of being behind*. Practitioners use such statements to challenge people within the organization, by showing they are "out of line" with the direction of the organization, even if this line is itself imaginary and does not direct institutional action. Documents do not simply have a referential or descriptive function: it is not simply that they describe principles that a university already has. Indeed, in a way, the documents might even perform a lie insofar as they represent the university as if it has principles that it does not have. But this can be a useful lie: by producing the university as if it was a subject with such principles, the documents then become usable as they allow practitioners to make members of the university as well as the university itself as an imagined entity subject to those principles. Statements of commitment then might do something, not in and of themselves, but because they enable the exposure of a gap between what organizations say they do, and what they actually do: indeed, they might "do something" insofar as they fail to describe what organizations do.

Performing Equality

So what work are these documents doing in their failure to bring about the effects that they name? Such documents arguably are forms of institutional performance. They are ways in which universities perform an image of themselves, to be sure, but they are also ways in which universities perform in the sense of "doing well." To return to my own experience of writing a diversity document: the document that documents racism becomes usable as a measure of good performance. What does it mean for "equality" and "diversity" to be seen as measurable in the first place? Are they becoming boxes to be ticked? Or a "paper trail" that goes nowhere?

Diversity and equality are increasingly discussed in the United Kingdom through an emphasis on good practice. Although good practice is often seen as "beyond the tick box" (or rather, the tick box approach is seen as bad practice), I would suggest that "the tick box" and the "good practice" are part of the same vocabulary. The tick box shows we have done it (whatever we do) while the good practice shows we have done it (whatever we do), where the "it" is taken as a sign of good performance. Good practice guides and tool-kits are produced based on the principle that the best way of improving institutional performance is to share good practice. These documents too move around. An example can be taken from the ECU toolkit on communications, "Good Talking: The HE Communicators Equality and Diversity Toolkit," which includes the following as an example of "general good practice": "University of Southampton has produced institutional equality and diversity gifts and novelties that are in great demand." For diversity novelties to become a sign of good practice is clear evidence of how diversity is being repackaged, as if it was a property of objects that can be passed around. So an organization even gets a "tick" for its novelties.

The RRAA signals a shift within the public sectors toward seeing equality and diversity as performance indicators, as things that can be measured. Heidi Mirza (2005) has described this as the "bureaucratisation of diversity." Indeed, the RRAA has encouraged the shift toward seeing diversity and equality work as auditable. Audit culture not only measures performance but it depends on the reliability of such measurements. It also associates good performance with accountability, efficiency, and quality, assumed goals for organizations (Powers 1994, 1). Race equality would be something that could be measured, such that doing well would become an indicator of institutional good performance. In other words, race equality would be a sign of accountability, efficiency, and quality.

Practitioners expressed mixed feelings about equality and diversity becoming auditable. Some suggested that to audit equality and diversity would be a good thing, as universities only take seriously the activities that are audited and attached to financial returns or penalties. As one interviewee describes, "I think it would be useful in the HE sector because it wouldn't have been done, just thinking about how they could operate and how they've been lagging behind, it was the push, you know you had to do it." Audit becomes here a "stick" that would compel action, as a compulsion that energizes or creates an institutional drive. Others suggested that audit would not necessarily work, given how audit culture works as a kind of awareness of itself. As one director of personnel elaborates:

> An audit can establish if we have gone through processes, it can't really determine whether we are altering culture here. It can perhaps show whether we are reaching various targets, say you know, the same teacher of leadership staff who come from various backgrounds over time. But the trouble is when dealing with audit you tend always to respond in terms of process you know, we've done this report, we've got a plan out and all that sort of stuff. And I could see that you could get a rough idea if universities were putting effort into diversity by doing that, but the trouble is that in universities we've got an audit-aware culture in administrations. And so people are practiced at how to show auditors that processes are being gone through.

So if diversity and equality were audited, then universities would be able to show they have gone through the right processes, however they define those processes. In other words, personnel can become good at audit by producing auditable documents, which would mean the universities that did well on race equality would be simply the ones that were good at creating auditable systems.

What it is important to note here is that audit culture too is very much about the politics of documentation. One does not audit something that is already in place. The audit generates a system by generating documents that are auditable. As Michael Powers argues, audit culture is what "makes things auditable" (1994, 33). Or, as Chris Shore and Susan Wright describe in their excellent account of audit in higher education: "The result has been the invention of a host of 'auditable structures' and paper trails to demonstrate 'evidence of system' to visiting inspectors" (2000, 72). The document is the paper in such a trail. The auditable document would be the document that "refers back" to the terms set up an in auditing system. Benchmarking works by generating documents that refer back to the benchmarks, produces a family of documents around the terms. It is not then that "diversity" and "equality" are simply in the documents: instead, they are terms used by documents, in reference to terms that have already been made. When we measure such documents, we might then be measuring how their terms correspond with other terms, such as those set up by the Race Relations Amendment Act itself. What does it mean for the correspondence of terms to be a measure of good performance? What is being measured when diversity becomes a measure of institutional performance?

I asked this question to one diversity practitioner whose university received an excellent rank for their race-equality policy, and she suggested that: "We are good at writing documents." I replied, without thinking, "Well yes, one wonders," and we both laughed. Our wonder is skeptical: we wonder whether what is being measured are levels of institutional competence in producing documents rather than what the university is doing in terms of race equality. As this practitioner further describes:

> I was very aware that it wasn't very difficult for me and some of the other people to write a wonderful aspirational document. I think we all have great writing skills, and we can just do that, because we are good at it, that's what we are expert at. And there comes with that awareness a real anxiety that the writing becomes an end in itself, the reality is being born

out by, say, for example, we were commended on our policies, and when
the ECU reviewed our Implementation Plans last year there were a number of quite serious criticisms about time slippages, about the fact that
we weren't reaching out into the mainstream and the issues hadn't really
permeated the institution and the money implemented in certain specific
areas. And it wasn't that there was hostility, it was much more of this
kind of marshmallow feeling.

In this fascinating statement about the politics of diversity as an institutional performance, the practitioner describes her skill and expertise in
terms of writing a "wonderful aspirational document." Being good at
writing documents becomes a competency that is also an obstacle for
diversity work, as it means that the university gets judged as good *because* of
the document. It is this very judgment about the document that blocks
action, producing a kind of "marshmallow feeling," a feeling that we are
doing enough, or doing well enough, or even that there is nothing left to
do.

Many practitioners and academics have expressed concerns that writing
documents or having good policies becomes a substitute for action: as this
practitioner goes on to say, "you end up doing the document rather than
doing the doing." The work that goes into writing the document ends up
blocking other kinds of action. Or, to make an even stronger argument: the
orientation toward writing good documents can block action, insofar as
the document then gets taken up as evidence that we have done the work.
As another practitioner describes, "Well I think in terms of the policies,
people's views are 'well we've got them now so that's done, it's finished.' I
think actually, *I'm not sure if that's even worse than having nothing*, that idea in
people's heads that we've done race, when we very clearly haven't done
race." The idea that the document is itself an action is what could allow the
institution to block recognition of the work that there is to do. The system
of rewarding organizations for their performance on diversity and equality
not only risks concealing forms of inequality and racism but also supports
forms of organizational pride, which reorient the politics of diversity work
away from challenging how institutions constitute their identity and
toward a promotion of that identity.

As one of my interviewees suggests, diversity work has become promo-
tional work, or what she calls a form of "R and R," that is, about risk and
reputation. Diversity involves promoting organizations through remaking

their image. In one of my interviews, we discussed a research project that had been funded as part of the university's commitment to race equality, which is described as "perception data" (data that gathers how people perceive an organization). This research project was a target met by the university under its action plan, so of course it is already a tick. What did the research reveal?

> OK yes. It was about uncovering perceptions, um, about the [xxx] as an employer. . . . [xxx] was considered to be an old boys network, as they called it, and White male dominated, and they didn't have the right perceptions of the [xxx] in terms of what it offers and what it brings to the academia. I think most of the external people had the wrong perceptions about the [xxx].
>
> . . .
>
> And I mean, quotes, there were such funny quotes, like librarians they were sitting there with their cardigans, you know. Um, and things like that, they were shocking reports to read, really, about how people, external people, perceive the [xxx] so we have to try to achieve, you know, we have to try to make the [xxx] an attractive employer.

The politics of diversity and equality has become about image management: diversity and equality work is about generating the right image and correcting the wrong one. According to this logic, people have the wrong perception when they see the organization as white, elite, male, and/or old-fashioned. In other words, what is behind the shock is a belief that the whiteness is in the image rather than in the organization. Diversity and equality work hence becomes about changing perceptions of whiteness rather than changing the whiteness of organizations. A good performance would then be about being perceived as a diverse and equal organization that is committed to diversity and equality. The perception itself would be the achievement and would be taken as a sign of good performance. The perception then becomes taken up as description: as if being perceived as diverse is what gives the organization such qualities.

Describing Diversity

Race-equality documents work as if they are descriptions: they describe the university not only as having certain principles, but also as having certain qualities, characteristics, and styles. They are often accompanied by images that give the university a face by adopting the diverse faces of its inhabitants. Through such images and documents, universities are constituted as if they have these qualities. One of the most obvious features of this descriptive purchase in the context of the RRAA is the use of the word "diversity." Diversity enters such documents not only as something the university is committed to but as a quality the university already has, by virtue of the kinds of staff and students that already exist within the organization. We can turn again to some opening sentences of race-equality policies.

> This Race Equality Policy has been published to inform all [xxx] staff and students and all other partners of our institutional commitment under the requirements of the RRAA 2000. [xxx] recognises that by embracing diversity it can achieve its ultimate goal to become a 'world class University' and pursue excellence in research, teaching and clinical service.
> . . .
> [xxx] values its diverse community and is opposed to racism in all its forms. The [xxx] is committed to the fair and equal treatment of all individuals and aims to ensure that no one in the [xxx] community is disadvantaged on the grounds of race, cultural background, ethnic or national origin or religious belief.

These are interesting documents to read in terms of showing the different ways that the university is imagined as a subject with commitments as well as characteristics. In the first sentence of the first quote, the word "equality" is associated with law and seems to point not to the university's commitment but to the force of law. The document then moves from equality to diversity. Diversity seems more readily embraced, as something that is both taken on and taken in within the constitution of the university as a subject community. We might note, then, that diversity is taken in precisely as it is associated with being a "world class university"; it functions in a way as a term that allows the university to measure up to its ego ideal or its ideal image. Diversity is taken in as an orientation toward the market, a way of being "world class." One way to rearticulate this statement might be, "We are committed to diversity insofar as we are committed to being world class." Diversity might even work through its proximity to the self-image of organizations.

The second quote begins with diversity as a property, as something the organization has. The discourse of valuing diversity is, of course, mainstream, and it lingers between discourses of economic value (the business case for diversity) and moral value (the social justice case). This model of diversity simultaneously reifies difference as something that already exists in the bodies of others ("we" are diverse because "they" are here). It also transforms difference into a property: if difference is something they are, then it is something we can have. It is this model of diversity as something others bring to the organization that we can see at work in the use of visual images of diverse organizations: images of colorful, happy faces, which show the diversity of the university as something it has embraced.

It is worth noting here the powerful critiques of the turn to diversity within higher education offered by feminist and critical management scholars. Such critiques have suggested that diversity enters higher education through "marketization": the term is seen as coming from management and from the imperative to manage diversity or to value diversity as if it were a human resource. Such a managerial focus on diversity, it has been argued, works to individuate difference and to conceal the continuation of systematic inequalities within organizations such as universities (Kandola and Fullerton 1994; Lorbiecki 2001; Kirton and Greene 2000). These important critiques attend to the word "diversity" itself, which has been attributed with a problematic genealogy, having not only dubious origins but also uncertain and potentially damaging effects. Deem and Ozga (1997) suggest that "the concepts of equity and equal opportunities imply an underlying concept of social justice for all," while "the notion of diversity invokes the existence of difference and variety without any necessary commitment to action or redistributive justice" (33). Similarly, Benschop (2001) suggests that "'diversity' does not so powerfully appeal to our sense of social justice" (1166). For Deem and Ozga, the word "diversity" invokes difference but does not necessarily evoke commitment to action or redistributive justice. What is problematic about diversity, by implication, is that it can be cut off from the programs that seek to challenge inequalities within organizations, and it might even take the place of such programs in defining the social mission of universities. We can certainly see this cut-off point. For these scholars, among others, the institutional preference for the term "diversity" is a sign of the lack of commitment to change and might even allow universities to conceal the operation of systematic inequalities under the face of diversity.

In light of these critiques, what does the word "diversity" do? It is because diversity does not seem to evoke such histories of struggle that many practitioners are critical of the institutional desire for this term. As one practitioner put it, "I think the concept of diversity, in the way that it is now used in equality, rather than 'diversity' as a word, which I don't really think it has much relationship to, I think it's used as a complete and utter cop-out. I think it's a dreadful concept." Indeed, this practitioner felt so strongly about the "cop-out" of diversity that she refuses to describe herself as an equality and diversity practitioner even though her job title involves both terms. She goes on to describe "diversity" as a "cuddly" concept that extends the university's self-image as being good:

> So now we'll talk about diversity, and that means everybody's different but equal and its all nice and cuddly and we can feel good about it and feel like we've solved it, when actually we're nowhere near solving it, and we need to, I think, have that, well, diversity as a concept fits in much better with the university's idea of what it's doing about being the great benefactor.

We could describe diversity as a politics of feeling good, which allows people to relax and feel less threatened, as if we have already "solved it" and there is nothing else to do. I asked another practitioner why she thinks that the word "diversity" is appealing. She argued that diversity appeals because "it obscures the issues. . . . It can, diversity is like a big shiny red apple right, and it all looks wonderful. This is an example actually a member of staff came up with in my focus group about gender issues, she says, but if you actually cut into that apple there's a rotten core in there, and you know that it's actually all rotting away and it's not actually being addressed. It all looks wonderful but the inequalities aren't being addressed."

Again, the suggestion here is that the appeal of diversity is about looking and feeling good, as an orientation that obscures inequalities like the obscuring of a rotten core behind a shiny surface. Diversity as a term has a marketing appeal: it allows the university to sell itself by presenting itself as a happy place, a place where differences are celebrated, welcomed, and enjoyed. Diversity becomes a form of organizational pride. Not only does this rebranding of the university as being diverse work to conceal racism but it also works to reimagine the university as being antiracist, even beyond race—as if the colors of different races have integrated to create a new hybrid or, even, a bronzed face.

And yet, this practitioner also acknowledges that there are some benefits to diversity in the sense it can "start to engage people." It is a given how diversity might make people feel good, that it can be a useful term, as it allows people in: once they are in, we can then do different things or even use a different set of terms. In other words, the word "equality," which is associated with the law, might be less useful as people turn away from it and/or are threatened by the work that it asks them to do. If we use the word "diversity," we might have a better chance of getting through. So it is precisely how diversity might work to conceal racism that might make it a term that can do things. In other words, what makes diversity useful is how it is appealing. If words do things, what they do depends on how they are being used and how they can hook people or bring them in. Indeed, most practitioners describe their work as a question of "what works," of using whatever language works for the different audiences to whom they speak. Diversity work is strategic, even if it has certain political principles behind it. So diversity is used by some precisely because it is a comfortable term that allows people to engage more easily with this kind of work. As a result, practitioners are positive about the term "diversity" for the very reasons some are critical of the term. As one interviewee describes:

> I think for me with equality, as I said, there is some legal framework, and I think sometimes overemphasised. There's a tension, really, because you need to make people aware of the legality, but you want to go beyond that don't you? You don't want it to be about compliance, so for me, I actually think "diversity" is actually a far more positive word than "equality" so for me it's about celebration. Whereas equality feels a bit more about, oh, you know, meetings, legal requirements almost, I don't know, that's just personal.

Here, diversity is something positive: it is about celebration or can be celebrated. This is why it is a useful term. "Equality" evokes compliance and meeting legal requirements. It is no accident that diversity is described as having an energizing effect. For many practitioners the question becomes then not so much whether to use the term "diversity" but how to use it. If the success of the term is that it can be detached from the history of struggle for equalities, then its success might paradoxically depend on being reattached to those very histories. Practitioners hence use the word "diversity" as a way of getting institutional attention, but then they use the word alongside other more worrisome words, or what I call elsewhere, "sticky signs," such as "equality and justice" (Ahmed 2004b, 89–92). As one practitioner suggests:

> I have gone for both equality and diversity, so as an institution we do not use the term "diversity" in isolation, nor do we use equality in isolation.

Equality is to do with compliance, diversity is more qualitative and can be internally driven and that premise suits us. There are pockets of the institution where diversity is more proactive than other areas and compliance is more of priority in some areas as well. And the both have to work together, they have to be married together, because if you just go down to the compliance level there's no reward in it for the institution and because of the positive images around equality and diversity that we project, it is important for us that both work together. And I think we have gone for that rather than just diversity. But I know some universities have just gone diversity and it depends how you package it.

So what the word "diversity" does might depend on the words it is placed alongside: using diversity with equality associates the political and legal challenge to inequalities with the qualities of feeling attached to the celebration of difference. The aim of such work would be to restick these words together so that when people hear the word "diversity," they hear a challenge to inequality.

At the same time, in order to be heard, practitioners also work by attaching the word "diversity" to the other words that are taken as key to the organization's strategic mission, whether it be excellence, internationalism, or widening participation. In other words, it is the proximity of the term "diversity" to the self-image of organizations that allows the term to accrue value. Take the following quotation:

For me, I think that the, well certainly, our aim in the diversity project is to help the organisation to see how diversity will help meet the strategic plans. So how can diversity help make us top ten in 2010? What will thinking about diversity enable a head of a school that is already very successful to be more successful? That would be my real aim and to live our vision for race, which is excellence through diversity.

Organizational pride gets translated into diversity pride by attaching diversity to the pursuit of excellence. As this practitioner goes on to describe, "[xxx] is very much, well, you know, it really does want to build a reputation and to be seen to be at the front, even if that's a bit risky." Doing diversity is not so much about putting diversity in front but about putting the organization in front and making diversity what follows. Indeed, another practitioner suggests that diversity is simply about getting the best people for the job, which for her is about the organizational mission of excellence: "People really care about excellence, they really get hacked off when somebody second rate is appointed to anything and they don't care what they look like." Interestingly, this practitioner works at an elite and White organization, which is perhaps so secure in its privilege that it does not have to defend itself against those who look different. Diversity can be taken in precisely insofar as it becomes a sign of indifference to difference: "They don't care what they look like."

In following the word "diversity" around, we can see that it gets embraced by organizations insofar as it is proximate to the ideal images organizations already have of themselves. To add "diversity" to a mission statement hence does not necessarily add anything, but, rather, it puts an educational mission in different terms. And yet this word still has baggage and still gets associated with people who look different. As Nirmal Puwar points out, "In policy terms, diversity has overwhelmingly come to mean the inclusion of people who look different" (2004, 1). Ironically, the hope of putting diversity into university documentation is that this word will keep these associations, however problematic they may be. The point would not be to constitute racial others as the origin of diversity, as what adds color to the White face of the university. Rather, insofar as diversity signifies the presence of racial others, then it might also point to how organizations are orientated around whiteness, around those who are already in place. The happy smiling face of diversity would not then simply rebrand the university but point instead to what gets concealed by this very image: the inequalities that are behind it and give it a surface appeal. In other words, the strategy of associating diversity with organizational pride is that the word might yet work to challenge the ideal image of the organization. It is pride, after all, which is the condition of the possibility for being shamed for exposing gaps between ideals and actions.

If we consider the politics of describing diversity, we can see that such descriptions create fantasy images of the organizations they apparently represent. The document says we are diverse, as if saying it makes it so. In a way, our task must be to refuse to read such documents as performatives, as if they bring into effect what they name. That is not to say that such documents do not matter, or that they do not do any work. They do. Indeed, this non-performativity is what makes them tools that can be used by practitioners as things that work insofar as they fail to describe or produce what is ongoing or going on within organizations. In other words, by putting commitments in writing—as commitments that are not followed by other actions—such documents can be used as supportive devices, by exposing gaps between words and deeds. This is not to say we should not be critical in the hope invested in such documents. We must be critical. At the same time, we must also consider how such documents circulate, how they move around, and how they get stuck. Following documents around begins with an uncertainty about what these documents will do. They might, at certain points, even cause trouble.

. . . .

Sara Ahmed is a feminist writer and independent scholar. She works at the intersection of feminist, queer, and race studies. Her research is concerned with how bodies and worlds take shape, and how power is secured and challenged in everyday life worlds as well as institutional cultures.

Note

Originally published in *Meridians* vol. 7, no. 1, 2006.

1   This paper develops the thesis on the nonperformativity of antiracism originally made in Ahmed (2004a).

Works Cited

Ahmed, Sara. 2004a. "Declarations of Whiteness: The Non-Performativity of Anti-Racism." *borderlands* 3, no. 4. http://www.borderlandsejournal.adelaide.edu.au/vol3no2_2004/ahmed_declarations.

———. 2004b. *The Cultural Politics of Emotion.* Edinburgh: Edinburgh University Press.

Austin, John Langshaw. 1975. *How to Do Things with Words.* New York: Oxford University Press.

Benschop, Yvonne. 2001. "Pride, Prejudice and Performance." *International Journal of Human Resources Management* 12, no. 7: 1166–81.

Butler, Judith. 1993. *Bodies That Matter: On the Discursive Limits of "Sex."* London: Routledge.

Deem, Rosemary, and Jennifer Ozga. 1997. "Women Managing Diversity in a Postmodern World." In *Feminist Critical Policy Analysis II: A Post-Secondary Education Perspective,* ed. Catherine Marshall, 25–40. London: Falmer.

Kandola, Rajvinder, and Johanna Fullerton. 1994. *Managing the Mosaic: Diversity in Action.* London: IPD.

Kirton, Gill and Anne-Marie Greene. 2000. *The Dynamics of Managing Diversity.* Oxford and Woburn, MA: Butterworth-Heinemann.

Law, Ian, Deborah Phillips, and Laura Turney, eds. 2004. *Institutional Racism and Higher Education.* Oakhill, CA: Trentham Books.

Lorbiecki, Anna. 2001. "Changing Views on Diversity Management." *Management Studies* 32, no. 3: 345–61.

Mirza, Heidi. 2005. "Race, Gender and Educational Desire." Inaugural Lecture, 17 May. http://www.mdx.ac.uk/hssc/research/cres/docs/heidi_lecture.pdf.

Modood, Tariq, and Tony Acland, eds. 1998. *Race and Higher Education*. London: PSI.

Pai, Hsiao-Hung. 2005. "Anxiety in the UK." *The Guardian*, 8 February. http:// education.guardian.co.uk/egweekly/story/0,,1407538,00.html.

Power, Michael. 1994. *The Audit Explosion*. London: Demos.

Puwar, Nirmal. 2004. *Space Invaders: Race, Gender and Bodies out of Place*. Oxford: Berg.

Shiner, Michael, and Tariq Modood. 2002. "Help or Hindrance? Higher Education and the Route to Ethnic Equality." *British Journal of Sociology of Education* 23, no. 2: 209–32.

Shore, Chris, and Susan Wright. 2000. "Coercive Accountability: The Rise of Audit Culture in Higher Education." In *Audit Cultures: Anthropological Studies in Accountability, Ethics, and the Academy*, ed. Marilyn Strathem. London: Routledge.

Joanne Barker

....

Gender, Sovereignty, and the Discourse of Rights in Native Women's Activism

Abstract: Drawing from Native feminist theories and sovereignty studies, this essay examines the 1983 and 1985 amendments and the activism that led to their development and passage as an instance of the co-constitutive relationship of gender and sovereignty. By looking at how the discourse of rights was mobilized from very different contexts to very different ends by various constituencies of Indian men, women, and their allies, this essay modestly opens the conflicts surrounding gender politics and women's rights in Native sovereignty movements. I hope to provide a forum for thinking about the kinds of social reformations that are needed to bring about social equity between and for men and women in Indian communities—an equity that is an essential aspect of decolonization and social justice for Native peoples in North America.

In 1876, the Canadian Parliament amended the 1868 Indian Act to establish patrilineality as the criterion for determining Indian status and all commensurate rights of Indian peoples to participate in band government, have access to band services and programs, and live on the reserves. In 1983 and 1985, several different kinds of Indian[1] women's constituencies and their allies secured constitutional and legislative amendments that partially reversed the 1876 criterion.[2]

The amendments were not passed easily. Male-dominated band councils and Indian organizations protested vehemently against the women and their allies. They were accused of being complicit with a long history of colonization and racism that imposed, often violently, non-Indian

MERIDIANS · feminism, race, transnationalism   Volume 19 Supplement 2020
DOI: 10.1215/15366936-8565968 © 2006 Smith College

principles and institutions on Indian peoples. This history was represented as being furthered by the women's appeals to civil and human rights laws, and more particularly to feminism, to challenge the constitutionality and human rights compliance of the Indian Act. Demonizing an ideology of rights based on selfish individualism, and damned for being "women's libbers" out to force Indian peoples into compliance with that ideology (Silman 1987, 178–89),[3] the women and their concerns were dismissed as embodying all things not only non- but anti-Indian. Indian women's experiences, perspectives, and political agendas for legal reform were dismissed as not only irrelevant but dangerous to Indian sovereignty. The dismissals perpetuated sexist ideologies and discriminatory and violent practices against Indian women within Indian communities. In doing so, they normalized and perpetuated an irrelevance of gender and the disenfranchisement of Indian women in Native sovereignty struggles.

Drawing from Native feminist theories and sovereignty studies, this essay examines the 1983 and 1985 amendments and the activism that led to their development and passage as an instance of the coconstitutive relationship of gender and sovereignty.[4] By looking at how the discourse of rights was mobilized from very different contexts to very different ends by various constituencies of Indian men, women, and their allies, this essay modestly opens the conflicts surrounding gender politics and women's rights in Native sovereignty movements. I hope to provide a forum for thinking about the kinds of social reformations that are needed to bring about social equity between and for men and women in Indian communities—an equity that is an essential aspect of decolonization and social justice for Native peoples in North America.

Of Rights Contingent

The discourse of rights—international, constitutional, civil, Native—deeply informed the Canadian political landscape in which the 1983 and 1985 amendments were developed and passed.[5] Through rights, various kinds of constituencies—immigrant, minority, women, Native—were able to claim an identity, assert its political significance, and articulate agendas for decolonization and social justice. Recognition of a particular identity by Canada and the international community implied the recognition of all associated rights under the law—that is, immigrants to human rights, minorities and women to constitutional rights, Natives to self-government and territorial integrity. Rights, then, governed the terms of multiple kinds of social relationships among variously situated groups and individuals, implicating such diverse issues as labor, health care, education, jurisdiction, and property.

Indian women mobilized a specific discourse of rights from the intersections of human and civil rights, feminism, and Native sovereignty politics to historicize and define their goals to end gender-based discrimination and violence within their communities. Rights to equality, made meaningful by the distinctive context of Native/women's histories of oppression, shaped how Indian women articulated their political perspectives and agendas for legal reform and social change. In a rights framework that was simultaneously about being Native and women, Indian women's groups contextualized their experiences of oppression within a particularly Indian history of colonialism and racism encapsulated by the Indian Act, strategically aligned themselves as women with feminists and immigrant and minority women in experiences of state-institutionalized discrimination and community-based violence, and asserted their unique collective rights as Indians in equality with Indian men as a matter of traditional, customary law. Rights, then, functioned for Indian women in defining themselves within multiple historical contexts and identities—as racialized Indians, as tribal, as women, as women of color, as feminists, as international and civil rights activists—with real political agendas and concerns. These rights reflected not only the principles of international human rights laws and feminism but Native women's cultural beliefs about gender equality, interdependence, and rights to self-governance and territories.

Band governments and prominent Indian organizations likewise mobilized a specific discourse of rights from international and constitutional law in efforts to be recognized as sovereigns with all commensurate rights to sovereignty. In terms of rights, they situated themselves within a particular history of colonialism and racism encapsulated by Canadian law (generally) and the Indian Act (in particular). They also aligned themselves with other Native peoples in struggles for rights to sovereignty. These rights reflected human rights principles of self-determination and Native agendas for decolonization and social justice against ongoing structures and practices of colonialism and racism in Canada.

While seeming to speak the same language, Indian women, band governments, and Indian organizations had very different histories, identities, and political agendas at work in their articulation of rights. These differences are at the heart of their political conflicts over the women's proposed amendments to the 1876 patrilineal criterion. Often constructed as adversarial concepts within Native sovereignty struggles and scholarship, gender and sovereignty are there—in those conflicts and in the amendments that resulted. Gender and sovereignty are in fact mutually definitive in consequential ways to the roles, rights, and identities of women and men in Native communities, and in Native struggles for self-government, lands, and cultural survival.

The Indian Act System: Structuring Inequalities

> *The woman, on marriage, must leave her parents' home and her reserve. She may not own property on the reserve and must dispose of any property she does hold. She may be prevented from inheriting property left to her by her parents. She cannot take any further part in band business. Her children are not recognized as Indian and are therefore denied access to cultural and social amenities of the Indian community. And most punitive of all, she may be prevented from returning to live with her family on the reserve, even if she is in dire need, very ill, a widow, divorced or separated. Finally, her body may not be buried on the reserve with those of her forebears.*
> —Kathleen Jamieson, Indian Women and the Law in Canada: Citizens Minus (1978)

Canada's Constitution Act of 1867 assigned "exclusive jurisdiction" to Parliament over "Indians, and Lands reserved for the Indians" (Section 91, 24). Canada's Indian Act of 1868 enumerated these powers by defining the laws and procedures of band governments as well as the terms of occupancy and use by bands of trust lands or reserves. It commissioned the Department of Indian Affairs and Northern Development (DIAND) to oversee band government operations and the management of reserve lands, resources, housing, and all related program and funding issues such as education and health care. DIAND agents were also given the authority to remove band officials from office if they felt that the officials had demonstrated that they were not qualified to carry out their duties. Generally, this meant that they had been seen drunk in public, were accused of adultery, or had otherwise broken the law or proven themselves to be of "unchristian character."[6] Related to this, DIAND had full authority over the Indian Registry that listed by band all of those individuals who were Indian according to the Indian Act. Those qualified as Indian had all commensurate rights as band members to vote in band elections, hold office in band government, live in reserve housing, be employed by the bands, and receive band services.

In an 1876 amendment to the Indian Act, "Indian status" was defined by patrilineal descent. Men with status passed on status to the women that they married, and their children; women with status could not. Status women had status in the band of their fathers until they married, if they did so. If a status woman married a non-status man, she lost status in the band of her birth. If a status woman married a status man, her status would be determined by his band; for example, if she were status Cree and married a status Mohawk, she would become Mohawk. Upon divorce, she would lose status as Mohawk and not be reinstated as Cree. The only way for a non-status woman to (re)gain status was by marriage. Consequently, many status women refused to marry.[7] The only way for children to gain status was if paternity was declared and the father was a status Indian.

Status men could marry non-Indian, non-status, or status women and extend status to them and their children. A status man, irrespective of whom he married, could never lose status based on who he married. A status man could lose status, however, under the Indian Act's enfranchisement provisions. Status men were automatically enfranchised as Canadian citizens and lost band status if they served in the Canadian military or were educated in a public school. If a status man was married and/or had children and was enfranchised, his wife and children would also lose band status and be made Canadian citizens (Jamieson 1978). A non-status man could not (re)gain status under any circumstance (Sprague 1995).[8]

The status provisions had a considerable and pervasive impact on Indian peoples.[9] Although the Indian Act defined band government and established the reserves in a seeming affirmation of band rights to self-government and territories, it was designed with the explicit intent of assimilating Indians into Canadian society as hard-working, tax-paying, Christian citizens. It anticipated the eventual and total dissolution of band governments and trust lands. As with all assimilation policies, it was based on an inherently racist and sexist assumption that Indian governance, epistemologies and beliefs, and gender roles were irrelevant and invalid, even dangerous impediments to progress. But in the process of undermining Indian law, land tenure, economics, cultural beliefs, and social relationships in the name of integration, the Indian Act and assimilation policies more generally ended up reproducing the social conditions of subordination and dependence that they promised to end since Indians were quite unwelcome in areas off-reserve.

Some of the most troubling consequences of the act were in the corrosion and devaluation, however uneven and inconsistent, of Indian women's inclusive participation within Indian governance, economics, and cultural life. This may seem an obvious intent and effect of the Indian Act, and its ideological predecessors in federal programs of "Christianization" and "civilization" that sought to make men heads of households and women subservient (Berger 1997). But the difficult issues to understand are how patriarchal, heterosexist, and homophobic ideologies came to characterize Indian attitudes and practices (Nicholas 1994) and how these attitudes and practices came to define the social conditions of oppression within Indian social and interpersonal relations.

The important conceptual challenge in understanding the impact of these ideologies on Indian peoples is the refusal of a social evolutionary framework in which Indian societies are mapped onto a historical trajectory from the utopic pristine to the tragically contaminated. Two things are true instead.

First, the Indian Act's provisions for status did not create gender-based inequalities or sexism within Indian communities. The provisions represented and perpetuated a much longer process of social formation in which Indian men's political, economic, and cultural roles and responsibilities were elevated and empowered while those of Indian women were devalued. Within this process, sexist ideologies and practices were normalized and not "for the first time"—patriarchy, sexism, and homophobia within Indian communities being much older than 1876. However, in conjunction with an entire social structure defined by colonialism, capitalism, Christianity, heteronormativity, and racism, gender inequalities, sexisms, and bigotries of various kinds had come to define Indian social and interpersonal relations by 1876 in consequential and lasting ways.

Second, the painful, confusing, and uneven adoption of these practices and attitudes by Indians is incredibly disconnected from their cultural histories, oral traditions, beliefs, and practices. Generally speaking, the majority of Indian societies were organized matrilineally. Gender norms were informed by a "separate but equal" value of the place of men, women, and other gendered identities within the community. Opportunities for Indian women and other gendered peoples in governance, ceremonial life, and trade afforded them a relatively public, empowered position within their bands and as diplomats and traders with others (Klein and Ackerman 1995).

These social relations and the cultural beliefs on which they were based were most directly targeted by colonization efforts, from the period of early missionization through assimilation. The systematic undermining of everything related to Indian cultural beliefs about gender took its toll on the structure of Indian societies, specifically social and interpersonal relations.

But even as Indian women's and other gendered people's roles were being maligned and devalued, men's were not, at least not within the confines of the bands or on the reserves. Although there was certainly much violence and discrimination directed at Indian men within Canada, the social roles and responsibilities of heterosexual Indian men within bands and on the reserves was systematically elevated over that of women and nonheterosexuals by the institutions of Christianity, capitalism, sexism, and homophobia.

The Indian Act's provisions for status encapsulated this social formation. With little opportunities for political power and economic self-sufficiency off of the reserve, heterosexual, status Indian men were given these opportunities in band government and reserve life. It is hardly surprising that they took advantage or would come to feel empowered and then entitled to these opportunities.

Thus, the provisions for status contributed to the normalization and legitimization of Indian male privilege within band government—land and resource access and use, social benefits and services, and social politics. The consequences of this privilege are embedded within the assumptions and expectations of status Indian men to the privileges that they were entitled to under the law. Status Indian men came to expect to be privileged and to rely on the material benefits of those privileges; over time they found the law "affirmed, legitimated, and protected" their expectations (Harris 1993, 1713). For even though relative to European Canadian men they were altogether disenfranchised and discriminated against as Indians, status Indian men found in the Indian Act system a relative position of power to which they came to feel and legally be entitled.[10] This is indicated in the myriad ways that the sexism of male privilege came to characterize band governments and reserve life. For instance, by the 1960s, only 6 percent of elected council chiefs and council members were women; and, certificates of possession, or the legal documents granting status Indians permission to live in reserve housing, were issued by bands and DIAND officials almost exclusively to men (Krosenbrink-Gelissen 1991; Goodwin 2002).[11]

More painful has been the systematic escalation of violence against Indian women.[12] In "Stolen Sisters: Discrimination and Violence against Indigenous Women in Canada," Amnesty International reports that now well over 60 percent of Indian women have had an experience of sexual violence (Amnesty International 2004; Smith 2005).[13] Further, "A shocking 1996 Canadian government statistic reveals that Indigenous women between the ages of 25 and 44, with status under the Indian Act, were five times more likely than all other women of the same age to die as the result of violence" (Amnesty International 2004, 1). Community-based and interracial violence against Indian women indicates a complex social matrix of oppression within and between Indian and non-Indian communities. This violence registers the prevalence of sexist ideologies and practices in band governments and Indian organizations that have chosen to ignore that it is Indian women who are most often the targets (Valencia-Weber and Zuni 1995).

Reclaiming Indian Women as Indian: Amending the Law

When Liberal Party Prime Minister Pierre Trudeau came into office in 1968, he promised Canadians a "just society." Drawing from international human rights and civil rights movements in North America, Trudeau's Canada was to be free of all state-sanctioned forms of discrimination on the basis of race, ethnicity, gender, sexuality, class, religion, and national origin. Coordinated by Jean Chrétien, Minister of DIAND, a series of public forums were held to hear Native peoples' perspectives on their experiences of discrimination and their recommendations for policy reform. Indians who gave testimony spoke almost unilaterally about the need for Canada to honor the terms of existing treaties, initiate negotiations with untreatied peoples, settle all land rights violations, and recognize Indian rights to self-government.

Ignoring the testimonies, Trudeau and Chrétien held to their preconceived conviction that the reported problems of poverty and crime on the reserves resulted not from Canada's violation of treaties, lack of recognition of Native rights, or ill-executed social programs but from the "special" status and benefits that Natives had under the law. They maintained that these laws produced racial segregation and a lack of viable access to housing, education, and jobs, which, in turn, resulted in Natives being excluded from the rights, privileges, and opportunities afforded to all Canadian citizens. Trudeau and Chrétien's plan for reform was entitled the "Statement of the Government of Canada on Indian Policy" (1969). It proposed the termination of all treaty obligations within five years, the repeal of the Indian Act, the transfer of all DIAND responsibilities to the provinces, and an affirmative action program to encourage employment opportunities in urban areas.

For Native peoples, the plan represented a stark return to a nineteenth-century anti-Indian assimilationist agenda that sought the total dissolution of band governments and reserves. Native organizations and governments mounted nationwide protests criticizing Trudeau and Chrétien. Within these protests, the National Indian Brotherhood (NIB) emerged as a leading voice because it represented status Indians who were perceived by Parliament, DIAND, and the majority of band governments as those with legitimate, legal claims to Indian status under the Indian Act and so those whose rights were immediately threatened by the proposal.[14]

The NIB's mandate crystallized in Harold Cardinal's *The Unjust Society* (1969). A Cree from Alberta and NIB president when the organization incorporated in 1969, Cardinal argued that the Indian Act provided the only mechanism in Canada for the recognition of the unique legal status and rights of Indian peoples. Consequently, he reasoned, Trudeau and Chrétien were threatening to take away the only means available to Indians to exercise their "sacred rights" as sovereigns (Cardinal 1969, 140). He and the NIB maintained that under no circumstances should the Indian Act or any related statute be amended or repealed and that any attempt to do so was indicative of a kind of throwback nineteenth-century colonialist, assimilationist, and racist effort to undermine Indian rights. Instead, Cardinal and the NIB argued that Parliament and DIAND should be working with band councils to turn over more control of reserve resources and social services in an affirmation of their rights to self-government.

The criticisms of Trudeau and Chrétien's proposal by the NIB, other Native organizations, and band governments were effective and garnered much media attention and public support. So much so, in fact, that Trudeau and Chrétien quickly withdrew it. Instead, Parliament and DIAND worked to build a relationship with the NIB in a public show of their commitment to Indian rights. They even allocated thousands of dollars to support the NIB and granted them an official advisory role to Parliament and DIAND. The NIB took the role on and succeeded in getting DIAND to begin transferring the administration of education, health care, and other social services to bands.

Responding to the dominance of men within the NIB and band governments and within national debates about Indian rights to self-government instigated by Trudeau and Chrétien's proposal, several local, reserve-based Indian women's groups mobilized to assert a role for Indian women within band governance, the debates, and any legal reforms that might result. The two primary groups that emerged were Indian Rights for Indian Women (IRIW) and the Native Women's Association of Canada (NWAC).[15] While both organized locally for cultural survivance through various programs aimed at revitalization and preservation, they focused nationally on securing a repeal of the status provisions of the Indian Act. This strategy resulted in three separate lawsuits—*Lavell v. Canada* (1971), *Bédard v. Isaac* (1972), and *Lovelace v. Canada* (1981). In each case, the women challenged the constitutionality and human rights' compliance of the patrilineal criterion for status in order to confront sexist ideologies and practices within band governments and Indian communities.

Jeannette Vivian Corbiere, a Nishnawbe woman from the Wikwemiking Reserve on Manitoulin Island of Ontario, was a founding member of the Ontario Native Women's Association and one of the elected vice presidents of NWAC. In 1970, she married David Lavell, a non-Indian journalist from Toronto. Almost immediately, she received notice from the local DIAND superintendent that she lost her status by marrying out and was consequently no longer entitled to live on the reserve. In 1971, Lavell filed suit. Her argument was that the Indian Act's status provisions violated Canada's Bill of Rights' prohibition against discrimination on the basis of sex. Judge Grossberg of the Ontario County Court dismissed the case on the grounds that Lavell, despite the loss of her status by marrying out, had acquired full and equal rights with all other Canadian women. As such, he found, Lavell was not deprived of any human rights or personal freedoms contemplated within the Bill of Rights and was actually fairing better than those Indian women who married in. Lavell petitioned to the Federal Court of Appeals and won. The appellate judges found that the Indian Act had resulted in different rights for Indian women than those for Indian men when they married out. They concluded that the status provisions of the Indian Act contravened the Bill of Rights and consequently recommended its repeal.

Meanwhile, Yvonne Bédard followed suit. Bédard, an Iroquois from the Brantford Reserve in Ontario, had married a non-Indian and lived with him off-reserve for six years until they separated, at which time she returned to the reserve to live in the house that she inherited from her mother. In 1971, Bédard was evicted by the Council of the Six Nations Indians, the ruling government of the reserve, although DIAND had informed them that under a 1951 amendment to the Indian Act, bands could make exceptions to the status rules for residency.[16] Making the same argument that Lavell made, Bédard secured an injunction from the Ontario High Court prohibiting her eviction from the reserve. The Supreme Court granted leave to an appeal. Bédard's case followed Lavell's to the Supreme Court (Goodwin 2002).

In the years pending the Supreme Court's ruling, fierce criticisms of Lavell and Bédard were made within Indian communities (Silman 1987) and by the NIB and band leaders (Jamieson 1978; Holmes 1987; Krosenbrink-Gelissen 1991; Nicholas 1994). Not only Lavell and Bédard but also their diverse supporters[17] were accused of being complicit and even conspiring with the kinds of colonialist, assimilationist, and racist ideologies and political agendas of the Canadian government and DIAND officials aimed at undermining Indian rights to self-government. In disturbing ways that echoed their criticisms of Trudeau and Chrétien's proposal, Indian men charged the women with being a part of a long history of colonization and racism that imposed, often violently, non-Indian ideologies and institutions on Indian peoples. This history was epitomized by the women's appeals to civil and human rights laws, and more particularly to feminist movements and principles of gender equality, to challenge the constitutionality and human rights compliance of the Indian Act.

Demonizing an ideology of rights perceived to be based on selfish individualism and personal entitlement, and damned for being "women's libbers" out to force bands into compliance with this ideology (Fiske 1990, 1993; Krosenbrink-Gelissen 1993; McIvor 1995; Silman 1987), the women and their concerns and experiences of discriminatory and violent sexist practices within their communities (Jamieson 1978; Holmes 1987; Monture-Okanee 1993; Krosenbrink-Gelissen 1994; Goodwin 2002) were dismissed as embodying all things not only non- but anti- Indian. Indian women's experiences, perspectives, and political agendas for reform were perceived as not only irrelevant but dangerous to Indian sovereignty movements. As the NIB and band governments continued on in their advisory roles with Parliament and DIAND while lobbying against Lavell and Bédard, the exclusion of women and their concerns from national politics and discussions of Indian sovereignty was represented as normal and necessary to the survival of Indian rights (Faith et al. 1991; Chiste 1994; Krossenbrink-Gelissen 1991; Crenshaw 1995).

Throughout, leaders of the NIB and band councils maintained that the Indian Act—the embodiment and guarantor of Indian rights to self-government—was not obligated to conform to either the terms or the principles of Canada's Bill of Rights. They shored up a definition of self-government that depended solely on the degree to which bands enjoyed governmental noninterference. The entire Indian Act system was made essential to establishing and protecting band government operations and so the single most important factor in the affirmation of Indian sovereignty. As Cardinal asserted:

> We do not want the Indian Act retained because it is a good piece of legislation, it isn't. It is discriminatory from start to finish. But it is a lever in our hands and an embarrassment to the government, as it should be. . . . We would rather continue to live in bondage under the Indian Act than surrender our sacred rights. (Cardinal 1969, 140)

Thus, any amendment to the Indian Act would completely contravene the means and abilities of bands to exercise their "sacred rights" to self-government under the Indian Act.

Cardinal's invocation of "sacred rights" within his assertion of band self-government is important. It associates rights, and the character of the bands from which they derive, with a sovereignty that is inherent and immutable. Rights derive not from international or constitutional law but from the character of the bands as integral, historical polities. In other words, the rights are sacred because the bands are sacred. It was an entirely transparent discursive move to make bands—and themselves as representatives of the bands—immune from political reproach. If bands did indeed possess "sacred rights," then Canada dared not play, even in jest, with the only law that preserved them. Indian women, by implication, were likewise put on notice. By challenging the Indian Act, they were undermining not only the rights of bands but also the sacred character of bands as sovereigns.

The rhetoric was successful. In March 1973, Canada's Supreme Court found that the provisions for status in the Indian Act were exempt from the Bill of Rights and ruled against Lavell and Bédard. This finding left Indian women with no legal recourse in Canada to challenge the Indian Act's provisions (Jamieson 1978; Holmes 1987; Silman 1987; Goodwin 2002). As a result, the United Nations' Human Rights Committee (HRC) agreed to hear a complaint against Canada by Sandra Lovelace, a Maliseet woman from the Tobique Reserve in New Brunswick.

Janet Silman's (1987) seminal collection of interviews with some of the Maliseet women of the Tobique Reserve shows how commonplace Indian women's experiences of poverty, domestic violence, and dismal housing conditions had become by the 1960s. The interviews with status and non-status women spanning three generations repeat incidents of their being kicked out of their homes by male partners claiming rights of occupancy against them; suffering physical and sexual abuse; being forced to live in overcrowded conditions with friends and relatives; being forced to live in debilitated structures and public buildings without water, heat, or proper insulation; and generally being without the financial means to support themselves and their children (Silman 1987, Part 1). These intolerable living conditions brought the women together to organize for change in the spring of 1977, on the specific occasion of a woman and her daughter's eviction from their home by a temperamental husband/father. Through the women's strategizing for fair and equal access to housing, they entered the international political arena as they realized (or remembered) that it was the Indian Act's provisions for status that were being used to justify the discrimination of housing by the DIAND, their council, and status men on the reserve. Reversing these provisions became the main objective of their organizing efforts (Silman 1987, Part 2).

Meeting with indifference at DIAND, opposition by their council, and open hostility at the reserve toward themselves and their children, the women decided to file a complaint against Canada with the HRC in the winter of 1977. Their immediate objective was to compel their own and other band governments to provide them with equal access to housing and social services, including health care, jobs and job training, and education on the reserves.[18] Their long-term goal was to get the provisions for status within the Indian Act repealed. To these ends, they persuaded Lovelace to be the one in whose name the complaint would be filed.

Lovelace had married a non-Indian, moved off of the reserve, and had a son with him. When she divorced and returned with her son, she found that she had lost status and that the band was unwilling to provide her with reserve housing as a non-status Indian. Because her family's situation was already crowded, she and her son lived in a tent on reserve lands, a particularly brutal situation given New Brunswick winters. In her complaint, Lovelace argued that through the enforcement of the Indian Act's criteria for status, Canada had discriminated against her rights to live and participate in the community of her birth on the basis of her sex. She claimed the status provisions were in violation of Canada's Bill of Rights and all relevant UN human rights accords that Canada had entered into as a signatory, including the International Covenant on Civil and Political Rights (Silman 1987, 176; Lovelace 1997, 26–28).

It was not until July 30, 1981, that the HRC was able to render a verdict, having finally received the requested documentation from Parliament and DIAND (Silman 1987, 176). The HRC found Canada in violation of the International Covenant on Civil and Political Rights because the Indian Act denied Lovelace equal treatment under the law. The ruling was felt to be a victory by the Tobique women because it shamed the band council and local DIAND superintendent, who were forced to account for questionable expenditures of federally allocated housing and other funds at Tobique and to address the needs of Indian women and their children. Both issues aggravated existing tensions among the women, the band council, and DIAND (Silman 1998, Part 2). But the ruling resulted in slow and incomplete changes at the reserve.

Lovelace v. Canada severely embarrassed Canadian officials as Canada was in the process of patriating from England. Had Canada not been so, Parliament would have probably paid only lip service to the HRC's conclusions. However, being found in violation of international human rights accords in their treatment of Indian women on the occasion of their patriation from the Crown and revision of their Constitution and Bill of Rights produced a unique situation in which Parliament and DIAND felt compelled to save face by pushing the NIB and band governments for an amendment to the Indian Act. This effort ran contrary to the agendas of the NIB and the majority of band governments, which did not want any such amendment as it had come to represent colonial, assimilationist, and racist agendas working to undermine Indian sovereignty. Serious political differences among Parliament, DIAND, the NIB, band governments, and Indian women's groups and their supporters defined the legal and social contexts in which the amendments to Canada's Constitution Act of 1982 and the Indian Act via Bill C-31 of 1985 were developed and passed.

These amendments were negotiated within the broader context of a series of First Ministers' Conferences held in Ottawa, Ontario, from 1983 to

1987. Commissioned by the Constitution Act, the purpose of the conferences was to provide a forum for the enumeration of Section 35(1), which provided that "the existing aboriginal and treaty rights of the aboriginal peoples of Canada are hereby recognized and affirmed." Incredibly important to defining the parameters of aboriginal and treaty rights in Canada, the conferences were to include participation from the prime minister, first ministers from each of the ten provinces, and invited "representatives of the aboriginal peoples of Canada" (Constitution Act [1982], Section 35 [1]a).

Band councils, the NIB, and organizations representing the Inuit and the Métis were invited as "representatives of the aboriginal peoples."[19] All aboriginal women's groups were excluded.[20] Two reasons were given. One was that they were "special interest" in membership and mandate, that is, they were not composed of representatives of all aboriginal peoples and were only concerned about "women's issues." The second reason was that Parliament and DIAND intended to address "women's issues" in the process of amending the status provisions of the Indian Act; by implication, the participation of women's groups in the conferences would be superfluous (Krossenbrink-Gelissen 1991, 2, 148).

While rejecting the government's position on the need for an amendment to the Indian Act, the NIB and majority of band government leaders agreed with Parliament's exclusion of Native women's groups from the conferences. Women and "women's issues" were negated as irrelevant to the serious political matters of "aboriginal and treaty rights" that the conferences were intended to address.

The dismissiveness by bands and the NIB over the need for the participation of Indian women within the conferences continued a particular intellectual genealogy of sovereignty. As Vine Deloria Jr. (Lakota), Glenn T. Morris (Shawnee), and S. James Anaya and Gerald Taiaiake Alfred (Mohawk) note in their respective works, sovereignty is rooted within European and North American ideologies and practices of colonialism and imperialism (Deloria 1979; Morris 1992; Anaya 1996; Alfred 1999). It was made meaningful within the historical contexts of the theologically inspired efforts of empire building. Through it, powerful nation-states "of the West" claimed rights of conquest over *terra nullius* and "infidels" in virtually every other part of the world. Ideologically, it was hierarchical, exploitative, and militaristic, and it defined a power that was based in force and a nation that was established by force.

Of course, meanings are never static. While Native peoples have certainly changed what sovereignty means over time, now linked in important ways to human rights principles of self-determination, its ideological origins make it impossible to forget that its significance cannot be assumed and is not innately benign or righteous. Its use is inherently political (Barker 2005).

Nowhere is this more apparent than in the simultaneity of band and NIB assertions of sovereignty, the dismissal of gender issues as irrelevant to matters of self-government, and the negation of the need for Indian women's participation within the conferences. Bands and the NIB defined a sovereignty that recalled its nationalist origins and absolutes while reinscribing its masculinist authority both in and as the wholly political (that is, in and as the public). The discursive links were positional and deliberate: they allowed bands to position themselves as sovereigns absolute in relationship to Canada, and of band leaders to represent themselves as masculine rulers in a political sphere that excluded women and femininity. Both positions deflected political and social accountability. Ironically, this sovereignty was embedded within the same ideologies that the bands and NIB were criticizing Canada and Indian women for as inherently colonialist and anti-Indian.

Undaunted by the bands and NIB'S assertion of the irrelevance of women's rights to self-government, Indian women's groups and their allies worked to secure a gender equity clause within Section 35 (1) and an Indian Act amendment. The aim was to ensure that any enumeration of "existing aboriginal and treaty rights" would be understood to apply equally to women and men (Krossenbrink-Gelissen 1991, 147–56). With the political momentum of the *Lovelace* decision behind them, the women garnered public support from Parliament, DIAND, and a range of international and national constituencies for their proposal. However, bands and the NIB stood fast against them. The argument, again, was that any women's rights qualification of Section 35(1) would undermine true Indian sovereignty. The women were criticized, again, for being anti-Indian and anti-sovereignty by trying to force non-Indian feminist and civil rights ideologies on the bands. As Maliseet elder Shirley Bear remembered, "They even stated. . . . 'It is our tradition and our culture if we want to discriminate against women'" (quoted, Silman 1987, 198–99).

This time, however, the NIB's and bands' polemics backfired. Instead of convincing Parliament, DIAND, the courts, and the public on the need to silence the women in the name of affirming Indian rights to sovereignty, government officials began to distance themselves from the NIB and band leaders who were being represented in the press and by multiple civil and human rights organizations as advancing sexist attitudes and discriminatory practices against women. The impact of this representation was reflected immediately in the NIB's name change. As the annual planning meetings were initiated in 1982 for the First Ministers' Conferences, "The Brotherhood," as it had come to be called, changed its name to the Assembly of First Nations (AFN). However, the AFN's continued rejection of gender and women's perspectives as irrelevant to matters of self-government failed to deflect government and public concerns about sexism within the organization and band governments. It ended up garnering further support for the women. Therefore, when the first conference took place March 15–16, 1983, at the Ottawa Conference Center, the only two items on the agenda were self-government and gender equality. Accordingly, the first day was devoted to self-government and the second to equality, a program mirrored at the 1984 and 1985 conferences.

Because of opposition from the majority of first ministers, the bands, Inuit, and Métis were not able to gain enough support on their proposal to entrench self-government as an "existing aboriginal and treaty right" (Constitution Act, Section 35 [1]; see Krosenbrink-Gelissen 1991, 150). However, they were able to secure the following two enumerations on a Constitutional Accord on Aboriginal Rights that would be signed by the majority of delegates and later ratified: "(2) In this Act, 'aboriginal peoples of Canada' includes the Indian, Inuit, and Métis peoples of Canada. (3) For greater certainty, in subsection (1) 'treaty rights' includes rights that now exist by way of land claims agreements or may be so acquired" (Ibid.). These amendments were made with the intent of qualifying who would be considered "aboriginal peoples" for purposes of being covered by Section 35 (1) and to allow for the possibility of additional land claims settlements that would need to fall under the same protections as those previously signed.

During the second day of the conference, and representing the diverse solidarities that the women had formed, elected representatives from NWAC spoke through the seats of the Native Council of Canada (NCC) and the provinces of Manitoba, Ontario, New Brunswick, Saskatchewan, and Québec. They maintained that gender equality was a self-government issue and that any true Indian self-government would not have a problem with the traditional principle of equality between men and women.[21] They proposed that any amendment to Section 35(1) ought to be made subject to the Charter on Rights and Freedoms of the Constitution Act, which guaranteed equality to all persons living within Canada.[22] Through several personal testimonies of their experiences of gender discrimination on the reserves, they made a compelling case that the reinstatement of those who had been unjustly disenfranchised by the Indian Act's status provisions ought to be explicitly provided for as a constitutional right (Krossenbrink-Gelissen 1991, 152–53; Fiske 1995).

While the Inuit and Métis delegates supported the women's arguments and their proposals, the AFN and band representatives did not (Krosenbrink-Gelissen 1991, 153–54). The AFN and bands upheld their position that equality would be sufficiently addressed by the affirmation of Indian self-government and that any further discussion of "women's issues" was irrelevant (Holmes 1987, 6; Krosenbrink-Gelissen 1991, 154). At the end of the second day, an AFN delegate made the following statement at a press conference:

> We would like to make it clear that we agree with the women who spoke so forcefully this morning that they have been treated unjustly. The discrimination they suffered was forced upon us through a system imposed by white colonial government through the Indian Act. It was not the result of our traditional laws, and in fact it would not have occurred under our traditional laws. We must make it perfectly clear why we feel so strongly that we must control our own citizenship. . . . The NIB maintains that "equality" does already exist within the traditional "citizenship code" of all First Nations peoples. (Krosenbrink-Gelissen 1991, 154)

The AFN attempted to indict the "white colonial government . . . imposed through the Indian Act" as the source and cause of gender inequalities within Indian communities. In a dizzyingly forgetful argument of their own position with regards to the "sanctity" of the Indian Act, the AFN argued that women were undermining Indian sovereignty by seeking a gender enumeration to Section 35(1) and amendments to the Indian Act that would force non-Indian ideologies on band governments (Holmes 1987, 6). They failed to convince. In a complicated response by Parliament and DIAND, informed by the *Lovelace* decision and government efforts to distance themselves from the histories of sexism then so firmly associated with the Indian Act, officials supported the women's proposals for a gender enumeration of Section 35 (1). Confronting mounting political pressure, the AFN and majority of band leaders relented. The resulting amendment was added: "(4) Notwithstanding any other provisions of this Act, the aboriginal and treaty rights referred to in subsection (1) are guaranteed equally to male and female persons" (Constitution Act, Charter on Rights and Freedoms, Section 28).

Lilianne E. Krosenbrink-Gelissen (1991) writes that despite their success in getting the amendment approved, the apparent sexism and political obstinacy of band and AFN representatives toward the women and with regards to women's rights left the women's groups and their allies feeling that the "equality clause" would not have the appropriate force it needed in changing the social conditions on the reserves for Indian women (Krosenbrink-Gelissen 1991, 156). The women, therefore, focused on securing further enumeration of Section 35 (1) that would define gender equality as an explicit aboriginal right applying to all other (156). Because of band and AFN opposition, they were not successful. The second conference took place March 8–9, 1984. On the first day, Parliament delegates agreed to delineate "aboriginal rights" by self-government. However, only the first ministers from Manitoba, Ontario, New Brunswick, and Nova Scotia agreed. All other provinces, representing the majority of Canada's population, rejected the proposal (157).

On the second day of the 1984 conference, gender equity was addressed. NWAC leaders spoke through the seats of the NCC, Ontario, Québec, and New Brunswick. The government made a second proposal based on the recommendations of NWAC and others to enumerate equality as an "existing" right that would cover all other rights. However, the AFN and band representatives objected so strenuously that no agreement could be reached, and the second conference closed without any resolution (158–59).

At some point during or immediately following the 1984 conference, it seems that the AFN realized that they would have to address the matter of gender before they could focus their attentions on securing support for a self-government enumeration of Section 35 (1). This change was informed in some measure by pressure from Parliament and DIAND, both of which wanted all discrimination of Indian women removed from federal statute before the Constitution Act's Charter on Rights and Freedoms became law on April 17, 1985. Because Section 35 (1) had been successfully enumerated to affirm gender equality, they pushed aboriginal organizations and bands for cooperation in getting an amendment to the Indian Act passed before April 17, 1985 (156–64).

In response to this pressure, the AFN began to work toward a compromise with NWAC. They invited NWAC to a Special Legislative Assembly in Edmonton, Alberta, in May 1984. The result was called the Edmonton Resolution, a joint resolution that affirmed the AFN's support of NWAC's proposal to remove the patrilineal requirement for status from the Indian Act and reinstate all women and their children who had lost their status or had never had it recognized as a result of its enforcement. For NWAC, the "first-generation cut-off rule" was a much compromised measure. They conceded to AFN fears that opening up the registries to everyone who had ever lost or been denied status as a result of the Indian Act had the potential of severely and negatively affecting band governments and their land rights. In exchange of the AFN's support of NWAC's efforts to secure an Indian Act amendment, NWAC agreed to support the AFN's efforts to secure an enumeration of Section 35(1) that would affirm aboriginal rights to self-government.[23]

The third conference took place April 2–3, 1985. The third, and final two conferences in 1986 and 1987, ended without any enumeration on self-government. Once joined, aboriginal peoples presented a strong case to the assembly but faced an equally strong resistance from the provinces to secure self-government as an "existing right" (Hawkes 1985, 28; Krosenbrink-Gelissen 1991, 190).

During the 1985 conference, Parliament expedited the process for an amendment to the Indian Act with the support of the AFN and women's groups (Holmes 1987, 7; Krosenbrink-Gelissen 1991, 159–60; Sanders 1983). The House of Commons Standing Committee on Indian Affairs held five weeks of public hearings in February and March to work out the specific provisions for Bill C-31. The bill was submitted to Parliament and given the Royal Assent on June 28. It took effect retroactively to April 17 in order to bring the Indian Act into compliance with the charter (Green 1985; Moss 1990; Sprague 1995).

Bill C-31 essentially provided for a "first-generation cut-off rule" for reinstatement. Those women who had lost their status as a result of marrying out, and their children, as well as those who had been automatically enfranchised as Canadian citizens, could apply to have their status reinstated.[24] As Joan Holmes observes in a study commissioned by the Canadian Advisory Council on the Status of Women, about 60 percent of those

registered by 1987 were first-time applicants; 40 percent were reinstate-
ments of those who had lost their status by marrying out or enfranchisement, with the vast majority of these applications being submitted by
women (Holmes 1987, 14–15; see also Manitoba Aboriginal and Northern
Affairs 2000). According to DIAND's Indian Registry, as of December 31,
2002, there are 704,851 status Indians in Canada.[25] About 17 percent are
those reinstated under the terms of Bill C-31 and about 60 percent live off-
reserve (Furi and Wherrett 1996).

The bill also allowed bands to assume control of their own membership
codes, with the effect of separating DIAND's Indian Registry (which
maintains a record of status Indians) and band registries (which records
members of bands). Individuals applying for reinstatement also have to
apply for band membership, as one does not secure the other.

As of 2002, 253 of 614 bands had established membership codes of their
own. In a 2000 study by Manitoba Aboriginal and Northern Affairs
(MANA), 15 percent of bands had adopted criteria for membership with
some form of unlimited one-parent inheritance, 11 percent with restrictive
two-parent inheritance rules, and 5 percent with some form of a blood
quantum criterion (MANA 2000).

Not all of those who have applied to be registered as status Indians
under Bill C-31 have wanted to return to the reserves. Many have families,
jobs, and educational opportunities off-reserve but have desired formal
status "so that they will have a recognized link with their band, and be able
to return if their circumstances change, when they retire, or for burial. It is
also important to them that their children have rights as band members"
(Holmes 1987, 18).

The lack of interest in returning or moving to the reserves was and is
owing to the intense political conflicts over "Bill C-31s" (the name given to
women who have been reinstated under the amendment). Since 1985, a few
bands have stopped providing services to non-status Indians and have
refused to extend those same services to newly registered women and their
children: "Women have been denied fishing licenses; their children have
been refused admittance to reserve schools; medical services have been
denied; and bands have refused to grant construction permits or permission to sell land to reinstated women" (Holmes 1987, 19).

Six bands in Alberta—Sawbridge, Sturgeon Lake, Ermineskin, Enoch,
Sarcee, and Blackfoot—challenged Bill C-31 in the Supreme Court, arguing
that the bill was in conflict with the Constitution's protection of "existing

aboriginal and treaty rights" because, by obligating membership codes to conform to Canada's Bill of Rights, it denied the rights of bands to determine their own laws as an act of self-government (Holmes 1987, 21).[26] The Supreme Court reminded the bands that Bill C-31 allowed them to maintain their own registries of members and upheld the constitutionality of the human and civil rights principles on which the bill was based. However, the challenge illustrates how divisive issues about women's rights and the relationship of women's rights to concepts of self-government remain within Indian communities (Faith et al. 1991).

From Rights to Reformation

Indian women, band governments, and Indian organizations articulated very different kinds of rights for themselves in working to achieve their different political ideas about and goals for sovereignty. The rights that resulted reflected deep political and cultural conflicts within Indian communities over issues of culture, identity, and tradition, particularly over what was considered to be traditional when it comes to women's roles and responsibilities. Oftentimes, within these conflicts, rights proxied for tradition. So that, the political debates over women's rights were simultaneously about the terms and social conditions of tradition. That is, debates over the kinds of rights Indian women and Indian men had as Indians were simultaneously debates about what traditions—what cultures and identities—were considered authentically Indian. So that, Indian women's assertions of their rights to everything from reserve housing and employment to full participation in band governance and national politics were an attempt to reclaim a particular kind of tradition that valued women's "separate but equal" place in Indian communities and politics. This countered the assertion of many Indian men, particularly those in band government and national Indian organizations, who wanted to claim a tradition that justified the exclusion of Indian women and the negation of gender issues within sovereignty politics. Men who wanted, in other words, to affirm the privileges of men in reserve, band, and national politics.

The rights that resulted from these different political perspectives and agendas reflected a conflicted social matrix of sexism within Indian communities. Therein, Indian women were disenfranchised and dismissed, their concerns represented as politically irrelevant and even dangerous to Indian self-government and territorial integrity. Indian sovereignty was defined likewise in troubling and troubled ways—as an absolute, as wholly unchallengeable, as sacred, as hyper-masculinist, with Indian men representing themselves as final authorities over Indian politics, both politically and culturally. The effect of such representations was that existing, exploitative relations of power between Indian women and Indian men were perpetuated as culturally authentic and integral, even traditional and certainly necessary to Indian sovereignty.

Patricia A. Monture (Mohawk) analyzes what she calls the "gender silence" within Canada's Supreme Court cases mitigating the application of the Constitution's Section 35(1). She asks:

> When your goal is protecting Aboriginal and treaty rights in a legal system that is not your own, do you choose to silence issues of gender difference if giving voice to your gendered cultural differences might further jeopardize (as in *Van der Peet*) your claim to Aboriginal and treaty rights? Do you ignore the place of your women for the sake of securing recognition of your claims to governance and land (as in *Delgamuukw*)? (Monture 2004, 53)[27]

Monture argues that these questions are a result of the colonialism of Canadian law. I would insist further that the questions are not merely a legacy of colonialism but that it is exactly the discourse that constructs gender and sovereignty as conceptual or political opposites that is at the heart of the problem. The argument that a choice has to be made between securing women's rights or Indian sovereignty has rationalized Indian women's disenfranchisement and disempowerment within Indian communities. The idea that by affirming Indian women's rights to equality, Indian sovereignty is irrevocably undermined affirms a sexism in Indian social formations that is not merely a residue of the colonial past but an agent of social relationships today.

Monture focuses her analysis of Supreme Court judgments on "the consequences of not taking gender into account in decisions that focus on First Nations governance and land relationships" (Monture 2004, 52). For her, this failure results from a lack of understanding about the centrality of gender in Native law, such as the fact that women had central roles within traditional forms of governance and agriculture. But gender is not silent or disappeared within these judgments. Rather, gender is made to appear in particular ways that reaffirms the sexist ideologies and practices that have established and maintained existing relations of power between Indian men and Indian women on the one hand, and between Indians and Canada on the other hand. In other words, because gender and sovereignty are co-constitutive, gender is a definitive aspect of the concepts, debates, arbitrations, and agendas of sovereignty even if Indian women are not a category of the discussion. Gender is always present, even if Indian women are silenced by insult or reduced to be proverbial audience members in the public forums of political debate.

In other words, the entire legal framework of the Indian Act has been based on ideologies of gender invested in establishing and protecting the status and rights of Indian men over Indian women. It does this even in places not specifically addressed to the status or rights of Indian men and Indian women. So, of course, women's concerns and activities are not going to be pronounced. But gender and women have not disappeared from the political or analytical scene; rather, gender and women have been made over to appear irrelevant in the normalization of the privileges, benefits, activities, and voices of status Indian men—so much so that, as Monture so rightly observes, Indian women's traditional governance roles and agricultural work are not protected under the law as are men's leadership and hunting and fishing practices. This does not mean that gender is absent; it means that the kind of gendering taking place is one that privileges and benefits the power and activities of men. Women are there, but they and their concerns are just being made over to appear complementary, subordinate, or irrelevant: as if in the provision of band government, Indian women are naturally being provided for; as if in the protection of band reserve rights, women are naturally being protected; as if in the affirmation of hunting and fishing rights, women's activities are naturally being affirmed.

The forced absorption of Indian women's experiences, perspectives, and agendas into the interests of status Indian men is exactly why the discourses of rights mobilized by Indian women, band governments, and Indian organizations during the 1983 and 1985 amendments articulated such conflicting notions of gender and sovereignty. They have continued to do so throughout the 1990s in a myriad of other legal cases, including *Courtois v. Canada* (1991), *Native Women's Association of Canada v. Canada* (1992), *Sawridge Band v. Canada* (1995), *Goodswimmer v. Canada* (1997), and *Corbiere v. Canada* (1999). The kind of sovereignty defined by bands and Indian organizations has taken for granted the fact that by entrenching Indian rights to self-government and lands, any possible concern that Indian women might have would obviously be taken care of. When Indian women have emphatically said no and asserted that it would not and has not been that way, band governments and Indian organizations have interpreted that to mean an anti-sovereignty perspective. Because gender has been understood to be subordinate to sovereignty, Indian women have been perceived as putting their own selfish, personal interests before those of the collective.

But Indian women have been saying something entirely different. They have been saying that the structure of inequalities produced by ideologies and practices of sexism are not okay. They have been saying that the normalization of their disenfranchisement is not okay—not okay because it does not reflect Indian cultural beliefs about gender and not okay because it does not reflect Indian women's agendas to (re)assume their public, participatory roles within the governance and social life of their communities.

The kind of political cross-talk over gender politics that took place most publicly in the 1983 and 1985 amendments has percolated throughout Canadian Native politics ever since.[28] The main impediment to any lasting legal reform for Native women seems to emerge and function within a discursive divide between gender and sovereignty. This has affected thinking about what rights mean for Native peoples in relation to Canada and the international community as well as the kinds of legal reforms necessary to entrench gender equality for Natives within federal, constitutional, treaty, and band law.

It has often been assumed within Native activism and scholarship that there is a fundamental, almost organic, conflict between individual and collective rights at the heart of these matters (Guerrero 1997). Marie Anna Jaimes Guerrero (Juaneño/Yaqui) argues that individual rights stem from ideologies of individualism defined by and imposed from European and North American colonialism, nationalism, and civil rights. She argues that individual rights, and the individualisms from which they derive, force the inclusion of Natives into a broader category of "American" as minorities or ethnic groups. This forced inclusion erases the unique political status of Native peoples as sovereigns by subsuming Natives as individual citizens with civil rights under the authority of colonial states such as Canada and the United States, where Native political freedoms are measured by individual experiences of civil rights. Guerrero argues that sovereignty, however, defines Native peoples as political collectivities with collective rights to sovereignty. This definition derives from international law and human rights accords that associate "peoples" with all commensurate rights to self-determination (Anaya 1996). Sovereignty and self-determination situate Natives under international law as "collective nonstate entities" (Wilmer 1993, 164) with measurable rights to self-government, territorial integrity, and cultural autonomy (Anaya 1996).

Val Napoleon (Cree/Saulteaux/Dunneza) posits that,

> The aboriginal political discourse regarding self-determination would be more useful to communities if it were to incorporate a practical and developed understanding of individual self-determination. In other words, an individual perspective on self-determination could perhaps shift collective self-determination between rhetoric to a meaningful and effective political project that engages aboriginal peoples and is truly inclusive of aboriginal women. (Napoleon 2005, 31)

Napoleon defines "individual self-determination" by the "freedom" and "autonomy" of individuals to be "self-making" and suggests that "manifestation of a person's self-determining autonomy is through relationships with others" (36). She argues that the dichotomy between the individual and the collective is false and has been used within Native communities to override the rights of Native women. For her, what is needed is an appreciation of the centrality of the individual to the collective, for the way that they constitute each other, and for a notion of "collective self-determination" that affirms the inclusion of all individuals and their rights to self-definition.

Guerrero's and Napoleon's writings open some interesting questions about Native conceptualizations of what it means to be a collective political entity, what defines the individual, what rights are implied by the collective and the individual, and the politics of gender throughout. Guerrero shows how discourses of ethnicity and civil rights have been mobilized to erase the unique political history of Native peoples as sovereigns.[29] What she does not do is trouble her concept of sovereignty.

Since the founding of the United Nations, sovereignty has been associated with the human rights of self-determination as a collective status and set of rights enjoyed by "peoples."[30] Within international and national politics, Natives have laid claim to their status as "peoples" with all of the legal implications for asserting their collective human rights to sovereignty as self-determination. Can Native groups claim and assert that status and those rights without any obligation to the principles of human rights on which the United Nations and international law is based? Can they assert their rights to self-government and territories under constitutional and federal law without any obligation to the principles of civil rights on which those constitutions are founded?

S. James Anaya (1996) observes that part of the difficulty in political debates over the nature and consequence of Native nationhood and citizenship has been about power, and perhaps more specific, about the power to govern. If the power to govern is located within the nation, the potential is for the affirmation of political and cultural distinction, but the danger is its evolution into totalitarianism. If the power to govern derives from citizens, then it is measured by the degree to which individual citizens enjoy real political, economic, and cultural freedom, equality, and participation. The discursive inflection of citizenship through ideologies of individualism, with all of the implications it has had for producing a masculine patriotic nationalism, has resulted in a problematic understanding of rights. Rights have assumed the entitlement, privilege, and prominence of men to the subordination of women. It is, after all, the self-made man who has dominated narratives of American politics. Napoleon argues that the individual is a key component of the collective. It is a collective that recognizes this cannot lay claim to a power that is absolute or that operates free of any ethical, moral, or humane obligations. It is grounded in a sense of shared political and cultural affiliation and so responsibility to all individuals within.

In the specific contexts of the 1983 and 1985 amendments, and in subsequent political activism by Native women in Canada, Indian women's groups such as NWAC did not define women's rights to equality to the exclusion or negation of the collective rights of their bands to self-government and territorial integrity or to the negation of the rights of Indian men. They asserted that fundamental to the character of their bands were women's issues and gender because the collective is only as sound as the status and rights of the individuals that comprise it. If the disenfranchisement or exploitation of women defines the collective, or is exercised in the name of the collective, then the collective will perpetuate sexist ideologies and practices.

Empowering Native women means not only extending rights of freedom, equality, and participation to them, or punishing institutions or individuals who discriminate against them. These strategies have proven to fall short of addressing the long-term realities of gender inequality. The 1983 and 1985 amendments, for instance, ended up working as mere additions and not reformations of the law or social conditions in Indian communities. They added women and their children as band members and added gender equality as a legal provision but into a preexisting legal and social structure that remained fundamentally sexist. They failed, therefore, to alter in any substantial way the political, economic, or social roles of Indian women within reserve and urban communities or to (re)empower the gender-based traditions and customs of Indian governance and territorial occupation.

I do not mean to imply that Indian women and their children should not have been reinstated as band members or that gender equality should not be incorporated into every aspect of the law. Rather, the failure of any real substantive transformation of women's social conditions is reflected in the definition, investment, and protection of the privileges of status Indian men within band governments and reserve lands and resources. "Additive reforms" cannot and do not change or transform these types of legal structures or social relations, as evidenced by the continued exasperation of Indian women's groups in Canada at the lack of any real changes in women's lives in the aftermath of the constitutional amendment of 1983 or post–Bill C-31 of 1985.

Real reformation must involve and result in a radical, affirmative repositioning of the legal and social status of women in respect to men. Men must be partners in this process. They must be willing to give up the assumptions, privileges, and benefits that they have inherited from a system based in sexism; take responsibility in their interpersonal relations for histories of discrimination and violence against women and children; and work to (re)empower women and their children within their communities and families. These are neither easy nor self-evident necessities within a legal system and social network that have worked so hard at subjugating Indian people to the still colonial powers of the state and negating gender as a non-issue and women's perspectives as irrelevant. The decolonization of Native governance and lands, therefore, must be concurrent. Only as viably self-determining communities will Native peoples be able to revitalize and reform their cultures and relationships with one another.

In sum, it is quite simple what must be done: (1) the affirmative empowerment of women in band government, Indian organizations, and on- and off-reserve communities; (2) the affirmative validation of gender-based traditions and inheritance customs in Indian governance and territorial occupation, including full participatory and property rights for women; and (3) the decolonization of Native governance and lands. The real measure of these affirmations—and women's and men's partnerships in them—will be the end of violence and discrimination against women and their children in Indian communities as well as the negation of any legacies of their tolerance in the law or in interpersonal relations. These will prove to be the hardest things ever done.

....

Joanne Barker is Lenape (a citizen of the Delaware Tribe of Indians). She is professor and chair of the American Indian Studies Department at San Francisco State University. In addition to her scholarly publications, Barker has cowritten and coproduced several documentary films and has published a short story collection and novellas. Her work focuses on indigenous feminism and the sovereignty and self-determination of indigenous peoples globally.

Notes

Originally published in *Meridians* vol. 7, no. 1, 2006.

1   *Indian, Métis,* and *Inuit* are the three legal categories of aboriginal or First Nation peoples in Canadian law. This essay is focused on the politics of *Indian* gender and sovereignty. I use the term *Native* when addressing all three and/or including all Native peoples in what is now Canada.

2   For the proliferation of scholarship on the amendments, begin with Fiske 1995; Grant 1994; Green 1985; Hawkes 1985; Holmes 1987; Jamieson 1978; Krosenbrink-Gelissen 1991, 1993, 1994; Leslie and Macquire 1979; McIvor 1995; Moss 1987, 1990; Native Women's Association of Canada 1984, 1985, 1992a, 1992b; Nicholas 1994; Pentney 1987; Rayner 1978; Sanders 1972, 1975, 1980, 1983; Sayers et al. 2001; Silman 1987; Sprague 1995; Tarnopolsky 1975; Turpel 1989.

3   See Fiske 1990, 1993; Krosenbrink-Gelissen, 1993; McIvor 1995.

4   For similar attempts, see Krouse and Howard-Bobiwash 2003, particularly Janovicek 2003.

5   Related historical moments include the debates surrounding the Charlottetown Accords in 1992 and the Report of the Royal Commission on Aboriginal Peoples in 1996. See Chiste 1994; Faith et al. 1991; Monture-Okanee 1993; Nahanee 1993.

6   See Harring (1998) for an excellent analysis of the development of Canadian law in the 1800s and its impact on the rights of Native peoples to self-government and lands. See Cook and Lindau (2000) for an uneven but solid comparative analysis of the long-term effects of European laws on Native self-government. See Chiste (1994) for an excellent review of Native women's roles in contemporary debates about the terms of Native self-government in Québec.

7   See Crossland (1982) for some provocative interviews with status Indian women who refused to marry for fear of losing status and all commensurate rights to live and participate in reserve life.

8   Under Section 6(2) of the Indian Act, the children of two successive generations of status and non-status parents are not entitled to become status Indians.

9   See Armitage 1995; Blackwood 1984; Bonvillain 1989; Bourgeault 1983, 1989, 1993; Brown 1981; Devens 1992; Etienne and Leacock 1980; Holly 1990; Klein and Ackerman 1995; Mitchell 1996; Smandych and Lee 1995; Van Kirk 1983.

10 Another layer of historical context is, of course, the way that the roles and responsibilities of Indian men had been so dramatically transformed by colonial processes. See, for instance, Nicholas (1994), who suggests that Indian men came to identify with patriarchy because of how colonialism had stripped them of their once empowered positions within Indian communities as leaders, traders, and providers.

11 As Goodwin (2002) observes, the consequences of the certificates being issued to men are that women seeking help for themselves and their children at shelters against abusive male partners are often punished by band councils, the women finding themselves evicted from their homes when they return.

12 Very little study or reporting has occurred on violence against other gendered peoples within Indian communities throughout North America.

13 Read about NWAC's Sisters In Spirit Campaign at http://www.sistersinspirit .ca/.

14 Treaty Indians, particularly organizations representing the Métis, were likewise mobilized into political action by the proposal. Their efforts paralleled those of the NIB's. See Miller 1991, 233. The NIB had origins in the National Indian Council (NIC), which represented all First Nation peoples in Canada. Apparently, the NIC experienced a period of contention among treaty Indians, Métis, and non-status Indians over the scope of its political objectives. The result was the reformation of the NIC into the NIB and the Canadian Métis Society (CMS), which later became the Native Council of Canada (NCC), representing non-status Indians and Métis (Miller 1991, 232). Other organizations that had nationwide prominence at the time included the Inuit Tapirisat of Canada (ITC) and the Inuit Committee on National Issues (ICNI), both representing Inuits, and the Métis National Council (MNC), representing Métis.

15 IRIW was incorporated in 1970; NWAC was incorporated in 1974. The Inuit Women's Association was founded in 1984 to "ensure their input on national issues of concern to aboriginal peoples in Canada, and to ensure their participation in federal policies and programs" (quoted from their Web site at http:/ /www .pauktuutit.ca/, accessed December 11, 2005). The Métis National Council of Women was incorporated in 1992 to address the unique legal and social issues confronting Métis women, including cultural preservation and treaty rights (see their mandate at http://www.metiswomen.ca/, accessed December 11, 2005).

16 The 1951 amendment to the Indian Act permitted bands to issue housing, or permit the continued occupancy of housing, to Indian women who lost status by marrying out. Bands almost never took advantage of the provision (Goodwin 2002).

17 The women found solidarity with multiple configurations of status/non-status, feminist, religious, student, and civil and human rights groups and individuals (see Silman 1987).

18 Bands were often the only employer on the reserves and as time went on became the sole administrator of certain social services and education programs.

19 Organizations for the Inuit and Métis included the Inuit Committee on National Issues, Inuit Tapirisat of Canada, Métis National Council, and the Native Council of Canada.

20 For an analysis of why women's issues were substantively central to the debates, see Native Women's Association of Canada 1992a, 1992b; McIvor 1995.

21 The Maliseet women's group and women from Québec not affiliated with NWAC were also present at the conference as delegates. Though they differed on the specifics of how the Indian Act ought to be amended, they shared the conviction that equality had to be entrenched within any enumeration of "existing aboriginal and treaty rights" in order to reverse the patterns of discrimination ingrained within band government practices (Silman 1987; Krosenbrink-Gelissen 1991, 152).

22 For analyses of Native women's rights in the charter, see Nahanee (1993) and Turpel (1989).

23 Their concession was apparently quite controversial, and several women publicly criticized them for giving in too quickly to the AFN (see Krosenbrink-Gelissen 1991, 156–61).

24 The bill did not address several important issues of discrimination within the status provisions. See Holmes 1987; MANA 2000.

25 See DIAND's Web site for updated information on the number of bands and registered Indians in Canada (www.ainc-inac.gc.ca).

26 What is interesting about these challenges, and something that Indian women's groups have not fully addressed, is that several of the bands involved in the suits were traditionally patrilineal. By amending the Indian Act in such a way that no gendered criteria can be used to determine membership, the law restricts the abilities of not only patrilineal but matrilineal bands from codifying criteria that reflect their own gendered traditions. The question becomes whether or not such a restriction is necessary given how entrenched men's privilege and women's disenfranchisement has become within band law and reserve politics, and what it means that in the political objectives of many women's groups cultural revitalization is still very much a part of the mandate.

27 R. v. Van der Peet (1996); Delgamuukw v. British Columbia (1997).

28 See also cases involving the politics of race, including *Raphael v. Montagnais du Lac Saint-Jean Band* (1975); *Desjarlais v. Piapot Bond No. 75* (1989); *Jacobs v. Mohawk Council of Kahnawake* (1998).

29 See also Wilkins 2002; Kauanui 2002; Barker 2002.

30 For a fuller analysis of the category of peoples in international law, see Barker 2004.

Works Cited

Alfred, Gerald Taiaiake. 1999. *Peace, Power, Righteousness: An Indigenous Manifesto.* Toronto: Oxford University Press.

Amnesty International. 2004. "Stolen Sisters: Discrimination and Violence against Indigenous Women in Canada: A Summary of Amnesty International's Concerns." October 4. Report Index: AMR 20/001/2004. http://web.amnesty.org /library/.

Anaya, S. James. 1996. *Indigenous Peoples in International Law.* New York: Oxford University Press.

Armitage, Andrew. 1995. *Comparing the Policy of Aboriginal Assimilation: Australia, Canada, and New Zealand.* Vancouver, BC: University of British Columbia Press.

Barker, Joanne. 2002. "Looking for Warrior Woman (Beyond Pocahontas)." In *This Bridge We Call Home: Radical Visions for Transformation,* ed. Gloria Anzaldúa and Ana Louise Keating. New York: Routledge, 314–25.

———. 2004. "The Human Genome Diversity Project: 'Peoples,' 'Populations,' and the Cultural Politics of Identification." *Cultural Studies* 18:4 (July), 578–613.

———. 2005. "For Whom Sovereignty Matters." In *Sovereignty Matters: Locations of Contestation and Possibility in Indigenous Struggles for Self-Determination,* ed. Joanne Barker. Contemporary Indigenous Issues Series. Lincoln: University of Nebraska Press, 1–32.

Berger, Bethany Ruth. 1997. "After Pocahontas: Indian Women and the Law, 1830–1934." *American Indian Law Review* 21:1, 1–62.

Blackwood, Evelyn. 1984. "Sexuality and Gender in Certain Native American Tribes: The Case of Cross-gender Females." *Signs: Journal of Women in Culture and Society* 10, 27–42.

Bonvillain, Nancy. 1989. "Gender Relations in Native North America." *American Indian Culture and Research Journal* 13:2, 1–28.

Bourgeault, Ron. 1983. "The Indian, the Métis and the Fur Trade: Class, Sexism and Racism in the Transition from 'Communism' to Capitalism." *Studies in Political Economy* 12, 45–79

———. 1989. "Race, Class, and Gender: Colonial Domination of Indian Women." *Socialist Studies* 5, 87–115.

———. 1993. "The Development of Capitalism and the Subjugation of Native Women in Northern Canada." *Alternate Routes* 6, 110–40.

Brown, Jennifer S. H. 1981. *Strangers in Blood: Fur Trade Families in Indian Country.* Vancouver: University of British Columbia Press.

Cardinal, Harold. 1969. *The Unjust Society: The Tragedy of Canada's Indians*. Edmonton: Hurtig Press.

Chiste, Katherine Beaty. 1994. "Aboriginal Women and Self-Government: Challenging Leviathan." *American Indian Culture and Research Journal* 18:3, 19–43.

Cook, Curtis, and Juan D. Lindau, eds. 2000. *Aboriginal Rights and Self-Government: The Canadian and Mexican Experience in North American Perspective*. Montreal: McGill-Queen's University Press.

Crenshaw, Kimberlé Williams. 1995. "Mapping the Margins: Intersectionality, Identity Politics, and Violence against Women of Color." In *Critical Race Theory: The Key Writings That Have Formed the Movement*, ed. Kimberlé Crenshaw, Neil Gotanda, Gary Peller, and Kendall Thomas. New York: The New Press, 357–83.

Crossland, Harvey J., director. 1982. *Somewhere Between*. The Hy Perspectives Media Group, Inc.

Deloria, Vine, Jr. 1979/1999. "Self-Determination and the Concept of Sovereignty." In *Economic Development in American Indian Reservations*, ed. Roxanne Dunbar Ortiz. Albuquerque: University of New Mexico Native American Studies, 1979. Reprinted in *Native American Sovereignty*, ed. John R. Wunder. New York: Garland Publishing, Inc., 118–24.

Devens, Carol. 1992. *Countering Colonization: Native American Women and Great Lakes Missions, 1630–1900*. Berkeley: University of California Press.

Etienne, Mona, and Eleanor Leacock. 1980. *Women and Colonization: Anthropological Perspectives*. New York.

Faith, Karlen, Mary Gottriedson, Cherry Joe, Wendy Leonard, and Sharon MacIvor. 1991. "Native Women in Canada: A Quest for Justice." *Social Justice* 17:3, 167–89.

Fiske, Jo-Anne. 1990. "Native Women in Reserve Politics: Strategies and Struggles." *Journal of Legal Pluralism and Unoffical Law* 30/31, 121–37.

———. 1993. "Child of the State/Mother of the Nation: Aboriginal Women and the Ideology of Motherhood." *Culture* XIII, 17–35.

———. 1995. "Political Status of Native Indian Women: Contradictory Implications of Canadian State Policy." *American Indian Culture and Research Journal* 19:2, 1–30.

Furi, Megan, and Jill Wherrett. 1996/2003. *Indian Status and Band Membership Issues*. Ottawa: Parliamentary Research Branch, Library of Parliament, originally prepared 1996, updated 2003.

Goodwin, Christine M. 2002. "Human Rights, Women's Rights, Aboriginal Rights: Indivisible and Guaranteed?" *Centrepiece: Newsletter of the Alberta Civil Liberties Research Centre* 8:2, 1–14 (www.aclrc.com/Newsletter/centrepiece8no2.htm1).

Grant, Agnes. 1994. "Feminism and Aboriginal Culture: One Woman's View." *Canadian Woman Studies* 14 (Spring), 56–57.

Green, Joyce. 1985. "Sexual Equality and Indian Government: An Analysis of Bill C-31 Amendments to the Indian Act." *Native Studies Review* 1:1, 81–95.

Guerrero, Marie Anna Jaimes. 1997. "Civil Rights versus Sovereignty: Native American Women in Life and Land Struggles." In *Feminist Genealogies, Colonial Legacies, Democratic Futures*, ed. M. Jacqui Alexander and Chandra Talpade Mohanty. New York: Routledge, 101–21.

Harring, Sidney L. 1998. *White Man's Law: Native People In Nineteenth-Century Canadian Jurisprudence*. Toronto: Osgoode Society for Canadian Legal History, University of Toronto Press.

Harris, Cheryl I. 1993. "Whiteness as Property." *Harvard Law Review* 106:8 (June), 1710–91.

Hawkes, D. 1985. "Negotiating Aboriginal Self-Government: Developments Surrounding the 1985 First Ministers' Conference." Kingston: Queen's University, Institute of Intergovernmental Relations.

Holly, Marilyn. 1990. "Handsome Lake's Teachings: The Shift from Female to Male Agriculture in Iroquois Culture. An Essay in Ethnophilosophy." *Agriculture and Human Values* VII: 3/4 (Summer–Fall), 80–94.

Holmes, Joan. 1987. *Bill C-31, Equality or Disparity? The Effects of the New Indian Act on Native Women*. Ottawa: Canadian Advisory Council on the Status of Women.

Jamieson, Kathleen. 1978. *Indian Women and the Law in Canada: Citizens Minus*. Ottawa: Advisory Council on the Status of Women/Indian Rights for Indian Women.

Janovicek, Nancy. 2003. "'Assisting Our Own': Urban Migration, Self-Governance, and Native Women's Organizing in Thunder Bay, Ontario, 1972–1989." In "Keeping the Campfires Going: Urban American Indian Women's Activism." Susan Applegate Krouse and Heather Howard-Bobiwash, eds. Special issue, *American Indian Quarterly* 27:3/4 (Summer/Fall), 548–65.

Kauanui, J. Kehaulani. 2002. "The Politics of Blood and Sovereignty in *Rice v. Cayetano*." *Political and Legal Anthropology Review* 25:1, 110–28.

Klein, Laura F., and Lillian A. Ackerman. 1995. *Women and Power in Native North America*. Norman: University of Oklahoma Press.

Krosenbrink-Gelissen, Lilianne E. 1991. *Sexual Equality as an Aboriginal Right: The Native Women's Association of Canada and the Constitutional Process on Aboriginal Matters, 1982–1987*. Saarbrücken: Verlag Breitenback.

———. 1993. "'Traditional Motherhood' in Defense of Sexual Equality Rights of Canada's Aboriginal Women." *European Review of Native American Studies* 7:2, 13–16.

———. 1994. "Caring Is Indian Women's Business, But Who Takes Care of Them? Canada's Indian Women, the Renewed Indian Act, and Its Implications for Women's Family Responsibilities, Roles, and Rights." *Law & Anthropology* 7, 107–30.

Krouse, Susan Applegate, and Heather Howard-Bobiwash, eds. 2003. "Keeping the Campfires Going: Urban American Indian Women's Activism." Special issue, *American Indian Quarterly* 27:3/4 (Summer/Fall).

Leslie, John, and Ron Macquire. 1979. *The Historical Development of the Indian Act*. Ottawa: Department of Indian and Northern Affairs Canada.

Lovelace, Sandra. 1997. "Award Address." In *Justice for Natives: Searching for Common Ground*, ed. Andrea P. Morrison. Monteal: McGill-Queen's University Press, 26–28.

Manitoba Aboriginal and Northern Affairs (MAMA), Province of Manitoba. 2000. "Aboriginal People in Manitoba 2000: Chapter 1: Demographics: Focus Bill C-31." http://www.gov.mb.ca/ana/apm2000/1/i.html (accessed March 10, 2003).

McIvor, Sharon. 1995. "Aboriginal Women's Rights as 'Existing Rights.'" *Canadian Woman Studies* 15 (Spring/Summer), 34–38.

Miller, James R. 1991. *Skyscrappers Hide the Heavens: A History of Indian-White Relations in Canada.* Toronto: University of Toronto Press.

Mitchell, Marybelle. 1996. *From Talking Chiefs to a Native Corporate Élite: The Birth of Class and Nationalism among Canadian Inuit.* Montreal: McGill-Queen's University Press.

Monture-Okanee, Patricia. 1993. "Reclaiming Justice: Aboriginal Women and Justice Initiatives in the 1990s." In *Aboriginal Peoples and the Justice System: Report of the National Round Table on Aboriginal Justice Issues.* Ottawa: Minister of Supply and Services, 105–32.

———. 2004. "The Right of Indian Inclusion: Aboriginal Rights and/or Aboriginal Women." In *Advancing Aboriginal Claims: Visions/Strategies/Directions,* ed. Kerry Wilkins. Alberta: Purich Publishers, Inc., 39–66.

Morris, Glenn T. 1992. "International Law and Politics: Toward a Right to Self-Determination for Indigenous Peoples." In *The State of Native America: Genocide, Colonization, and Resistance,* ed. M. Annette Jaimes. Boston: South End Press, 55–86.

Moss, Wendy. 1987. "History of Discriminatory Laws Affecting Aboriginal People." Ottawa: Library of Parliament Research Branch, 1–29.

———. 1990. "Indigenous Self-Government in Canada and Sexual Equality under the Indian Act: Resolving Conflicts between Collective and Individual Rights." *Queen's Law Journal* 15 (Fall), 279–305.

Nahanee, Teresa. 1993. "Dancing with a Gorilla: Aboriginal Women, Justice and the Charter." In *Aboriginal Peoples and the Justice System: Report of the National Round Table on Aboriginal Justice Issues.* Ottawa: Minister of Supply and Services, 359–82.

Napoleaon, Val. 2005. "Aboriginal Self-Determination: Individual Self and Collective Selves." *Atlantis* 29:2, 31–46.

Native Women's Association of Canada. 1984. *Contemporary Issues: Information Kit.* Ottawa: NWAC.

———. 1985. *A Voice of Many Nations.* Ottawa: NWAC.

———. 1992a. "Our Voices Must Be Heard." *Women in Action* 2, 18–19.

———. 1992b. "Aboriginal Women and the Constitutional Debates: Continuing Discrimination." *Canadian Woman Studies* 12 (Spring), 14–17.

Nicholas, Andrea Bear. 1994. "Colonialism and the Struggle for Liberation: The Experience of Maliseet Women." *University of New Brunswick Law Journal* 43, 223–39.

Pentney, William. 1987. "The Rights of the Aboriginal Peoples of Canada in the Constitution Act, 1982." *University of British Columbia Law Review* 22, 207.

Rayner, Linda. 1978. *The Creation of A "Non-status" Indian Population by Federal Government Policy and Administration.* Ottawa: Native Council of Canada.

Sanders, Douglas. 1972. "The Bill of Rights and Indian Status." *University of British Columbia Law Review* 7.

———. 1975. "Indian Women: A Brief History of Their Roles and Rights." *McGill Law Journal* 21:4, 656–72.

————. 1980. "Indian Status: A Woman's Issue or an Indian Issue?" *Canadian Native Law.*

————. 1983. "The Rights of the Aboriginal Peoples of Canada." *The Canadian Bar Review* 61:1, 314–38.

Sayers, Judith F., Kelly A. MacDonald, Jo-Anne Fiske, Melonie Newell, Evelyn George, and Wendy Cornet. 2001. *First Nations Women, Governance, and the Indian Act: A Collection of Policy Research Reports.* Ottawa: Status of Women Canada.

Silman, Janet. 1987. *Enough Is Enough: Aboriginal Women Speak Out.* Toronto: The Women's Press.

Smandych, Russell, and Gloria Lee. 1995. "Women, Colonization and Resistance: Elements of an Amerindian Autohistorical Approach to the Study of Law and Colonialism." *Native Studies Review* 10:1, 21–46.

Smith, Andrea. 2005. *Conquest: Sexual Violence and American Indian Genocide.* Boston: South End Press.

Sprague, D. N. 1995. "The New Math of the New Indian Act: 6(2) +6(2)=6(1)." *Native Studies Review* 10:1, 47–60.

Tarnopolsky, Walter. 1975. *The Canadian Bill of Rights.* Toronto: McClelland and Stewart.

Turpel, Mary Ellen. 1989. "Aboriginal Peoples and the Canadian Charter of Rights and Freedom." *Canadian Woman Studies* 10:2/3, 149–57.

Valencia-Weber, Gloria, and Christine Zuni. 1995. "Domestic Violence and Tribal Protection of Indigenous Women in the United States." *St. John's Law Review* (Winter-Spring).

Van Kirk, Sylvia. 1983. *Many Tender Ties: Women in Fur-Trade Society, 1670–1870.* Norman: University of Oklahoma Press.

Wilkins, David E. 2002. *American Indian Politics and the American Political System.* Maryland: Rowman & Littlefield Publishers, Inc.

Wilmer, Franke. 1993. *The Indigenous Voice in World Politics.* Newbury Park: Sage Publications.

Daphne A. Brooks

"All That You Can't Leave Behind"

Surrogation and Black Female Soul Singing in the Age
of Catastrophe

Abstract: As numerous scholars have shown, Hurricane Katrina exacerbated
the already-ongoing precarity of African American communities in New
Orleans. The crisis demanded a reckoning with the afterlives of slavery at
the national and global level. This article focuses on the work of Black
women popular music artists whose early twenty-first century recordings
and stirring performances addressed the traumas, the challenges, and the
spectacular subjugation of Black women who fell victim to brutal disenfranchisement in the midst of the disaster. Beyonce's B-Day album and Mary J.
Blige's history-making Katrina telethon performance are central to this discussion. The original title of this article was "'All That You Can't Leave
Behind': Black Female Soul Singing and the Politics of Surrogation in the
Age of Catastrophe."

It has been more than a decade since Black feminist cultural critic Hazel
Carby (1992, 738) explored the early-twentieth-century phenomenon of
"policing the black woman's body in an urban context." In her groundbreaking essay, Carby illuminates the myriad ways in which postbellum
and Gilded Age Black female migrants wrestled with sexually and morally
pathologizing labels imposed on them by social and political institutions.
In search of new work in northern cities, these women found themselves
the subject of a "moral panic," one that resulted in stringent forms of cultural surveillance and institutional efforts to control and discipline their
collective behavior in a shifting industrial environment (Carby 1992).[1]

MERIDIANS · feminism, race, transnationalism   Volume 19 Supplement 2020
DOI: 10.1215/15366936-8565979 © 2008 Smith College

Ring the Alarm

One could make a claim that a curious new version of this phenomenon—
call it "policing the upwardly mobile Black woman's body in a high-profile
context"—has taken shape at the turn of this new century. The year 2006
alone featured a range of media events in which working Black women were
spectacularly punished and policed in the media's eye. The spring of that
year unfolded with former Georgia Congresswoman Cynthia McKinney
allegedly striking a capitol police officer who tried to stop her from entering a House office building (supposedly for failure to present proper identification). One week later, New York state senator Ada L. Smith was
charged with third-degree assault for allegedly having thrown hot coffee at
a staff member in the workplace. We might think of these women as on
their way to or presumably in the midst of "work" and yet not looking and/
or acting the (proper) part.

By summer, the focus had shifted to a dubious martyr at work: Star Jones
fought to preserve a semblance of dignity in the midst of being banished
from her workplace on the kaffeeklatch gossip bowl *The View* (presumably
for having extensive work done *on* herself). Further down the B-list ladder,
the phenomenal R&B singer-songwriter Angie Stone failed to toe the line
on VH1's reality series *Celebrity Fit Club*, refusing to work to shed unwanted
pounds for most of the season and sparking the ire of former *Love Boat*
bartender Ted Lange. Even Oprah Winfrey and Gayle King, women who
often revel in showcasing the work of grand and sumptuous "legends," by
fall had stumbled into situations on their "road trip" across America in
which cranky bigots in backwater towns lashed out at them for trespassing
unwanted into their territory (e.g., "there goes Oprah, that n** b**!").
Hard at work on television, even the "Queen of All Media" was chastised for
supposedly bringing her work to forbidden spaces.

Certainly these lesser cultural events should remind us of the 1990s and
the very high/low points in public memory when upwardly mobile, putatively successful Black women were punished and policed for their supposed transgressions. From Anita Hill to Lani Guinier to Jocelyn Elders, the
middle years of that decade read like a roll call of over-achieving, rigorously
educated Black women who nonetheless found themselves attacked and
"on trial," at the center of hearings and media scrutiny in the midst of
simply trying to do their jobs.[2]

Perhaps this is why mega-superstar Beyoncé Knowles's video for her hit
single "Ring the Alarm" is in fact so disturbing. Under the direction of

veteran video director Sophie Muller, the stunning Knowles, dressed in a caramel-colored trench coat to match her glistening skin, is dragged away by policemen in riot gear, locked in a padded cell, dressed in army fatigues, and restrained by interrogators in a scene that overtly references Sharon Stone's leg-crossing moment in *Basic Instinct*.[3] Knowles is no Hollywood femme fatale, though, and these images that catalogue her in severe distress and entrapment while staring the camera down and calling for someone to "ring the alarm! I'll be damned if I see another chick on your arm!" remind us less of Michael Douglas's misogynistic oeuvre and more of not only the powerful Black women who have been chastised and punished for "misbehaving" in recent years, but also of the growing number of Black women who are or have been in lock-down with little opportunity for recourse or rehabilitation (the much less adventurous recording artist Alicia Keys nonetheless gave mention to this dilemma in her breakthrough 2001 video for "Fallin'").

In the custody of the police, Beyoncé struggles and writhes, is brought to her knees, and is dragged by her arms and legs. The image no doubt sounds an alarm of its own, one that should make us think too of Diana Ross and her image-shattering star turn in the opening scene of 1972's *Lady Sings the Blues*, in which Ross's fictionalized Billie Holiday character turns up in jail on drug charges with smeared eyeliner and tousled hair, desperately in need of a fix. And while the comparisons between Ross and Beyoncé were in abundance not long ago as the latter jettisoned her Supremes-inspired vehicle Destiny's Child for a full-fledged solo career, as well as the Ross-inspired role of Deena Jones in *Dreamgirls*, the Beyoncé of the "Ring the Alarm" video is perhaps an entirely misleading representation of the artist and the highly theatricalized character who emerges in the 2006 classic that is *B-Day*, one of the oddest, most urgent, dissonant, and disruptive R&B releases in recent memory.

Equally concerned with work (romantic, sexual, and physical as well as monetary) as it is with questions of Black women's access to property, ownership, and modes of production, *B-Day* is the post-Hurricane Katrina answer to southern Black women's spectacular disenfranchisement in the wake of that natural disaster. It is a record that documents the sheer virtuosic mastery of a singer-songwriter-performer's claims to owning and controlling her own work, property, and much-lauded body. Likewise, it is probably the most high-profile musical effort by a Black female entertainer who has made no bones about embracing and affirming her own class privilege by birthright with roots that run deep in New Orleans as well as Houston familial history.

Below I explore the critical work of Beyoncé's second solo recording, and I place it in conversation with yet another under-theorized yet equally dissonant R&B performance by her "hip-hop soul queen" contemporary Mary J. Blige in order to examine the politics of Black women's pop music culture in relation to the Gulf Coast catastrophe and the spectacular marginalization of African-American women in American sociopolitical culture. I suggest that we look closely at the musical performances of Beyoncé as well as of Blige, as each artist's work creates a particular kind of Black feminist surrogation, that is, an embodied cultural act that articulates Black women's distinct forms of palpable sociopolitical loss and grief as well as spirited dissent and dissonance. Their combined efforts mark a new era of protest singing that sonically resists, revises, and reinvents the politics of Black female hypervisibility in the American cultural imaginary.

"I Hold No Grudge": Black Feminist Dissent in Song

Much has been made of how the Beyoncé of recent years is a far cry from what pop-culture critic David Swerdlick calls the "sistah grrrl power" of early Destiny's Child recordings (Swerdlick 2007). On those records, and particularly on the multi-platinum *The Writing's on the Wall*, Knowles and her fellow "children" belted out densely arranged urban anthems with *Waiting to Exhale* themes of romantic distrust, material disillusionment, and "ne'er do well" scrub boyfriends who are roundly criticized and kicked to the curb. And while much credit was given to a then-teen-aged Knowles for having penned or co-written the lyrics to chart-topping hits such as the Grammy-winning "Say My Name," Beyoncé has herself claimed that large portions of her song-writing inspiration and the vivid detail that infuses some of these early songs came as a result of having ventriloquized the intimate "woman-talk" coursing through the aisles of Houston's Headliners salon, a successful business run by über-mom and clothing-designer Tina Knowles (Weiner 2006, 79).

But just as Destiny's Child's early classics—"Bills, Bills, Bills," "Bugaboo," and "Independent Women, part I" among them—document Beyoncé's emergence as a popular late-twentieth-century Black female songwriter, one could easily make a case that her newer material marks her arrival as an artist unafraid of complicating and disturbing her well-regarded cultural persona in less conventional ways than the straitjacketed patriarchal models afforded most contemporary pop divas (see, for instance, the ways in which pop culture represents Christina Aguilera's "virgin-whore-virgin" transformations, Britney's "virgin-whore-whore" dissolution, or even Madonna's "whore-to-mother" moves).

To be sure, the Beyoncé on *B-Day* is a far cry from the "daddy's girl, naughty-but-nice" icon who came bounding onto the scene with her first solo effort, 2003's monstrously successful *Dangerously in Love*. Rather than mistaking "edge" (the MTV marketers' much-overused term to reference the allure of "pushing the envelope") for dirty raunch, Beyoncé's latest recording imagines her growth as an artist by stretching (until it's taut) the emotional register of her lyrical and musical content. Although she returns time and again to conflicts between love and money, the material on *B-Day* examines an ever-sophisticated range of emotions tied to Black women's personal and spiritual discontent, satiation, self-worth, and agency. From this standpoint, rather than dismissing *B-Day* as the arrival of a new unemancipated diva figure in danger of miming (through her singles and videos) a "Mariah/Mimi-size" breakdown or an unhinged and wholly incoherent Whitney meltdown, we might do well to consider the shrewd and complicated articulation of rage, "resentment" (the title of *B-Day*'s closing track), desperation, and aspiration that Beyoncé's album charts at a time when public and sociopolitical voices of Black female discontent remain muted, mediated, circumscribed, and misappropriated.

Crafting a voice of Black female discontent in Black female popular culture is, however, a slippery slope if one aims to avoid the caricature of "the angry Black woman"—immortalized by everyone from Hattie McDaniel's simmering and contemptuous cinematic characters to the sour squint of genius comic LaWanda Page, or of late, the wickedly "sick and tired" stand-up of Wanda Sykes.

In contemporary pop music, Black female (sociopolitical) discontent is even trickier to trace. Certainly eclectic performer Nina Simone's songbook ranged from the sly, oblique, and ironic critique in classics such as "I Hold No Grudge" ("I hold no grudge/There's no resentment und'neath/I'll extend the laurel wreath and we'll be friends/But right there is where it ends") to the searing political satire of civil rights "showtune" "Mississippi Goddam." But while Simone and Odetta remain forebears of a certain kind of critical voice that emerged as the cultural arm of the civil rights and anti-war movements, twenty-first-century Black female pop stars—save for folkies like Tracy Chapman, bohemian rebels like Me'Shell Ndegeocello, or sharp and powerful emcees like early MC Lyte, Lauryn Hill, and Jean Grae—are more likely to couch their dissatisfaction in domestic, romantic, and/or gospel-religious R&B zones.[4]

No wonder that the most adventurous and provocative R&B female singers who traffic in articulating material, quotidian discontent have roots, like Beyoncé herself, that run deep in the confrontational aesthetics of hip-hop. Envelope-pusher Kelis, a frequent crooner and collaborator on singles by the late Ol' Dirty Bastard and Busta Rhymes, burst into the mainstream with her coarse and vituperative single "Caught Out There," a PJ-Harvey-smoking-blunts-with-the-Neptunes-sounding breakup song most memorable for its nails-on-a-chalkboard refrain of "I hate you so much right now!" Likewise, the brilliant upstart singer Keisha Cole, an artist with a hardscrabble upbringing in Oakland, California (which gave her instant street cred), released one of the most brutally visceral, emotionally assertive, and convincingly combative R&B records of the decade, The Way It Is, ushering in a new generation of Black female recording artists who are willing to do battle with lovers and friends in order to gain some kind of personal agency. Both of the aforementioned singers owe much (if not nearly everything) to the inroads made by the woman oft-regarded as the "Queen of Hip-Hop Soul," Mary J. Blige, who, it seems, is the iconic "sister-spirit" of sorts, hovering in the background of Beyoncé's B-Day.

Since her rise in the early 1990s, Blige has cultivated a beloved pop persona as the fighting survivor from Yonkers, New York. As rock critic Jessica Willis notes of Blige: "everything about her appearance . . . gives her the aura of a sexy outlaw with a rough past" (Willis 2003, 19). Increasingly, Blige has cultivated an image as something of the Fannie Lou Hamer of hip-hop R&B, a woman who's "sick and tired of being sick and tired" but who nonetheless rallies the energy to deliver show-stopping, James Brown-Live-at-the-Apollo stage histrionics to declare the end of "drama" in her personal and public life.

Not surprisingly, Blige was the ideal figure to emerge in the wake of Hurricane Katrina as the (singing) voice of Black female testimony and social critique. As political scientist and Black feminist scholar Melissa Harris-Lacewell cogently observes in her forthcoming study on the disaster: "It is on the bodies, lives and minds of Black women that the story of Hurricane Katrina was written. Their suffering became the conduit through which a conversation on race, class and vulnerability was initiated. They were literally the bridge over the deadly waters that gave the rest of

America a place to cross into the agonizing realization of how unequal the country remained at the dawn of the 21ST century" (Harris-Lacewell forthcoming, 3).

It is fitting, then, that Blige (and not the attention-grabbing Kanye West) would stage the most cogent political coup of the airwaves during a telethon performance of U2's 1990s elegy-anthem "One," turning what could have been an awkward duet with frontman-activist Bono into a metanarrative, a staged musical dialogue of sorts that brought to light the emotional dimensions of Black female disenfranchisement and White patriarchal and legislative power, arrogance, and humility.[5]

Candles in the Wind: Surrogation and (Collective) Grief in the Age of Pop Protest

Within the first two and a half weeks after Hurricane Katrina struck New Orleans, a stunning four separate relief benefit telethons aired on major networks across the country. During the weekend of September 9 alone, NBC, ABC, CBS, and other networks jointly aired the commercial-free benefit concert special titled *Shelter from the Storm*, while MTV, VH1, and the Country Music Channel followed with their own respective televised-relief events; Black Entertainment Television (BET) offered a separate program as well. Each of the specials raised money for blanket "relief efforts" directed at assisting Katrina survivors, and each featured a carefully selected mix of pop music veterans (Randy Newman, Rod Stewart), MTV mainstays (Alicia Keys, Mariah Carey), and activist musicians (Stevie Wonder, Neil Young).

Alicia Keys's performance of "Father I Stretch My Hand to Thee" alongside Shirley Caesar, Alvin Slaughter, and Bishop Daniels, and Mariah Carey's "Fly Like a Bird" were, for instance, suggestively offered up as articulations of collective grief, anguish, and spiritual catharsis. *New York Times* critic Ned Martel characterized these performances and others as examples of "the power of songs to transcend generational and ethnic boundaries." As Martel keenly observed, many of the shows, but particularly *Shelter from the Storm*, "could be seen to have lasting value: as a teaching tool, as a meditation on American expression, and as a pop-political jazz funeral—a wake—the dead march for the whole New Orleans musical scene. It was a tribute that reflected history as much as it tried to shape it" (Martel 2005). As sites of mythical collective healing, the Katrina telethons repeatedly aimed to create a kind of cultural renewal across the body of the singing pop star, who provided the occasion for communities in crisis to register loss, outrage, and melancholia in the space of a four-minute song with big hooks, heavy string arrangements, and a wall of Pottery Barn candles burning brightly in the background.

"Into the cavities created by loss" stepped pop artists, figures whose words, bodies, and songs were intended to do the work of what performance studies theorist Joseph Roach has influentially characterized as "surrogation." In the wake of both a horrific natural disaster and a shameful government-led response to social catastrophe, the (in)tense emotional occasion of these telethons demanded that various entertainers "perform effigies to evoke an absence, to body something forth, especially something from a distant past" (Roach 1996, 2). To be sure, rock culture has often been the pop cultural site where musicians and entertainers repeatedly and ritualistically traffic in "performances" that "so often carry within them the memory of otherwise forgotten substitutions—those that were rejected and even more invisibly, those that have succeeded" (Roach 1996, 36; 5). But the impossibility of adequately responding to communal loss during the Katrina telethons presented a particularly poignant surrogation for the spiritual and existential opacity generated by the phenomenon of the hurricane itself.

No doubt *Shelter from the Storm* and other benefit concerts were seeking to follow in the endless stream of protest songs, benefit songs, and tribute songs that erupted out of rock culture in the second half of the twentieth century, but that took a particularly commercial shape in the 1980s when Boomtown Rats lead singer Bob Geldof called together his British musical brothers-in-arms to create the "Band Aid" benefit record to raise funds to fight African hunger. Geldof's effort, "Do They Know It's Christmas" begat "We are the World," which begat Farm Aid and a slew of concert events in which, as members of the agit-prop English rock group Chumbawumba recently put it, celebrities essentially instructed people with "less money than them to donate to causes," in turn potentially reinforcing the very inequality these events ostensibly sought to extinguish. Certainly, with the 2005 release of the parody-novelty record "Do They Know It's Halloween" (a single that mocks the obtuse condescension of Geldof's twenty-year-old song), the political power and the social utility of protest pop music activism seems in peril of slipping all too easily into the jaws of ironic lack of interest.[6]

Indeed, while many heaped praise on rapper-producer Kanye West for his skill at social agitation and for reminding the nation of just what George Bush thought of Black people, less public note was made of what was perhaps the most provocative performance aired on any of the tele-thons. It was a performance that pushed beyond merely evoking spectacu-lar absence as a kind of protest, instead playing with the historically dense liminality of the Black female performer singing her way through rock memory and the national imaginary.

Few critics talked much about Mary J. Blige and U2's duet of the band's memorial anthem "One," but we might look to that performance as a cogent site of pop music historical recuperation as well as a space for the production of history wherein the work of memory, absence, presence, collective desire, substitution, sacrifice, and expenditure get worked out through the voice and "kinesthetic imagination" of Blige, the "Queen of Hip-Hop Soul."

By drawing from Roach's critical discussions of memory and perfor-mance, I want to examine the ways that rock memory collided with the Katrina catastrophe in the fall of 2005, and how the Black female soul and R&B heroine emerged with her own circum-Atlantic "displaced transmis-sion, rising like a Phoenix, from the ashes of diaspora and genocide on wings of song" (Roach 1996, 66), in turn paving the way for Beyoncé's deceptively slick, re-packaged protest on *B-Day*.

The Testimony of "One": Recovering Black Female Citizenship in Rock Culture

When the Irish pop prophet Bono appeared on stage during the multi-network Katrina relief concert with a big straw cowboy hat and a severely furrowed brow, he seemed destined to deliver a repeat performance of the band's post-9/11 network telethon gig, a somber affair shot in Black and white as a dirge-like wake. But the transformation of one of the group's most recognizable anthems, "One," into a duet with Yonkers's hard-scrabble, hard-singing, sometimes-hard-on-the-ears Mary J. Blige, opened up a space to make rich, powerful, multi-layered references to the complex intersections of race, gender, and class embedded in the Katrina catastro-phe. Called by one fan in the wake of the performance "the most intrigu-ing and wistful cover tune since Johnny Cash covered Nine Inch Nails' 'Hurt,'" Blige's *Shelter from the Storm* version of U2's "One" is perhaps the most insurgent political work of a Black female pop singer since Nina Simone's "Four Women" and "Mississippi Goddam."

A song that has retained its place in contemporary rock culture for its multiple and intersecting meanings, "One" has been interpreted by critics as a narrative of a conversation between a father and his queer, HIV positive son. Others have described it as the documentation of an emotionally abusive relationship coming undone. The band itself has recounted it as the pivotal song that was inspired by an effort to find aesthetic resolution and peace while they recorded their identity-transforming 1991 album *Achtung Baby*.

But Blige's performance of this song in this context at this moment in time opens up the historical value of Bono and company's lyrics and musical arrangements. Easing her way around guitarist The Edge's *Exile on Main Street*, *Beggar's Banquet*-era Rolling Stones riff, Blige steps into the rock pantheon here in a moment that musically resonates with exposed erasures and absences—the erasure of Black female artists from rock genealogies, the erasure of Black female sexual exploitation in rock memory (see the Stones' "Brown Sugar" for instance),[7] and most critically and urgently, the absence conjoined with the spectacular presence of Black female suffering in America, what some might call the ur-text of this national disaster.

As Harris-Lacewell makes plain in her work on the politics of Black female citizenship in American culture:

> Black women were at the center of this literal and rhetorical storm. Photographs of black mothers carrying their infants as they waded through filthy, chest-high waters became the enduring images of this disaster. Television news and popular news magazines used images of desperate, frightened and suffering African American women to dramatize the tragedy facing the residents of New Orleans as they battled the aftermath of the hurricane with little assistance from official authorities. (Harris-Lacewell forthcoming, 3)

Within this brutally charged context, Blige's surplus performance highlights the unheralded position of Black women in rock, the unheralded position of Black women in America, the violence of White patriarchal political neglect and discrimination, the violence of White patriarchal sexuality in rock—all of this comes to the surface in her performance. *Off key.*

Never before (nor perhaps since) have Mary J. Blige's tonal eccentricities been put to more powerful use. Here I am suggesting that we pay close attention to Blige's trademark bent voice, the voice—as Roach might describe it—"of African-American rhythm and blues [that] carries awesomely over time and distance, through its cadences, its intonations, it accompaniment, and even its gestures." As he observes,

> the degree to which this voice haunts American memory, the degree to which it promotes obsessive attempts at simulation and impersonation, derives from its ghostly power to insinuate memory between the lines, in the spaces between the words, in the intonation and placements by which they are shaped, in the silences by which they are deepened and contradicted. By such means, the dead remain among the living. (Roach 1996, 69)

In the midst of the *Shelter from the Storm* telethon, Blige's performance reminds us of the ways that the Black singing voice is not confined to the ethereal netherworld (as techno-shaman Moby would have it). Indeed, her rendition of this song gives living voice to the mythically-driven, over-determined, under-theorized scapegoat figure (an accretion of caricatures, as Hortense Spillers has shown), allowing her instead to enter *in the flesh* into the public conversation to which she has been denied access (Spillers 1987). Blige here majestically reinforces Lindon Barrett's powerful conten-tion that "the singing voice sounds of the most enduring of African Amer-ican testimonies to the exigencies of our presence in the Americas" (Barrett 1999, 65). In this regard, Blige's duet-cover performance marks a particular kind of Black female resistant vocal presence where previously there had been a putative silence in the era of post-Katrina relief and recovery. As Simon Reynolds might suggest in his Barthes-inspired ruminations on the singing voice, we should listen for the noise in Blige's embodied voice, and we should hold still to catch "the way she chews and twists language" in this performance, "not for any decipherable, expressive reason . . . but for the gratuitous voluptuousness of utterance itself. In [Blige's voice] you can hear a surplus of form over content . . . of 'telling' over 'story'" (Reynolds 2004, 58).[8]

Blige's performance thus complicates the pop-cultural constructions of Black female Katrina survivors, women who were—as Harris-Lacewell contends—"framed as distant foreigners [but who] retained the power to 'shame the nation' through their suffering. These Black women were shameful to the nation," she argues, "because their vulnerability indicated the continuing existence of poverty and racism. As women and mothers they retained a power to represent victimization in a way that male survi-vors were less able to embody" (Harris-Lacewell forthcoming, 9).

In contrast, this rendition of "One" deploys an emotionally charged dialogue between Black female soul singer Blige and White male celebrity-politico Bono. Their duet stages a sage, sobering, brutally honest summit between two figures who are iconographically conjoined in America's miscegenated history, and it underscores repeated rehearsals of that brutal history of White patriarchal power and Black female abjection—here rewritten and recast in the voice of Black female difference and resistance. "Did I disappoint you," Blige begins, "or leave a bad taste in your mouth?" That trademark, rough-around-the-edges, is-my girl-really-singing-off-key? delivery serves Blige most powerfully in this tale where the Black female voice of dissonance and disappointment observes wryly of the man who conserves his compassion that "you act like you never had love, and you want me to go without."

Blige plays here the role of the fighting survivor, a character she's crafted into her persona over her decade-plus career. As critic Willis notes of Blige, her physical aesthetic, "her come hither-step back stare, her big tattoos and the scar under her left eye" effectively accessorize her urban survivor image. No doubt she has cultivated a "loner-in-high-heels persona with great care," and here in "One" she channels that iconography, something of a palimpsest of Simone's "four women," into an interventionist anthem that champions the preservation of difference and specificity as a fecund site for coalition-building: "We're one but we're not the same/We get to carry each other/Carry each other." Blige here rejects "crawling" in the temple of love, the temple of democracy, demanding instead recognition of her worth as a citizen in this "contract with America."

Like Curtis Mayfield, who, English rock critic Charles Shaar Murray argues, perfected "the seamless fusion of form and political content" by "secularizing gospel and lyrically anchoring it here and now [and declaring that] salvation is [of] this world" (Murray 2005), Blige recycles "One"—a song that mainlines the twice-removed blues of the Mississippi Delta by way of Keith Richards and the Edge—re-placing it and replaying it as the soundtrack for the Louisiana Gulf Coast women who, in this moment in time, on this night, at this benefit, will—through this act of soulful surrogation—indeed have their say.

Diary of a Dissenting Black Woman: Beyonce's B-Day and the Politics of Evacuation and Ownership

For some, it may be a stretch to associate Beyoncé's fierce, two-in-the-morning club beats with Blige's poignant wake of a performance and the natural (and national) disaster that has come to define twenty-first-century race relations in this country. But I want to suggest there are ways to listen to B-Day on another frequency so as to hear the register of post-Katrina, Blige-esque discontent in pop music culture, as well as the ways in which Beyoncé Knowles reconfigures this sort of dissent as fleet, urgent desire, and aspiration. Listen closely and one can hear the sounds and words of Knowles the artist imagining ways for her character on the album to transcend despair through a sharp attendance to work, her own property, and the attainment of her own version of "control," one that recalls, rivals, and outpaces Janet Jackson's two-decade bid for autonomy.

B-Day arrived in stores on September 5, 2006, coinciding both with the artist's own birthday (9-4-81—a date she chants at the opening and close of the album) as well as the much-publicized one-year anniversary of the storm that damaged and destroyed large swaths of the Gulf Coast. That week, in addition to news retrospectives and Spike Lee's stunning Wagnerian documentary *When the Levees Broke*, music video outlets like MTV (and BET earlier in the summer) showcased tributes to Katrina survivors in their awards show telecasts. Beyoncé appeared at both the MTV and BET awards and yet was never overtly involved in any of the Katrina tributes. Nevertheless, Knowles and her fellow Destiny's Child group members Kelly Rowland and Michelle Williams joined in with other Black pop stars in particular to make charitable contributions to hurricane survivors (the group's "Destiny's Village," was organized in December 2005 to house 100 displaced families for the holidays).

There are more metaphorical than literal ties to Katrina on B-Day though, the visual imagery being just one of several ways that the album invokes the specter of Gulf Coast culture. Images of a glistening, bronze Knowles, looking like a hard yet luscious *Jet* magazine centerfold, adorn the back cover and inner photos of the CD, which also find her lifting a leg in a thigh-high juke joint mini on the dock of the bay, navigating twin crocodiles by the leash through verdant wetlands in high heels and a cutout swimsuit, and walking the path of dusty railroad tracks in a leather and frills bodice. Whether showcasing the singer as sexually titillating against a landscape that resonates with (Eve's?) bayou imagery is a purely provocative move or one that offers compelling (or perhaps confounding?) social commentary may be hard to glean in the end. But the consistent ways in which B-Day's marketing remains linked to recognizable visual markers of southern bayou culture is undeniable. One need look no further than the controversial video for the album's first single, "Déjà vu," in order to find images of a historical déjà vu of sorts, a tricked-out plantation setting with Knowles alternately draped across ornate Victorian furniture and dashing haltingly through everglades and (cotton?) fields looking like a deer in headlights, or perhaps more accurately, like a fugitive (house) slave on the run (Beyoncé 2006a).

Online message boards and pop music critics alike expressed shock and disappointment with this lead single (called "flat" by some)—both at its video promotion of a southern heroine who waxes paranoid and obsessive over her desire for on- and off-screen love interest rap mogul Jay-Z, and at the song itself, which on the surface does little more than reproduce both the best of the horn-driven arrangements that made Knowles's biggest single to date, "Crazy in Love," such a worldwide smash, and which seems also to merely reiterate the virtuosic gangsta-flow and "dough" of Jay-Z at the expense of showcasing Knowles (who, in one famous frame of the video, tugs longingly at her lover's belt buckle while writhing on her knees).

Dismissing the album for "Déjà vu's" seemingly retrograde gender politics would, however, miss the point of the song entirely, since the track clearly serves as a "decoy" single of sorts. In the wake of two previous top-ten songs recorded together (2003's "Bonnie & Clyde '03" as well as "Crazy in Love"), an endless stream of paparazzi photos detailing their every move, and a shrewd unwillingness to discuss their relationship in public, Knowles and her "jigga" man were wise to draw on this notoriety in ushering in the release of B-Day. The allure of their "hush-hush" relationship creates its own aura around the single. Likewise, the rap solo at the core of "Déjà vu" celebrates the capital and genius of rapper-turned-record executive Jay-Z, his "Hova's flow so unusual" who "just make the hits like a factory" (Beyoncé 2005).

On this lead track of the album, if one listens closely, one can hear the early traces of a different Beyoncé voice from previous recordings—one that vocally belies the submissiveness or the paranoia of her video persona. Co-written by Knowles (as are all of the tracks on B-Day) and co-produced by the singer in collaboration with Rodney "Darkchild" Jerkins (the man who gave us J. Lo's first single and a reconstructed Whitney "It's Not Right But It's Okay" Houston), "Déjà vu" initially opens—before any of the bluster and braggadocio of her "partner"—with the diva emerging as the conductor—calling for bass, hi hat, and 808 drum machine.

And while the would-be savvy utterances of pop songstresses "calling out," as it were, to their bands, disc jockeys, mix masters, and backup singers to get in line is as old as the era of the blues queens and as tired, in some ways, as the most derivative Christina Aguilera track—Beyoncé's lead-off roll call here still nonetheless gives us a taste of what is to come on the album: a vocalist who urgently and masterfully traverses dense sonic arrangements and who fully controls space—musical, lyrical, and metaphorical—in deft and unprecedented ways throughout the album. (It may be worth mentioning too that the artist expanded the reach of female-centered space when she assembled an "all-female band" to accompany her on her worldwide 2006–07 tour.) Even as Knowles's voice escalates to arch, sky-scraping ranges at a rapid, hysteria-inducing pace on "Déjà vu," one is reminded of how hard, in fact, the singer is working here and how much effort—physical and aesthetic—it takes to dash at breakneck speed through Knowles's trademark wordy-verses, jam-packed lyrics that threaten, as their very content suggests, to break "out of control" (one need only recall Destiny Child's last great hit "Lose My Breath" to get a sense of how prevalent these tropes of urgency and excess are in Knowles's work). So on the one hand, while "Déjà vu" details the singer's inability to "get over" her lover, while it details the ways that Jay is all-consuming, filling up her senses, trapping his lover in a haze, really it is Knowles whose power-house vocals increasingly command space on the song, dwarfing Jay-Z's harmless rap at the center of the track. Watch as Knowles takes the reins on "Déjà vu" and leads her listeners into provocatively controlled and control-ling spaces on the rest of B-Day.

Nothing else on B-Day sounds quite like "Déjà vu." Knowles abruptly shifts gears and alters the tempo of the record entirely from the second track forward. "Get Me Bodied," a Swizz Beatz-produced, dancehall track, combines Rasta percussions with double-dutch syncopations and gor-geous vocal harmonies (by Knowles herself) to celebrate once more the joys of girls' night out: Beyoncé and "three best friends" on the town in a "vin-tage Rolls" with plenty of money to spend. Yes, the young-women-clubbing anthems are, on the one hand, ubiquitous right now with everyone from Red-State fave Gretchin Wilson getting "all-jacked up," to Us Weekly cover girl Jessica Simpson glorying in her flaccid "Public Affair." There is, how-ever, something particularly provocative about Knowles's reworking of this theme on B-Day, inasmuch as the song reaffirms Knowles's control of her space on this album. "Get Me Bodied" is a track that is both more percus-sively oriented than "Déjà vu" and more resonant with the sounds of Black girls' play—rope-twirling, hand-clapping, and improvised cheers—games that, as ethnomusicologist Kyra Gaunt reminds us, are the backbone of Black popular music culture (Gaunt 2006).

The militaristic pace of "Get Me Bodied" yet again signals that fierce beat that Knowles has called attention to at the opening of the album. She is, in fact, the leader of the "drumline" on this record. Think of her as a majorette or impresario of sorts who takes center stage again and again on tracks that find her openly controlling the pace of the arrangements (on the irresistible "Freakum Dress," a "desperate-housewife" Knowles halts the beat like many a dance diva so as to "fix her hair" before launching into her sartorial seduction anthem). This role of the conductor overseeing a frantically paced environment is an image that Knowles herself has marketed as a part of making the album.

Indeed, the current and carefully crafted legend behind the making of B-Day is how short a time the artist took to record the tracks, and how Knowles herself oversaw a studio dynamic that heightened its urgent sound. Recorded in what was reportedly a mere two weeks and in the wake of the Dreamgirls shoot, B-Day has been described by Knowles as an effort to put down on record the feelings conjured up by playing her doomed diva character (in her "hidden" address to the "fans" at the close of the record, Knowles—perhaps in a Freudian slip—alludes to Dreamgirls as "the film of my life"). Allegedly recorded in "secrecy" from both her Svengali-manager father Matthew Knowles and from Knowles's Columbia label, B-Day has been repeatedly defined in interviews by the artist herself as a Beyoncé-orchestrated endeavor (Amber 2006, 174). This is a rather unusual and remarkable spin story for a female R&B artist's album (whether we believe it or not in this age of publicist-driven image control), if only in light of the fact that everyone from Mariah Carey to Blige to Aguilera have, at one point or another, aggressively centered the "making" of their recordings around narratives that involve the centrality of producer figures.

For her part, Knowles makes use of her own impressive array of production wizards (everyone from the old stand-bys the Neptunes to Norwegian hitmakers Stargate to youthful soul revivalist Ne-Yo). But what's interesting about their presence is how Knowles has discussed her own involvement in arranging and conducting their multiple roles in the production process. If the recording of B-Day is unique in its abbreviated session time that recalls, at the very least in spirit, the kind of mythical aura of "performance authenticity" (fewer takes; a raw, "live" feel) of indie rock and hiphop albums, it is equally fascinating how Knowles arranged for her producers to work in multiple studios simultaneously reportedly so as to capture the feel of "battling" emcees so prominent in the making of her Roc-A-Fella partner's records (Amber 2006, 174).[9] B-Day is an album, then, that sounds like a battlefield—or at the very least a race of sorts—in which Beyoncé emerges victorious as a co-producer and entrepreneur engaged in multiple forms of "redress" that are, on the surface, couched in domestic and romantic terms, but that consistently make metaphors of the exigencies and the emotional and material stress of post-millennium and perhaps post-Katrina life as well.

No track sums up this theme more startlingly than "Suga Mama," a song that marks the evolution of Beyoncé's relationship with the (dollar) "bill" and her search for a partner who fits the bill. On "Suga Mama," Knowles promises to her baby that she "won't let no bills get behind," effectively assuming the role that her Destiny's Child-era lover of her "Bills, Bills, Bills" days cannot fulfill. Producer Rich ("Crazy in Love") Harrison yokes a gut-bucket-blues-guitar lick from J Wade and the Soul Searchers into an easy pickup-truck-on-a-back-road beat as Knowles claims purchase of a nubile lover whose services are worthy of the gift of a "short set." The slinky retro blues chorus coursing through this track holds a special resonance of sorts inasmuch as it recalls the sexual candor and assertiveness of blues legends such as Ma Rainey and Bessie Smith. All the same, Knowles's pickup line here is thoroughly 2006 in its emphasis on the purchasing power of the singer herself, whose love is seemingly not for sale but who is capable of providing the bling, the "new whip," the "new heavy on the wrist" to satisfy her lover's needs.

On a broader level, this is a song that sheds light on the phenomenon of sponsorship in the wake of (emotional) evacuation and (domestic) disaster, and it forces the post-catastrophe question of what does it mean to sponsor someone and to provide redress (literally and figuratively)? What does it mean to be a "Suga Mama" with an "accountant waiting on the phone"? What does it mean to be a woman who proudly claims to be the "type to take care of mine" in an age of gross federal (read patriarchal) failure to serve and to protect? There is something remarkable, almost parodic, about this track with its sinuous chorus ("Sit on mama lap/Hey, hey/Come sit on mama lap"), and its insistence on acknowledging the power and the allure of the maternal entrepreneurial figure, of which Knowles's own mother Tina has clearly set a life-long inspirational example.

Again and again on B-Day, Knowles assumes the role of the female entrepreneur, the conductor, just as capable of assembling heavyweight producers at once in multiple studios as she is of (re)assembling the best traits of her lover. "Upgrade U," the second track that features Jay-Z, finds Knowles once again playing the role of the producer of sorts. Jay and Knowles "do battle" like emcees throughout the track, as the singer makes a bid to refine and reform her partner, "switch [his] neckties to purple labels." It is, on the surface, an astoundingly retrograde song, one in which the Beyoncé of Destiny's Child's controversial track "Cater 2 U" re-emerges and offers to "take care" of the home and her man. There is, though, per-haps a bit more to this track with its cowboys "out-on-the-range" horns and synthesizer arrangements. Even in a line as ludicrously overblown as "I can do for you what Martin did for the people," Knowles's fixation on uplift, upgrade, and enlightenment steers the track toward the broader concerns of redress that hang over B-Day. The song assures that uplift will take the form of the material as Knowles flips the Svengali script in the latter verses, announcing to her lover that "you my project celebrity." Rather than assuming the role of the helpless "dreamgirl," Knowles declares her gift at turning Jay-Z into good product, declaring that "Unless you're flawless/ Then ya dynasty ain't complete without a chief like me."

If anything, "Upgrade U" is a track that reinforces the tenor of B-Day as an album focused on ownership and personal property. It also returns time and again to modes of evacuation and our heroine's efforts to maintain spatial control in various circumstances. This is why the lyrics to the album demand special attention. For, on the one hand, while the "Ring the Alarm" video threatens to replay hackneyed images of a "girl gone Fatal Attraction wild," the song itself is a far more complicated narrative than that of the familiar "woman scorned." Like "Bills, Bills, Bills," it would be easy to misread "Ring the Alarm" as a result of the chorus alone, an abrasive, in-your-face mantra in which Beyoncé yells a refrain that's punctuated by red alarm sirens: "I been through this too long!/But I'll be damned if I see another chick on your arm."

If the cathartic outrage that shapes "Ring the Alarm" recalls the kind of carefully crafted breakup ire voiced by the likes of pop songstresses such as Alanis Morrissette and Kelly Clarkson, Knowles is carving out a very particular kind of palpable female R&B anger, one that sounds more like Kelis's debut single, yet one that lyrically is much more concerned with property and ownership than any other song of its kind. "Ring the Alarm" gives loud, burning-down-the-house voice to a woman more concerned with losing her property, her "chinchilla coats," the "house off coast," "everything I own" than she is with love itself. Relationships, in Beyoncé's cold, class-act world, are, in fact, for much of this record, business trans-actions. If "Déjà vu" charts a kind of obsessive love, the intimacy of "Ring the Alarm"—a song that rhythmically has more in common with the shifts in tempo found on "Get Me Bodied" and "Upgrade U"—conveys a narrative reduced to a woman's relationships to her goods. Female discontent is rooted in lost "things" on "Alarm": "I don't want you but I want it/And I can't let it go/To know you give it to her like you gave it to me, come on, . . . " The "it" that Beyoncé laments losing—sex, money, power—is cause for starting a fire. As empty as this relationship is, Knowles is clearly wary of reminding her listeners of the alienating effects of the material on intimacy itself: "How can you look at me/And not see all the things that I kept only just for you? Why would you risk it baby?/This is my show and I won't let you go/All has been paid for, and it's mine."

Even a seemingly knock-off sexual innuendo track like "Kitty Kat," in which the singer declares that she and her feline "pet" are leaving an uncaring lover, is infused with the rhetoric of evacuation and the repos-session of (sexual) property. Lyrics that point to the fact that the singer and her lover are "at two places but different paces" and that declare that "we in trouble but you won't meet me at the bridge" perhaps point to more com-plicated images of stress and the stinging recognition of being devalued in a relationship (the "bridge" imagery even brings to mind the many bridges that hurricane evacuees were forced to wait on and, in some cases, were not allowed to cross at the height of the disaster). If this is a song about getting out, about evacuating a relationship, "Kitty Kat," with its refrain of "What about my body, body?/You don't want my body, body/Acting like I'm nobody," also underscores a longing to revalue the self in real, corporeal ways. In the end, there is something poignant that pulses beneath the sur-face of this euphemistic attention-grabber, something that reinforces the deeper social and emotional dimensions of the record as a whole.

More often than not, then, the Beyoncé on *B-Day* does battle with lovers who need upgrading, who betray, and who fail to fulfill. By the time the euphoric crescendo of the Neptunes' signature bass-driven "Green Light," this heroine has emerged in full boast-and-toast mode, encouraging her (ex)-lover to recognize the "green light" and go rather than "holdin up traffic." Once again conducting, setting the pace, morphing into the arbi-ter of flow, Knowles orders her lover to "move along" and acknowledges her

own "pimpish" worth that "gets no older." "Green Light" signals the liberation of her character and transitions the album into its final "unpretty"
act, "Irreplaceable," the hook-driven, number-one smash akin to some of
TLC's most successful crossover pop material. With so many orchestrated
movements throughout the record, it's fitting that this track would find
Knowles once again efficiently directing an ex-lover "to the left, to the
left . . . Everything you own in the box to the left/Yes, if I bought it, then
please don't touch." Evacuation is once again afoot here as Knowles
reminds him that it's her "name that's on that jag/So go move your bags, let
me call you a cab." The purchase(d) power of "Suga Mama" has turned sour
here as Knowles informs her boyfriend-product that he should never "for a
second get to thinkin'" that he's "irreplaceable."

The cordial disillusionment of that track, however, comes undone in
"Resentment," B-Day's dissonant, closing number proper (the album
includes an additional, product-placement track, "Listen," from the film
Dreamgirls, which debuted later that year, as well as a reprise of "Get Me
Bodied") that loops a sample of Curtis Mayfield's melancholic "Think"
with gospel and doo-wop-tinged harmonies to convey the pure depths of
romantic bile that lead the singer to a hard, grief-stricken nadir. With shrill
vocals stretched to the very extreme, "Resentment" is a difficult, visceral
track on which to officially end the record. In many ways it delivers the retro
arrangements of En Vogue's 1990s smash cover, "Giving Him Something
He Can Feel," but re-outfits electric sexual "feeling" here as shards of pain.
The "feeling" of resentment is rushed, off-center, arched, and surfeiting
with emotion that sounds as though it is at the crossroads of a choir solo
and juke-joint nightclub abandon. It's an extraordinarily uncomfortable
crescendo, a jagged little pill for fans of the 40/40 club dreamgirl-covergirl
to swallow, and one that reminds us, as pop critic Jody Rosen argues, that
this is indeed a "tough record" produced by "a storm system disguised as a
singer" (Rosen 2006).

Rosen's allusion reminds us too of the Gulf Coast roots in Beyoncé's
own familial past. Born and raised in Houston, Knowles is nonetheless the
product of a maternal line that hails from New Orleans. Indeed, that one-
of-a-kind first name is in fact a variation on her mother's maiden name,
"Beyince," the mark of a proud Creole heritage as well as an example of her
parents' self-inventive spirit. Embedded in Knowles's family history, then,
is a tale of migration from New Orleans to Houston as well as one of
resourceful self-styling. Knowles herself has reiterated the importance of

her upper-middle class roots, her father's got-to-know-how spirit that propelled him from working as an executive in medical sales at Xerox to managing her career and, likewise, her mother's solid example as a Black female entrepreneur. And although this privilege, this recognition that for her there is "no pressure, because" her parents "are going to be successful regardless of what they do" (Toure 2004, 44) would seem to set Knowles at utmost odds with the women who survived the storm, the sheer sense of entitlement and the rejection of disenfranchisement on B-Day is perhaps a subtle yet powerful emotional statement about the politics of Black women's property in the wake of that national crisis. It is a record whose visceral dimensions around the subject of ownership challenge century-old American myths about race, class, and gender—ones that, as Carby once argued, still imagine Black women as lazy, feckless, "degenerate," and unwilling to work (Carby 1992). Knowles's album asserts a willed response to Black women's social dislocation in the wake of yet another massive migration, and it imagines a language of socioeconomic autonomy that is, in every way, troubling in its fixation on materialism and yet provocative as well in light of the gross loss of property endured by so many African Americans and particularly by female-headed households in the wake of the storm.

Beyoncé's steady chart success and, perhaps more importantly, her still vaulting iconicity represent the extent to which the social, political, and cultural desires of R&B music fans—and especially female R&B music fans—still remain largely overlooked and under-theorized in popular music studies. Save for the likes of Mark Anthony Neal, few critics have analyzed the ways that both female R&B performers and the fans who love them are actively and consistently producing a public record of cultural expression that affirms the intersecting personal and political questions and concerns of women of color in the early twenty-first century. Their musical subcultures should remind us of the point that Neal has often made, that popular R&B demands that we take it more seriously since it articulates overt as well as latent desires pulsating through contemporary African-American culture (Neal 2003).

B-Day makes many of these desires manifest. It is an album that articulates the questions and concerns of Black women who are wary of having their movements controlled and policed in the public eye—from Sojourner Truth to Super Bowl Janet. In the post-Hurricane Katrina era, both Beyoncé's B-Day and Blige's stirring duet with U2 mark the emergence of resolutely off-center, surrogated performances of discontent and dissent.

Taken together, Beyoncé's urgently paced album and Blige's pointed, methodical-as-a-heartbeat cover song score an R&B response of sorts to this long history of Black women who have been stripped and stressed and displaced and denied, and each artist's performance imagines new ways of moving and singing under duress.

....

Daphne A. Brooks is the William R. Kenan, Jr. Professor of African American Studies, American Studies, and Women's, Gender, and Sexuality Studies at Yale University. She specializes in African American literary studies, cultural performance studies, sound studies, and Black feminist theory. Brooks is the author of numerous articles and several books, including *Liner Notes for the Revolution: The Intellectual Life of Black Feminist Sound* (forthcoming 2021). She is also the cofounder and codirector of Yale University's Black Sound & the Archive Working Group.

Notes

Originally published in *Meridians* vol. 8, no. 1, 2008, as "'All That You Can't Leave Behind': Surrogation and Black Female Soul Singing in the Age of Catastrophe."

1   Portions of this article appeared previously in Brooks 2006. Many thanks to Christine Smallwood, Eric Weisbard, and Reginald Jackson for their helpful suggestions and feedback during the writing and revision of this essay.

2   For more on the politics of race, gender, class, and 1990s media spectacles, see Lubiano 1992.

3   *Basic Instinct* 1992; Beyoncé 2006b.

4   Much work has yet to be done on the culture of Black women's popular protest and dissent music. Of the major works on this topic, most have focused on the work of Blues and jazz pioneers. See, for instance, Carby 1994; see also Davis 1999; Griffin 2001; and Feldstein 2005. Alice Echols is currently working on a study of Black women's social and political aesthetics and identifications in 1970s disco, soul, and funk culture (Echols 2010). For studies of Black women and rock and roll cultural dissent, see Mahon 2004; Wald 2007; Hobson 2008.

5   We might heed the fact that the moment was quickly co-opted by Blige for her forthcoming album and later staged and re-staged—in effect "watered down"—at a string of awards shows, variety specials, and sporting events. In this regard, the staging and re-staging of the song led to a kind of tragic evacuation of the meaning of this stunning, original performance.

6   See Mayshark 2005, 3.

7   For a study of Black satirical and critical responses to the Rolling Stones's "Brown Sugar," see Brooks 2004, 124–46.

8   See also Barthes 1977, 179–89. For more on the currency, cultural appropriations, and trans-historical resonance of the Black female singing voice, see Griffin 2004, 102–25.

9   See also Weiner 2006, 75–84.

Works Cited

Amber, Jeannine. 2006. "A Fashionable Life." *Essence Magazine* (September): 174.

Barrett, Lindon. 1999. *Blackness and Value: Seeing Double.* New York: Cambridge University Press.

Barthes, Roland. 1977. "The Grain of the Voice." In *Image, Music, Text,* translated by Stephen Heath, 179–89. New York: Hill and Wang.

Basic Instinct. 1992. Directed by Paul Verhoeven. Canal +.

Beyoncé. 2005. *B-Day.* Sony Records.

———. 2006a. "Déjà vu." Sony Music Studios.

———. 2006b. "Ring the Alarm." Directed by Sophie Mueller. Sony Music Studios.

Brooks, Daphne A. 2004. "Burnt Sugar: Post-Soul Satire and Rock Memory." In *This is Pop: Critical Essays from the First Annual Experience Music Project Conference on Popular Music,* edited by Eric Weisbard, 103–23. Cambridge, MA: Harvard University Press.

———. 2006. "Suga Mama Politicized." TheNation.com (18 December). http://www.thenation.com/doc/20061218/brooks (accessed November 26, 2007).

Carby, Hazel. 1992. "Policing the Black Woman's Body in an Urban Context." *Critical Inquiry* 18, no. 4: 738–55.

———. 1994. "'It Just Be's Dat Way Sometime': The Sexual Politics of Women's Blues." In *Unequal Sisters: A Multicultural Reader in U.S. Women's History,* edited by Ellen DuBois and Vicki Ruiz, 330–41. New York: Routledge.

Davis, Angela. 1999. *Blues Legacies and Black Feminism: Gertrude Ma Rainey, Bessie Smith, and Billie Holiday.* New York: Vintage.

Echols, Alice. 2010. *Upside Down: Disco and the Re-making of American Culture.* New York: Norton.

Fatal Attraction. 1987. Directed by Adrian Lyne. Paramount Pictures.

Feldstein, Ruth. 2005. "'I Don't Trust You Anymore': Nina Simone, Culture, and Black Activism in the 1960s." *Journal of American History* 91, no. 4 (March): 1349–79.

Gaunt, Kyra. 2006. *The Games Black Girls Play: Learning the Ropes from Double-Dutch to Hip Hop.* New York: New York University Press.

Griffin, Farah Jasmine. 2001. *If You Can't Be Free, Be A Mystery: In Search of Billie Holiday.* New York: Free Press.

———. 2004. "When Malindy Sings: A Meditation on Black Women's Vocality." In *Uptown Conversation: The New Jazz Studies,* edited by Robert G. O'Meally et al. New York: Columbia University Press.

Harris-Lacewell, Melissa. Forthcoming. "Introduction." *For Colored Girls Who Have Considered Politics When Being Strong Wasn't Enough.*

Lubiano, Wahneema. 1992. "Black Ladies, Welfare Queens, and State Minstrels: Ideological War by Narrative Means." In *Race-ing Justice, En-gendering Power: Essays on Anita Hill, Clarence Thomas, and the Construction of Social Reality,* edited by Toni Morrison, 323–63. New York: Pantheon.

Mahon, Maureen. 2004. *The Right to Rock: The Black Rock Coalition and the Cultural Politics of Race.* Durham, NC: Duke University Press.

Martel, Ned. 2005. "On a Telethon Weekend, Restraint from an Unlikely Source." *New York Times* (September 12).

Mayshark, Jesse Fox. 2005. "In a Send-Up of Charity Songs, the Elite of Indie Rock Take on Halloween Revelry." *New York Times* (October 5): section E.

Murray, Charles Shaar. 2005. As quoted in "Get Up, Stand Up: The Story of Pop and Protest" (PBS), produced by Rudi Dolezal and Hannes Rossacher. September.

Neal, Mark Anthony. 2003. *Songs in the Key of Black Life: A Rhythm and Blues Nation.* New York: Routledge.

Reynolds, Simon. 2004. "Noise." In *Audio Culture: Readings in Modern Music,* edited by Christopher Cox and Daniel Warner, 55–58. New York: Continuum.

Roach, Joseph. 1996. *Cities of the Dead: Circum-Atlantic Culture.* New York: Columbia University Press.

Rosen, Jody. 2006. "Party Girl: Beyoncé's B-Day." *Entertainment Weekly* (September 1).

Shelter from the Storm, ABC, CBS, NBC, September 9, 2006.

Spillers, Hortense. 1987. "Mama's Baby, Papa's Maybe: An American Grammar Book." *Diacritics* 17, no. 2: 64–81.

Swerdlick, David. 2007. "Six Degrees of Beyoncefication." Creative Loafing.com, January 3. http://charlotte.creativeloafing.com/gyrobase/Content?oid=oid%3A114268 (accessed November 26, 2007).

Toure, 2004. "A Woman Possessed." *Rolling Stone Magazine* (March 4): 38–44.

Wald, Gayle. 2007. *Shout, Sister, Shout!: The Untold Story of Rock-and-Roll Trailblazer Sister Rosetta Tharpe.* Boston: Beacon Press.

Weiner, Jonah. 2006. "The Ice Princess." *Blender Magazine* (October): 75–84.

When the Levee Broke. 2006. Directed by Spike Lee. HBO Films.

Willis, Jessica. 2003. "Sadly, Mary J. Blige is Happy At Last." *New York Times* (August 24): section 2.

Lourdes Torres

....

Queering Puerto Rican Women's Narratives
Gaps and Silences in the Memoirs of Antonia
Pantoja and Luisita López Torregrosa

Abstract: While in the last decades there has been a proliferation of writings by
Latina lesbians who theorize issues of intersectionality, missing still are the
voices and analyses of Puerto Rican lesbians who articulate the specificity
of Puerto Rican sexual, racial, national, and class dynamics. It is within this
context that the author examines *Memoir of a Visionary* (2002) by Antonia
Pantoja and *The Noise of Infinite Longing* (2004) by Luisita López Torregrosa;
the article considers how these recent memoirs engage with intersecting
issues in the lives of Puerto Rican women and suggest how shame implicitly
conditions the articulation of Puerto Rican identity.

As a closeted Nuyorican lesbian attending graduate school in the Midwest,
I remember the joy I felt in the early 1980s when a friend gave me a copy of
This Bridge Called My Back. For the first time ever I encountered writings by
Latina lesbians and other lesbians of color. The work of writers such as
Cherríe Moraga and Gloria Anzaldúa made visible the realities of lesbian
lives, and documented how the personal is always political; their powerful
narratives resonated for me at many levels. They broke the silence about the
impact of sexuality, race, and class on the lives of Latina lesbians, and
documented the myriad ways in which Latina lesbians across the Americas
resist interlocking oppressions. This public recognition of the complex
struggles of communities to which I belonged legitimized our concerns; it

MERIDIANS · feminism, race, transnationalism   Volume 19 Supplement 2020
DOI: 10.1215/15366936-8566001 © 2009 Smith College

gave me the courage to come out in the Latina, feminist, and academic communities in which I participated, even as associates and friends in some of these communities encouraged me to hide or at least to minimize my lesbianism or my ethnicity in an effort to avoid upsetting straight or White community members. The groundbreaking work of Latina lesbian writers helped me battle the shame connected to aspects of these identities and the homophobia and racism I had internalized throughout my life. It helped me to resist the impulse to silence aspects of myself to avoid making others uncomfortable. While I had the benefit of this work to support me in my journey, the same was not true for those who came before me for whom such revelations could have been devastating on public and private fronts.[1]

In the last few decades a proliferation of writings by Latina lesbians has theorized issues of intersectionality; however, missing still are the voices and analyses of Puerto Rican lesbians who articulate the specificity of Puerto Rican gender, sexual, racial, national, and class dynamics similarly to the way that writers such as Moraga and Anzaldúa and others have done for the Chicana lesbian experience. It is within this context that I examine *Memoir of a Visionary* (2002), by Antonia Pantoja, and *The Noise of Infinite Longing* (2004), by Luisita López Torregrosa. I consider how these recent memoirs engage with intersecting issues in the lives of Puerto Rican women, and suggest how shame implicitly and explicitly conditions the articulation of Puerto Rican identity.

All memoirs are projects of self-invention.[2] I am interested in how these two Puerto Rican women enacted strategies of passing and covering in order to manage their queer sexualities in relation to their nationality, race, and class. Clearly, the language and political context that writers have access to in a particular time and place exert significant influence on how they represent sex and sexuality in their work. In this case, it is perhaps not surprising that given their coming of age in Puerto Rico during the mid 1940s and 1960s respectively, neither Pantoja nor López Torregrosa uses the "L" word to describe herself;[3] for the most part, they both use euphemisms and indirect language when they discuss their relationships with women. Of all aspects of their identities, their sexuality is the most understated. I do not seek to privilege sexuality as the primary or exclusive frame for self-identification or political action; rather, I believe that analyses that dissect the multiple and intersecting systems of power that condition the life chances of women of color are the most insightful (Crenshaw 1991; Cohen 2005). However, given the dearth of writing by openly lesbian[4] Boricua[5]

writers, and the general lack of discussion of sexuality and especially lesbianism[6] in Puerto Rican culture, I am interested in how sexuality is negotiated in these two recent memoirs in relation to race, nationality, and class
and the shame associated with aspects of these identities. Shame is commonly defined as a powerful emotion that often emerges when one feels
that she or he has transgressed moral or social norms. Feelings of self-
doubt, unworthiness, and low self-esteem often embody shame. Negrón-
Muntaner argues that given Puerto Rico's particular history of colonial
domination and mass migration (Negrón-Muntaner 2004),[7] Puerto Ricans
are placed in a context where we are perpetually responding to shame.
Additionally, the flood of social-science literature emerging in the early
twentieth century, which pathologized Puerto Ricans both on the island
and stateside (perhaps best exemplified by Oscar Lewis's racist yet award-
winning study, *La Vida: A Puerto Rican Family in the Culture of Poverty—San Juan
and New York*),[8] helps explain why Puerto Rican attempts to value ourselves
are often "staged through spectacles to offset shame" (Negrón-Muntaner
2004, viiii). Negrón-Muntaner's reading of shame is framed as a social
phenomenon circumscribed by political realities rather than as an exclusively psychological condition. It is important to stress these social dimensions since shame responds to a fear of being stigmatized or losing a social
bond. "A sense of shame," then, is a powerful tool of social control.[9] In this
regard, Arnaldo Cruz-Malavé cites novelist's Luís Rafael Sánchez's assertion that all Puerto Rican writers are haunted by a sense of guilt or shame
because we are always afraid of "harming our communal ties, lest we supply the terms—and the weapons—for our own demise, lest we feed that
machine, that greedy, human-eating machine with our own blood, all the
worse because it's not ours, but the blood of those whom we love most"
(Cruz-Malavé 2007, 111).

The memoirs by educator and activist Antonia Pantoja and journalist
Luisita López Torregrosa, with their silences, understatements, and selective revelations, provide a site from which to consider how shame influences the articulation and/or silencing of sexuality, race, nationality, and
class. Intimately connected to shame is the idea of uncovering, particularly
of those things that remain unstated although they exert a significant
influence on our lives. In *Defacement: Public Secrecy and the Labor of the Negative*,
Michael Taussig defines a "public secret" as "that which is generally known
but cannot be articulated" (Taussig 1999, 5). He argues that such secrets are
the foundation of most of our institutions, including the state, the family,

and the workplace. In these memoirs, tensions and shame around public secrets and their potential uncovering hold much power. The authors grapple with how much information to reveal, and their ambivalence around issues of race, nationality, and sexuality creates an uncomfortable position for the reader who seeks to position them in familiar paradigms.

Queering Boricua Lives

While they resist categorization as standard coming-out stories that perhaps would please some lesbian and gay readers, Pantoja and López Torregrosa certainly queer the tradition of Puerto Rican women's narratives in more ways than just their struggles around sexuality.[10]

Both of these women can be described as queer in the sense that they do not conform to Puerto Rican conventions for women in effect when they were coming of age (Pantoja was born in 1921, and López Torregrosa in 1945), and therefore they trouble or "queer" these gendered traditions. Pantoja and López Torregrosa destabilize the gender norms that are associated with women in mainstream Puerto Rican culture in many ways. Historically, Puerto Rican women have been defined in the heteronormative national imaginary as submissive wives and mothers. Anticolonialist, nationalist movements have also positioned women in this way, and have claimed that any deviations from this model are the result of foreign imperialist influences.[11] Defying gendered expectations for their time period, both women left the island as young single women. As Crespo-Kebler explains, women born during the early years of U.S. rule experienced a period of rapid transformation. Given the industrialization of the island, as well as the introduction of compulsory education, new options other than marriage and motherhood became available for women of this period who participated in the paid labor force and gained financial independence. Pantoja left Puerto Rico in 1944 at the age of twenty-three because of economic and emotional pressure. She writes, "I was so overburdened, carrying the major financial responsibility for the family. I was suffocating with emotions and responsibilities. I needed to find my own life. I felt that the culture was oppressive, demanding that I take care of my mother's family because I was unmarried" (Pantoja 2002, 48). Likewise, López Torregrosa left Puerto Rico at the age of sixteen to attend college, and did not return until the death of her father thirty-five years later. Both women were highly educated and never married. While López Torregrosa comes from an upper-class White background, Pantoja was a Black, working-class woman. They both led unconventional lifestyles and achieved noteworthy career success, Pantoja as an educator and activist primarily around education issues, and López Torregrosa as a journalist for the *New York Times*. In addition to these unconventional characteristics, both women engaged in long-term relationships with other women. Manuel Guzmán coined the term "sexile" to refer to Puerto Rican men and women who left the island for the United States in order to escape condemnation as queers. Both Pantoja and López Torregrosa could be identified as sexiles although they do not explicitly claim this identity. Their memoirs reveal how race, class, and gender shaped their experiences, and suggest why sexuality is broached so tentatively.

Dr. Antonia Pantoja, who passed away in 2002 at the age of eighty, was a powerful activist and educator. She made many important contributions to the Puerto Rican community throughout her life. She is best known as the founder of Aspira, a national organization that creates opportunities for young Puerto Ricans through education and leadership training. Pantoja was also a co-founder of The National Puerto Rican Forum and the Puerto Rican Association for Community Affairs. Throughout her career she received many honors, including the Presidential Medal of Freedom in 1996. In an online column in GLAAD (Gay and Lesbian Alliance Against Defamation), activist Andrés Duques describes his pleasure as a Latino gay man at seeing public recognition of her lesbian relationship in *The New York Times*, which in its obituary following Pantoja's death reported that, "She is survived by her partner, Dr. Wilhelmina Perry."[12] Not many of the tributes that followed her death and celebrated her activism in the Puerto Rican and Latino communities mentioned Pantoja's sexual preference or her long-term partner. Perhaps this should not be a surprise given that Pantoja herself makes scant reference to her emotional and sexual relationships with women in her life story, *Memoir of a Visionary*, which she completed a few years before her death. On the last page of her memoir, dedicated to "my friend and partner, Wilhelmina Perry," Pantoja addresses this glaring absence,

> Although I have not discussed directly my sexuality, I am also at peace with this part of me. I have decided not to discuss it in this book because I have always drawn a line between my private and public life. However, I wish to eliminate the possibility of being misinterpreted and being described as secretive about this matter, I claim it at various points in the book.[13] (Pantoja 2002, 197)

Indeed Pantoja does mention her relationships with women at various places in her memoir. But only the reader who is looking for evidence of a lesbian life will connect the dots that Pantoja provides since she does not focus on her intimate relationships. Pantoja, briefly and without elaboration, does mention three women who were close to her and who lived with her for many years: Helen Lehew, Barbara Blourock, and Wilhelmina Perry.[14] The reader of her memoir learns that these women are in her life and that they are important, but the nature of the relationships is not revealed. For example, Pantoja reports that she lived with her friend Helen Lehew from the late 1940s to the early 1950s. She mentions that Helen accompanied her to many events, but then they had a big disagreement, and Helen moved out (Pantoja 2002, 94). No further explanation is offered to explain why they parted ways. Barbara Blourock was her companion in the 1960s; she traveled with Pantoja as she moved from New York to Puerto Rico, Washington, and California. Pantoja mentions that she, Blourock, and Perry worked on many projects together. Then there is no further mention of Blourock in the narrative, and Perry is referenced as her companion for over twenty-five years, until the end of her life.

Ironically, Pantoja's memoir unmistakably demonstrates how, in fact, it is impossible to separate the "private" from the "public." When accounting for the fact that she never ran for office despite her long-established leadership skills and the encouragement of her political allies, she explains that she refused to subject herself to the media scrutiny that inevitably exposes the lives of candidates. She states, "Also, I had never married. I had led a bohemian life in my early years, and since then, I had had a number of female companions. I felt that all these things could have been the subject of personal attacks because I knew that political campaigns used low tactics" (Pantoja 2002, 131). Pantoja acknowledges that her relationships with women kept her from pursuing an elected position. In her many official capacities in her lifelong political work, she was very discreet, and thus was able to maintain the public secret about her sexuality and pass as heterosexual, thanks to the well-known, "don't ask, don't tell" policy characteristic of Latino/a and other communities.

Like Pantoja's memoir, *The Noise of Infinite Longing* is not marketed as a lesbian story in the mainstream press. The memoir chronicles the story of Luisita López Torregrosa's family in Puerto Rico and in the United States. Starting with the death of her mother, which brings the scattered siblings together, López Torregrosa traces the history of the family and their connections with one another. While López Torregrosa provides much information about her parents' marriage and the relationships of her siblings, she reveals little about her own intimate partners until the end of the text. She mentions women who shared her life, but she offers few details about these connections, and their secrecy is the most recurring issue concerning these relationships. Recalling her childhood, she mentions that as a child she often became obsessed with other girls. While there are hints about her love of women throughout the memoir, it is not until almost the end of the book that this issue is explicitly named. López Torregrosa makes clear that throughout her life she avoided conversations about her relationships with women with most of the people in her family and at her workplace. Discussing her relationship with her deceased mother, she laments how little her mother knew about her life. She writes:

> I never talked to my mother about it, about my love for women, and she never asked me. That silence ran deep. And it was perhaps more than any other thing what kept me away—I was afraid she would ask, and at the same time, I resented that she did not want to know, that a whole part of my life was unacknowledged and not talked about with the ease she talked about my sisters' husbands and children. The tacit understanding was not enough; the silence set me apart from the others. (López Torregrosa 2004, 249)

Similarly to the case of Pantoja's story, the gay media foregrounds sexuality in their analysis of López Torregrosa's memoir. A review of the book in *The Advocate* is titled "My mother, myself: a lesbian daughter provides a rare glimpse into Puerto Rican family life . . . " (Marler 2004). The subtitle for an article on the book in the *Gay City News* is "Lesbian newspaper editor chronicles growing up the oldest in a Puerto Rican family" (Kennerley 2004). These references occur despite the fact that like Pantoja, López Torregrosa never claims the lesbian label in her memoir.

Passing and Covering

In their memoirs, Pantoja and López Torregrosa discuss their lives as professional women in narratives that disrupt expectations of heterosexual coupling and motherhood as the inevitable paths for Puerto Rican women. However, the issue of same-sex desire is tentatively approached but concurrently understated and minimized by these authors. Neither woman self-identifies as lesbian or bisexual, nor discusses her nontraditional sexuality in terms of gay and lesbian political or cultural movements.[15] In fact, same-sex relationships are to differing degrees understated and quietly integrated into the life stories of these women. In their memoirs, Pantoja and López Torregrosa engage in a tentative dance around the issue of sexuality that underscores the tension between striving to avoid potentially alienating heterosexual readers while at the same time acknowledging same-sex desire.[16] Meanwhile, those Puerto Rican queer readers yearning to claim these powerful, unconventional women as queer Boricua icons must acknowledge the reality that both Pantoja and López Torregrosa shun an openly lesbian identity.

Debates among some queer Latino/as center on whether or not to claim women such as Pantoja or López Torregrosa as Puerto Rican lesbian heroes. In a related argument concerning the reading of autobiographies of women, Hallet points out that lesbian readers are "hungry readers," and seeking out evidence of lesbianism is "an occupational habit of lesbians" (Hallet 1997, ix). Nonetheless, the ethics and politics of proclaiming and promoting a closeted or reluctant figure as a queer icon is a familiar debate in mainstream gay and lesbian communities forever eager to identify queer role models.

This hunger, in fact, has led to the outing of public figures (dead and alive) who have never directly acknowledged their sexuality (for example, Virginia Woolf, Rock Hudson, Ricky Martin, and so on). Queer Latino/as, even more starved for public figures to celebrate as our own, cannot be blamed for yearning to claim as queer "respectable" figures such as activist Pantoja or journalist López Torregrosa. However, critic José Quiroga cautions against the impulse to "out" Latin American writers who declined to take on a queer public identity. He points out that we should not assume a one-size-fits-all, progressive, homosexual continuum from the closet to visibility. He cautions us against mapping Anglo paradigms onto Latin American writers. Rather than outing writers who do not position themselves as publicly queer, Quiroga argues that it is more important to consider how they negotiated their sexuality in the private and public spaces they moved through (Quiroga 2000).

On the other hand, Andrés Duques asserts that following the "outing" of Pantoja in the New York Times obituary, now her lesbianism has been acknowledged in public, so we can legitimately celebrate Pantoja as a Puerto Rican lesbian. He discusses conversations he has had with Dr. Pantoja's friends, who maintain that she kept her sexuality a secret because she felt it would jeopardize her advocacy work for Puerto Rican children. He imagines that she would not be averse to being claimed by queer activists at this time. Nonetheless, Pantoja and López Torregrosa are questionable queer icons since neither publicly embraced a queer identity. And Pantoja, despite speaking out and organizing on a wide range of social and political inequities, apparently never publicly advocated for gay and lesbian human rights.[17]

The argument could be made that since both these women came of age before or at the dawning of the gay and lesbian liberation movement, they belonged to generations that faced enormous risks if they came out, especially if they were public figures. Gay men and women born before the 1960s could be criminalized or subjected to medical intervention if their sexual identities were revealed. A nascent homophile moment existed in the U.S. in the 1950s that challenged discrimination against gays and lesbians, especially in fields such as psychology, law, and medicine. While organizations such as the Mattachine Society and Daughters of Bilitis worked to transform mainstream views of gays and lesbians, they tended to seek accommodation, and encouraged the assimilation of their members into mainstream society.[18] Pantoja was in New York in the late 1960s as more radical activism around gay and lesbian issues was just gaining visibility. She was in her late forties at that time and very active working on issues of educational reform. She also was involved in projects involving community empowerment. She worked to form coalitions among Puerto Ricans, African Americans, and Jews to share resources and create opportunities. López Torregrosa was in her twenties in the late 1960s and was also in the United States trying to break into the racist and homophobic world of journalism. As a Puerto Rican woman she had confronted considerable obstacles as she struggled to find a place in the White masculine terrain of print journalism. In addition, she was far removed from the world of social movements or activism in many of the rural areas where she lived. Whatever they felt while observing the unfolding of the gay and lesbian movement in the 1970s and beyond, neither woman seems ever to have spoken out publicly on the rights of gays and lesbians, nor to have publicly acknowledged her same-sex intimate partnerships. Since the mainstream gay and lesbian movement was (and arguably still is) a single issue, middle-class movement run primarily by White men, it is perhaps not surprising that it did not speak to Pantoja's activism or López Torregrosa's interests. Unlike White male memoir writers who came of age before the advent of contemporary social movements for gay rights, yet who write from a perspective that acknowledges the social movements that have transpired since the 1960s and explain how these movements have helped them recast their lives, Pantoja and López Torregrosa are silent about any impact these movements may have had on their lives.[19]

Both Pantoja's and López Torregrosa's memoirs suggest a lifetime of "discretion shame" around their same-sex desires and of passing as heterosexuals. Carl Schneider makes a distinction between "disgrace shame" and "discretion shame" (Schneider 1977). While the former concerns a response to perceived misdeeds, discretion shame is a type of self-monitoring that is necessary to maintain social order, and motivates the individual to keep private those things that a society deems should not be opened up to social scrutiny. Silence about a subject can have many meanings. I argue that the Pantoja and Lopez Torregrosa's oblique management of public statements about same-sex desire in their memoirs at one level suggests discretion shame about their non-normative sexuality, while simultaneously serving as a mode of resistance and a strategy for survival. Given heteronormative conventions and homophobia, it is almost impossible to disengage same-sex desire from its associations with stigma and shame. Both Pantoja and López Torregrosa apparently felt that their sexual and emotional relationships with women could not be publicly acknowledged. At the same time, they resisted contemporary expectations; they lived their lives with female companions, and found acceptance in their communities as long as the nature of their relationships with women was not verbalized. While in their memoirs, both women do confront the issue of their sexuality, however understatedly, it is clear from their narratives that much of their lives involved sexual passing. López Torregrosa directly addresses the fact that she did not discuss her relationships with her family. She also states that she and one of her partners, another journalist, were deeply concerned that their colleagues would guess the nature of their relationship. They took great care to avoid any behavior that would elicit suspicion. Pantoja mentions various women in her life and their work and travel together, but does not explicitly name the fact that these women were her lovers. She and her companions seem to have chosen to pass in many instances of their public lives.

Passing is a recurring theme in Boricua lesbian narratives, not only in those that center on closeted sexuality, but also in those that engage contested racial and national identities.[20] It can be read as a response to shame about possessing a stigmatized identity. While passing is commonly associated with deception, particularly in terms of race and sexuality, recent readings of passing reveal this practice to be much more nuanced and complex.[21] Passing strategies can serve to allow a measure of freedom in racist and homophobic contexts at the same time that they inhibit identifications and associations with marginalized communities. Passing is sometimes an intentional act; at other times it is imposed from the outside and may or may not be challenged. A light-skinned person read as White, or a gay person read as straight, may opt not to make their "true" identity known. For some thinkers, passing can result only in loss and tragedy. For example, Leslie Feinberg writes in *Stone Butch Blues* that "passing didn't just mean slipping below the surface, it meant being buried alive" (Feinberg 1993, 213). However, Linda Schlossberg acknowledges its negative associations but also suggests how passing can be potentially liberating:

> Passing is not simply about erasure or denial, as it is often castigated but, rather, about the creation and establishment of an alternative set of narratives. It becomes a way of creating new stories out of unusable ones, or from personal narratives seemingly in conflict with other aspects of self-presentation. (Schlossberg 2001, 4)

Since both Pantoja and López Torregrosa eventually reveal their sexual preference in their memoirs, and many who had close contact with them probably knew about their sexuality, perhaps the concept of "covering" more appropriately captures how they managed their sexuality. In his recent book, *Covering*, legal scholar Kenji Yoshino complicates the idea of passing by distinguishing it from the concept of covering. The term "covering" is derived from sociologist Erving Goffman's book *Stigma*, where he defines it as a strategy used by those with stigmatized identities to "tone down" shameful aspects of problematic identities, even when they are known to the world (Goffman 1974). Yoshino describes how covering is a form of assimilation that can operate along the parameters of appearance, affiliation, activism, and association. The boundary between passing and covering is not clear-cut, and often the two strategies may overlap. Yoshino explains that "passing pertains to the *visibility* of a particular trait, while covering pertains to its *obtrusiveness*" (Yoshino 2006, 18), so that passing refers to concealing difference while covering has to do with minimizing differences and not calling attention to them. Clearly, in their memoirs Pantoja and López Torregrosa strive to ensure that issues of their sexuality do not overshadow other aspects of their lives. Surely, there must have been suspicion and whispers about their sexual preferences given their nontraditional lifestyles. However, in the absence of public acknowledgment, their sexuality remained a public secret until the publication of their memoirs. Pantoja tentatively placed her foot out of the closet door on the last page of her memoir. And López Torregrosa cautiously raises the issue of her sexuality in an understated, unobtrusive, and arguably assimilationist manner in the last chapters of her book.

Every day in numerous spaces and interactions, gays and lesbians decide how gay or how out to be; we determine when to uncover, when to cover, and when to pass. Debates in the gay and lesbian community position those who think that the political goal of lesbian and gay movements should be to assimilate into mainstream society against those who advocate emphasizing queer differences from a heterosexist society and dismantling heteronormative assumptions and conventions. These differences are sometimes referenced in regard to a shift from a homophile movement to a more radical gay and lesbian rights movement, but both views can be found within contemporary gay and lesbian communities. Yoshino identifies these two camps as the normals (or those who argue for integration) and the queers (those who think straight society should accept queer culture in all its diversity). With these terms, Yoshino captures long-standing arguments in the gay and lesbian community about visibility, perhaps best exemplified in *Virtually Normal* by Andrew Sullivan (1995) and *The Trouble with Normal* by Michael Warner (1999). Sullivan argues for the assimilation of gays into straight culture, and argues that legitimizing gay marriage is the most important issue for gays and lesbians; on the other hand, Warner advocates for a transformation of the status quo; he argues against practices that promote heteronormative values to the detriment of all queer practices. Pantoja's and López Torregrosa's strategy of minimizing their sexual identities seems to place them squarely in the "normal" camp. They subscribe to an assimilationist creed that states that it is okay to be gay as long as one is not blatant about it. They tentatively acknowledge their lesbianism, but make an effort, as Erving Goffman states, to "keep the stigma from looming large" so they will be embraced by their Puerto Rican community and by mainstream society.

Pantoja and López Torregrosa may be responding to homophobia in their communities by avoiding any mention of their same-sex relationships, and/or they may be signaling that other issues, other identifications, are more important to them. Marlon Ross argues that the out-of-the-closet paradigm serves to define gay politics almost exclusively, and is the central metaphor through which the world is understood (Ross 2005). However, people of color who are already marked as other and marginalized in many communities have to consider multiple levels of repercussions when making their queerness visible in family, community, classroom, and workplace. Many queer writers of color have argued that the coming-out paradigm does not structure queer of color communities as it does White communities.[22] They suggest that in many cases queers of color coexist with heterosexual community members, and are accepted (or tolerated) without a coming-out moment. In a recent intervention into these debates, Carlos Decena introduces the idea of the tacit subject (*sujeto tácitio*); he argues that for the Dominican immigrant male community in New York that he examines, coming out may not be spoken but is understood within the realm of the community and social relationships that the subject inhabits (Decena 2008). Manolo Guzmán makes a similar argument, suggesting that the practice of male homosexuality in Puerto Rico does not require a verbalization of homosexual identification (Guzmán 2006). Both Decena and Guzmán argue that silence around same-sex desire should not be understood as repression or homophobia since others in the community know without being told, and a complex form of expression beyond a verbal proclamation can manifest same-sex desire. Yolanda Chávez Leyva also proposes a more complex reading of silence, since for Latina lesbians, historically and currently, silence has meant not only repression but also protection, survival, and resistance (Chávez Leyva 1998).[23] While I concur with these analyses that discern the multiple meanings and nuances of silence, I also agree with Chávez Leyva when she concludes that, "This is not, however, a call to continue the silence, nor to justify it. Naming ourselves, occupying our own language, is essential to our continued survival, particularly in these times of increasing violence against us as Latinas and lesbians" (Chávez Leyva 1997, 432). In the case of Puerto Ricans, one would have to assess the degree to which island and mainland Puerto Ricans subscribe to coming-out paradigms. As in all other cases, issues of race, class, and gender as well as social and political relationships and context will affect whether individuals adhere to expectations about coming out. Given the historical period when these two women assumed public roles, it is not surprising that they were quiet about their personal relationships.

Pantoja and López Torregrosa experienced a Puerto Rican culture that until recently rendered lesbianism invisible, and in fact tended to silence discussion of any kind of nonreproductive female sexuality. In a study of the construction of heterosexuality in the Puerto Rican penal code since U.S. control, Crespo-Kebler demonstrates that there is scant reference to women's sexuality even in its transgressive mode, to the degree that while the trafficking of prostitutes is addressed and sanctioned by the legal system, it was not until 1983 that the penal code codified the act of prostitution as a crime, and thus for the first time named women as potential agents of sexuality, albeit a "deviant" sexuality (Crespo-Kebler 2003). This silence is also apparent in other parts of Puerto Rican society where male sexuality was endorsed but female sexuality was contained and rendered invisible. As Crespo-Kebler explains, "Female sexuality was associated with sin, witchcraft and classist notions of the supposed promiscuity and immorality of black and poor women" (Crespo-Kebler 2003, 197). Crespo-Kebler argues that the segregation of women and the absence of discussion about female sexuality may in fact have created a space for the generation of women born before 1940 to explore same-sex relations within their closed communities (198). Such relationships, however, were hidden and largely invisible.[24]

Repression of gay and lesbian sexuality was also prevalent in the mainland context. This is perhaps best evidenced by the fact that it was not until 1989 that a gay and lesbian contingent first marched in the Puerto Rican Day parade in New York City. The first gay and lesbian parade took place in Puerto Rico in 1991 amid great controversy. Parades are important because they provide symbolic evidence that queer issues are on the public radar. Negrón-Muntaner and La Fountain-Stokes argue that the development of queer Puerto Rican activism on both the island and stateside must be analyzed side by side, given the colonial situation that binds Puerto Rico and the United States (Negrón-Muntaner 1992; La Fountain-Stokes 1999). Negrón-Muntaner asserts that the queer movement that emerged in Puerto Rico was heavily influenced by the mainstream U.S. gay movement (Negrón-Muntaner 1992). There is little record of pre-1970s gay activism in Puerto Rico, and the movement seems to have really taken off in 1974 in response to the rearticulation of Article 103, which criminalized sodomy between same-sex persons and added a ten-year mandatory sentence to the law. Interestingly, prior to the 1974 revision of the statute, only men could be charged with sodomy; the revision now specified that the statute referred to "sexual relations with persons of the same sex," thus also including and applying to women (Crespo-Kebler 2003, 203). This revision was significant since for the first time it rendered lesbianism visible in Puerto Rican culture at the same time that it criminalized female same-sex behavior.

Feminist movements that evolved in the 1970s began to question more vigorously the silence around sexuality and the rigid construction of femininity and masculinity on the island.[25] While gays and lesbians have always been participants in civil rights work in the Puerto Rican community stateside, it was not until the 1980s that gay and lesbian Puerto Ricans demanded that queer issues be considered part of the Puerto Rican political agenda (Aponte-Parés 2001). The 1990s saw more public discussion about gay issues, thanks largely to political organizing around AIDS. Before that, public disclosure of Puerto Rican gay and lesbian sexuality could be grounds for removing someone from a political organization.

As an activist, Pantoja was most certainly well aware of the pervasive homophobia in political circles, and this may have influenced her decision to stay away from public declarations of her sexuality. López Torregrosa likewise was not interested in publicizing her sexual preference to her family or workmates. External sanctions against homosexuality as well as internalized homophobia seem to have contributed to their decision to downplay their same-sex relationships. These two high-profile women lived in a heterosexist culture that policed queer sexuality through explicit and implicit social controls. One powerful element of this social control that is suggested in these memoirs is discretion shame, specifically fear of exposure of a stigmatized sexual identity. Living in a Puerto Rican context during a historical period when any discussion of sexuality was considered taboo, discretion shame could have conditioned Pantoja and López Torregrosa's silence around sexuality. In addition, as Gopinath suggests is the case for non-Western women (Gopinath 2005), and Quiroga suggests is true for many queer Latin American writers (Quiroga 2000), both Pantoja and López Torregrosa seem to reject the idea that women who love women should present themselves as visible, public lesbians.[26] Rather, other aspects of their identities assume center stage in the telling of their stories.

Race, Class, Nationality, and Shame

While the intersection of nationality, race, class, and sexuality manifests quite differently in the two autobiographies, given Pantoja's and López Torregrosa's divergent racial identification and socioeconomic status, profound feelings of shame affected both their lives. Shame is implicitly suggested in their treatment of sexuality in their memoirs, but is directly named in relation to race, class, and nationality. Pantoja is very conscious of the impact of skin color on her extremely poor family's life. It is not uncommon for Puerto Ricans to argue that race has not been a contentious issue among Puerto Ricans, since Puerto Ricans span a range of phenotypes from White to Black, and thus the argument goes that people of all colors are part of "la gran familia puertorriqueña" (the great, all encompassing Puerto Rican family). However, much scholarship debunks this myth,[27] and documents that while not premised on the Black/White paradigm that characterizes racism in the U.S., Puerto Rican culture has its own racist hierarchy that includes a large, intermediate mixed category.

In Pantoja's memoir, secrets surface, particularly around race and paternity. Her childhood was marked by shame: her mother was unwed and Pantoja did not know for sure who her father was. Pantoja's grandparents disowned their daughter but raised her child. Pantoja bemoans the fact that she never discussed her "illegitimate" birth with her mother. She states, "To this day, I regret not having this conversation with her. I still feel angry at myself for having resorted to the indirectness and mendacity that is so prevalent in the Puerto Rican culture that prevents the asking of questions considered embarrassing to others" (Pantoja 2002, 3). Meanwhile, her dark-skinned mother harbored shameful feelings about her race. The author identifies herself as a "grifa," a light-skinned person with kinky hair (Pantoja 2002, 53). Her mother's anxieties about race led her to fear that one day Antonia, her lighter-skinned daughter, would reject her. Mother and daughter never resolved either issue. Pantoja explains that racism exists in Puerto Rico, but claims that Blacks were never discriminated against as blatantly as she learns is the case in the U.S.; she does not examine the specific context of racism on the island that might explain her mother's fears. For Pantoja, as well as for other Puerto Ricans, racism on the island and in the community is an unexamined, open secret. Pantoja states that she became acquainted with U.S. racism in 1944 during her first trip away from Puerto Rico; she and her friends were humiliated and refused service when they went to a New Orleans café that did not serve Blacks or Mexicans (Pantoja 2002, 53). While critiquing the shame, secrecy, and lack of conversation about issues of race and paternity in her family, Pantoja remains uncritical about silences concerning sexuality, and she does not delve too deeply into the specificity of systemic racism on the island.

López Torregrosa grew up as a privileged child in Puerto Rico, and although she acknowledges this situation, in her memoir she does not seriously interrogate its meaning in her life or in the life of Puerto Ricans who do not enjoy her status. Although her childhood was wracked by her father's violence and her parents' unhappy marriage, she was brought up with the trappings of wealth as the daughter of a doctor and lawyer and as a descendant of an important political family in Puerto Rico. Her childhood included trips abroad, boarding school, and debutante balls. While she recognizes her privilege, unlike her sister Angeles who is a leftist, López Torregrosa proclaims that she is not very interested in politics. She first confronted racism when she moved to New York and struggled to make it on her own without the assistance of her family. She writes, "In a few months in New York, I had learned shame, had learned that being Puerto Rican meant the back kitchen, the bottom, something I had not felt in the Deep South or in Pennsylvania" (López Torregrosa 2004, 225). When an employer at the library where she was working insulted her by lumping her with poor Puerto Ricans despite her class status and education, she seemed more disturbed by the fact that she was placed in this category than by the insult against Puerto Ricans. Rather than articulating a position against the racism leveled at Puerto Ricans in New York, she seemed embarrassed by working-class Nuyoricans.[28] She, along with the rest of her family, was dismayed when her brother married a Nuyorican woman and moved with her to the South Bronx. Given their privileged lifestyles, they wondered how he could become accustomed to the kind of marginal existence they imagine he must be experiencing in the Bronx. While Negrón-Muntaner argues that acknowledging and confronting shame is a precursor to transformation (Negrón-Muntaner 2004), the shame Pantoja and López Torregrosa discuss in relation to their families is named but little scrutinized or linked to systems of oppression. Their feelings of shame and unease around their nationality are explored at greater length.

Both Pantoja and López Torregrosa struggled with ambivalent feelings about their culture and homeland, and both chose a life as exiles in New York. While both women identify as Puerto Rican, their relationship to the nation is complicated by their frustration with the restrictions they felt on the island. They well understood that Puerto Rican women were expected to adhere to conventional expectations of women as wives and mothers, and felt that they had to leave the island in order to live fuller lives. Their ambivalence about Puerto Rico surfaces in various moments in myriad ways. For example, Pantoja explains that she hated the very common form of respect expected from Puerto Rican children, "Bendición," since her mother would expect her to say this to a man she was taken to meet as a young child. The man may have been her father, and Pantoja was embarrassed when she and her mother went to his workplace to request financial support. On the one hand, she critiques the class structure that caused her and others to suffer many humiliations in their attempt to survive and become educated. On the other hand, she accepted some of the social conventions involving conduct because they connoted order and respectability. From childhood on, she was concerned with displaying proper behavior because she understood that lacking money and status, poor people could garner respect based only on their appearance and manners; thus she worked hard to show that she was "bien educada" (well-mannered). This was perhaps more important to her because she must have been aware of the racist associations linking poor Black women to a lack of respectability in Puerto Rico.[29]

Pantoja tried again and again to reconcile her feelings about the island. As someone deeply committed to Puerto Rican people, she tried to make the island her own, but seemed to find Puerto Rico somewhat inhospitable during her several attempts to live there. She returned to the island in the 1970s when she was ill and needed to recuperate in a warm climate. Given all of her education, leadership experiences, and many skills in community-building, she attempted to secure a position in the government. Unfortunately, a conservative political party was in office, and despite her connections, because of her progressive politics she was unable to attain a position. When she set up a business—a guesthouse—with one of her female companions, the obstacles to getting anything done frustrated her. She left the island, disgusted. Toward the end of her life, she and her partner, Wilhelmina Perry, retired to Puerto Rico and got involved in community activism. After living there for fourteen years, they left, convinced that things could not change in Puerto Rico given its colonial status and the dependency that it fosters in the Puerto Rican community. Toward the end of her life Pantoja declared herself a Nuyorican, or someone born or living in the United States but firmly identified with Puerto Rican culture. Interestingly, this is a term that Puerto Ricans born and raised on the island originally used in a disparaging manner in order to differentiate themselves from Puerto Ricans born and raised in the U.S., who were therefore viewed as not "authentic" Puerto Ricans. While it is often Nuyoricans who have had to fight to be considered "real" Puerto Ricans, Pantoja queers this dynamic and claims the term for herself with the affirmative connotation that it has come to have for U.S.-based Puerto Ricans. Her choice to define herself as a Nuyorican, even though she was born in Puerto Rico, is not a rejection of the island but expresses a desire for mobility and freedom from the gender, social, cultural, and sexual repression that she experienced in Puerto Rico, as well as a reflection of her identification with the Nuyorican communities in the U.S. that she dedicated her life to serving.

It is significant that López Torregrosa, absent from Puerto Rico for thirty-five years, returned only when her father died. The last time she had seen her father, when she was in her late twenties, had been a disaster as he had offered to give her 10,000 dollars if she would get married. Shipped off to boarding school in Pennsylvania at fourteen, she sensed herself changing. She didn't miss the island, loved New York (and its "beautiful women"), and claimed that at this time she stopped thinking in Spanish. At sixteen, deciding where to go to college, she realized that she must leave the island to live her own life. She states that she left because she didn't want to live in her parents' shadow, and because she did not want to marry and have children. She continually equates her status-conscious family—especially her father—and the island with stifling repression. She laments, "The island was my family, what I had known, and now the island seemed very small, isolated, too crowded, noisy and dirty, always living in dreams, believing its own lies" (López Torregrosa 2004, 198). As a teenager, she knew that she had to leave the island because of the shame that her sexuality would have caused for her family. Although she does not state it directly, it is clear that even though, unlike Pantoja, López Torregrosa enjoyed class and white-skin privilege, these did not afford her the protection or space to live her own life and enact her same-sex preference on the island. Since she did not share Pantoja's desire to work for the Puerto Rican community, or to live in Puerto Rico, her disconnection from the island seems largely unexamined for most of her life. It is only toward the end of her narrative that she takes up her relationship to Puerto Rico in a way that seems to be largely romantic. In "Imaginary Homelands," Salman Rushdie points out that writers in exile or those who have emigrated are often haunted by the loss of their homeland, and feel a strong desire to reclaim it through their writing. Pantoja does appear to come to terms with her relationship to the island in her memoir, in an arguably queer manner, when she claims the identity of a Nuyorican. López Torregrosa also attempts to work out this relationship, but in her case the connection to the island seems unresolved and nostalgic. At one level López Torregrosa feels the loss of her association to her birthplace and attempts to work this out in her writing. However, as Rushdie cautions, the exile's separation from the homeland inevitably "means that we will not be capable of reclaiming precisely the thing that was lost; that we will in short, create fictions, not actual cities or villages, but invisible ones, imaginary homelands. . . . " (Rushdie 1991, 10). It is only at the end of her book, when López Torregrosa returns for her father's funeral, that she directly considers her relationship to the island and her identity as a Puerto Rican. The feelings she discusses, the longing for the island and the recognition that despite her long absence her roots are in the island, ring hollow given her decades-long absence from Puerto Rico and from her family and her repeatedly proclaimed apathy about the island. Her tribute to the island in the memoir's last pages comes across like unexamined nostalgia, almost like a formula to close the book.

Ultimately, as sexiles, both women felt more at home in New York. In reconfiguring their Puerto Rican identities as New Yorkers, both women queer expectations of Puerto Rican women's narratives. Pantoja proclaims that after a lifelong search for a home, she realizes that she is a Nuyorican. López Torregrosa, while not identifying as a Nuyorican, also identifies New York as home; she says of the city, "I feel totally belonging here and that's difficult for me to feel anywhere" (Kennerley 2004, 4).

Conclusion

However much I, or other queers of color, may want to claim Pantoja and López Torregrosa as our own, we have to acknowledge that they do not position themselves as queer. While we might have hoped that in writing about their queer lives at the beginning of the twenty-first century, they would have viewed their lives from the vantage point of the social changes that have occurred as the result of gay and lesbian activist movements of the last few decades, that is not the story they chose to tell. Perhaps as Quiroga suggests, more important than outing resistant queers is examining how they queered the multiple spaces they moved in. Moreover, he reminds us that it is probably more politically useful to destabilize identity categories than to essentialize them. Crespo-Kebler likewise cautions against setting up normative categories of lesbians, and she invites us to imagine a whole range of possible sexualities and identities. Neither Pantoja nor López Torregrosa embraced a public lesbian identity. López Torregrosa wants her memoir to be read as a "universal story," not a queer example. In an interview with *Gay City News* she clarifies that in her book, she did not want to focus on sexuality and produce a "coming out, tell-all." She states, "I believe this is a universal story, it's not a Latino story, it's not a gay story." Asked about her identity for the same interview, she states: "First, I am a woman. Second, I am a writer. Third, I am an American. Fourth, I am a Puerto Rican. Fifth, I am gay. I am proud of all my identities" (Kennerley 2004). Clearly as persons who occupy multiple identity categories, Pantoja and López Torregrosa can prioritize different identities for strategic reasons depending on the context; not everyone may be comfortable with their choices.

Pantoja makes it clear to her readers that she understands her legacy to be her advocacy work for the Puerto Rican community; this is the imperative that guides her life and her writing.[30] She wants to be remembered as someone who "has spent her life trying to improve the conditions and life chances of people in my community who do not enjoy the rights or respect of other citizens in the society. I wish to be remembered as a person who has lived according to her philosophy, a person who is not a fake" (Pantoja 2002, 137). The last part of this quote, "a person who is not a fake," seems curious in this sentence, and lends itself to a reading in the context of the strategies she employs in her narrative to cover and reveal her private life. However reluctantly, Pantoja chose to reveal her sexuality; she states she did this because she was concerned with being "misinterpreted" and seen as "secretive" (197). In many ways however, these are the repercussions of choosing the strategy of covering. Clearly the shame surrounding the open secret of a queer sexuality had great power over the lives of these two women.

The two memoirs underscore the weight of public secrets and shame, as they complicate the idea of identity that may be expected in a Puerto Rican woman's memoir. The memoirs suggest the intricacies of negotiating multiple identities in public and private contexts. Furthermore, these memoirs compel readers to question our desire to position the authors in conventional categories as prototypical Puerto Rican or lesbian as they queer the space of Puerto Rican women's narratives in multiple ways and around issues beyond sexuality.

. . . .

Lourdes Torres is the Vincent de Paul Professor in Latin American and Latino studies and critical ethnic studies at DePaul University. Her research and teaching interests include sociolinguistics, Spanish in the United States, and Queer Latinidades. She has been the editor of *Latino Studies* since 2012.

Notes

Originally published in *Meridians* vol. 9, no. 1, 2009.

I would like to thank the anonymous readers of this essay for the rich and generous feedback they offered. I am also grateful to Amina Chaudhri and Ann Russo, who provided very helpful comments and suggestions.

1   I do not mean to imply that coming out is entirely risk-free in the present day. The high rate of teen suicide for young people of all colors struggling with issues of sexuality attests to the reality that we still live in a homophobic country. But things have changed, and there is support today in many places for young people who are dealing with queer identifications.

2   Autobiographical works provide a window into the socially and historically constructed world of a community, and help to illuminate the conditions that its members inhabit and transform. Memoirs, particularly memoirs by women of color who are multiply positioned in complex worlds, provide an alternative to mainstream masculinist conceptions of culture and politics. See Smith and Watson 1998 for a history of the development of women's life-writing. The essays in this collection explore the historical significance of women's autobiographical writing, specifically how this genre challenges masculine autobiographical theories and models. They document how recent theories of postcolonialism, postmodernism, agency, and identity-formation have complicated the idea of life-writing. The essays additionally document that self, community, identity, and nation are complex ideas, and that subjectivity and identification are provisional and contested notions.

3   They were most probably both aware that, as La Fountain-Stokes (1999; 2005) describes, non-normative sexuality has been identified as harmful to the national character during many periods in the twentieth century. This viewpoint is expressed in a range of foundational Puerto Rican historical and literary texts, such as the work of Antonio S. Pedreira and René Marques. See also Cruz-Malavé 1995, which discusses the absence of queer writers in Puerto Rican literary history.

4   In this paper I use the terms "lesbian" and "queer" as identity markers. Lesbian is an important term that specifically names women's same-sex desire. Queer is often used as an all-encompassing term that includes those who identify as lesbians, gay men, bisexuals, transgendered, and intersexed. Queer is also a contested term that is ambiguous and unstable, and thus can usefully be deployed to question the categorizing of sexualities itself and as a way of challenging both heteronormative and homonormative constructions of sexuality.

See Rodríguez 2003 for an extensive discussion of the politics of naming and identity practices in the Latino/a queer community.

5   "Boricua" is a term we Puerto Ricans use to identify ourselves. It derives from "Boriken," which was the word that the Taíno Indians used to refer to the island of Puerto Rico before the Spanish colonization. "Boricua" is used by both stateside and island Puerto Ricans.

6   A recent (2007) issue of the *Centro Journal* edited by Luís Aponte-Parés et al. is dedicated to the subject of Puerto Rican queer sexualities; however, as is also the case for most of the literature on Hispanic or Latino sexualities, the majority of the articles address male sexualities. Exceptions to this rule in the case of queer Puerto Rican studies are Fiol-Matta 1986 and Muñiz Couto 1988. Other important work that focuses on Puerto Rican lesbians includes the essays in Hidalgo and Hidalgo-Christensen 1976; Negrón-Muntaner 1992; Crespo-Kebler 2003, as well as Ramos 1994, an anthology of oral histories of Latina lesbians that includes many Puerto Rican lesbian voices. Important Puerto Rican lesbian poets include Liliana Ramos Collado, Nemir Matos, Aixa A. Ardín Pauneto, Ivonne Ochart, and Luz María Umpierre. Agosto, Acevedo, and Negrón 2008 is a groundbreaking collection that includes the work of Puerto Rican queer writers from the island and the diaspora. It features the work of many of these poets and other queer-identified women.

7   Puerto Rico has been a U.S. colony since it was invaded by the United States during the Spanish American War in 1898. Puerto Ricans were granted U.S. citizenship in 1917. This is a second-class citizenship since Puerto Ricans residing on the island do not have voting representation in Congress and cannot vote for president. In 1952, Puerto Rico's status was modified to that of a commonwealth (technically the constitution declares that Puerto Rico is a Free Associated State, although it is neither free nor a state.). As citizens of the United States, Puerto Ricans are free to move back and forth from the island to the mainland. The greatest migration of Puerto Ricans to the U.S. took place in the 1950s and 1960s. Puerto Ricans were encouraged to come to the U.S. to ease unemployment on the island. By 1970, 1.5 million Puerto Ricans lived in the United States. Between 1990 and 2000, the Puerto Rican population in the U.S. grew by 12.5%, from 3.2 to 3.6 million. As of 2005 there were more Puerto Ricans residing stateside than on the island. The colonial relationship between the U.S. and Puerto Rico still obtains, and it is the subject of ongoing debate by Ricans on the island and stateside.

8   See Briggs 2003 for a review of the social-science literature of the 1950s and 1960s that argued that Puerto Ricans were basically immoral, overly sexed, and pathological people whose sexuality had to be controlled and managed.

9   Scheff 2000 reviews theories of shame, and highlights its importance in maintaining social order. See also Probyn 2005 for an exploration of the usefulness of shame across cultures. Probyn writes, "Shame just is. How it is experienced and theorized varies, but nonetheless it is a fact of human life. It is productive in how it makes us think again about bodies, societies, and human interaction.

That shame is both universal and particular, universalizing and particular should be a resource, not a point of division" (Probyn 2005, xviii).

10   See Jolly 2001 on other "queer" autobiographical writing that challenges the expectations of the Western lesbian and gay coming-out story.

11   Colón Warren 2003 provides an extensive overview of feminism and feminist studies in Puerto Rico.

12   See Hallet 1997 for a discussion of how obituaries can work to erase, obscure, or make visible lesbian lives.

13   One of the places where Pantoja does covertly claim her sexuality is in the epilogue of the book. Pantoja declares that she regrets not having time to develop her interest in writing poetry. She includes several poems that she wrote when she was still on the island. One poem with strong lesbian connotations, "Possessing the Virgin Image," was written in 1942 when she was twenty years old. In it the poetic voice is soliciting a virgin lover. She desires that the virgin give in to her urges to deflower her so that her desire will be satisfied. The narrator takes on the persona of an aggressive lover (Pantoja 2002, 194).

14   Pantoja is very close-mouthed about personal relationships. Every now and then she mentions that she spent most of her time working and that she was lonely. She talks about missing the love of a special person in her life. She states that she missed commitment to a special person (Pantoja 2002, 125). In the early part of the narrative she mentions dating some men. Mostly, however, her companions were women.

15   In other words, these are not lesbian coming-out narratives. In such narratives authors emphasize their sexual conversion and the stories focus on sexual identity. According to Plummer 1995, coming-out stories share three elements: suffering, a crisis that precipitates a revelation, and a transformation. Additionally, they are all premised on the idea of a secret that is revealed in the course of the narrative. While secrecy about sexuality is certainly a component of their stories, Pantoja's and López Torregrosa's narratives are not focused on enacting a coming-out ritual. See Martin 1998; Hallet 1999; and Jolly 2001 for discussions of lesbian autobiographies and the significance of coming-out stories.

16   These narratives are very different from life stories of other lesbians of color, such as Moraga 1981 or Lorde 1982, which place lesbian sexuality at the center of their self-narrations, and explore it in the context of race, ethnicity, and class. See Torres 1991 for a discussion of queer sexuality in the autobiographies of Latinas.

17   Apparently Wilhelmina Perry has recently (June 2006) spoken out in favor of gay rights. In a sermon on a website (http://www.rutgerschurch.com/Sermons /sermon061106.html [accessed September 19, 2007]) Reverend Dr. Byron E. Shafer reports that Perry gave testimony at Riverside Church concerning problems she and Pantoja had when Pantoja was close to dying from cancer. Pantoja's family was claiming the right to make final decisions concerning Pantoja's burial place without consulting her partner of thirty years. Perry and Pantoja had to rush to secure legal documents while Pantoja was on her deathbed to

enable Perry to make the decisions that are automatically assumed in the case of married, heterosexual couples.

18   See D'Emilio 1983 for a history of the gay and lesbian movement from the 1940s to the 1970s, and Gallo 2006 for a history of the Daughters of Bilitis.

19   Cohler 2007 examines how many gay writers born in the 1940s and 1950s explain how narratives of shame and silence were replaced with more positive life stories following gay activism in the 1960s and subsequent decades. Fewer narratives seem to exist from women recasting their lives in similar ways. Factors such as race, class, and gender have certainly mitigated the impact of gay radical movements in the lives of women, especially women of color, and have conditioned the likelihood that they might publicly articulate the impact such movements may have had on their lives.

20   See Torres 2007 for a discussion of various forms of passing in a series of Puerto Rican queer texts.

21   See Robinson 1994; Ginsberg 1996; Muñoz 1999; and Schlossberg 2001 for provocative and multidimensional analyses of racial and sexual passing.

22   See, for example, Guzmán 1997; Quiroga 2000; Manalansan 2003; Gopinath 2005; and Guzmán 2005.

23   See also the much-cited Ludmer 1985, which outlines how Sor Juana Inés de la Cruz uses silence as a tactic against repression. Ludmer explores how Sor Juana manipulates silence and turns it against those who seek to muzzle her.

24   Crespo-Kebler (2003) interviewed women born between 1920 and 1940 in Puerto Rico who reported having lesbian relationships while participating in female segregated spaces, such as girls and women's associations, or while being married to men. In all cases women kept these relationships hidden.

25   See Crespo-Kebler and Rivera Lassén 2001 for a history of feminist organizations and mobilization in Puerto Rico during the 1970s.

26   It is clear that neither woman wanted to declare herself publicly a lesbian during her life or while looking back on her life as she wrote her memoir. See Tzu-Chun Wu 2001 for an interesting discussion of Margaret Chung (1898–1959), the first Chinese American woman to become a physician. Tzu-Chun Wu explains that Chung was an unconventional gender bender who had homoerotic relationships but never claimed an identity as a lesbian because she feared losing her stature in the Chinese community.

27   See, for example, Zenon Cruz's classic volume on racist images in Puerto Rican literature and historiography (Zenon Cruz 1975) and Betánces 1972; 1973. For a discussion of race and gender in the Puerto Rican context, see Quiñones Rivera 2006. Godreau (1998; 2000) discusses the range of terms used to refer to race in Puerto Rico and how these terms change in response to the social context. She also discusses how ideologies of whitening (*blanquamiento*) and race-mixing function at the popular and national levels. Duany (2005) suggests that the denial of blackness is a ubiquitous feature of Puerto Rican society, and explores how both Puerto Ricans and Anglo Americans have represented Puerto Rican racial identity over the years.

28 "Nuyorican" is the term that Puerto Ricans from the island use to identify Puerto Ricans who were born and raised in the U.S. While the term originally had negative connotations, in the 1960s and 1970s U.S. born poets and writers such as Pedro Pietri, Tato Laviera, Victor Hernández Cruz, Sandra María Esteves, and Miguel Algarín co-opted Nuyorican as a positive, affirming name for the community.

29 Súarez Findlay (1999) explores the intersectionality of race and class, and examines how class and gender power relations were mediated through race in Puerto Rico at the turn of the century.

30 She states that (at the time of her writing) Puerto Ricans had been in U.S. just over fifty years, and had made important contributions. Because she is well aware that the contributions of Latinos to their community-building efforts are largely ignored in mainstream publications, Pantoja states that she writes to make visible her efforts and those of other Puerto Ricans who have struggled to improve their community (Pantoja 2002, 136).

Works Cited

Agosto, Moisés, David Caleb Acevedo, and Luís Negrón, eds. 2008. *Los otros cuerpos: Antología de temática gay, lésbica y queer.* Río Piedras: Librería Isla.

Aponte-Parés, Luís. 2001. "Outside/In Crossing Queer and Latino Boundaries." In *Mambo Montage,* edited by Agustin Laó-Montes and Arlene Dávila. New York: Colombia University Press.

———et al., eds. 2007. *Puerto Rican Queer Sexualities. Centro Journal* 19, no. 1.

Bátances, Samuel. 1972. "The Prejudice of Having No Prejudice in Puerto Rico." Part 1. *The Rican* 2: 41–54.

———. 1973. "The Prejudice of Having No Prejudice in Puerto Rico." Part 2. *The Rican* 3: 22–37.

Briggs, Laura. 2003. *Reproducing Empire: Race, Sex, Science, and U.S. Imperialism in Puerto Rico.* Berkeley: University of California Press.

Chávez Leyva, Yolanda. 1997. "Listening to the Silence." In *Living Chicana Theory,* edited by Carla Trujillo. Berkeley: University of California Press.

Cohen, Cathy. 2005. "Punks, Bulldaggers, and Welfare Queens: The Radical Potential of Queer Politics." In *Black Queer Studies: A Critical Anthology,* edited by E. Patrick Johnson and Mae G. Henderson. Durham, NC: Duke University Press.

Colón Warren, Alice. 2003. "Puerto Rico: Feminism and Feminist Studies." *Gender and Society* 17, no. 5: 664–90.

Cohler, Bertram. 2007. *Writing Desire: Sixty Years of Gay Autobiography.* Madison: University of Wisconsin Press.

Crenshaw, Kimberlé. 1991. "Mapping the Margins: Intersectionality, Identity Politics, and Violence against Women of Color." *Stanford Law Review* 43, no 6: 1241–99.

Crespo-Kebler, Elizabeth. 2003. "'The Infamous Crime Against Nature': Constructions of Heterosexuality and Lesbian Subversions in Puerto Rico." In *The Culture of Gender and Sexuality in the Caribbean,* edited by Linden Lewis. Gainesville: University Press of Florida.

Crespo-Kebler, Elizabeth, and Ana Irma Rivera Lassén. 2001. *Documentos del feminismo en Puerto Rico: Facsímiles de la historia, Volumen 1 (1970–1979)*. Río Piedras: University of Puerto Rico.

Cruz-Malavé, Arnaldo. 1995. "Toward an Art of Transvestism: Colonialism and Homosexuality in Puerto Rican Literature." In *¿Entiendes? Queer Readings, Hispanic Contexts*, edited by Emile Bergman and Paul Julian Smith. Durham, NC: Duke University Press.

———. 2007. *Queer Latino Testimonio, Keith Haring, and Juanito Xtravaganza*. New York: Palgrave.

Decena, Carlos Ulises. 2008. "Tacit Subject." *GLQ: A Journal of Lesbian and Gay Studies* 14, no. 2–3: 339–60.

Duany, Jorge. 2005. "Neither Black nor White: The Representation of Racial Identity among Puerto Ricans on the Island and in the U.S. Mainland." In *Neither Enemies nor Friends: Latinos, Blacks, Afro-Latinos*, edited by Anani Dzidzienyo and Suzanne Oboler. New York: Palgrave MacMillan.

D'Emilio, John. 1983. *The Making of a Homosexual Minority in the United States, 1940–1970*. Chicago: University of Chicago Press.

Duques, Andrés. 2002. "She is Survived by Her Partner: An Op-Ed Piece." *GLAAD*. August. http://www.glaad.org/publications/resource_doc_detail (accessed September 15, 2005).

Feinberg, Leslie. 1993. *Stone Butch Blues*. Ithaca, NY: Firebrand Books.

Fiol-Matta, Lía. 1986. "Análisis sobre el control de la sexualidad de la mujer: Estudio del lesbianismo en Puerto Rico." M.A. thesis, Universidad de Puerto Rico, Río Piedras.

Gallo, Marcia. 2006. *Different Daughters: A History of the Daughters of Bilitis and the Rise of the Lesbian Rights Movement*. New York: Seal Press.

Ginsberg, Elaine. 1996. *Passing and the Fiction of Identity*. Durham, NC: Duke University Press.

Godreau, Isar. 1998. "Missing the Mix: San Anton and the Racial Dynamics of 'Nationalism' in Puerto Rico." Ph.D. dissertation, University of California, Santa Cruz.

———. 2000. "La semantica fugitiva: Raza, color y vida cotidiana en Puerto Rico." *Revista de Ciencias Sociales* 9: 52–71.

Goffman, Erving. 1974. *Stigma: Notes on the Management of Spoiled Identity*. New York: Jason Aronson, Inc.

Gopinath, Gayatri. 2005. *Impossible Dreams*. Durham, NC: Duke University Press.

Guzmán, Manuel. 1997. "'Pa'La Escuelita con Mucho Cuida'o y por la Orillita'o': A Journey through the Contested Terrains of the Nation and Sexual Orientation." In *Puerto Rican Jam: Essays on Culture and Politics*, edited by Frances Negrón-Muntaner and Ramón Grosfoguel. Minneapolis: University of Minnesota Press.

Guzmán, Manolo. 2006. *Gay Hegemonies/Latino Homosexualities*. New York: Routledge.

Hallet, Nicky. 1999. *Lesbian Lives: Identity and Auto/biography in the Twentieth Century*. London: Pluto Press.

Hidalgo, Hilda, and Elia Hidalgo-Christensen. 1976. "The Puerto Rican Lesbian and the Puerto Rican Community." *Journal of Homosexuality* 2 (Winter): 109–21.

Jolly, Margaretta. 2001. "Coming Out of the Coming Out Story: Writing Queer Lives." *Sexualities* 4, no. 4: 474–96.

Kennerley, David. 2004. "One Woman's Elegy to Her Destiny." In *Gay City News*. http// www.gaycitynews.com/gen_318/asoundtrackforthe.html (accessed September 20, 2005).

La Fountain-Stokes, Lawrence. 1999. "1898 and the History of a Queer Puerto Rican Century: Gay Lives, Island Debates, and Diasporic Experiences." *Centro Journal* 11, no. 1 (Fall): 91–109.

———. 2005. "Cultures of the Puerto Rican Queer Diaspora." In *Passing Lines: Sexuality and Immigration*, edited by Brad Epps, Keja Valens, and Bill Johnson Gonzalez. Cambridge, MA: The David Rockefeller Center Series on Latin America.

Lewis, Oscar. 1966. *La Vida: A Puerto Rican Family in the Culture of Poverty—San Juan and New York*. New York: Random House.

López Torregrosa, Luisita. 2004. *The Noise of Infinite Longing: A Memoir of a Family — and an Island*. New York: HarperCollins.

Lorde, Audre. 1982. *Zami, A New Spelling of My Name*. Watertown, MA: Persephone Press.

Ludmer, Josefina. 1985. "Las tretas del débil." In *La Sarten por el mango: Encuentro de escritoras Latinoamericanas*, edited by Patricia Elena González and Eliana Ortega. San Juan: Ediciones Huracán.

Manalansan IV, Martin. 2003. *Global Divas*. Durham, NC: Duke University Press.

Marler, Regina. 2004. "My Mother, Myself: A Lesbian Daughter Provides a Rare Glimpse into Puerto Rican Family Life in a Somewhat Disconnected Memoir." *The Advocate* (March 30): 38.

Martin, Biddy. 1998. "Lesbian Identity and Autobiographical Differences." In *Woman, Autobiography, Theory: A Reader*, edited by Sidonie Smith and Julia Watson. Madison: University of Wisconsin Press.

Moraga, Cherríe. 1981. *Loving in the War Years*. Boston: South End Press.

Muñiz Couto, Doris. 1988. "Análisis de las experiencias y dificultades de mujeres lesbianas en Puerto Rico en un grupo de discussion: Hacia un vision liberadora del lesbianismo." M.A. thesis, Universidad de Puerto Rico, Rio Piedras.

Muñoz, José. 1999. *Disidentifications: Queers of Color and the Performance of Politics*. Minneapolis: University of Minnesota Press.

Negrón-Muntaner, Frances. 1992. "Echoing Stonewall and Other Dilemmas: The Organizational Beginnings of a Gay and Lesbian Agenda in Puerto Rico, 1972–1977." *Centro Journal* 4, no. 1: 77–95.

———. 2004. *Boricua Pop*. New York: New York University Press.

Pantoja, Antonia. 2002. *Memoir of a Visionary*. Houston: Arte Público Press.

Plummer, Ken. 1995. *Telling Sexual Stories: Power, Change and Social Worlds*. London: Routledge.

Probyn, Elspeth. 2005. *Blush: Faces of Shame*. Minneapolis: University of Minnesota Press.

Quiñones Rivera, Maritza. 2006. "From Trigueñita to Afro-Puerto Rican: Intersections of the Racialized, Gendered, and Sexualized Body in Puerto Rico and the U.S. Mainland." *Meridians* 7, no. 1: 162–82.

Quiroga, José. 2000. *Tropics of Desire*. New York: New York University Press.

Ramos, Juanita, ed. 1994. *Compañeras: Latina Lesbians*. New York: Routledge.

Robinson, Amy. 1994. "It Takes One to Know One: Passing and Communities of Common Interest." *Critical Inquiry* 20 (Summer): 715–36.

Rodríguez, Juana María. 2003. *Queer Latinidad: Identity Practices, Discursive Spaces*. New York: New York University Press.

Ross, Marlon. 2005. "Beyond the Closet as Raceless Paradigm." In *Queer Black Studies*, edited by E. Patrick Johnson and Mae G. Henderson. Durham, NC: Duke University Press.

Rushdie, Salman. 1991. *Imaginary Homelands: Essays and Criticism 1981–1991*. London: Granta.

Scheff, Thomas. 2000. "Shame and the Social Bond: A Sociological Theory." *Sociological Theory* 18, no. 1 (March): 84–99.

Schlossberg, Linda. 2001. "Introduction: Rites of Passing." In *Passing: Identity and Interpretation in Sexuality, Race, and Religion*, edited by María Carla Sánchez and Linda Schlossberg. New York: New York University Press.

Schneider, Carl. 1977. *Shame, Exposure, and Privacy*. Boston: Beacon Press.

Smith, Sidonie, and Julia Watson, eds. 1998. *Women, Autobiography, Theory: A Reader*. Madison: University of Wisconsin Press.

Súarez Findley. 1999. *Imposing Decency: The Politics of Sexuality and Race in Puerto Rico*. Durham, NC: Duke University Press.

Sullivan, Andrew. 1995. *Virtually Normal*. New York: Vintage Press.

Taussig, Michael. 1999. *Defacement: Public Secrecy and the Labor of the Negative*. Palo Alto: Stanford University Press.

Torres, Lourdes. 1991. "The Construction of Self in U.S. Latina Autobiographies." In *Third World Women and the Politics of Feminism*, edited by Chandra Mohanty, Ann Russo, and Lourdes Torres. Bloomington: University of Indiana Press.

———. 2007. "Boricua Lesbians: Sexuality, Nationality, and the Politics of Passing." *Centro: Journal of the Center for Puerto Rican Studies* 2, no. 2 (Spring 2007): 230–59.

Tzu-Chun Wu, Judy. 2001. "Was Mom Chung a 'Sister Lesbian'? Asian American Gender Experimentation and Interracial Homoeroticism." *Journal of Women's History* 13, no. 1: 58–82.

Warner, Michael. 1999. *The Trouble with Normal*. Cambridge, MA: Harvard University Press.

Yoshino, Kenji. 2006. *Covering: The Hidden Assault on Our Civil Rights*. New York: Random House.

Zenón Cruz, Isabelo. 1975. *Narciso descubre su trasero: El negro en la cultura puertorriqueña*. Humacao, Puerto Rico: Furidi.

Laurie Ann Guerrero

How I Put Myself through School

There is a label specifically for organic meats and caviar
on the refrigerator shelf of the woman whose house I clean.

Another on a rack for the well-traveled chardonnays and sauvignons,
below the crystal champagne flutes, reminding me what goes where.

I systematize her cupboards and nail-clipping-infested junk drawer,
while her children, the underweight, disobedient *darlings*, stare

as I reshelve their dolls and brand-new books. Stare as their mother
stares. Stare as I pour the ajo y cebolla of my blood into a pot of rice

that will end up in the trash because of its spice. Stare as I shake
the wrinkles out of faded cotton panties and boxer shorts—

the lingering heat of the dryer taking me to a bedroom
I never wanted to be in. Sweat beading at the bridge of my nose,

I accept the clothes she collects in trash bags for my daughters
who are younger but much bigger, knowing they will never fit,

and wonder, if she could, would she pierce the skin of my gut,
scrape the eggs from my womb, spread them like a good Beluga,

MERIDIANS · feminism, race, transnationalism Volume 19 Supplement 2020
DOI: 10.1215/15366936-8566012 © 2009 Smith College

eliminating me and any other chance at adding to the fiery Chicanitas
who ask, *Why do you take her used things, Mama?*

. . . .

Laurie Ann Guerrero was born and raised in the Southside of San Antonio. She was
an Ada Comstock Scholar at Smith College and took her MFA from Drew University.
A CantoMundo fellow and member of the Macondo Writers Workshop, Guerrero has
served on the faculty at the University of the Incarnate Word, University of Texas–El
Paso, Palto Alto College, and Gemini Ink, a community-centered literary arts organization in San Antonio. She was appointed poet laureate of San Antonio in 2014, and
poet laureate of the state of Texas in 2016.

Note

Originally published in *Meridians* vol. 9, no. 1, 2009. A revised version of this
poem was subsequently published in Guerrero's chapbook *A Tongue in the Mouth
of the Dying* (2013).

Nancy Marie Mithlo

....

"A Real Feminine Journey"
Locating Indigenous Feminisms in the Arts

Abstract: Despite the prevailing acceptance of homogenized global sensibilities in media productions, many American Indian and other indigenous artists continue to articulate a sovereign, bounded, and discrete identity based on land, family, and memory. Both material (embodied knowledge) and ideological (the interconnectedness of people, the earth, and culture) constructs enable communal paradigms rather than individualistic or gendered identities to rise to the fore. Given these parameters, how can the testimonies of native women's lives as artists inform debates of indigenous feminisms? Drawing from Native women artists' narratives, transnational feminist scholarship, and ethnographic and historical texts, the author demonstrates how indigenous communities become gendered communities as a result of colonialism.

Can Gender Exist outside of Culture? Sites of Struggle

I've been talking about pottery-making as a real feminine journey. And I've been talking about my ties to my community as a very feminine, symbolic connection. It's all about . . . I don't know what it's all about, but it has to do with femaleness in a big way. Femaleness, femaleness. My community is female. My culture is female. I'm female. My art-making is female. Everything is female and it's very interesting and important to me that you can crown it all with one big bow by saying, "Yeah, I've got this cord that I'm symbolically tied to my community, and by the way, my

MERIDIANS · feminism, race, transnationalism   Volume 19 Supplement 2020
DOI: 10.1215/15366936-8566023 © 2009 Smith College

artwork is a part of that symbolic cord, and I can't ever stray from it because I know where I belong." In the most . . . I don't want to get away from it. Because I know who I am, and I know where I'm at, and I know where I've got to be. (Naranjo 1991)

Tessie Naranjo's poetic description of herself as a female, an artist, and a cultural person resonates with a certainty, a sense of place and belonging. Her narrative creates a bounded space; a gendered assertion of identity tied to place, process, and community. This simultaneous claiming of the feminine and of tribal responsibility signals a sensibility that runs counter both to implied requisite freedoms of the modern artist as well as to societal resistances championed by Western feminist ideologies (Okin et al. 1999). Naranjo's symbolic cord presents an image that is representative of female fertility and reproduction (as in the umbilical cord), while also claiming recognition of that which sustains life—the larger community of Santa Clara pueblo. She does not resist association with the consumer of her work in the style of a contemporary artist, nor does she oppose her community of origin as an oppressive structure. This uncompromising allegiance to community appears to challenge feminist demands for equal rights against the "unequal power arrangements in society, in particular, a societal system in which men and masculine qualities are more highly valued and privileged than women and femininity" (Williams 2000, 9).

Naranjo's text collapses the feminine and community in ways that resist standard binaries in arts practice (artistic freedom vs. commercial success) and feminist dialogues (male control, female subordination). How do the variables of gender and culture inform indigenous identity in the arts? Referencing Naranjo's passage, can gender even be said to exist outside of, or dissociated from, culture? Both the cognitive categories employed (such as the standard conceptual frameworks of individual and community allegiances as separate and alienated categories) and the social and political aims championed (Native American arts as expressive of Native identity as well as providing income) demand inquiry. Naranjo's holistic orientation tells of the challenges inherent in interpreting contemporary Native women artists' lives. Although their experience is grounded in the realities of indigenous womanhood and arts commerce, Native women in the arts are not easily defined either as fine artists or feminists. In fact, the women I interviewed generally dismissed any form of labeling altogether.[1]

Susan M. Williams and Joy Harjo note, "Feminism is not a word found in tribal languages" (Williams and Harjo 1998, 198). Although the assertion that feminism is not compatible with indigenous values has more recently been questioned by aboriginal scholars who find increasing similarities with other feminists of color, the critical debates about this intersection are far from being mapped or fully developed as theory. The assumption that traditional gender relations (characterized as egalitarian, complementary, or matriarchal) have survived colonialism is now fully exposed as a questionable assertion (St. Denis 2007), yet the parameters of this overlap remain largely unarticulated.

In my conceptualization of these questions, I have been challenged by other women of color scholars to assign feminist identities to my research, even when Native American women did not self-describe as such. Although I have benefited greatly from my exposure to transnational feminist discourse,[2] ethically I feel I cannot pursue this type of labeling. Legacies of appropriations in Native communities (appropriations of land, language, spirituality, even human bodies) dictate that respect be shown to people's own self-designations. I can and do, however, explore how multiple forms of feminist ideologies may be viewed as variously applicable or inaccurate in understanding indigenous worldviews.

Given these multiple conceptual challenges, why do I choose to pursue an inquiry specific to Native American women in the arts? What can be drawn from this privileged positioning? I argue that if contemporary Native arts are to be considered as a political manifestation of cultural identity, communal referents (tribal, pan-tribal, family) therefore take precedence over individual achievements (prestige, individual advancement). In this respect and according to these frames of reference, contemporary Native women artists exhibit an uncompromising allegiance to their extended lives as mothers, tradition-bearers, and wage-earners. As image-makers, Native women who refuse to dissociate themselves from their identities as women and as tribal members are positioned to make more salient social and political commentaries than are either their non-Native or male Native peers.

I argue that in Native arts, a denial or diminishing of community allegiances in an effort to be considered a fine artist ("Artist First, Indian Second") does not simply affect agency but also reinforces false paradigms of artistic freedoms that are applied unequally to artists of color. The assumption that indigenous artists must choose one role over another (artist or Indian) evidences racist typecasting of one-dimensional, historical, and non-contemporaneous identities. Likewise, the dismissal of common female attributions, including fertility, softness, or domesticity (relegation to craft) does not erase these qualities from the public's imagination nor does it necessarily empower women who may choose to distance themselves from overt expressions of tribal sensibilities. The cultural values of gender and economics in the arts are both constitutive of and reactive to established paradigms of knowledge. These multiple sites of knowledge have the opportunity to be contested in the social arena of arts production and consumption, thereby allowing for highly charged articulations of identity claims. Qualities such as femaleness, maleness, isolation, belonging, and community find voice in these moments where conflicting ideologies meet.

The privileging of a tribal identity as more relevant than other descriptive terms such as educational status, gender, or age is illustrated in the following passage from Naranjo's interview in 2000. My interview trajectory with artists followed my experience as an American Indian student, and later researcher, professor, and museum director at the Santa Fe, New Mexico-based Institute of American Indian Arts, a tribal college. Over a twenty-year period, I established relationships with Native artists in the urban arts hub of Santa Fe that formed the basis of my dissertation research in cultural anthropology at Stanford University in 1993. In the ten years since I had previously interviewed her, Naranjo had completed a Ph.D. in sociology at the University of New Mexico. Our relationship was in part defined by our shared experience of working on graduate degrees concurrently, and I was curious as to how her academic achievements may have informed her ideas of self-identity.

> **NM:** I was wondering, do you now call yourself something different, like if someone says, you're giving a paper at a conference and they want you to put something in parentheses, do you now choose to say, sociologist, artist, tribal person, woman, how do you handle that?
>
> **TN:** How do I define myself?
>
> **NM:** Yeah.
>
> **TN:** Um, (pause) it's neat that you ask that question. And people have asked me, every time there's a presentation to be made they say "How do I introduce you?" And I say I have a passion for community, I have a passion for family. Please tell in your introduction that I am from the community and I am very much a part of my extended family. So that's what they'll do. In terms of the labeling, the Ph.D. thing, I almost never use it to define myself. I just say that I'm Tessie Naranjo and as

far as a sociologist is concerned, almost never do I say that but I do
know that privately they have impacted my life so, so significantly, but
that's my private experience. For the public world, I don't need to; I
don't need to define myself in that way. In fact, I almost . . . well, for
sure, I prefer not to. I prefer not to because it is almost as if you are
(sigh) depending on those labels to define you and I don't need to have
those labels define me. But I do need to let the rest of the world know I
am from Santa Clara Pueblo and I am a woman who treasures the wisdom of our past and who treasures the wisdom of what we still have,
and those are the ways that I work. (Naranjo 2000a)

I heighten Naranjo's narratives to explore how the multiple identities of
tribal person, artist, and woman intersect in meaningful ways. I am careful
to delineate the manner in which these connections appear to contradict
prevailing intellectual trends in feminist theory, art criticism, and cultural
studies. For example, although hybridity is heralded as a normative reference for contemporary arts dialogues, tribal communities claim segmented spaces. Art historian Lucy Lippard's Mixed Blessings claimed that
"Faced with the facts of nomadism and displacement, many artists are
trying to form a new hybrid cultural identity and to locate themselves
therein," adding that tribalism in its exclusive sense "is a perverted,
embattled form of community" (Lippard 1990, 153). More recently, Native
theorists have championed similar post-Indian sentiments in the curation
of contemporary art exhibits (Mithlo 2007). By comparison, Naranjo writes
of tribalism as an organic philosophy of life, "The notion of the container is
crucial to the worldview of the pueblo. The lower half of our cosmos is a pot
that contains life, the womb of the mother. The notion of containment also
is evident in the pueblo plaza, which contains outdoor community activities and is bounded by the house forms and the hills and the mountains"
(Naranjo 2000b).

Despite the prevailing acceptance of homogenized global sensibilities
in media productions, many Native American and other indigenous artists
continue to articulate a sovereign, bounded, and discrete identity based on
land, family, and memory. A continued sense of separateness prevails, fully
positioned in the unique status of tribal nations and their special relationship to the federal government. This boundedness, however, cannot be
interpreted as static; belonging is not enforced but rather is employed
according to political, technical, economic, and educational developments

and changes in the world at large. Both material and ideological constructs enable communal paradigms rather than individualistic or gendered identities to rise to the fore.

If gendered identities are conceptualized as part of the totality of communal identity, then what relevance can feminist theory have for Native women? Given the separate ideological constructs of how gender "works" in tribal communities, can the experience of Native women ever be comprehensible to feminist inquiries that often premise their arguments on the universal oppression of women? Adopting Naranjo's perspective, if the whole world is feminine then how relevant can feminist thought be?

This essay will track certain moments when feminist theory has drawn from Native women's experience to see what aspects of Native women's lives seemed to have relevance for feminist thought. Similarly, indigenous women's narratives will be assessed for indications of feminist ideologies and their relevance to indigenous rights. My research suggests that the crossover applications between feminist theory and indigenous knowledge systems for which productive theory-making may be structured include: intersectionality (often defined as holism in Native contexts), universality (or community values), and identity claims (including art-making and performance).

My parameters locate this discussion in light of ethnography, feminist literature, indigenous rights discourses, and cultural theory. Although parallel developments in feminist art history may be pertinent to this exercise, the field's current lack of sustained engagement with indigenous communities at this time positions this body of literature outside of my present inquiry. I have therefore situated my discussions in places that are both inclusive of indigenous content and that advance a politically engaged and thus highly contextual inquiry. A traditional art-historical analysis of form alone cannot accomplish my goal of advancing an embodied theoretical analysis. Likewise, although the major geographical focus of this essay is Native North America (where the majority of my research is based), the voices of theorists whose works have become central to American Indian studies discourses—voices from Mexico, Hawaii, New Zealand, Africa, Bolivia, and Canada—are included as well. My field of inquiry is not defined by existing academic disciplines, geography, or nationhood, but by the logic of contemporary theorists committed to a just and politically salient indigenous research methodology.

Appropriations, Exclusions, Self-segregations

Henrietta L. Moore defines feminist anthropology as "more than the study of women"; it is rather "the study of gender, of the interrelations between women and men, and the role of gender in structuring human societies, their histories, ideologies, economic systems and political structures" (Moore 1988, 6). Moore describes how the deconstruction of the social category of "woman" led feminist anthropology to "formulate . . . theoretical questions in terms of how economics, kinship, and ritual are experienced and structured through gender, rather than asking how gender is experienced and structured through culture" (9). Contrary to the inseparable identities of femaleness and culture demonstrated by Naranjo's opening passage, within this construct gender concepts are prioritized.

The lack of a critical inclusion of racial identities in early hegemonic feminist theory led Black feminist scholars such as Irma McClaurin-Allen to charge that feminist debates of the 1970s acknowledged the influence of race and class in the production of gender, but often treated them as " 'epiphenomenal,' ignoring the fact that the particular way in which women define themselves and experience gender oppression arises out of a cultural history shaped and determined by race, class, and particular events." Importantly for my argument, McClaurin-Allen describes these identity attributes as "inextricable from one another" (McClaurin-Allen 1990, 316). Black feminist ideology of this period argued for a consideration of "dialectical interrelations of race, class, and gender," and in particular how forms of social inequality are "created, manipulated, and incorporated into individual identities" (316). A concern with individual experience rather than institutions of dominance was advocated as a way to gain new perspectives on the contradictions within systems of social inequality.

My inquiry finds affinity with McClaurin-Allen's impulse to locate the intersections of various identity constructs within individual women's lives, yet the experience of individual Native women's lives alone problematically marginalizes communal rights inherent in nationhood and fails to recognize the unique history of genocidal practices exercised in policies of colonialism. Andrea Smith argues for the agency of indigenous women in an account of feminist history that begins in 1492 when Native women collectively resisted colonization (Smith 2005).

Although Black feminist paradigms have become central to a genealogy of feminist theoretical developments over time (including the use of intersectionality and positionality described above), indigenous ideologies have remained largely outside of the feminist mainstream. I believe that this separate narration of Native women's experiences is attributable to both internal self-segregation and external exclusion. By exclusion, I refer specifically to the lack of serious engagement with Native American intellectual traditions with respect to gender analysis.

Native women's lives and bodies have historically been incorporated into the Western feminist movement as an expedient means of advancing predetermined theoretical aims, but not often as a viable alternative dimension of gender analysis. In a related manner, Native American activists and scholars have often themselves claimed a unique space apart from a totalizing gender discourse that appeared unwilling or unable to accommodate an interrogation of central feminist tenets.[3] For example, when I questioned Santa Clara Roxanne Swentzell about her conception of her career trajectory over the past decade, she responded by imparting an appreciation of lived knowledge over abstract thought:

> The last ten years . . . (long pause) I think more clearer [sic] on what it is that I'm doing. And what I find . . . when I was younger . . . I thought I knew more than I know. And I suspect that as I get older I'll even feel that more. And, life seems to be of those very, very mundane small things that happen and it becomes more and more that way, stronger and stronger to me. So it's like when you talk about a male mind vs. a female mind, it's almost like, to me it's proving itself too, that it's less and less ideal. It's more like these really little things.

> Like I noticed, instead of these big goals that I have in life, even as a woman, a goal looks like, "I'm going to make this home for my kids," or women's goals, whatever; it gets more and more like, I'll stop and pick up a little piece of trash, even if I'm in a hurry. And before, "I'll pick those up when I get, next week, we'll go around the yard picking up trash, all of us." No, it's almost like, no, it's right now. I'll just stop and pick up that gum wrapper. And that's real significant to me, like it's never been. And if anything changed, that was really changed. It's very now. And it's just these tiny little things because I can't put my life on my kids, I can't put my life on my art, my name. I can't put . . . it's just these very, very little things (Swentzell 2000).

In this passage, a life fully lived is a life that is noticed, experienced in the *now*, rather than in an abstracted knowledge, separate from the business of living and appreciating each moment. But even beyond this hesitancy to disassociate oneself from the immediacy of life, there is concurrent recognition of identity that goes beyond the typical variables of home, children, career, and even gender. Identity in this respect is a holistic experience of thought, presence, and being, enacted in a physical location, in this case the Santa Clara pueblo. This very sophisticated ideology cannot be easily accommodated within existing frameworks of feminism, gender, or the arts. This multiple way of being present in the world is accessible only through careful attention to the intersections of these approaches, with indigenous voices as primary knowledge conveyors, as central subjects rather than objects of study.

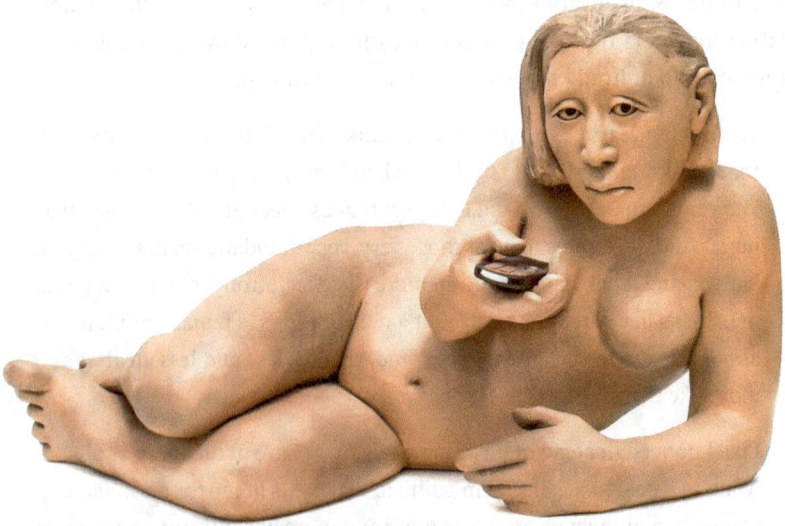

Roxanne Swentzell, *Remote Woman—I'm Getting That Far Away Feeling Again* (1996). Ceramic, 12×12×14 in. Photograph by Walter BigBee, The Big Picture.

Julia Emberley describes how aboriginal women's literature in Canada resists alignment with "the colonialist assumptions in academic feminist theory," claiming that feminist theory of the 1980s "failed to consider what Aboriginal women said about their particular concerns within the movement" (Emberley 1996, 100). This problem is characterized as one of inequality—the "academically privileged" exercise imperialist, "first worldist" feminist practices such as "elitist lament for the marginality and dispossession of Aboriginal women," while aboriginal peoples who have systemically been excluded from higher education serve as the ground—

the oppressed (102). Likewise, Andrea Smith charges that "even within feminist circles, the colonial logic prevails that women of color, indigenous women, and women from Global South countries are only victims of oppression rather than organizers in their own right" (Smith 2005, 25). Lee Maracle writes, "Until white women can come to us on our own terms, we ought to leave the door closed. Do we really want to be part of a movement that sees the majority as the periphery and the minority as the centre?" (Maracle 1996, 138–39).

This character of exploitation thus seems to form a circular pattern of exclusions whereby indigenous women serve as raw data for feminist theorizing (and at times, political gain) while concurrently, indigenous knowledges (in large part due to exclusionary academic hierarchies) remain unincorporated. Subsequently, Native women themselves withdraw or mark clear boundaries outside of perceived elitist feminist spheres of belonging.

Contemporary critiques of hegemonic feminisms reflect the broadening of the field to include transnational feminist ideologies and increasing consideration of indigenous values and activism, rather than tribally specific histories. Sylvia Marcos examines the dominant discourse of urban feminism in Mexico that "portrays indigenous women as passive, submissive subjects, bound to inevitable patriarchal oppression springing from their cultural background" (Marcos 2005, 81). She cites two contradictory phenomena emerging in Mexican social movements. Although the Mexican feminist movement has participated more in international women's movements due to globalization, a new recognition and reappraisal of the indigenous (as evident in the Zapatista uprising) has developed concurrently. Marcos identifies the tensions resulting from "a new breach between elite feminists who travel, consult, interact, and negotiate with the international feminist voices (frequently from the 'North') and the grassroots poor and/or indigenous women" (84–85).

In a similar manner, Obioma Nnaemeka critiques the "intellectual gymnastics and empty theorizing in feminist scholarship" and its lack of engagement with social utility (Nnaemeka 2003, 64). She specifically notes the epistemological divide between African women as "knowledge producers and as subjects/objects for knowledge production" (66). Nnaemeka argues that third-world women are often banished in gender and international rights publications to case-study and country-specific locations, which implies that "these women can speak only to the issues pertaining to the specific countries from whence they come and do not have the capacity to dabble in the intricacies of theory as an intellectual, scientific abstraction." She charges that this allocation of tasks is "colonial both in intent and execution" (67).

Nnaemeka advocates "building on the indigenous" by locating feminisms in Africa as dynamic acts—as a "third space" where negotiation, compromise, and balance are mobilized—as opposed to Western feminisms that tend toward challenging, deconstructing, and disrupting normative sexual politics. She illustrates the third space in her description of the women's studies department at Makerere University, Uganda that functions in a gendered context ("a healthy mix of men and women") rather than the feminized environment of women's studies in the West ("all/almost all female"). She notes how complementarity as an indigenous concept informs everyday practice for African women as a "willingness and readiness to negotiate with and around men even in difficult circumstances" (Nnaemaka 2003, 79–80).

Dorothy Goldin Rosenberg suggests that traditional cultural paradigms (especially women's indigenous knowledges) be "reclaimed" within ecological feminisms. Rosenberg's advocacy for moving away from patriarchal biomedical models, militarism, and environmental racism and toward holistic health and traditional well-being is politically progressive yet lacking in a nuanced reading of an indigenous-knowledge-systems approach. Indigenous knowledges in this example are highly generalized: "The spiritual traditions of native peoples, Africans, Asians, and other cultural groups, and the pre-Christian traditions that survived in Europe, shared a common world view in which the sacred was seen as a part of the living world" (Rosenberg 2000, 140). Although transnational inquiries are often effective in challenging globalized systems of inequality, the inclination to enter totalizing paradigms diminishes the overall weight of these arguments.

A review of these data reveals that Native American women (and by extension in recent scholarship, indigenous women) have historically been represented as cultured, exotic others, inserted into existing feminist paradigms for the political, social, and intellectual advancement of non-Natives. Early blatant examples of appropriations from the suffragist movement and second-wave feminisms suggest that recognition of these selective borrowings or even a formal apology may offer a productive route for reconciliation between mainstream elite feminists and Native American communities.[4] However, contested spaces and conflicting ideologies appear remarkably persistent even in recent scholarship.

When contemporary theorists suggest that they can "build upon" (Nnaemeka), "draw from" (Rosenberg), and "help" (Marcos) indigenous women, a danger zone of active and passive participation is created. The writings of each of these contemporary feminist scholars reflect a deep concern and engagement with indigenous communities; each recognizes the liabilities of encompassing Native realities into hegemonic, urban, elite feminist movements. Yet there is a sense of distance, of token engagement rather than a deep, prolonged exchange between equals. Nnaemeka's isolated reference of the Igbo spirit figure *nmanwu* as an illustration of indigenous wisdom and complexity accomplishes too little; Rosenberg's totality of holistic religions assumes too much. Marcos's confession that the Zapatismo indigenous women's law was for her "like a dream come true" because it bridged her own interests in indigenous and feminist practices appears hopelessly self-referential (Marcos 2005, 86).

Given the complexities of exchange and interactions too easily interpreted as appropriative, what models of analysis might yield some of the depth conveyed in Naranjo's opening statements of "Femaleness, femaleness. My community is female. My culture is female. I'm female. My art making is female" (Naranjo 1991)? Returning to Nnaemeka, it is apparent that her analysis relies upon the division of theory and practice, with mainstream feminists overly concerned with theory and African communities too often referenced only as data. How can the intersections of feminist inquiry and indigenous knowledges reach rapprochement, given the limited conceptual repertoires available? Is the comparative method (the West and the Rest) a useful and productive approach for an articulation of conceptually distinctive approaches to gender and community?

"A Commonality of Difference": Searching for Indigenous Feminisms in Ethnographic Accounts

Searching for an adequate theoretical method with which to describe Native women's lives, Choctaw scholar Devon Abbott Mihesuah asserts the primacy of self-narratives and self-naming. Her argument draws from Black feminist theorist Patricia Hill Collins's *Black Feminist Thought: Knowledge, Consciousness, and the Politics of Empowerment* in advocating for an experiential, lived knowledge as a basis of theoretical positioning (Collins 2000). Mihesuah states, "Native women—and there are many, many different world views, values, and traditions represented in those words—are the ones who can best describe what it means to be Indigenous women, because, like African American women, they are 'those who live it'—not non-Native theorists" (Mihesuah 2003, 29). This advocacy asserts the primacy of experiential knowledge while diminishing disembodied, cognitive theorizing.

Cherokee scholar Rayna Green's 1983 contextual bibliography *Native American Women* cites the "persuasiveness of testimony" by Native women leaders and writers writing about their own lives. Comparing these works to those of mainstream scholars, Green notes, "I know of no Indian woman preparing systematic studies of puberty rites, for example. Women may believe in them, honor them, and participate in them but they do not, for the most part, document them or wish to do so. They do not document change, they make change. Their focus remains on strategies to address problems, rather than on the descriptive analysis of problems" (Green 1983, 12).

Although self-narratives as a legitimate knowledge base hold promise for avoidance of the theory/practice divide, the case for Native American communities is somewhat more complex. Mihesuah qualifies her advocacy of personal narrative by citing the problematic of tribal diversity (the "extraordinary differences in cultural audience, geographic location, blood quantum, appearance, and reliable memory"), concluding, "There certainly can be no theory that encompasses all these voices, except maybe that Indigenous women share what I call a 'commonality of difference'" (Mihesuah 2003, 30). Green cites the difficulties for non-Natives gaining research access and a lack of interest for Natives, "given the hostile climate for discussion of any theory applied to Native people, I doubt that feminist theory of any stripe would be well received. For Indian feminists, every woman's issue is framed in the larger context of issues pertinent to Native peoples" (Green 1983, 14).

Although these Native scholars do not dismiss theory altogether, the inherent problems appear insurmountable. The rejection of theory, however, is unproductive in light of the continued marginalization of Native women purely as sources for field data. Following Mihesuah's desire to embrace both commonalities and differences and Green's emphasis on agency and sovereignty, it would appear that ethnographic research that attends to both communal and individualist structures would find the most relevance in advancing the holistic community imperatives of embodied research. An ethically informed ethnographic research methodology also importantly allows for the long-term, reciprocal, mutually meaningful criteria that are demanded in indigenous research methodologies (Smith 1999).

I will briefly examine two contemporary ethnographies of Native American women that are not straight personal narratives or segregated case studies in academic volumes. The ethnographies proactively engage feminist theories and attempt to address the problems inherent in semiotic and ontological differences. My aim is to examine what alternative patterns of analysis may possibly yield in clarifying intersecting feminisms and tribal women's knowledges as a productive basis for application to Native women in the arts. Both studies are authored by women: one Native one non-Native. Although not specific to the arts, a consideration of these ethnographies renders competing paradigms available for discussion. In particular, attention will be paid to how identity claims are structured in communal paradigms.

Lillian Ackerman's study, *A Necessary Balance: Gender and Power among Indians of the Columbia Plateau* (Ackerman 2003) asserts that gender equality existed among all Plateau groups of the past and is likely to be present among all Plateau Indians today. Ackerman claims a prior existence of gender equality, terming it an "indigenous trait" and a "legacy from the past" that predates Euro-American culture (Ackerman 2003, 229). She bases her findings on her extensive study of the Colville Indian Reservation of north-central Washington state from 1979 through the 1990s. Combining historical archival research with participant observation and interviews with fifty-one men and women, Ackerman adopted a definition of gender equality authored by Alice Schlegel that stresses balanced access to power, authority, and autonomy by males and females (Schlegel 1977).

Ackerman's ethnography aims to "portray gender equality on the Colville Reservation sufficiently well so that no one can deny the existence of gender equality somewhere in the world" (Ackerman 2003, 239). Specifically, Ackerman notes, "I hope this study will contribute to the demise of the notion of universal male dominance" (239). The Colville (and by extension, Plateau) data reveal that women retained equal status even after Euro-American colonialism and capitalism, due largely to the women's continued prominence in economic activities as well as the important role women played in the survival of the family and tribe. Ackerman notes these traits make women's equality "necessary" and "structural," noting that women are "so integrated into the everyday mechanism of life that to make them unequal would make the society unworkable" (249).

Ackerman's findings are congruent with the following description by Joy Harjo and Susan Williams writing on American Indian feminism: "In recognition of the importance of women in sustaining tribal cultures, community takes precedence over individual women's rights yet conversely there are no human rights until femaleness is respected and venerated" (Williams and Harjo 1998, 198–99). These interpretations of gender as an integral component of community, inextricable from consideration of other cultural values, echoes the concerns of second-wave women of color feminists (womanists) who advanced intersectionality as a theoretical methodology.

Ackerman openly rejects a reading of her Colville Reservation data as feminist, noting that gender differences are less important to Plateau people than to Euro-Americans. "Colville roles are complementary; Euro-American roles are opposite. The Colville define people as individuals first, then as a particular gender. Euro-Americans tend to see a particular gender first and individuals second" (Ackerman 2003, 250).

Thus, both complementarity and intersectionality (Crenshaw 1991) emerge as potentially productive theoretical bridging concepts. Phyllis Fast's ethnography *Northern Athabascan Survival: Women, Community, and the Future* (Fast 2002) explores Northern Athabascan ontologies and epistemologies in relationship to theories of gender, history, wellness, and social relations with outsiders. Both Fast and Ackerman describe Euro-American hegemonies in direct opposition and conflict with indigenous theories (re: the West and the Rest). While Ackerman seeks to assertively confront and dispel feminist theories of universal gender oppression and asymmetry, Fast pursues a more nuanced analysis. The tension between individual actions and collective norms finds relevance throughout Fast's work in what she describes as a "cultural contradiction" among Athabascans, that is, "they become socially and emotionally independent of others while at the same time weaving intricate fabrics of social independence within their society." Fast describes these activities as bordering on nationalism— there exists the tendency to "denounce otherness"—yet the institutional structures of a nationalist movement are absent (Fast 2002, 181).

I suggest that the concepts of subordination and equality in gender relationships so commonly referenced in the feminist literature are constitutive of a hierarchical structure of power as well as a belief in the individual as separate from society. The overlay of these generalized categorical assumptions onto Native American cultural traditions inhibits an accurate

reading of Native theoretical orientations that are not so easily compart-
mentalized. For example, Fast draws from oral traditions to demonstrate
how group survival through independent action is an ideal in Athabascan
culture; consequently, gender status was not traditionally forefronted as a
cultural theme in survival situations.

Today, Gwich'in women exercise gendered responses in their
approaches to social healing, utilizing an Athabascan model of cultural
survival while their male counterparts pursue political courses defined by
United States government policies. The women's "mental codes" for healing are characterized by independence and social aloofness while simultaneously teaching social interdependence within their society (Fast 2002,
181–82). In this way, "women are the primary instruments of shaping
Athabascan social identity and solidarity" (225). Does this indicate that
women therefore exercise more or less power than men in these situations?
Clearly, not only indigenous models of leadership and authority need to be
examined thoroughly, but rapid social changes occurring in response to
colonialism and capitalism must be considered as well.

In this regard, Fast's analysis importantly pays particular attention to
the "addictive infrastructure" of drugs, alcohol, and gambling (including
related social crises such as rape, child abuse, and poverty), noting how
these social disruptions are part of a larger global addictive economy. Fast
estimates $11 million a year circulates through the town of Gwichyaa Zhee
related to these addictive behaviors, from health-care services, law
enforcement, and state and federal administration, to the alcohol and drug
products themselves. She defines this addictive system as "the biggest
business in Athabascan territory and one whose prosperity renders impo-
tent ideas about removing it from Gwichyaa Zhee or elsewhere" (Fast 2002,
277).

Transnational Indigenous Feminisms:
Productive or Misleading?

Clearly, a productive theoretical inquiry into the status of indigenous
women's roles must utilize a transnational model that accounts not only for
the existence of indigenous cognitive patterns for right living but also the
brutal impacts of environmental, political, and social oppressions fueled
increasingly by corporate capitalism. Examples of this theoretical methodology may be found in Andrea Smith's work, *Conquest: Sexual Violence
and American Indian Genocide*, as she advocates building transnational

relationships in the fight to end violence against women. Citing the ability of the prison industrial complex as well as the non-profit industrial complex to manage and control dissent by incorporating it into the state apparatus, Smith argues for adopting alternative models of social change utilized throughout Latin America and in India. These social movements have created accountability strategies that do not rely on the state. Nonhierarchical leadership, constituent-funded organizing projects, and family rather than individual participation are some of the strategies she identifies as alternatives to state-run domestic violence programs (Smith 2005, 164–68).

In *Feminism without Borders: Decolonizing Theory, Practicing Solidarity*, Chandra Talpade Mohanty advocates a transnational, anti-capitalist feminist critique that centralizes racialized gender as the most inclusive paradigm for thinking about social justice (Mohanty 2003, 231). Like Green, Mihesuah, and Collins, Mohanty privileges experiential, epistemic knowledges, linking her work to post-positivist realists (Moya and Hames-García 2000) by stating, "I believe there are causal links between marginalized social locations and experiences and the ability of human agents to explain and analyze features of capitalist society" (Mohanty 2003, 231–32). Mohanty's call to "read up the ladder of privilege" is centered specifically on the lives and interests of marginalized communities of women; she notes that women and girls are seventy percent of the world's poor and the majority of the world's refugees (231). Mohanty writes, "It is especially [on] the bodies and lives of women and girls from the Third World/South—the Two-Thirds World—that global capitalism writes its script, and it is by paying attention to and theorizing the experiences of these communities of women and girls that we demystify capitalism as a system of debilitating sexism and racism, and envision anticapitalistic resistance" (235).

The transnational feminist strategy of originating both theoretical and activist agendas with women, based on their status as the world's most disenfranchised population, provides a productive platform for consideration of how indigenous feminisms may work in the context of the arts. The "experiential and analytic anchor" (Mohanty 2003, 231) that Mohanty cites appears to offer an inclusive point for Native North American women to enter into dialogue with feminists, rather than serve as objects of study.

Yet, in what ways can this transnational feminist approach then engage with the realities of Native North America, poised geographically as it is outside of the scope of what is being termed the Third World South? How do anti-capitalist resistances speak to the efforts of Native Americans fighting for the right to establish casinos as a means of providing an economic infrastructure for their members? How then to account for Native American sovereignty efforts within a global, anti-nationalist construct? Is this another missed opportunity, similar to Green's early lament that the abundance of feminist consciousness in Native women's struggles is too often only a "rhetorical recognition of the similarities" with feminism? Does Green's conclusion that American Indian women's writing of the 1980s "bears little resemblance to conventional feminist analysis of the status and circumstances of women's lives" still hold? (Green 1983, 13).

Summarizing the question of productive theoretical avenues for bridging feminist and Native women's concerns, these studies suggest that the comparative methodology presents a useful model for identifying unique cultural values, yet also confines discussions to a level of analysis that is ultimately insufficient for conveying the intricacies of unique, indigenous worldviews. Ethnographic works that particularize on the level of the individual, while accounting for tribal, regional, and even transnational patterns do, I think, hold promise for conveying some of the intricacies and "commonalities of difference" that Mihesuah recognizes. Within this format, feminist theory has proven to be both productive and potentially misleading, as ethnographers struggle to relate theoretical stalemates to the Native American material. Debates such as domestic vs. public status, individualism vs. communal identity, and even theory vs. practice do not seem to guide contemporary discussions in a deeply meaningful manner. The complexity of interpreting sovereign nationhood demands more than mainstream feminist theoretical approaches have to offer. This assessment follows Green's conclusion noted some twenty years earlier that "feminist rhetorical consciousness is used, only in part, by Native women to be explanatory and activating, but not to encompass the sum total of interest or concern" (Green 1983, 231).

I noted earlier that the concepts of intersectionality and complementarity appeared to have parallel applicability to Native American values of holism, multiple identity referents, and the inclusion of men in gender research and practice. Although these terms offer useful cross-cultural referents, they do not address either the question of how Native communities engage individualism or the quandary of theory and practice perceived as separate and distinct sites of knowledge-production. I hope to resolve these oversights by returning to my discussion of Native women in

328 MERIDIANS · 20th Anniversary Reader

the arts, and in particular to the salience of gender constructs in Native imagery and image production. As Native women artists navigate intersections of access, assimilation, and confrontation, they articulate unique identity claims based on simultaneous references to their individual, tribal, and gendered statuses. These "social arenas" enable women to make "political claims and initiate personal strategies" (Moore 1988, 37).

An Indigenous Knowledge Systems Approach:
Colonialization, Communalism,
and Embodied Knowledge

In an interview in 2000, Navajo (Diné) painter Emmi Whitehorse stated:

> I live with another male artist who happens to be European. When people walk into our spaces, they would look at his paintings, and then they would look at my work. And people would automatically go, OK, he's the male, the real male, his work really shows the male side and your work is very feminine. I don't know, with native artists, but I think there is to some degree that female, male.
>
> You know, my work, I tend to be very low key, there's not very much bravado. When it comes to the work, when you look at the work, it's very inward, it's very reclusive. You really have to kind of follow the work. And then it releases itself to you or it opens up these secrets to you. It's not something that says, "Here I am" or just hit you over the head with its message. I think with Native male artists you do get a sense of that, there is a lot of bravado.
>
> But as in life, I think there is definitely a difference between how males and females treat each other in life and it's much different than the Western ideal where male and female relationships are so very different, as much as we try, or tell yourself that they're enlightened . . . it's still very permanent. It's still very male, always dominant. The female is always domestic, stay at home, always lower than. . . . I say that now because (my mother) heading out of the whole husband thing as soon as she started becoming financially secure and went out and got a job, he had a very hard time with that, (to) handle that, and (he) just divorced her. And in my case, the same thing happened. I was way much too successful, too independent. . . . So I guess it just depends on the maturity of people. I think we always, we all pretty much suffer from . . . those stereotypical tendencies when it comes to male-female relationships. (Whitehorse 2000)

Black feminist scholars Johnnetta Cole and Beverly Guy-Sheftall write about the power of discovering that what was assumed to be particular to an individual woman was in reality a common experience in the lives of women—the personal is political (Cole and Guy-Sheftall 2003, 5). The disconnect between the personal read as woman's domain and the political read as man's sphere allowed for the naturalization, privatization, and individualization of women's experiences that could be directly attributed to societal and structural forms of oppression. It is at this personal level that the interconnections between competing ideas of womanhood, both symbolically (the reading of the painting as female) and in practice (the meaning of women's economic autonomy) become apparent.

On the symbolic level, Whitehorse's painting is interpreted by consumers as clearly female (no bravado). Whitehorse does not claim that her painting is demarcated as female; the work is "inward," "reclusive," and "low-key," not as gendered attributes, but simply as a non-gendered description of her genre. In this realm, although she has control over the material work (how it is executed), she cannot exert control over the interpretation of her work in a gendered fashion. The artistic symbolism is in many ways colonized by the preconceptions of the viewer as to Whitehorse's racial, ethnic, and gendered identity. On the level of arts practice, Whitehorse's role as an accomplished female artist is also read in a colonizing fashion. Her ability to sustain a career in the arts as a woman makes her "way too successful" for her male non-Native partner. This gender bias is importantly intergenerational; her mother's experience was similar. Ethnicity in this narrative is collapsed under the weight of gender. Male artwork, White and Native, demonstrates the "Here I am!" aesthetic. Males both White and Native resent women who are economically successful and independent. Whitehorse's analysis of ethnicity cites traditional Navajo culture today as fairly restrictive in its assumptions about female domesticity and subservience.

Gender as a primary reference in this passage complicates indigenous ideologies. Indigenous patterns of complementarity are nonexistent here. We do not find an anti-capitalist agenda. In a reverse of hierarchical tendencies, non-Natives appear less domineering than Natives. What the passage does evidence is the Westernization of the Native male, compared to the relative cultural orientation of Native females. As demonstrated elsewhere in my research, Native women continue to exercise their economic independence, prioritize communal obligations, and embrace their role as educators, even as they experience the impact of patriarchy, capitalism, and colonialism.

I wish to be careful about how independence is read in this context, as too often independence is taken to connote individual autonomy and rejection of social mandates. In a hegemonic feminist reading, freedom to earn money may commonly be interpreted as an exercise of female agency. For many Native American women, the ability to earn an income is a necessity, not a choice. The type of autonomy I am referring to is similar to Fast's description of Athabascan ideal behavior: group survival through independent action. Commonly, freedom in these contexts references the freedom to act and think in terms of collective, not individual, rights.

I suggest that the arts as a profession exemplifies the bridge between the individual and society in symbolic and engaged ways: symbolic, because the concept of woman has applicability to related referents of family and community, engaged due to the enacted roles, both generative and destructive, that a gendered analysis of Native arts reveals. I wish to theorize the practice of the arts as a component of indigenous knowledge systems utilizing the concepts of culture and gender as variables. Universalistic ideas of individualism and change are forwarded as key platforms of analysis. As useful as a comparative methodology (the West and the Rest) is in highlighting identity claims and enabling communication across conceptual chasms, I suggest that the deconstruction of these divides by way of a gendered inquiry enables a nuanced reading of indigenous knowledge practices. An example of this indigenous response is characterized by Gloria Emerson, Navajo (Diné) painter and educator, who attributes the Westernization of Navajo men to their participation in the armed services. A woman eighteen years older than Whitehorse, Emerson relates the impact of World War II on traditional Navajo matriarchy and notes how women have responded:

> Navajo society, well it used to be, was matriarchal and there is a lot of ownership of our own property, of our this and that, and the men's roles were almost secondary. And it's changed, flip-flopped it seems with the return, the men returning from the wars, with their attitudes about gender roles and such. With Westernization processes, education and so on. And maybe there are a lot of conflicts yet. I don't know. I think a lot of kitchen art is created that way, art around the kitchen table, clear the table to cook, to feed and then when everybody is sleeping that's the time

they can take the table back for their own work. And it's just not . . .
there's very little give and take, I think. (Emerson 2002)

Here, the idea of "kitchen art" is forwarded as a dynamic illustrative of
Westernization. Commerce is suggested by the production of crafts; wom-
en's roles are apparently marginalized. In a standard feminist critique, this
account of women's apparently secondary status would surely be followed
by a call for change based on a social-justice agenda, including organized
resistance and direct confrontation with oppressive gender practices. If we
consider the multiple readings of this imaginative feminist intervention for
a moment, it becomes clear that separate value systems are at play. The
variables of racism, ways of belonging, and concepts of time and tradition
find differing relevance in classic feminist ideology and in indigenous
ideology. Native American women and men continue to respond to the
legacy of colonialism based on their race, not primarily on their gender.
Native men and women were systematically killed, tortured, enslaved, and
imprisoned by foreign nations at contact; these histories continue in
struggles for present-day sovereignty, rendering race and ethnicity
primary.

Hawaiian scholar Haunani-Kay Trask visualizes the apparently competing concepts of gender and culture by referencing lateral and vertical
divides:

> [O]ur efforts at collective self-determination mean that we find solidarity
> with our own people, including our own men, more likely, indeed prefer-
> able, to solidarity with white people, including feminists. Struggle with
> our men occurs laterally, across and within our movement. It does not
> occur vertically between the white woman's movement and indigenous
> women on one side and white men and Hawaiian men on the other
> side. . . . [W]e have more in common, both in struggle and in contro-
> versy, with our own men and with each other as indigenous women than
> we do with white people, called *haole* in Hawaiian. This is only to make
> the familiar point that culture is a larger reality than "women's rights."
> (Trask 1993, 264–65)

Trask summarizes this prioritization of culture by stating, "At this point in
our struggle, race and culture are stronger forces than sex and gender"
(265).

Gender, however, cannot be dismissed as a central consideration, for the ways in which Native American men and women have experienced the genocide of the past 500 years has been and continues to be uniquely informed by rigidly defined Western male and female roles. Native communities became gendered communities as a result of colonialism, disrupting other intellectual traditions of leadership and the uses of power. This "gendering" of the community was evident in how Hawaiian statehood developed in 1959: "As our men sought power in the Americanized political system, they internalized the values of that system: politics is a man's world, family life is a woman's world. While some of our men, the most educated and articulate, rose up in the ranks of the political system, our women tended the home" (Trask 1993, 120).

The resultant economic and cultural exploitation of post-statehood Hawaii is characterized by Trask as "beyond imagining. Our Hawaiian people have been further marginalized, our living conditions and general health diminished, our lands developed and poisoned" (120). Yet in the 1970s a self-determination movement led by Native Hawaiian women activists ("articulate, fierce, and culturally grounded") emerged. A new form of power based on traditional Hawaiian beliefs developed with "women asserting their leadership for the sake of the nation." Nation in this instance is not strictly conceived in the sense of a bounded political entity alone, but as an extension of a holistic belief system including family and land. "Caring for the nation is, in Hawaiian belief, an extension of caring for the family, the large family that includes both our lands and our people. Our mother is our land, *Papa-hānau-moku*—she who births the islands. This means that Hawaiian women leaders are genealogically empowered to lead the nation" (121–22).

The Hawaiian example that Trask provides illustrates the problematic nature of conceiving gender and therefore feminism in indigenous contexts. Gender does and does not exist. Gender does exist as a colonial development—an imposition of typical male and female roles with males exercising political and therefore public power and females exerting only private power in domestic contexts. This strict definition of gender cannot be said to exist, however, in more accurate and culturally aware readings where the responsibility of protecting land and family resides holistically with women. Trask's example importantly conveys this indigenous-knowledge-systems reading as living and enacted—an embodied knowledge—that can and does occur in contemporary settings—not an imagined, historical, authentic belief system alone. This impulse is centrally characterized as a communal imperative.

The communal-individualistic variable in feminist discourses is exposed in a similar critique by Frédérique Apffel-Marglin and Loyda Sánchez's discussion of developmentalist feminism in Bolivia. Their analysis interrogates the state agenda that promotes birth control for indigenous women under the rubric of self-determination. Here, the concept of a self apart from the community or the land is a misreading of indigenous realities:

> The world for which women are being prepared is emphatically not that of their campesino native communities. They are being prepared to be individuals and citizens with their autonomous access to "resources," decision-making, services, education, their bodies, etc. . . . The State uses a developmental feminist discourse to create individual female citizens. Such a discursive move is at once creative and destructive; the female individual citizen emerges from the destruction of the *comunera* and of her world. (Apffel-Marglin and Sanchez 2002, 6)

This transnational perspective demonstrates that the concept of gender is not only a separate and inaccurate reading of indigenous worldviews, but gender as an imposition of individualism actually destroys a communalistic indigenous life. A feminist perspective can be said to then dangerously replace the ability to enact—to embody—an indigenous world. This prohibition problematically impacts the survival of indigenous peoples, attacking as it does the reproductive ability of women to produce a future generation.

Apffel-Marglin and Sánchez continue their essay by interrogating essentialist notions of the body and gender, concluding, "the term 'gender' (*género* in Spanish) has forced itself on many Andean peasant communities . . . " (19).

> The unicity of the biological body is taken by developmentalist feminists as a universal given, thus holding constant the correlation between an unchangeable biological body and a variable socio/cultural "gender" (the sex/gender differentiation). Although "gender" is recognized as variable across time and place, what is not variable is gender's anchoring in a universally given biological body and with it the notion that gender is

something that characterizes *individual* human men and women. . . .
When deployed by developmentalist feminism in an Andean context it
becomes a (neo)colonialist move (17–18).

So while individualism may be clearly demarcated as a foil of indigenous knowledge systems (defined variously as communal or nationalistic),
gender as a variable continues as a marked but not explicitly demarcated
reference. In other words, gender has multiple and contradictory referents;
the term may be dismissed as not accurately representing indigenous cos-
mologies (such as the notion of the body discussed by Apffel-Marglin and
Sánchez) or variously assigned utility in charting a colonial trajectory
(Trask's discussion of nationhood); as an overarching frame of reference,
however, gender serves to obscure rather than clarify. A holistic and
nuanced worldview as described by these authors and artists emerges as
having more utilitarian and theoretical worth than the over-determined
connotations of gender referenced in standard feminist discourses.

One manner in which we might conceptualize these divergent readings
(gender as a product of colonialism and gender as an inaccurate reading of
complementarity) is a temporal approach. As Trask described in pre- and
post-statehood Hawaii, can a meaningful analysis emerge from interrogating historically situated frames of reference? Specifically, what utility
does the notion of social change hold for uncovering possible forms of
indigenous feminist orientations? Does a call to pre-colonialization norms
(or pre-World War II, in Emerson's example) provide more clarity?

The concept of change in many social-justice movements indicates a
type of linear progress whereby tradition is viewed negatively. How many
times have we heard of progressive politics as social-change movements?
Yet, if we start from the standpoint of marginalized communities of
women, as Mohanty suggests, then change in the Native American context
would most often connote assimilation; assimilation by boarding-school
practices, assimilation by conversion, assimilation by forced relocation to
cities. The genocide of Native North America was accomplished by forced
rejection and cessation of traditional religions, economies, languages,
arts, social customs, child-rearing practices, and politics, rendering the
rhetoric of change suspect.

For example, Louise Lamphere's 1989 article "Historical and Regional
Variability in Navajo Women's Roles" indicates that Navajo men's and

women's roles changed drastically with the influx of capitalism (Lamphere 1989). The sexual division of labor was altered under an enforced wage-system economy, with wage labor in the immediate postwar period being generally male-dominated. Lamphere notes how various residence patterns established under government programs may negatively impact the ability of women to engage in female exchange networks, an important indicator of Navajo women's agency.

Conflicting ideas of gender hierarchies, social change, and the constitution of community are often encapsulated in the comparative ideology of Western and indigenous traits. Classically, under this rubric, feminism is identified as a Western conceptual framework due to its emphasis on individual change and agency as well as its often ahistorical orientation. The variables of history, time, and, most importantly, community must be considered primary if an indigenous feminist analysis is to find relevance. Consider for example, Emerson's passage below that illustrates how traditional gendered orientation enables collective response.

> NM: What is an issue that you have to address in your work because you're a woman? Are there things that come up that are unique for you, that you have to negotiate?
>
> GE: Time, I think time. I think time on women, women's time is owned by others. You're not, you don't belong to yourself. You belong to your family, your clan, your mother, your parents, your relations. In Navajo, it's even stronger, that sensibility of belonging to a community of relations, clan, family. They all have demands on you and you have to respond if you want to maintain your place in that social fabric. If you want to be honored and respected, you have to respect others, too. And part of respecting others is giving up your time. Right? (Emerson 2002)

Emerson demonstrates the centrality of an embodied knowledge—a lived and experienced reference that has utility and applicability. This engaged site of knowledge is not an abstracted ahistorical framework, but is an enacted knowledge. It is, in Green's words cited earlier, a form of testimony by doing. For Roxanne Swentzell, it is about embracing "the now." Santa Clara artist Nora Naranjo-Morse (sister of Tessie Naranjo) similarly describes how a woman's responsibility enhances her grounding as a tribal person:

I come from Pueblo people who still have an ideology of community and what community does. Because of the choices I have made, I live on the periphery. I don't know if the people who live in the community understand that I am learning how to be a contemporary Native woman. What they do understand is that I make really good chili. And that I had not one, but two children. To be a mother, a nurturer, is how I'm valued by my people. It has nothing to do with what you've achieved in the outside world, or what your name is. When my son was dancing for the Deer Dance, I made a whole feast where I fed about one hundred people. I felt I was a very important person—even though I was slaving over the stove. Maybe feminists would deem this a step backwards, but I had a role in my community. I was happy because I was nourishing my son through his spiritual journey, and, on a different level, I was being nourished through his dance and his energy. (Naranjo-Morse 1998, 86)

In what ways has a gendered experience of change, place, and belonging informed Native women's experiences in the arts specifically? These narratives help theorize the practice of the arts as a component of indigenous knowledge systems and specifically offer possible readings for indigenous feminist ideologies. This essay has suggested that although various forms of feminist approaches to indigenous lives have been unevenly applied over time, feminist perspectives are not altogether irrelevant. Central feminist paradigms of intersectionality and complementarity provide useful constructs for interpreting diffuse power dynamics in Native contexts. Specific to this study, the arts provide a channel for assessing modes of embodied knowledges and communal values. A gendered personhood in these contexts is not separate from, but may also be essential to, conveying a holistic, complex framework of indigenous knowledge construction. As in Naranjo's opening statement "My community is female. My culture is female. I'm female. My art making is female. Everything is female," a totality reading of gender emcompassed within a larger knowledge system can be altogether different, but parallel to the equally materially constructed application of gender as a product of colonialism. This historicized deconstruction of unique knowledge fields exists alongside and in concurrence with indigenous frames of reference. Thus, colonized genders as well as more culturally appropriate gendered feminisms may concurrently be at play in feminist discourses, confounding discussions and possible rapprochements of American Indian Studies and feminist discourses. The weighty variable that must be attended to is the possibility that one frame of reference may be premised on the marginalization or even destruction of the other. The field of contemporary arts serves as a useful platform for considering these intersections of indigeneity and feminisms.

....

Nancy Marie Mithlo (Chiricahua Apache) is a professor of gender studies and faculty advisor for the American Indian Studies Interdepartmental Program at the University of California, Los Angeles. In 2017, she was a George A. and Eliza Gardner Howard Foundation Fellow at Brown University and a Getty Research Institute guest researcher. Mithlo's curatorial work has resulted in nine exhibits at the Venice Biennale. Her most recent book is *Knowing Native Arts* (2020).

Notes

Originally published in *Meridians* vol. 9, no. 2, 2009.

I dedicate this piece to my friend, Sue Ann Ritter DelRios, the wild woman of Stone Mountain, North Carolina, whose spirit fed mine in so many ways.

1 The research presented here is part of my larger project, documented in Mithlo 2009.

2 I was fortunate to be chosen as a Future of Minority Studies fellow for the 2005 summer institute "Feminist Identities, Global Struggles," taught by Beverly Guy-Sheftall, Anna Julia Cooper Professor of Women's Studies and English, Spelman College, and Chandra Talpade Mohanty, professor of Women's Studies and the Dean's Professor of the Humanities, Syracuse University. I am grateful to the instructors, guest presenters, and the other participants for the many inspirational conversations that emerged in that setting.

3 However, this marginalization is now more often contested. Note the recent conference and proceedings in Canada that resulted in Green 2007.

4 Formal apologies as a mechanism of dispute resolution have been utilized in other circumstances where historical oppressions have occurred. See the Kevin Gover (Assistant Secretary-Indian Affairs Department of the Interior) apology at the ceremony acknowledging the 175th anniversary of the establishment of the Bureau of Indian Affairs, September 8, 2000: http://www.tahtonka.com/apology.html (accessed May 12, 2009).

Works Cited

Ackerman, Lillian A. 2003. *A Necessary Balance: Gender and Power among Indians of the Columbia Plateau.* Norman: University of Oklahoma Press.

Apffel-Marglin, Frédérique, and Loyda Sanchez. 2002. "Developmentalist Feminism and Neocolonialism in Andean Communities." In *Development or Post-Development: Which Way for Women and Development?*, edited by Kriemild Saunders. London: Zed Books.

Cole, Johnetta B., and Beverly Guy-Sheftall. 2003. "The Personal is Political." In *Gender Talk: The Struggle for Women's Equality in African American Communities*. New York: Random House.

Collins, Patricia Hill. 2000. *Black Feminist Thought: Knowledge, Consciousness, and the Politics of Empowerment*, 2nd ed. New York: Routledge.

Crenshaw, Kimberle. 1991. "Mapping the Margins: Intersectionality, Identity Politics, and Violence against Women of Color." *Stanford Law Review* 43, no. 6: 1241–99.

Emberley, Julia. 1996. "Aboriginal Women's Writing." In *Women of the First Nations: Power, Wisdom, and Strength*, edited by Christine Miller and Patricia Chuchryk. Winnipeg: University of Manitoba Press.

Emerson, Gloria. 2002. Interview with author. December 7.

Fast, Phyllis. 2002. *Northern Athabascan Survival: Women, Community, and the Future*. Lincoln: University of Nebraska Press.

Green, Joyce, ed. 2007. *Making Space for Indigenous Feminism*. New York: Zed Books.

Green, Rayna. 1983. "Introduction." In *Native American Women; A Contextual Bibliography*. Bloomington: Indiana University Press.

Lamphere, Louise. 1989. "Historical and Regional Variability in Navajo Women's Roles." *Journal of Anthropological Research* 45, no. 4: 431–56.

Lippard, Lucy. 1990. *Mixed Blessings: New Art in a Multicultural America*. New York: Pantheon Books.

Maracle, Lee. 1996. *I Am Woman: A Native Perspective on Sociology and Feminism*. Vancouver: Press Gang Publishers.

Marcos, Sylvia. 2005. "The Borders Within: The Indigenous Women's Movement and Feminism in Mexico." In *Dialogue and Difference: Feminisms Challenge Globalization*, edited by Marguerite Waller and Sylvia Marcos. New York: Palgrave Macmillan.

McClaurin-Allen, Irma. 1990. "Incongruities: Dissonance and Contradiction in the Life of a Black Middle-Class Woman." In *Uncertain Terms: Negotiating Gender in American Culture*, edited by Faye Ginsburg and Anna Lowenhaupt Tsing. Boston: Beacon Press.

Mihesuah, Devon Abbott. 2003. *Indigenous American Women: Decolonization, Empowerment, Activism*. Lincoln: University of Nebraska Press.

Mithlo, Nancy Marie. 2007. "The New Thing is Old News: Why Post-Identity Claims Are Regressive." A paper given at the Eiteljorg Fellowship for Native American Fine Art 2007, Eiteljorg Museum, Indianapolis, IN. November 10.

———. 2009. *"Our Indian Princess": Subverting the Stereotype*. Global Indigenous Politics Series. Santa Fe, NM: School for Advanced Research Press.

Mohanty, Chandra Talpade. 2003. *Feminism without Borders: Decolonizing Theory, Practicing Solidarity*. Durham, NC: Duke University Press.

Moore, Henrietta L. 1988. *Feminism and Anthropology*. Minneapolis: University of Minnesota Press.

Moya, Paula M. L., and Michael R. Hames-Garcia, eds. 2000. *Reclaiming Identity: Realist Theory and the Predicament of Postmodernism*. Berkeley: University of California Press.

Naranjo, Tessie. 1991. Interview with author. April 18.

———. 2000a. Interview with author. September 18.

————. 2000b. "Pueblo Pottery Remains Down to Earth." *The Santa Fe New Mexican* (January 1).

Naranjo-Morse, Nora. 1998. "Nora Naranjo-Morse speaks . . . " In *Reservation X: The Power of Place in Aboriginal Contemporary Art*, edited by Gerald McMaster. Seattle: University of Washington Press.

Nnaemaka, Obioma. 2003. "Negro-Feminism: Theorizing, Practicing, and Pruning Africa's Way." *Signs: Journal of Women in Culture and Society* 29, no 2: 357–85.

Okin, Susan Moller, Joshua Cohen, Matthew Howard, and Martha Craven Nussbaum, eds. 1999. *Is Multiculturalism Bad for Women?* Princeton, NJ: Princeton University Press.

Rosenberg, Dorothy Goldin. 2000. "Towards Indigenous Wholeness: Feminist Praxis in Transformative Learning on Health and the Environment." In *Indigenous Knowledges in Global Contexts: Multiple Readings of Our World*, edited by George J. Sefa Dei, Budd L. Hall, and Dorothy Goldin Rosenberg. Toronto: University of Toronto Press.

St. Denis, Verna. 2007. "Feminism is for Everybody: Aboriginal Women, Feminism, and Diversity." In *Making Space for Indigenous Feminism*, edited by Joyce Green. New York: Zed Books.

Schlegel, Alice. 1977. "Toward a Theory of Sexual Stratification." In *Sexual Stratification: A Cross-Cultural view*, edited by Alice Schlegel. New York: Columbia University Press.

Smith, Andrea. 2005. *Conquest: Sexual Violence and American Indian Genocide*. Cambridge, MA: South End Press.

Smith, Linda Tuhawai. 1999. *Decolonizing Methodologies: Research and Indigenous Peoples*. New York: Zed Books.

Swentzell, Roxanne. 2000. Interview with author. September 12.

Trask, Haunani-Kay. 1993. *From a Native Daughter: Colonialism and Sovereignty in Hawai'i*. Monroe, ME: Common Courage Press.

Whitehorse, Emmi. 2000. Interview with author. September 18.

Williams, Christine. 2000. "Preface." In *Feminist Views of the Social Sciences*, edited by Christine Williams. *The Annals of the American Academy of Political and Social Science*. Thousand Oaks, CA: Sage Publications, Inc.

Williams, Susan M., and Joy Harjo. 1998. "American Indian Feminism." In *The Reader's Companion to U.S. Women's History*, edited by Wilma Mankiller et al. New York: Houghton Mifflin Company.

Kimala Price

. . . .

What Is Reproductive Justice?
How Women of Color Activists
Are Redefining the Pro-Choice Paradigm

Abstract: Frustrated by the individualist approach of the "choice" paradigm used by the mainstream reproductive rights movement in the United States, a growing coalition of women of color organizations and their allies have sought to redefine and broaden the scope of reproductive rights by using a human rights framework. Dubbing itself "the movement for reproductive justice," this coalition connects reproductive rights to other social justice issues such as economic justice, education, immigrant rights, environmental justice, sexual rights, and globalization, and believes that this new framework will encourage more women of color and other marginalized groups to become more involved in the political movement for reproductive freedom. Using narrative analysis, this essay explores what reproductive justice means to this movement, while placing it within the political, social, and cultural context from which it emerged.

Frustrated by the individualist approach of the pro-choice framework, a growing movement created and led by women of color has emerged to broaden the scope of reproductive rights. Calling itself the reproductive justice movement, this coalition of women of color activists and their allies are using a human rights and social justice framework to redefine choice. Focus group research has shown that women of color and low-income women do not identify with the pro-choice message; in fact, the choice rhetoric is almost meaningless (PEP 1997; 2004). Reproductive justice activists believe that this new framework will encourage more women of

MERIDIANS · feminism, race, transnationalism   Volume 19 Supplement 2020
DOI: 10.1215/15366936-8566034 © 2010 Smith College

color and other marginalized groups to become more involved in the political movement for reproductive freedom.

The main goal of the reproductive justice movement is to move beyond the pro-choice movement's singular focus on abortion. The Oakland-based advocacy group Asian Communities for Reproductive Justice (ACRJ) defines reproductive justice as:

> the complete physical, mental, spiritual, political, economic, and social well-being of women and girls, and will be achieved when women and girls have the economic, social and political power and resources to make healthy decisions about our bodies, sexuality and reproduction for ourselves, our families and our communities in all areas of our lives. (ACRJ 2005, 1)

As the above definition suggests, the reproductive justice framework recognizes the importance of linking reproductive health and rights to other social justice issues such as poverty, economic injustice, welfare reform, housing, prisoners' rights, environmental justice, immigration policy, drug policies, and violence. The movement's three core values are: the right to have an abortion, the right to have children, and the right to parent those children. Women must be able to freely exercise these rights without coercion. Although reproductive justice activists acknowledge that an emphasis on gaining legal rights, lobbying, and electoral politics is not necessarily a bad thing, they argue that there has to be an intersectional analysis and the acknowledgment of oppression in order for women to truly gain freedom.

Using narrative analysis, I will discuss this emerging movement and the concept of reproductive justice: What is reproductive justice? How does it differ from "choice"? What is the political, social, and cultural context from which this "reproductive justice" framework emerged? In order to address the questions posed, I gathered and analyzed the stories of the individuals and organizations who are actively involved in building the reproductive justice movement; specifically, I focus on the activities of SisterSong and many of its member organizations. I will show how reproductive justice activists have rhetorically created space for women of color, low-income women, women with disabilities, and other women who have been marginalized not only within the mainstream reproductive rights movement, but also in society at large. This particular project is well-suited for narrative analysis, as reproductive justice activists have consciously used

storytelling as an organizing tool; that is, storytelling is used as a pedagogical tool for consciousness-raising within their respective communities. Although we normally associate storytelling with the telling of *personal* stories, this essay focuses on the collective *public* stories that activists
and advocacy groups tell about reproductive justice organizing and the
histories of women of color and their communities. In other words, this
essay is not grounded in the personal stories of *individuals*, but in the collective stories of *communities*.

Reproductive Justice in Context

A rich legacy in reproductive activism within communities of color is
increasingly being documented by feminist scholars and the activists
themselves. From Jennifer Nelson, we have learned how women of color in
the Black and Puerto Rican Nationalist movements worked to get feminist
issues, particularly abortion and reproductive rights, onto their respective
movements' agendas (Nelson 2003). Jael Silliman and her co-authors have
documented the history of women of color creating their own reproductive
health organizations in the 1980s and 1990s; some of the groups profiled
include the National Black Women's Health Project (now known as the
Black Women's Health Imperative) in 1984, the National Latina Health
Organization in 1986, Asians and Pacific Islanders for Reproductive Health
(now known as Asian Communities for Reproductive Justice) in 1989, and
the Native American Women's Health Education Resource Center in 1988
(Silliman et al. 2004).

Loretta Ross has shown how African American women were actively
involved in the birth control movement in the early part of the twentieth
century (Ross 1992). College-educated, middle-class African American
women were actively involved in their communities with the sole purpose
of racial uplift. They felt that it was their duty to help their impoverished
brethren and believed that access to birth control was the key to the economic and social mobility and self-determination of the African American
community as a whole (Davis 1983; Ross 1992). Moreover, African American women established abortion clinics, such as the Gainesville Women's
Health Center in Florida, which was founded in 1974 by Byllye Avery and
four of her colleagues.

Prominent African American women such as politician Shirley Chisholm and feminist lawyer and advocate Florynce "Flo" Kennedy were
involved in abortion politics in the 1960s and 1970s. Chisholm was the first

president of NARAL (then known as the National Association for the Repeal of Abortion Laws), and in 1969 Kennedy was one of the lawyers representing the Women's Health Collective and 350 plaintiffs in a lawsuit challenging New York State's law prohibiting abortion (Davis 1983; Ross 1992; Nelson 2003; Silliman et al. 2004).

In the 1970s, advocacy groups founded and led by women of color, such as the National Black Feminist Organization (NBFO), the Third World Women's Alliance, and the Committee for Abortion Rights and Against Sterilization Abuse (CARASA), included abortion and reproductive rights and sterilization abuse on their political agendas (Davis 1983; Ross 1992; Springer 1999; Nelson 2003; Silliman et al. 2004). Specifically, these groups exposed federal government-sanctioned sterilization campaigns targeting African American, Puerto Rican, Mexican American, and Native American women in the 1950s, 1960s, and 1970s (Davis 1983; Roberts 1997; Silliman and Bhattacharjee 2002; Smith 2005b). In the words of Silliman et al.:

> CARASA saw the mainstream pro-choice organizations as narrow at best and, at worst, as taking positions that undermined the reproductive freedom of many women. In this regard, they specifically cited hostility [from the mainstream pro-choice movement] to regulations regarding sterilization abuse and the use of population control arguments for abortion rights. Following the lead of women of color, CARASA placed opposition to sterilization abuse on par with support for abortion rights. (Silliman et al. 2004, 33)

Women of color have been active as members and staffers in traditional reproductive rights organizations, such as the National Organization for Women (NOW) and NARAL. In fact, many of the mainstream groups developed programs that specifically targeted women of color, such as NOW's Women of Color Program and the Religious Coalition for Abortion Rights' (RCAR; now known as the Religious Coalition for Reproductive Choice) Women of Color Partnership Program. In 1987, NOW hosted the first national conference on women of color and reproductive rights; it coincided with the 1987 March for Women's Lives. Some smaller prochoice organization such as the Reproductive Rights National Network (R2N2) placed race, class, and LGBT issues at the center of their mission (Fried 2007).

Nevertheless, many women of color activists have expressed their frustrations with working within majority-White, pro-choice organizations. In her book of essays, long-time African American activist Marcella Howell writes:

> During my 30 years in the women's movement, I have watched young
> black women come into women's and reproductive rights organizations
> with idealistic hopes of what they could achieve. By the time they leave,
> usually within a few years, they are disillusioned with these organiza-
> tions in particular and with the women's movement in general. In many
> cases, these young women found themselves in inhospitable and often
> hostile environments. (Howell 2007, 7)

The disillusionment stemmed from the perceived lack of attention to issues that were of concern for many women of color, such as the repeal of the Hyde Amendment, which prevented federal monies (for example, Medicaid) and facilities (for example, military hospitals) from being used for abortions (NAPAWF 2008). This frustration also partly stems from the "choice" rhetoric of the movement, which is problematic because it is based on a set of assumptions that applies only to a small group of women who are privileged enough to have multiple choices. Although the "choice" message tactic may have worked in the short run in response to the actions of the conservative anti-abortion countermovement, many reproductive rights activists, especially women of color, believe that choice should not be the long-term or sole goal of the reproductive rights movement.

Early reproductive justice activists were strongly influenced by international human rights discourse. Beginning in the early 1970s, a global, transnational women's movement that placed human rights at the core of its organizing activities emerged. Many U.S. feminists were arguing that women should be involved in the international human rights scene (Silliman et al. 2004). As Charlotte Bunch argued, "The separation of women's rights from human rights has perpetuated the secondary status of women" (Bunch 1995). This transnational movement was centered on several of the international women's and human rights conferences held by the United Nations. There were the two decades of women's conferences: Mexico City, Mexico (1975), Nairobi, Kenya (1985), Copenhagen, Denmark (1980), and Beijing, China (1995). There were also other UN conferences such as the Convention to Eliminate All Forms of Discrimination Against Women (CEDAW) in 1979; the World Conference on Human Rights held in Vienna, Austria in 1993; and the International Conference on Population and

Development held in Cairo, Egypt in 1994. Many women of color activists were involved in these international conferences and were radically influenced and inspired by the human rights framework employed at these conferences:

> [T]he term Reproductive Justice was coined in 1994 by women of color shortly after [the United Nations International Conference on Population and Development in Cairo, Egypt]. We were envisioning from the perspectives of women of color engaged in both domestic and international activism, and attempting to create a lens applicable to the United States with which to interpret and apply the normative (but not universally agreed) understandings reached at Cairo. . . . As activists in the U.S., we needed an analysis to connect our domestic issues to the global struggle for women's human rights that would call attention to our commitment to the link between women, their families, and their communities. (Ross 2006, 6)

Reproductive justice activists were particularly inspired by how the United Nations conceptualizes human rights, as simply stated in Article 3 of the Universal Declaration of Human Rights: "Everyone has the right to life, liberty and the security of person" (*Universal Declaration of Human Rights* 1948). The UN delineates three broad categories of human rights: 1) civil and political rights; 2) economic, social, and cultural rights; and 3) sexual, environmental, and developmental rights (OHCHR 1996). The first category includes rights that provide for liberty and equality, freedom from discrimination, and the right to participate in the political life of our communities, whereas the second category provides for the material well being of individuals, the right to live and participate in communities, and the preservation of one's cultural identity. The last category refers to bodily integrity, community self-determination, and rights to land and other natural resources. Human rights doctrine has taken center stage in the reproductive justice framework.

There have been several attempts to create a national reproductive rights coalition for women of color, such as the Women of Color Coalition for Reproductive Rights, which was launched in 1992 by six organizations (Silliman et al. 2004). The SisterSong Women of Color Reproductive Health Collective (known simply as SisterSong) is the latest attempt to create a national network. Comprised of over eighty national and local women of color and allied organizations, boasting hundreds of individual members, and headquartered in Atlanta, SisterSong was formed in 1997 by sixteen organizations with funding from the Ford Foundation.

In 1997 and 1998 under the leadership of Luz Rodríguez, director of the Latina Roundtable for Health and Reproductive Rights (New York), the Ford Foundation hosted a series of meetings. Although the original purpose of these gatherings was to focus on reproductive-tract infections among women of color, the participants shared the belief that women of color have the right and responsibility to represent themselves and their communities (Ross et al. 2001). As a result, the group developed a plan to create a collective vision and coordinated effort among women of color groups. The Ford Foundation would eventually provide the seed money SisterSong needed to launch itself as a viable advocacy organization. In fact, the initial support from Ford was channeled through an unprecedented funding model; not only did SisterSong receive funding, but several of the founding organizations also received funding for their individual projects and programs. Loretta Ross, a veteran women's rights, civil rights, and human rights activist, would become SisterSong's national coordinator, a position comparable to being an executive director.

In keeping with its mission of creating and maintaining a multicultural movement that acknowledges, respects, and supports a diversity of voices and perspectives, the collective is organized into five principal caucuses representing ethnic and indigenous groups in the United States: 1) African American/Caribbean/African, 2) Arab American/Middle Eastern/North African, 3) Asian/Pacific Islander, 4) Latina, and 5) Native American/ Indigenous. Over the years, other caucuses have formed, including ones for the LGBTI/queer community, young women under the age of twenty-four, and women of color who work in majority-White, reproductive rights organizations. Last, the member organizations also represent specific issue niches. Besides representing specific racial and ethnic communities, SisterSong organizations work on a range of issues, including, but not limited to, HIV/AIDS, anti-poverty policy, violence against women, disability rights, gay and lesbian rights, environmental rights, biotechnology, and immigration rights. It has also incorporated human rights principles in its organizing educational efforts, especially in its national and regional trainings and workshops. In fact, the organization often distributes free copies of the Universal Declaration of Human Rights to its grassroots constituency.

Many social movement theorists have typically focused on resource mobilization and participation in the political process in their evaluations of the impact and effectiveness of social movements (Staggenborg 1991). However, Francesca Polletta and James Jasper argue that the construction of a collective identity is just as important for assessing the impact of movements as well as understanding what mobilizes people to participate in movements and accounts for the tactical choices that activists make (Polletta and Jasper 2001). In its attempts to map out space for itself within the social and political landscape, part of SisterSong's strategy is to develop a strong collective identity, which is important for recruiting individual and organizational members, especially women of color, economically disadvantaged women, and other women who have felt marginalized by the pro-choice movement. Doing so is also part of its political vision and mission. Moreover, collective identity-formation is important for distinguishing the movement from other social movements, mainly the pro-choice movement. Is the reproductive justice movement merely an outgrowth of the pro-choice movement? Is it a countermovement? Or is it a parallel movement in its own right that is distinctive from the pro-choice movement? Storytelling aids in this process of collective identity-formation.

SisterSong and Narrative Analysis

This essay is based on a narrative analysis of a range of written and oral texts. I specifically focus on the activities of and documents produced by SisterSong and its member and allied organizations. Stories serve multiple purposes. They can be documentary in nature; they can provide information about a person, project, situation, event, or any other set of circumstances. Second, stories construct reality, or at least provide a glimpse into the storyteller's version of reality. We cognitively make sense of the world around us by telling stories; storytelling is how we give meaning to our experiences and convey those interpretations to others (Stone 1989; Czarniawska-Joerges 1998; Feldman and Skoldberg 2002; Czarniawska-Joerges 2004; Feldman et al. 2004). Third, stories can create space; that is, storytelling can be a means by which those who are marginalized within society or in a specific community can create a reality that includes and addresses their experiences, perspectives, and concerns, that is, their reality. Last, stories can serve as consciousness-raising tools for grassroots, political organizing. Reproductive justice activists consciously use storytelling as a form of activism to document the experiences, history, thoughts, and emotions of women of color and other marginalized groups before these stories are lost or erased from official, public memory.

Narrative analysis is most often associated with the analysis of data collected from oral interviews; however, stories can be collected from a variety of primary and secondary documentary sources. Stories can be collected from media sources such as newspaper articles, magazines, and blogs, especially if one is interested in analyzing the public discourse on a particular social or political issue. Social movement organizations produce a variety of materials, including pamphlets, brochures, reports, press releases, flyers, and congressional testimony, all of which are rich sources for gathering narratives.

For this project, I gathered narrative data using several strategies. First, I gathered information from my participation and observation in several reproductive justice movement activities, such as meetings and conferences. These included four annual meetings of the SisterSong Women of Color Reproductive Health Collective (2004–2006, 2009), the national conferences held by SisterSong in 2003 and 2007, and a national policy conference (entitled "Reproductive Justice for All") convened by the Planned Parenthood Federation of America and Smith College in 2005. Participant observation provided a great deal of context that aided in the interpretation of the documents that I collected.

I collected and analyzed documents produced by reproductive justice organizations, including websites, reports, mission statements, fact sheets, newsletters, and meeting transcripts. Ultimately, I collected stories from over 100 documents and seventeen websites. The following groups are represented in this project: SisterSong; Asian Communities for Reproductive Justice; Center for Genetics & Society; California Latinas for Reproductive Justice; National Latina Institute for Reproductive Health; National Asian Pacific American Women's Forum (NAPAWF); African American Women for Reproductive Freedom; California Black Women's Health Project; Black Women's Health Imperative (formerly NBWHP); African American Women Evolving (AAWE); Wise Women Gathering Place; Justice Now; Committee on Women, Population, and the Environment (CWPE); Planned Parenthood Federation of America (PPFA); Mothers Movement Online; Population and Development Program (Hampshire College); and Advocates for Youth. I collected many of these documents from archival organizational records at the Sophia Smith Collection at Smith College.

Last, I collected interview transcripts from the Voices of Feminism Oral History Project, which is housed at the Sophia Smith Collection. Many of the feminist activists interviewed are the "founding mothers" of the reproductive justice movement, including Byllye Avery, Loretta J. Ross, Luz Martínez, Luz Rodríguez, Marlene Fried, Katsi Cook, Nkenge Toure, and Carmen Vazquez.

I coded the texts for specific narrative themes. From the analysis, three categories of stories emerged: origin stories, opposition stories, and cautionary tales. For the rest of this essay, I will discuss these different categories of stories and how they contribute to the construction of the reproductive justice framework.

Origin Stories: Establishing a Movement

In the early stages of an emerging social movement, it is crucial to gain as much momentum as possible at the grassroots; a movement must construct an identity that not only reflects what it stands for, but also establishes it as a viable and effective political contender. The process of constructing a social movement identity includes the repeated telling of origin stories. Origin stories are the collective narratives that a culture uses to explain how other things came into being, such as the beginning of the world or the creation of the human race. Emerging social movements often tell stories about their founding and purpose in their grassroots organizing activities, such as membership meetings, conferences, training workshops, and other related events. The following is an example of an origin story about SisterSong:

> Throughout our herstory in the United States, women of color have been engaged in individual and collective struggles to save our lives. Our reproductive and sexual rights have always been an integral part of this movement. Now, newer generations of women are continuing this legacy. Its [sic] important for them to understand "herstory" and on whose shoulders they [stand]. Despite evidence of our resistance, women of color in the United States remain disproportionately affected by reproductive health concerns and related human rights violations. The Sister-Song Collective emerged at a crucial time in this herstory, a time when the women's and civil rights movements were both experiencing critical backlash. SisterSong is the fifth and longest-lived attempt to organize a national coalition of women of color health organizations. The previous

efforts were in the late 1980s and early 1990s, but did not last due to lack of funding to build the capacity of women of color organizations to support a national collaboration. (SisterSong 2003, 8)

For reproductive justice activists, the purpose of continually retelling this and similar stories is not only to relate the founding of the collective, but also to remember and honor the "herstory" of the foremothers of the movement. These stories dispel the misconception that reproductive rights is a White women's issue and that women of color have not been involved in this type of activism at all. Examples of past achievements and struggles are meant to educate young women of color and to *inspire* them to become the future leaders of reproductive justice activism.

In establishing the identity of the movement, reproductive justice activists tell origin stories explaining the meaning behind the name "SisterSong." According to SisterSong lore, the organization's name is attributed to Juanita Williams, a founding member of the collective who serves on the management circle (that is, the collective's board of directors). The collective wanted a name that reflected the commonality in struggle of all racial and ethnic groups and recognized the specific needs of each community.

SisterSong and the reproductive justice movement were formed at a time when a lot of women of color organizations were struggling to stay afloat, and many of the women of color projects that had been established within the mainstream pro-choice groups were also struggling. Many of these organizations had limited funding, small staffs, no computers, and no non-profit, tax-exempt status, and as a result, they felt isolated from one another and ineffective. One woman of color activist lamented:

Resources and efforts on reproductive health ceased in communities of color. In the late 80s, it was in vogue to fund women of color projects within white women's organizations. In the early [1990s], because of the lack of cultural competency within those white organizations and tokenism, the trend was to fund women of color organizations. Now they have gone back to funding women of color projects in white organizations, because many of these organizations are not in existence or no longer addressing those issues. . . . The [1980s] was when these organizations flourished, but there [were] no cultural competencies. These organizations—NBWHP, NLIRH, and NAWHO—were doing the organizing in their communities. There was a lack of presence of communities of color in public events. So some people began to question their effectiveness and began to ask, "Why are we funding you?" We are still seeing the same issue, but when we had our meetings, people were showing up. (NLIRH 2001)

According to Juanita Williams at the 2007 SisterSong conference in Chicago, "we're singing the same song, but we are not singing in harmony." Along with the name came the tagline, "doing collectively what we cannot not do individually" (SisterSong 2007). The founding of SisterSong was a move for survival as well as unity, as these organizations were about to pool their energy and resources to support one another. The collective's name reflects the unity of the many voices of the groups.

Opposition Stories: Moving beyond Choice

In the creation of its own identity, a movement not only defines itself by what it is, but also by what it is not. That is, it defines itself by its opposition. I call these sets of narratives opposition stories. Borrowed from semiotics, the term "opposition" refers to the meaning-making process. An object or entity (that is, a sign) derives its meaning not solely by what it is, but also by what it is not (that is, its signifier) (Feldman and Skoldberg 2002). In other words, an object has meaning because of another object that is its opposite.

In early 2003, the "big four" reproductive rights groups in the country—Planned Parenthood, NOW, the Feminist Majority Foundation, and NARAL Pro-Choice America—met to discuss the current state of affairs. They ultimately decided to hold a march to call attention to the endangerment of reproductive rights, deciding to call it the "March for Freedom of Choice." Little did they know that getting people at the grassroots level revved up and excited to participate was going to be a challenge. Loretta Ross, the national coordinator of SisterSong and a former organizer for national NOW, recalls:

But we women of color felt that the abortion framework, the choice framework, was just too narrow a vessel to talk about the threat to women's lives. We're dealing with the Bush administration, an immoral and illegal war in Iraq, the Patriot Act, poverty—I mean, all these things would not be challenged by just talking about freedom of choice. I mean, if we made abortion totally available, totally accessible, totally legal, totally affordable, women would still have other problems. And so reducing women's lives down to just whether or not choice is available, we felt was inadequate. . . . It was really about choice and abortion. Not the right to have a child, but the right to terminate a pregnancy. That's all they wanted to talk about. And so, we had dissatisfaction with the name of the march. We had dissatisfaction with the fact that there were no women of color involved in the decision-making about the march. And then, if they wanted women of color to significantly participate in the march, then they had to build our capacity to do so. We're representing organizations that have one, two, three staff people, so which one of our projects are we going to drop so that we could participate in their agenda? That was not a tenable solution for us. And so, we had the plenary and then the march organizers sponsored a post-plenary discussion caucus dinner where we sat around, about twenty of us sat around, and hashed it out with them. (Ross 2005)

As Ross's story suggests, the march was not gaining any momentum among grassroots constituencies in the early stages of the planning. Many activists were resentful that the "big four" had decided to plan a march without any significant input from them and were dissatisfied that the march would address only abortion rights. Eventually, SisterSong, the Black Women's Health Imperative, and the National Latina Institute for Reproductive Health would join the planning team of the 2004 march. These three groups are credited with broadening the march's message beyond abortion and having it renamed the March for Women's Lives. Not only did the revamped march draw more than one million participants, it was endorsed by over 140 women of color and people of color organizations out of a total 1,400 organizations; only twenty women of color groups had endorsed the march at the beginning (Cassie 2004; Otis 2004; Kashef 2005). Significantly, the NAACP publicly endorsed the reproductive rights march, which was the first time ever for the ninety-five-year-old civil rights organization. Its endorsement resolution simply stated, "A woman denied the right to control her own body is denied equal protection under the law" (Cassie 2004).

This story echoes similar stories that emerged from previous reproductive rights marches hosted by NOW in the 1980s and 1990s. In previous marches, women of color were not only concerned that their perspectives would not be included; they also expressed fears that the mainstream pro-choice groups would co-opt their political perspectives once they were included in the organizing for these marches (Martínez 2004). The story reflects the precarious nature of the relationship between women of color activists and the mainstream, pro-choice groups.

Ross's story also alludes to the ambivalence that many women of color activists have felt toward the pro-choice framework. As Andrea Smith argues, the pro-choice/pro-life framework marginalizes many groups of women, including women of color, poor women, and women with disabilities, as it is not an accurate reflection of the experiences of these communities (Smith 2005a). For example, Native American women are not just concerned about the criminalization or decriminalization of abortion, but also about fighting for the life and self-determination of their communities, including the issues of sovereignty rights and the increased incarceration of people of color. The focus on life should not be concerned just with the birth of children, but also about the quality of life for those who already exist. The "right to life" is an empty rhetorical phrase if it is not also focused on addressing social issues such as poverty and drugs that contribute to poor living conditions and crime-related activity—which have a significant impact on reproductive freedom.

When I use the term "opposition stories," I do not mean to imply that the reproductive justice movement is a countermovement to the pro-choice movement, that is, a movement created to directly oppose the political agenda of the pro-choice movement. After all, many pro-choice groups, such as the Planned Parenthood Federation of America, NARAL ProChoice America, and Choice USA, are affiliated (allied) groups of SisterSong. Moreover, the reproductive justice movement supports keeping abortion legal and advocates for women's right not to have children, but also for women's right to to *have* children and to *parent* the children that they have, which have not traditionally been a central component of the pro-choice agenda. On the other hand, it would be a misstatement to say that the reproductive justice movement is a subset of the pro-choice movement, even though many reproductive justice activists have been involved in pro-choice groups as members, staff, and board members. It is a movement in its own right; the difference is that intersectional politics are at the center of its political mission and vision. Intersectional politics informs its political agenda. These sets of stories are the means through which the movement establishes its political territory.

The reproductive justice movement forms its identity partially by setting itself apart from the mainstream pro-choice movement; we make sense of the identity and the goals of reproductive justice because of its difference from the mainstream pro-choice movement. Part of this process includes critiquing the concept of choice and arguing why it is problematic, while also presenting an alternative framework. It is through the telling of opposition stories that reproductive justice activists reveal how the intersections of race, class, sexuality, and other markers of difference affect reproductive freedom not only for individuals but also for entire communities; that is, "choice" does not exist in a vacuum. There are systemic, structural obstacles that can limit the options that exist for individuals and communities.

Cautionary Tales: The Specter of Eugenics

In addition to telling stories about the origins of the movement and the limitations of the concept of "choice," reproductive justice activists also tell cautionary tales in their consciousness-raising activities. Cautionary tales are stories that have a moral message and often warn the audience of the negative consequences of a particular transgression, character flaw, or objectionable situation. Reproductive justice activists are particularly cautious when new reproductive and genetic technologies are approved the U.S. Food and Drug Administration (FDA) and introduced into the consumer market.

In an interview, a Latina reproductive justice activist explained her organization's stance on controversial contraceptive drugs and devices:

> We did need more options for women. There was the boom and bust of Norplant—which was promoted as a miracle contraceptive technology, the way it was utilized, forced on disenfranchised communities— dispensed to poor women, African American women, and Latina women. The government would pay for the implant, but only for a percentage of the removal—so there was a coercive mechanism in place through policy in the public health system. Women get it in, but the side effects were not good, but then they couldn't get it out because they did not have the money for that and the federal government would not pay for it. Physicians were eager to implant these devices, but were not well-trained to remove them. These are two separate [issues]. Yes, it was a good thing to have more technologies available. However, we need to give some thought to the different possible scenarios where policy makers may react or overreact in the utilization of those technologies. (NLIRH 2001)

The specter of eugenics looms in the backdrop of reproductive justice discourse. Popular in the early half of the twentieth century and based on social Darwinism, eugenics is a pseudoscientific theory that promotes the improvement of the human species by encouraging or permitting reproduction among individuals who are deemed to have the desirable genetic profile for breeding. Under the eugenics framework, only the fit shall reproduce. Those who were considered unfit to reproduce or parent have included the poor, the disabled, the mentally ill, criminals, gay men, and lesbians. Federal and state laws, policies, and court cases promoted, supported, and upheld eugenics practices. State institutions routinely sterilized "feebleminded" individuals on the premise that mental health and low IQs were inherited traits and should not be transmitted to future generations; these practices were upheld by the U.S. Supreme Court, particularly in *Buck v. Bell* (1927) in which the court ruled that the forced sterilization of a woman in a mental hospital was constitutional (Roberts 1997; Cushman 2001; Baer 2002).

Some reproductive justice activists would also argue that seemingly beneficial family planning programs may not be as innocuous as they may appear to be. Asian Communities for Reproductive Justice argues:

> Though highly problematic from an anti-racist and anti-imperialist perspective, population control discourse was politically successful in increasing the visibility and acceptance of birth control in the first half of the 20th century. At the same time, African American women who made connections between race, class, and gender joined the fight for birth control in the 1920s as much from Black women's experience as enslaved breeders for the accumulation of wealth of White slave-owners as for realization of gender empowerment. In the 1960s, the federal government began funding family planning both in the United States and internationally as part of a strategy for population control, rather than women's empowerment. Population control has been defined as externally imposed efforts by governments, corporations or private agencies to control (by increasing or limiting) population growth, usually by controlling women's reproduction and fertility. Other forms of population control include immigration restrictions, selective population movement or dispersal, incarceration, and various forms of discrimination. (ACRJ 2005, 3)

Given the troubling history of sterilization abuse and eugenics practices, many reproductive justice advocates are cautious not to rush into embracing newer reproductive and genetic technologies, including Norplant and Depo Provera, without examining the potential consequences to their communities. Judges around the country began using the devices in sentencing not long after their approval by the FDA. Norplant and Depo Provera were often offered as alternatives to prison for women of childbearing age who were convicted of felony possession or distribution of cocaine, crack, or heroin as well as pregnant women with a history of drug use. In many states legislation had been proposed that would make the device a condition for continuation of welfare payments to beneficiaries (Rees 1991; Samuels and Smith 1992; Arras and Bluestein 1995; Chavkin and Breitbart 1996; Roberts 1997; Campbell 2000; Paltrow 2002; Roberts 2006). For instance, some states, such as Kansas, Louisiana, and North Carolina, have proposed legislation in which financial incentives would be given to welfare recipients to obtain Norplant. This was usually in the form of a "bonus" of up to $500. There have been reports of the systematic implantation of Norplant in Native American women through the Indian Health Services (Smith 2005b).

These policies were modeled after a program implemented by C.R.A.C. K. (Children Requiring a Caring Kommunity), a private organization founded by homemaker Barbara Harris in Anaheim, CA in 1994. The organization offers poor women with substance addictions $200 to undergo surgical sterilization or use a long-acting contraceptive such as Norplant or Depo Provera, which essentially are temporary sterilization. The program has expanded to Chicago, Florida, New Hampshire, and Washington State (BWHI 2001; CWPE 2006). The Committee on Women, Population, and the Environment (CWPE) has been diligent in monitoring and counteracting the activities of C.R.A.C.K.

Concern about reproductive technologies has informed the political agenda of several reproductive justice organizations. To address the legacy of involuntary sterilization, for example, the CWPE has begun a campaign to get state legislatures to pass resolutions to publicly apologize for those and other eugenics campaigns. They were successful in getting the Georgia state legislature to introduce and pass a resolution in 2007. The resolution states:

BE IT RESOLVED BY THE SENATE that the members of this body express their profound regret for Georgia's participation in the eugenics movement and the injustices done under eugenics laws, including the forced sterilization of Georgia citizens. BE IT FURTHER RESOLVED that the members of this body hereby support the full education of Georgia citizens about the eugenics movement in order to foster a respect for the fundamental dignity of human life and the God given rights recognized by our Founding Fathers. (Georgia General Assembly 2007, 2)

Last, this set of stories allows the reproductive justice movement to deal with political issues in which the pro-choice rhetoric is insufficient and a nuanced understanding of the reproductive experiences of communities of color is needed. In early 2010, members of the Georgia State Assembly introduced a bill, entitled the OB/GYN Criminalization and Racial Discrimination Act, that would categorize abortions performed on fetuses based on race, color, or sex as a form of discrimination, and it would criminalize medical practitioners who performed such abortions (SisterSong 2010b). This legislation was accompanied by large billboards that proclaimed that "black children are an endangered species," tapping into long-standing fears of genocide among many African Americans. By fighting the passage of this bill, SisterSong created a coalition of reproductive justice and allied organizations, including SPARK Reproductive Justice NOW!, SisterLove, Inc., Feminist Women's Health Center (GA,) and Planned Parenthood Southeast, and garnered national support from civil rights leaders and clergy. Because of its acumen in understanding the right of all women to have access to abortion and the history of fertility control targeting communities of color, SisterSong was able to counter the genocidal arguments of the bill's anti-abortion supporters and eventually prevent the passage of the bill (SisterSong 2010b).

Creating Space, Building a Movement

SisterSong is not the entirety of the reproductive justice movement, but it serves as a good stand-in for the movement given the sheer number of organizations involved in it. As a movement organization, SisterSong is continually constructing its collective identity through the process of telling stories. These stories are repeatedly told at membership meetings, conferences, workshops, rallies, and other events as well as in various written materials.

As I have shown in this essay, three types of stories dominate the identity-construction process. Collectively, these stories serve the purpose of not only defining SisterSong, and consequently the movement, but also setting it apart from the mainstream pro-choice movement. This strategy allows the movement to reach out to constituents that traditionally have never felt a part of the pro-choice movement. Indeed, many individual activists involved in the reproductive justice movement, including founding mother Luz Rodríguez, were not previously involved in pro-choice organizations, but were veterans of other social justice activism, such as environmental justice, economic justice, prison reform, and civil rights. Some of these non-traditional reproductive freedom activists have expressed, and continue to express, some ambivalence toward the pro-choice movement.

These stories also create the space that the movement needs in order to advance its more holistic agenda. This was evident at a recent membership meeting held in Washington, DC in December 2009, when the health-care reform bill was on the floor of the U.S. House of Representatives for debate and final vote. Although the planners and participants initially thought that it would be a routine membership meeting, that sentiment quickly changed when it was discovered that several amendments had been introduced that could be detrimental to women of color and immigrant women (SisterSong 2010a). Several amendments proposed to restrict immigrants' access to healthcare. Another, the Stupak-Pitts amendment, would prevent federals funds from being used to pay for abortions, including private plans that cover subsidized customers; the amendment would explicitly codify the 1976 Hyde amendment in the health bill. Drawing upon their narrative threads, SisterSong was able to rally the 400+ participants to action by sending impromptu state delegations of women of color, who visited their respective representatives in their congressional offices, to urge them to vote against these proposals. Although some of these amendments, including the Stupak-Pitts amendment, passed, the lobbying experience energized the participating activists, as many of them had no previous legislative lobbying experience. This moment also marked the political coming of age of the movement; this was the first coordinated congressional lobbying effort of the organization.

The goal of the reproductive justice framework is to transform the way in which we all conceptualize and understand reproductive freedom. Will this new framework catch on? A Google search in June 2007 of the term "reproductive justice" yielded over 1.2 million hits, which suggests that the term is gaining some momentum. In fact, some of the mainstream pro-choice organizations have adopted the term. For example, in 2005 the Planned Parenthood Federation of America hosted a national policy conference entitled "Reproductive Justice for All" at Smith College in Northampton, Massachusetts, and even the national group Choice USA, co-founded by Gloria Steinem, hosts a "Reproductive Justice Organizing Academy" for young activists (PPFA 2005). Although Choice USA uses the term "reproductive justice" in its political and grassroots activities, it has still retained the term "choice" in its name (for examples, visit its website http://www.choiceusa.org). Reproductive justice activists warn that the term "reproductive justice" is not meant to be a substitute or interchangeable term for other terms such as abortion rights, family planning, pro-choice, population control, or even reproductive rights. It is a different way of conceptualizing reproductive freedom that is broader in scope than its predecessors.

The next step in understanding the impact of the reproductive justice movement is to focus on reproductive activism at the grassroots level, especially on how the organizing efforts of reproductive justice activists at this level contribute to the national political and policy agenda. After all, much of the national agenda is based on issues that arise from the community level and depends upon the activities of grassroots activists, especially coalition-building with other social justice movements. For instance, the network of reproductive justice organizations in California have worked successfully with groups representing other social justice movements, such as immigrants' rights and traditional African American civil rights groups, to defeat voter ballot initiatives that could have had a negative impact on women's ability to access reproductive health services in the state. These efforts have served as models for reproductive justice groups in other regions of the country.

....

Kimala Price is associate professor and graduate advisor of women's studies at San Diego State University (SDSU). Additionally, she is a codirector of the Bread and Roses Center for Feminist Research and Activism at SDSU. She holds a doctorate in political science and a graduate certificate in women's studies from the University of Michigan, Ann Arbor. Her research focuses on reproductive policy and politics, the reproductive justice movement, interpretive research methodology, and community-engaged research.

Note

Originally published in *Meridians* vol. 10, no. 2, 2010.
This essay began as a series of invited talks I gave in 2006 and 2007 at Georgetown University Law School, the Feminist Forum of the George Washington

University Law School, the Harvard School of Public Health, and the Department of Women's Studies at San Diego State University. A version of this paper was presented at the 2008 Feminism(s) and Rhetoric(s) conference. The project was partially funded by a fellowship from the American Association of University Women (AAUW).

Works Cited

ACRJ. 2005. "A New Vision for Advancing Our Movement for Reproductive Health, Reproductive Rights and Reproductive Justice." Oakland, CA: Asian Communities for Reproductive Justice.

Arras, John D., and Jeffrey Blustein. 1995. "Reproductive Responsibility and Long-Acting Contraceptives." *The Hastings Center Report* 25: S27–29.

Baer, Judith A. 2002. *Historical and Multicultural Encyclopedia of Women's Reproductive Rights in the United States.* Westport, CT: Greenwood Press.

Bunch, Charlotte. 1995. "Transforming Human Rights from a Feminist Perspective." In *Women's Rights, Human Rights: International Perspectives,* ed. J. S. Peters and A. Wolper. New York: Routledge.

BWHI. 2001. "Comments on C.R.A.C.K. (Children Requiring a Caring Kommunity): Discrimination in Disguise." Washington, DC: Black Women's Health Imperative.

Campbell, Nancy Duff. 2000. *Using Women: Gender, Drug Policy, and Social Justice.* New York: Routledge.

Cassie, M. Chew. 2004. "Black Women Shape Their Own Message at March for Women's Lives." *The Crisis* 111, no. 4:14–15.

Chavkin, Wendy, and Vicki Breitbart. 1996. "Reproductive Health and Blurred Professional Boundaries." *Women's Health Issues* 6, no. 2: 89–96.

Cushman, Clare. 2001. *Supreme Court Decisions and Women's Rights: Milestones to Equality.* Washington, DC: CQ Press.

CWPE. 2006. "CRACK Uses Unethical Tactics to Stop Women with Substance Abuse Problems." Atlanta, GA: Committee on Women, Population, and the Environment.

Czarniawska-Joerges, Barbara. 1998. *A Narrative Approach to Organization Studies.* Thousand Oaks, CA: Sage Publications.

———. 2004. *Narratives in Social Science Research.* London: Sage.

Davis, Angela Yvonne. 1983. *Women, Race, & Class.* New York: Vintage Books.

Feldman, Martha S., et al. 2004. "Making Sense of Stories: A Rhetorical Approach to Narrative Analysis." *Journal of Public Administration Research and Theory* 14, no. 2: 147–70.

Feldman, Martha S., and Kaj Skoldberg. 2002. "Stories and Rhetoric of Contrariety: Subtexts of Organizing (Change)." *Culture and Organization* 8, no. 4: 275–92.

Fried, Marlene Gerber. 2007. Interview by Joyce Follet. Transcript of video recording, August 14 and 15, 2007. Voices of Feminism Oral History Project, Sophia Smith Collection. Northampton, MA: Smith College.

Georgia General Assembly. 2007. Senate Resolution SR 247. "Eugenics; Express Profound Regret for Georgia's Participation." March 27. http://www.legis.state.ga.us/legis/2007_08/sum/sr247.htm (accessed September 7, 2010).

Howell, Marcella. 2007. *Walk in My Shoes: A Black Activist's Guide to Surviving the Women's Movement.* Washington, DC: Advocates for Youth.

Kashef, Ziba. 2005. "Toward Reproductive Freedom." *Colorlines* 7, no. 4: 30.

Martínez, Luz Alvarez. 2004. Interview by Loretta Ross, Transcript of video recording, December 6–7, 2004. Voices of Feminism Oral History Project, Sophia Smith Collection. Northampton, MA: Smith College.

NAPAWF. (National Asian Pacific American Women's Forum). 2008. "Hyde Amendment – 30 Years is Enough!" (Briefing Paper) (January).

Nelson, Jennifer. 2003. *Women of Color and the Reproductive Rights Movement.* New York: New York University Press.

NLIRH (National Latina Institute for Reproductive Health). 2001. Interview with Representative. Washington, DC, December 12.

OHCHR. 1996. "The International Bill of Human Rights (Fact Sheet)." Geneva: Office of the United Nations High Commissioner for Human Rights, United Nations.

Otis, Ginger Adams. 2004. "Racism and Reproductive Rights." *The Nation,* http://www.thenation.com/doc/20040510/otis (accessed April 22, 2004).

Paltrow, L. M. 2002. "The War on Drugs and the War on Abortion: Some Initial Thoughts on the Connections, Intersections and Effects." *Reproductive Health Matters* 10, no. 19: 162–70.

PEP. 1997. "An Exploration of Young Women's Attitudes toward Pro-Choice." New York: The Pro-Choice Education Project.

———. 2004. "She Speaks: African American and Latino Women on Reproductive Health and Rights." New York: The Pro-Choice Public Education Project.

Polletta, Francesca, and James M. Jasper. 2001. "Collective Identity and Social Movements." *Annual Review of Sociology* 27: 283–305.

PPFA. 2005. "Reproductive Justice for All: A Policy Conference, Summary Report." November 10–13, 2005, at Smith College, Northampton, MA.

Rees, Matthew. 1991. "Shot in the Arm: The Use and Abuse of Norplant: Involuntary Contraception and Public Policy." *The New Republic* (December 9): 16–17.

Roberts, Dorothy E. 1997. *Killing the Black Body: Race, Reproduction, and the Meaning of Liberty.* New York: Pantheon Books.

———. 2006. "Feminism, Race and Adoption Policy." In *Color of Violence: The Incite! Anthology,* ed. Incite! Women of Color Against Violence. Cambridge, MA: South End Press.

Ross, Loretta. 1992. "African-American Women and Abortion: A Neglected History." *Journal of Health Care for the Poor and Underserved* 3, no. 2: 274–84.

———. 2005. Interview by Joyce Follet. Transcript of video recording, November and December 2004, February 2005. Voices of Feminism Oral History Project, Sophia Smith Collection. Northampton, MA: Smith College.

———. 2006. "Understanding Reproductive Justice." (Briefing paper) Atlanta, GA: SisterSong Women of Color Reproductive Health Collective, May.

Ross, Loretta J., et al. 2001. "The 'SisterSong Collective': Women of Color, Reproductive Health and Human Rights." *American Journal of Health Studies Special Issue* 17, no. 2: 79–88.

Samuels, Sarah E., and Mark D. Smith. 1992. *Norplant and Poor Women.* Menlo Park, CA: Henry J. Kaiser Family Foundation.

Silliman, Jael, and Anannya Bhattacharjee. 2002. *Policing the National Body: Race, Gender and Criminalization in the United States.* Boston: South End Press.

Silliman, Jael, et al. 2004. *Undivided Rights: Women of Color Organize for Reproductive Justice.* Cambridge, MA: South End Press.

SisterSong. 2003. "SisterSong Reproductive Health and Sexual Rights National Conference Program Book." Atlanta, GA: SisterSong Women of Color Reproductive Health Collective.

———. 2007. SisterSong Women of Color Reproductive Health Collective website. http://www.sistersong.net (accessed September 7, 2010).

———. 2010a. "SisterSong Collective Continues Fight for Women's Health Care Rights." (press release). January 10. http://www.sistersong.net (accessed September 7, 2010).

———. 2010b. "SisterSong, Spark, and SisterLove Defeat SB 529." (press release). April 30. http://www.sistersong.net (accessed September 7, 2010).

Smith, Andrea. 2005a. "Beyond Pro-Choice Versus Pro-Life: Women of Color and Reproductive Justice." *NWSA Journal* 17, no. 1: 119–40.

———. 2005b. *Conquest: Sexual Violence and American Indian Genocide.* Cambridge, MA: South End Press.

Springer, Kimberly, ed. 1999. *Still Lifting, Still Climbing: Contemporary African American Women's Activism.* New York: New York University Press.

Staggenborg, Suzanne. 1991. *The Pro-Choice Movement: Organization and Activism in The Abortion Conflict.* New York: Oxford University Press.

Stone, Deborah A. 1989. "Causal Stories and the Formation of Policy Agendas." *Political Science Quarterly* 104, no. 2: 281–300.

Universal Declaration of Human Rights. 1948. Office of the High Commissioner for Human Rights, United Nations. December 10.

L. Ayu Saraswati

....

Cosmopolitan Whiteness

The Effects and Affects of Skin-Whitening Advertisements
in a Transnational Women's Magazine in Indonesia

Abstract: Previous scholarship on the immense popularity of skin-whitening
frames this practice as revealing women's desire to emulate whiteness and
upper class White populations. Others have focused on whitening practices
to highlight the working of racialized color hierarchy and European/Euro-
American hegemony in local and global contexts. This article breaks away
from these established theoretical trajectories by arguing that desire for
"whiteness" is not the same as desire for "Caucasian whiteness." Examining
advertisements for skin-whitening products in the Indonesian version of
Cosmopolitan and skin-tanning products in the American version of Cosmopolitan, the author points out the construction of "cosmopolitan whiteness." Whiteness is not simply racialized or nationalized as such, but transnationalized. Whiteness is represented as "cosmopolitanness," embodying
transnational mobility.

Skin-whitening advertisements dominate the landscape of Indonesian
women's magazines. Often, these whitening advertisements appear on the
first page of such magazines. In the June 2006 edition of the Indonesian
Cosmopolitan (hereafter referred to as *Cosmo*), Estée Lauder's "Cyber White"
ad appeared on the inside front-cover spread of the magazine. In the following issue of the Indonesian *Cosmo* (July 2006) Kosé's Sekkisei whitening
ad with the slogan "Skin of Innocence" appeared as the front-cover gate-
fold. Neither of these transnational ads employs Indonesian models: a
Caucasian woman models the "Cyber White" ad, and a Japanese woman

MERIDIANS · feminism, race, transnationalism   Volume 19 Supplement 2020
DOI: 10.1215/15366936-8566045 © 2010 Smith College

models the Sekkisei ad. These skin-whitening ads, modeled by women of different racial backgrounds and facial features, beg the question: what kind of whiteness is being marketed in transnational women's magazine such as the Indonesian *Cosmo*?

Existing studies on skin-whitening phenomena in a variety of countries fall short of answering this question because these studies operate under the assumption that whiteness is an ethnic or racially based category, however marked it may be by biological, social, and visual signifiers (Burke 1996; Peiss 1998; Kawashima 2002; Hall 2005; Hunter 2005; Rondilla and Spickard 2007; Pierre 2008; Glenn 2009; Parameswaran and Cardoza 2009). For example, when cultural studies scholar Radhika Parameswaran and journalist Kavitha Cardoza point out that whitening advertisements in contemporary Indian media do not necessarily reveal women's desire to be racially White, they are equating "White" with racially Caucasian people (Parameswaran and Cardoza 2009). Similarly, when historian Timothy Burke notes that women's consumption of skin whiteners in modern Zimbabwe was considered as a sign of (re)colonization and "selling-out" to the White regime, he also positioned "white" as a racial category (Burke 1996). Indeed, the term "white-privileging subject position" that Asian studies scholar Terry Kawashima coined in her analysis of contemporary anime, skin-whitening ads, and hair-coloring phenomena in Japan also rests on the same assumed White racial category: Caucasian (Kawashima 2002).

Other important studies on the racial politics of beauty that challenge body-altering practices as merely revealing people's desires for the White beauty norm nonetheless refer to Caucasian whiteness as a frame for referencing "whiteness." Kathleen Zane, although providing us with a different way of reading Asian women's eyelid surgeries that goes beyond Asian women's desire to "imitate a Caucasian appearance" (Zane 1998, 355), still attaches the category of "Caucasian" whiteness to the meaning of a "White" beauty norm. Kobena Mercer has demonstrated the complex "inter-culturation" of so-called "artificial" and "natural" techniques of hairstyling among Black people (as well as among people in "White subcultures"), and asked "who in this postmodern mêlée of semiotic appropriation and counter-creolization, is imitating whom?" (Mercer 1987, 52). Yet he also refers to Caucasian whiteness when he highlights this complexity of whiteness as an embodied racial category. Thus, although critical scholarship on the racial politics of beauty convincingly debunks the myth of racially authentic bodies and points to the unstable quality of "looking

White," these studies nonetheless still subscribe to the very notion of Caucasian whiteness as the point of theoretical reference in challenging such whiteness.

This article breaks away from these theoretical trajectories by arguing that desire for "whiteness" is *not* the same as desire for "Caucasian whiteness." By examining skin-whitening advertisements in the Indonesian *Cosmo*[1] published during the months of June, July, and August, 2006–2008,[2] I argue that in contemporary Indonesia it is what I am calling "cosmopolitan whiteness" that is being marketed through these whitening ads. By cosmopolitan whiteness, I refer to whiteness when represented to embody the "affective" and virtual quality of cosmopolitanism: transnational mobility. In using the term "affect," I am drawing on Theresa Brennan's definition of the term as "physiological shift accompanying a judgment" (Brennan 2004, 5). Here affect is understood as preceding emotions, yet also involving "sociality or social productivity" (Wissinger 2007, 232). In this article I position these ads as a socially productive site where affective qualities about white-skinned women are produced, represented, and circulated.

I propose the notion of cosmopolitan whiteness as a mode for rethinking whiteness beyond racial and ethnic categories and for thinking about race, skin color, and gender as "affectively" constructed. To think about whiteness beyond a racial or ethnic category is not to argue that race and racialization are irrelevant in thinking about whiteness, of course. Rather, I argue that whiteness is *also* affectively constructed as cosmopolitan and that race and racialization operate in concert with cosmopolitanism in these whitening advertisements.

Redefining whiteness as cosmopolitan whiteness allows me to reveal yet another aspect of cosmopolitanness *and* whiteness that is not often discussed: its virtuality. Virtuality here is understood as occupying the space between the real and the unreal: the virtual. This notion of virtuality is important in understanding cosmopolitan whiteness because virtuality highlights the lack of "traditional physical substance" (Laurel 1993, 8). I argue that cosmopolitan whiteness is a signifier without a racialized, signified body. Cosmopolitan whiteness can and has been modeled by women from Japan to South Korea to the United States. There is no one race or ethnic group in particular that can occupy an authentic cosmopolitan White location because there has never been a "real" whiteness to begin with: whiteness is a virtual quality, neither real nor unreal.

This article anchors the analysis of skin-whitening advertisements in affect theories and cultural studies of emotion; in doing so, it aims to advance our understanding of the ways in which race, gender, and skin color are not only socially and visually constructed but also affectively, virtually, and transnationally constructed. As such, this article operates at the intersection of affect theories and cultural studies of emotions and theories of gendered racialization, transnationalization, and cyberculture studies. For this particular study, a privileging of affect theories is important because key studies on race, skin color, and racialization that highlight the ideological work and material consequences of race (Omi and Winant 1994; Winant 1994; Dyer 1997; Winant 2001; Hunter 2005) have yet to pay careful attention to the affective structures through which gender and race are constructed. This is problematic because racialization processes rely on how people feel about others: "feeling" is where the structural and the individual collide. Moreover, although much has been written on how people and objects that travel across national boundaries help transform the racial, political, physical, cultural, social, and financial landscape of the places they have traveled to and from (Appadurai 1996; Shohat 1998; Ong 1999; Sarker and Niyogi De 2002), little attention has been paid to how circulations of people and ideas across national boundaries influence the production of affects and the affective construction of race, skin color, and gender. The few exceptions and exceptional works that have charted affect and emotions in a global context do not focus on Indonesia (Grewal 2005; Freeman 2007; Harding and Pribram 2009). The two works that discuss emotions in the Indonesian context do not focus on racialized beauty (Wieringa 2008; Lindquist 2009). Additionally, although cyberculture scholars have addressed issues of race in cyberspace (Ebo 1998; Kolko, Nakamura, and Rodman 2000; Ebo 2001; Nakamura 2002; 2008), they have yet to link notions of virtuality and race with emotions.

In the following pages, I provide two essential contexts for this study. The first context provides a brief historical overview of gendered, racialized beauty in Indonesia. The second context addresses the politics of the transnational circulation of *Cosmo* from the United States to Indonesia. Such a context will help demonstrate how "a racially saturated field of visibility" (Butler 1993, 15) has limited the readings of skin-whitening ads as merely reflecting desires for Caucasian whiteness. This contextual grounding leads us directly into the analysis of these whitening ads, focusing on both the construction of cosmopolitan whiteness and on the ads as a site for the production of a cosmopolitan whiteness as something that is good and desirable. I do the latter by focusing on one exemplary ad, Estée Lauder's "Cyber White," to provide evidence for my argument that the construction of cosmopolitan whiteness contributes to the production of "positive" affects toward white-skinned women, that virtuality is an important aspect of cosmopolitan whiteness, and that the production of these "good" affects relies on the ads' "facialization" process. Finally, I will end this article with a twist. That is, rather than reiterating my argument by way of repeating my reading of whitening ads, I will draw my examples from a different type of skin-coloring ad: tanning ads.

Transnational Contacts and Cosmo Contexts
The Racialized Beauty Ideal in Transnational Indonesia

In Indonesia, a country of 300 ethnic groups, the formation of beauty ideals, articulated through racial, skin color, and gender discourses, has historically been transnational. As seen in some of the oldest surviving Indonesian literature, such as *Ramayana*, light-skinned women were the dominant beauty norm of the time. The Indonesian (or so-called Old-Javanese) version of *Ramayana* was adapted from its Indian origin in the late ninth century. In both the Indian and Indonesian versions of *Ramayana*, beautiful women are described as having white shining faces, like the full moon. This evidence suggests that: 1) preference for light-skinned women in Indonesia predates European colonialism; and 2) the light-skinned beauty standard in precolonial Indonesia should not be read as merely a "local" or "indigenous" construction. Rather, this idea of light skin color as beautiful is already a "transnational" construction, *avant la lettre*—from India to Indonesia.[3]

This transnational construction of beauty ideals has continued from Dutch and Japanese colonial times into the present day. During the early twentieth century, when Dutch colonialism fully matured in colonial Indonesia (then called the Indies) preference for light (decoded as Caucasian White) skin color was strengthened. Images of Caucasian White beauty represented the epitome of beauty in the beauty ads published in women's magazines during this time. When the Japanese took over as the new colonial power in Indonesia from 1942 to 1945, they propagated a new Asian beauty ideal: white was still the preferred color but not the preferred race. In postcolonial Indonesia, particularly since the late 1960s when the pro-American president Suharto reigned in Indonesia, American popular

culture has become one of the strongest influences against which the
Indonesian white beauty ideal is articulated and negotiated. In contemporary Indonesia, as Indonesian feminist Aquarini Prabasmoro points out, it
is light-skinned "Indo" or "mixed-race" women who embody the beauty
ideal (Prabasmoro 2003). She argues that it is precisely the ability of the
Indo woman's body to be read as "white in a non-white culture," but not
white enough "to be white in the global context" that positions her as
desirable (Prabasmoro 2003, 91). After all, desiring Caucasian whiteness is
objectionable for it suggests a sign of European recolonization (Prasetyaningsih 2007).

With a light-skinned beauty standard being cultivated throughout different historical periods, it is not surprising that skin-whitening products
are the most popular products in the cosmetics industry in Indonesia. This
is so regardless of the Indonesian Badan Pengawas Obat dan Makanan's
(BPOM—equivalent to the U.S. Food and Drug Administration) public
warning, issued on September 7, 2006, that listed whitening products that
contain illegal ingredients such as mercury or hydroquinone beyond the
allowable two-percent limit. These ingredients are deemed dangerous
because they could cause skin irritation, brain and kidney damage, fetal
problems, lung failure, and cancer. The Indonesian BPOM recalled and
destroyed 1,002 products (produced not only in Indonesia but also
imported from Taiwan, Hong Kong, China, the Philippines, England, and
Thailand) that had been sold in various cities across Indonesia such as
Bengkulu, Denpasar, Kendari, Lampung, Padang, Pekanbaru, Pontianak,
Samarinda, and Jayapura. Regardless of these recalls, however, whitening
products containing banned ingredients continue to be marketed in Indonesia, and whitening ads continue to flourish in the Indonesian market,
particularly in women's magazines.

The Cosmo Politics of Transnational Circulation:
From the United States to Indonesia
U.S. popular culture, from its films and magazines to its consumer products, has become one of the most powerful "nodes" (Appadurai 1996) in
shaping the terrain of contemporary Indonesian pop culture. Particularly
since 1998,[4] there has been a major boom in Indonesian adaptations of
American magazines such as *Cosmo, Good Housekeeping,* and *Esquire.* Hence,
although my focus in this article is on examining skin-whitening ads
in the Indonesian *Cosmo,* in this section, I am also looking at U.S. *Cosmo*

magazines during the same months (June–August of 2006–2008) to chart the circulation of beauty, racial, and gender discourses through this transnational magazine. Moreover, examining the United States as a site where whiteness is articulated as "desirable," my analysis makes visible how transnational circulations of whiteness from the United States to Indonesia depend on the ways in which whiteness is capable of maintaining its currency globally (hence the notion of cosmopolitan whiteness).

The magazine I examine here, *Cosmopolitan*, is one of the most popular transnational women's magazines in Indonesia. It originated in the United States in 1886 as a literary/fiction magazine. It underwent a significant transformation in 1965 when its new editor, Helen Gurley Brown, then the well-known author of *Sex and the Single Girl*, took a daring step by shifting the magazine's focus to women's sexuality and, as well as in, the workplace (McMachon 1990; Spooner 2001). With the slogan, "fun . . . fearless . . . female," U.S. *Cosmo*'s strategy of marketing to and advocating for sexually independent women saved it from almost certain bankruptcy. Prior to 1965, sexuality was rarely discussed in U.S. women's magazines, which at that time were focused more on women's place in the home (Nelson and Paek 2005). In Indonesia as well, when *Cosmo* (originally called *Kosmopolitan Higina*) first began publication in September 1997, promoting sexually assertive women (albeit in a much subtler way compared to the 2006–2008 editions that I analyzed for this article) meant breaking new ground. Although some Muslim groups in Indonesia sent letters to the editor protesting that the magazine was "helping Indonesian women love sex too much" (Carr 2002), nonetheless, the strategy of putting forth women's independence through sexuality was what made *Cosmo* one of the most successful magazines in the world. It has fifty-eight international editions, is published in thirty-four languages, and is circulated in over one hundred countries, including Indonesia. *Cosmo* is indeed the most popular transnational women's magazine in Indonesia, with a circulation of 139,000. In the Indonesian context, marketing specialist Hermawan Kartajaya applauded its marketing strategy, arguing that *Cosmo*, by carefully formulating and consistently encouraging women to adopt a "cosmopolitan woman" identity, provided a space for Indonesian women to reject society's masculine domination (Kartajaya 2004).

From the eighteen issues of the Indonesian and U.S. *Cosmo* that I analyzed, I found that most articles and images in the two versions were different, although they seemed to be similarly structured and drew from similar sources. This is so because *Cosmo* is a transnational magazine having its own confidential "50–page manual, which dictates criteria in selection of cover models and editorial focus" (Nelson and Paek 2005, 372). For example, when both versions featured American celebrity/actress Brittany Murphy on their cover (July 2006 of American *Cosmo* and August 2006 of Indonesian *Cosmo*), she was photographed wearing different dresses. The Indonesian version shows her in a sexy, tight-fitting, red dress. The American version represents her in a colorful, floral-print tropical dress. Hence, although at first glance the two covers seem the same with the same celebrity and even connect to articles on the same topic, the Indonesian *Cosmo* is not simply a direct translation of U.S. *Cosmo*. Names are changed from American to Indonesian, and local examples or commentary by local experts are added in the Indonesian version. Based on research by David Machin and Joanna Thornborrow (2003), Michelle Nelson and Hye-Jin Paek (2005), and Jui-Shan Chang (2004) that examined *Cosmo* in several countries around the globe, this is not unique to the Indonesian case. From her work on Taiwan, for example, Chang concludes that the production of *Cosmo*

> is both centralized and localized: the various editions can borrow materials from the "central bank"—that is the New York headquarters—or from "sister" issues in other countries, as well as producing their own articles. Consequently, each issue of *Cosmopolitan*, in Taiwan and in its sister countries, contains a unique blend of global and local cultural ingredients on topics concerning modern womanhood. (Chang 2004, 363)

As such, the magazine not only uses the word "cosmopolitan" as a label to address its reader, the "cosmo" woman, it also embodies the very notion of cosmopolitanism by producing its magazines transnationally.

It is these cosmopolitan meanings, deployed in various ways by *Cosmo*, in addition to the transnational formation of a racialized beauty ideal, that provide me with the context within which I read these whitening ads published in the Indonesian *Cosmo*.

The Construction of Cosmopolitan Whiteness in Skin-Whitening Ads

Within its theoretical trajectories, the word "cosmopolitan" is understood to be rooted in the Greek "*kosmos*," which means "world," and "*polites*," meaning "citizen" (Cheah 1998, 22). It conveys the aura of a "citizen of the world." Eighteenth-century French philosophers used the term to highlight "an intellectual ethic, a universal humanism that transcends regional particularism" (Cheah 1998, 22). For Steven Vertovec and Robin Cohen, cosmopolitanism refers to "something that simultaneously: (a) transcends the seemingly exhausted nation-state model; (b) is able to mediate actions and ideals oriented both to the universal and the particular, the global and the local; (c) is culturally anti-essentialist; and (d) is capable of representing various complex repertoires of allegiance, identity and interest. In these ways, cosmopolitanism seems to offer a mode of managing cultural and political multiplicities" (Vertovec and Cohen 2002, 4). Moreover, the way the magazine deploys the word "cosmopolitan" also falls within these theoretical trajectories insofar as the magazine seems to make meanings of cosmopolitan, as Bruce Robbins explains it: "the word *cosmopolitan* . . . evokes the image of a privileged person: someone who can claim to be a 'citizen of the world' by virtue of independent means, expensive tastes, and a globe-trotting lifestyle" (Robbins 1998, 248). Here, cosmopolitanism is framed within consumer culture to mean consuming the other's exoticized and commodified culture (Vertovec and Cohen 2002, 7). Indeed, Indonesian *Cosmo*, in constructing an imaginary *Cosmo* woman, often suggests that readers should buy expensive gourmet cakes at elite hotel pastry shops and invites readers to travel abroad. "Cosmopolitan" therefore refers to embodying the possibility of transnational mobility (the slogan's "fearless"/adventurous aspect), leisure, and pleasure through the consumption of these advertised products (the slogan's "fun" aspect), and certainly "female"-ness—the essence of *Cosmo*, a magazine for women.

My close reading of skin-whitening ads published from 2006 to 2008 attests to this: these whitening ads were "transnational" and "cosmopolitan" in nature. First, almost all of the whitening ads advertised transnational brands. Except for Unilever's "local-jewel" brand, Citra, that is now also available in a few other Asian countries (and is therefore becoming transnational) and another product, Viva, all brands were transnational. Advertised brands originated in France (Dior, Biotherm, L'Oréal), the United States (Estée Lauder and Clinique), Japan (Bioré, Kosé, Kanebo, and SK-II), South Korea (Laneige), The Philippines (SkinWhite), Germany (Nivea), and the Netherlands (Pond's).

The cosmopolitanness of these ads was further emphasized by featuring non-Indonesian models. In 2006–2008, unlike only a few years prior when whitening ads typically featured local, light-skinned, Indonesian women, ads featured international models such as Choi Ji Woo (a South Korean actress/celebrity) advertising the France-based "DiorSnow Pure White"; Sammi Cheng (a Hong Kong actress/singer) modeling for Japanese SK-II's "Whitening Source Skin Brightener"; Michele Reis (a Hong Kong supermodel) advertising L'Oréal Paris's "White Perfect" and "White Perfect Eye"; Ploy Chermarn (Thai actress) modeling for L'Oréal Paris's "White Perfect Eye"; Gong Li (a Chinese movie star) posing for L'Oréal Paris's "Revitalift White"; and even a few Caucasian (perhaps American) White models. Interestingly, the Caucasian White models' names are not printed in the ads. This hints at the ways in which Caucasian white models need not be qualified to represent the face of beauty, unlike the Asian White models whose celebrity status is needed to justify their presence in these ads. Moreover, because these models are hired to advertise the products in several countries, these women are constructed as "cosmopolitan," since their images travel transnationally. The meanings of these "cosmopolitan" models are then transferred to the product that is now embodying the model's cosmopolitanness. This process invites the reader, positioned as a cosmopolitan woman, to consume a product coded as cosmopolitan. Moreover, these ads, published in *Cosmo*, also capitalize on and rely on the cosmopolitanness of the magazine's editorial contents to provide a cosmopolitan meaning to the advertised products. Using a Japanese model in these whitening ads does not suggest that they are selling or relying on Japanese-ness to sell their (at times non-Japanese) products; rather, these international models' cosmopolitanness, their ability to be popular beyond their local boundaries, as well as the meanings provided by the editorial contents of *Cosmo* magazine—representing whiteness as a desirable commodity across the globe—encode these products as cosmopolitan.

The cosmopolitanness of these ads is also signified by their use of English; all of these ads use English, though in varying degrees. At the very least, English is used in the products' labels. The use of English in ads and in magazines functions to flatter the audience's superior status: fluency in English signifies the reader's educated and middle/upper-class position in Indonesian society. It is also used to signify that the magazine and its readers are part of the worldly *Cosmopolitan* women.

And, if not Indonesian, why English? Remember, it was Dutch, not English, that was the colonizer's language in Indonesia. It is English, however, that has become the dominant foreign language in today's Indonesia, and in the world. And it is in English that whitening products' brands and labels are displayed in whitening ads. With only two exceptions—the French ad for "Laneige" and the Japanese ad for "Sekkisei"—all the others are in English: Bioré's "Whitening Scrub," Citra's "White Milk Bath," Clinique's "Derma White," Estée Lauder's "Cyber White," Garnier's "Light Whitening Moisturizer," L'Oréal's "White Perfect" and "Revitalift White," Menard's "Fairlucent," Nivea's "Face Sun Block Whitening Cream," Pond's "White Beauty," "White Beauty Detox," and "Complete Care Whitening," SK-II's "Whitening Source Skin Brightener," "Whitening Source Dermdefinition," and SkinWhite's "Whitening Hand and Body Lotion." That English is used in almost all whitening labels raises the question: why does English become an appealing language to market these whitening products in a postcolonial country, and what are the consequences of such a strategy?

Within the discourse of postcolonialism, as postcolonial theorist Ngugi Wa Thiong' O points out, English functions as a carrier of culture and a means of spiritual subjugation (Thiong' O 1986). As a carrier of culture, the English in these labels therefore represents Western culture. This means English, as it carries the culture of a Western White empire, is embedded within the racist structure of its own society and its own color symbolism. "White" in the U.S. is not simply a color in a box of Crayola crayons. The word "White" in English represents a racist ideology at work. The word *putih*, which is the Indonesian translation of the word, cannot fully capture this. Nor does *putih cantik* invoke the cultural meaning of that which in the West is imbricated in a history of racialized color: "White beauty" is not "putih cantik." This is to say that English is effective in signifying racial categories that are embedded in this language, specifically in U.S. culture. Moreover, as demonstrated in one of these whitening ads, "Pond's White Detox," non-whiteness is constructed as "toxic," as something that needs to be "detoxed." Hence in using English, a signifier for cosmopolitanness, these ads help to maintain the imperial power of the West.

However cosmopolitan these models or the language used in these magazines, white remains the dominant and desired color in these ads. The Indonesian *Cosmo*, like the U.S. *Cosmo*, circulates biased, gendered representations of skin color and race that privilege whiteness (oftentimes Caucasian White encoded as cosmopolitan White) in their magazines. Images of African Americans rarely appear in the Indonesian *Cosmo*. Even when African Americans' images appeared in the U.S. and Indonesian *Cosmo*, their numbers were significantly lower than those of Caucasians.

For example, out of 308 pages in the August 2006 Indonesian *Cosmo*, only four pages have images of African Americans (1.5%). In comparison, out of 242 pages in the August 2006 U.S. *Cosmo*, only twenty-three pages (10%) contain images of African Americans. The numbers are significantly even lower for images of Asian Americans in the U.S. *Cosmo*. Indonesians or women with stereotypical Southeast Asian features rarely appear in the U.S. *Cosmo*. Indeed, in analyzing thirty-eight issues of U.S. *Cosmo* from 1976–1988, Kathryn McMachon pointed out how models, "if third-world, which is not often the case, are represented in codes which signify difference as the culturally exotic. Paradoxically, actual differences between third-world or minority women and White women in the United States are denied, while racial and ethnic stereotypes are exploited" (McMachon 1990, 383). Conversely, Caucasian women dominate advertisements and images that accompany editorial content in U.S. and Indonesian editions. Having Caucasian White women dominate the Indonesian *Cosmo* highlights the ways in which, within a transnational setting, not only do U.S. citizens travel elsewhere more freely, compared to Indonesian citizens, but their images (mostly of Caucasian Americans) are also circulated more frequently across the globe and therefore are thought to have more value than those of Indonesians.

The circulation of these images cannot be detached from the structure that governs which images can travel—white-skinned women of various races have easier access to transnational (visual) mobility. Framed in such a way, the transnational circulation of images of white-skinned women contributes to the production of a racially saturated field of visibility (Butler 1993). This field of visibility shapes not only which images can travel, or which images have more currency in a transnational setting, but also how we make meanings of these traveling images.

Looking White, Feeling Good: Race, Gender, and Color as Affectively Constructed

My argument that whiteness is cosmopolitan and transnationalized (transcending race and nation) leads us to this article's larger theoretical claim: gender, race, and skin color are "affectively" constructed. Cosmopolitan whiteness is more than just an embodiment of certain phenotypes and vaguely defined skin color, that is, Caucasian Whites as having white skin color, big round eyes, and so on. It is *also* affectively constructed. Moreover, what is also interesting about cosmopolitan whiteness is that anyone can be cosmopolitan and White—cosmopolitan White, that is. Anthropologist Peter Van der Veer argues that "the racial distinction between natives and metropolitan has become obsolete and is replaced with the notion that anyone can be cosmopolitan, as long as one remains open, mobile, and improvising, and forgets about one's traditions" (Van der Veer 2002, 169). Expanding on his argument, I argue that access to whiteness, in its cosmopolitan sense, and to cosmopolitanness, in its White sense, relies on one's ability to embody the affective identities constructed as cosmopolitan White. Whiteness here is not simply coded as embodying specific biological features or originating from a specific place, let alone "race," but also as involving feelings of cosmopolitanness.

At the heart of these ads lie powerful cultural narratives of how happiness is achieved by consuming specific products. As media scholar Sut Jhally argues, "Fundamentally, advertising talks to us as individuals and addresses us about how we can become happy. The answers it provides are all oriented to the marketplace, through the purchase of goods or services" (Jhally 2003, 251). Similarly, Kartajaya emphasizes that the "feel benefit," the benefit of reaching consumers' emotions and promising happiness over rational explanations, rather than the "think benefit," plays a significant role in helping consumers make their choices. As he succinctly points out, "people's actions are rooted in 'feelings'" (Kartajaya 2004, 34). Inciting the audience's feelings and promising them happiness through the consumption of the "right" commodity is important in the advertising world.

In these whitening ads, happiness is offered via the route of whitening practices. Feminist cultural studies scholar Sara Ahmed argues, "some objects more than others embody the promise of happiness. In other words, happiness directs us to certain objects, as if they are the necessary ingredients for a good life" (Ahmed 2007, 127). In these skin-whitening ads, skin-whitening products become the objects necessary for a good life. Happiness is coded as cosmopolitan whiteness.

In these ads, White is embedded with positive affective qualities such as sophistication, beauty, or, as one of the whitening ads' slogans puts it, "skin of innocence." One of the mechanisms that the ads deploy to produce these positive affective meanings (such as desirability, beauty, and cosmopolitanness) of whiteness is employing certain models and organizing their faces to embody certain affects. These models, as Wissinger argues, become one of the nodes in the circulation of these affects (Wissinger 2007, 247).

The circuits of affect indeed rely on how the models perform particular affects in these ads. Advertisements function to provide the advertised products with positive (that is, desirable) affects. They do so by employing models with a particular look to deliver the product's positive affects. Simultaneously, these models are also instilled with positive affects. Ahmed argues, "to be affected by an object in a good way is also to have an orientation towards an object as being good" (Ahmed 2007, 124). That is, as the audience feels good looking at beautiful pictures, they will have an orientation toward these beautiful women as being good. In all of these ads, the models have white skin color, even if they are not considered Caucasian women themselves. And because as Wissinger argues in her analysis of affect circulation through a model, "affective value accrues to an image as it moves in circulation . . . her affective capacity increased in accordance with the number and places her image appeared" (Wissinger 2007, 239–40), the more these White women appear in these transnational magazines, the more they accrue affective capital. These images of "good" and beautiful white-skinned women produce positive affects about women with white skin color. This then functions as an apparatus through which the audience reads their encounter with others in their lives. As Ahmed argues, the meanings of these "stranger" others are already constructed prior to our encounter with them (Ahmed 2000). In other words, these ads help "rehearse" (Massumi 2002, 66) the audience's perceptions of the other. Hence when the audience members encounter these white-skinned women in their lives, they tend to have positive affects toward these women even when they do not know them beyond their visually and affectively constructed selves. For example, in Estée Lauder's "Cyber White" ad, the Caucasian White model is represented as a goddess-like figure. Her blonde hair is tied in the back. Her blue eyes match the blue background and the blue bottle of "Cyber White" cream. Her white face looks perfect, without any pores. Here, her goddess look is deployed to capture the ultimate beauty offered by the "Cyber White" cream and to evoke a positive affect about the product. (This transfer of values can easily be seen from the white light emanating from the whitening bottle to her face.) Simultaneously, she becomes the point of positive affective identification: she looks good; she makes the reader feels good; the reader will feel good if she has her good looks and good skin, achievable by consuming the advertised cream. What happens here is the deployment of White women's bodies to evoke a positive affect, which is similar to the ways in which, as Paul Gormley argues, Black bodies are used in new-brutality Hollywood films to evoke negative affects—that is, fear—in the spectators (Gormley 2005). This reminds me of Frantz Fanon's argument that the fear in the White child's body when seeing Fanon's Black body, as evidenced from the White child's utterance, "Mama, see the Negro! I'm frightened!" is related to the ways in which the historico-racial schema structures how the White child *felt* about his Black body (Fanon 1952/1967, 111). Building on these theorists, I argue that ads are a part of the historico-racial schema that shapes how we are *affected* by and feel certain affects toward others and ourselves. This is what I call an affective structure.

Facialization and the Affective Structure

One of the most salient features of skin-whitening ads in the Indonesian *Cosmo* is its emphasis on the model's face. All but five whitening ads (Estée Lauder's "Re-Nutriv Ultimate White Lifting Serum," Lux's "White Glamour," Nivea's "Night Whitening Milk," SkinWhite's "Whitening Hand and Body Lotion," and Viva's "White") consist of close-up images of the model's face, which fill almost the entire page. This begs the question: what affective work does this magnification of the face in whitening ads do? I will answer this question by turning once again to the "Cyber White" ad.

In the version of the "Cyber White" ad published in the June 2007 issue of the Indonesian *Cosmo*, as in other whitening ads, the face is the focal point. The face of a blonde-haired, blue-eyed, stereotypical Nordic woman fills the left side of a two-page spread. Her close-up face is magnified. A large, ice-crystal necklace fits perfectly on her smooth, white neck. The neatly arranged light blue ice bricks provide a sense of cool aura to the ad's background. The spectator is invited to feel the "cool"-ness of the ad, of the model, and of the product through the process of a transfer of meanings among these signs (a blue bottle with a white cap, blue ice bricks, a transparent ice-crystal necklace, and the model's blue eyes). She does not smile, which is often requisite in beauty ads. This lack of a smile, however, actually adds to her innocent presence. She peers deep into the spectator's eyes with her sharp and superior look. After all, she is a goddess, or is supposed to make us recall such a mythical figure.

This return to the mythical figure of the Greek goddess is not surprising. In the visual culture world, the color white is often used as a vehicle that "takes us to the place that was held to be both the origin of Western art and its highest known form, Greek and Roman sculpture" (Mirzoeff 1999, 58).

This evocation of Greek and Roman art to endorse whiteness is racially suspect, however. This is all the more so when we know that whiteness has also been used in the visual culture world to "convey an intense physical beauty in itself' (59). After all, racism works, as philosophers Gilles Deleuze and Félix Guattari argue, "by the determination of degrees of deviance in relation to the White-Man face" (Deleuze and Guattari 1987, 178).

Moreover, in this ad the model's face is represented as surreal in its state of "flawless," poreless, ultra-white brilliance. Here, the "Cyber White" ad positions whiteness as occupying the space in between real and unreal—the virtual. Thus, the invocation of the mythological Greek goddess who looks quite modern in the ad's rendition also makes visible the realness and the unrealness of her whiteness, "Cyber White."

Cyberdiscourse, according to cyber culture scholar Susanna Paasonen, "revolves around notions of mobility and freedom in terms of identity and self-expression" (Paasonen 2005, 2–3). This certainly reminds us of cosmopolitanism: the sense of a globe-trotting lifestyle and the luxury of making claims about multiple (virtual) homes. In this sense, the virtual and the cosmopolitan bleed into each other. However, as some cyberculture scholars have noted, cybercitizens have often been constructed as "White" (here, "White" usually refers to Caucasian White) (Kolko, Nakamura, and Rodman 2000; Ebo 2001; Nakamura 2002; Paasonen 2005; Nakamura 2008). Hence whiteness becomes one's access to experiencing cosmopolitanness (even if at times only virtually), and cosmopolitanness becomes one's access to experience whiteness.

Virtuality, as it reverberates with cosmopolitan whiteness, also brings to the surface the issue of "real" (authentic) vs. unreal (inauthentic). According to Brenda Laurel, "the adjective virtual describes things—worlds, phenomena, etc.—that look and feel like reality but lack the traditional physical substance" (Laurel 1993, 8). This provides us with yet another understanding of cosmopolitan whiteness: whiteness as lacking the traditional physical substance, traditionally (and discursively) known as Caucasian whiteness. Cosmopolitan whiteness can never be "real" or authentic, nor can any race occupy an authentic White location because there has never been a "real" whiteness to begin with.

Visual studies scholar Nicholas Mirzoeff points out that adding to this lack of authenticity, virtual space is a space that "is not real but *appears* to be" (Mirzoeff 1999, 91; emphasis mine). Thus, cosmopolitan whiteness is not about claiming a form of real whiteness. Rather, it is about appearing White—these creams can only make you *appear* White but cannot make you *become* a "real" White. The body can only be virtually White. The product's label, "Cyber White," therefore captures and exemplifies the cosmopolitanness of the whiteness that is being marketed in this ad. In some sense, this notion of virtuality—real but not real—bears a resemblance to post-colonial theorist Homi Bhabha's notion of colonial mimicry in which Whiteness is read as White but not quite (Bhabha 1994).

The question, however, remains: why is the face emphasized in whitening ads? The term "face-to-face conversation" is used to signify the presence of bodies involved in the conversation. This hints at the importance of the face in relation to one's body and its subjectivity. In his analysis of webcam sex Dennis Waskul argues,

> Clearly the face occupies a supreme position in connecting or disconnecting the self with the body. One's face is the most identifiable feature of one's body and self; it is the single human physiological feature that concretely conjoins the corporeal with the self. (Waskul 2002/2004, 51)

Here, the face matters because it links the body and the self. The face becomes, to build on Deleuze and Guattari's argument, a "loc[us] of resonance" (Deleuze and Guattari 1987, 168) that allows us to make meanings out of forms of subjectivity played out in these ads. The face is a source of information through which we approximate the other's subjectivity. The wrinkled old face, the mad person's face, the evil face, the feminine face, the "Asian" face, or the beautiful face could tell us something about the person and how we would feel about them. The meanings of their faces seem so evident that we rarely question where or how these ideas arise, or why certain faces evoke particular feelings in us; that is, a beautiful face may evoke our desire or the mad person's face may incite our fear.

However, another question still remains: how are affective meanings of the model's face produced in this ad? In other words, in what way does the face evoke certain affects in others? I argue that through the organization of face, or what Deleuze and Guattari call "facialization," these skin-whitening ads function as an "abstract machine of faciality" (Deleuze and Guattari 1987, 168) that encourages the audience to feel positive affects toward these faces. Here, I refer to an "abstract faciality machine," as Deluze and Guattari define it:

This machine is called the faciality machine because it is the social production of face, because it performs the facialization of the entire body
and all its surroundings and objects, and the landscapification of all
worlds and milieus. The deterritorialization of the body implies a reterri-
torialization on the face; the decoding of the body implies an overcoding
by the face; the collapse of corporeal coordinates or milieus implies the
constitution of a landscape. The semiotic of the signifier and the subjective never operates through bodies. It is absurd to claim to relate the signifier to the body. At any rate it can be related only to a body that has
already been entirely facialized. . . . Never does the face assume a prior
signifier or subject. . . . That is why we have been addressing just two
problems exclusively: the relation of the face to the abstract machine that
produces it, and the relation of the face to the assemblages of power that
require that social production. The face is a politics. (Deleuze and Guattari 1987, 181)

Here, they suggest that the social production of face is implicated within
social relations of power. It is produced at the moment of re/deterritoriali-
zation of the body and the face—here the linkage between the body and
face is established: when the body can provide meanings for the face and
vice versa. This process of re/deterritorialization relies on an apparatus of
abstraction and facialization. This process allows the model to *affect* us in a
certain way.

In this era of Photoshop, literally everything is up for alteration. Color is
an option. Every pixel's color serves certain (affective, if not aesthetic) purposes. The easiest way to uncover the meanings of these images, according
to media scholar Katherine Frith, is to alter the image of the ads and see
what different meanings are produced (Frith 1997). For example, would we
feel differently about the ad had the model's face been colored red and
organized to look angry, that is, instead of having her lips represented as
delicate, the model would show her clenched teeth to demonstrate her
rage? Of course! These ads hence function as part of the faciality machine
because they help the audience "rehearse" (Massumi 2002, 66) their perception of women with white skin color. Moreover, they also help maintain
relations of power in which whiteness holds the supreme position. This ad
feeds into the reconstruction of *her* white-skinned face as beautiful, desirable, and positive-affect generating. These are the faces we are "educated"
to desire (Stoler 1995). This matters because the micro-management of

desire is central to the maintenance of power (Stoler 2002). In other words, whose face we desire is always implicated in the relations of power.

I do not argue, however, that when we look at a white-skinned face, we are *always* positively *affected* by it. This would rob the spectators of their own agency and discount the different degrees of "intensity" (Massumi 2002, 14) that the same face may evoke in different people. This is where I agree with Stoler, who argues that there is "a space for individual affect [to be] structured by power but not wholly subsumed by it" (Stoler 1995, 192). After all, as Terry Kawashima has pointed out, the work of labeling others based on established racial categories involves an active visual reading (Kawashima 2002). That is, readers often dismiss certain parts of the body and simultaneously privilege other parts to claim that a certain figure looks "White"—in this case the Japanese anime Sailor Moon (a blonde-haired, blue-eyed, small-nosed, petite, young girl). This is what she calls a "white-privileging subject position." (Note that once again, White here is assumed to be Caucasian White.) Kawashima's article is of significance to my analysis because it convinces us of the way in which certain parts of the body (for the purposes of this article, the face), are privileged over other parts in order to construct the subjectivity of the other. Taking this a step further, I point out that facialization not only reveals how the face is privileged and socially produced to project various social relations of power within which this facialization process is implicated, it also shapes how we feel toward women with certain racialized and "colored" faces.

Cosmopolitan Whiteness and Hegemonic White Supremacy

I wish to end this article with a twist. I would like to preempt a particular question, perhaps unnecessarily. However, it is a question that is almost always raised after I share my reading of these skin-whitening ads in conferences, seminars, or lectures: what about skin-tanning ads? Don't all of these ads simply expose the human desire to want what they don't have? My answer is no: skin-tanning ads actually perpetuate and further strengthen the notion of "cosmopolitan whiteness." Hence in this conclusion, I will provide a succinct reading of these tanning ads to demonstrate how both skin-whitening ads *and* skin-tanning ads function to provide positive affects toward white-skinned women and help construct "cosmopolitan whiteness."

Tanning ads published in the U.S. *Cosmo* during the months of June–

August of 2006–2008 provide us with evidence that even in these tanning ads, the color "tan" is advertised *without* undermining the supremacy of the Caucasian White race. Instead, these ads merely affirm positive affects toward women with white skin color and "race," and, of course, their cosmopolitan whiteness. First, unlike whitening ads, none of these tanning ads use the word blackening or browning—words that have racial connotations in the U.S. context. Rather, ads for Banana Boat and L'Oréal, for example, use the word "tan" or "bronze." "Deepest bronze," a surreal color—a color that is not often used to describe skin color—is used to describe the darkest skin tone that these women could achieve by using these tanning products. This suggests that these tanning ads do not even flirt with desires of racial transformation or desires to have black skin, let alone to *be* Black.

Second, whereas none of the whitening ads hint at one's ability to take control of how white one's skin can be, these tanning ads explicitly employ the language of choice and control, an apparatus of White supremacy. Aveeno, for example, sells "moisturizer that lets you customize your color." Olay puts it even more strongly by advertising "the color you control." Hence here, the anxiety of getting too dark is eliminated because Caucasian women can control how "bronze" their skin can be. After all, as Sarita Sahay and Niva Piran found after surveying one hundred South-Asian Canadian undergraduate students and one hundred Euro-Canadian undergraduate students at the University of Toronto, even as Euro-Canadian women desire to have skin that is darker than their current skin color, this "darker skin" still falls within the "white-skin-color-category" (Sahay and Piran 1997, 165). This demonstrates that White skin is indeed the desired norm in North America.

Third, in these ads, tanning is represented within a specific temporal (and therefore contained) context. Most of these ads, such as Aveeno ("you choose the shade for the perfect summer radiance for you"), Dove ("gradually builds a beautiful summer glow in just one week"), and Jergens "a gradual healthy summer glow, just by moisturizing"), use summer as the timeframe for their products. As such, tanning registers within the realm of postmodern playfulness. It invokes temporality, the changing nature of one's skin color, rather than the permanence of desire for darker skin tone. This certainly is not the normative convention of whitening ads that do not highlight any specific time frame in their ads.

Fourth, in these tanning ads, no one is advised to "detox" their white skin color. Whereas in whitening ads we are told that white is "perfect" and that it is a signifier for beauty, in tanning ads, one is advised to simply "enhance" one's skin color. L'Oréal, for example, offers a moisturizer that functions as a "natural skin tone enhancer." This is also the case for Jergens ("natural glow face") and Banana Boat ("natural looking color"). None of these ads insult the white-skinned audience because none of these ads tell them that brown is perfect and their White skin color is toxic.

Last, some of the tanning brands in these ads suggest that tanning is a form of cosmopolitan whiteness insofar as it articulates a sense of "imperialist nostalgia." Renato Rosaldo coined the term "imperialist nostalgia" to mark the colonial's "innocent yearning" for the native's precolonial life imagined as "pure" that had been transformed because of processes of colonialism (Rosaldo 1989). The imperialist nostalgia that haunts these ads can be seen through, for example, the "Hawaiian Tropic" ad, which at a glance resembles a tourism brochure. In this ad an almost fully-naked woman with medium-tanned skin stands seductively displaying her curves. We only see one half of her body, positioned on the right side of the ad, occupying only one third of the page. We see her lips, part of her nose, and one of her eyes, enough to sense that she's smiling coyly. In the background, there is a shadow of a man who is holding a surfboard and is seen walking on the beach. The gender narrative in this ad is too obvious: the man is surfing; the woman is posing for the audience. The colonial narrative, however, lingers subtly in the ad's text: "Hawaiian Tropic sunscreen pampers you with its luxurious tropical moisturizers, exotic botanicals and alluring island scent. . . . With protection up to SPF 70, you can embrace the sun and fully experience the pleasures of the Tropic." Here, tanning practices become a way for White female consumers to inhabit "the exotic other" (Williamson 1986). The Tropic, with a capital T, becomes a colonial site that exists for the purpose of pampering cosmopolitan White consumers. This "going native," the glorification of the exotic other for the consumption of the White self, or "imperialist nostalgia," frames cosmopolitanism as a trope of "colonial modernity"—a mode of engaging the other in the colonizing context (Van der Veer 2002). Hence cosmopolitan whiteness, I argue, is at once a form of longing for the purity of the past and of belonging to the un-rooted and re-routed world culture simultaneously. Hence, I argue that although tanning ads register differently from whitening ads, they both have the same positive affective effects (that is, cosmopolitan, fun, fearless, and beautiful) toward women with white skin color. In whitening ads the English word "white" and foreign models function to infuse whiteness with a cosmopolitan flair. Skin-tanning ads in the U.S.

Cosmo, by using the word "tanning" or "bronze" instead of "blackening," urge women to bask in the postmodern desires of playful color transformation while freeing them from the accusation of emulating blackness and hence still privileging (cosmopolitan) whiteness in its ability to travel and consume exoticized others.

In conclusion, in this article I argue that positive affective effects toward women with white skin color are the problematic effects of a transnational women's magazine that circulates within a racially saturated field of visibility. Rather than challenging any racial hierarchies, these skin-whitening (and tanning) ads simply affirm them even if in much more nuanced ways. Moreover, cosmopolitan whiteness illustrates that whiteness works in hegemonic ways. That is, whiteness adapts, mutates, and co-opts new forms of whiteness to maintain its supremacy. As Ahmed points out, "freedom involves proximity to whiteness" (Ahmed 2007, 130). I further argue that the freedom to move transnationally involves proximity to whiteness—and this is the essence of a non-essentialist, "virtual," cosmopolitan whiteness.

....

L. Ayu Saraswati is an award-winning author, award-winning teacher, engaging speaker, innovative consultant, and associate professor and chair of the Department of Women's Studies at the University of Hawai'i. She teaches gender, sexuality, race, and new/media studies from a transnational perspective. Prior to her current position, she was an assistant professor in women's studies at the University of Kansas, and a postdoctoral fellow in women's studies at Emory University. Saraswati is also a meditation and academic writing retreat cofacilitator.

Notes

Originally published in *Meridians* vol. 10, no. 2, 2010.
The author wishes to thank the anonymous reviewers for their immensely helpful comments, as well as the following people, who have all provided insightful comments at various stages of the article's development: Claire Moses, Christina Lux, Sherrie Tucker, Shawn Parry-Giles, Tanya Golash-Boza, Jessica Vasquez, Akiko Takeyama, Hannah Britton, Ann Schofield, the students in her seminar class, participants in both the Globalization Seminar and the Hall Center's Gender Seminar at the University of Kansas, and the members of her writing group at the University of Kansas.

1   *Cosmopolitan* costs Rp. 35,000 (US$4) and targets upper-middle-class Indonesian women. Class is a significant aspect that begs a more comprehensive analysis, which is beyond the scope of this article.

2   Whitening ads are published throughout the year in the Indonesian *Cosmo*. For
     this article, I focus on thirty-four whitening ads published in the summer
     months (June, July, and August) of 2006, 2007, and 2008. This is so because in
     the larger project from which this article stems, I also provide a comprehensive
     analysis of a total of nine tanning ads published in the U.S. *Cosmo* (usually pub-
     lished during the summer months).

3   For a thorough racial history of Indonesia from the precolonial to the postcolo-
     nial period, see Prasetyaningsih 2007.

4   In 1998, Suharto, who had been Indonesia's president for thirty-two years, vol-
     untarily stepped down from his presidency following large-scale protests and
     the collapse of the economy. His decision was influenced in part because he lost
     the U.S. government's support. Since 1998 Indonesia has been undergoing a
     democratization process, one that includes a more open environment for vari-
     ous forms of expressive media that had been repressed under his regime.

Works Cited

Ahmed, Sara. 2000. *Strange Encounters: Embodied Others in Post-Coloniality*. London:
    Routledge.

———. 2007. "Multiculturalism and the Promise of Happiness." *New Formations* 63:
    121–37.

Appadurai, Arjun. 1996. *Modernity at Large: Cultural Dimensions of Globalization*. Minne-
    apolis: University of Minnesota Press.

Bhabha, Homi. 1994. "Of Mimicry and Man: The Ambivalence of Colonial Dis-
    course." *October* 28: 125–33.

Brennan, Teresa. 2004. *The Transmission of Affect*. Ithaca, NY: Cornell University Press.

Burke, Timothy. 1996. *Lifebuoy Men, Lux Women: Commodification, Consumption, and Clean-
    liness in Modern Zimbabwe*. Durham, NC: Duke University Press.

Butler, Judith. 1993. "Endangered/Endangering: Schematic Racism and White Para-
    noia." In *Reading Rodney King: Reading Urban Uprising*, edited by Robert Gooding-
    Williams. New York: Routledge.

Carr, David. 2002. "Romance, in *Cosmo's* World, is Translated in Many Ways." *New
    York Times*, May 26. http://tiny.cc/t12ks (accessed August 16, 2010).

Chang, Jui-Shan. 2004. "Refashioning Womanhood in 1990s Taiwan: An Analysis of
    the Taiwanese Edition of *Cosmopolitan* Magazine." *Modern China* 30, no. 3: 361–97.

Cheah, Peng. 1998. "Introduction Part II: The Cosmopolitical—Today." In *Cosmopo-
    litics: Thinking and Feeling beyond the Nation*, edited by Peng Cheah and Bruce Rob-
    bins. Minneapolis: University of Minnesota Press.

Cosmopolitan (American). 2006–2008. (June, July, August).

Cosmopolitan (Indonesian). 2006–2008. (June, July, August).

Deleuze, Gilles, and Félix Guattari. 1987. *A Thousand Plateaus: Capitalism and Schizophre-
    nia*. Trans. Brian Massumi. Minneapolis: University of Minnesota Press.

Dyer, Richard. 1997. *White*. New York: Routledge.

Ebo, Bosah, ed. 1998. *Cyberghetto or Cybertopia?: Race, Class, and Gender on the Internet*.
    Westport, CT: Praeger.

———. 2001. *Cyberimperialism?: Global Relations in the New Electronic Frontier*. Westport, CT: Praeger.

Fanon, Frantz. 1952/1967. *Black Skin White Masks*. Trans. Charles Markmann. New York: Grove Press.

Freeman, Carla. 2007. "Neo-liberalism and the Marriage of Reputation and Respectability: Entrepreneurship and the Barbadian Middle Class." In *Love and Globalization: Transformations of Intimacy*, edited by Mark Padilla and Jennifer Hirsch. Nashville, TN: Vanderbilt University Press.

Frith, Katherine, ed. 1997. *Undressing the Ad: Reading Culture in Advertising*. New York: Peter Lang.

Glenn, Evelynn, ed. 2009. *Shades of Difference: Why Skin Color Matters*. Stanford: Stanford University Press.

Gormley, Paul. 2005. *The New-Brutality Film: Race and Affect in Contemporary Hollywood Culture*. Bristol, UK: Intellect.

Grewal, Inderpal. 2005. *Transnational America: Feminisms, Diasporas, Neoliberalisms*. Durham, NC: Duke University Press.

Hall, Ronald. 2005. "The Euro-Americanization of Race: Alien Perspective of African Americans vis-à-vis Trivialization of Skin Color." *Journal of Black Studies* 36, no. 1: 116–29.

Harding, Jennifer, and E. Deidre Pribram, eds. 2009. *Emotions: A Cultural Studies Reader*. London: Routledge.

Hunter, Margaret. 2005. *Race, Gender, and the Politics of Skin Tone*. New York: Routledge.

Jhally, Sut. 2003. "Image-Based Culture: Advertising and Popular Culture." In *Gender, Race, and Class in Media*, edited by Gail Dines and Jean Humez. Thousand Oaks, CA: Sage.

Kartajaya, Hermawan. 2004. *Marketing in Venus*. Jakarta: Gramedia.

Kawashima, Terry. 2002. "Seeing Faces, Making Races: Challenging Visual Tropes of Racial Difference." *Meridians: feminism, race, transnationalism* 3, no. 1: 161–90.

Kolko, Beth, Lisa Nakamura, and Gilbert Rodman, eds. 2000. *Race in Cyberspace*. New York: Routledge.

Laurel, Brenda. 1993. *Computer as Theater*. Reading, MA: Addison-Wesley.

Lindquist, Johan. 2009. *The Anxieties of Mobility: Migration and Tourism in the Indonesian Borderlands*. Honolulu: University of Hawaii Press.

Machin, David, and Joanna Thornborrow. 2003. "Branding and Discourse: The Case of *Cosmopolitan*." *Discourse and Society* 14, no. 4: 453–71.

Massumi, Brian. 2002. *Parables for the Virtual: Movement, Affect, Sensation*. Durham, NC: Duke University Press.

McMachon, Kathryn. 1990. "The Cosmopolitan Ideology and the Management of Desire." *Journal of Sex Research* 27, no. 3: 381–96.

Mercer, Kobena. 1987. "Black Hair/Style Politics." *New Formations* 3: 33–55.

Mirzoeff, Nicholas. 1999. *An Introduction to Visual Culture*. London: Routledge.

Nakamura, Lisa. 2002. *Cybertypes: Race, Ethnicity, and Identity on the Internet*. New York: Routledge.

————. 2008. *Digitizing Race: Visual Cultures of the Internet*. Minneapolis: University of Minnesota Press.

Nelson, Michelle, and Hye-Jin Paek. 2005. "Cross-Cultural Differences in Sexual Advertising Content in a Transnational Women's Magazine." *Sex Roles* 53, no. 5/6: 371–83.

Omi, Michael, and Howard Winant. 1994. *Racial Formation in the United States: From the 1960s to the 1990s*. New York: Routledge.

Ong, Aihwa. 1999. *Flexible Citizenship: The Cultural Logics of Transnationality*. Durham, NC: Duke University Press.

Paasonen, Susanna. 2005. *Figures of Fantasy: Internet, Women and Cyberdiscourse*. New York: Peter Lang.

Parameswaran, Radhika, and Kavitha Cardoza. 2009. "Melanin on the Margins: Advertising and the Cultural Politics of Fair/Light/White Beauty in India." *Journalism and Communication Monographs* 11, no. 3: 213–74.

Peiss, Kathy. 1998. *Hope in a Jar: The Making of America's Beauty Culture*. New York: Metropolitan Books.

Pierre, Jemima. 2008. "'I Like Your Colour!' Skin Bleaching and Geographies of Race in Urban Ghana." *Feminist Review* 90, no. 1: 9–29.

Prabasmoro, Aquarini. 2003. *Becoming White: Representasi Ras, Kelas, Femininitas dan Globalitas Dalam Iklan Sabun*. Yogyakarta: Jalasutra.

Prasetyaningsih, L. Ayu Saraswati. 2007. "The Maze of Gaze: The Color of Beauty in Transnational Indonesia." Ph.D. diss., Department of Women's Studies, University of Maryland, College Park.

Robbins, Bruce. 1998. "Comparative Cosmopolitanisms." In *Cosmopolitics: Thinking and Feeling beyond the Nation*, edited by Peng Cheah and Bruce Robbins. Minneapolis: University of Minnesota Press.

Rondilla, Joanne, and Paul Spickard. 2007. *Is Lighter Better?: Skin-Tone Discrimination among Asian Americans*. Lanham, MD: Rowman & Littlefield.

Rosaldo, Renato. 1989. *Culture and Truth: The Remaking of Social Analysis*. Boston: Beacon Press.

Sahay, Sarita, and Niva Piran. 1997. "Skin-Color Preferences and Body Satisfaction among South Asian-Canadian and European-Canadian Female University Students." *Journal of Social Psychology* 137, no. 2: 161–71.

Sarker, Sonita, and Esha Niyogi De, eds. 2002. *Trans-Status Subjects: Gender in the Globalization of South and Southeast Asia*. Durham, NC: Duke University Press.

Shohat, Ella, ed. 1998. *Talking Visions: Multicultural Feminism in a Transnational Age*. Cambridge, MA: MIT Press.

Spooner, Catherine. 2001. "Cosmo-Gothic: The Double and the Single Woman." *Women: A Cultural Review* 12, no. 3: 292–305.

Stoler, Ann. 1995. *Race and the Education of Desire: Foucault's History of Sexuality and the Colonial Order of Things*. Durham, NC: Duke University Press.

————. 2002. *Carnal Knowledge and Imperial Power: Race and the Intimate in Colonial Rule*. Berkeley: University of California Press.

Thiong 'O, Ngugi Wa. 1986. *Decolonizing the Mind: The Politics of Language in African Literature*. London: James Currey Ltd.

Van der Veer, Peter. 2002. "Colonial Cosmopolitanism." In *Conceiving Cosmopolitanism: Theory, Context, and Practice*, edited by Steven Vertovec and Robin Cohen. New York: Oxford University Press.

Vertovec, Steven, and Robin Cohen. 2002. "Introduction: Conceiving Cosmopolitanism." In *Conceiving Cosmopolitanism: Theory, Context, and Practice*, edited by Steven Vertovec and Robin Cohen. New York: Oxford University Press.

Waskul, Dennis. 2002/2004. "The Naked Self: Body and Self in Televideo Cybersex." In *Readings on Sex, Pornography, and the Internet*, edited by Dennis Waskul. New York: Peter Lang.

Wieringa, Saskia. 2008. "'If There is No Feeling': The Dilemma between Silence and Coming Out in a Working-Class Butch/Femme Community in Jakarta." In *Love and Globalization: Transformations of Intimacy*, edited by Mark Padilla and Jennifer Hirsch. Nashville, TN: Vanderbilt University Press.

Williamson, Judith. 1986. "Woman is an Island: Femininity and Colonization." In *Studies in Entertainment: Critical Approaches to Mass Culture*, edited by Tania Modleski. Bloomington: Indiana University Press.

Winant, Howard. 1994. *Racial Conditions: Politics, Theory, Comparisons*. Minneapolis: University of Minnesota Press.

———. 2001. *The World is a Ghetto: Race and Democracy since World War II*. New York: Basic.

Wissinger, Elizabeth. 2007. "Always on Display: Affective Production in the Modeling Industry." In *The Affective Turn: Theorizing the Social*, edited by Patricia Clough with Jean Halley. Durham, NC: Duke University Press.

Zane, Kathleen. 1998. "Reflections on a Yellow Eye: Asian I(\Eye/)Cons and Cosmetic Surgery." In *Taking Visions: Multicultural Feminism in a Transnational Age*, edited by Ella Shohat. Cambridge, MA: MIT Press.

Shoba Sharad Rajgopal

. . . .

"The Daughter of Fu Manchu"
The Pedagogy of Deconstructing the Representation
of Asian Women in Film and Fiction

Abstract: Courses regarding race, gender, and representation are not easy to teach under any circumstances, but even more so in predominantly White classrooms in the post 9/11 United States, where the masses have been fed a diet of xenophobic, anti-Asian propaganda inculcating an "us" versus "them" mentality. This article analyzes the discourse of empire, a metaphor that has been used time after time to construct a mythical and menacing Other. In contrast, the portrait of Asian women in cinema and television news as traditional, veiled, and inhabiting a separate sphere adds to this representation of Asian cultures as premodern and irrevocably opposed to the West, much as portrayed in Samuel Huntington's "clash of civilizations" theory. The author illustrates this transnational feminist critique with a documentary used in Women's Studies classes, Deborah Gee's landmark film *Slaying the Dragon* (1988).

. . . .

I have a vision. Of the Orient. That, deep within its almond eyes, there are still women.
Women willing to sacrifice themselves for the love of a man . . .
Rene Gallimard, in M. Butterfly. (Hwang 1986, 92)

. . . .

I teach ethnic and gender studies courses concerning Asian women predominantly to White students on the east coast, and have found that most of them find it very difficult to comprehend how both race and gender oppression continue to influence them on a daily basis. Many of them acknowledge that things "were really bad" for women and people of color

MERIDIANS · feminism, race, transnationalism   Volume 19 Supplement 2020
DOI: 10.1215/15366936-8566056 © 2010 Smith College

in the past, but feel that now, in light of the current occupant of the White House, things have all changed for the better.

Interestingly, this is the case not just with my White students but with many of my Asian students too, predominantly those from the east coast, where they are not as much a presence as they are in the west, and who do not have the tools to recognize that certain patterns of behavior are not the norm but are in fact ways in which non-White populations are perceived within the dominant discourse. My pedagogy is thus guided by theorists such as Patricia Hill Collins, bell hooks, Chandra Mohanty, and Ella Shohat, who articulate the principles of White hetero-patriarchal privilege that grants not only explicit but unspoken levels of access to social and institutional power. I also provide texts by other South Asian scholars whose location, like mine, privileges issues pertaining to transnationalism, such as the crossing of boundaries and confronting difference. These include Uma Narayan, Kum-Kum Bhavnani, Gayatri Chakravorty Spivak, and Inderpal Grewal.

I find that one of the most effective means of raising the consciousness of my students is to utilize film documentaries that demonstrate how images from Hollywood have been used in the past century to further the "Othering" of a specific, immigrant population. I will discuss both Asian and Arab women in this study, since they have much in common, both from a shared history of persecution in the U.S., and from the fact that many people in the West are often unable to distinguish between Arabs and South and Central Asians, leading to several attacks on Sikhs from South Asia in the immediate aftermath of 9/11.

The primary documentary I use in my class is Deborah Gee's *Slaying the Dragon* (1988). Produced by Asian Women United, the film was originally made in the late 1980s, but, if used with supplementary films and readings in Asian American Studies and feminist film theory, and with documentary and feature films as well as YouTube videos, the film remains very effective as an icebreaker, to get students talking to enable them to confront racial and gender stereotypes and move into the complexities of international geopolitics behind such representations.

Much of feminist film theory has been concerned with film as a signifying practice, as a locus of pleasure and entertainment, and as an instrument of dominant ideology, or conversely as a tool for political resistance and subversion. It brings to the forefront things that are often ignored in dominant or mainstream popular cinema. These things are centered not just on *presences* but also in *absences*, where presences include explicit ways in which women are portrayed in cinema, while absences imply the ways in which women do not appear in film at all (Chatterjee 1998, 4). But if the representation of White women in cinema was perceived by feminist theorists as the signifier not of woman, but of the absent phallus (Johnston 1975), what about the non-White woman, how was she represented? Interestingly, this was even more repressed or ignored by much of Western feminist theory until the 1980s and 90s, with the publication of critiques by women scholars of color (Anzaldua 1987; Collins 1990; hooks 1996).

Indeed, the problem of this representation is compounded by the White woman's complicity in the construction of the discourse of empire and the civilizing mission of colonialism. It fell to theorists of color to critique this representation with the publication of the landmark anthology of cultural studies by the Birmingham Centre for Contemporary Cultural Studies, *The Empire Strikes Back: Race and Racism in Seventies Britain* (Gilroy 1982). However, it was only much later that theorists began to deconstruct the representation of these marginalized groups and link it to the discourse of empire (Spivak 1988; Marchetti 1993; Hamamoto 1994; Shohat and Stam 1994; Hamamoto and Liu 2000; and Hirabayashi and Xing 2003).

Gee's film can be regarded as a celluloid version of this critique of Hollywood as the discourse of empire through its representation of Asian women as ahistorical and frozen in time, a composite of the many wars of empire that the West was engaged in, with the Asian woman playing the role of the spoils of war.

Gee uses the Dragon to symbolize the representation in cinema and fiction, a usage that is interesting in that the Dragon is associated with the cultures of the East, and indeed, many Eastern cultures have been represented in the mainstream cinema of the West as dangerous (to the West, that is), devious and evil, all characteristics in the West of the mythical being, the Dragon. It first appeared to Western audiences as Fu Manchu in the early decades of the twentieth century. The character Fu Manchu has been described in these words:

> Imagine a person, tall, lean and feline, high-shouldered, with a brow like Shakespeare and a face like Satan . . . one giant intellect, with all the resources of science past and present. . . . Imagine that awful being, and you have a mental picture of Dr. Fu-Manchu, the yellow peril incarnate in one man. (Rohmer 1913)

Gee demonstrates how the representation of the evil genius's female incarnation in *Daughter of Fu Manchu* (1931) is no less Machiavellian. If anything, she is perceived as even more of a danger because she is so beautiful. Examining the cover of the first version of the book *Fu Manchu's Daughter* by Collier publishers, it is curious to note the blatant obscuring of the multitude of different cultures in the developing world, where women from cultures as distinct and different as India and China and the entire "Middle East" are all collapsed into one, all-encompassing representation of "the Oriental woman." Chandra Talpade Mohanty describes this as the reductive and homogeneous notion of "Third World difference," that stable, "ahistorical something that oppresses most, if not all women in these countries" (Mohanty 2003, 19). I shall examine subsequently whether this mass media representation of women from the Global South has changed in recent times and the implication of such representations in Western mass media.

The representation of Asian men has changed a great deal from the emasculated Indian *sepoy* Gunga Din in the Hollywood film of the 1930s and the Chinese cook Hop Sing in the Cartwright household of *Bonanza* (NBC, 1959–1973). The pot-smoking, comedic duo of recent times, Harold and Kumar, are now seen, at least by their own generation, as being as "American" as any Caucasian males could be. But has the representation of Asian women changed as much? To study this question I examine recent Hollywood films and mass-media representations of Asian female characters in the U.S. Gina Marchetti's landmark book of the 1990s on the representation of Asians in Hollywood starts with the statement, "Hollywood has long been fascinated by Asia, Asians, and Asian themes. Mysterious and exotic, Hollywood's Asia promises adventure and forbidden pleasure" (Marchetti 1993, 1). This brings us to the concept of Orientalism and how it continues to operate in the world today, a concept that has become a powerful analytical tool for many postcolonial scholars in our study of literature and the media. Central to Edward Said's concept of Orientalism is its role in helping the West define itself by constructing an "Other" whose characteristics were understood as being in opposition to the West (Said 1978).

The enduring value of Said's text lies in its unmasking of the machinations of empire by demonstrating how culture and discourse actually worked in tandem with the military industrial complex of its time to secure a seamless, Western reality that was assured and confirmed while negating everything the supposed "Oriental" stood for. Said, moreover, represents both Arabs and South Asians as falling within the purview of the panoptical representations of Orientalism, and this fact adds fuel to my argument that Arab and Asian women are represented in similar ways in the Western media. In fact, both these groups are most often represented in much of Western media as traditional, veiled, and inhabiting a separate sphere, and the images of women from these different regions of Asia, the Middle East, and Africa often coalesce in Orientalist fashion, as seen in a recent (1999) adaptation of the *Arabian Nights* by Hollywood director Steve Barron, which opens with a scene of an Arab dancing girl pirouetting on the genie's hand. But as I continued to watch, it was clear to me that the supposed Arab dancing woman was performing a traditional dance form from India, was attired in traditional Indian clothes, and finally, was enacted by an actress from the Bollywood film industry. In this sense it is truly representative of the repertory of images that conjure up the Asian woman as "the sensual woman who is there to be . . . used by the man, the East as a kind of mysterious place full of secrets and monsters" (Jhally 1998).

These differences between South Asian and Arab cultures are evidently lost on mainstream Western audiences, which cannot distinguish between them anyway. Such misrepresentations only add to the perception of their different cultures as backward and irrevocably opposed to the West, much as portrayed in Samuel Huntington's "clash of civilizations" theory (Huntington 1996). Never do we see a nuanced historical perspective in which they were ruled by progressive rulers, like Muhammad Mossadegh of Iran, rather than by totalitarian theocrats. Indeed, such binary demarcations between East and West serves what Uma Narayan calls "the colonialist stance," which presents Western cultures as dynamic, progressive, and egalitarian, while portraying non-Western cultures as backward, barbaric, and patriarchal. This project involves a certain historical amnesia, for the West ignores its own complex past engaged in slavery and colonization, and refusing civil rights to large parts of its own people, including women (Narayan 1997, 15). As such, mass culture and cinema in particular plays a crucial role in constructing the categories that reinscribe racial hierarchies, and the process of racialization is often gendered. Moreover, the racialized female body is a particularly contested site, with women of different races pitted against each other in order to best serve the heteronormative patriarchies of imperialism.

Lane Hirabayashi and Marilyn Alquizola discuss an excellent method of utilizing *Slaying the Dragon* in classrooms in the U.S. They suggest that before showing the first episode of the film, about twenty minutes or so, instructors give students a set of questions to consider before the film is screened to help them key into certain information or points they might otherwise miss. These include questions regarding the kinds of stereotypes held by mainstream Americans of Asian women, as well as whether they are consistent over time or shift over the decades (Hirabayashi and Xing 2003, 158). I have utilized this approach myself, asking students to come up and write words or phrases on the board that describe Asian women, and discovered that most American students often continue to carry stereotypes of Asian women in their heads. Although they said these came from the media, they could not recollect exactly which films they were thinking about. Words and phrases that revealed the surviving stereotypes include *subservient, traditional, mysterious, exotic, dangerous, veiled,* and so on. Most of the films discussed in the documentary are from an earlier era, and current students may not have seen many of these films. Yet when they viewed the video, they sat up and commented that they had heard the names of some of the films, especially popular films from the 1970s and 80s such as the *Rambo* series and *Year of the Dragon* (1985). Moreover, they agreed for the most part with articles I presented to them by Asian American theorists who have observed that Asian women have been represented in Hollywood cinema of the past as either the demure, devoted butterfly exemplified by characters like Katsumi in *Sayonara* (1957) or Suzy Wong, the hooker with the heart of gold (1958), or the sinister and crafty siren Fah Lo Suee, the daughter of Fu Manchu. But the fact did not dismay them, as most American students appear to believe that things have changed greatly in today's world with the spread of multiculturalism.

In his landmark work on race relations in the U.S, *Race Matters*, Cornel West has described the flaws of American society as flaws rooted in historical inequalities and longstanding cultural stereotypes (West 1994). As far as Asian Americans are concerned, these stereotypes were created by the media as far back as the mid-nineteenth century, when the first large groups of Asian immigrants began to arrive on American shores. These, the Chinese immigrants, were the first group of non-Whites against whom legislation would be enacted by the U.S. Congress to prevent them from being naturalized, as were other workers of European descent, including the "probationary Whites" of Italian and Irish descent. Not too long after the enactment of the racist legislation of 1882, Asians began to be depicted in a distinctly unfavorable light in the American media, first in poems and short stories, and later in American films as well, as delineated in Gee's documentary. The most striking of these stereotypes was undoubtedly the notorious Fu Manchu, the brilliant but crazed Machiavellian Asian super-villain, out to destroy the West. The character of Fu Manchu was created by the British writer Sax Rohmer in 1913, but it was in the U.S. that Rohmer's books found most acceptance followed by the series of films on Fu Manchu's nefarious activities. This was no doubt because it was in the Americas that early Chinese immigrants had first appeared, seeking the splendid "Gam Saan" (Gold Mountain) in California. Many failed to find it, finding only the depths of humiliation to which they would be plunged as they were singled out for racial degradation in the heady days of the mid to late nineteenth-century Gold Rush. Yet this history had been ignored for many years until the rise of ethnic studies in the 1970s, which called into question not just the historical amnesia involved, but the actual historical erasure of minority communities from the pages of American history. Zillah Eisenstein puts it succinctly in her critique of imperialism: "Remembering at this moment is subversive and stands against the erasure of political history" (Eisenstein 2004, 149).

Gee's film demonstrates the changing attitudes toward Asians starting with the "Yellow Peril" era when the Chinese exemplified the menace of the Asian Other. Thus the sinister opening strains as the evil Asian vamp sashays onto the screen in the films of the 1920s and 1930s, plotting to destroy the hero. Gee's film goes on to show the changing face of Asians from "bad" to "good" to "bad" again, mirroring the political climate of the day, from the Flash Gordon films of the 1950s, which saw the evil Asian villain Ming pitted against the all-American hero Flash Gordon, to well into the 1960s, as Hollywood found it easy to pick on Asian Americans, even in such light-hearted comedies as *Breakfast at Tiffany's*, where the buck-toothed, squint-eyed Mickey Rooney in "yellow face" would pander to the lowest common denominator to raise a laugh. But it was earlier, during the World War II years, that the Japanese were depicted in an openly negative light in Hollywood films. Until then it was the Chinese who were seen as the quintessential Asian villains. Gee delineates how the transformation of the Chinese from "bad Asian" to "good Asian" is accomplished through the release of Hollywood films like the 1937 film version of Pearl Buck's famous novel, *The Good Earth*. The screen reality coincided with the rewarding of the good Asian, as the Chinese Exclusion Act of 1882 was finally repealed in

1943. But this changed again with the Communist takeover of China in 1949, and the Chinese became once more the favorite Hollywood whipping boy, along with the Viet Cong.

If "good" Asians are shown at all, it is those who played a "Gunga Din" role, betraying their own people to save their White masters. A true Indian hero, on the contrary, would be one vilified by the British as a traitor, such as the *sepoy* Mangal Pandey, who attacks his colonial masters instead of saving them, as a Gunga Din would have done. But only Indian cinema would dare to cast Mangal Pandey as a hero; the imperialist cinema of the West definitely would not have done so. In the case of Asian and Asian American women—for the two were often collapsed—the representation was even worse, because they were seen as henchwomen to the evil Asian men, or as pathetic "Madame Butterflies" who could easily be cast aside and forgotten or who committed suicide upon being parted from their White lovers, as in films like *The Barbarian and the Geisha* (1958). Thus the "good" Asian women are those who serve the White protagonist against her own people, often sleeping with him in the process. As David Henry Hwang points out, the neocolonial notion that good elements of a native society, like a good woman, desire submission to the masculine West speaks precisely to the heart of our foreign policy blunders in Asia and elsewhere (Hwang 1986, 99).

Gee demonstrates how the racism of mainstream American cinema is revealed in its treatment of Asian actors as well. In the 1932 film *Shanghai Express* the great Asian American actress Anna May Wong enacts a wicked Asian vamp, but when it came to playing a good Chinese woman such as O-Lan in *The Good Earth* (1937) from Nobel Prize-winning author Pearl S. Buck's book, Wong was not permitted to play the role even though she was the most famous Asian American actress of her time. Instead it was Luise Rainier, a White woman in yellow face, with her eyelids taped back, who played the Chinese peasant woman and won the coveted Oscar. The 1944 film *Dragon Seed* likewise had Katherine Hepburn, also in yellow face, playing the Chinese woman despite the fact that there was no dearth of Asian American actresses longing to play roles in Hollywood. The rationale behind these bizarre decisions taken by the Hollywood moguls was not hard to understand. Miscegenation laws were still in effect all over the country, and no Asian actress could play a lead role opposite a White man. Thus Asian American actresses played only negative roles, such as the evil henchmaiden to the Asian villain. This pattern has continued to this day, for the Dragon Lady stereotype remains alive even in popular TV soap operas of the 1990s like *Ally McBeal*, where the sultry Asian siren Ling was often shown literally baring her fangs and growling.

If the Asian woman is not a cold and dangerous villain, she is a mindless, simpering doll, as seen in the Suzie Wong character of the 1960 film. By the early 1960s, the Korean and Vietnam wars had resulted in scores of Asian women being exploited sexually by the American GIs stationed in those countries. Despite a somewhat more humane portrayal in films like *Sayonara* (1957), Asian women remained coquettish, pretty dolls, eager to please their White lord and master. Scenes from *Year of the Dragon* (1985) make this clear. Gee cuts from scenes of Tracy Tzu, the young Asian American news reporter on the streets with her TV crew, giving the impression that she is a smart professional, to one of her being manhandled and dominated by the Caucasian hero, Stanley White, as he overpowers her and carries her off to bed like a trophy. As Richard E. Lee points out, Tzu's ambivalent position as both object of desire and seductive destroyer of the family is redeemed only by her collaboration with White and her ultimate devotion to him (Lee 1999, 202). Gee's film makes it clear, too, how these cinematic representations of Asian women as exotic creatures who were eager to please the men who owned them has fed into common perceptions of Asian American women even today, contributing to the risk of sexual assault upon them. For, despite the apparent improvement in the cinematic depiction of Asian women, there was also, simultaneously, a representation of them as being somehow "asking for it," and not quite as decent as the wholesome white woman. Gee points out the irony of this through interviews with Asian American women, which bring out the fact that this picture of the worldly, passionate, and exotic Asian woman, skilled in the wiles of carnal knowledge, is a world away from the reality of most Asian women, who are brought up to lead sheltered lives with little contact with the opposite sex until they are married.

It is evident that these media depictions are intended to serve a purpose, that of brainwashing the American public, especially at a time when the nation is at war with Asian countries such as Iraq and Afghanistan. At such a time Asian women are perceived literally as the spoils of war, which the White man has the right to seize, much as he does the Asian country that the woman represents. But of course he seizes in order to "liberate," not to destroy; that is the discourse of empire. Graham Greene says as much in his brilliant expose of the imperialist mindset in *The Quiet American* (1955), where we perceive the seduction of Phuong, the beautiful Vietnamese woman whose sole role in the book appears to be to serve as mistress to both of the White men who covet her favors, much as the two imperial nations coveted her nation. Its critique of empire resulted in the more recent version of the film (Miramax, 2002) being delayed after 9/11 and finally released in 2002 only due to the direct intervention and political clout of the lead actor, Michael Caine. Evelyn Yoshimura had dissected this issue as early as the 1970s, connecting such portrayals to the rationale behind it being easy to slaughter Asian people in the wars in Asia, for they were seen as somehow not part of the norm, always somehow alien. The image of "a people with slanted eyes and slanted vaginas" enhances the feeling that Asians are other than human and therefore much easier to kill (Yoshimura 1971, 28).

The wars in Iraq and Afghanistan have only made things worse, with Asian women being once again in the eye of the storm. Robert G. Lee claims that this history of wars against Asian countries has been successfully effaced from American history in schools and universities, and hence the people belonging to these communities have remained in public perception as "perpetual aliens" (Lee 1999).

The humanity of Asian and Arab women as daughters, sisters, and mothers, and often as professionals—doctors, lawyers, and teachers—is hardly ever represented in the Western media. Where they do appear, it is as mindless, persecuted victims of their own culture who need to be rescued, as faceless, brainwashed figures clad in all-encompassing dark robes, thereby justifying Gayatri Spivak's famous description of the White men trying to save brown women (persecuted by) their own brown men syndrome (Spivak 1988). This representation is far from incidental as it serves to reify the Orientalist portrait of women from the global South as victims of their own cultures. It serves to represent them as victims of their own hyper-patriarchal societies, which in turn serves to justify the neocolonial dreams of empire, as these cultures are seen as desperately in need of intervention and the "*mission civilisatrice.*"

Indeed, although many of my students do acknowledge that sexism exists in the world, they locate it as outside of themselves, and in fact, outside of the West as a whole, and located especially in the Middle East, which in their mental spectrum, as I discovered to my amazement, does not follow national boundaries but extends all the way from Iraq and Saudi Arabia to Afghanistan and even Pakistan. Interestingly, parallel to this story of mistreatment and abuse is the story of hyper-sexuality and eroticism associated with Arab women, so much so that contradictory images of sensuous, half-naked, belly-dancing sirens co-exist along with the suffering, burqa-covered victims of the Taliban. This has indeed been the dominant Western narrative about the status of Islamic women for the past couple of centuries, and Hollywood has played a key role in this representation of an entire region, as demonstrated in numerous studies (Said 1997; Shaheen 2001). Ella Shohat points out how, in a classic splitting operation, the third world is both demonized and infantilized, with evil adult males and innocent, childlike women who are preyed upon by their own men, calling for Indiana Jones to ride in and rescue them (Shohat and Stam 1994). As such, students in much of the West perceive Arab/Asian women as badly in need of rescue from their own bizarre and brutal cultures, masking the reality behind the invasion of Asian countries like Iraq and Afghanistan.

Anthropologist Lila Abu-Lighod demonstrates that the U.S. "war on terror" has taken this approach, presenting First Lady Laura Bush's November 17, 2001 address to the nation where she links the "fight against terrorism" to the "fight for women's rights," thereby enlisting women to justify the U.S. bombings in Afghanistan and the Middle East. "Projects of saving other women depend on and reinforce a sense of superiority by Westerners, a form of arrogance that deserves to be challenged" (Abu-Lighod 2002, 789). Transnational feminists like Cynthia Enloe (2004; 2007), Zillah Eisenstein (2004), Alison Jaggar (2005), Chela Sandoval (2004), and Chandra Talpade Mohanty (2003) critique the hypocrisy of the U.S., which claims to be defending women's rights via their invasions of Afghanistan and Iraq, arguing that women in countries across the world are struggling to create their own lives and not be crushed by either fundamentalist patriarchs at home or capitalists abroad.

To this I add that in the case of Afghanistan, when the Bush regime rushed into the fray, guns blazing, claiming to liberate Afghani women, the fact was conveniently glossed over that the women had been suffering for over a decade from the onslaught of the Taliban and before them, the various warlords that made up the Northern Alliance, while the West turned a Nelson's eye upon them after the retreat of the former USSR from Afghanistan. Moreover, the fact that most of the women's organizations such as RAWA that had been functioning in Afghanistan were totally against Western bombings and occupation was also completely ignored. But most of all, what was completely overlooked was the financial support given to the Taliban by the U.S. Indeed, the role of the U.S government in supporting the Islamic militants needed to be ignored, for only then could Afghan women be exploited in order to justify the imperial mission of the neocolonial power.

This background information is needed to give a complete picture of the entire debacle. I utilize Spivak's tongue-in-cheek analogy to state that the wars waged by White men on brown men serve to make the condition of brown women much worse than prior to this ostensibly benevolent intervention to save them from their own misogynistic culture. It would bode well if more people in the West were to acknowledge their own roles in creating chaos in the Third World as the transnational feminists admit. "Rather than simply blaming Amina Lawal's culture, we should begin by taking our own feet off her neck" (Jaggar 2005).

In the late twentieth century, however, women of color claimed some of the principles of modern feminism in their efforts to define themselves and control their representation, wresting their image from the classic stereotypes of the Mammy, the hot-blooded Latina, and the Asian Butterfly and Dragon Lady, both. Despite their growing influence in mass culture, however, these representations remain resilient, often reappearing in new forms that serve to confuse the average viewer and lull him/her into a delusion that things have changed completely from the days of Fu Manchu's diabolical daughter. For instance, it may be argued that Asian women appear far more in Hollywood films today, from Lucy Liu in *Kill Bill* (2003) to Scottish actress Katie Leung as Harry Potter's love interest, Cho Chang, in *Harry Potter and the Goblet of Fire* (2005), or even the giggly Patil twins duo in the same. Television is not far behind with Sandra Oh's brilliant but humorless surgeon Christina Yang in *Grey's Anatomy* (ABC) and Lucy Liu's rendition of Mia Mason in *Cashmere Mafia* (NBC), which follows four female executives struggling to balance family and career in New York City. However, the question remains, has the manner in which Asian women have been represented changed much?

In the popular Hollywood thriller *The Transporter* (2002), the character played by actress Shu Qi is not even given a last name; unlike in films starring Caucasian actresses, she is just "Lai." Mohanty's contention that third-world women are represented in the U.S. media as weak and defenseless, needing to be protected from their own brutal culture, is seen here, for Lai's father is a brute and gangster, as with Tracy Tzu in *Year of the Dragon* (1985), and it is the macho White hero who steps in to rescue her from him. Gee describes the stereotypical representation of Asian women in Hollywood films over the years, starting with *Sayonara* (1957), in which a Japanese performer wins the heart of "Ace Gruber," a macho U.S. Air Force officer. When the White officer woos the Japanese artist, her demure whispered response is, "I shall love you if you so desire." American GI Kelly in the same film, while devoted to his Japanese wife Katsumi, treats her like a small child, and indeed she appears to be one, alternately cajoling and cosseting her husband, scrubbing his back in the bath and catering to his every need. Soon after the release of the film, the country saw a spate of Asian brides being brought to the country by American men eager to have a wife who would tend to their every whim and fancy. Indeed, that appears to be the message of the film as well, for Major Grover dumps his independent-minded Caucasian fiancée for his exotic Japanese paramour.

It may be argued that *Sayonara* was after all a product of its time, and things have changed substantially for Asian women today. But I posit that this representation of the Asian woman continues into our era with the Asian woman remaining subordinate, as in the Hollywood film *The Transporter* (2002) where you see Lai fawning over her taciturn White hero the morning after, trying to prepare a special meal for him, preparing both tea and coffee for him in case he preferred one over the other. How similar this is to *Sayonara's* Katsumi's desire to please her White husband in any way possible, even if necessary by undergoing an operation to remove the epicanthic folds on her eyelids in order to have "round eyes" that are more pleasing to Western men. The Transporter's curt response that he prefers silence in the morning while he has his breakfast adds to his macho image even as it cements the Asian woman's subordinate status. The film ends with Lai disappearing into the sunset much as Bond women do, for in the film's sequel there is not even a mention of the woman, she is so obviously a disposable commodity. Recalling her father's dour warning that he does not want the White man getting involved with his daughter, can we be surprised?

Some may argue that things have changed greatly in today's U.S. media and that the portrayal of Ling Woo by actress Lucy Liu, the sultry lawyer in the popular 1990s TV series *Ally McBeal* (Fox TV, 1997–2002) is a step in the right direction with regard to the representation of Asian/Asian American women in the visual media. But as Ling purrs and growls and slithers her way up the corporate ladder, the question remains: was this role a fair and accurate portrait of Asian women? Moreover, has it changed much from the days when the great Asian American actress Anna May Wong played a wicked vamp in the 1932 film *Shanghai Express* opposite the Caucasian heroine, Marlene Dietrich? Liu earned an Emmy nomination and a Screen Actors' Guild award for the role of Ling Woo, but Asian American activists wondered whether the character's aggressiveness challenged the stereotype of Asian women as meek and submissive, or merely continued the stereotype of the Asian woman as the hypersexual Dragon Lady who seduces and then destroys. Some critics allege that the character of Ling Woo changes as she is gradually humanized, but this is hardly sufficient to erase the caricature. Ling does occasionally show a glimpse of a more humane side, as in the episode where she defends a boy dying of cancer, but she reverts to her "inscrutable Oriental" image all too soon, making that the quality the viewer most associates with her. A quote from the actor on a celebrity website reveals as much: "It's so much fun playing Ling, but I have this fear that people are going to run away from me in terror on the streets. They think I'm going to bite their heads off or something."[1]

Asian American media theorists and activists, such as Helen Liu, media consultant for the Asian American Resource Workshop in Boston, support this observation. Liu calls Ling Woo "the '90s version of all the old stereotypes wrapped up in one. She's a Suzie Wong; she has sex secrets. . . . People say, 'It's OK if she has this kind of weird and kinky side because she's also a powerful and central character.' But you have to look at what people are really being drawn to. They're not being drawn to the fact that she's powerful or central. They're drawn to her because of her stereotypical qualities" (Chihara 2000).

Liu's role in *Kill Bill Volumes 1 and 2* (2003, 2004) had her playing the role of Asian Dragon Lady O-Ren Ishii, a brutal assassin, Queen of the Tokyo Underworld and leader of the Crazy 88 Fighters, who decapitates men with the drop of a hat, not too much of a stretch from her earlier role as Pearl, the sadistic dominatrix and mafia hit woman in *Payback* (1999). Tarantino's depiction of unmitigated violence is entwined with the exploitation of the female body as spectacle, and it is not coincidental that the body that controls the action and eventually triumphs is the White body, represented by the Bride, while the Asian Dragon Lady is vanquished. Indeed, the Bride, resplendent in her whiteness, is humanized through her maternal role, with her violence being justified, while that of the Asian Dragon Lady is perceived as aberrant, making her defeat and death inevitable. The stereotype of the beautiful but cold Asian siren continues with Liu's role as a sexy executive in the *Cashmere Mafia* and *Dirty Sexy Money* (ABC, 2008) where she plays the role of Nola Lyons, a powerful attorney. Korean American actress Sandra Oh's representation of the brilliant but cold surgeon Dr. Christina Yang in the popular soap opera *Grey's Anatomy* (ABC, 2007) is a similar case in point. The women concerned are beautiful and competent professionals, but devoid of the more humane, "normal," and feminine qualities represented by the Caucasian women in the show, Dr. Isobel (Izzy) Stevens and Dr. Meredith Grey. Asian women as represented in these popular soaps remain remote, exotic, enigmatic, and unfathomable, "inscrutable Orientals" to the end.

As far as South Asian, Muslim, and Arab women are concerned, the post 9/11 world has increased their feelings of misperception by much of the mainstream U.S. Tram Nguyen, executive editor of *Colorlines Magazine*, discusses the impact of the attacks of September 11, 2001 on immigrant communities of color. In an ironic reversal of the American dream, a shocking 20,000 members of the community known as little Pakistan voluntarily left the U.S. after 9/11 in order to escape the climate of suspicion. She quotes one woman, "For women who wear the hijab, it's like they have a bull's eye on their forehead" (Nguyen 2005, 51). Ironically, this is similar to the attacks in New York City on South Asian Hindu women in the late 1980s by the self-proclaimed "Dot Busters," who homed in on women wearing the traditional Hindu *pottu* or *bindi* on their foreheads. Indeed, the time for a renewed attack on people of color from this area appears to have returned, coinciding, not unsurprisingly, with a new climate of economic uncertainty calling for new scapegoats to target. South Asian filmmakers have not been slow to respond to the renewed persecution of their communities either. Independent films like *Brick Lane* (2003) and *American East* (2007) describe the discrimination faced by South and Southwest Asian communities in the West post 9/11. Those two well-known independent films were made by Asian filmmakers in the West, whereas films like *New York* (2009) and *The War Within* (2005) are from the Bollywood and Pakistani film centers and represent the perception of ordinary people from India and Pakistan respectively.

As South Asian writer Mohsin Hamid's character in his book wryly observes, "America was gripped by a growing and self-righteous rage. . . . It was a time when South Asian cabdrivers were being beaten within an inch of their lives" (Hamid 2007, 94). Indeed, this bore an eerie similarity to the climate of fear that afflicted Japanese Americans in the days immediately following the attack on Pearl Harbor, leading to the mass incarceration of Japanese Americans in the euphemistically named relocation camps. At such a time it is very easy for dominant cinema to play into people's fears and create portraits of entire races and cultures as dangerously foreign, inassimilable, and even the enemies within. Even films as sensitive as *Crash* (2006) have been unable to shake off the xenophobic lens of Hollywood. Margaret Rhee points out that although many other races are redeemed by the conclusion of the film, Asian Americans are not. *Crash* enforces racist ideologies through its portrait of Asians as greedy, shrilly yelling, inhuman, foreign characters with thick Korean accents, incapable of even a moment of compassion (Rhee 2009, 43). They are seen as doing anything to get ahead, even human trafficking through the sale of other Asian people, such as Thai and Cambodian slaves. Film theorist bell hooks puts it succinctly, "Whether we like it or not, cinema assumes a pedagogical role in the lives of many people. It may not be the intent of a filmmaker to teach audiences anything, but that does not mean that lessons are not learned" (hooks 1996, 2).

Like hooks, I learned too that my students learned more from movies than from all the literature I was urging them to read. But getting students who have absolutely no background in this media manipulation of reality to comprehend the power of these media images in distorting reality is far from easy. The merging of standpoints in some films makes it difficult for students to critically read the overall cinematic narrative. Moreover, instructors who belong to the specific races or regions under scrutiny face even more of an uphill task, as being of Asian descent in the post 9/11 world in the U.S. turns out to be a complex position to navigate. Indeed, however much they have tried to "fit in," people of color in this country have never been able to shake off what sociologist Robert Park described as their "racial uniform" (Takaki 1998). Given this, Gee's film *Slaying the Dragon* is very important indeed. She demonstrates how through stereotypical images, generalizations about people of color have passed into "common sense," making it possible for dominant society to establish control over what passes as truth. Literature and cinema thus become insidious, political forces of mass deception whereby the public is robbed of its ability to see the substance for the shadow, and comprehend the reality behind the stereotype. Indeed, dominant Hollywood cinema is seen as constructed according to the unconscious patriarchy, which means that "film narratives are constituted through a phallocentric language and discourse that parallels the language of the unconscious" (Kaplan 2000, 120).

The problem is not just that "the male gaze" remains intact, to utilize Laura Mulvey's famous critique, but that it is also an imperial, patriarchal gaze wherein the colonized Asian figure is reduced to a caricature. The 1957 film *Sayonara*'s Katsumi's devotion to her White husband Airman Kelly is all-consuming: she cooks for him, cleans for him, even bathes him. But what is disturbing is that this representation continues today; it recurs every decade. Arthur Golden's best-selling novel *Memoirs of a Geisha* (1997), filmed by Rob Marshall in 2005 and nominated for six Academy Awards, is a case in point. The beautiful geisha protagonist Sayuri is what Asian American theorist Noy Thrupkaew calls "a white man in geishaface." For as she reveals in her incisive essay for the progressive journal *Zmag*, many who have never been to Japan or spoken to a geisha have marveled at Golden's ability to capture the voice of a geisha so accurately. "Some readers even told me they liked it more because Golden is a white man—why would it be interesting if it was written by a Japanese woman?" (Thrupkaew 2001). It is interesting that this representation of a geisha is taken by many to be authentic, even though it is an American film directed by an American Caucasian director from a novel by a male American author that uses Chinese actors to portray Japanese characters.[2] Would it have been perceived as being so authentic had it been the other way round, an Asian film by an Asian author, assuming the identity of a White American male? Indeed, what E. Ann Kaplan calls "the imperial gaze," the gaze of the colonist that refuses to acknowledge its own power and privilege (Kaplan 1997, 79), is the only gaze that has authority in the West to this day.

Things only seem to get worse in more recent films, even in supposed award-winning, art-house films such as *The Civilization of Maxwell Bright* (2005), where the Asian mail-order bride of misogynist Bright caters to his every whim, stopping short only of disrobing in front of his male friends when he orders her to do so. Said's original Orientalism thesis of the collapsing of every Asian group into one monolithic entity appears initially to be mocked in the scene where Bright first meets his Chinese bride and greets her in Japanese, saying "Arigato." But the Asian wife's transformation of her misogynist husband is also a reification of the Confucian dictum of the dutiful wife who refuses to desert even the worst husband as she considers it her duty to help him discover his "Buddha nature." In this sense the film renews the worst stereotypes of Asian women as the oriental version of steel magnolias who stand by their men to the bitter end, and reinscribe the binary demarcation of subjugated Asian woman vs. liberated Western woman. Indeed, Bright orders his mail-order bride precisely to escape from the liberated White women he has dated, and the film's supposed progressive bent is negated through the very stereotypes it claims to deconstruct.

I posit further that the average American viewer is so accustomed to inaccurate and outdated representations of Asians in the media that it is startling to hear them speak in complete, syntactically correct sentences, as in films by Asian American directors that challenge the Orientalist paradigm. Films like M. Butterfly from the play by David Henry Hwang (1986) and The Namesake (2007) by Mira Nair demonstrate that these populations are fully capable of representing their own lives and experiences in a manner that is far more authentic. This being so, it is evident that in denying the humanity of these communities by restricting them to narrowly socially defined roles, the gatekeepers of the mass media deprive the American public of the vitality and genius of the diverse Asian groups that have contributed so much to the building of the nation (Hamamoto 1994, 252). Molly Haskell's famous description of Hollywood as "the propaganda arm of the American Dream machine" (Haskell 1987, 1) is true enough, but I add that not only is the big gender lie perpetuated on Western society, as she posits, but also that of race. Gee's film encourages students to question these stereotypical representations of an entire people by delineating the reality behind the politics behind the cinematic representations. Although Slaying the Dragon was originally made in the late 1980s, if used with supplementary films and readings, it is still very effective as an icebreaker to get students to confront racial and gender stereotypes and move confidently into the sociopolitical complexities behind such representations. This "reversing of the lens," to utilize the concept of Lane Hirabayashi and Marilyn Alquizola (Hirabayashi and Xing 2003), serves to help viewers to confront the stereotypes in order to destroy them.

One of the one major problems that I had with the film, however, is that there is no mention in it of South and Central Asians, bringing out the critique of many Asian theorists that South and Central Asians are marginalized by American theorists who often do not even acknowledge that these groups are Asians too. One needs, therefore, to supplement the Gee film screening with other readings and more recent films that critique the representation of South and Central Asians in Hollywood as well. One such documentary I have found to be an extremely useful tool to be utilized along with the screening of Gee's film is Sut Jhally's interview with Edward Said, titled *On Orientalism* (1998), brought out shortly before the eminent scholar's demise by the Media Education Foundation of Northampton, Massachusetts. This documentary film contains video clips from the visual media on the repertory of European and American Orientalism and the contemporary understanding in the U.S. of "the Orient." It is only through an examination of such films that students can learn to develop what hooks calls "an oppositional gaze," a critical gaze, one that "looks" in order to document, which realizes that looking at is not a mere acceptance of the images and stereotypes represented, but can also be a process of contestation and confrontation (hooks 1996). Best of all, it enables students of all races to examine anew the power of the myth machines to fashion our portraits of ourselves and our fellow citizens.

....

Shoba Sharad Rajgopal is professor and chair of the Department of Ethnic and Gender Studies at Westfield State University, and holds a PhD in communication. Her research and teaching areas are in postcolonial and transnational feminist theories; Queer movements and identities; South Asian cinema, globalization, and religion; and gender conflicts in the Subcontinent. Dr. Rajgopal has worked as a television news norrespondent based in Bombay (Mumbai) for Indian television networks and CNN International focusing on the rights of women, and indigenous and marginalized communities in India.

Notes

Originally published in *Meridians* vol. 10, no. 2, 2010.

1   See http://www.celebritybazar.com/lucy_liu/quotes.shtml (accessed September 13, 2010).

2   Interestingly, after the publication of *Memoirs of a Geisha*, Arthur Golden was sued by the geisha on whom he had supposedly based his character, Mineko Iwasaki. Eventually, in 2003, Golden's publisher settled with Iwasaki out of court for an undisclosed sum. Iwasaki later went on to write her own autobiography, which shows a very different picture of twentieth-century geisha than the one shown in Golden's novel. The book was published as *Geisha, a Life* in the U.S. and *Geisha of Gion* in the UK, but it was never in the spotlight in the way Golden's portrait of a geisha was. Apparently, a Western account of a Japanese tradition is considered more authentic to fellow Occidentals than that of somebody actually from the country and tradition concerned.

Works Cited

Abu-Lighod, Lila. 2002. "Do Muslim Women Really Need Saving? Anthropological Reflections on Cultural Relativism and Its Others." *American Anthropologist* 104, no. 3: 783–90.

Anzaldua, Gloria. 1987. *Borderlands La Frontera: The New Mestiza.* San Francisco: Aunt Lute.

Chatterjee, Shoma. A. 1998. *Subject: Cinema, Object: Woman: A Study of the Portrayal of Women in Indian Cinema.* Calcutta: Parumita Publications.

Chihara, Michelle. 2000. "There's Something about Lucy: Casting a Cold Eye on the Rise of Asian Starlets." *Boston Phoenix* (February 24–March 2). http://www .bostonphoenix.com/archive/features/00/02/24/ASIAN_BABES.html (accessed September 13, 2010).

Collins, Patricia Hill. 1990. *Black Feminist Thought: Knowledge, Consciousness, and the Politics of Empowerment.* New York: Routledge.

Eisenstein, Zillah. 2004. *Against Empire: Feminisms, Racism, and the West.* New Delhi: Women Unlimited.

Enloe, Cynthia. 2004. *The Curious Feminist: Searching for Women in a New Age of Empire.* Los Angeles: University of California Press.

———. 2007. *Globalization and Militarism: Feminists Make the Link.* Boulder, CO: Rowman & Littlefield Publishers, Inc.

Gilroy, Paul. 1982. *The Empire Strikes Back: Race and Racism in '70s Britain.* London: Hutchinson, in association with the Centre for Contemporary Cultural Studies.

Greene, Graham. 1991. *The Quiet American.* New York: Penguin Classics.

Hamamoto, Darrell. 1994. *Monitored Peril: Asian Americans and the Politics of TV Representation.* Minneapolis: University of Minnesota Press.

Hamamoto, Darrell, and Sandra Liu. 2000. *Countervisions: Asian American Film Criticism.* Philadelphia: Temple University Press.

Hamid, Mohsin. 2007. *The Reluctant Fundamentalist.* New York: Harcourt.

Haskell, Molly. 1987. *From Reverence to Rape: The Treatment of Women in the Movies.* Chicago: University of Chicago Press.

Hirabayashi, Lane Ryo, and Jun Xing, eds. 2003. *Reversing the Lens: Ethnicity, Race, Gender, and Sexuality through Film.* Boulder: University Press of Colorado.

hooks, bell. 1996. *Reel to Real: Race, Sex, and Class at the Movies.* New York: Routledge.

Huntington, Samuel P. 1996. *The Clash of Civilizations and the Remaking of World Order.* New York: Simon & Schuster.

Hwang, David Henry. 1986. *M. Butterfly.* New York: Plume, Penguin Books.

Jaggar, Alison. 2005. "Saving Amina: Global Justice for Women and Intercultural Dialogue." *Ethics & International Affairs* 19, no. 3: 85–105.

Jhally, Sut. 1998. Producer/director. *Edward Said: On Orientalism,* Northampton, MA: Media Education Foundation.

Johnston, Claire. 1975. "Women's Cinema as Counter-Cinema." In *Notes on Women's Cinema,* ed. Claire Johnston. London: Society for Education in Film and Television, reprinted in: *Feminist Film Theory. A Reader,* ed. Sue Thornham. Edinburgh: Edinburgh University Press 1999.

Kaplan, E. Ann. 1997. *Looking for the Other: Feminism, Film, and the Imperial Gaze.* New York: Routledge.

———. 2000. *Feminism and Film.* New York: Oxford University Press.

Lee, Robert G. 1999. *Orientals: Asian Americans in Popular Culture*. Philadelphia: Temple University Press.

Marchetti, Gina. 1993. *Romance and the Yellow Peril: Race, Sex, and Discursive Strategy in Hollywood Fiction*. Berkeley and Los Angeles: University of California Press.

Mohanty, Chandra Talpade. 2003. *Feminism without Borders: Decolonizing Theory, Practicing Solidarity*. Durham, NC: Duke University Press.

Narayan, Uma. 1997. *Dislocating Cultures: Identities, Traditions, and Third World Feminism*. New York: Routledge.

Nguyen, Tram. 2005. *We Are All Suspects Now: Untold Stories from Immigrant Communities after 9/11*. Boston: Beacon Press.

Rhee, Margaret. 2009. "Chink, Chinaman, and Celestial: Inhumanity in Crash." In *Crash Course: Reflections on the Film for Critical Dialogues about Race, Power, and Privilege*, ed. Michael Benitez, Jr. Emeryville, CA: The Institute for Democratic Education and Culture.

Rohmer, Sax. 1913. *The Insidious Dr. Fu Manchu*. New York: McBride, Nast & Company.

Said, Edward. 1978. *Orientalism*. New York: Pantheon.

———. 1997. *Covering Islam: How the Media and the Experts Determine How We See the Rest of the World*. New York: Vintage.

Sandoval, Chela. 2004. *Methodology of the Oppressed*. Minneapolis: University of Minnesota Press.

Shaheen, Jack G. 2001. *Reel Bad Arabs: How Hollywood Vilifies a People*. New York: Olive Branch Press.

Shohat, Ella, and Robert Stam. 1994. *Unthinking Eurocentrism: Multiculturalism and the Media*. London: Routledge.

Spivak, Gayatri Chakravorty. 1988. "Can the Subaltern Speak?" In *Marxism and the Interpretation of Culture*, ed. Cary Nelson and Lawrence Grossberg. Urbana: University of Illinois Press.

Takaki, Ronald. 1998. *Strangers from a Different Shore: A History of Asian Americans*. Boston: Little, Brown and Company.

Thrupkaew, Noy. 2001. "Going Geisha." http://www.zmag.org/zspace/commentaries/770 (accessed September 13, 2010).

Yoshimura, Evelyn. 1971. "GIs and Asian Women." In *Roots: An Asian American Anthology*, ed. Amy Takaki, Eddie Wong, and Franklin Oda. Los Angeles: UCLA Asian American Studies Center.

West, Cornel. 1994. *Race Matters*. New York: Vintage Books.

Jennifer Cho

....

Mel-*han*-cholia as Political Practice
in Theresa Hak Kyung Cha's *Dictée*

Abstract: Turning to extant theories of melancholy, this article uses Theresa
Hak Kyung Cha's *Dictée* to reevaluate the linear trajectory of Asian American
identity formation in the United States. In particular, the author develops
the term mel-*han*-choly—a hybrid form of melancholy and Korean *han* (a
culturally specific grief)—to show how Cha uses it as a subversive political
tool to defer historical closure and to refuse her quiet assimilation. Cha's
remembrance of the histories of Japanese colonialism in the Korean peninsula and the Korean War defies the expectation that minority populations
somehow transcend their grievous pasts in becoming model American citizens. The author claims that Cha's mel-*han*-cholic gestures disrupt the
United States' discursive power in narrating Korean history, especially as
one contingent on accepting America's "liberating" charge. This article also
proposes that mel-*han*-choly serves a healing function within the diasporic
Korean community, offering transnational connectivity through the shared
experience of grief.

....

"[Y]our han calls out to me, animating me, making me present in your past, making
me present in your consciousness. Even though I was not born yet, I am there inside
your experience. I remember these things happening to you."
—Suji Kwock Kim, Notes from the Divided Country
....

Published by Tanam Press in 1982, Theresa Hak Kyung Cha's Dictée returns
to the enmeshed histories of colonization, war, and migration on the
Korean peninsula, suggesting that the traumatic past and its attendant

MERIDIANS · feminism, race, transnationalism   Volume 19 Supplement 2020
DOI: 10.1215/15366936-8566067 © 2011 Smith College

grief are still very much alive.[1] These histories erupt intermittently through the personal stories of Cha's narrator, a Korean immigrant-turned-U.S. citizen, and her mother, a Korean transplant in Manchuria during Japan's imperial reign. This intergenerational overlay of immigrant and postcolonial subjectivities reveals how both subjects have undergone a similar series of disciplinary measures assessing loyalty to the nation-state. Although immigrant and postcolonial experiences are certainly not mutually exclusive and can overlap, they both demonstrate that the state can command visibly different bodies to behave acceptably for national inclusion. How these bodies remember, too, can confirm their allegiance to dominant practices of memory.

By sustaining grief over Korea's colonial and wartime past, *Dictée* challenges the U.S.'s reliance on linear, historical time to manage the grieving processes of its minority subjects. I suggest that *Dictée* depicts historical temporality as the straight, teleological time of the nation-state, used to measure how far it has come since the traumas of the past. In such a conception of time, national subjects may be expected to quickly "get over" their traumatic pasts for the reason that the U.S. may refuse to acknowledge minority histories as grief-worthy. Additionally, the U.S. may be able to gloss over its own participation in producing grievous histories among its subjects. Recall Foucault, who claimed that biopolitical power seeps into and shapes those institutions meant to rehabilitate or normalize otherwise aberrant bodies (the hospital or prison, for example) to guarantee the exceptional fortitude of the larger body politic. As Foucault insisted, "deployments of power are directly connected to the body—to bodies, functions, physiological processes, sensations, and pleasures" (Foucault 1990, 151–52). This dissemination of state power through disciplined bodies may then legitimate familiar patterns of remembrance. In the U.S., the grief of racialized others is managed through the expectation that they relinquish those oppressive histories around which minority identity is often organized. Histories of hurt, oppression, and struggle are dramatically whisked away into the past, where traumatic histories bear no tangible effects in the present.

Rather than taking history down verbatim, *Dictée* urges us to pause in the silent gaps and furious dins that might exist between dominant American discourse and the cultural memory of diasporic Koreans in the U.S. This is because the history of the Korean peninsula cannot be recalled without sparking memory of American intervention. Cha reminds us to pursue a kind of conscientious historical practice, in which we examine not so much the validity of one's grief over another's, but the state's institutional apparatuses, which simultaneously produce and manage the grief of inassimilable minority groups. Whereas society at large might pathologize melancholia, condemning its obstruction of an idealized national future, such unresolved grief might, as David Eng suggests, serve as "a model of group formation" (Eng 2000, 1278). Eng writes that a minority group's recognition of and internalization of their symbolic loss can, in fact, shape the collective ego: "This ambivalent attachment to devalued objects, like ressentiment, comes to define—indeed, to produce—minoritarian subjectivities" (1278).

In *Dictée*, Cha suggests that dominant understandings of Korea's colonial and wartime history in the American imaginary have relegated the Korean peninsula (and its displaced populations who have arrived in the U.S.) to the realm of subjugated knowledge. As I employ it here, the meaning of the term "subjugated knowledge" is twofold. It refers not only to alternative or dissenting historical knowledge that has been purged from the official U.S. historical record, but also the knowledge of one's subjugation. The U.S. seeks to quiet such eruptions of historical memory that expose the nation's reliance on the subjugation of minority others. In other words, the past histories that have shaped Eng's "minoritarian subjectivities" are subjugated by the unquestionable "truths" of official American discourse.

In this essay, I argue that Cha's narrator assumes a series of mel-han-cholic postures in response to the oppressive nature of official history. My term, mel-han-choly, hinges on Freud's conception of melancholy, defined as a state of unfinished mourning. Freud suggests that the subject can't or is reluctant to replace the lost object; rather, she internalizes it as part of her ego, so that the self emerges from and is constituted by loss. Mel-han-choly, however, diverges from Freud's conception of melancholy, as it integrates *han*.

According to scholars such as John Lie and Elaine Kim, *han* is a communal, affective bond within the Korean diaspora. Loosely translated by Lie as "ressentiment" resulting from the "accumulation of human tragedies—physical and spiritual anguish," *han* bears melancholic inflections through its formulation of a cultural identity around the prevalence of loss (Lie 1998, 114). Elaine Kim defines *han* as "the sorrow and anger that grow from the accumulated experiences of oppression shared among the Korean people" (Kim 2000, 270). *Han*, in Lie's and Kim's renderings, represents an irreducible, intergenerational feeling of communal grief, suggesting that the pervasive memories of foreign invasion and coloniza- tion, civil war, and internal division in Korea continue to impinge upon and redefine the safe boundaries of the present.

Han also presents the possibility of using grief toward mobilizing polit- ical action. As *han* points us to the social and cultural institutions that have produced grief, or cause for mourning among the U.S.'s minority popula- tions, it draws attention to a shared group consciousness formulated around a history of oppression. The mutual recognition of this shared his- tory might, as Kim suggests in her reading of the L.A. riots, generate social action to address and resolve institutional injustices and race- and class- based discrimination that might otherwise remain hidden.[2] The impossi- bility of ever fully evacuating diasporic Korean consciousness of *han* speaks to its shape-shifting qualities. Unresolvable by nature, *han* can constantly rework and redefine itself to escape an impending moment of final resolu- tion and translation in the symbolic register of the nation—one that works toward the healing and erasure of cultural difference.

This is not to say that *han* communicates a kind of true Korean identity, or that Korean identity can even be essentialized or recuperated around this shared affective response to a sense of culturally inherited history. Rather, *han* can mobilize a dispersed people around shared political and cultural struggles, resisting the kind of forgetting on which the rise of new national subjectivities depends.[3] The reminders of oppression and despair, posed by this shared cultural affect, dispel the possibility of full redress.

For Cha, mel-*han*-choly emerges as a subversive political practice, as she refuses to surrender knowledge of Korean history and of her symbolic lack as a Korean immigrant in the U.S. This move is clearly evidenced as Cha employs the Korean past to simultaneously comment on the struggles she experiences as a Korean immigrant expected to speak and perform the signs of successful American citizenship. Cha's compulsion to return to Korea's traumatic history can be read as an attempt to craft cultural belonging in the U.S. where she has been previously excluded due to her racial and linguistic estrangement.

Informing my understanding of Cha's mel-*han*-choly is Juliana Chang's belief that the promise of melancholia lies in its "state of nonclosure" (Chang 2004, 245). As Chang weds melancholy to unresolved grief due to trauma, she suggests that melancholy's appearances can defy the belief that trauma has been overcome through its integration into the symbolic narrative of the U.S. Similarly, Cha's mel-han-choly derives its political effect from its capacity to protest the U.S.'s reified modes of remembering the traumatic histories it incurred in distant places like the Korean peninsula. The value of mel-han-choly—a cultural and racialized permutation of melancholy—can burst open seemingly closed historical discourses of the U.S. from the inside.

Starting with a theoretical discussion of racial melancholy, I aim to reevaluate the accepted, linear trajectory of Asian American identity-formation in the U.S. In particular, Korean American identity far exceeds the boundaries of the continental U.S. As Dictée reveals, it can span multiple histories, geographies, and generations. I trace how Cha employs mel-han-choly as a kind of political gambit to defer closure to the processes of assimilation and post-traumatic recovery that enable a threatening outsider to be transformed and disciplined into a docile national citizen. While full assimilation and recovery from trauma can certainly be rewarding processes and are necessary for one's personal survival and social inclusion, I am interested in how they reflect the U.S.'s inclination to link national progress to a symbolic relinquishing of some detrimental past. Rather than demonize these processes of assimilation and recovery, Dictée shows how they cannot be detached from the larger ideologies of the modern U.S. nation. Cha suspends herself in a prolonged state of mel-han-choly to prevent post-traumatic recovery and national assimilation from becoming regimented processes that leave the values and ideologies of the U.S. unchallenged. Ultimately, Cha's examinations of immigrant experience in the U.S. lead us to reexamine American military and political activity on the Korean peninsula.

By drawing attention to the explicit and the less obvious imbrications between Korean and American histories beginning as early as 1905, and deferring Korean history's complete assimilation into American history alone, Cha produces a parallel critical examination of the assimilatory process that frames Asian immigrants and Asian Americans' entrance into mainstream American culture. While Japanese colonialism in Korea and the subsequent decolonization of South Korea under American sponsorship are by no means equivalent, Cha shows that the political, economic, and military transition from one order to the next enabled the U.S. to reassert its exceptional national character. In Dictée, Cha provides a renewed understanding of the values that secure American national identity. These values are especially challenged by the melancholic histories that the U.S. has produced for other nations and its internal populations due to their inassimilable differences.

Racial Melancholy and the State of Mourning

Represented by her circular obsessions with Korea's traumatic past and the painful struggles with narrative fidelity and expression, Cha's narrator is plagued by a sense of loss from the recognition of her inassimilable difference. As a Korean immigrant to the U.S., she exhibits a strain of "ethnic malaise," which David Palumbo-Liu describes as a state of psychological sickness that Asian immigrants experience due to the awareness of both their alien presence and their lack of symbolic capital (Palumbo-Liu 1999, 396). This "ethnic malaise" can be cured through the immigrant's labored attempts to transcend her racialized past by integrating into the linear, future-bent trajectory of the state. One way that Asians and Asian Americans have historically been able to mimic the progress narrative of the U.S. is through their achievement of model minority status.

Palumbo-Liu articulates that the model minority myth is the belief that Asian Americans' "success lies in their ability to adapt Asia to America as well as to transform America through the application of a Confucian ethos" (Palumbo-Liu 1999, 21). Under the simplistic one-to-one exchange of Asia for America and past for future, Asian immigrants and Asian Americans are expected to cure the "ethnic malaise" by which they are afflicted. This American adaptation of Asia also speaks to Johannes Fabian's suggestion, as quoted by Juliana Chang: "Temporal distancing relegates the racial and colonial Other to an Other time, an Other order" (Chang 2004, 253). If the immigrant must assimilate through her acknowledged subjection to majority discourses about the kind of identity (or memory) she must perform, she may also be expected to surrender any lingering remnants of cultural grief for national inclusion, particularly if such grief over the past attunes us to the U.S.'s violent creation of "an Other time, an Other order."

By transcending individual difference, the subject can be integrated into majority culture. Expected to overcome the recurring symptoms of her "ethnic malaise" so she can function effectively within the social fabric, the immigrant might achieve national belonging only by renouncing the past of her departed homeland and entering the future of her adopted nation. Yet, Cha's text reveals the limitations of this national narrative of healing.

Cha examines the refusal to adapt to the conditions of U.S. citizenship. Rather than concentrating on the future signified by American citizenship, *Dictée* returns to a Korean past discovered to run parallel to, and at times convergent with, the historical time of the U.S. Cha implicates the U.S. in various traumatic moments of the Korean peninsular past, from its colonization to its (post)war history. As these tangled histories of domination and suppression are remembered, Cha withholds the kind of narrative and psychological closure that would enable readers to see traumatic Korean history as past, or overcome.

In its repetitive compulsion toward remembering Japanese and American presences in the Korean past, *Dictée* performs the inassimilable and language-defying symptoms of trauma. Its disjointed presentation mimics the temporal confusion of traumatic memory itself, as narrative fragments and decontextualized images flare up unexpectedly. The text refuses narrative coherence, escaping categorizations of genre, closed textual interpretations, and proper conventions of language and form. Even the multiple modes of representation (print, visual, aural) and languages (French, English, Korean, Chinese) presented in *Dictée* speak to the impossibility of parsing the text into any singular meaning. The estranged personal and historical leftovers that appear in *Dictée* (as stuttering fits, handwritten and crossed-out words, blank pages, uncredited images, or indecipherable voices) defy narrative linearity. The structural arrangement of Cha's work conveys how traumatic experiences reside outside the range of verbal representation.

As trauma's etymology suggests a wound created by some external force, the division of the Korean peninsula—imposed by the U.S. and the Soviet Union in September 1945—is rendered as a physical and psychic wound in *Dictée*. A map of the severed Korean peninsula appears in the section called "Melpomene Tragedy" (Cha 1995, 78). In this map, Korea appears to be detached from the rest of the world, as its only signs of orientation are provided through its tangential boundaries with China, the Sea of Japan, and the Yellow Sea. The Demilitarized Zone (DMZ) situated along the 38th parallel appears as a darkened line of severance across the country, and Patti Duncan reminds us that this national division attunes us to memories of Korea's serial colonization: "To point repeatedly to the partition of Korea, then, is to refuse any denial of the colonization of Korea by both Japan and the United States" (Duncan 2004, 169). As Duncan suggests, Cha's map of a divided Korea visualizes the messy histories of linked imperial projects in the Korean peninsula, although they, of course, vary widely in degree and intention.

Trauma, in Chang's view, not only erupts within the symbolic to expose its fantasy of wholeness, but it also troubles the authoritative reign of national, historical time. Chang writes, "Trauma is that which the subject is unable to assimilate into her symbolic universe. . . . Thus overwhelmed and immobilized, the traumatized subject cannot place herself into a symbolic narrative such as that of history; she is displaced from normative historical time" (Chang 2004, 242). In this sense, Dictée's narrative obscurity and the frustrations it might create for its readers refuse to offer a teleological moment of interpretive mastery. Departing from "normative historical time," the narrator never moves into a future where she achieves the kind of full national subjectivity that one expects with the American bildungsroman.

The text departs from the traditionally conceived American bildungsroman, which equates its telos with what Lowe calls "the individual's relinquishing of particularity and difference through identification with an idealized 'national' form of subjectivity (Lowe 1996, 98). It also reveals how Cha as an Asian American writer employs and subverts the genre of the bildungsroman, since she is unwilling to relinquish those histories that conflict with her American identification.

The narrator's inability to free herself from the entangled histories of Japanese colonialism, the Korean War, and American neocolonialism shows the failure of U.S. citizenship to redeem her from the Korean past. She has refused to synchronize with the U.S.'s sense of historical time. Since she cannot achieve national belonging without relinquishing some of the particularities of her individual story, she faces temporal paralysis. She remains unable to move forward with historical time and, therefore, incapable of achieving the alleged emancipating fullness of American subjectivity.

In order for the distant foreigner to become an assimilated American, she must relinquish the unmodern past. Yet for Cha, there is never a moment of fully handing over her immigrant identity. In the section entitled "Calliope/Epic Poetry," Cha recounts the process of becoming an American citizen as one's identity is extracted and replaced with its expected image. As evidenced in the following lines, acquiring citizenship follows a temporal schema similar to that of mourning. It also involves the consignment of one's personal history to the past:

I have the documents. Documents, proof, evidence, photograph, signature. One day you raise your right hand and you are American. They give you an American passport. The United States of America. Somewhere someone has taken my identity and replaced it with a photograph. The other one. Their signature their seals. Their own image. And you learn the executive branch the legislative branch and the third. Justice. Judicial branch. It makes the difference. The rest is past. (Cha 1995, 56)

Cha's physical and symbolic mobility as an immigrant endowed with personal subjectivity are severely limited, since newly minted American citizenship depends upon the uncontested acceptance of "[t]heir own image" of the model and obedient immigrant. As she enters the future of a meticulously documented American subject who must consider "[t]he rest is past," Cha remains skeptical of the neatness of this process. She questions and challenges the officiated time of the state instead.

National citizenship fails to synchronize with one's geographic repositioning, and Cha's immigrant body manifests the failures of subject formation when it refuses to make "[t]he rest . . . past." Cha writes, "They search you. . . . Their authority sewn into the stitches of their costume. Every ten feet they demand to know who and what you are, who is represented. . . . You smell filtered edited through progress and Westernization" (Cha 1995, 57). Cha depicts the invasive marks of "progress and Westernization" as parallel processes enacted on the site of the immigrant body. The production of identity, suggests Cha, always involves the "filter [ing]" and "edit[ing]" of any prior identifications and memories in contrast to American identity. This excerpt not only serves to critique the progressive narrative of Westernization, particularly as it appears as a symptom on the body—as "smell"—it also demonstrates how the assimilation of racialized histories into a nation's dominant memory culture produces the fantasy of a homogeneous, nationalized collective. In Cha's case, memories of Korea's colonial histories, which implicate the U.S., serve to disrupt this narrative of progress. Rather than evacuate her Korean past of significance, Cha unveils its potential to agitate the seemingly fixed pathway to American citizenship. Though she is expected to transcend traces of *han* after being recuperated as a U.S. citizen, Cha finds that the teleological narrative of the American bildungsroman allows for the possibility of self-determination only within narrowly prescribed limits.

As Anne Anlin Cheng suggests, opportunities for minority self-determination can arise only when histories of oppression have been relegated to the past where they have little or no real effect on the present. Cheng builds upon Freud's original theory of melancholy, as she explores how the nation itself might produce a sense of incommensurable lack among its racialized subjects. Examining melancholia as an institutional production, Cheng identifies a particular "American melancholia" stemming from the irrefutable fact that "America is founded on the very ideals of freedom and liberty whose betrayals have been repeatedly covered over" (Cheng 2001, 10). According to Cheng's model of melancholy, racialized minorities' experience of these "betrayals" is most amplified when they begin to internalize the deficiency of their symbolic value.

Racial melancholy is double-edged for Cheng, as she defines it as the "internalization of discipline and rejection—and the installation of a scripted context of perception" (Cheng 2001, 17). Cheng asserts that to demonstrate American citizenship, racialized minorities must undergo an unending series of disciplinary and systematic checkpoints that measure their national loyalty. In addition to internalizing the boundaries of social viability, such groups also see the impossibility of ever being recognized as part of the defining majority. The fantasy of equal validation and inclusion for racialized minorities is maintained by the obscured knowledge of their permanent exclusion, and it is this denied access to the institutional structures that legitimate those practices that Cheng believes creates a kind of collective melancholy among racial and cultural others. Cheng views this version of melancholia as harmful, since it wields the power to define an entire minority group's subjectivity as well as the limits within which collective identity can be performed. If this collective, racialized identity is already scripted around constant reminders of its national exclusion, then Cheng seems to hint that the state's denial of others' grief has enabled a kind of racial melancholia to persist.

This suggestion emerges in Cheng's claim that "Asian immigrants are denied grief about the traumatic histories that precipitated their migration but also about their traumatic beginnings in a country whose national ideals are sustained by the exclusion-yet-retention of racialized others." In their need to come up to speed with the state's sense of historical temporality, these "racialized others" are not given time to work through their grief. Their culturally specific histories and experiences are excluded from American subjectivity. Although Cheng, in this case, might too eagerly use trauma to claim that American democracy necessarily excludes its racialized minority populations, her discussion of melancholy opens up a way of thinking about Cha's conceptualization of mel-*han*-choly as a generative, political practice for directly responding to the ways in which the state produces racial melancholia among its minority subjects.

Cha's reclamation of a kind of collective, cultural grief, emanating from the traumatic experiences of the homeland and immigration to the U.S., can be read as a subversive move. As Cha exposes persisting grief, we find that the U.S. continues to subjugate its racialized subjects by pathologizing their melancholia. By making melancholy a personal, subjective experience, in which subjects are expected to deal with unresolved grief on their own, the U.S. is saved from confronting its own involvement in the production of minority grief. Glossed over are the built-in exclusions of minority groups on which the ideologies and institutional apparatuses of the U.S. nation rely. In this sense, one's grief—even an entire group's experience of melancholy—becomes a responsibility outside of the U.S. context. Minorities are expected to transcend past oppressions based on their racial and cultural differences, instead fully embracing the healing opportunities presented by American citizenship.

In representing Japanese colonialism, American neocolonialism in South Korea, and the processes of American citizenship for the Korean immigrant, *Dictée* recovers grief that was never worked through in the first place. It complicates the historical immigration story in the U.S. that imagines migration as unidirectional, causing traumatic histories to be left behind at points of departure. These traumatic histories instead possess physical and imagined mobility, moving with diasporic populations through intergenerational memory, their literal returns to original locations of departure, and more specifically, through the conjuring of *han*.

Whereas melancholy remains a pathological presence in Cheng's analysis, other scholars have considered its potential for opening up new directions in cultural and literary studies. For example, David L. Eng and David Kazanjian claim that while with mourning "the past is declared resolved, finished, and dead," melancholy leaves space for the past to flare up in the present, as it "creates a realm of traces open to signification, a hermeneutic domain of what remains of loss" (Eng and Kazanjian 2003, 3–4). The sudden temporal confusion that arises from the contemporary appearance of a past thought to be dead, as Eng and Kazanjian argue, effects an opening or shifting of meaning in an otherwise closed system of symbolic representation. This opening in signification is particularly important, given Cha's compulsions to thwart reader accessibility and to defer interpretive closure in her text.

Following Eng and Kazanjian, Heather Love calls for an openness to "negative affects" and "backward feelings" like melancholy within a marginalized community. Love's focus is on the queer community, and she is wary of the dominant trend to empty the painful and difficult queer past through recent advancements in social justice. Love worries that if the queer past is valorized as a thing overcome, its complexities and material struggles might be easily replaced with a socially viable, hegemonic version of queerness. Love calls for a return to these "backward feelings," which have had little warranted place in narratives of queer progress. She argues that they "serve as an index to the ruined state of the social world," and constantly reevaluate the significations of a queer history (Love 2007, 27). Love continues to call for openness toward "unproductive" affects like shame, grief, and melancholy by raising the provocative claim that "mourning can be another name for forgetting" (42). If Freud understands that the melancholic, unlike the one in mourning, involves "an extraordinary diminution in his self-regard, an impoverishment of his ego on a grand scale," then what Cheng, Love, Eng, and Kazanjian move us toward in their analyses are the social infrastructures that continue to "impoverish" minority egos and refuse their assimilation in a way that maintains (rather than homogenizes) their differences.

"Backward feelings" and negative affects pose a powerful ethical challenge to the way we choose to remember certain histories. Momentarily, we can reconsider if we have a choice in remembrance at all, or if institutional forces have already mapped out our methods of historical recollection. We might begin to imagine alternatives to replacing the material histories of Asian immigrants and Asian Americans with the triumphant, self-determining (and self-deceptive) narratives of individuals who rise above the past, expected to master their symptoms of grief as they join the nation's future. *Dictée*, however, shows the extent to which a Korean immigrant's recollections of the homeland's colonial and wartime history can confuse and splinter the linear time of the U.S. Denied opportunity to grieve, Cha confronts the failed substitution of one's Korean past for the future guaranteed under American citizenship—a replacement of loss that should swiftly put her on the path to assimilation.

"Circle within a Circle, a Series of Concentric Circles": Japanese and U.S. Imperialisms

Dictée examines the intersection of perceivably separate colonialisms from the transnational perspective of a Korean female immigrant writing from within and in reaction to Western understandings of modern history. In the past, both Japan and the U.S. have viewed access to Korea as a geopolitical necessity for warding off perceivable foreign threats and influences and, even more so, for preventing the infiltration of dangerous doctrines that could redistribute international balances of power. While Japan viewed its official annexation of the Korean peninsula in 1910 as a strategic move to defend the Asian continent from white, Euro-American encroachment, it still endorsed the rhetoric of Euro-American colonization to justify its seizure of Korea (as well as other Asian countries). In fact, Ian Buruma cites "overcoming modernity" and "overcoming the West" as popular phrases deeply entrenched in selling colonial Japan's agenda to its people (Buruma 2003, 87). Moreover, Japan, through its formal establishment of the Greater East Asian Co-Prosperity Sphere in 1940, attempted to justify its colonization of other Asian countries by promoting the fantasy of pan-Asianist solidarity. Viewing themselves as "the only Asians who could progress to a higher level of civilization along with white Westerners," Japan took it upon itself to defend the Asian continent from the modern West (Koshiro 1999, 10). After the end of World War II and the U.S. occupation of South Korea, the Korean War would define South Korea as a pivotal American geopolitical asset during the Cold War and the U.S. as South Korea's appointed guardian.

While the Japanese occupation of Korea (1905–1945) stands as the most obvious and oppressive regime to which Cha assigns both memorial significance as well as serious reevaluation, *Dictée* also critiques American involvement in Korea's history of colonization. This long history of external domination, according to Nam-hee Lee, has been the "epicenter of the contemporary ideological, social, political, and intellectual fault lines intersecting all the variegated dimensions of Korean life" (Lee 2003, 557). Elaine Kim and Chungmoo Choi have suggested that modern Korea reads as "a palimpsest of multiple layers of Japanese colonialism and neo-imperial domination, especially by U.S. hegemony, which superimposed its systems on the political and social infrastructures of Japanese colonial rule" (Kim and Choi 1998, 3). It is this history of colonial rule, foreign occupation, war, and division that has injected *han* with all its emotional force.

Lee's, Kim's, and Choi's observations that Korea has been subjected to various forms and degrees of imperial projects reveal the imbalance of memory regarding the country's traumatic history and the lingering permutations of *han* in postcolonial, diasporic Korean populations. U.S. hegemony has also affected patterns of memory regarding Korean history, as Grace Cho reiterates. She claims that from the American perspective, the "official script of U.S.–Korea relations" is framed around the "narrative of Korea as successful rescue mission restor[ing] the United States' dominance in the patriarchal family of nations" (Cho 2008, 58–59).

As Cha returns to moments of Japanese colonialism and American domination in Korea, she sets out to question this script of American patriarchal rescue. The Korean subject is never fully healed, as she repeatedly circles back to the past and the past to her. Departing from the linear narration of history, Cha's fragmented and deviant language practices refuse institutional disciplining, and reveal the failure of the U.S.'s patriarchal rescue of its immigrants. As Cha's spelling errors, grammatical errors, and opaque sentence constructions suggest, there is no visible transformation of the incomprehensible immigrant into an improved, superseded version of herself—a metamorphosis expected of an immigrant subject at the center of an American bildungsroman.

The text also reveals how the U.S. might organize and pervade subjugated bodies through its disciplining of collective, nationalist memory. In other words, the U.S. can guide the nation's memory in directions that confirm its all-inclusive, benevolent mantras, thereby leaving racial exclusion an impossible reality of the past. As the U.S. might extend its biopolitical reach through the shaping and perpetuation of a nationalized collective memory, it does so by pathologizing melancholy. Dissenting traumatic memories that run counter to official discourse threaten to undermine a future in which the traumatic past is completely demystified and integrated into the historical narrative of the U.S.

Like mourning, which depends on the successful replacement of one lost object by another, more attainable object, the subject's collective inclusion is contingent on her ability to replace her material past with the promised future of American identification. Cha denies the immigrant body's complete capitulation to the dominant social order. Gifted with new citizenship, Cha's narrator might prove her gratitude by recalling the Korean past not for its traumatic consequences but for its signification in American memory as a site of rescue.

As Cha turns to the possibility of indirect American involvement in Korea's colonization, she sets out to expose the limitations of the American narrative of rescue—one that posits that Korea was liberated from the Japanese, the perceived "enemy people" of the Allied Forces during World War II. Even though Cha has not personally experienced this history for herself, a fact that suggests the possibility of intergenerational trauma, she continues to lament Korea's loss of independence and language with Japanese rule. She inserts herself in the plural first person, claiming the collective "our" to describe a colonial history she feels compelled to transmit across time and national identifications. Cha professes, "There is no people without a nation, no people without ancestry. There are other nations no matter how small their land, who have their independence. But our country, even with 5,000 years of history, has lost it to the Japanese" (Cha 1995, 28–29).

Cha complicates the colonizer position by introducing an implicit American presence as early as 1905—the same year that the Taft-Katsura Pact, or the Gentlemen's Agreement, was signed between the U.S. and Japan. In the Taft-Katsura Pact, Japan agreed to resist meddling in U.S. investments in the Phillipines as long as the U.S. did not interfere with Japan's colonial venture in Korea (Cumings 1998, 142). This agreement is indirectly evoked in Cha's inclusion of a "PETITION FROM THE KOREANS OF HAWAII TO PRESIDENT ROOSEVELT," dated July 12, 1905. This letter clearly reads as a request for American intervention from Korean subjects positioned in the liminal space between the American mainland and the Korean peninsula, though recognized as neither American nor Korean. Still, they view themselves as directly connected to their homeland's political struggles and transformations, and address Roosevelt on behalf of their subjected "countrymen." Addressed "To His Excellency," the petition begins, "We, the Koreans of the Hawaiian Islands, voicing the sentiments of twelve millions of our countrymen, humbly lay before your Excellency the following facts . . . " (Cha 1995, 34). Not only does Cha's inclusion of this petition affirm her larger intent to reimagine Japanese and American systems of domination from a transnational perspective, it also critiques American inaction in dealing with the Japanese presence in Korea due to its own colonial agenda in the Philippines.

Cha hints, through the inclusion of this petition, that American assistance arrived a little too late, and the seeds of American influence were planted in its previous condoning of Japanese rule. By "gifting" the former colony of Japan with liberation and, ironically, the trauma of internal division, the U.S. has held onto discursive authority to produce historical knowledge about these events. Cha resists forgetting the Korean past, an act contingent on her acceptance of U.S. citizenship. Instead, she evokes the ellipses of Korean history in American discourse:

> To the other nations who are not witnesses, who are not subject to the same oppressions, they cannot know. . . . They exist only in the larger perception of History's recording. . . . To the others, these accounts are about (one more) distant land, like (any other) distant land, without any discernable [sic] features in the narrative, (all the same) distant like any other. (Cha 1995, 32–33)

Cha's doleful rumination on the ways that Korea's history simply becomes "(one more) [from a] distant land" reenacts the distancing of American culpability from Korea's colonization in dominant retellings. Also revealing about these lines is Cha's use of parenthetical text, as this subordinate positioning of (one more), (any other), and (all the same) performs the necessary evacuation of Korean memory from American "History's recording." What Cha's erratic flights between past and present, and South Korea and the U.S., drive us toward, however, is that diasporic migrations and recollections complicate the assimilation of distant foreigners into the future of mainstream American culture.

"From One Mouth to Another": A Community of Grief

Cha's inability to mourn in synchronization with the linear time of the U.S. challenges the demands of American citizenship upon a Korean foreigner. She breaks out of the mold of the obedient immigrant, whose past hurts and oppressive histories should be mastered in her movement toward future American subjectivity. Departing from this future, Cha circles back to past grievous histories that the U.S. has simultaneously produced for (South) Korea and refused to view as histories worthy of mourning.

The earlier documentation scene where Cha's narrator becomes an American citizen features the immigrant's inability to mourn properly and consider the "rest [a]s past." This disavowal of the past as irreversibly past is especially difficult when Cha continues to bear tangible connections to her nation of departure through literal returns and metaphorical ones in memory. After the immigrant's identity has been seemingly replaced by its model version, Cha invalidates the return home:

You return and you are not one of them, they treat you with indifference. All the time you understand what they are saying. But the papers give you away. Every ten feet. They ask you identity. They comment upon your inability or ability to speak. Whether you are telling the truth or not about your nationality. They say you look other than you say. As if you didn't know who you were. You say who you are but you begin to doubt. . . . You leave you come back to the shell left empty all this time. . . . They check each article, question you on foreign articles, then dismiss you. (Cha 1995, 56–58)

Though documented as an American citizen, Cha remains suspended between conflicting national loyalties. She has yet to fulfill the expectation that she overcome *han*, the grief associated with an enduring Korean history of invasion, division, exploitation, and subjugation. Yet her return to South Korea demonstrates not only the suspicion that her U.S. citizenship sparks, but also her disappointment in finding no more traces of national belonging there than in the U.S. Cha's mel-*han*-cholic stance is left unresolved by her return to the homeland, suggesting the loss at the core of her melancholy is not the loss of the homeland itself. Rather, her grief results from the homeland's inassimilable and untranslatable traumatic histories.

Cha's generational distance from the Korean colonial past is doubled by her physical and emotional distance from her mother. The daughter's abortive attempt to recuperate the Korean nation, once torn apart by Japanese colonialism and later by externally imposed national division, reveals how the individual subject resides in grief, denied the opportunity to mourn effectively. This earlier scene of Cha's disappointing return to the homeland can also be read in tandem with the narrator's unanswered letters to her mother. Cha's beckoning to the mother arrives with little surprise, since colonial discourse often relies on gendered, material representations of involved nations. But the mother represented in *Dictée* fails to respond to her daughter's letters and pleas, instead leaving the narrator to dwell in the overwhelming absence of any response. Both the narrator's disappointing return to the "motherland" and her unrealized reunion with the estranged mother signal the failure of the maternal figure to recuperate loss and restore fullness to the fractured self.

The section "Calliope Poetry" is bookended by two photos of the narrator's mother, one as a young woman and the other as an aged woman. The themes of the narratives in this section shuffle between Japanese colonialism and American citizenship, as they are represented through the personal experiences of the narrator's mother and the narrator herself. "Calliope" begins with the narrator's direct address of her mother, yet the mother is never allotted space to respond. Her mother is cut off from communication, alienated in memory. Instead, only the static image of her mother-in-the-past receives the daughter's correspondence, which is left undated: "Mother, you are eighteen years old. You were born in Yong Jung, Manchuria and this is where you now live. You are not Chinese. You are Korean. But your family moved here to escape the Japanese occupation. . . . You live in a village where the other Koreans live. Same as you. Refugees. Immigrants. Exiles" (Cha 1995, 45).

The anguish of physical, geographical displacement as a result of Japanese rule is further exacerbated by the mother's insertion into colonial language—a process that violently roots itself in the body. She continues, in her address to her mother: "[Y]ou speak the tongue the mandatory language like the others. It is not your own. . . . The tongue that is forbidden is your own mother tongue. You speak in the dark. In the secret. The one that is yours . . . Mother tongue is your refuge. It is being home" (Cha 1995, 45–46). In a similar way that Cha's desire for the mother parallels her desire for the homeland, the "Mother tongue" in this case is equivalent to "being home" for the narrator's mother.

The figure of the mother exposes how modernity has been historically aligned along gender lines, as her stories of colonial rule, once denied narrative space and legitimacy due to mandates of language, recall the immigrant daughter's own struggles to speak as a foreigner in the U.S. The narrator's own "cracked" and "broken tongue" emits strange sounds later in Dictée, aiming to connect with the mother's "forbidden tongue." Beside diagrams of internal organs responsible for speech ("Side View of Air Passages and Lungs," "Position of the Larynx in the Neck," "Front View of the Larynx," and "Superior View of Larynx and Vocal Folds"), the narrator's frustrating attempts toward speech appear: "Stop. Start. Starts. / Contractions. Noise. Semblance of noise. / Broken speech. One to one. At a time. / Cracked tongue. Broken tongue. / Pidgeon. Semblance of speech. / Swallows. Inhales. Stutter. Starts. Stops before starts" (Cha 1995, 75).

Even more striking in the narrator's letter to her mother is the ensuing presence of the past, evidenced by Cha's decision to employ the present tense. Like a dream running contiguous to present reality, Cha's vision of her mother in 1940 occurs in tandem with other historical moments called to attention in *Dictée*: "You suffer the knowledge of having to leave. . . . They take from you your tongue. . . . You write you speak voices hidden masked you plant words to the moon you send word through the wind. . . . From one mouth to another, from one reading to the next the words are realized in their full meaning" (Cha 1995, 45–48). The mouth from where a tongue was taken, here, also becomes an eroticized site of narrative connection and exchange. Clearly, Cha returns a kind of bodily dynamism to those very mouths once asked to feed on the colonial language. It is also in the site of the oppressed mouth, manipulated to speak in a way that confirms one's allegiance to her assumed national identification, where Cha finds potential for social connectivity.

Though disparate, the experiences of the postcolonial mother and immigrant daughter share narrative space in this section, suggesting that their respective experiences of national exile, internal displacement, and international migration establish a communal sense of mel-*han*-choly. In other words, we glimpse the beginnings of a transnational community forged around grief, confirming trauma theorist Kai Erikson's belief that collective trauma, or a shared history of trauma, can incite the formation of unexpected community: "[T]raumatic wounds inflicted on individuals can combine to create a mood, an ethos—a group culture, almost—that is different from (and more than) the sum of the private wounds that make it up" (Erikson 1995, 185). Missing in Erikson's conception, however, is the potential for such a "group culture" to pose a challenge to the processes of national assimilation, particularly at the level of collective memory. In terms of the Korean diaspora, the formation of a transnational community around *han* disrupts the progress narrative of the U.S. and its continued dependence on the denial of others' grief. It also postpones the homogenization of cultural memory that is expected as one assimilates herself (and her prior histories) into the dominant memory practices of the U.S., therefore demonstrating her unwavering loyalty to the state.

Cha's representation of a troubled mother–daughter relationship is a metaphor for broaching the history of Korea since the end of World War II. It comments on the role of American militarism in dividing and re-subjugating a newly liberated country. Cha's narrator addresses this communication gap with her mother through a visual image of Korea's division: "We are severed in Two by an abstract enemy an invisible enemy under the title of liberators who have conveniently named the severance, Civil War. Cold War. Stalemate" (Cha 1995, 81). Though she never names the enemy, instead referring to it as "abstract" or "invisible," Cha is critical of the rhetorical plays used to justify the Korean peninsula's division and the Korean War, which would later expedite installations of American military bases, economic policies, and American-sponsored presidencies—all under the narrative of liberation.

Cha's intention is not necessarily to weigh the actual decision of the U.S. to establish the DMZ or enter the Korean War. What seems to concern her is the privileged location of discursive authority in representing these moments in official historical memory, both in South Korea and in the U.S. Claiming the "title of liberators," the U.S. has access to this kind of prolonged discursive authority, justified by its exceptional moral privileges. Thus, the conflation of Cha's experience of immigration to the U.S. and transformation into an American subject, and her mother's experiences of Japanese and American systems of domination (albeit non-equivalent), occurs around the discursive and didactic relations of power understood between the U.S. liberator and the liberated minority. It could be said that in her simultaneous inability and refusal to step in time with emergent American national consciousness, Cha views the narrative of liberation as another kind of oppressive national fantasy used to tame those who have been deemed incapable of historical consciousness.

Dwelling in mel-han-choly, Cha refuses to be liberated from her past. She contests the kind of assimilation required of her as an immigrant looking to the future signified by the gift of American citizenship. Such a future frames "the teleology of 'Americanization' undergirding the conceptualization of immigrant cultures in the U.S. [which] figures racial-ethnic difference as largely a matter of something 'left behind'" (Kang 1998, 250).

Her mother (and the Korean nation whose colonial past and national division are embodied through maternal representation) are denied full recuperation in Cha's own narrative. This move on Cha's part highlights the failures of Korean history to service and be fully incorporated into American liberation narratives so common throughout the Cold War. As Cheng says, "Cha disturbs the faith in either the 'history lesson' or the narrative of redemption" through the guaranteed closure and finitude she withholds from her readers (Cheng 2001, 145). Rather than emancipate the postcolonial and/or immigrant subject from the oppressive past, Cha provides "for the reader, a relation to the world that is melancholic: a trace of something lost that cannot be named" (147). A question Cheng's analysis of

Dictée seems to neglect, however, is what to do with this recognition of an inexpressible and irreplaceable loss—one that escapes symbolic representation and is instead registered as desire for belonging in a diasporic community linked by shared experiences of hungry mouths and stolen tongues. If defining that "trace of something lost" is an impossible feat, then why name it at all?

As much as Japanese and English, respectively, create the "pain of speech the pain to say" in a "foreign" tongue for Cha's narrator and her mother, the mouth functions as an orifice expressive of desire for narrative contact and community (Cha 1995, 3). If memory of the mother (as well as the memory of her mother's recollections) enables Cha to feel a kind of lost proximity to the homeland tarnished by experiences of colonialism and war, then perhaps she contributes to the formation of cultural memory beyond national identification. Instead, national belonging is cultivated around han. As an affective bond, han can establish collective solidarity around the melancholy of national exclusion. It can be channeled toward social justice, addressing past and continuing cases of systemic discrimination based on racial, ethnic, class, and cultural differences.

Elaine Kim reiterates the possibilities of political resistance that han offers despite its emphasis on past and continuing histories of Korean oppression, since the recognition of the institutional processes that create hierarchies of discursive power and racialized difference reveal other practices of subjugation that might be concurrently taking place. Kim validates "the rich and haunted lode of Korean national consciousness" as an imagined site where "we struggle to understand how our fate is entwined with the fate of others lying prostrate before the triumphal procession of the winners of History" (Kim 2000, 284).

Cha reverses the trajectory of the assimilation paradigm that insists national belonging trumps the melancholy of the past. Even in the absence of the mother/the homeland, Cha does not surrender to melancholy alone, understanding that prolonged, inward introspection is not the most politically viable solution. Fully succumbing to melancholy would serve only to refashion the discursive relations, which have defined melancholy as a pathological threat to the future well-being of both the individual and the nation to which s/he must claim loyalty. Instead, I find that Cha's mel-han-cholic eruptions challenge the hegemonic discourses that shape her identity as a Korean immigrant in the U.S.

Conclusion

Cha reveals in a statement from her personal notes that her designated responsibility as an artist was to bring awareness of the "Korean plight."[4] She had hoped to "lessen the physical geographical distance as well as the psychological distance of the Asian people from other ethnic cultures." Language is one pathway through which Cha attempts to collapse this distance, evidenced in her commitment to writing against "real time," which I read as the linear, straight time of the state. The "you" in Cha's subsequent address refers to someone either expunged from or not yet written into memory, perhaps someone who returns with the reminder to continuously write within the existing public record to challenge its discursive reign: "I write. I write you. Daily. From here. If I am not writing, I am thinking about writing. I am composing. Recording movements. You are here I raise the voice. Particles bits of sound and noise gathered pick up lint, dust. They might scatter and become invisible. Speech morsels. Broken chips of stones" (Cha 1995, 56).

Language, for Cha, functions as both sustenance ("speech morsels") and ruin ("Broken chips of stones"), yet she also professes that "the pain not to say. To not say" is far more intense than the pain of speech (Cha 1995, 3). This desire for human connectivity across time, space, and nation is played out in the oppressed mouth, again directing our attention to the ways in which the losses associated with historical traumas like colonialism, war, and geographical displacement do not have to be immediately dumped into the prehistoric past, only to be recuperated under the victorious marks of Western humanism.

Cha, along with those scholars who have previously written on the rewards of a melancholic practice, are confronted with a formidable ethical dilemma—one that emerges when "pathological" inhibitors of the future like melancholy are embraced. This bind is, of course, a serious one since a perpetual state of melancholy has real effects on a person's mental well-being and her capacity to live beyond the emotional suffering in which she feels trapped. A full turn toward melancholy can also undoubtedly inspire social paralysis and self-endangerment, since the melancholic figure observes no real alternative to the object of loss, nor does she find any respite from her suffering through the possibility of communal bonds and social connectivity.

As an experimental, part-fictional work, though, *Dictée* is able to momentarily depart from "real time" and imagine mel-han-cholic practices in a way that returns Cha and her readers to a Korean past seemingly removed and separate from the immediate American present. Interested in "collective reminiscing," Cha admits in her personal notes that "[her] work until now . . . ha[d] been a series of metaphors for the return, going back to a lost time and space, always in the imaginary." While Cha does not necessarily believe in the full recuperation of the Korean past, recognizing how it may be selectively remembered depending on one's national allegiance, her constant returns to lost traumatic memories imagine an alternative to their complete substitution.

Cha's pursuit of "a lost time and space" sets off remembrance of another kind, drawing attention to the institutional apparatuses of the U.S. that have marginalized these other times and spaces for their measured lack. Additionally, the reevaluation of the muted proximity of Korean history to U.S. history enables Cha to reassess the nationalizing processes through which Asian immigrants and Asian Americans become recognized citizens. Despite the larger expectation in American majority culture, histories of oppression based on race, class, and cultural differences can neither be surrendered at their points of departure nor fully assimilated into dominant American memory.

....

Jennifer Cho is a lecturer in the English Department of the University of California, Berkeley, and specializes in twentieth and twenty-first-century American and global literatures, critical theory (particularly related to memory, trauma, and history), ethnic and cultural studies, and composition pedagogy.

Notes

Originally published in *Meridians* vol. 11, no. 1, 2011.

1　*Dictée*'s current status as a seminal Asian American literary and political work is due largely to *Writing Self, Writing Nation* (Kim and Alarcon 1994). This edited collection of essays on *Dictée* seeks to return an ethnic focus to Cha's work, especially as it comments on dominant practices of othering, legitimated by the state. *Writing Self Writing Nation* has undoubtedly opened up discussion of *Dictée* as a powerful political text examining the logics of discursive power involved in the colonial, postcolonial, and/or immigrant subject's acquisition of citizenship and national belonging.

2　Thanks to Patricia P. Chu for pointing out that *han* can also appear even in seemingly mundane struggles. For example, a Korean student working to pass his college entrance exams might be said to channel *han*. I would also venture to claim that *han* fueled the recent fervor surrounding South Korean figure skater Kim Yu-Na, when she competed against Japanese rivals Mao Asada and Miki Ando during the 2010 Winter Olympics. Jeré Longman writes, "More than a half-century later, South Korea's nationalistic fervor and sense of victimhood still inform sporting rivalries between the two nations" (Longman 2010). The article also cites political scientist Kyung-ae Park, who suggested that Kim Yu-Na's "loss or her winning [would] be perceived as a national loss or a national winning." Park continues, "If she wins the gold medal . . . I think it will be a great boost for national pride for Koreans. In a way, it will work as compensation for past humiliations." Although in these examples it is difficult to grasp *han's* political appeal, they reveal the extent to which its traces have permeated everyday scenarios and inform Korean subjectivity on many different and nuanced levels.

3   An example of this trend toward forgetting emerges when we consider how the U.S. has referred to the Korean War as the "Forgotten War," while, clearly, the same war continues to be a significant mnemonic touchstone within the intergenerational diasporic Korean community.

4   The Theresa Hak Kyung Cha archive is housed at the Berkeley Art Museum and Pacific Film Archive in Berkeley, CA.

Works Cited

Buruma, Ian. 2003. *Inventing Japan 1853–1964*. New York: Random House.

Cha, Theresa Hak Kyung. 1995. *Dictée*. Berkeley: Third Woman Press.

Chang, Juliana. 2004. " 'I Cannot Find Her': The Oriental Feminine, Racial Melancholia, and Kimiko Hahn's *The Unbearable Heart*." *Meridians: Feminism, Race, Transnationalism* 4, no. 2: 239–60.

Cheng, Anne Anlin. 2001. *The Melancholy of Race: Psychoanalysis, Assimilation, and Hidden Grief*. Oxford: Oxford University Press.

Cho, Grace. 2008. *Haunting the Korean Diaspora: Shame, Secrecy, and the Forgotten War*. Minneapolis: University of Minnesota Press.

Cumings, Bruce. 1998. *Korea's Place in the Sun*. New York: W.W. Norton.

Duncan, Patti. 2004. *Tell This Silence: Asian American Women Writers and the Politics of Speech*. Iowa City: University of Iowa Press.

Eng, David. 2000. "Melancholia in the Late Twentieth Century." *Signs: Journal of Women in Culture and Society* 25, no. 4: 1275–81.

Eng, David L., and David Kazanjian. 2003. *Loss: The Politics of Mourning*. Berkeley: University of California Press.

Erikson, Kai. 1995. "Notes on Trauma and Community." In *Trauma: Explorations in Memory*, edited by Cathy Caruth. Baltimore: Johns Hopkins University Press.

Foucault, Michel. 1990. *The History of Sexuality, Volume 1: An Introduction*. Translated by Robert Hurley. New York: Vintage Books.

Kang, Hyun Yi. 1998. "Re-membering Home." In *Dangerous Women: Gender and Korean Nationalism*, edited by Elaine Kim and Chungmoo Choi. New York: Routledge.

Kim, Elaine H. 2000. "Home Is Where the Han Is: A Korean American Perspective on the Los Angeles Uprisings." In *Asian American Studies: A Reader*, edited by Jean Yu-wen Shen Wu and Min Song. New Brunswick, NJ: Rutgers University Press.

Kim, Elaine, and Norma Alarcon, eds. 1994. *Writing Self, Writing Nation*. Berkeley: Third Woman Press.

Kim, Elaine, and Chungmoo Choi. 1998. "Introduction." In *Dangerous Women: Gender and Korean Nationalism*, edited by Elaine Kim and Chungmoo Choi. New York: Routledge.

Koshiro, Yukiko. 1999. *Trans-Pacific Racisms and the U.S. Occupation of Japan*. New York: Columbia University Press.

Kim, Suji Kwock. 2003. *Notes from the Divided Country: Poems*. Baton Rouge: Louisiana State University Press.

Lee, Nam-hee. 2003. "Between Indeterminacy and Radical Critique: Madang-guk, Ritual, and Protest." *Positions* 11, no. 3: 555–84.

Lie, John. 1998. *Han Unbound: The Political Economy of South Korea*. Stanford: Stanford University Press.

Longman, Jeré. 2010. "Balanced on a Skater's Blades, the Expectations of a Nation." *New York Times*, February 22. http://www.nytimes.com/2010/02/23/sports/olympics/23longman.html (accessed May 30, 2011).

Love, Heather. 2007. *Feeling Backward: Loss and the Politics of Queer History*. Cambridge, MA: Harvard University Press.

Lowe, Lisa. 1996. *Immigrant Acts: On Asian American Cultural Politics*. Durham, NC: Duke University Press.

Palumbo-Liu, David. 1999. *Asian/American: Historical Crossings of a Racial Frontier*. Stanford: Stanford University Press.

Myriam J. A. Chancy

. . . .

Under/Water

Memorial Day, May 31, 2010

For the departed
For Haïti
And in reference to Asako Narahashi's 'half awake and half asleep in the water'
(photograph, 2001)

. . . under water,
sinking, eyes
closed, listening
to the voices
the sea, hopeful
not to drown
remembering,
arms wide, mantra:
the body is but water
and salt
. . . will float up
. . . sooner or later

. . . deep under,
sky water,
salt swimming
open
eyes. . . . the ocean murmurs

MERIDIANS · feminism, race, transnationalism   Volume 19 Supplement 2020
DOI: 10.1215/15366936-8566078 © 2011 Smith College

from the depths
her belly
broken, to jagged shore:
"this time,
I would gladly have taken them
in my womb
for all eternity"
. . . arms stirring blue light
staying afloat . . .
listening to waves
drumming eulogy . . .

. . . remaining under
as long hold of breath, possible
. . . in fear of . . . surfacing
. . . . in fear of . . . the angry aria
of the nameless dead
riding the gales,
tumbling down
defiled mountains over,
in defense of
wreckage
of hurricanes . . .
the sheet of sheen above
like ice
to break . . .

treading water, invisibly, slowly, methodically

. . . waters embracing
like folds of blankets . . .
treading the dark, pensively
. . . what could be the answer
to the riddle
tectonics, shifts . . .
if movement
could stop time,
turn back

clocks,
tread she would
for seven and a day
. . . to reach the hour of before,
when an afternoon
of slumber
meant nothing more
than heat, sweat, flies buzzing,
the rooster's cry, thirst
for the sea
. . . bracing under . . .

. . . descending
to the nether,
to *Vilokan*, to dance
the dead, the living
gods, our ancestors
. . . . never to utter, "I'm swamped"
. . . . "I'm buried alive"
mindless phrases
swimming
against the ether
. . . . all limbs
intact to brace
against the never
. . . to be ever . . .
ever again. . . .
the never
of again . . .

moving
very slowly . . .
this
is what the sea sung:
to carry the dead,
as our mothers
carried us,
not to remain

submerged, enfolded
in her layers
pulsing waters
.... push ... the lullaby
... push, push up ...

what remains on shore
is for us all
to bear ...
the air, fresh of despair,
the stale hope:

Let us carry
our mothers
as they
have carried us. ...

....

Myriam J. A. Chancy is Hartley Burr Alexander Chair of the Humanities at Scripps College. She is the author of eight books, including *Autochthonomies: Transnationalism, Testimony and Transmission in the African Diaspora* (2020) and *The Loneliness of Angels* (2010), winner of a 2011 Guyana Prize. She was an editorial advisory board member for PMLA from 2010 to 2012 and Editor of *Meridians* from 2002 to 2004, for which she garnered the 2004 Phoenix Award for Editorial Achievement from the Council of Editors of Learned Journals.

Note

Originally published in *Meridians* vol. 11, no. 1, 2011.

Jennifer C. Nash

Practicing Love
Black Feminism, Love-Politics, and Post-Intersectionality

Abstract: This article studies love as a distinct, transformative, and radical Black feminist politic. By closely sitting with the work of Alice Walker, June Jordan, and Audre Lorde, this article treats love-politics as another political tradition that has emerged from within the parameters of Black feminist thought, one that challenges the political tradition most closely associated with Black feminist thought: intersectionality.

....

"I often talk about love as one of the few places where people actually admit they want to become different."[1]

— Lauren Berlant

....

By the summer of 1972, Roberta Flack and Donny Hathaway's eponymous album had already produced two Billboard hits. But it was the album's third single, "Where Is the Love?" that was its biggest success. Flack and Hathaway's harmonies earned them comparisons to Marvin Gaye and Tammi Terrell, and the song's catchy chorus—"where is the love you said was mine, all mine, to the end of the time, was it just a lie? Where is the love?"—helped make "Where is the Love?" one of the summer's most memorable hits.

Six years later, June Jordan delivered her "Where is the Love?" speech at Howard University's National Black Writers Conference. Jordan said, "It is here, in this extreme, inviolable coincidence of my status as a Black feminist, my status as someone twice stigmatized, my status as a Black woman

MERIDIANS · feminism, race, transnationalism   Volume 19 Supplement 2020
DOI: 10.1215/15366936-8566089 © 2013 Smith College

who is twice kin to the despised majority of all the human life that there is, . . . it is here, in this extremity, that I ask, of myself, and of anyone who would call me *sister. Where is the love?*" (Jordan 2003, 270–71; italics in original). In the years to come, her plea for love would become widely anthologized, included in Gloria Anzaldúa's edited collection *Making Face, Making Soul/Haciendo Caras: Creative and Critical Perspectives by Feminists of Color*, and republished in *Essence Magazine*. Jordan's "where is the love?" refrain—like the chorus of a catchy song—was instantly popular in Black feminist circles. This paper uses Jordan's query—*where is the love?*—as a window into a much longer, and largely unanalyzed, Black feminist tradition of love-politics, a tradition marked by transforming love from the personal (epitomized by Flack and Hathaway's song about romantic love gone wrong) into a theory of justice.

Of course, Jordan was not the first to put love at the center of her Black feminist project; a few years earlier, the Combahee River Collective Statement noted that its proto-intersectional politics "evolve[s] from a healthy love for ourselves, our sisters, and our community which allows us to continue our struggle and work" (Combahee River Collective 1983, 267). Nor has Black feminist love-politics been confined to "second-wave" Black feminist organizing; in fact, it remains a political and rhetorical trope even in contemporary Black feminist scholarship.[2] Joan Morgan asserts that "black-on-black love" is the centerpiece of her hip-hop feminism (Morgan 1995, 152), Gwendolyn Pough argues that the labor of contemporary Black feminism should be articulating a "message of self-love" (Pough 2003, 241), and bell hooks reminds us that "all the great movements for social justice in our society have strongly emphasized a love ethic" (hooks 2000, xvii).

Although Black feminist love-politics has been expressed in distinctive ways in different periods, this paper focuses on a "second-wave"[3] Black moment when pleas for love were consolidated into a sustained call for a Black feminist love-politics, a moment that set the stage for later women of color feminist scholarship—including work by hooks, Traci West, Chela Sandoval, and Patricia Hill Collins—grappling with love. This particular moment has long been celebrated for its advocacy of love as a resistant ethic of self-care. If "bein alive & bein a woman & bein colored is a metaphysical dilemma"—to borrow Ntozake Shange's oft-quoted lines—then Black feminism's insistence on love, particularly self-love, might be read as a practice of self-valuation (Shange 1977, 45). Collins captures this reading of Black self-love, arguing that, "Loving Black people . . . in a society that is so dependent on hating Blackness constitutes a highly rebellious act" (Collins 2004, 250). According to this scholarly tradition, love is a politics of claiming, embracing, and restoring the wounded Black female self.

My interest in Black feminist love-politics departs from interpretations of love as simply a practice of self-valuation. Instead, I analyze "second-wave" Black feminism's pleas for love as a significant call for ordering the self *and* transcending the self, a strategy for remaking the self *and* for moving beyond the limitations of selfhood. Moreover, this paper reads Black feminist love-politics' insistence on transcending the self and producing new forms of political communities as a kind of affective politics. My use of the term *affective politics* draws on work by scholars including Sara Ahmed, Lauren Berlant, José Muñoz, and Ann Cvetkovich, who invite us to ask: "how do emotions work to align some subjects with some others and against other others? How do emotions move between bodies?" (Ahmed 2004, 118). I use the term *affective politics* to describe how bodies are organized around intensities, longings, desires, temporalities, repulsions, curiosities, fatigues, optimism, and how these affects produce political movements (or sometimes inertias). I am particularly interested in reading Black feminism's affective love politics as a departure from the kind of political work that Black feminism is often associated with: *identity politics*.

Reading Black feminist love-politics as an affective project serves three important purposes. First, this paper intervenes in scholarly conversations advocating the emergence of a "politics of love" by highlighting Black feminism's long labor of love-politics. Michael Hardt and Antonio Negri, for example, bemoan a culturally narrow view of love, and advocate the dawning of a political era marked by public love. They argue, "The modern concept of love is almost exclusively limited to the bourgeois couple and the claustrophobic confines of the nuclear family. Love has become a strictly private affair. We need a more generous and more unrestrained conception of love" (Hardt and Negri 2004, 351). Yet their plea for a "generous and more unrestrained conception of love" ignores the long history of Black feminism's love-politics, a politics marked by a broad activist conception of love. My work asks how a consideration of Black feminism's love-politics might enable us to rethink the very contours of a "generous" love-politics.

Second, this paper endeavors to center Black feminism in affect theory's intellectual genealogy. The "affective turn"[4] in critical theory (Staiger, Cvetkovich, and Reynolds 2010, 5) has produced a rich body of scholarship invested in "public feelings," in the ways that "global politics and history manifest themselves at the level of lived affective experience" (Cvetkovich 2007, 461). This work problematizes the boundaries between private and public, and draws intimate connections between the subjective and the social, between the emotional and the political.

This scholarly tradition generally roots itself in queer theory. Ann Cvetkovich's description of the Public Feelings project—a group of scholars working at the intersections of academia, political action, and performance—is emblematic of this genealogical work. She notes:

> It's impossible to imagine the Public Feelings project without the inspiration of queer work. Our interest in everyday life, in how global politics and history manifest themselves at the level of lived affective experience, is bolstered by the role that queer theory has played in calling attention to the integral role of sexuality within public life. Moreover, our interest in negative affects draws inspiration from the depathologizing work of queer studies, which has made it possible to document and revalue non-normative ways of living. (Cvetkovich 2007, 461)

Cvetkovich goes on to argue that affect theory helps to make queer studies "intersectional" (462), and notes the importance of work emerging from African American Studies, particularly on the violent trauma of the Atlantic slave trade, to affect studies (465). Her work, then, gestures to the intimate relationship between affect studies and African American studies. My article continues the labor she begins: locating affect theory within Black feminist studies.

Finally, and most important, my paper reveals that Black feminism has long engaged in political work that transcends—or, at the very least, circumvents—identity politics and its at-times problematic elisions and lapses into essentialism (Brown 1995). In a moment in which Black feminism is increasingly imagined as synonymous with intersectionality, and in which intersectionality is increasingly scrutinized, underscoring Black feminism's nonidentitarian political labor is particularly significant (Kwan 1997; Ehrenreich 2002; Puar 2005). Indeed, in this post-identitarian—or at least identity-skeptical—theoretical milieu, feminists regularly craft narratives about feminist history that relegate Black feminism to the past (Lee 2000; Hemmings 2010) precisely because of its imagined attachment to identity-work, an attachment that has been "vilified by feminists of many different persuasions" (Hekman 2000, 289). My investment in tracing Black feminism's non-identitarian work is animated by a commitment to underscoring the myriad political traditions that have long been part of Black feminism, but that are often ignored because of the extent of intersectionality's institutionalization.

To be clear, I am not indicting intersectionality and celebrating love-politics; instead, I am interested in heeding Muñoz's call to "imagine a position or narrative of being and becoming that can resist the pull of identitarian models of relationality" (Muñoz 2006, 677), and in foregrounding Black feminist work that imagines "relationality" outside of the elisions of identity politics. Moreover, I am not suggesting that intersectional labor is inherently opposed to affective work, particularly in a moment in which intersectionality is practiced across the humanities and social sciences, and is inflected differently by each intersectionality practitioner. Instead, this paper is undergirded by the belief that the task of tracing Black feminism's multiple and heterogeneous political traditions is of the utmost importance in a moment in which Black feminist labor is increasingly reduced to the status of a relic because of its affiliation with intersectionality's identitarian work.

What do I mean when I describe intersectionality as an identitarian project? In this article, I argue that intersectionality is inextricably linked to the production and maintenance of identity categories. Its primary intervention, I argue, is to add complexity to existing identity categories, not to jettison identity categories altogether. As Robyn Wiegman notes, intersectionality "promises . . . a critical practice that gives difference to identity in order to discern identity's multiple and proliferating intensities, inequities, and political agencies" (Wiegman 2012, 240). That is, the "promise" of intersectionality, a theoretical innovation that is now regularly championed as "the most important theoretical contribution that women's studies . . . has made so far" (McCall 2005, 1775), is "particularity, specifically through the critical location attributed to both black women and black feminism, and in such a way that no configuration of identity as a constructed social relation of power and subordination is thought to be beyond its analytical reach" (Wiegman 2012, 240). Intersectionality's investment in "particularity" is evident in its investment in using Black women's experience to problematize the rigid distinction between race and gender while maintaining a fundamental faith in both categories as meaningful, legible, and coherent.

My reading of intersectionality as an identitarian project underscores that it emerged both as *juridical intervention* and as a *restoration of identity politics* crafted in a moment—not unlike the one we inhabit now—when identity politics was increasingly critiqued for eliding intragroup difference. As a juridical intervention, intersectionality problematizes an antidiscrimination regime that always presumes the mutual exclusiveness of race and gender. By recognizing as cognizable (and legally actionable) only discrimination claims that are *either* race-based or gender-based, antidiscrimination law often, though not always, ignores Black women's injuries because:

> Black women can experience discrimination in ways that are both similar to and different from those experienced by white women and Black men. . . . [O]ften they experience double-discrimination—the combined effects of practices which discriminate on the basis of race, and on the basis of sex. And sometimes, they experience discrimination as Black women—not the sum of race and sex discrimination, but as Black women. (Crenshaw 1989, 149)

Kimberlé Crenshaw's intervention reveals that the architecture of antidiscrimination doctrine, with its insistent *or* formation—race-or-gender—ignores the "and" that captures many Black women's experiences. Crenshaw's juridical intervention, then, was not to abandon antidiscrimination law's reliance on categories both for redressing injuries and for granting relief. Rather, she sought to reveal the injuries that antidiscrimination's logic necessarily elides or ignores, and to show the necessity of judicial attention to injuries that occur "in the intersection" of race and gender.

If intersectionality emerged as a legal intervention, it also sought to rehabilitate identity politics. Crenshaw's point of departure is that identity politics "frequently conflates or ignores intragroup difference" (Crenshaw 1991, 1242), and that intersectionality can restore complexity to identity politics by insisting on a recognition that race and gender are heterogeneous categories.[5] To say it another way, Crenshaw seeks to dismantle the logic that Barbara Smith, Gloria T. Hull, and Patricia Bell Scott called attention to with their aptly titled anthology *All the Women are White, All the Blacks Are Men, But Some of Us Are Brave* (Hull, Scott, and Smith 1982). Crenshaw notes, "the intersectional experiences of women of color marginalized in prevailing conceptions of identity politics does not require that we give up attempts to organize as communities of color. Rather, intersectionality provides a basis for reconceptualizing race as a coalition between men and women of color. . . . Recognizing that identity politics takes place at the site where categories intersect thus seems more fruitful than challenging the possibility of talking about categories at all" (Crenshaw 1991, 1299). For Crenshaw, intersectionality allows for identity-politics practitioners to perform identity work with a new attention to the heterogeneity of the categories they labor with.

This is not to say that intersectionality neglects the contextuality and contingency of identity. At times, intersectionality has usefully analyzed how one's experience of subjectivity or domination depends on location and moment. Evelyn Brooks Higginbotham's now-canonical work on the "metalanguage of race," for example, recognizes that race "lends meaning" to gender, sexuality, and class in historically specific ways, effectively "impregnating the simplest meanings we take for granted. It makes hair 'good' or 'bad,' speech patterns 'correct' or 'incorrect'" (Higginbotham 1992, 255). Higginbotham's intervention reveals that race, gender, class, and sexuality intersect—to borrow Crenshaw's vocabulary—in context-specific ways. My interest, though, is in how categories remain fixed, legible, and knowable, even as scholars attend to how context shifts our experiences of our selves and the structures of domination that constrain us.

This paper begins by arguing that Black feminism's recurring interest in love can be interpreted as an advocacy of a particular kind of self-work, one that encourages the Black feminist subject to transcend the self. The paper then asks how this politics so focused on a labor of the self might also be the vanguard of a promising form of nonidentitarian Black feminist politics, one that we might fruitfully consider "postintersectional" (Kwan 1997; Hutchinson 2001; Chang and Culp 2002). Prefixes like *post* are always misleading temporally and politically; the labor of "postintersectionality," at least as I use the term, is not to suggest that intersectionality is no longer useful. Instead, I use "postintersectionality" as an invitation to problematize the interdisciplinary fetishization of intersectionality's "complexity" (Nash 2010; Wiegman 2012), as part of a larger endeavor to uncouple Black feminism and intersectionality (Nash 2011), and as a move toward recognizing Black feminism's other political traditions. In suggesting that love-politics might help us think about Black feminist politics outside of—or beyond—intersectionality, I hope to show that Black feminism's political tradition is rich and heterogeneous, that it has reflected and unleashed myriad "freedom dreams" (Kelley 2003).

Self-Love as a Practice of Freedom

In 1983, Alice Walker began *In Search of Our Mothers' Gardens* with a two-page definition of womanism (Walker 1983). In the years that followed its publication, Walker's definition would become the subject of vibrant interdisciplinary debate as scholars routinely asked: what is womanism? How is it different from feminism, and from black feminism? What is the value of a new name for Black feminism? Does womanism contain a viable and distinctive politics?[6] Walker's "feminist, Afrocentric, healing, embodied, and spiritual" (Razak 2006, 100) definition is at times quite specific—referring to "a black feminist or feminist of color"—and at times it defines womanism "associatively" by connecting the womanist subject to a set of practices and beliefs (Torfs 2007, 20). Though the definition moves from the specific to the general, from the material to the spiritual, it emphatically stakes out womanism as a political project separate from feminism.

For Walker, womanism is distinct from mainstream feminism because it emerges from an imagined Black woman's standpoint, from the collective and particular experience of Black women's gendered and racialized oppression. As such, womanism is imagined to "describe black women's historical responses" to conditions of patriarchy and White dominance (Collins 1996, 16). Although Walker documents the social and historical context from which womanism emerges, she also differentiates womanism from mainstream feminism: if womanism is serious, grounded, universal, and purposeful, feminism is its opposite, somehow trivial, diminished, selective, silly. Where womanism is a vibrant, deep "purple," feminism is a quiet, muted "lavender."

Yet Walker's definition does far more than distinguish a womanist practice from a mainstream feminist practice; it crafts an episteme from Black women's imagined experiences. Walker's womanism amplifies the centrality of love to Black feminist politics. Although love had long been foundational to Black feminist thought—from members of the Black women's club movement advocating the "power of love" (Fannie Barrier Williams, quoted in Hendricks 1998, 19) to Audre Lorde's claim that "what was native has been stolen from us, the love of Black women for each other" (Lorde 1984, 175)—Walker's womanism is both one of the clearest Black feminist attempts to stake out a particular Black feminist politics and one of the clearest articulations of love as Black feminist politics. Love is central to the very definition of the womanist subject who feels love for other women ("loves other women, sexually and/or nonsexually"), for humanity ("committed to survival and wholeness of entire people"), for the spiritual world ("Loves the moon. *Loves* the Spirit") for celebration ("loves music. Loves dance. . . . Loves love and food and roundness"), and, most important, for her self.

Scholars have long noted the importance of love to womanism's "ethical or ideal vision," but have tended to celebrate certain loves that Walker champions, and to downplay others (Collins 1996, 16). Walker's universalistic appeal, her call for a love "that embraces everyone for the purposes of healing, change, and liberation," is often a celebrated portion of womanism (Sanders et al. 2006, 152). In its broad humanistic appeal, the grounded, "serious" Black womanist subject is "traditionally universalist." Walker writes, "As in: 'Mama, why are we brown, pink and yellow, and our cousins are white, beige, and black?' Ans: 'Well, you know the colored race is just like a flower garden, with every color flower represented.'" Walker's womanist subject is invested in the preservation (and representation) of "every color flower," a gesture that shows that the political project of womanism is a radical investment in difference. For Walker, womanism's universality is rooted in Black women's particular experiences. She notes, "Part of our tradition as black women is that we are universalists. Black children, yellow children, red children, brown children, that is the black woman's normal, day-to-day relationship. In my family alone, we are about four different colors" (Bradley 1984, quoting Walker). The embrace of difference becomes a way of connecting womanism to Black women's imagined experiences and traditions.[7]

Yet I am particularly interested in what I read as the most novel, underanalyzed, and transgressive portion of Walker's definition: her call for the womanist subject's unwavering self-love. Walker's womanist subject "loves herself. *Regardless*." The italicized "*regardless*" reveals that self-love is absolutely essential, that it persists in spite of everything else. Although Walker's call to self-love is certainly an "artful advocacy of unconditional love that starts with our acceptance of ourselves as divinely and humanly lovable," it is also far more (Sanders et al. 2006, 152). With "regardless" modifying "loves herself," Walker suggests that self-love stands at the heart of the womanist project, and functions as a prerequisite for the other kinds of humanistic, sensual, erotic, and spiritual loves that the womanist embodies. Self-love, it seems, is the only love that must *always* exist; it is the love that enables the other loves Walker's womanist embodies, engenders, and relishes. It is also the love that allows for the pleasures the womanist subject enjoys—the pleasure in the Folk, in the moon, in roundness, in music and dance.

At its broadest, Walker's plea for self-love articulates a relationship between self and politics, revealing that womanist politics requires a particular orientation of self, and that ethical management of the self might even *prefigure* the political and creative projects that the womanist subject engages in.[8] But what does this arrangement of the self look like? If, as Elizabeth Povinelli argues, love is a "political event," what kind of "political event" is the womanist call for self-love? (Povinelli 2006, 175).

For Walker, love is a strategy of orienting the self away from the frivolous, from the insignificant, and toward what she describes simply as the "serious." Walker asserts that the womanist subject wants "to know more and in greater depth than is considered 'good' for one. Interested in grown up doings. Acting grown up. Being grown up. . . . Responsible. In charge. *Serious.*" The womanist subject is "grown," she orients her self toward "grown up doings," toward "knowing more," toward a kind of social engagement that transcends the self. Being grown describes a self prepared to move beyond itself, a self that recognizes the limitations of selfhood, a self prepared for a certain kind of radical curiosity about the social world. The politics of womanism is an active working on the self, preparing it for the labor of social engagement, and for the task of advocating for the "survival and wholeness of entire people." To put it another way: womanist politics requires subjects to work on their selves in order to transcend their selves; it is, then, a radical articulation of the political limitations of selfhood.

Walker's "serious" womanist subject orders her self to transcend her self; other Black feminists have suggested that a commitment to love means training the self in other ways, in ways that extend and challenge the self. For some Black feminists, love-politics has been amplified as a call to orient the self *toward* difference, even in the face of fear or anxiety. Lorde writes, "I urge each one of us here to reach down into that deep place of knowledge inside herself and touch that terror and loathing of any difference that lives there. See whose face it wears. Then the personal as the political can begin to illuminate all our choices" (Lorde 1984, 113). For Lorde, Black feminist love-politics requires turning the self away from "terror and loathing," from a fear of "any difference that lives there." Indeed, Lorde implies that all subjects have a "deep place of knowledge" where fear abides; this is the place that has to be "touch[ed]" to realize the feminist goal of allowing "the personal as the political . . . to illuminate all our choices." Though the labor of training the self might be taxing, the result is productive: Black feminists can learn to "value recognition within each other's eyes as well as within our own, and seek a balance between these visions" (173). Lorde, then, is making an implicit claim about the untrained self (that it "fears" difference) and urging her Black feminist subjects to embrace a politics that names that fear, and actively labors to topple it.

Like Lorde, Jordan treats love as a configuration of the self that labors to transcend the fear of difference. She asks, "If I am a Black feminist serious in undertaking self-love, it seems to me that I should gain and gain and gain in strength so that I may without fear be able and willing to love and respect, for example, women who are not feminists, not professionals, not as old or as young as I am, women who have neither job nor income, women who are not Black" (Jordan 2003, 271). For Jordan, the political act of "undertaking self-love" is the process of embracing difference, of becoming more expansive in one's conception of political community. Both Lorde and Jordan suggest that the labor of crafting a collectivity constructed around difference requires a "serious . . . undertaking," the task of working on—or perhaps even against—the self. The self is then able to recognize the possibility of a politics organized not around the elisions (and illusions) of sameness, but around the vibrancy and complexity of difference.

What Walker, Lorde, and Jordan share is a fundamental conception that love is a labor of actively reorienting the self, pushing the self to be configured in new ways that might be challenging or difficult. The three also explicitly resist rooting love-politics in romantic love, something that some contemporary hip-hop feminists have not been able to avoid. Hip-hop feminist Joan Morgan, for example, imagines hip-hop feminism as a response to the peculiarly contemporary problem of Black lovelessness.[9] For Morgan, the tasks of hip-hop feminism are to treat hip-hop as a productive archive that records and amplifies Black male pain, and to answer Black male pain with an unwavering—though not self-destructive—love. Morgan argues, "As black women, we've got to do what any rational, survivalist-minded person would do after finding herself in a relationship with someone whose pain makes him abusive. We must continue to give up the love but *from a distance that's safe*" (Morgan 1995, 155; italics in original). For Morgan, love is not a strategy of self-labor or a transformative practice of reorienting the self; instead, it is something that is "given up" for the preservation of an imagined Black community. More than that, Morgan suggests that Black women should "give up the love" to avoid loneliness. She ends her piece with a haunting warning: "At the end of the day, I'd prefer the love to the empty victory of being right and alone anyway. Wouldn't you?" (157). By evoking the specter of Black female loneliness, Morgan reveals that her concept of love is not about the transformation of self but instead about romance.

Although Morgan's call for love wears the guise of a radical politics, it is actually a departure from the long labor of Black feminist love-politics consolidated during the "second wave." In fact, Black feminist love-politics practitioners rejected the notion that the political call to love is simply a call to love *others*. Although scholar-activists like Walker carved out space within their conception of love-politics for loving others (Walker, for example, notes that the womanist might "love other women sexually and/ or nonsexually. . . . Sometimes loves individual men, sexually and/or non-sexually"), the political thrust of their notion of love is that it is a labor of the self, not a romantic attachment to an Other. Part of what makes the work of second-wave love-practitioners so radical is a fundamental invest-ment in love as a practice of self-work.

Love and Politics/Loving Politics

If Black feminism's commitment to love has been amplified as an interest in a transformative labor of the self, it has also manifested itself through an advocacy of the formation of affective political communities. My analysis focuses on two aspects of love-politics that render it a distinctive, noni-dentitarian *political* tradition: first, Black feminist love-politics stakes out a radical conception of the public sphere; second, Black feminist love-politics maintains a new relationship to temporality generally, and to futurity specifically. In both regards, Black feminist love-politics offers a sharp departure from the identitarian labor of intersectionality revealing the existence—indeed, vibrancy—of multiple Black feminist political traditions.

My investment in locating a distinctive, affective, Black feminist politics emerges, in part, in response to strong—and important—critiques of intersectionality amplified by a host of scholars, most notably Jasbir Puar. For Puar, intersectionality—at least as it is currently practiced—is too eas-ily adapted into liberal regimes of inclusivity, too easily works as a strategy of "difference management," and too often gets taken up as "a tool of diversity management, and a mantra of liberal multiculturalism . . . [which] colludes with the disciplinary apparatus of the state—census, demography, racial profiling, surveillance—in that 'difference' is encased within a structural container that simply wishes the messiness of identity into a formulaic grid" (Puar 2005, 128). In place of intersectionality, Puar advocates theorizing "assemblage," which "underscores feeling, tactility, ontology, affect, and information" (Puar 2007, 215). Puar treats assemblage as opposed to intersectionality (though later she would note they are not opposed but "rather frictional"); if intersectionality can be a technology of liberalism invested in inclusion and diversity, assemblage is invested in movement, futurity, and affect. Puar's intervention is significant because, I argue, Black feminist love-politics constitutes a Black feminist tradition *deeply* invested in "feeling, tactility . . . [and] affect," and in crafting political communities constituted by heterogeneity and variety, rather than homogeneity and fixity. So how might we read Black feminist love-politics as performing precisely the kind of work that Puar suggests is opposed (or "frictional") to intersectionality, a kind of affective politics that transcends the pitfalls of visibility, inclusion, and liberalism associated with intersectionality? What is the affective political work that Black feminism's call to love performs, and how is it different from the identitarian work of intersectionality?

First, Black feminism's love-politics offers a powerful reconception of the public sphere. My understanding of the public is indebted to Cvetkovich, who suggests that we keep the definition of "public culture" expansive to make space for "forms of affective life that have not solidified into institutions, organizations, or identities" (Cvetkovich 2003, 9), and to Lauren Berlant and Michael Warner, who "support forms of affective, erotic, and personal living that are public in the sense of accessible, available to memory, and sustained through collective activity" (Berlant and Warner 1998, 562). My understanding of "public culture" is also indebted to the interdisciplinary work on the "black public sphere," which treats an expansive archive—from "street talk and new musics, radio shows and church voices"—as part of a "wider sphere of critical practice and visionary politics" (Black Public Sphere Collective 1995, 3).[10] I draw on this interdisciplinary body of scholarship to ask how Black feminist love-politics engenders new publics, new forms of relationality, even if tenuous and fleeting, marked by forms of collective sentiment rather than by identity.

If "communal affect" constitutes the "ties that bind utopian communities," then Black feminism's love-politics creates a public culture based on a collective "public feeling" of love, or what Jordan calls "a steady-state deep caring and respect for every other human being, a love that can only derive from a secure and positive self-love" (Jordan 2003, 272). Love, then, is a practice of self, a labor of the self, that forms the basis of political communities rooted in a radical ethic of care. In her "Where is the Love?" speech, Jordan asserts, "I am entering my soul into a struggle that will most certainly transform the experience of all the peoples of the earth, as no other movement can, in fact, hope to claim: because the movement into self-love, self-respect, and self-determination is the movement now galvanizing the true, the unarguable majority of human beings everywhere" (270). Jordan's claim—that she is participating in a struggle of like-minded subjects, an "unarguable majority"—reveals that the public sphere she wants to create is one rooted in a shared commitment to "self-love, self-respect, and self determination." What her "unarguable majority" shares is a commitment to a utopian vision, a commitment to "transform[ing] the experience of all the peoples of the earth." Jordan's political community is not based on the elisions of identity or a shared (imagined) sameness, but on a conception of the public rooted in affiliation and a shared set of feelings. It is this affiliation—however tenuous, however momentary, however fragmentary—that allows Jordan to shift from a minoritarian politics to a conversation about an "unarguable majority."

This is not, of course, to argue that Jordan does not recognize profound social inequalities and how they are allocated in ways that coincide with race, gender, class, and sexuality. Indeed, Jordan is one of the great theorists of racial and gendered violence and their effects on the material, social, and psychic lives of those who are subjected to brutality. Instead, I am interested in how a radical ethic of care, rather than an assertion of shared injury (when, of course, the great insight of Black feminist theory has been to showcase that injury is never *really* shared; identity-work always requires elisions), can form the basis of a public. By jettisoning identity as the foundation of her public sphere, Jordan's plea for love transcends the "logic of pain" that Wendy Brown identifies as lying at the heart of many calls for identity politics (Brown 1995, 64). Brown argues that a conception of injury is central to identity politics because "politicized identities generated out of liberal, disciplinary societies, insofar as they are premised on exclusion from a universal ideal, require that ideal, as well as their exclusion from it, for their own perpetuity as identities" (408). But for Jordan, the public is not a site for articulating—or displaying—wounded Black flesh; instead, it is the site where selves laboring to love—to orient their selves toward difference, toward transcending the self—join in a form of relationality. In so doing, Black feminist love-politics "shed[s] new light on the possibilities of the public sphere," imagining the public sphere as a site organized around a shared utopian vision rather than around a wounded, shared identity that demands recognition of the wound (Pough 2004, 166).

Black feminist love-politics also reshapes the public sphere by offering a distinctive conception of remedy. Rather than looking to the state for remedy—as intersectional projects often do in their sometimes ambivalent call for doctrinal remedy[11]—Black feminist love-politics asks how affective communities can themselves be a site of redress. This is not to say that naming injury isn't important or that minoritarian subjects do not need the state to redress harm; instead, I read this turning away from the state as a critique of the state's shortcomings, particularly its unwillingness to adequately name and redress Black women's injuries. By insistently looking *away* from the state, love-politics practitioners perform frustration, revealing their understandings of the limitations of a regime that is not committed to redressing their harms. For example, Jordan asks, "*Where is the love?* How is my own lifework serving to end these tyrannies, these corrosions of sacred possibility? How do the strong, the powerful, treat children? How do we treat the aged among us? How do the strong and the powerful treat so-called minority members of the body politic? How do the powerful regard women? How do they treat us?" (Jordan 2003, 270). Jordan's queries suggest that although the "unarguable majority" cannot undo "tyranny," the "majority" can critically analyze its role in the perpetuation of injustice, and labor to unlock itself from the hold of hegemony. More than that, affective communities can consider the "sacred possibilities" they can unlock *even under* conditions of patriarchy and white-dominance. By insisting on analyzing both how the powerful "treat so-called minority members of the body politic" and how political communities can organize around unlocking the connections between subjects, Jordan argues that the labor of unlocking the "sacred possibility" among us comes from examining our own engagement with power, and locating ways to remove ourselves from its seductive hold. By focusing on how the public sphere can be a site of redressing the "spirit-murder" of racism and sexism—through conventional activism and through practices that reveal that "customary forms of political response, including direct action and critical analysis are no longer working either to change the world or to make us feel better" (Cvetkovich 2007, 460)—Black feminist love-politics implicitly offers a critique of the state and its capacity (or incapacity) to ever adequately remedy injuries.

Although love-politics reformulates public culture and organizes it around affect and new conceptions of redress, love-politics also orients public culture toward a different sense of temporality, one that Jordan gestures to in her call for a recognition of "sacred possibility." Recent years have been filled with interdisciplinary calls toward thinking about the possible, from Muñoz's conceptualization of queerness as an embrace of "futurity," (Muñoz 2009) to Robin D. G. Kelley's celebratory belief that "the map to a new world is in the imagination" (Kelley 2002, 2) to Wendy Brown's plea to move toward "claims which, rather than dispensing blame for an unlivable present, inhabited the necessarily agonistic theater of discursively forging an alternative future" (Brown 1995, 408) to Kathi Weeks's interest in "a horizon of utopian possibility" (Weeks 2011, 30). Indeed, critical theory's recent preoccupation with temporality—particularly queer theory's interest in conceptualizing queerness as a critique of normative time—has led some scholars to champion a "politics of the open end" (Puar 2007, 215).

Black feminist love-politics, though, has long been invested in the "open end," in radical possibility, orienting itself toward a yet-unknown future. Black feminist love-politics constantly evokes what "has yet to be known, seen, or heard" (Puar 2007, 216) or what Kelley calls the labor of "talk[ing] openly of revolution and dream[ing] of a new society, sometimes creating cultural works that enable communities to envision what's possible with collective action, personal self transformation, and will" (Kelley 2002, 7). To put it another way, Black feminist love-politics is staunchly utopian; rather than the presentism of a visibility politics like intersectionality, which calls for legibility and recognition in "the here and now," Black feminist love-politics, like Muñoz's reading of queerness, chooses "the future" as its "domain" (Muñoz 2009, 1).

The traces of the what-might-be are present in Lorde's rumination on "the future of our earth" that "may depend upon the ability of all women to identify and develop new definitions of power and new patterns of relating across difference" (Lorde 1984, 123) and in her description of the virtues of anger, where she notes "we *are* moving on. With or without uncolored women. We use whatever strengths we have fought for, including anger, to help define and fashion a world where all our sisters can grow, where our children can love, and where the power of touching and meeting another woman's difference and wonder will eventually transcend the need for destruction" (123). Lorde's project is, at its simplest, world-making, it is "moving on" toward a future that is not yet here but is unfolding; her interest is in what Muñoz would call the "could." It is a project strategically disinvested in remedying the present (or the possibility that the present could be remedied), and wholeheartedly invested in the future as a locus of possibility. This orientation toward the "could" echoes what Muñoz terms "feeling revolutionary," a sentiment he describes as a "feeling that our current situation is not enough, that something is indeed missing and we cannot live without it. Feeling revolutionary opens up the space to imagine a collective escape, an exodus, a 'going-off script' together. . . . Practicing educated hope is the enactment of a critique function. It is not about announcing the way things *ought* to be, but, instead, imagining what things *could* be" (Muñoz and Duggan 2009, 278). It is the interest in "collective escape," in the visionary dreaming about "going off script" that distinguishes Black feminist love-politics' utopian impulse from the presentism of identitarian politics like intersectionality.

In describing intersectionality as present-oriented, I do not mean to deny intersectionality's commitment to a just social world, which is, of course, a visionary project, or to discount its normative project: reconfiguring legal doctrine, insisting on the inherent value of Black women's experiences, reformulating feminist and antiracist theory. What I mean, though, is that intersectionality relies on an attachment—perhaps even a cruel attachment[12]—to the present in two ways: first, it insists that redress can be crafted *within the confines* of the social moment as it now exists. Legal doctrine can be reformed to make cognizable race-and-gender-based discrimination claims; feminism can be recrafted to "include" Black women's experiences; antiracist work can be transformed to take seriously Black women's injuries. Second, intersectionality's very conception of identity, which treats race and gender as fixed, coherent, and legible, "presupposes identity and thus disavows futurity, or, perhaps more accurately, prematurely anticipates and thus fixes a permanence to forever" (Puar 2005, 216). Although intersectionality fixes identity, presuming that race and gender are stable categories that interact in particular and knowable ways, it also aspires to make visible those identities and their intersections in the "here-and-now."

Black feminist love-politics suspends this attachment to the present, recognizing that changing the grammar of our contemporary political moment will not remove us from the script that is always already in place. Instead, love-politics practitioners dream of a yet unwritten future; they imagine a world ordered by love, by a radical embrace of difference, by a set of subjects who work on/against themselves to work for each other. This dreaming, of course, does not suspend labor; Black feminist love-politics practitioners have always been attached to the idea that the radical future requires certain kinds of very hard work, pushing beyond our investments in selfhood and sameness, and reaching toward collectivities and possibilities. Nor does this vision neglect the host of ways that power and structures of domination work on and against bodies in quotidian and spectacular ways. It is a critical response to the violence of the ordinary and the persistence of inequality that insists on a politics of the visionary.

Ultimately, Black feminist love-politics proposes a departure from the identitarian political work that is so often associated with Black feminism. Where proto-intersectional groups like the Combahee River Collective insisted that "we believe that the most profound and potentially the most radical politics come directly out of our own identity" (Combahee River Collective 1983, 16), a sentiment that Crenshaw would share a decade later when she coined the term "intersectionality," Black feminist love-politics responds with its own "radical politics." Black feminist love-politics crafts a political community that eschews the wounded subject that lies at the heart of identity politics. In its place, it crafts a collectivity marked by "communal affect," a utopian, visionary, future-oriented community held together by affiliation and "public feeling" rather than an imagined—or enforced—sameness.

Thinking Love, Doing Love

Kelley argues, "Freedom and love may be the most revolutionary ideas available to us, and yet as intellectuals, we have failed miserably to grapple with their political and analytical importance" (Kelley 2002, 11–12). My paper takes up Kelley's challenge and examines how Black feminists have treated love as a "revolutionary idea." Indeed, this paper has endeavored to show that Black feminism's long tradition of love-politics—particularly as it was consolidated during the "second wave"—has effectively amplified a "material and political" conception of love (Hardt and Negri 2004, 352). For the scholar-activists at the center of my analysis—Alice Walker, June Jordan, Audre Lorde—love acted as a *doing*, a call for a labor of the self, an appeal for transcending the self, a strategy for remaking the public sphere, a plea to unleash the radical imagination, and a critique of the state's blindness to the violence it inflicts and enables.

Love, of course, is not wholly unproblematic political terrain: it can be deployed to shore up heteronormativity, to re-energize dominant narratives of romance, and to advance claims to power. Sara Ahmed's work, for example, invites scholars to examine how the claim to be acting *in* or *through* love can enable the exertion of particular kinds of power. She asks, "How has politics become a struggle over who has the right to name themselves as acting out of love? What does it mean to stand for love by standing alongside some others and against other others?" (Ahmed 2003). Her work reveals that the "language of love" operates, at least at times, by concealing animus and renaming it love.

Though it is important to consider how claims to acting in love are often claims to power as well, this paper celebrates Black feminist love-politics as producing a number of critical shifts: first, studying Black feminism's long labor of love-politics reveals an under-studied Black feminist political tradition, and underscores the importance of not reducing Black feminist work exclusively to intersectional work. In so doing, the paper aspires to counter a larger trend in feminist theory to relegate Black feminism to the category of feminisms-past, feminisms problematically (and anachronistically) attached to identity. Second, reading Black feminism's long-standing interest in affect exposes that the roots of the "affective turn" are far more varied than often theorized. Although affect theory and queer theory are inextricably intertwined, the labor of constructing political communities around "public feelings" and "communal affect" has been a Black feminist investment for decades. Finally, reading Black feminism's love-politics takes up the challenge that Hardt and Negri advocate when they champion a "politics of love." Indeed, Black feminism's visionary love-politics effectively and hopefully uses a refrain like "where is the love?" and transforms it from a personal question about romantic love into a political call for transcending the self and transforming the public sphere.

Jennifer C. Nash is associate professor of African American studies and gender and sexuality studies at Northwestern University. She is the author of *The Black Body in Ecstasy: Reading Race, Reading Pornography* (2014) and *Black Feminism Reimagined: After*

Intersectionality (2019). She has also published articles in *GLQ, Signs, Feminist Theory, Feminist Studies,* and *Social Text.*

Notes

Originally published in *Meridians* vol. 11, no. 2, 2013.

Thanks to Amber Musser and Libby Anker for thoughtful feedback on earlier drafts, and to Amin Ahmad, always.

1   See Berlant and Hardt 2011.

2   I use the term "second-wave Black feminism" with analytical suspicion, mind-ful of the host of critiques of wave metaphors. See, for example, Springer 2002; Henry 2004; Snyder 2008.

3   This is not to say that all second-wave Black feminist politics was love-politics; indeed, second-wave Black politics was a moment that was also marked by a proliferation of identity politics. Rather, I am interested in how calls for love-politics were amplified and organized in this moment.

4   Jasbir Puar parses the "affective turn" more finely, suggesting that we might think of it in two particular strains; the first are a set of scholars "who deploy affect as a particular reflection of or attachment to 'structures of being' or feel-ing that otherwise remains unarticulateable. In many cases affect in these works is situated in a continuum or becomes interchangeable with emotion, feeling, expressive sentiment." The other is, she argues, part of a "Deleuzian frame whereby affect is a physiological and biological phenomenon, signaling why bodily matter matters, what escapes or remains outside of the discursively structured and thus commodity forms of emotion, of feeling" (Puar 2007, 207).

5   Crenshaw echoes this in her article "Race, Reform, and Retrenchment: Trans-formation and Legitimation in Antidiscrimination Law" when she asserts, "History has shown that the most valuable political asset of the Black commu-nity has been its ability to assert a collective identity and to name this collective political reality" (Crenshaw 1988, 1336).

6   For examples of some of this debate, see Collins 1996, 9–17; Coleman 2006, 85–89; and Phillips 2006.

7   Less celebrated, and less analyzed, is Walker's interest in Black women's love for each other—an imagined spiritual *and* sexual connection between Black women. Although other scholar-activists have theorized psychic and erotic con-nections between women, including Adrienne Rich's lesbian continuum and Audre Lorde's plea for resurrecting and celebrating the erotic, Walker's explicit investment in the *sexual* and nonsexual love between women is explicitly racial-ized. Although Walker "gives a primacy to the sexual love between women," she also "gives a primacy" to the sexual love between *Black* women (Coleman 2006, 86). And yet the sexual love portion of Walker's womanism continues to be under-theorized.

8   Walker's definition gestures to much earlier philosophical traditions, including Plato's *Republic*, which argues that the soul—consisting of rational, appetitive, and spirited portions—has to be correctly ordered for an individual to be

oriented toward justice (Plato 1992). The just subject, according to Plato, is the one governed by rationality; the rational self tempers both the appetitive and spirited facets of the self, ensuring that the self is governed fairly. It is only when the self is fully balanced—governed by rationality—that it can act virtuously.

9   Sociologist Orlando Patterson echoes these claims, arguing "the simple, sad truth is that Afro-Americans are today the loneliest of all Americans—lonely and isolated as a group; lonely and isolated in their neighborhoods, through which they are often too terrified to walk; lonely as households headed by women sick and tired of being 'the strong black woman'; lonely as single men fearful of commitment; lonely as single women wary of a 'love and trouble' tradition that has always been more trouble than love" (Patterson 1998, xii).

10   My interest in publics is informed by work like Houston Baker's, which is critical of Jürgen Habermas's work on the "bourgeois public sphere." According to Baker, "Habermas [is] eager to enter a time machine and return to the good old days of London coffee houses and literary societies: things long ago and far away" (Baker 1995, 11).

11   Intersectionality practitioners, although invested in seeking redress from the state in the present, also noted that state redress was not their ultimate goal. Crenshaw writes, "the civil rights constituency cannot afford to view antidiscrimination doctrine as a permanent pronouncement of society's commitment to ending racial subordination. Rather, antidiscrimination law represents an ongoing ideological struggle in which the occasional winners harbor the moral, coercive, consensual power of law. Nonetheless, the victories it offers can be ephemeral and the risks of engagement substantial" (Crenshaw 1988, 1335).

12   Here I am referencing Berlant 2011.

Works Cited

Ahmed, Sara. 2003. "In the Name of Love." *Borderlands E-Journal* 2, no. 3. http://www
.borderlands.net.au/vol2no3_2003/ahmed_love.htm (accessed December 4, 2012).

———. 2004. *The Cultural Politics of Emotion.* New York: Routledge.

Baker, Houston A. 1995. "Critical Memory and the Black Public Sphere." In *The Black Public Sphere: A Public Culture Book*, edited by the Black Public Sphere Collective. Chicago: University of Chicago Press.

Berlant, Lauren. 2011. *Cruel Optimism.* Durham, NC: Duke University Press.

Berlant, Lauren, and Michael Hardt. 2011. "No One is Sovereign in Love: A Conversation Between Lauren Berlant and Michael Hardt." *Amour No. 18.* http:
//nomorepotlucks.org/article/amour-no-18/no-one-sovereign-love-conversation
-between-lauren-berlant-and-michael-hardt (accessed August 25, 2012).

Berlant, Lauren, and Michael Warner. 1998. "Sex in Public." *Critical Inquiry* 24, no. 2: 547–66.

Black Public Sphere Collective. 1995. *The Black Public Sphere: A Public Culture Book.* Chicago: University of Chicago Press.

Bradley, David. 1984. "Novelist Alice Walker Telling the Black Woman's Story." *New York Times,* January 8.

Brown, Wendy. 1995. *States of Injury.* Princeton, NJ: Princeton University Press.

Chang, Jerome, and Robert Culp. 2002. "After Intersectionality." *University of Missouri Kansas City Law Review* 71: 485–91.

Coleman, Monica. 2006. "Must I be a Womanist?" *Journal of Feminist Studies in Religion* 22, no. 1: 85–96.

Collins, Patricia Hill. 1996. "What's In a Name: Womanism, Black Feminism and Beyond." *Black Scholar* 26, no. 1: 9–17.

———. 2004. *Black Sexual Politics: African Americans, Gender, and the New Racism.* New York: Routledge.

Combahee River Collective. 1983. "The Combahee River Collective Statement." In *Home Girls: A Black Feminist Anthology,* edited by Barbara Smith. New York: Kitchen Table Press.

Crenshaw, Kimberlé. 1988. "Race, Reform, and Retrenchment: Transformation and Legitimation in Antidiscrimination Law." *Harvard Law Review* 101, no. 7: 1331–87.

———. 1989. "Demarginalizing the Intersection of Race and Sex: A Black Feminist Critique of Antidiscrimination Doctrine, Feminist Theory, and Antiracist Politics." *University of Chicago Law Forum:* 139–68.

———. 1991. "Mapping the Margins: Intersectionality, Identity Politics, and Violence against Women of Color." *Stanford Law Review* 46, no. 3: 1241–99.

Cvetkovich, Ann. 2003. *An Archive of Feelings: Trauma, Sexuality, and Lesbian Public Cultures.* Durham, NC: Duke University Press.

———. 2007. "Public Feelings." *South Atlantic Quarterly* 106, no. 3: 459–68.

Ehrenreich, Nancy. 2002. "Subordination and Symbiosis: Mechanisms of Mutual Support between Subordinating Systems." *University of Missouri Kansas City Law Review* 71: 252–310.

Hardt, Michael, and Antonio Negri. 2004. *Multitude: War and Democracy in the Aye of Empire.* New York: Penguin.

Hekman, Susan. 2000. "Beyond Identity: Feminism, Identity, and Identity Politics." *Feminist Theory* 1, no. 3: 289–308.

Hemmings, Clare. 2010. *Why Stories Matter: The Political Grammar of Feminist Theory.* Durham, NC: Duke University Press.

Hendricks, Wanda. 1998. *Gender, Race, and Politics in the Midwest: Black Club Women in Illinois.* Bloomington: Indiana University Press.

Henry, Astrid. 2004. *Not My Mother's Sister: Generational Conflict and Third-Wave Feminism.* Bloomington: Indiana University Press.

Higginbotham, Evelyn Brooks. 1992. "African American Women's History and the Metalanguge of Race." *Signs* 17, no. 2: 251–74.

hooks, bell. 2000. *All About Love: New Visions.* New York: William Morrow and Company, Inc.

Hull, Gloria T., Patricia Bell Scott, and Barbara Smith, eds. 1982. *All the Women Are White, All the Blacks Are Men, But Some of Us Are Brave*. New York: Feminist Press.

Hutchinson, Darren L. 2001. "Identity Crisis: 'Intersectionality,' 'Multidimensionality,' and the Development of an Adequate Theory of Subordination." *Michigan Journal of Race and the Law* 6, no. 2: 285–317.

Jordan, June. 2003. *Some of Us Did Not Die*. New York: Basic Books.

Kelley, Robin D. G. 2003. *Freedom Dreams: The Black Radical Imagination*. Boston: Beacon Press.

Kwan, Peter. 1997. "Intersections of Race, Ethnicity, Class, Gender, and Sexual Orientation: Jeffrey Dahmer and the Cosynthesis of Categories." *Hastings Law Journal* 48: 1257–92.

Lee, Rachel. 2000. "Notes from the (non)Field: Teaching and Theorizing Women of Color." *Meridians* 1, no. 1: 85–109.

Lorde, Audre. 1984. *Sister Outsider*. Berkeley: Crossing Press.

McCall, Leslie. 2005. "The Complexity of Intersectionality." *Signs: Journal of Women in Culture and Society* 30, no. 3: 1771–800.

Morgan, Joan. 1995. "Fly-Girls, Bitches, and Hoes: Notes of A Hip-Hop Feminist." *Social Text* 45: 151–57.

Muñoz, José. 2006. "Feeling Brown, Feeling Down: Latina Affect, the Performativity of Race, and the Depressive Position." *Signs* 31, no. 3: 675–88.

———. 2009. *Cruising Utopia: The Then and There of Queer Futurity*. New York: New York University Press.

Muñoz, José, and Lisa Duggan. 2009. "Hope and Hopelessness: A Dialogue." *Women & Performance: A Journal of Feminist Theory* 19, no. 2: 275–83.

Nash, Jennifer C. 2010. "On Difficulty: Intersectionality as Feminist Labor." *Scholar & Feminist Online*. http://sfonline.barnard.edu/polyphonic/nash_01.htm (accessed December 11, 2012)

———. 2011. "'Hometruths' on Intersectionality." *Yale Journal of Law and Feminism* 23, no. 2: 445–70.

Patterson, Orlando. 1998. *Rituals of Blood: Consequences of Slavery in Two American Centuries*. New York: Basic Civitas Books.

Phillips, Layli. 2006. "Womanism on its Own." In *The Womanist Reader: The First Quarter Century of Womanist Thought*, edited by Layli Phillips. New York: Routledge.

Plato. (380 BCE) 1992. *Republic*. Indianapolis: Hackett.

Povinelli, Elizabeth. 2006. *Empire of Love: Toward a Theory of Intimacy, Genealogy, and Carnality*. Durham, NC: Duke University Press.

Pough, Gwendolyn D. 2003. "Do The Ladies Run This? Some Thoughts on Hip Hop Feminism." In *Catching a Wave: Reclaiming Feminism for the 21ST Century*, edited by Rory Dicker and Alison Peipmeier. Boston: Northeastern University Press.

———. 2004. *Check it While I Wreck It: Black Womanhood, Hip-Hop Culture, and the Public Sphere*. Boston: Northeastern University Press.

Puar, Jasbir. 2005. "Queer Times, Queer Assemblages." *Social Text* 23, nos. 3–4: 121–39.

————. 2007. *Terrorist Assemblages: Homonationalism in Queer Times*. Durham, NC: Duke University Press.

Razak, Arisika. 2006. "Response." *Journal of Feminist Studies in Religion* 22, no. 1: 99–107.

Sanders, Cheryl, et al. 2006. "Roundtable Discussion: Christian Ethics and Theology in Womanist Perspective." In *The Womanist Reader: The First Quarter Century of Womanist Thought*, edited by Layli Phillips. New York: Routledge.

Shange, Ntozake. 1977. *For Colored Girls Who Have Considered Suicide, When the Rainbow is Enuf: A Choreopoem*. New York: MacMillan.

Snyder, R. Claire. 2008. "What is Third-Wave Feminism? A New Directions Essay." *Signs* 34, no. 1: 175–96.

Springer, Kimberly. 2002. "Third Wave Black Feminism?" *Signs* 27, no. 4: 1059–82.

Staiger, Janet, Ann Cvetkovich, and Ann Reynolds. 2010. "Introduction: Political Emotions and Public Feelings." In *Political Emotions*, edited by Janet Staiger, Ann Cvetkovich, and Ann Reynolds. New York: Routledge.

Torfs, Elisabeth. 2007. "Alice Walker's Womanism: Theory and Practice." M.A. Thesis, Katholieke Universiteit Leuven.

Walker, Alice. 1983. *In Search of Our Mothers' Gardens*. New York: Harcourt Brace.

Weeks, Kathi. 2011. *The Problem with Work: Feminism, Marxism, Antiwork Politics, and Postwork Imaginaries*. Durham, NC: Duke University Press.

Wiegman, Robyn. 2012. *Object Lessons*. Durham, NC: Duke University Press.

Vivian M. May

....

Under-Theorized and Under-Taught
Re-examining Harriet Tubman's Place in Women's Studies

Abstract: Interpretive approaches to Black women's insurgency can stifle as much as they reveal. Harriet Tubman is deservedly remembered for her sustained resistance to multiple forms of oppression. Yet, she is often made visible in ways that distort, rendering her invisible. Scholars often warp Tubman's contributions by presenting her as an exceptional but lone figure, by animating stereotypes of Black women's unparalleled strength, or by fragmenting her activism via single-issue lenses. Critics also draw on maternal or salvific frames to soften Tubman's militancy or enfold her into the nation's triumphal narrative (misrepresenting Tubman and erasing how systems of oppression she challenged continue today). Unfortunately, such forms of "checking" Tubman go relatively "unchecked" in feminist scholarship, where Tubman's work is often not viewed as relevant to core feminist theories, concepts, methods, or curricula. However, Tubman's contributions should be understood as pertinent to women's studies, particularly from within women of color theoretical traditions.

Introduction

As an iconic figure of U.S. history, and specifically of Black women's history, Harriet Tubman is deservedly remembered for her sustained resistance to multiple forms of oppression. For instance, to underscore Tubman's position in the history of Black feminist consciousness, Darlene Clark Hine argues that "slavery, and resistance to it, were the defining

MERIDIANS · feminism, race, transnationalism   Volume 19 Supplement 2020
DOI: 10.1215/15366936-8566100 © 2014 Smith College

moments of the birth of black women's oppositional consciousness" (Hine 1993, 343). Tubman's role in this history is also, in part, what Barbara Smith sought to underscore when explaining how the naming of the Combahee River Collective was a conscious naming of Black feminist selfhood and of history—"a way of talking about ourselves being on a continuum of . . . Black women's [collective] struggle" (quoted in Harris 1999, 10).

However, such outright claiming of Tubman's insurgency as pivotal to her legacy remains relatively unusual—this aspect of her contributions tends either to be overlooked or softened. Generally speaking, evidence of Black feminist radicalisms and histories of overt militancy are, if not wholly suppressed, usually stifled by other means. As Joy James argues, for example, "The revolutionary remains on the margin, more so than any other form of (black) feminism" (James 1999, 92). Thus, Black women's radicalism is often disassociated from feminism altogether, either via polite distance or via vilification (for example, militancy may be condescendingly disparaged as rash or misguided, or more overtly pathologized as monstrous or dangerous). Alternatively, radicalism may be brought into the fold of history, but only by first being rendered more amenable to conventional frameworks. Recognition, therefore, often has, at its heart, a kind of concealment—meaning that many forms of historical visibility, and not just invisibility, can entail insidious forms of erasure.

Nonetheless, insurgency has a long and central tradition in Black feminist history, as Carole Boyce Davies's recent biography of Claudia Jones[1] underscores, for instance. Via the example of Jones's life and writings, Davies documents how Black women's political militancy has often developed organically: from confronting multilevel forms of structural exploitation, nationally and internationally, and also personally, and from struggling with political allies to have the multidimensionality of Black women's lives acknowledged, not fragmented or ignored. Davies also stresses, in her exploration of how Jones is (and is not) remembered, how this effort also entails a deep representational struggle—not only for Black women radicals to be recognized and heard in their own time, but also to be remembered in the historical, intellectual, and political records (Davies 2008, 7–19). However, Jones's radicalness, whether in the present day or in her own time, if not wholly overlooked, has often been downplayed or coopted as symbolic of Black power conceived on androcentric terms. In this way, though acknowledged, the most radical aspects of Jones's work, such as her analyses of the interconnected, global workings of capitalism, gender, and race (2, 24), are suppressed and tend to disappear from historical memory.

I pause to mention Jones for a few reasons. First, though she is a much more recent example of Black feminist radicalism than is Tubman, Jones is rarely referenced, even nominally, in most feminist and Black feminist political genealogies. As with Tubman, fragmented politics and reductive historical categories have cordoned Jones off from her rightful place in our intellectual and political frameworks. I also focus on Jones here because she invokes Tubman as part of her own journey. For example, she references Tubman when delineating her own views about Black women's role in fighting super-exploitation in the global economy, while simultaneously battling White supremacy on the part of White women allies and patriarchy on the part of Black male allies (Davies 2008, 50). Tubman offers Jones evidence of a tangible longer history of Black feminist radical resistance to draw on in the present day, of a genealogy of insurgency in which Black women engaged in concerted efforts to be recognized as agents of liberation and as freedom's central subjects, not as mere helpmeets of others' leadership and liberation.

To clarify, unlike the countless Black women who remain anonymous and are in many ways lost to history, Tubman as a figure certainly is not eclipsed or erased from the record. However, she is often made visible as a historical figure piecemeal, within narrow frameworks and in attenuated ways. In fact, stories of Tubman's overall life and life's work tend to be relatively curbed, both presently and historically. Unfortunately, various forms of "checking" Tubman's contributions have gone more or less "unchecked" in feminist scholarship: Tubman's narrative and political curtailment has been under-theorized, despite the fact that feminist and antiracist scholars have been committed to identifying reductive interpretive frames that distort questions of Black women's roles as knowers, political organizers, and historical agents.

Thus, although many Black feminist intellectuals and activists have sought to approach Tubman as part of a larger trajectory, providing context for her as an individual actor and for the development of Black feminisms more widely (see, for example, Taylor 2010), Tubman is more often remembered in ways that misrecognize, distort, or flatten. As Patricia Hill Collins argues, for example, Tubman is often embraced by being treated as so unusual as to be without equal and then folded into masculinist Black history frameworks (Collins 1998, 175). Rendered an anomalous Black heroine, she is then incorporated into an androcentric narrative of Black history: Tubman, argues Collins, is lauded in such contexts by zeroing in on only some aspects of her life story, particularly those that align effortlessly with androcentric notions of protest. Tubman, in other words, is "incorporated" into ready-made political and historical frames (an alignment that is really only possible when Tubman's longer life's work is fragmented and, to a great degree, decontextualized).

In short, Collins argues, Afrocentric historians are often only willing to fold in "the work of a few clearly exceptional Black women . . . if these Black women worthies do not challenge preexisting Afrocentric assumptions. For example, Harriet Tubman . . . meets a [preconceived] standard of greatness derived from male experience, namely, military leadership in warfare" (Collins 1998, 175). In women's studies, on the other hand, in contrast to the kinds of distortion that can result from "folding" Tubman into conventional or established lenses, the distortion results more from omission or absence, not tokenism or assimilation. In other words, Tubman is generally overlooked entirely in the field: rather than being made to conform to prevailing feminist frameworks or historical timelines, Tubman tends to just be left out.

This double-edged dynamic of simultaneous recognition/misrecognition is an epistemological pattern that must be considered when tracing Black feminist histories, one that plays out in specific ways with each individual subject. Examining how Tubman is and is not remembered, or is and is not imagined, helps illuminate how interpretive tools used to document and examine resistance can stifle as much as they reveal. In essence, seemingly positive analytic lenses, when applied to radical Black women's histories, can animate epistemological violence. I discuss herein three intertwined approaches that artificially delimit Tubman's legacy and must be reconsidered.

- First, though Tubman's resilience frequently is hailed and even celebrated, doing so can present Tubman as an exceptional but lone figure and can animate stereotypes of Black women's unparalleled strength. When showcased positively in U.S. history, Black women tend to enter the historical record primarily as superhuman, anomalous individuals.
- Second, Tubman's lifelong resistance is often fragmented (and large periods of her life's work totally ignored), meaning that her longer

history of activism and the varied forms of coalition-building she engaged in remain both under-theorized and under-recognized.

- Third, via lenses of the maternal and salvific, Tubman's militancy is often made over or made ready to be embraced into the folds of the nation's progress narrative, a triumphal tale of our having fully broken from the past that erases the ongoing, tenacious nature of many forms of systemic oppression Tubman fought against and sought to transform.

I conclude by discussing Tubman's relative absence in women's studies, even though her life's work can readily be understood as pertinent to the field's analytics and themes, particularly from the angle of women of color theoretical traditions. To counter perceptions that Tubman's life and contributions merit only passing reference (if that) in feminist scholarship and curricula, I also delineate how Tubman is relevant to a wide range of current theoretical issues and political frameworks.

Tubman as an Icon of Strength

Thinking about Tubman requires examining how the iconic as a lens functions, since, when applied to Black women's lives and bodies, it often taps into controlling images of superhuman psychological and physical strength. Moreover, as I have argued with regard to Anna Julia Cooper, pedestals of historical greatness created by the iconic gaze also separate figures like Tubman and Cooper from their wider communities of resistance (May 2007, 39–44). Michelle Wallace therefore finds deploying the iconic risky because its focus is singular, on the lone historical figure "meant to stand in for the whole. Its primary function is to distract us from the actual debate and dilemma with which black feminists, intellectuals, and activists are really engaged" (Wallace 2004, 155). Additionally, she contends, it further distorts by rendering Black women "devoid of history and context" (175).

In this vein, many popular narratives of Tubman portray her as a lone militant and martyr: she seems ahistorical, selfless, and without equal, not someone who worked within long-established networks of communication and resistance. Though many enslaved women "plotted for insurrections" (Ellison 1983, 56), for example, these wider patterns of resistance and insurrection are rendered invisible by individualist heroic portraits of Tubman. As a historical celebrity apparently sprung from nowhere, who rose up and revolted, thanks seemingly only to her unique personal merits, Tubman has indeed been rendered a "superwoman." But, as Wallace explains, "The problem with the myth of the superwoman . . . was that it . . . [covered] up an inexorable process of black female disenfranchisement, exploitation, oppression, and despair." She therefore asks us to consider how "the dominant culture perpetuates the myth not in order to celebrate [black women] but [to be used] as weapons against them" (Wallace 1990, 61).

Wallace challenges us to acknowledge the consequences of romanticizing strength and of lionizing historical figures in acontextual, individualist ways. One can still acknowledge what Angela Davis and others have argued: that "she who accepted her lot as a slave was the exception rather than the rule" (Davis 1983, 20). Davis clarifies that, although "Tubman was indeed an exceptional individual," it is also the case that "what she did was simply to express in her own way the spirit of strength and perseverance which so many other women of her race had acquired" and which led countless other enslaved women to express themselves through "acts of resistance" (22). However, at the same time, it is imperative to understand that references to Tubman as exceptional can also indirectly buttress hegemony and serve to further pathologize those who could not resist in the same manner, or with the same toughness of mind, spirit, and body.

The heroic rhetorics and individualist lenses frequently applied to Tubman ignore much painstaking research that has been done to render visible less overt, though equally persistent, forms of gendered resistance within the contexts of slavery. As Stephanie Camp contends, for instance, "Turning our attention to the everyday, to private, concealed, and even intimate worlds, is essential to excavating bondwomen's resistance to slavery because women's history does not merely add to what we know; it changes what we know and how we know it" (Camp 2004, xi). Methodologically, Camp asserts, "Studying bondwomen's opposition has demanded creative approaches: a shift from the visible and organized to the hidden and informal, as well as rigorous attention to personal topics that, for enslaved women, were also political arenas" (3).

In general, icon-of-strength heroic frameworks neither account for these wider contexts nor acknowledge within-group differences among Black women in terms of available or chosen modes of resistance. Stories highlighting Tubman's resilience and strength can therefore have an unexpected utility: they can buttress mindsets that render Black women's historical roles invisible or insignificant and can also reinforce logics of subjugation, even as they may be intended to commemorate insurgency. For instance, narratives of Tubman's strength can animate ideologies of savagery, dominant imaginaries Nell Irvin Painter has described as forms of "nineteenth-century primitivism and romantic racialism" (Painter 1990, 10; see also Painter 1997). Furthermore, since, "as a 'technology' of racialized gender, . . . strength has the dual status of a tool of exploitation and a marker of virtue" (Beauboeuf-Lafontant 2009, 42), celebrating physical and psychological strength can essentially bolster the very ideas used to rationalize and naturalize Black women's systemic exploitation.

As Tamara Beauboeuf-Lafontant explains, "Taking race, class, and gender domination as givens, the discourse asserts that the intertwined problems that Black women know well . . . are not grounds for social outrage but acceptable tests of individual mettle. . . . [S]trength celebrates Black women's heroic actions and deflects attention from their circumstances. . . . It is a claim of exceptionality that draws on Black women's bodies and minds to defend a flawed social order" (Beauboeuf-Lafontant 2009, 42–43). The "strength" motif, while seeming to honor Tubman's insurrection, albeit on solo terms, can do more than erase the coalition politics and strategies she both forged and worked within: it can also function to safeguard the supremacy and exploitation that Tubman, in concert with others, rose up against.

Fragmenting Tubman

Focusing on parts of Tubman's life in isolation distracts from a wider historical view of her contributions and thwarts more nuanced understandings of communities of struggle. For example, she is often remembered solely in reference to her childhood in slavery and her contributions to the Underground Railroad (however, the fact that she was, in the logics of the state, a criminal because of those labors is not commonly referenced and is generally ignored).[2] Celebrated for escaping slavery, her relevance seems, paradoxically, artificially confined to that era. What does it mean to, effectively, restrict Tubman to a system and to a period she did not see as defining her person, as determining her life's course, or as the be-all and end-all of her life's contributions?

Even immediately proximate historical periods, including her Civil War participation, are under-recognized, meaning her work as a healer schooled in herbal medicine, who went to the Sea Islands to cure dysentery;

and her role as a savvy military strategist, including her brilliant leadership in the Combahee River campaign, which freed more than 750 enslaved people, are less well known. Furthermore, her decades of engaging in activist organizing thereafter are generally ignored altogether. Tubman's work in alliance with the Black women's club movement and her labors for women's suffrage are under-acknowledged, as is her advocacy against economic exploitation on multiple fronts, a vision that shaped her work around poverty, housing, schooling, and aging. Her unflagging efforts as a fundraiser and community organizer are generally overlooked; likewise, her political practice of solidarity is under-theorized.

Even more rare are discussions of Tubman as a knower, though Angela Davis (1983), Tiya Miles[3], and Ann Petry[4] are among those who take up this question in part. Tubman's epistemic role as storyteller and performer, wherein she used narrative to reach toward a changed future and participated in creating a Black feminist public sphere, is rarely examined. Importantly, Jean Humez considers the educational and rhetorical strategies Tubman used in her public speeches and storytelling, such as her rhetorical use of metaphor and parable and her performative use of emotion, dramatic climax, and song (Humez 2003, 133–39).

Similarly infrequent are analyses of how Tubman sought to intervene in public memory, shaping others' perceptions regarding her own life and legacy, within the means available to her. Just as Sojourner Truth carefully composed her photographic portraits so as to counter prejudiced perceptions of her as unlettered and crude (see Painter's discussion of Sojourner Truth in this regard [Painter 1997, 151–280]), we should consider more fully the different ways in which Tubman composed and performed her stories, dictated her correspondence, and asked others to tell her story and also revise or reissue it. In addition, Tubman regularly negotiated historical memory in other ways, by insisting, for instance, that other political rebels not be forgotten—for example, by naming the home she founded in Auburn for the elderly, orphaned, and poor after John Brown.

Remembering Tubman piecemeal, we relinquish multifaceted understandings of her work and of resistance politics more broadly. Her varied forms of action across time and place, and her ability to fight the state and work within it, and to work across and within the bounds of race and gender politics, slip away. Tubman must be approached as an agent of history who fought for dignity and rights in part by crafting a public self—a shifting, multifaceted self, working in coalition with others. Notably, in a blog space dedicated to Tubman and to Black women in diaspora, Cheryl Clarke invokes this aspect of Tubman by underscoring that "Itinerancy is a cardinal characteristic of black feminists. . . . We don't settle emotionally, physically, intellectually, or politically. . . . We are constantly in motion" (Clarke 2008).

With this legacy of itinerancy in mind, we also need to recognize more fully that the Underground Railroad was an international endeavor, as Dann Broyld's discussion of female fugitives and Ontario/British Canada suggests (*Meridians* vol. 12, no. 2). Tubman was not held by national boundaries, and thinking about her methods and geographical maneuverings should not be constrained by the bounds of nation either. Tubman's and others' strategic uses of the U.S./Canadian border means that a transnational analytic lens is vital for understanding the Underground Railroad and for thinking through the history of cross-racial and cross-border solidarities.

In short, fragmenting Tubman's activism and life is a violation: it draws attention away from the varied issues she addressed and the differing tactics she used in so doing. Lionizing her contributions to the Underground Railroad and even to the Civil War can have an unexpected effect: significant lessons we might draw about the intricate, shifting nature of struggle over time slip away. Instead, we must remember her lifetime of differently courageous acts of working in solidarity with others on multiple fronts. Tracing Tubman's ideas about personhood, freedom, solidarity, and change is important, as is reflection about how her organizing and political strategies shifted due to changing historical circumstances, geographical locations, and varied local political networks of resistance.

Reshaping Tubman: From Militant Outlaw to Maternal Savior

In addition to celebratory (but distorting) rhetorics of the heroic, or truncated (and fragmenting) historical lenses, Tubman's radical acts are often made "safer" in other ways, particularly by means of two interwoven narrative frames: rhetorics of redemption and veneration by means of the maternal. Evidence of Tubman as an "inspirational and edifying" (Humez 2003, 121) figure is certainly apparent, for instance, in curricular approaches to her. Since she appears far more widely in children's literature and in elementary school curricula than in high school or college coursework, Catherine Clinton asserts Tubman has been turned into a nurturing figure, "maternalized . . . as one of the most popular heroines of the elementary school set" (Clinton 2004). A cursory glance at primary, secondary, and college curricula supports Clinton's general claim: indeed, Tubman is regularly taught (in rather constrained ways) in K–6 curricula, but slowly disappears from the majority of course content thereafter, other than in specialized (and often special-topics, rather than general or core) courses.

In the contexts of U.S. nationalism, "taming" Tubman's militancy usually occurs via a salvific lens (often tacitly relying on the controlling image of the Mammy, forming part of the particular raced-gendered logics connecting the maternal and the salvific when it comes to the history of Black women in the U.S.). In this vein, Tubman's lifetime of insurgency is made over into a life defined by selflessness and caregiving. Often, her motives for her life's work (whether on the Underground Railroad or, much later, in founding the John Brown Home in Auburn, New York) are attributed above all to her dedication to family—that is, her own relatives as well as the wider family of the Black community.

For instance, Humez describes how, early on, "Tubman had seized the opportunity to do dangerous work to emancipate her family and establish them in the North." Humez then describes how, later in life, in Auburn, New York, Tubman "found a new partner, made a living for herself and her dependents, and made herself available to help a large extended family whenever they needed her. She also raised funds to help support the displaced and impoverished and brought to fruition the ambitious John Brown Hall project—charitable work that clearly had roots in family feeling" (Humez 2003, 118–20). As Humez's comments suggest, Tubman is consistently portrayed as acting primarily on behalf of family values. Given the pathologizing discourse about Black families (historically and presently), this rhetorical frame can be seen, on the one hand, as strategic: it contravenes racist logics. However, as with the pitfalls associated with strict adherence to a politics of respectability when it comes to refuting and refusing dehumanizing representations of Black womanhood, the costs of portraying Tubman's motives as primarily induced by family values need to be considered.

Family values analytics are used to fold Tubman into the nation's embrace as well, for Tubman is also seen as having nurtured and rescued the family of the nation at large. Joy James discusses how "outlaw" women like Tubman have usually only survived in historical memory via this kind of interpretive twist: they are "accepted into an American society that claims their resistance by incorporating or 'forgiving' their past revolutionary tactics [by recasting them as] humanitarian goals. Tubman's antebellum criminalized resistance to slavery . . . typifies a rebellion that later became legitimized through American reclamation acts" (James 1999, 232). In this vein, Tubman's "outlaw" legacy has been recuperated and idealized by both White and Black audiences alike. For instance, in 1914, when dedicating a bronze memorial tablet for Tubman in Auburn, New York, Booker T. Washington celebrated her "law-abiding" nature and asserted that her "devotion to duty" was exemplary of "the best types of our race," in contrast to "the criminal Negro" Washington made a point to disparage (Washington, in Humez 2003, 122).

However, such rhetorics insist that we remember Tubman by forgetting her. To accept Washington's assertions, for instance, we must overlook that Tubman *broke the law* and was *not devoted to duty*, at least not to the duties laid out for her by the status quo: she refused to be servile to the duties of enslavement (or to her first marriage, if it meant staying within slavery), or to bow before the law of the land. Rhetorics of forgiveness and enfolding also direct attention away from ongoing contradictions between these "family" rhetorics of nationhood and issues of asymmetrical life opportunities, endemic criminalization, increased militarization, and omnipresent violence. James contends that "the nation's racial progressivism seeks to reclaim black women who bore arms to defend themselves and other African Americans and females against racial-sexual violence in a culture that continues to condemn black physical resistance to political dominance and violence while it supports . . . the use of weapons in the defense or expansion of the nation-state, individual and family, home, and private property" (James 1999, 232).

Tubman's historical "makeover" transforms her radical vision and resistant (and at times illegal) actions into benign symbols of progress and family values: this interpretive shift aligns her organized resistance to fit with narratives of the nation's deliverance from its past sins and to render a tender family portrait of the United States. The salvific also reinforces problematic ideas about the state as an otherwise perfect system—with its central tragic flaw, slavery, and its tragically flawed central characters, White citizens—healed, thanks to Tubman. It is imperative to consider how such "deliverance" models draw attention away from the tenacious nature of the oppressions Tubman fought against in her lifetime and how they persist to this day in new forms (that is, we as a nation are still not "delivered" from them).

The invocation of the maternal *within* Black feminist histories, as in the moniker "Mother Tubman" used at the 1896 inaugural convention of the National Association of Colored Women (NACW), for example, is quite complex. Both Rosalyn Terborg-Penn and Gayle Tate identify a nationalist feminist impetus in the history of Black feminism, particularly in the club movement (Tate 1995; Terborg-Penn 1998). We must consider whether a Black feminist nationalism may also have played a part in generating softened perceptions of figures like Tubman, turning historical memory away from militancy toward respectable, representative Black womanhood. Public recognition and celebration of "Mother Tubman" at the 1896 NACW convention could be seen, from this angle, as aligning Tubman with an uplift model of Black womanhood (rather than an armed resistance model, for example). In other words, the NACW audience's celebration of Tubman, cheering her speech and applauding her contributions, prompts consideration of how the title "Mother Tubman" may signify a reverent yet possibly maternalizing reshaping of Tubman's image or legacy to support a politics of respectability.

At the same time, if we recall Angela Davis's analysis of how, in slavery, many Black women formed and led "household[s] of resistance" (Davis 1972, 90), and use that lens to examine the 1896 NACW convention, then the application of the title "Mother" for Tubman can, alternatively, be interpreted as celebrating and supporting a wholly different impetus, that of fostering insurgent households. From this standpoint we could view Black feminist counter-memory at work: the "Mother" in "Mother Tubman" may have functioned to recall this radical legacy, operating as a form of rhetorical dissemblance, as much as it may have signaled a nationalist impetus and historical makeover.

Whether in U.S. nationalist contexts, or in Black feminist contexts, it is imperative that we remember that although the salvific may pull at the heartstrings with its vision of healing progress, it may also, and simultaneously, distract us from its more deceptive or distorting qualities. Though different on the surface, redemptive portraits that use Tubman and her legacy to persuade us to take up nationalist frameworks (often by denying or erasing her radicalness) are not all that conceptually different from examples of outright cooptation of Tubman in service of the state's interests, even its carceral logics. For instance, naming a juvenile prison facility for girls the "Tubman Residential Facility" (at the New York State prison in Auburn, New York—not far from Tubman's own home), or calling a series of New Deal public housing complexes the "Tubman Homes" or "Tubman Terraces," implies these newer forms of containment, alongside escalating incarceration and criminalization, are fitting tributes to her memory, rather than flagrant violations of it. Instead of naming prisons after Tubman, a more fitting tribute would be to take up the call for prison abolition (Davis 2003).

Conclusion: Tubman and Women's Studies

These wider rhetorical contexts, where Tubman is celebrated yet made safe, recognized but flattened, have affected how she is (and, in all honesty, is not) meaningfully examined in women's studies, where she is both under-taught and under-theorized. A survey of syllabi quickly reveals her absence other than in topical courses focused on Black women's history or in other specialized curricula, as in the coursework once offered at the Tubman juvenile facility in Auburn.[5] In asserting Tubman's relevance to women's studies, I do not mean in a token or "cosmetic" (Alarcón 1990, 357) way, such that Tubman would just be "added and stirred" into a research project or a course. Rather, the question is one of asking how women's studies lenses might change if we start from what we know (and don't) of Tubman's long life.

Moreover, it is imperative to note that, if one's feminist frameworks already *begin from within* women of color feminist theorizing, Tubman's organic place in the field is in many ways readily apparent. For instance, Tubman's life of advocacy and change-making can be illuminated by drawing on Barbara Christian's emphasis on kinetic action and change. Christian focuses on theorizing as a verb, rather than as a noun (as an inert thing, as property or commodity); furthermore, she values ways of thinking and writing that are difficult to control or map out in conventional terms (Christian 1990, 336, 341). Gloria Anzaldúa's call to combat the psychological toll of oppression, both in terms of individual and collective consciousness, is likewise relevant when thinking about Tubman, as is her discussion of the hidden distortions embedded in the politics of address and interpretation (Anzaldúa 1990, xvii–xxvii).

Equally relevant are Alice Walker's (1983) and Toni Morrison's (1995) insights that marginalized communities frequently have no archive, meaning we must both read history skeptically and craft new archives of memory, often via the creative imagination (in this case, fiction) (Walker 1983; Morrison 1995). If available materials and records fall short, what have Black feminist and other radical artists imagined or conjured with regard to Tubman? Walker, Morrison, Christian, Anzaldúa, and others have taught us well that the creative and the critical, the artistic and the political, and the dreamscape and the historical are interwoven and do not adhere to the false dichotomies of Western epistemes.

Finally, María Lugones's work, beckoning us to develop the skills to recognize resistance in myriad and often coded forms (Lugones 2005; 2011), is equally imperative, for she reminds us that although figures like Tubman will be continually misread, it is nevertheless possible to read them against the grain of normative and co-opting interpretations. In fact, Lugones argues, we must do so since oppression is rarely 100 percent successful or fully determining—meaning resistance, and resistant figures, exist alongside and against oppression. Discussing Anzaldúa, with regard to the question of "borderland" dwellers and agency, Lugones writes: "Even though every move she makes will have a status quo interpretation that reads her as an alien, an outlaw, reduced, her meaning co-opted in the direction of servility or incompetence, those interpretations do not hold her captive" (Lugones 2005, 90). The same could be said for Tubman. In short, as these few examples should begin to illustrate, to draw on Tubman's contributions more substantively would require women's studies scholars to meaningfully shape and derive the field's key questions, core themes, and analytic methods from *within* women of color histories, theories, politics, and analyses from the start.

Thinking about Tubman more adequately also requires confronting how historical knowledge about her is highly mediated (in that her activist work and her words, from her life story to her correspondence, are preserved in "as told to" accounts, for instance). Certainly, contemporary feminists working within various theoretical approaches, whether in standpoint or postmodern traditions, underscore the value of recognizing how knowledge is filtered and knowers are situated. Yet such philosophical excitement seems missing when it comes to thinking about Tubman, whose life is so *overtly* mediated. Indeed, many of her words are left to us in dialect, weighed down by White writers' ideas about "authentic" Black vernacular speech. Sarah Bradford's biography of Tubman is laden with biased perceptions and troubling stereotypes from the period, for example. Despite her political sympathies and what could be seen as an open-minded, even politicized consciousness, Bradford's race and class standing muddle her portraits of Tubman and muddy her syntax, and contemporary readers are left to wade through the rhetorical and historical muck.

Yet these questions of Tubman's historical obfuscation and linguistic caricature, even by supportive allies, can illuminate a range of debates around the knowledge/power nexus, the politics of transparency, and norms of objectivity. These issues are often claimed as pivotal or core questions for the field of women's studies (and are usually debates considered as "recent," even as individuals like Tubman had to negotiate them long ago). For instance, although it is a valuable teaching tool, Peggy McIntosh's discussion of White privilege does not have to be the sole source turned to in order to illustrate this concept (McIntosh 2001). Furthermore, current philosophical questions of epistemic distortion and violence (Dotson 2011), testimonial injustice (Fricker 2007), and the authorization/ dis-authorization of marginalized knowers are all relevant to examining Tubman's life's work and to assessing the interpretive frames (and obstacles) surrounding her life story. Indeed, Tubman could easily have a central place in analyses of the impact of past biases on current knowledge practices, illuminating how "hegemonic imaginaries" (Code 2006) can become "settled" mindsets (Campbell 1999) that live on.

Tubman is also pertinent for those interested in unearthing and understanding social-change organizing, as women's studies certainly is (in fact, a social justice orientation is often claimed as central to the field). Beyond developing more nuanced histories of activism, examining Tubman's organizing strategies also provides opportunities for considering the obstacles to so doing: studying "underground" resistance movements may well require different methods and strategies. Nuanced resistance networks and covert communication strategies on the Underground Railroad, for instance, were, of necessity, shrouded in secrecy: these grids of communication, alternative maps, and forms of intra- and interracial collaboration (and also international coalitions) had to remain imperceptible to White (and state) surveillance. Furthermore, such systems of insurrection were not only secretive but were also consigned to the private realm, and thus ironically under-recognized as political action, as Frederick Douglass underscored in his August 29, 1868, letter to Tubman.

Highlighting connections between them, in terms of vision, he emphasized gendered differences that must be noted when comparing their public visibility. Douglass related this asymmetry in part to a public/private dichotomy that delegitimizes Tubman's contributions even as it functions to celebrate his work. Douglass also raised the issue of poverty as another factor, suggesting that because Tubman had consistently attended to those with the least access to power or money, as bondspeople, her public image had become, ironically, more diminished than had his own. Douglass wrote:

> The difference between us is very marked. Most that I have done and suffered in the service of our cause has been in public, and I have received much encouragement at every step of the way. You, on the other hand, have labored in a private way. I have wrought in the day—you in the night. I have had the applause of the crowd and the satisfaction that comes of being approved by the multitude, while the most that you have done has been witnessed by a few trembling, scarred, and foot-sore bondmen and women, whom you have led out of the house of bondage. (Douglass, in Bradford 1869, 7)

Here again several fruitful issues emerge for women's studies, including questions about how public/private dichotomies *differently* impact perception and documentation of people's lives and historical roles,[6] as well as the issue not merely of biased or incomplete archives, but absent ones, at least in the conventional sense, when dealing with resistance movements. Moreover, what is interesting in thinking about Douglass and Tubman together is that, on the one hand, his women's rights advocacy has been generally forgotten, just as, on the other hand, her women's rights allegiances and suffrage advocacy have been overlooked or downplayed (Guy-Sheftall 2013). If we are to rethink the archive, look anew at evidence of resistance, and reimagine what historical agency looks like, we must acknowledge that the *missing* Harriet Tubman stories, and the lesser-told ones, are as relevant to deepening our understanding as reading the extant archive against the grain.

To conclude, I have begun to sketch out some additional ways that Tubman "fits" *and* changes the boundaries of common feminist analytics: this list, below, is intended to be evocative of what a more adequate approach to Tubman could entail, to provoke us, collectively, to think of more ways Tubman's life contributions can be understood as pertinent to contemporary debates and issues. To start this conversation, I contend that thinking critically about Tubman is relevant to:

1. Contemplating what it means, in everyday life, to forge resistant selves and to develop (and help others to foster) oppositional consciousness within or despite wider contexts of constraint and systemic oppression;

2. Rethinking the parameters of feminist "theorizing" and reassessing who (and who is not) considered a knower and what genres or forms of knowledge "count" as theoretical work;

3. Reconsidering where history lies, and understanding how radical legacies have been crafted in alternative spaces (for example, in oral, literary, or other artistic realms, rather than in traditional archives) and how these legacies have, at the same time, also been suppressed, or, if not totally ignored, rendered safer and more acceptable;

4. Examining solidarity politics and coalitional practices in a sustained way—delineating their histories and varied forms and tracing the use of diverse strategies to combat oppression on multiple fronts;

5. Reframing what "counts" as activism and who "counts" (and how) as a historical agent;

6. Questioning distortions at work in seemingly positive interpretive lenses, including notions of the iconic, the salvific, and the maternal;

7. Historicizing the politics of embodiment and considering how multiple systems of oppression affect the lived body (for example, for Tubman, the interdependence of race, gender, geography, disability, and "illegal" or outlaw status all come to mind);

8. Examining how marginalized knowers navigate unequal cognitive authority and maneuver within structural domination to get their ideas across and their lives documented;

9. Considering how knowledge is mediated and how knowers are situated within and across asymmetries of power;

10. Recognizing that working with or within the state is not always equivalent to accepting its logics—such labors can stem from outrage and transformation efforts since agitation must take place on multiple fronts;

11. Understanding that some of the key issues raised by feminists engaged in contemporary "borderlands" thinking and politics, as articulated by Anzaldúa, for instance, have had earlier iterations, in different contexts (for example, Tubman's movement between slave-

state/non-slave state, U.S./Canada, and so on). This means not only
that questions of border politics (and the criminalization of migra-
tion/immigration) can be connected to earlier periods, but so can
several related concepts (for example, epistemologies of crossing,
cross-border coalitions, and living with/forging identities across the
violent separations inherent to border formations);

12. Examining Tubman's efforts against institutionalized poverty as a
persistent legacy of slavery underscores that poverty agendas and
capitalist exploitation should be central to women's studies; and

13. Questioning what activities and which groups of people are criminalized requires: breaking from carceral logics, working collectively to
decriminalize poverty or immigrant status, and thinking more fully
about prison abolition—both in terms of why it's necessary to a multidimensional liberation politics and how to achieve it.

....

Vivian M. May is director of the Humanities Center and professor of women's and
gender studies at Syracuse University, where she also leads the Central New York
Humanities Corridor, an eleven-institution consortium supported by an award from
the Andrew W. Mellon Foundation. May has published over three dozen articles and
chapters in Black feminist thought, feminist philosophy, and African American literary studies. She is author of *Anna Julia Cooper, Visionary Black Feminist* (2007), which
documents Cooper's groundbreaking contributions to a Black feminist public
sphere, and *Pursuing Intersectionality, Unsettling Dominant Imaginaries* (2015), which
calls for meaningful engagement with intersectionality's radical ideas, histories, and
justice orientations.

Notes

Originally published in *Meridians* vol. 12, no. 2, 2014.
I would like to thank Janell Hobson, Paula Giddings, and the *Meridians* anonymous reviewers for their insight and feedback.

1   A pivotal figure in Black liberation and communist organizing, Jones had a
major impact, as a journalist and activist, on anticolonial, antiracist, feminist,
and workers' justice movements in the Caribbean, the United States, and the
United Kingdom. Arrested during the McCarthy era, sentenced to federal
prison, and later deported, she moved to England, where she was offered residency on humanitarian grounds (Davies 2008).

2   As I discuss later, accounts of Tubman's Underground Railroad work generally
avoid reference to, much less examination of, the fact that her actions were
criminalized, such that today she would likely be characterized as a terrorist
threat to national security. Her "outlaw" status during this period is usually
downplayed or muffled in our current "law and order" cultural moment.

3   Miles offers an astute reading of Tubman in this regard. She asserts, "when Tubman is living in Philadelphia, where she works to try to earn money to fund her rescue missions, a group of people invite her to come see a stage production of *Uncle Tom's Cabin*. She says that she will not go, she has no need to go, because *Uncle Tom's Cabin* can in no way capture the reality of the experience of slavery, which she herself already knows. So this is a form of cultural criticism. She is saying that as popular as this novel was, . . . that as a former slave . . . she had a more accurate version of slavery than Harriet Beecher Stowe" (Miles [2012]).

4   Petry wrote a biography of Tubman as an alternative to high school curricula and textbooks, which she found wholly unsatisfactory. Petry underscores how the young Tubman was schooled in various forms of knowledge and also schooled in resistance on the plantation: she presents not only Tubman as a knower but also the wider community of enslaved people as knowers. For example, she discusses how Tubman learned to read the weather, to study plants and herbal medicines, to scan the sky for the North Star, and to appear compliant, as necessary, for self-protection (Petry 1955/1983, 20–22).

5   Information on the Tubman residential facility at the New York State prison in Auburn, New York (closed in 2011 due to state budget cuts), including the women's studies curriculum, can be found at http://www.ojjdp.gov/pubs/principles/pro7.html (accessed June 2, 2014).

6   For instance, here, the public/private dichotomy, though gendered, is gendered in a particular way with regard to Tubman. Rather than consigned to invisibility for being at/in the home, as the argument usually goes with regard to how "women" are erased from history and political memory via consignment to the home (thereby homogenizing and treating as isolatable the gendered category, women, *and* homogenizing the domestic space, the home, without regard to asymmetries of power among and between women), the dichotomy works here to erase Tubman for her work in *leaving* or *escaping* from "home."

Works Cited

Alarcón, Norma. 1990. "The Theoretical Subject(s) of *This Bridge Called My Back* and Anglo-American Feminism." In *Making Face, Making Soul/Haciendo Caras: Creative and Critical Perspectives by Feminists of Color*, edited by Gloria E. Anzaldúa. San Francisco: Aunt Lute.

Anzaldúa, Gloria E. 1990. "Haciendo Caras, Una Entrada." In *Making Face, Making Soul/Haciendo Caras: Creative and Critical Perspectives by Feminists of Color*, edited by Gloria E. Anzaldúa. San Francisco: Aunt Lute.

Beauboeuf-Lafontant, Tamara. 2009. *Behind the Mask of the Strong Black Woman: Voice and the Embodiment of a Costly Performance*. Philadelphia: Temple University Press.

Bradford, Sarah. 1869. *Scenes in the Life of Harriet Tubman*. Auburn, NY: W.J. Moses.

Broyld, Dann J. 2013. " 'We Prefer to Live in the Land of a Queen': Harriet Tubman, Female Fugitives, and their Quest for British Canada in the Late Antebellum." *Harriet Tubman: A Legacy of Resistance* (symposium). March 8–9. Albany, NY.

Camp, Stephanie M. H. 2004. *Closer to Freedom: Enslaved Women and Everyday Resistance in the Plantation South*. Chapel Hill: University of North Carolina Press.

Campbell, Sue. 1999. "Dominant Identities and Settled Expectations." In *Racism and Philosophy*, edited by Susan E. Babbitt and Sue Campbell. Ithaca, NY: Cornell University Press.

Christian, Barbara. 1990. "The Race for Theory." In *Making Face, Making Soul/Haciendo Caras: Creative and Critical Perspectives by Feminists of Color*, edited by Gloria E. Anzaldúa. San Francisco: Aunt Lute.

Clarke, Cheryl. 2008. "Why Harriet Tubman Project." http://www.blogster.com /cherylclarke/why-harriet-tubman-project-black-feminist-blog-041008102104 (accessed June 2, 2014).

Clinton, Catherine. 2004. "Epilogue: Harriet Tubman's Legacy." In *Harriet Tubman: The Road to Freedom*. New York: Little Brown/Hachette.

Code, Lorraine. 2006 "Negotiating Empiricism." In *Ecological Thinking: The Politics of Epistemic Location*. New York: Oxford.

Collins, Patricia Hill. 1998. *Fighting Words: Black Women and the Search for Justice*. Minneapolis: University of Minnesota Press.

Davies, Carole Boyce. 2008. *Left of Karl Marx: The Political Life of Black Communist Claudia Jones*. Durham, NC: Duke University Press.

Davis, Angela Y. 1972. "Reflections on the Black Woman's Role in the Community of Slaves." *The Massachusetts Review* 13, no. 1–2: 81–100.

———. 1983. *Women, Race, and Class*. New York: Vintage.

———. 2003. *Are Prisons Obsolete?* New York: Seven Stories Press.

Dotson, Kristie. 2011. "Tracking Epistemic Violence, Tracking Practices of Silencing." *Hypatia* 26, no. 2: 236–57.

Ellison, Mary. 1983. "Resistance to Oppression: Black Women's Response to Slavery in the United States." *Slavery & Abolition* 4, no. 1: 56–63.

Fricker, Miranda. 2007. *Epistemic Injustice: Power and the Ethics of Knowing*. New York: Oxford.

Guy-Sheftall, Beverly. 2013. Commentary. Harriet Tubman: A Legacy of Resistance (symposium). March 8–9. Albany, NY.

Harris, Duchess. 1999. "'All of Who I Am in the Same Place': The Combahee River Collective." *Womanist Theory and Research* 2, no. 1: 1–26.

Hine, Darlene Clark. 1993. "'In the Kingdom of Culture': Black Women and the Intersection of Race, Gender, and Class." In *Lure and Loathing: Essays on Race, Identity, and the Ambivalence of Assimilation*, edited by Gerald Early. New York: Penguin.

Humez, Jean M. 2003. *Harriet Tubman: The Life and the Life Stories*. Madison: University of Wisconsin Press.

James, Joy. 1999. *Shadowboxing: Representations of Black Feminist Politics*. New York: St. Martin's Press.

Lugones, María. 2005. "From within Germinative Stasis: Creating Active Subjectivity, Resistant Agency." In *Entremundos/Among Worlds: New Perspectives on Gloria Anzaldúa*, edited by Analouise Keating. New York: Palgrave.

———. 2011. "Toward a Decolonial Feminism." *Hypatia* 25, no. 4: 742–59.

May, Vivian M. 2007. *Anna Julia Cooper, Visionary Black Feminist: A Critical Introduction*. New York: Routledge.

McIntosh, Peggy. 2001. "White Privilege and Male Privilege: A Personal Account of Coming to See Correspondences through Work in Women's Studies." In *Race, Class, and Gender: An Anthology*. 4th ed., edited by Margaret L. Anderson and Patricia Hill Collins. Belmont, CA: Wadsworth.

Miles, Tiya. [2012]. Transcript of video interview with Miles about Sarah Bradford's 1869 biography of Tubman, *Scenes in the Life of Harriet Tubman.* http:/ /teachinghistory.org/best-practices/examples-of-historical-thinking/25379 (accessed June 2, 2014).

Morrison, Toni. 1995. "The Site of Memory." In *Inventing the Truth: The Art and Craft of Memoir*, edited by William Zinsser. Boston: Houghton Mifflin.

Painter, Nell Irvin. 1990. "Sojourner Truth in Life and Memory: Writing the Biography of an American Exotic." *Gender & History* 2, no. 1: 1–14.

———. 1997. *Sojourner Truth: A Life, A Symbol*. New York: W.W. Norton.

Petry, Ann. 1955/1983. *Harriet Tubman: Conductor on the Underground Railroad*. New York: Harper Collins.

Tate, Gayle T. 1995. "Black Nationalism." In *Black Women in America*. 2d ed., edited by Darlene Clark Hine. New York and Oxford: Oxford University Press.

Taylor, Ula Y. 2010. "Black Feminisms and Human Agency." In *No Permanent Waves: Recasting Histories of U.S. Feminism*, edited by Nancy A. Hewitt. Piscataway, NJ: Rutgers University Press.

Terborg-Penn, Rosalyn. 1998. *African-American Women in the Struggle for the Vote, 1850–1920*. Bloomington: Indiana University Press.

Walker, Alice. 1983. "Saving the Life that Is Your Own: The Importance of Models in the Artist's Life." In *In Search of Our Mother's Gardens*. New York: Harcourt Brace.

Wallace, Michelle. 1990. "Variations on Negation and the Heresy of Black Feminist Creativity." In *Reading Black, Reading Feminist: A Critical Anthology*, edited by Henry Louis Gates, Jr. New York: Meridian.

———. 2004. *Dark Designs and Visual Culture*. Durham, NC: Duke University Press.

Basuli Deb

....

Cutting across Imperial Feminisms toward Transnational Feminist Solidarities

Abstract: Photography, not only by imperial men but also by imperial women, has played a significant role in portraying the Muslim woman as the apolitical exotic of orientalist fantasies, its legacies haunting the media of the global North even today. Imperial feminist representations about Muslim women have also marked the rhetoric of Hillary Clinton, Laura Bush, Cherie Booth, and Condoleezza Rice. In contrast, this article draws on various photographic counter-narratives, among them "the girl in the blue bra," that transnational feminists circulated through social media during the 2011 people's uprising in Egypt as well as on the iconic pan-Arab feminist leader Huda Shaarawi to evoke powerful images of Muslim women. Finally, the essay turns to transnational feminists such as Angela Davis, Trinh T. Minh-ha, Cynthia Enloe, Miriam Cooke, and Zillah Eisenstein for cross-border feminist work that cuts across imperial feminist practices.

In June 1985 the cover of the *National Geographic* featured the photograph of "The Afghan Girl." Her head and torso were wrapped in a red *chaadar* (long scarf), a traditional symbol of modesty in South Asian women's attire. Her piercing green eyes were complemented by the green background and the green of her dress that peeked from underneath the tatters of her red shawl. The caption read: "Haunted eyes tell of an Afghan refugee's fears."

As her nameless face stared at the reader, this girl from a refugee camp near Peshawar in Pakistan became iconic of the Afghan people's helplessness under the Soviet occupation (1979–1989). Captured by American photojournalist Steve McCurry (McCurry 1985), this photograph would be

MERIDIANS · feminism, race, transnationalism   Volume 19 Supplement 2020
DOI: 10.1215/15366936-8566111 © 2016 Smith College

widely used by Amnesty International, calendars, brochures, and posters, and would become one of *National Geographic's* most recognized photographs. However, "the First World's Third World *Mona Lisa*" would remain unidentified for the next seventeen years (Hesford and Kozol 2005, 1). In 2001, when the war in Afghanistan had the world's attention, McCurry returned to trace her again and identified her as Sharbat Gula. She was around thirty, and this time, on its April 2002 cover, the *National Geographic* featured her in a violet *burqa*, the traditional attire worn by Muslim women that covers the body from head to toe (McCurry 2002). The piercing green eyes were covered by the densely netted eye covering of the *burqa*, and her *burqa* clad hand held the famous 1985 photograph of "The Afghan Girl." The big, bold caption underneath in red screamed, "Found." Beneath it in smaller white the cover declared, "After 17 Years An Afghan Refugee's Story." The silent, apolitical, exotic Muslim woman, the "victim" of Cold War rivalry, of both Soviet and US occupation, for seventeen years stood by and stared at it all—first with her open piercing gaze as a girl and later from behind the veil. She is indeed the radical *other* of the American nationalist imaginary, in fact, of the Euro-American colonial imaginary.

However, Sharbat Gula is not a new phenomenon. As the cultural arm of imperialism, the first-world media has circulated the images of many Sharbat Gulas, most of whom have remained nameless icons of orientalist fantasies. The legacy of European colonial photography vis-à-vis the Muslim woman indeed haunts the media of the global North today.[1] This article refuses to forget the violent legacy of gendering that the past left behind, not only by the empire's men but also by imperial women, that conditions Islamophobic representations of the *other* today, benefiting imperial women immensely at the cost of women of the *elsewhere*. Nonetheless, this article probes for possibilities of transnational feminist alliances between women of the global North and South that continue to be forged in the present as they recognize the political subjectivity of Muslim women. Such traces can be gleaned from the archives of history, no matter how fraught those alliances are.

Images from the Colonial Harem

With its discovery in 1827 and its subsequent popularity from the 1870s onward, photography became an important part of colonial technology in the nineteenth and twentieth centuries. Malek Alloula's study of the colonial fantasy around the Algerian woman in picture postcards sent home by the French in the first three decades of the twentieth century has become iconic of such pictorial orientalism. The obsession of the colonial gaze with penetrating the veiled native women in their inaccessible harems finds closure in its access to bare-breasted, poor, native models and their enactment of exotic rituals in costumes provided by the photographer in exchange for money (Alloula 1986, xiv). The sexual excesses of the harem in the occidental imagination are constituted through the orchestrated performances of "oriental sapphism" in the harems, glaringly captured in the homoerotic image of two young Moorish women with floral headgear, beaded necklaces, and bangles; their torsos are bare, and they are dressed in native costumes that hang from their waists (103). Their heads conjoined in performed intimacy, the women raise their arms to lift their very differently shaped breasts. As one woman drapes her arm around the waist of her companion to touch her right breast while her breast touches the left breast of her companion, it is French colonial pornography of the harem at its voyeuristic best. The colonial photographer's ability to lay bare the body of the women of the elsewhere also marks the orientalist fantasy of British colonialism. Poor women of British Egypt and French North Africa breastfeeding their children in public became a favorite of imperial photographers (Graham-Brown 1988, 106). In fact, these images are rife with a play on exposure and concealment, as in the image of the Egyptian mother, her entire body covered in a burqa except for a succulent breast. A two-year-old holds the nipple close to its mouth, making the image all the more exotic because of the practice of breastfeeding children until age two (107). Then there is the 1896 image of naked Egyptian children and their mothers clothed in rags in "Degenerate Egypt," distributed widely in the US and Europe, justifying British colonial presence as messianic to the Egyptians since their economic poverty is rooted in their "degenerate" morality and culture (108).

The violence of the colonial gaze is especially striking in the image of the Egyptian woman with sorrowful eyes peeking from underneath her burqa that covers her cleavage but exposes her breasts. The stark contrast between the rest of her covered body and her bare breasts hyper-eroticizes this image of the raided body (136). A war trophy, the Arab woman becomes a study in impotence before the colonial gaze.

Imperial Women Photographers, the Burqa, and the Mythical Other

Photography, not only by imperial men but also by imperial women, has played a significant role in portraying the Arab woman as the apolitical exotic of orientalist fantasies. The legacy of colonial photography in the Middle East by European women travelers has contributed to a colonial visual culture. Here the subtext of the image establishes an imperial feminist discourse through the striking contrast between the "liberated" mobile European woman behind the lens and her "less fortunate" Arab sisters behind the *burqa*. For instance, a 1937 photograph taken by the British explorer Freya Stark, who traveled widely in the Middle East and Afghanistan, captures the diminutive figure of a Kuwaiti woman in a black *burqa*, rendered even more minuscule against the high walls of the buildings and long shadows against them (Graham-Brown 1988, 76). Similarly, lesser-known British travelers like Marjorie Armstrong replicate the same fetish with the *burqa* and the camera angles, which are deliberately designed to diminish the women attired in them. Armstrong's 1932 image of five Iraqi women by a train station renders them into a conglomeration of black, the figures indistinguishable from one another; the woman sitting on the sand bypasses the perspective of the onlooker and becomes invisible and nonhuman because she looks like a black bundle similar to the ones lying nearby. These imperial women photographers and their images literally turn Arab women into still-life objects subjected to violent representation, to be archived as social history of the Arab people. In the absence of the voices of the natives speaking back, the imperial gaze undergirded by a secular humanist philosophy constructs a feminist epistemology about the *burqa* as the ultimate yardstick of women's oppression, with complete disregard for the intense structural violence that colonialism inflicts on these women. Lila Abu-Lughod has underlined that, despite the intensity of violence unleashed by secular humanism "over the last couple of centuries, from world wars to colonialism, from genocides to slavery," secular humanism has not come under fire (Abu-Lughod 2002, 788). The *burqa*, in fact, serves to legitimize colonial presence as imperial women generate a visual epistemology that screams of the empire's humanitarian need to *save* the Muslim woman from the Muslim man, as Gayatri Spivak famously articulated in the colonial triangulation of "white men saving brown women from brown men" (Spivak 1988, 297). For this the liberated sisters from Europe have to take on the *White woman's burden* of raising these newfound creatures of the empire—"half devil and half child" (Kipling 1899)—freeing them from the *burqa* to offer them a modicum of the independence of *adult* life through destruction of their people and cultures.

Similarly, Freya Stark's 1938 photograph of a young Yemeni girl in her native attire and jewelry evokes something, in Stark's own words, "'very ancient, very remote and very beautiful, which may pass for ever from our world'" (Graham-Brown 1988, 122). The Yemeni girl is then forever frozen as a fossilized piece of romanticized humanity in a mythical past far removed from the modernity of the British woman behind the camera. In this timeline Britain comes to signify a dynamic society that is forever progressing, whereas Yemen is eons behind. In this colonial ethnography there is no place for Yemeni women to talk back to the epistemological violence of the imperial archive, underlining the absurd assumptions about racial others that are foundational to the colonial project. Yemeni women cannot push Britain to access Yemen through a paradigm of *difference*, where, in an ideological overturning, they can intercept the colonial gaze to assert that the outfit that Stark wears appears equally exotic to them as markers of British subjectivity defined by British tradition. In fact, this kind of colonial anthropology is even more pronounced when imperial women photographers enter the frame of the photograph in an explicit encounter with the colonial subject. This is portrayed in the image of a European woman dressed in a white blouse, long black skirt, hat, and sunglasses, holding a camera in her left hand as she stares at the Egyptian woman in black head-covering and a long dress, filling a pitcher at the shallow end of a body of water. Trapped between the gaze of the colonial camera and that of the imperial woman in the photograph, the Egyptian woman becomes an object of patronizing surveillance (Graham-Brown 1988, 66). The insinuation is that because Egyptian women's lives are not like those of their British "sisters," Egypt does not have the right to be sovereign.

Power-Dressing Women, Discursive Continuities, and Neo-imperial America

Colonial discourses justifying European presence in Islamic countries in the name of the Muslim woman have been boldly reiterated in the twenty-first-century American colonial War on Terror. In an unprecedented media gimmick on November 17, 2001, Laura Bush took over the president's weekly radio speech to launch a transnational project against the violence inflicted on Afghan women and children espoused by al-Qaeda and the Taliban regime. She asserted: "Civilized people throughout the world are speaking out in horror—not only because our hearts break for the women and children in Afghanistan, but also because in Afghanistan we see the world the terrorists would like to impose on the rest of us." She reminded other nations of sharing in a "common humanity" that demands a global alliance with the US War on Terror: "The fight against terrorism is also a fight for the rights and dignity of women" (Bush 2001). In a similar gesture at Downing Street, Tony Blair's wife, Cherie Booth, brought a group of Afghan women refugees to meet with her and women cabinet ministers, and taking the podium ahead of the international development secretary, Clare Short, and the education secretary, Estelle Morris, declared: "We need to help them free that spirit and give them their voice back" (Ward 2001). Gargi Bhattacharya has pointed out certain theatrical gestures that came to justify domination:

> In the famous press conference that Cherie Booth and Laura Bush give together, Cherie Booth gives this terrible (hand motions indicating two cupped hands around the eyes). Her explanation of why we have to invade Afghanistan to save these women is done through this gesture, what I am calling the "Burqa eyes" gesture. (Bhattacharya 2007)

This joint appearance of Cherie Booth and Laura Bush at the 2003 press conference at the White House spells out the feminist alliance within a transatlantic Euro-American White empire where women, through heterosexual marriages to political decision-makers for the war, eke out their share of power. Liberating women from the *burqa* here becomes a battle cry in the name of a global sisterhood that simultaneously defines its sisters through gestures that render them as choiceless aliens without recognizing that *burqa*-clad women might have other notions of liberation, such as freedom not to be invaded and conquered by an alien people. When in 2005 Secretary of State Condoleezza Rice was asked about the new Iraqi constitution that could potentially deny the rights that Iraqi women had had during Saddam Hussein's time and where the US stood with regard to it, Rice dismissed the claim that there could have been any rights for any Iraqis before the US occupation (Lehrer 2005). Likewise, Secretary of State Hillary Clinton in her December 2011 announcement of the National Action Plan on Women, Peace, and Security at Georgetown University did not acknowledge the myriad sexual and gendered atrocities committed by the United States during the War on Terror in Iraq and Afghanistan. Instead, with typical imperial feminist benevolence, she stated, "The United States will help build the capacity of foreign militaries, police forces, and justice systems to strengthen the rule of law and ensure that protecting civilians and stopping sexual and gender-based violence in particular is a shared priority" (Clinton 2011). In the context of the Arab uprising across North Africa and the Middle East in 2010, the Egyptian military and political parties came under sharp criticism from Secretary Clinton for shutting out Egyptian women from decision-making by military authorities as well as by the major political parties. She underlined how women protesters had experienced humiliation and violence by both security forces and extremists:

> Marchers celebrating International Women's Day were harassed and abused. Women protesters have been rounded up and subjected to horrific abuse. Journalists have been sexually assaulted. And now, women are being attacked, stripped, and beaten in the streets. This systematic degradation of Egyptian women dishonors the revolution, disgraces the state and its uniform, and is not worthy of a great people. (Clinton 2011)

What is forgotten in the process is that disgracing of "the state and its uniform" is not a monopoly of the *elsewhere*. Abu Ghraib, Guantanamo, Bagram, and the many US secret prisons across the world disgrace the state and its uniform as well. The Association of Humanitarian Lawyers, in their report to the UN, revealed how Abu Ghraib women prisoners, among them pregnant women, were forced to strip and were raped by US guards (McNutt 2005, 1). This was confirmed by Major General Antonio Taguba, who headed the US military's inquiry commission. The report to the UN had pointed out that among the 1,800 digital images taken inside Abu Ghraib, many were of naked women detainees being sexually abused. The Taguba Report underlined that those images were shared with Congress, but the Bush administration refused to release them (McNutt 2005).

However, cutting across the feminism that stands at the service of imperialism—a global feminism symbolized by the Laura Bushes, Cherie Booths, Condoleezza Rices, and Hillary Clintons of our time—is a transnational feminism deeply cognizant of the urgent need to resist violence against women everywhere. At the same time, rather than using the rhetoric of gender violence as a ruse to forge alliances with "foreign militaries, police forces, and justice systems," as Hillary Clinton outlined (Clinton 2011), such cross-border feminisms focus on what kind of manifestos—public declarations of political principles, purposes, and programs by a collective—women in contexts of violence want to forge. Such alliances recognize that the representations of the personas of these women send out strong messages about their political subjectivities that counter the orientalist stereotypes of Muslim women as the silent, apolitical, exotic *other*.

Feminist Manifestos from Tahrir Square

It can be argued that transnational feminist alliances led to the circulation of such women's manifestos during the Arab uprising that began in 2010. These feminist manifestos were rather different from traditional manifestos that were political scripts written after systematic deliberations about political missions with distinct governing structures. Banned, burned, and censored in many capitalist countries, Marx and Engels's *The Communist Manifesto* of 1848, commissioned by the Communist League, is one such example. Nonetheless, it is vital to recognize the orientalist premise of Marxism that theorizes colonization as a historical necessity that laid out the possibility of social revolution in America, the Cape, East India, and other feudal societies,[2] critiqued as a "Romantic Orientalist vision" by Edward Said's colonial discourse-analysis that resists the imperial gaze: *Orientalism* (Said 1978, 153–56). Nevertheless, *The Communist Manifesto* has remained iconic of liberation from extractive and settler colonialism as well as neo-imperialism because of its philosophy of class warfare and victory of the oppressed. However, today's feminist manifestos are different. In an age when cellphones and social media are integral parts of activism, images documenting the revolution are generated and disseminated exponentially. These images elude the control that governments have exercised over more traditional forms of "dangerous" political information such as books, traditional manifestos, and pamphlets. The feminist manifestos of the Arab uprising, made up of images of revolutionary women, formed what I call "a political visual" rather than a political script. They came into being through a vastly different mode of production marked by sudden outbursts of dissidence rather than through a highly organized, revolutionary structure. When read in conjunction with one another as a collage, they nonetheless encoded the principles of the movement, signifying dissident thinking that challenged existing political systems. Such manifestos remain archived on the Internet, facilitating strong transnational feminist alliances that bear witness to the revolutionary consciousness of Arab women, as did the images from Egypt's Tahrir Square in downtown Cairo.

On December 17, 2010 a poor Tunisian vendor, Mohamed Bouazizi—

whose supplies his local municipality had confiscated—immolated himself in protest, providing the initial impetus to what would become a people's revolution that toppled Tunisian President Ben Ali's twenty-four-year-long dictatorship.

The revolution spread to Tahrir Square in Egypt, galvanized by the June 6, 2010 death of a twenty-eight-year-old Egyptian man, Khaled Said, dragged out of a café in Alexandria and publicly beaten to death by the Egyptian police (Kraidy 2012). The Facebook page "We are all Khaled Said" with a profile picture of Said's smashed face, created on July 19, 2010, generated thousands of supporters (Society/Culture 2010).

In the aftermath of the tremendous dissidence against his government, President Hosni Mubarak, who had ruled Egypt from 1981, resigned on February 11, 2011. On February 13, the military takeover of Egypt dissolved the constitution and the parliament. On November 28 the first parliamentary elections in thirty years took place. It is against this background that we see how Egyptian women came to create a political manifesto premised on three principles, through the use of their bodies. First, the participation of women in nation-building despite gendered bodily vulnerabilities, second, their refusal to be defined politically by gendered dress codes, and third, inclusive notions of collaborative politics with different bodies on the line. Transnational feminists were quick to seize powerful images of such body politics and to circulate these images through social media. This ensured that the uprising celebrated Arab women as distinctive icons of political dissidence along with the likes of Bouazizi.

Exactly a year from the day Mohamed Bouazizi set himself on fire in Tunisia, "the girl in the blue bra," as she has come to be called, made world headlines. Images and YouTube clips of Egyptian military police dragging and stripping a protester in Cairo's Tahrir Square went viral. Her *abaya*—the black robe worn by Muslim women—was ripped off, exposing her midriff and bright blue bra as a soldier stomped on her stomach.

This image became iconic not only of violent military crackdown on protesters, but in particular on women protesters. As its transnational circulation became a rallying feminist cry against the gagging of the dissenting voice through sexual humiliation and physical violence, the Lebanese blog *Beirut Spring* created an intriguing collage.[3] It was called *Blue-Bra Egyptian Girl as Modern Day Hypatia* (Mustapha 2011). The collage offered an uncanny analogy by juxtaposing the image of the woman in the blue bra, which it called "Egypt Today," with a painting of Hypatia, called "Egypt

Then." Hypatia was a Greek neo-Platonist philosopher in Roman Egypt who was dragged along the streets of fifth-century Alexandria by a fanatical Christian mob into a church, where they stripped her and brutally killed her with roofing tiles before tearing her body apart and burning it. Hypatia's crime, like that of the woman in the blue bra, was that of dissident views (Zielinski 2010). The Web also offered active testimonies of women from Tahrir through YouTube clips, such as the one provided by twenty-seven-year-old media editor-in-chief Hanna Kemal to Code Pink—a women-led grassroots organization working to end US wars and militarism. Kemal described anti-Mubarak activists like herself as "the young pharaohs," and criticized the United States, Israel, and other countries from the global North for supporting Mubarak's thirty-year-long dictatorship. She eloquently spoke of a slogan she created, which the revolutionaries were chanting: "Mubarak, go! Go out! Let Egypt see the light!" (Kemal 2011). About the role of women in the revolution in another testimony to Code Pink from Tahrir, circulated globally through YouTube, another fierce activist, Nadia Magdashahi, asserts: "It's huge . . . You can see a lot of women here on the streets . . . I have kids, and I left them with my mother, . . . and she is with the revolution but she cannot go on the streets because she has to care for the kids. . . . It's not only the people on the streets. It's the people who are protecting our interests and our properties at home that are also supporting what's happening here" (Magdashahi 2011). During the peak of the uprising in Egypt, a feminist blogger from Spain—Leil-Zahra Mortada—created the now well-known Facebook collage with a 181 images of Egyptian women demonstrating in the face of military-police violence at Tahrir Square (Mortada 2011). Examining specific images from this album in conjunction with the image of the "girl in the blue bra" serves to vividly illustrate how the dissemination of such images generates political messages about the mission of Arab women in the revolution. The first of these images shows a young woman in black; her forefinger is raised in a defiant gesture, as she appears to join in chanting the slogans of the revolution. Behind her stands a whole regiment of helmeted military police in bulletproof uniforms with protective shields raised in front of themselves—a sharp contrast to the woman's light clothing, underneath which her body is obviously vulnerable to state violence.

In this context it is important to remember that Isobel Coleman has pointed out that the woman in the blue bra has come under criticism from bloggers and tweeters "for being out in public protesting in the first place" and "being provocative for not wearing more clothes under her abaya" (Coleman 2011). Contesting such misogyny, lightly clad, unarmored bodies of dissident women in the face of hyper-masculine militarized state structures resisting popular dissent can be interpreted as a political statement that the people refuse to be cowed by the physicality of state power. These images assert that a different physics of power can transform Egypt: the power of the people to steer Egypt through the strength of their political vision rather than the might of arms. In this frame of reference, women do not feel the need to protect their bodies. Neither women's fear nor their shame, on which the state believes it can capitalize to terrorize and cordon them off, will prevent them from being active participants in the nation-building process. Here is the first principle of the manifesto: Women protesters recognize that fear and shame are the basis of patriarchal state sanctions on women's mobility in violent zones where state power is redistributed. Women protesters declare that being vulnerable to danger, fear, and shame around their bodies being violated will not deter them from actively staking out their own claims in the reconstruction of the state.

A cluster of three other images from Mortada's Facebook collage is useful in arriving at what I call the second principle of the women's manifesto. In one of these images an *abaya*-clad woman is confronting a troop of military police with her back to the camera as her right hand holds the Egyptian flag high up in the air. In a similar image, a woman in a headscarf shouts slogans and raises a victory sign at the representatives of state power, with her carefully manicured hand adorned with a bangle and a beautiful finger ring. In these images, the forcefulness of women's truth-telling power successively scales up. In the third image the camera captures the face of a policeman with eyes closed in an intense encounter with a visibly irate woman in a blue headscarf. Her warning finger is really close to his face as she rebukes him, and her eyes dilated with anger are visible through the tinted lenses of her big sunglasses. Another policeman looks at her askance with a weary look in his eyes.

The three images of head-scarved and *abaya*-clad women bring us to the second principle of the women's manifesto: Speaking truth to power or entering the public order has nothing to do with what women wear or can wear. Such a principle shakes the very foundations of state power based on a masculine ethos of public order. In this order, women who enter politics are transgressive, and such tainted women deserve the kind of public humiliation that was meted out to the "woman in the blue bra." Stripping her of her *abaya* literally un-genders her, foregrounding the message that *abayas* are meant only for women who accept the status quo of patriarchal sanctions for women with respect to the public order.

Examining two other images helps in further defining the women's manifesto. One shows the jubilant celebration of Egyptian women in Tahrir Square after they hear that Mubarak had resigned. With fists and signs of victory flung in the air to express the power of the people, and joyous and serene expressions on their faces, these women carry among them a child. In another image the Egyptian feminist Nawal El Sadaawi stares with a smile at the camera from Tahrir, where the octogenarian had been squatting in alliance with other women against Mubarak. In Sadaawi's photograph, four men are in the background; one of them has a bandaged chin, probably as a result of skirmishes with the police at Tahrir. With these two images, we arrive at the third principle of the women's manifesto: As opposed to state power that is premised on the principle of excluding people from sharing power based on their identities, as we have seen in the case of the "girl in the blue bra," women's common-front politics is inclusive and based on power-sharing. Children, the aged, and men are all invited into their circle of allies. Thus, these photographic counter-narratives of the Arab uprising trace a feminist iconography of the revolution that directly talks back to the empire and its toxic legacies of Islamophobic representations of Muslim women.

Bodies on the Line

It is important to emphasize that much as cellphones and social media have facilitated transnational, feminist common fronts against Islamophobic imperialism, it is vital for a feminist understanding of the revolution to refrain from techno-fetishizing. Such fetishism forgets about the very different political valence that bodies took up when they put themselves in harm's way in the real space of Tahrir Square. This is what activist Miral Brinjy meant when she testified from Tahrir Square during the protest against Mubarak: "even though they shut down the Internet, this is not just a Facebook revolution or an Internet revolution. As you have seen, hundreds of thousands of people on the streets" (Van Langendonck 2011). In fact, the Arab uprising was ignited in Tunisia through the "spectacle of burnt flesh" in Mohamed Bouazizi's self-immolation (Jadaliyya Reports 2013). In Egypt, as the military terrorized and tortured dissident bodies to mold them into passive subjects of the state, "revolutionaries transformed

disfiguration into badges of political maturity. Eye patches became ubiquitous; even the venerable lions of Qasr al-Nil bridge donned them as
symbols of the deformed but steadfast body" (Jadaliyya Reports 2013). This
is the kind of steadfastness Samira Ibrahim demonstrated when she took
the Egyptian military to court for subjecting her, along with a group of
other women protesters at Tahrir, to virginity tests along with beatings,
electric shocks, and strip-searching in detention in March 2011. Her powerful act defies the state's ability to claim her flesh as a terrain to exercise its
brutal authority. Sherene Seikaly has highlighted how Ibrahim ruptures the
dominant discourse that marks the bodies of women revolutionaries: "We
have all been in one way or another on this very disturbing line where we
are sort of asked are you a girl or are you a woman, where our ethics, our
status, our social meaning is tied to our flesh" (Jadaliyya Reports 2013).
Ibrahim's power lies in being "able to say I reject this question. I answer this
question by saying I am a revolutionary" (Jadaliyya Reports 2013). In this
context the French Algerian feminist Nabila Ramdani has reminded us that
"the protection of civilian lives" that became a justification for lethal
intervention in Libya somehow escaped European and American leaders in
the face of the Egyptian army's excesses against civilian lives. Ramdani
argues, "Those who try to justify this triumph of military power are inevitably those who believe that martial force is the desired default position of
any Arab country" (Ramdani 2013b). According to Turkish British feminist
scholar Deniz Kandiyoti, the precarity of women's rights in the successor
regimes of the Arab uprising lies in a complex set of internal and external
influences that can be broadly categorized under democratic paradox and
hijacking of women's rights. Kandiyoti argues how the projects of nation-
building in the post-independence states in the region resulted in a "state
feminist compact" through the expansion of women's access to education,
labor, and public space for a greater good: "the creation of a stronger, more
productive nation that enlisted enlightened mothers and sisters-in-arms
to the project of national development" (Kandiyoti 2012). In the wake of
subsequent economic liberalization and privatization policies, this social
compact was between authoritarian states, and women's rights gave way to
Islamist opposition to and grassroots class activism against the emergent
phenomena of dynastic rule and crony capitalism. Kandiyoti has argued
that particularly in Egypt "the encouragement of apolitical, pietistic forms
of conformism, especially in the realms of gender and the family, 'normalized' an ethos of social conservatism co-opted by the Islamist parties"—a
structure intensified by the international donor-funded organizations and

NGOs for women's rights in the region that became a "'democratic' fig-leaf for dictatorial regimes" (Kandiyoti 2012). A discussion of the body as a revolutionary political and expressive medium in the Egyptian uprising remains incomplete without addressing Alia al-Mahdy, who posted a naked picture of herself on her blog in 2011 in protest against societal violence and discrimination. Drawing on his "performative-contentious model of the Arab public sphere" where the human body plays a major role as both the "bone of contention and medium of expression," Marwan Kraidy has argued that al-Mahdy's act of "semiotic self-immolation" needs to be read on a continuum with Mohamed Bouazizi's ultimate bodily performance of self-immolation with which the Arab uprisings began—"both provocative yet sacrificial acts" of communication igniting public discourse across a huge political spectrum (Kraidy 2013). Critiquing the media's unfavorable comparison of al-Mahdy with Nawal El Sadaawi, Kraidy asserts that feminists like the latter are acceptable because they play to "the reasoned, disciplined and cerebral deployment of words," unlike "al-Mahdy's radical speech act" that refuses to abide by the rationalist-deliberative ideal of acceptable public discourse. Along with her call to Egyptian men to wear the *hijab* in solidarity with women, which threatened the socio-religious order of gendered boundaries and hierarchies, al-Mahdy's picture led to death threats against her, and it is believed that al-Mahdy was kidnapped and threatened with rape, while the nude male body of her partner posted alongside her came under no censure and was in fact ignored in public discourses (Kraidy 2012, 68). In this, her virtual activism spills into the material world where her body becomes ubiquitously recognizable as transgressive, and hence vulnerable to violence. In fact, she had to relocate from Egypt to seek asylum in Sweden, where she joined the "sextremist" FEMEN movement in which women use their topless and nude bodies to protest against patriarchy, particularly the sex industry, dictatorships, and religion. Al-Mahdy has come under severe criticism for becoming a handmaiden of the global North because FEMEN is based on an imperial feminist assumption that women's liberation is tied to what women wear. Hence, enabling Muslim women to free themselves from their religion, the *burqa*, and strip naked has become a measure of FEMEN's benevolence toward their less fortunate "sisters." Sara Mourad has pointed out:

> the staged unveiling of Alia, sponsored by her European sisters, bears an unsettling resemblance to the symbolic unveiling of Algerian women by their French sisters in public squares to the cries of "Vive l'Algerie

Française!" FEMEN's call "Muslim women unveil!" is an invitation that is
at the same time a prescription for what these women should want.
(Mourad 2013)

Thus, Alia who protests naked alongside her FEMEN sisters represents the
possibilities for Muslim women to enjoy the liberties of European womanhood. Nineteenth- and twentieth-century colonial feminism that marks
the images of Freya Stark and Marjorie Armstrong is recycled here as
twenty-first-century Islamophobic feminist body politics, while global
structural inequalities shored up by racism and imperialism remain under
the radar of FEMEN. But if it is crucial to interrogate FEMEN's appropriation of the bodies of Muslim women and nude bodies of atheist women like
Alia through a transnational feminist lens, it is also deeply significant to
bring such a lens to Alia's nude body in Egypt. Alia's transgressive body and
its political enunciation, condemned by many across the political
spectrum—Islamists, secularists, liberals, leftists, and feminists—take on
very different valences in this context of religious and social conservatism
from that of Sweden, marked by Islamophobia and orientalism (Mourad
2013) However, just as FEMEN does not have the right to appropriate the
body of Alia in the service of an imperialist feminism, similarly the diverse
political factions in Egypt do not have the right to claim Alia's flesh to further their own political agendas. If they do, sexual terrorism against
women protesters that reached its peak between June 28 and July 3, 2013—
when the military in a coup d'état removed the democratically elected
President Mohammad Morsi in response to public protest against his dictatorial style—would be naturalized. These attacks have been described as
organized crimes where a group of five or six formed a tight circle around
the targeted woman, groping her, tearing off her clothes, while the circle
swelled as more predators join the group (Kholaif 2013). However, while
Alia defended the integrity of her body by defiantly baring it in the face of
socio-religious conservatism, similarly these women defended the integrity of theirs with the 8,000 mattress needles distributed free among
female protesters.

Huda Sha'arawi, Anti-Colonial Protest, and Transnational Negotiations

The media of the global North has portrayed the uprising in Egypt as a
novel historical moment that would politicize and liberate the women in

Egypt, since before this they had been the silent, mythical beings of orientalist fantasies. This transnational feminist critique remains invested in tracing the revolutionary heritage of Egyptian women of this century—another move that will write back to the empire and its legacies of misrepresentation bequeathed to Muslim women. Such a critique attempts to trace how Alia's foremother, the Egyptian feminist Huda Sha'arawi (1879–1947), in her encounter with the hyper-masculine authoritarian state and in forming transnational feminist alliances with women of the global North, rejected appropriation by both. The British ruled Egypt from 1882 to 1952. In March 1919 Sha'arawi led the largest women's demonstration against the British colonial state, using her alliance with the Sa'ad Zaghlul, leader of the Wafd—the nationalist movement—to form solidarities with the men. Sa'ad Zaghlul's wife, Safiyya Zaghlul, was also part of the leadership of this nationalist feminist movement against British imperialism. Shouting "Down with the protectorate!" the demonstration marched "towards the foreign missions and other administrative offices, where organisers aimed to deliver tracts stating their demands" (Ramdani 2013a, 48). As the British troops aimed their weapons at the women, Sha'arawi drew parallels to her own advantage between British colonial violence on Egyptian women and the violence on British women martyrs by Axis powers. Invoking the English nurse Edith Cavell, who was killed in 1915 by German soldiers after helping Allied prisoners of war to escape, Sha'arawi retorted: "Let me die so Egypt shall have an Edith Cavell." One hundred and eighteen women signed a petition to various consulates in Egypt aimed at building transnational pressure against Britain. In their petition to the US Consul General, the women relied on President Woodrow Wilson's principles of self-determination in his Fourteen Points speech to Congress at a joint session of Congress on January 1, 1918 (Ramdani 2013a, 49). Shrewdly referring to the US War of Independence, the petition "condemned the British for using machine gun fire against unarmed women and children" (49). The success of 1919 led to the formation of the Wafdist Women's Central Committee (WWCC) in 1920, but after 1922, when Egypt was partially decolonized and women found themselves marginalized in the liberation struggle, Huda Sha'arawi founded the Egyptian Feminist Union (EFU) in 1923 and became its president (50). The 1919 women marchers have come under criticism for being an exclusionary movement of elite women (50). Though peasant women were engaged in anticolonial work such as the destruction of railway lines and other acts of sabotage, it was only after 1919 that elite women and working-class women started marching together against imperialism. In 1935 Huda Sha'arawi became the vice-president of the International Alliance of Women for Suffrage and Equal Citizenship (IAW). However, Sha'arawi's attempt at a genuine transnational feminist alliance between women of the global North and the global South, cutting across centuries of colonial bias, was met with an imperialist feminism that disenfranchised Arab women. Soon she became dissatisfied with the international women's movement and with IAW, whose board she sat on, for not addressing Euro-American imperialism and Zionist support (Fleischmann 2003, 188). In response to the vested interests of women of the global North in maintaining the oppressive status quo against populations of color, Huda Sha'arawi convened the 1938 Eastern Women's Conference in Cairo. The Palestine issue was the central focus of this conference, and strengthened the ties between Palestinian women and the larger Arab feminist movement. In 1944 Sha'arawi led the Arab Women's Congress in Cairo, and in 1945 became the founding president of the Arab Feminist Union.

Angela Davis and Women in Egypt: Transnational Feminist Solidarity Politics

This opens up the question about whether there are possibilities of cutting across imperial legacies and moving toward transnational feminist alliances between women of the global North and the global South that recognize Arab women's political subjectivities. Angela Davis, in her discussion of women in Egypt in her book *Women, Culture, and Politics* (Davis 1989), offers a transnational feminist trajectory that can potentially move us forward on a path of solidarity politics: where women of the global North learn to listen to voices from the global South rather than speaking for them. This is what I call "learning to unlearn" the legacies of the past, "learning to unlearn" the lessons of the empire. Davis's 1985 visit to Egypt was hosted by the Arab Women's Solidarity Association (AWSA) to celebrate the UN Decade for Women (1976–85) in Nairobi. Right at the outset, she admitted she did not know that her sponsors in the US wanted her trip to revolve around a discussion of women's sexual rights, including clitoridectomy—something she did not know till it was too late. Davis foregrounds how, as an African-American woman in transnational feminist solidarity with women in Africa, she was familiar with the "hidden dynamics of racism" underlying "the myopic concentration on

female circumcision in U.S. feminist literature on African women"
(Davis 1989, 117). It was believed that women on whom this practice was
exercised

> would magically ascend to a state of equality once they managed to throw
> off the fetters of genital mutilation—or rather, once white Western femi-
> nists (whose appeals often suggest that this is the contemporary "white
> woman's burden") accomplished this for them. (118)

Davis underlines the double standard in feminist thinking in the United
States when college students who are horrified by the practice of genital
mutilation are not disturbed by the lengths to which women in the US go to
surgically alter their own bodies to fit in with male supremacist standards
of beauty (119). Emphasizing the need to contextualize women's lives
within a larger context of global patriarchy and its unequal international
division of economic and political power, Davis states that Egypt's stronger
ties to the United States and Israel through President Anwar Sadat's open-
door policy served to intensify economic, political, and sexual oppression
in the lives of Egyptian women (122). Although the photographs of European women travelers became important tools for the project of imperialism, Davis's writing becomes an instrument for antiimperialist activism
as she intersperses her writing with direct quotes from Egyptian women,
carrying their voices and perspectives on a sponsored discussion of Egyptian women's sexuality back to US feminists. She cites women who speak
back to the empire through this transnational solidarity politics—women
who feel such a discussion renders them into guinea pigs in sexual experi-
ments and into lists in catalogs in the interest of the global North (124–25).
However, Davis is also careful to address the issue in all its complexity,
underlining that women in Egypt are not a homogeneous community; they
have a diverse range of political ideologies around genital mutilation that
enable them to politically engage with one another. There are women like
activist-writer-medic Nawal El Sadaawi, who has written about her own
difficult experience with female circumcision, and Azziza Hussein, the
then-president of the Family Planning Association, with her direct-action
campaign to eradicate genital mutilation (130). What is important to Davis
in this transnational solidarity politics is letting the other of the imperial
imaginary speak for herself. In the face of the vehement outburst of the
women against Davis for her social location as a woman from the United
States who might misrepresent them, she asks:

After all, was I not in Egypt to learn about the way Egyptian women themselves interpreted the role of sexuality in their lives and their struggles?
And was I not especially interested in their various responses to the
unfortunate chauvinism characterizing attitudes in the capitalist countries toward the sexual dimension of Arab women's lives? (124)

In the same spirit as she learns about female genital mutilation, Davis
learns about the veil, both having become iconic of the *woman of the elsewhere*
in the Euro-US imagination. She learns about the "class character of the
veil": that peasant women and factory women did not practice seclusion
because it became an impediment to their work. She cites the many voices
with their various positions on the veil—among them voices criticizing
aristocratic women in the women's movement for focusing their energies
on abolishing the veil, with complete disregard for the need of working
women to address economic issues (Davis 1989, 138). Some Egyptian
women see the veil as denying the multidimensionality of women and
reducing them to sexual beings, whereas others see it as iconic of resistance to imperialism. Still others see it as a mark of their deep personal
faith. Davis ends her discussion by foregrounding the organizational work
of highly politicized Egyptian women of the progressive coalition Tagamo
and the National Culture Defense Committee, many of its members having
undergone repeated imprisonments and death threats. Thus, Davis
through her writing constantly disrupts the epistemological violence of
imperialistic discourse that has generated an Islamophobic understanding
about women in Muslim-majority countries. This is the kind of feminist
disruption that the Vietnamese-American filmmaker and writer Trinh T.
Minh-ha addresses in an interview with the British-Asian queer feminist
filmmaker Pratibha Parmar in the context of the publication of her 1989
book *Woman, Native, Other*. Minh-ha argues: "In a context of marginalization, at the same time as you feel the necessity to call yourself a feminist
while fighting for the situation of women, you also have to keep a certain
latitude and to refuse that label when feminism tends to become an occupied territory" (Parmar 1990, 66). Occupied territory here refers to epistemological violence: the proclamation of authority over feminist knowledge
by the global North. By refusing the label of feminism in such contexts, the
marginalized redefine agency and subjectivity beyond the imperial gaze by
pushing the limits of feminist epistemology itself, and enabling the field
to grow toward new knowledge about the other and new definitions of

transnational feminist solidarity politics. In the context of the War on Terror, a plethora of feminist scholars from the US, among them Cynthia Enloe, Miriam Cooke, and Zillah Eisenstein, have made the same attempt at cutting across Islamophobic imperialist feminism toward a transnational feminist solidarity politics. Enloe has argued how the war entrusted the Northern Alliance with guardianship of Afghan femininity, and intensified the disempowerment of women (Enloe 2004, 285). She highlights the extreme gender imbalance in the coalition's Iraqi governing council and the lack of gender-security planning in post-invasion Iraq (293–94). Cooke highlights how the imperial feminist discourse of saving Muslim women has erased the role of Afghan women as fighters and martyrs in their opposition to Soviet occupation in the 1980s, the Mujahideen in the 1990s, and the Taliban from the mid 1990s until 2001 (Cooke 2002, 228–29). Eisenstein demonstrates the pernicious effects of the militarization of women's lives across the world—both for women who are targets of war and women who perpetrate war as agents of the empire, thereby refuting both the claim that war can liberate women in the global South through the rescue mission of the empire, as well as the claim that war can redistribute gender power for women of the global North (Eisenstein 2008). In the end, a plethora of feminist scholars engaging with the problematic of women of the global North benefiting from wars on women of the global South will generate a more rigorous epistemology and praxis of transnational feminist solidarity.

This article is about archives—both pictorial and written. It traces archives of the nineteenth, twentieth, and twenty-first centuries to plot the trajectories of imperialist feminisms as well as transnational feminist solidarities that contest the ideologies about the global South maintained by the global North. Using colonial discourse-analysis to examine colonial and neoimperial images as well as texts enables us to see how such ideologies come to be shaped. The vital significance of this article lies in its attempt to map the failures and possibilities of transnational solidarity politics between women of the global North and South in the face of the brutal legacies of empire.

....

Basuli Deb is a Visiting Scholar at Columbia's Institute for the Study of Human Rights, Global Scholar at Rutgers' Institute for Research on Women, and CUNY faculty. She teaches/mentors undergraduate/graduate students; has published a monograph, multiple peer-reviewed articles, and three co-edited volumes; delivered feminist keynotes at international conferences; and advised the UN on gender violence. She is also a creative writer, media artist, and the founder-director of *iSights Media & Communications*.

Notes

Originally published in *Meridians* vol. 13, no. 2, 2016.

1   As evidentiary testament to the long and enduring history of the imperial gaze in structuring the European imaginary, it is particularly important to contextualize it within the long history of European Orientalist art—paintings by Antoine-Jean Gros, Jean-Leon Gerome, Eugene Delacroix, Jean-Auguste Dominique Ingres, Paul Gauguin, among others—and its official sponsorship through Napoleon's royal patronage and the French academy. For instance, Gros's *Napoleon in the Plague House at Jaffa* depicts Napoleon healing a plague-afflicted person with the divine touch of kings during the siege of Jaffa. Similarly, Delacroix's *Massacre at Chios* (1824) and *Death of Sardanapalus* are depictions of the brutality of the oriental Other, and the signature paintings of Ingres, who, like Gros, had never traveled to the East, revolved around the genre of harems filled with female slaves and concubines objectified either in the nude or in exotic dress.

2   *The Communist Manifesto* argues: "The discovery of America, the rounding of the Cape, opened up fresh ground for the rising bourgeoisie. The East-Indian and Chinese markets, the colonisation of America, trade with the colonies, the increase in the means of exchange and in commodities generally, gave to commerce, to navigation, to industry, an impulse never before known, and thereby, to the revolutionary element in the tottering feudal society, a rapid development" (Marx and Engels 1998, 35–36).

3   Here it is useful to articulate the difficulty in naming the pan-Arab revolutions from December 2010, and the problematic around the putative "Arab Spring" as if the Middle East were a fossilized region, a relic of a mythic past that is now catching up with the "West." I have instead used the term "Arab uprising."

Works Cited

Abu-Lughod, Lila. 2002. "Do Muslim Women Really Need Saving? Anthropological Reflections on Cultural Relativism and Its Others." *American Anthropologist* 104, no. 3: 783–90.

Alloula, Malek. 1986. *The Colonial Harem*. Minneapolis: University of Minnesota Press.

Bhattacharya, Gargi. 2007. "Transcript of all the Speakers' Presentations." Transnational Feminism–Terrorism: A Round-Table Discussion between Scholars from the USA and Europe, May 7. http://www.darkmatter101.org/site/2007/05/07/transnational-feminism-terrorism/ (accessed January 8, 2016).

Bush, George W. 2001. "Radio Address by Mrs. Bush," edited by Gerhard Peters and John T. Woolley. *The American Presidency Project*, November 17. http://www.presidency.ucsb.edu/ws/?pid=24992 (accessed January 8, 2016).

Clinton, Hillary Rodham. 2011. "Secretary Clinton's Remarks on Women, Peace, and Security." US Department of State, December 19. http://www.state.gov/secretary /20092013clinton/rm/2011/12/179173.htm (accessed January 17, 2016)

Coleman, Isobel. 2011. "'Blue Bra Girl' Rallies Egypt's Women vs. Oppression." CNN *Opinion*, December 11. http://www.cnn.com/2011/12/22/opinion/coleman-women -egypt-protest/ (accessed January 8, 2016).

Cooke, Miriam. 2002. "Islamic Feminism Before and After September 11TH." *Duke Journal of Gender Law & Policy* 9: 227–35.

Davis, Angela Y. 1989. *Women, Culture, and Politics*. New York: Random House.

Eisenstein, Zillah. 2008. "Resexing Militarism for the Globe." In *Feminism and War: Confronting US Imperialism*, edited by Robin Riley, Chandra Talpade Mohanty, and Minnie Bruce Pratt. London and New York: Zed Books.

Enloe, Cynthia. 2004. *The Curious Feminist: Searching for Women in a New Age of Empire*. Berkeley: University of California Press.

Fleischmann, Ellen. 2003. *The Nation and its "New" Women: The Palestinian Women's Movement, 1920–1948*. Berkeley: University of California Press.

Graham-Brown, Sarah. 1988. *Images of Women: The Portrayal of Women in the Photography of the Middle East 1860–1950*. New York: Columbia University Press.

Hesford, Wendy S., and Wendy Kozol. 2005. "Introduction." In *Just Advocacy?: Women's Human Rights, Transnational Feminisms, and the Politics of Representation*, edited by Wendy S. Hesford and Wendy Kozol. New Brunswick, NJ: Rutgers University Press.

Jadaliyya Reports. 2013. "The Body as a Site of Contest: Sherene Seikaly on the Gendered Exercise of Power and Resistance." *Jadaliyya*, June 11. http://www.jadaliyya .com/pages/index/12162/the-body-as-a-site-of-contest_sherene-seikaly-on-t (accessed January 8, 2016).

Kandiyoti, Deniz. 2012. "Disquiet and Despair: The Gender Sub-Texts of the Arab Spring." *Open Democracy*, June 26. https://www.opendemocracy.net/5050/deniz -kandiyoti/disquiet-and-despair-gender-sub-texts-of-arab-spring (accessed January 8, 2016).

Kemal, Hanna. 2011. "Interview with Hanna—Women Activists at Tahrir Square in Cairo, Egypt." YouTube. *Code Pink Action*, Feb. 2. https://youtu.be/zhT_SPsIEu0 (accessed January 8, 2016).

Kholaif, Dahlia. 2013. "Sexual Harassment Taints Egypt's Euphoria." *Aljazeera*, July 6. http://www.aljazeera.com/indepth/features/2013/07/20137617131125427.html (accessed January 8, 2016).

Kipling, Rudyard. 1899. "The White Man's Burden." http://historymatters.gmu.edu /d/5478/ (accessed January 8, 2016).

Kraidy, Marwan M. 2012. "The Revolutionary Body Politic: Preliminary Thoughts on a Neglected Medium in the Arab Uprisings." *Middle East Journal of Culture and Communications* 5, no. 1: 66–74.

Kraidy, Marwan M. 2013. "New Texts Out Now: Marwan M. Kraidy, The Revolutionary Body Politic." *Jadaliyya*, Jan 2. http://www.jadaliyya.com/pages/index/9321/new -texts-out-now_marwan-m.-kraidy-the-revolutiona. (accessed January 8, 2016).

Lehrer, Jim. 2005. Interview with Condoleezza Rice. Transcript. PBS *Newshour*, July 28. http://www.pbs.org/newshour/bb/white_house-july-dec05-rice_7–28/ (accessed January 8, 2016).

Marx, Karl, and Frederick Engels. 1998. *The Communist Manifesto*. New York: Verso.

Magdashahi, Nadia. 2011. "Interview with Egyptian Pro Democracy Activist, Nadia— Women Activists at Tahrir Square." YouTube. *Code Pink Action*, Feb. 2. https:/ /youtu.be/YUOluXFoZTI (accessed January 8, 2016).

McCurry, Steve. 1985. "The Afghan Girl." *The National Geographic*, June. https:/ /thepowerofthefrontcover.wordpress.com/1985/06/28/1985–the-afghan-girl-the -national-geographic-2/ (accessed January 8, 2016).

———. 2002. "Found: After 17 Years An Afghan Refugee's Story." *The National Geographic*, April. http://ngm.nationalgeographic.com/2002/04/afghan-girl/index -text (accessed January 8, 2016).

McNutt, Kristen. 2005. "Sexualized Violence against Iraqi Women by US Occupying Forces." Association of Humanitarian Lawyers. A Briefing Paper of International Education Development. Geneva: United Nations Commission on Human Rights. http://www.uruknet.info/?p=11094 (accessed January 8, 2016).

Mortada, Leil-Zahra. 2011. "Women of Egypt." Facebook. https://www.facebook.com /leilzahra/media_set?set=a.493689677675.268523.586357675&type=1 (accessed July 3, 2014).

Mourad, Sara. 2013. "The Naked Bodies of Alia." *Jadaliyya*, January 1. http://www .jadaliyya.com/pages/index/9291/the-naked-bodies-of-alia (accessed January 8, 2016).

Mustapha. 2011. "Blue-Bra Egyptian Girl as Modern Day Hypatia." Blog. *Beirut Spring*, December 28. http://beirutspring.com/blog/2011/12/22/blue-bra-egyptian-girl-as -modern-day-hypatia/ (accessed January 8, 2016).

Parmar, Pratibha. 1990. "Interview with Trinh T. Minh-ha." *Feminist Review* 36: 65–74.

Ramdani, Nabila. 2013a. "Women in the 1919 Egyptian Revolution: From Feminist Awakening to Nationalist Political Activism." *Journal of International Women's Studies* 14, no. 2: 39–52.

———. 2013b. "The Arab Spring is Being Stifled by the Force of Arms." *The Guardian*, July 27. http://www.theguardian.com/commentisfree/2013/jul/27/arab-spring -stifled-by-armies-and-militias (accessed January 8, 2016).

Said, Edward. 1978. *Orientalism*. New York: Vintage Books.

Society/Culture. "We Are All Khaled Said." 2010. *Facebook*. https://www.facebook.com /elshaheeed.co.uk/ (accessed January 8, 2016).

Spivak, Gayatri Chakravorty. 1988. "Can the Subaltern Speak?" In *Marxism and the Interpretation of Culture*, edited by Cary Nelson and Lawrence Grossberg. Urbana and Chicago: University of Illinois Press.

Van Langendonck, Gert. 2011. "Interview with pro-democracy activist Miral at Tahrir Square." YouTube for documentary *Zero Silence*, Feb. 1. https://youtu.be /RtLJpzUp2Z8 (accessed January 8, 2016).

Ward, Lucy. 2001. "Cherie Blair Pleads for Afghan Women: Call for Government Role and Education for Girls." *Guardian*, November 20. http://www.theguardian.com /politics/2001/nov/20/uk.septembern (accessed January 8, 2016).

Zielinski, Sarah. 2010. "Hypatia, Ancient Alexandria's Great Female Scholar." *Women's History Month*, March 15. http://www.smithsonianmag.com/womens-history /hypatia-ancient-alexandrias-great-female-scholar-10942888/ (accessed January 8, 2016).

Sonia E. Álvarez

....

'Vem Marchar com a Gente'/Come March with Us[1]

Figure 1. *Marcha* logo, designed by Afro-Bahian artist J. Cunha.

The cover to volume 14, number 1, of *Meridians* features a powerful photograph of Dona Tiana (Sebastiana Geralda Ribeiro da Silva), a grassroots activist from the historically Black territory *Quilombo* Carrapatos da Tabatinga in the state of Minas Gerais, delivering an impassioned speech during the first-ever national *Marcha das Mulheres Negras contra o Racismo e a Violência e pelo Bem Viver* (Black Women's March against Racism and Violence and for Living Well, hereafter the *Marcha*), held in Brasília on November 18,

MERIDIANS · feminism, race, transnationalism   Volume 19 Supplement 2020
DOI: 10.1215/15366936-8759876 © 2016 Smith College

2015.[2] The actual march on the nation's capital, which drew between 5,000 and 20,000 women and a few hundred men from across Brazil, was the culmination of an unprecedented nationwide mobilizational process spanning several years (beginning in late 2011, the U.N.'s International Year for People of African descent) and encompassing all regions of this country of continental proportions. Considered a major turning point and veritable watershed in Afro-Brazilian women's activism by organizers, participants, and observers alike, the Marcha involved every conceivable sector of Afro-descendant women's organizing and many women from the mixed-gender Brazilian Black movement as well. It therefore merits a special place in Part I of our special issue on Afro-descendant Feminisms in Latin America.

Though many Black Brazilian feminist and women's movement activists and organizations form part of national networks such as the Articulação de Organizações de Mulheres Negras (Articulation of Black Women's Organizations), the Fórum de Mulheres Negras (Black Women's Forum), the Federation of Domestic Workers, the Black Lesbian National Seminar, and the National Front for Women in Hip Hop, the Marcha sought to reach out to all Black women involved in all sorts of social change efforts in an exceptionally wide range of places and spaces, urban and rural, governmental, religious, trade union, academic, and artistic sites, and many more. As captured in their slogan, "Vem Marchar com a Gente" (Come March with Us) and spelled out in the "call to action" or "Manifesto" released in July 2014 and reproduced in translation in this issue, Marcha organizers worked especially to draw in women "who had never attended a meeting of hegemonic feminism" to engage in "constructing the Marcha," starting from wherever they were situated, no matter where they worked and wherever they were active, in whatever ways, forms, and venues they were organizing for racial, gender, and social justice. (Group interview with Black feminist organizers of the Marcha, Salvador, Bahia, 11 May 2014.)[3]

The Marcha process explicitly called on the full range of both organized and heretofore unorganized sectors of Afro-Brazilian women and their allies (of whatever genders and races) to join them in loudly proclaiming Black women as subjects of their own lives, of a transformed racially and gender conscious citizenship, of new forms of "living well" with nature, the environment, and one another. The Marcha's recognition of diversity within racialized, gendered difference was central to its strategy and is vividly illustrated in the following excerpt from one of their earliest outreach messages:

We are especially interested in mobilizing: Black girls, adolescents, and young women, from the cities and the rural areas; Black nurses, teachers, domestic workers, *quilombolas* [quilombo/maroon community residents], Black prostitutes, Black women doctors, those linked to religions of African origin . . . Black women whose sons and daughters have been assassinated by the police, Black washerwomen, cooks, construction workers . . . nerds, punks, *emos*, Black women athletes, artists, atheists . . . rappers, *funkeiras* [participants in funk music culture], DJs, graffiti artists, Black women street cleaners, businesswomen . . . Black lesbians, bisexuals, transsexuals, Black fashion models, Black landless women, those affected by dams, homeless Black women. . . . That is, all Black women, including, and principally, all who are or have been discriminated against by neighbors, doctors, dentists and others, and who have felt powerless in the face of such enormous oppression.

The exquisite images from the Brasília event included below, taken by Brazilian feminist photographers Claudia Ferreira and Adriana Medeiros, provide just a glimpse, and, we hope, a poignant one, into the multiplicity of expressions of Afro-Brazilian women's activism that came into dialogue through this unparalleled process.

The *Marcha's* success in reaching tens of thousands of Black women and their allies throughout Brazil, in all their heterogeneity, entailed exceptionally creative organizing and outreach strategies, including women's arts festivals, turban-wrapping and hair-braiding workshops, sambas, *saraus* (alternative artistic/cultural/performance events), *xirês* (dances used to summon the African religious deities Orixás or Orishas), blogs, Facebook pages, chats, spoken poetry, and hip hop events. These events took place along with the more standard fare of lectures, debates, conferences, demonstrations, gatherings of domestic and sex workers, and other "sectoral" meetings of Black (cis- and trans-) women activists, in literally every corner of the country, particularly during 2014 and 2015. State and municipal *Marcha* promotional-organizing committees (*Comités Impulsores*) were created in dozens of cities and towns; like the national coordination committee, most included representatives from diverse Afro-Brazilian women's groups and networks as well as from mixed-gender Black organizations, trade unions, and other networks—who, in accordance with *Marcha* bylaws, had to be represented by women members.

Some localities where contemporary Black feminist organizing dates back to the 1970s, such as Rio de Janeiro, held their own "Pre-Marchas," with highly visible demonstrations drawing thousands of participants. Black feminist activists from Salvador, in the Northeastern state of Bahia, who were involved in the national coordination for the *Marcha*, transformed *Julho das Pretas* (Colored Women's July), the month-long series of events and celebrations they had inaugurated earlier in the 2000s, into a nationwide phenomenon that reached miniscule towns and large metropoles alike, marking the commemoration the International Day of Afro-Latin American and Caribbean Women (July 25). Younger activists in the mostly European-descendant Southern state of Santa Catarina organized an "Afro-Divas" fashion and music event in Florianópolis; a "I *Encontro de Arte e Cultura Negra: Mulher Negra em Foco*" (First Meeting of Black Art and Culture: Focus on Black Women) in German-immigrant dominant Joinville; and, in Bahia, the state with the largest Black population, they held a *Feijoada de Jovens Negras* (Young Black Women's Feijoada).[4] These are but a few examples of the broad range of activities that typified that *Marcha* process.

The significant, if not majoritarian, participation of Black women activists from the North and Northeast—Brazil's blackest/darkest and, not coincidentally, poorest regions—was a particularly noteworthy dimension of the *Marcha*. Historically, the wealthier South and Southeast, with their institutionalized and better-resourced Black movement NGOs, have often overshadowed their organizational counterparts in the North and Northeast. But the extraordinary organizing efforts of *Odara—Instituto da Mulher Negra* (Odara—Black Women's Institute), and the *Rede de Mulheres Negras do Norte e Nordeste* (the North and Northeast Network of Black Women) it helped found in 2013, brought tens of thousands of poor and working class rural and urban women into the *Marcha* process. Their participation made poverty, regional inequalities, and alternative development central dimensions of the *Marcha*'s agenda, as reflected in the inclusion of "*Bem Viver*" (Living Well) in its name. Black feminist socio-environmentalists from the Northern region of Brazil who regularly work transnationally with women in other countries of the Amazon—such as Nilma Bentes, one of the founders of the *Centro de Estudos e Defesa do Negro do Pará* (Center for the Study and Defense of Blacks of the state of Pará) and a key national organizer of the *Marcha*—are widely credited with bringing the idea of *Bem Viver* to the *Marcha* process. The notion of "living well" evokes decolonial discourse, which is very significant in activist and scholarly circles in the Andean region and other parts of Latin America, and is also gaining adherents among some Black women theorists, activists, and indigenous women in

Brazil. Valdecir Nascimento, core organizer of the national *Marcha* process and veteran Bahian feminist and Odara coordinator, explained that Black women "gave the term our own meaning, signaling the need for a new civilizational pact" (Group interview with Black feminist organizers of the *Marcha*, Salvador, Bahia, 11 May 2014).

Organizers have been re-grouping in the aftermath of the Brasília event, redesigning the website, consolidating their organizational structures, and building on this successful, decentralized, horizontal model of organizing and articulation to plan further events in the future. We join them in hoping that the 2015 *Marcha* process will indeed prove a critical turning point in Afro-Brazilian women's quest for gendered, class, and racial justice.

....

Sonia E. Álvarez is Leonard J. Horwitz Professor of Latin American Politics and Society at the University of Massachusetts Amherst. She is the author or editor of eight books and dozens of essays, many authored collaboratively and published in Portuguese and Spanish as well as English. She is a committed intellectual-activist who for over three decades has been deeply connected with feminist movements in Brazil and Latin America, while conducting research on and with them.

Notes

Originally published in *Meridians* vol. 14, no. 1, 2016.

1   These brief reflections are based on my participation in the Black Women's March on Brasília on 18 November 2015, informal and formal interviews with organizers and participants, and an overview of materials about the *Marcha* available on the web.

2   November 20th is National Black Consciousness Day, now an official national holiday in Brazil, and in 2015 marked the 20th anniversary of another notable march on the nation's capital: the "*Marcha Nacional Zumbi dos Palmares contra o Racismo,*" named after the legendary leader of Brazil's largest and longest-lived maroon society, which lasted from 1605 until its suppression in 1694. *Marcha* organizers set the date for the 18th so those participating could also take part in local *Zumbi + 20* actions.

3   For detailed information on the March, please see http://mulheresnegrasmarc .wix.com/marchamulheresnegras; https://www.facebook.com/search/top/ ?q=marcha%20das%20mulheres%20negras%202015; and select posts at http:/ /www.geledes.org.br/.

4   *Feijoada* is the prototypical national dish, a black-bean stew of Afro-Brazilian origin. It is a celebratory, shared meal.

Claudia Ferreira and Adriana Medeiros

. . . .

March against Racism and Violence and in Favor of Living Well (*bem viver*), Brasilia 2015[1]

National Black Women's March November 18

Abstract: These three brief pieces formed part of a two-part special issue (vol. 4, nos. 1 and 2, 2016) on Afro-Descendant Feminisms in Latin America. The unprecedented nationwide mobilizational process that culminated in the first-ever Marcha das Mulheres Negras contra o Racismo e a Violência e pelo Bem Viver (Black Women's March against Racism and Violence and for Living Well), which brought tens of thousands of Black women to Brasília on November 18, 2015, is described in an opening essay by Alvarez. It is followed by one of the several Manifestos produced by Marcha organizers, which captures the core political and theoretical issues discussed in hundreds of events across every sector of Afro-descendant women's activism and women from the mixed-gender Brazilian Black movement as well. Finally, a photo essay by Brazilian photographers Claudia Ferreira and Adriana Medeiros offers a vivid glimpse into what many consider a watershed moment in the Afro-Brazilian feminist movement.

MANIFESTO

We are 49 million Black women—in other words, 25 percent of the Brazilian population. We experience the most perverse racism and sexism by virtue of being Black and women. We face daily White supremacy and patriarchy and sexism, which constitute a system of oppressions that prompt Black women to fight for their own survival and the survival of their communities.

MERIDIANS · feminism, race, transnationalism   Volume 19 Supplement 2020
DOI: 10.1215/15366936-8566122 © 2016 Smith College

We struggle for land and for the demarcation of the *quilombola* territories, which is our source of sustenance and a connection to our ancestral lines.

Despite our contributions, we have been the targets of all kinds of discrimination for generations and generations, which has not allowed us to enjoy the fruits of our labor.

We have been and continue to be the basis for the economic and political development of Brazil, and yet the wealth generated by our labor has not been returned to us.

Even with the prospect of social mobility via consumerism, which has been perceptible in recent years, gender and racial inequality that allows for the concentration of power has kept us, Black women, from developing our full potential and from disputing spaces of power as should be the norm in a just, solidary, and democratic society.

We summon all Black women to join us and to get organized, wherever they happen to live, and to join us for this march on behalf of our citizenship.

Imbued with our ancestral force, our freedom of thought, and political action, we rise from the five regions of this country to form the Black Women's March against Racism and Violence and in Favor of Living Well (*bem viver*) to that demand our right to live free from discriminations in all stages of our lives be ensured.

We do not accept being seen as objects for consumption or guinea pigs for the cosmetic industry, fashion, or pharmaceutical industries. We want to put an end to the dictatorship of White European beauty standards and we want respect for our cultural diversity and Black aesthetics.

We are marching to demand the end of racism in all its manifestations, including in the fields of health care, where maternal mortality is due to the lack of access to proper health care and the low quality of care combined with the lack of training for health professionals regarding the issues that affect Black women; and of public safety, where public safety agents decide who should live and who should die while the state and the society remain negligent.

We denounce the solitary battles against drug addiction, the criminalization of our people, and the elimination of our sons and daughters in the war against drugs that has been happening for a long time. We denounce the lawless imprisonment of our bodies, as we represent 60 percent of the incarcerated women in this country.

As we engage in solitary battles for justice in the middle of extreme racial violence, we also denounce the cruelty of domestic violence, which causes abuse and death among Black women and goes unmentioned in official data. We fight to put an end to institutionalized racism and patriarchy, which prevents the public power and society from facing the extermination of our Black population.

We are marching to demand the freedom to worship our deities of African origin without being persecuted and without having profanities directed at us or our temples desecrated.

We are marching against the racist removal of populations from the places they inhabit. We fight for housing rights, for cities that do not limit our right to come and go, to put an end to the racial segregation between urban and rural spaces, for high-quality public transportation, and for decent working conditions for us to exercise our professions. We value our immaterial patrimony of our *terreiros* (places of worship), samba schools, Afro carnival blocs, *carimbó* (a dance from the northern region of Brazil), literature, and all other cultural manifestations that define our Black identity.

We are marching because we are the overwhelming majority raising our children alone as heads of the household with limited resources and only the sweat generated by our labor.

We are marching:

- to end Black women's femicide, to create visibility, and to guarantee our lives;
- for the investigation of all cases of domestic violence and homicides against Black women with prosecution of guilty parties;
- to end racist and sexist representations produced by the media, which promotes physical and symbolic violence against Black women;
- to end racist and sexist practices and criteria for selection in the work environment;
- to end vexing body searches in prisons and the summary aggression against Black women in detention centers;
- to guarantee access to quality health care for Black women and to prosecute racial and sexual discrimination by health providers at health care centers;
- to guarantee title of ownership to a *quilombola's* land and especially to place the title in women's names, because that is our source of livelihood and what connects us to our ancestors;

- to end religious disrespect and to guarantee the reproduction of our culture and ancestral practices of African origin;
- for our effective participation in public life.

Through our leadership, we aim to place our agenda with our demands at the center stage in this country. This is our starting point and the beginning of a new journey to take place on November 18, 2015 amidst the activities to commemorate Black Consciousness Month.

Images from the 2015 March of Black Women in Brasília

The following mini photo essay shows some of the most striking images captured during the 2015 March, as captured by photojournalists Claudia Ferreira and Adriana Medeiros.

Firure 1. Cordon of Mães de Santo (the highest authorities of Afro-Brazilian religions such as Candomblé) leading off the the Black Women's March on Brasilia. Photo by Adriana Medeiros.

Figure 2. March participants from the Northern state of Pará, which has dozens of *quilombo* communities—rural Black settlements often inhabited by descendants of for slaves or settled and cultivated by generations of Black families. Photo by Adriana Medeiros.

Figure 3. "Black Panthers" (from right to left) Valeria Monã, Sinara Rúbia and Ludmila Almeida. Photo by Claudia Ferreira.

Black Panthers are a group of women who got together to invoke The Black Panthers, the U.S. organization formed in the 1960s for the self-defense of Black folks, who suffered egregious acts of brutality from the police and the White population and were routinely assassinated. Taking into consideration that the same reality extends into the present day in Brazil and elsewhere in the diaspora, where the Black population is still victimized by racism, with the slogan "Even during Carnaval we don't lose our focus," the group in this photograph has, since 2014, enacted urban interventions during Carnaval revelries, marching through the streets and presenting unparalled performances that are contagious to all who hear their marching orders.

Figure 4. Protester aesthetically prepared to march in the 2015 March of Black Women in Brasília. Photo by Claudia Ferreira.

Figure 5. Scene from the March. Photo by Adriana Medeiros.

Claudia Ferreira was born in Rio de Janeiro. During the 1980s, she worked as a photographer for various newspapers, and was a Rio de Janeiro correspondent for the French news agency *Sipa Press*. Toward the end of the 1980s, she began dedicating herself to photographing social movements, and feminist movements in particular.

Adriana Medieros is a Brazilian documentary photographer. She contributes to media and editorial venues in defense of human rights. Medeiros develops documentation projects on social movements—especially Black culture, women, housing, labor movements, and movements for dignified childbirth. Her work has been featured in several national and international exhibitions.

Notes:

Originally published in *Meridians* vol. 14, no. 1, 2016.

1   See http://www.marchadasmulheresnegras.com/#!manifesto/c15t1; accessed on November 16, 2015.

Lena Palacios

Challenging Convictions
Indigenous and Black Race-Radical Feminists Theorizing
the Carceral State and Abolitionist Praxis
in the United States and Canada

Abstract: This essay, with accompanying lesson plan, explores how race-radical
Black and Indigenous feminists theorize and resist the carceral state violence of White settler nations of Canada and the United States. It focuses
on the theoretical interventions driven by Indigenous and Black race-
radical feminists and how this has placed these activists at the forefront of
anti-violence movement-building. Such an intervention specifically upholds
the tensions within and refuses to collapse political approaches of Indigenous movements for sovereignty and Black race-radical traditions. Its transnational, comparative focus helps us to not only identify but to create multiple strategies that dismantle the carceral state and the racialized
gendered violence that it mobilizes and sustains. Proceeding from the argument that both prison abolitionist praxis and race-radical feminist praxis
are inherently and primarily pedagogical, the lesson plan explores the ways
we learn, teach, and organize in a manner that teaches against the grain of
carceral common sense.

Prologue
My formal introduction to the feminism of Indigenous and Black race-
radical women of color was violent due to my own life experience as a survivor of sexual and state violence and my social location as a queer Chicana
from an urban working-class/working-poor background, and to the wider

MERIDIANS · feminism, race, transnationalism   Volume 19 Supplement 2020
DOI: 10.1215/15366936-8566133 © 2016 Smith College

political conjuncture that was taking place when I was introduced to this activist tradition. Like many poor and working-class youth of color growing up in the "shadow of the prison" in the '80s and '90s in "Golden Gulag" (Gilmore 2007) California, feminism—or what I thought at the time was feminism—didn't speak to me or to anyone else in my 'hood. It didn't help me to understand why and how California became comprised overnight of more than nine hundred miles of concrete prisons overflowing with the caged bodies of the "surplus population" of young men and women of color victimized by "The War on Drugs" and by other horrors that start with the letter "D": devolution, downsizing, deindustrialization, and dehumanization. What I would later understand to be "whitestream" hegemonic feminism just didn't do it for me like queer Black and Chicana feminisms and "This Bridge Called My Back" (Moraga and Anzaldúa 1983) feminist praxis would. While "a principled sense of mortal urgency" (Gilmore 2007, 251) has continued to propel me to act, the feminist thought of race-radical women of color has continued to teach me to act strategically and tactically; to possess a healthy distrust of easy, instantaneous solutions; and—as Audre Lorde reminded us in her 1995 poem "A Litany for Survival"—"to speak, remembering, we were never meant to survive."

Introduction

This essay, with accompanying lesson plan, explores how race-radical women of color feminist activists—in particular, Black and Indigenous feminists—identify, conceptualize, theorize, and resist the carceral state violence of White settler societies in both Canada and the United States (Palacios 2014). When I refer to "Indigenous and race-radical feminists," I do so to reference both girls and women of color and Indigenous girls and women who experience gender-based state violence and who identify as women, queer, Two-Spirit, lesbian, bisexual, gender queer, or gender nonconforming, whose interventions are generally marginalized by both "whitestream feminist" (Grande 2004, 148) anti-violence movements as well as more radical (male-dominant, nationalist) movements resisting both interpersonal and state violence. My analysis of state violence enables an exploration of the ways that girls and women of color are assaulted, manipulated, unprotected, and hyper-criminalized by the institutions and the individuals who speak/act on their behalf, and of the development of corresponding Indigenous and race-radical feminist praxis. As I argue throughout my research and teaching, it is long past time that feminist anti-sexual violence activism, anti-prison abolitionism, and anti-police brutality movements integrate and address the particular experiences of girls and women of color—not just as mothers, partners, and children of men of color targeted by systemic state violence and the criminal legal and punishment systems, but as both targets of state violence and agents of resistance and theoreticians in our own right. Lastly, we need to interrogate our own complicity in policing and silencing other women of color and Indigenous women, especially their particular enactments of resistance against gendered, sexualized, and carceral state violence.

This essay focuses on the theoretical interventions driven by Indigenous and Black race-radical feminists and how this has placed these activists at the forefront of anti-violence movement-building in Canada and the United States. Such a critical ethnic studies intervention "is not a melting pot for diverse racialized identity-based groups; it is a coalitional intellectual project that seeks to assess the intersecting logics of White supremacy, settler colonialism, and capitalism" (Simpson and Smith 2014, 13). Such an intervention specifically upholds the tensions within and refuses to collapse the radical and revolutionary political traditions and approaches of Indigenous movements for sovereignty and Black race-radical liberatory traditions. This transnational, comparative focus helps us to not only identify and understand but to create multiple strategies that dismantle the carceral state and the racialized gendered violence that it mobilizes and sustains. Importantly, the politics of prison abolition are fundamentally shaped by each group's particular relationship to racial slavery and settler colonialism. While this essay does not focus on the particulars of Latina migrants, for example, who are increasingly targeted for captivity (see Escobar 2009), it does provide a context to understand the phenomenon, since the various forms of containment to which they are subjected (for example, reproductive control strategies) are integrally related to the history of captivity experienced by Black and Indigenous women in North America (see Roberts 1997; Smith 2005).

Importantly, Indigenous and race-radical feminisms advocate for a justice outside the normative neoliberal politics of justice and the mechanisms of the state. This justice aligns more with a politics of refusal: on the one hand, a race-based refusal that understands—consistent with an Afropessimist approach or intellectual disposition (Hartman 1997; Sexton 2011; Wilderson 2010)—how social death and Blackness are fungible and how the struggle for "abolition of slavery unsettles both colonial and decolonial forms of sovereign determination" (Sexton 2014, 1); and on the other, with an Indigenous politics of refusal that rejects statist relations of sovereignty in favor of self-determination informed by Indigenous knowledges. While the aims of Indigenous sovereignty movements are to bring about the repatriation of Indigenous lands and resurgence of Indigenous life, the politics of abolition (of racial slavery) that "consists in the affirmation of the unsovereign slave" rejects the restoration of sovereignty and refuses "a politics of resurgence, recovery, or recuperation" (Sexton 2014, 11). I say all this not to rank oppressions—as "to be anti-black is also to be fundamentally anti-indigenous" (Jackson 2014) and vice versa—but to trace some of the different positions and approaches that are available from which to critique and potentially dismantle necropolitical logics (Mbembe 2003).

To this end, I pose the following set of questions throughout this essay and in the accompanying lesson plan: How have Indigenous and race-radical feminists identified and theorized the legitimized violence of the carceral state? What questions have those diverse identifications and theoretical understandings led activist scholars currently theorizing the carceral state to ask? And what insights have those critiques generated in the activist scholarship on social movements dedicated to anti-racist, feminist anti-violence, Indigenous decolonial, and anti-prison abolitionist praxis? These questions move beyond introspection or interrogation of texts about violence into compelling conversations that highlight the interlocking nature of interpersonal, sexual, and carceral state violence.

Indigenous and Race-Radical Women of Color Feminisms

> Black feminism performs a double refusal: the refusal to disappear and the refusal to comply.
> —Denise Ferreira da Silva (Barnard Center for Research on Women 2015)

I reference Indigenous and race-radical women of color feminism as an analytic to clearly demarcate a radical and revolutionary tradition and standpoint that is separate from, and oppositional to, one that embraces hegemonic feminism and a liberal politics of recognition. The radicalizing potential of Indigenous and race-radical feminism is based on integrative analyses and incisive critiques of heteropatriarchy and racialized and gendered violence within structures of settler colonialism and White supremacy; autonomy from mainstream bourgeois feminism; independence from heteropatriarchal anti-racism; activism that connects with grassroots and non-elite objectives and leadership; movement-building based upon Indigenous politics of decolonization, sovereignty, and nationhood that rejects the given-ness of the nation-state system or state-like forms of governance; and a marked distaste for overreliance on corporate philanthropy and liberal rights- and reform-based politics in lieu of confronting corporate power, state authority, and policing.

Like race-radical Black feminists, Indigenous feminism centers anti-racist and anticolonial praxis within its anti-violence organizing and challenges the heteronormative and patriarchal nation-state. Currently, numerous Indigenous feminist organizations led by Indigenous girls and women have been challenging calls for a Canadian-based national inquiry on missing and murdered Indigenous women. Instead of conveniently sidestepping outlaw logics and discourses that resist state intervention and litigation out of respect for the family members of murdered women who wish to engage the state, radical Indigenous community organizers foster a politics of Indigenous resurgence to respond to both racialized gendered and carceral state violence. Indigenous renaissance and resurgence is about reclaiming Indigenous contexts (e.g., knowledge, interpretations, values, ethics, processes) for their own political cultures and refocusing Indigenous-led organizing work "from trying to transform the colonial outside into a flourishment of the Indigenous inside" (Simpson 2011, 17; emphasis in the original). As Indigenous feminist Leanne Simpson further elaborates,

> We need to rebuild our culturally inherent philosophical contexts for governance, education, health care, and economy. We need to be able to articulate in a clear manner our visions for the future, for living as Indigenous Peoples in contemporary times. To do so, we need to engage in Indigenous processes, since according to our traditions, the processes of engagement highly influence the outcome of the engagement itself. We need to do this on our own terms, without the sanction, permission, or engagement of the state, western theory, or the opinions of Canadians. (2011, 17; emphasis in the original)

Indigenous feminists embrace this politics of resurgence and are interested in nurturing self-determined and community-led responses to racialized gendered violence targeting Indigenous girls and women rather than relying on colonial nation-states by further engaging with and appealing to state institutions and government bodies.

Black race-radical, Indigenous, and revolutionary women of color feminisms all explicitly challenge liberalism as expressed by dominant liberal feminism and official liberal multiculturalism, which have explained (away) the racialized and gendered violence inherent in carceral states. Despite ideological fluidity and border crossings between and within liberal, radical, and revolutionary women of color feminisms, one can make some valid and useful generalizations. For example, liberal women of color feminisms accept the legitimacy of corporate state institutional and police power, but posit the need for humanistic legal reform, whereas race-radical feminisms view oppression as stemming from capitalism, White supremacy, colonialism, heteropatriarchy, and the neoliberal corporate and carceral state that reinforces all forms of subjection (James 2000; Melamed 2011). Those race-radical and revolutionary feminisms explicitly challenge the carceral settler state itself, not just by protesting its violent excesses—solitary confinement, prison exploitation, and torture—but by connecting grounded political theory for radical transformation with political action to abolish capitalism and the nation-state. As Joy James argues, "radical black feminists' liberation theories address their nemesis: political violence, in both its private and public manifestations; counter-revolutionary state police repression, and a liberal anti-revolutionary discourse that seeks to contain Black feminism by portraying it as an idealistic maverick" (2000, 249). Race-radical and revolutionary Black feminist formations arose from an intersectional analysis of interlocking systems of oppression, including the relations between gender and sex regulation and global capital's new regimes of racial exploitation, of which mass incarceration is but one iteration.

Mass incarceration is bluntly reconstituting and revivifying North American productions of gendered racial citizenship and White supremacy, as well as targeting a large and permanent group of Indigenous women and women of color for legal elimination and social death. These women are, as Lisa Cacho argues, "*ineligible for personhood*—as populations subjected to laws but refused the legal means to contest those laws, as well as denied both the political legitimacy and moral credibility necessary to question them" (2012, 6; emphasis in the original). The "metastasizing carceral state" has helped to legitimize a new mode of "governing through crime" that has spread well beyond the criminal justice system to other core institutions (Gottschalk 2008, 237). In North America, the ascendance of the carceral state has coincided with neoliberal cuts in welfare, public health provision, and social services, alongside increased state policing and surveillance of Indigenous communities and communities of color, which simultaneously struggle with heightened economic insecurity and vulnerability.

The reach of the carceral state extends far beyond the more than one million women currently under the supervision of the criminal justice system—including those women on probation or parole—in the United States (The Sentencing Project 2007). While the U.S. and Canadian prison systems do not operate in the same ways, in Canada, the number of adult female admissions to provincial/territorial custody and federal custody has increased by 55 percent between 1999/2000 and 2008/2009 (Mahony 2011, 33). In addition, women of color are significantly overrepresented in the U.S. criminal justice system. Case in point: Black women represent 30 percent of all incarcerated women in the United States, although they represent only 13 percent of the female population generally (American Civil Liberties Union 2016). Running parallel to mass incarceration of Black girls and women in the United States, Canada is an avid incarcerator of Indigenous women, sharing a pattern of phenomenal growth mirrored in other White settler societies (Balfour and Comack 2014). According to the Correctional Investigator of Canada, more than 36 percent of women in federal prison are of Aboriginal descent, and 2011 statistics show a jump to 41 percent when examining women in provincial custody. Aboriginal people make up just over 4 percent of the overall Canadian population (Sapers 2015, 2). As further lessons will explore, the intrusive reach of punitive carceral controls into the everyday lives and onto the marked bodies of perpetually criminalized Indigenous women and Black women are transcarceral—forming beyond the walls of prisons—and therefore constitute what I and other race-radical feminist activist-scholars call a transcarceral continuum. The transcarceral continuum manifests itself primarily in the guise of localized mental health agencies, welfare and child protective services, and professionalized social services, as well as in individualizing, pathologizing, and self-responsibilizing educational and therapeutic projects. This continuum blurs the boundary between the prison's "outside" and "inside," extending its control through stigmatization and the embodied markers of imprisonment of criminalized girls and women who have spent the majority of their lives under some form of state control.

The interlocking interpersonal, sexual, and carceral state violence targeting Indigenous and Black girls and women in White settler societies is an issue that has rarely been analyzed in dominant, hegemonic feminist explorations of women and violence or heteropatriarchal explorations of prisons and policing. Indigenous feminists and race-radical Black feminists, however, have engaged in a sustained critique of such framings that evacuate carceral state violence from any critical analysis of or activist engagement with gendered, sexualized, and racialized violence. The historical legacies and activist genealogies of Indigenous and race-radical women feminists continue to guide feminist anti-violence activists in strengthening contemporary movements capable of dismantling both race-based and gender-based violence sustained and perpetuated by the carceral state.

Theorizing the Carceral State and Abolitionist Praxis

We cannot live without our lives.
—Banner held by Combahee River Collective members protesting the sexual assault and murder of twelve Black women in the Boston area in the first six months of 1979 (Combahee River Collective 1979)

As Angela Davis and Gina Dent (2001) argue in their seminal essay "Prison as Border," the political economy of North American prisons, policing, and the punishment industry in the Global North brings the intersections of gender, race, colonialism, and capitalism into sharp focus. The Prison-Industrial Complex (PIC) is defined by Critical Resistance as a "complicated system situated at the intersection of governmental and private interests that uses prisons and policing as a failed 'solution' to social, political and economic crisis" (Critical Resistance 2012). The PIC depends upon the oppressive systems of racism, classism, sexism, and homophobia operating within White settler societies such as the United States—the world's largest purveyor of state violence, both militarily and in the scale of its prison system. As Davis and Dent argue, "find[ing] that the prison is itself a border . . . is an important interpretation that undoes the illusions of powerful nation-states on the one hand and the seeming disorganization and chaos of capital's travels on the other" (2001, 1236–37). Similar to how the factories and workplaces of local and transnational corporations discipline the labor of immigrant women of color, the prisons of White settler societies disproportionately incarcerate large numbers of Indigenous people and people of color.

Furthering this analysis which identifies borders and prisons as shaping this moment of global crisis, Ruth Wilson Gilmore argues that prison expansion and mass incarceration of populations deemed surplus or redundant to racial capitalism is the newest iteration of White supremacism and heteropatriarchal regimes and racism. She defines racism as "the state-sanctioned and/or extralegal production and exploitation of group-differentiated vulnerabilities to premature death, in distinct yet densely interconnected political geographies" (Gilmore 2002, 261). Gilmore's definition of racism relates closely to postcolonial scholar Achille Mbembe's conceptualization of necropolitics as politics defined as a "work of death" in that it identifies "who matters and who does not, who is disposable and who is not" based upon race and the logic of racism and colonial domination (2003, 12 and 27). Mbembe argues that the meanings of death in necropolitics emerge through interpretations of embodiment: of corpses, of who kills, and of who is targeted for death. As will be further explored throughout my curriculum, in North America, necropower is most visible in the hyper-criminalization, mass incarceration, deportation, and extermination of Indigenous nations and Black communities.

Employing a critical intersectional analysis, race-radical Black feminists like Angela Davis, Assata Shakur, Joy James, Cathy Cohen, Ruth Wilson Gilmore, Beth Richie, and Julia Sudbury (Oparah) have both embraced and critically departed from Michel Foucault's seminal analysis in *Discipline and Punish* of the "birth of the prison" in order to discuss how the particular formation of the North American carceral state emerges, functions, and reproduces itself. Foucault's term "carceral" refers to a network of regimentation and discipline, a prison without walls in turn made up of social networks of surveillance. Since it is, according to Dylan Rodríguez, "the prison regime that possesses and constitutes the state," (2006, 43) and not the other way around, the analysis of state violence presented by race-radical women of color theorists necessarily centers a race-radical women of color feminist standpoint from which to challenge the expanding, transnational, and transcarceral prison regime. The idea of the PIC as a regime underscores how the cultural and institutional site of prison is no

longer "some building 'over there' but a set of relationships that undermine rather than stabilize everyday lives everywhere" (Gilmore 2007).

The metanarrative of Foucault's *Discipline and Punish* has been uniformly
contested by Indigenous and race-radical women of color feminists who
have critiqued Foucault for universalizing the White, propertied, male
body and erasing the spectacle of state-sanctioned racialized and gendered
violence targeting Black and Indigenous bodies throughout Africa and the
Americas. If the "art of punishing, in the regime of disciplinary power" is
designed not to expiate or repress but to "normalize" (1977, 182–83), as
Foucault argues, then one must recognize, as Joy James in turn argues,
"that some bodies cannot be normalized no matter how they are disciplined, unless the prevailing social and state structures that figuratively
and literally rank bodies disintegrate" (1996, 27). Race-radical feminists
have departed from "Foucauldian erasures," which, by arguing that nothing exists outside the carceral, fail to explore the reality of resistance to
White supremacist, carceral state violence.

I now turn to examine briefly those Black and Indigenous anti-prison
abolitionist communities who view political life outside and beyond the
carceral in an effort to analyze and dismantle racialized state violence and
the carceral state.

Poignantly stressing the devastating economic and affective effects that
incarceration has on the children and communities that incarcerated people leave behind, Ruth Wilson Gilmore explains that prisons, "wear out
places by wearing out people, irrespective of whether they have done time"
(2007, 17). In response to the intensity with which the carceral state was
locking their children, of all ages, into the criminal punishment system,
working-class Black and Indigenous women have been establishing
important grassroots abolitionist collectives and statewide campaigns to
challenge the carceral state on a number of fronts, from mandatory minimum three-strikes laws to the siting of new prisons. Gilmore traces how
the organization Mothers Reclaiming Our Children (ROC), founded in
California in the early 1990s, evolved from being a cooperative self-help
group that formed in response to racist police murders of young Black men
in deindustrializing South Central Los Angeles into a social movement
built to challenge what she calls "domestic militarism" (Gilmore 2007,
239). Mothers ROC (whose members are known as "ROCers") open up the
possibility of identification by "critically deploy[ing] the ideological power

of motherhood" to challenge the legitimacy of the changing carceral state and by emphasizing that all prisoners are somebody's children, and children are not alienable (Gilmore 1999, 27). Neither a non-profit service agency nor a liberal reformist organization, Mothers ROC rejected a liberal politics of recognition, visibility, and inclusion. This cadre of mothers of color, who first encountered one another in the interstices of the carceral state, has focused on making power through organizational capacity building, political education, coalition building, and direct action driven by "a principled sense of mortal urgency" (Gilmore 2007, 251).

Driven by a similar urgency, grassroots, volunteer-led local and transnational groups like Families of Sisters in Spirit (FSIS), No More Silence (NMS), and the Native Youth Sexual Health Network (NYSHN) embrace a politics of Indigenous resurgence and are interested in nurturing self-determined and community-led responses to racialized gendered violence targeting Indigenous girls and women rather than relying on the Canadian nation-state by further engaging with and appealing to state institutions and government bodies for justice. In their joint statement, "It Starts With Us," which lays the groundwork to support the resurgence of community-based responses to violence, these three Indigenous-led organizations name specific forms of state violence and identify the harms of going through "the proper channels" of state-led interventions, ranging from providing testimonies to British Columbia's Missing Women Commission of Inquiry to making recommendations to the United Nations Committee for the Elimination of Discrimination against Women (CEDAW) (Families of Sisters in Spirit, No More Silence, and Native Youth Sexual Health Network 2014). Heightened calls for a national inquiry into the phenomenon of missing and murdered Indigenous women have been made in the wake of the disappearance and murder of Loretta Saunders, a pregnant young Inuk graduate student who was writing her thesis on the murders of three Nova Scotia Indigenous women (CBC News 2014; Leroux 2014); to these organizations, however, such calls are a waste of time.

Moreover, beyond being a waste of time, Robyn Bourgeois argues, an inquiry "allows the Canadian state to *appear* that it is doing something about violence against women *without ever having to actually do anything*" (2012; emphasis in the original). Establishing an inquiry or special committee to examine an issue that has successfully been defined in mainstream media and civic fora as a social problem has historically been a common strategy by the state to silence the voices of opposition. After warning other Indigenous women who are advocating for the inquiry about how the "colonial government can, and will, define, dictate, and decide the purpose, mandate, process, and outcome of that inquiry," Andrea Landry deploys an outlaw discourse that delegitimizes an inquiry "established by a structure meant to murder, rape, and annihilate the Indigenous self" (2014). Landry writes, "if the colonial government were to put the dollars in to 'fix' an issue that they continuously create and justify, and if we were to agree to work together, we would be shaking hands with and embodying the oppressor" (Landry 2014). Landry powerfully equates Indigenous women's falling prey to the "assimilative lure of the statist politics of recognition" (Coulthard 2007, 456) in the form of a national inquiry to that of the visceral pain induced by internalized oppression and violent victimization at the hands of the White-settler state. While nothing can be gained from engaging in a liberal politics of recognition, inclusion, and visibility, for Indigenous women, in particular, everything can be lost. Instead of engaging with carceral and settler states, these radical Indigenous feminists are "call[ing] attention back to ourselves; we have the answers and solutions . . . we always have" (Families of Sisters in Spirit, No More Silence, and Native Youth Sexual Health Network 2014). The solutions in which communities are already actively engaged range from Indigenous resurgence, teach-ins and critical education, media-arts justice, community accountability and transformative justice, supporting Indigenous people in the sex trades and street economies, centering Indigenous youth leadership and intergenerational organizing, and Annual February 14TH Memorial Marches for Missing and Murdered Women (Native Youth Sexual Health Network 2013a; 2013b; 2014), to the "countless acts of hidden resistance and kitchen table resistance aimed at ensuring their children and grandchildren could live as *Indigenous* Peoples" (Ladner and Simpson 2010, 8; emphasis in the original).

The new abolitionism of anti-prison movements, such as that advanced by Mothers (ROC), and of resurgent, decolonial Indigenous movements like those advanced by the Indigenous feminists of FSIS, NMS, and NYSHN put into practice a pragmatic intersectional analysis in affinity with the work of Indigenous and race-radical women of feminism in that abolitionist activists examine how processes of race, class, gender, and sexuality and transnational economic forces aggregate and interlock to create the everyday lived conditions of the carceral state. Indigenous and race-radical women of color in White settler societies have created a number of prison abolitionist tools: First, they developed the analytic ability to understand how seemingly disconnected institutions of carceral state violence—citizenship, incapacitation, and punishment, for example—work together to produce and police social difference and to legally consign entire groups of people to precarious futures and premature deaths. Second, their organizing points to the centrality of gender politics within anti-racist, anticolonial abolitionist struggles and therefore rejects heteropatriarchal racial nationalism espoused within their own communities. Relatedly, and as will be discussed in further detail in later lessons in the proposed course, Indigenous and race-radical women of color feminists who are both prison abolitionists and anti-domestic and -sexual violence activists have built a strong critique of how the mainstream U.S. feminist and anti-violence movements have been complicit in building up the carceral state (see Bumiller 2008; Collective 2008a; Gottschalk 2006; Richie 2012; Smith 2005a). Lastly, because prison abolition is both a practical organizing tool and a long-term goal, Indigenous and race-radical women of color feminists have also crafted and honed inclusive organizing strategies and tactics capable of challenging both racialized gendered violence and systemic carceral state violence waged against Indigenous girls and women, communities of color, and trans people of color.

Because the PIC in White settler societies is not an isolated system, abolition is a necessarily expansive and broad decolonial project—a project that is in line with the "holistic anti-violence agendas" engendered most centrally by Indigenous and race-radical women of color feminists (Sudbury 2003). As Angela Davis (2003) demonstrates, a prison abolitionist project is a positive rather than a negative or reactive project; the way out is not to simply keep pushing back against carceral state policies of social control and criminalization that contribute to violence, but rather to proactively build grassroots antiviolence mobilizations. Working with this analysis, the Critical Resistance "CR10 Publications Collective" argues, prison abolition is "not simply about tearing down prison walls, but . . . about building alternative formations that actually protect people from violence, that crowd out the criminalization regime" (CR10 Publications Collective 2008a, 5). Relatedly, Fred Moten and Stefano Harney offer the following musings on prison abolition:

> What is, so to speak, the object of abolition? Not so much the abolition of prisons but the abolition of a society that could have prisons, that could

have slavery, that could have the wage, and therefore not abolition as the elimination of anything but abolition as the founding of a new society. (2004, 114)

In summary, prison abolitionist praxis is a political vision with the goal of eliminating imprisonment, policing, and surveillance—and the ideological structures of White supremacist capitalist heteropatriarchy that shape institutional violence—and creating lasting alternatives to the nation-state, citizenship, militarized policing, mass incarceration, and border fortification. The next section will argue that prison abolitionist praxis engages not only political commitments but also pedagogical ones. In other words, race-radical feminist praxis is inherently and primarily pedagogical.

The Lesson Plan for Indigenous and Race-Radical Feminist Prison Studies

Arguing that the "massive carceral-cultural form of the prison has naturalized a systemic *disorientation of the teaching act*," Dylan Rodriguez suggests that our primary task as radical teachers is to ask, "whether and how the act of teaching can effectively and radically displace the normalized misery, everyday suffering, and mundane state violence that are reproduced and/or passively condoned by both hegemonic and critical/counter-hegemonic pedagogies" (Rodriguez 2010, 8; emphasis in the original). The following lesson plan asks: What would happen to the "disoriented teaching act" if it were reoriented to challenge students—particularly those learners who have a firsthand experience of the criminal legal and injustice system—to question their assumptions about the necessity of prisons and the blithe acceptance of societies that use prisons and policing as "a failed 'solution' to social, political and economic crisis" (Critical Resistance 2012)? In other words, how do we learn, teach, and organize about carceral logics and prison abolition in the classroom in a manner that teaches against the grain of carceral common sense?

The attached lesson plan continues to build from the literature to underscore how Indigenous and race-radical women of color feminist epistemology lays the necessary theoretical and activist groundwork to make possible a rejection of a liberal politics of recognition and fosters an unwavering commitment to the abolition of the carceral state. The felt theory and activist-scholarship of Indigenous feminist and race-radical women of color feminist formations have offered us a roadmap of how to: 1) denaturalize White settler colonialism, carceral feminisms, and their genealogies; 2) challenge our complicity in upholding carceral logics; and 3) model an affective economy in stark opposition to that proffered by the carceral state.

Future lessons will explore the prescient work undertaken by race-radical Black and Indigenous feminist scholar-activists that have advanced important insights into the relationship between systematic racialized, gendered, and sexualized violence and White settler colonialism. The project of the state in perpetuating violence in Indigenous, Black, and Chicana/Latina communities through genocide, slavery, prisons, and border patrols is well documented by race-radical feminist scholars (Bhattacharjee and Silliman 2002; Davis 1983; Díaz-Cotto 2006; Ross 1998; Smith 2005). These race-radical women of color feminists have served as "radical bridge-builders" between a multiplicity of social movements, such as the antiwar, prison abolitionist, political prisoner, police brutality, racial profiling, and domestic violence and sexual assault movements (Sudbury 2003, 135). Their activist praxis points to the manner in which the work to dismantle the carceral state will advance the feminist anti-violence agenda in fundamental and critical ways.

Lesson Plan:

Are the Cops in Our Heads and the Prison in Our Hearts?:
Starting at the Place Where You Stand

....

"[T]he prison is not some building 'over there' but a set of relationships that undermine rather than stabilize everyday lives everywhere."
– Ruth Wilson Gilmore (2007a)

....

Introduction

Echoing Gilmore's acknowledgement that our bodies and political imaginations have been captured by the carceral state and White settler imaginaries, Paula X. Rojas asks: "Are the Cops in Our Head and Hearts?" Rojas (2007) is one of the collective members and co-founders of the Sista II Sista Collective—a group of young women of color in Brooklyn, New York, working to end intimate and state violence against women and girls of color. In her article, Rojas explores how in their transformative justice work, grassroots, volunteer-based collectives and social movements "develop short-term strategies for protecting and supporting survivors of racialized gendered and carceral state violence as they organize to end the societal structures that enable violence to happen in the first place" (Rojas 2007, 200). When these collectives and movements focus on organizing as part of everyday life—making power instead of taking power (as though the entire political setup were only a matter of "it" (structure) versus "us" (agency)—the process becomes as important as the final product. Thus, communities of Indigenous and race-radical women of color feminists seek not merely to intervene after violence happens, but also to create a world in which violence becomes unimaginable. Learning, teaching, and organizing about carceral logics and prison abolition both inside and outside of the classroom in a manner that goes against the grain of carceral common sense means putting on the table transformative examples of communities and movements that are actively working to confront racialized, gendered, and sexualized violence without automatically turning to or over-relying on the prison industrial complex (PIC) (INCITE! Women of

Color Against Violence 2005) and the non-profit industrial complex (NPIC) (Gilmore 2007b). I bring these radical and revolutionary alternatives into college classrooms and community-based teaching/learning spaces by centering non-state resources, organizations, and examples that practice radical harm reduction and transformative justice (see list of resources below). The targeted audience is other activist-scholars who are working with and alongside these nascent organizations and movements and teacher-learners who understand themselves and their communities to be directly impacted by the PIC.

In order to begin to imagine the unimaginable, activist-scholars and teacher-learners must strive to mutually build community so as to explore how we have all been socialized within, touched/targeted/punished by, resistant to, and/or complicit with maintaining the carceral state. Acknowledging that "the cops" have burrowed their way into our minds and our hearts, we must engage with—and most importantly, produce our own—activist-scholarship pushing back against a purist politics that mistakenly believes that there is a clearly demarcated and pure "outside" to the current system. As Indigenous feminist Dian Million reminds us, "we dance in a politically electrified field most of our lives" (2011, 316). Indigenous feminist conceptualizations of sovereignty and decolonization, as well as Black race-radical feminist political claims to what Black feminist Saidiya Hartman would call statelessness, homelessness, and motherlessness (Hartman 2007) have, however, furnished new ways for breaking the stranglehold of carceral state necropower, as well as provided answers to the questions that have weighed most heavily throughout this course: To whom (and to where) do we run for cover from the carceral state? What do these political formations and autonomous spaces that do not rely on the nation-state look and feel like? Can we actually achieve a freedom from interpersonal, sexual, and carceral state violence?

The goal here is not to craft and share ready-made, clear-cut strategies for teaching and learning abolition "the right way." Rather, in excavating the emotional and affective charges connected to the carceral state and its attendant logics, I have some directions and questions that are worth experimenting with. As Jessi Lee Jackson and Erica R. Meiners argue in their aptly titled article "Feeling Like a Failure," teaching/learning abolition necessitates that we not only critically examine our investments in viewing people as either innocent or guilty, good or bad, but that we examine experiences of shame and fear, "especially the fear of 'going too far' with prison abolition, a feeling we identify as linked to how experiences of trauma and social rejection can limit how much we are willing to ask for" (Jackson and Meiners 2010, 21). Incorporating and building first-person narratives of trauma and social rejection can provide oppositional and alternative models of confronting the trauma of living in the "shadow of the prison" and providing care to others. Inspired by these words, the point is not to fixate on our failures (as there will be many) or to strive for resolution (as there will be none) but to heighten the conflicts and embrace the contradictions that emerge when we begin to honestly assess our complicities with maintaining and commitments to abolishing the carceral state.

Learning Objectives

By the end of this lesson, you will have:

- Explored how you have been socialized within, touched/targeted/punished by, resistant to, and/or complicit with maintaining the prison regime;
- Thought about what it means—for yourself, your family, and your community—to be *simultaneously* privileged by, oppressed by, *and* complicit with carceral systems of domination, control, and violence; and,
- Created meaningful connections between race-radical, Indigenous, and transnational feminist prison studies and your own social location in order to begin crafting your own auto-ethnographic narrative.

Before you start this lesson, you will have previously:

- Practiced reading and interrogating primary texts closely to develop a nuanced understanding of the central concepts and issues, as well as historical and contemporary debates within the still-burgeoning field of transnational, race-radical feminist prison studies;
- Analyzed how transnational, race-radical feminist prison studies has evolved from its roots in Indigenous, race-radical, and critical race feminist scholarly engagements with feminist anti-violence and anti-prison praxis in White settler societies;
- Contributed your own emergent, yet rigorous, feminist analysis of racialized and gendered violence in White settler societies, trans-

carceral state violence, and global prison regimes to the field of transnational feminist prison studies scholarship;

- Assessed multiple forms of anti-racist feminist activism and activist-
scholarship in terms of their argument, assumptions, implications,
benefits, and limitations; and,
- Created meaningful connections between race-radical, transnational
feminist prison studies and methodologies and your own field or area
of interest/discipline/practice.

Learning Activities

This lesson plan outline can be adapted for an upper-division undergraduate course or community-based course, as there are many systemic and
structural barriers that would prevent this lesson from being offered in a K-
12 school system. It can be condensed into a single three-hour lesson
(shown here) or extended over two or three lessons.

Time	Activity	Description
10 minutes	Introduction (Part 1)	• Grounding exercise and review of our collective discussion about triggers and trauma
20 minutes	Introduction (Part 2)	• Watch the auto-ethnographic film *Shadow Boxing: A Chicana's Journey from Vigilante Violence to Transformative Justice* (Palacios 2013)
30 minutes	Individual Activity #1	• Free-write and provide your reactions and critiques of the film
15 minutes	Stretch, Exercise, and Break	• Shadowboxing and deep breathing exercises • 10-minute break
45 minutes	Small-Group Activity	• Share free-writing activity and discuss readings for the day • Guided reading questions provided 1 week/session prior to class
45 minutes	Large-Group Activity	• Report-backs and open discussion facilitated by professor • Discussion of assignment
5 minutes	Stretch and Exercise	• Shadowboxing and deep breathing exercises
10 minutes	Individual Activity #2	• Closure and short overview of today's lesson • Free-write and provide your questions and comments about today's lesson • Preview of next week's lesson

On Shadowboxing

Twice throughout the lesson, I engage with deep breathing and shadowboxing exercises that can be done either sitting or standing. When

shadowboxing, boxers spar with an imaginary opponent as a form of training. I encourage this form of grounding exercise not only to relieve stress and promote presence but to confront traumatic material in ways that mirror how Indigenous and race-radical Black feminists work with and through the trauma brought on by experiencing racialized, gendered, and sexualized violence. An Indigenous race-radical woman of color feminist standpoint is constituted in and through the politics of continuous interplay between activism and violent repression—what Joy James alludes to as revolutionary Black women's learned capacity to navigate daily life as if "shadowboxing" (James 2002)—an apt metaphor for the "outsider within" struggle to both "fight the authoritative body casting one off, while simultaneously struggling with internal conflict and contradictions" (James 2000, 255). Militant antiracist feminists, in particular, have had to negotiate the "internal" opposition of antiradicalism among liberal feminists and anti-racists as well as the counter-feminism evident among radicals—all while fighting carceral state power.

On Collective Models of Learning and Accountability

I strongly believe that class should be structured in such a way that all learners can have ample opportunities to talk back and can feel free to articulate opinions or political perspectives that they think I and others will disagree with. When learners can make their voice public, it is possible for me and for other students to converse with these views. It is only through open, honest, substantive, and respectful dialogue that we can change our minds, and that cannot happen if learners do not feel free to share what they really think and feel. I only ask that students be at least be open to hearing new ideas, even if they are not immediately convinced by them. So that all learners have a voice in shaping the classroom experience itself, at the beginning of the course—usually during the second week of class—we will collaboratively discuss in-class and online dynamics and come up with some agreements about how we hold each other accountable (how we can "call each other in" instead of merely "calling each other out") and collectively deal with discomfort, conflict, triggers, trauma, unequal participation (e.g., when someone is dominating discussions), "devil's advocate" positions, "speaking for" and "speaking over," racism, sexism, homophobia, transphobia, heterosexism, ableism, ageism, Islamophobia, classism/elitism, etc.

This class is intended for us to learn; we have both the collective right and responsibility to change the classroom culture if it does meet our individual and collective needs. I will conduct periodic oral and written evaluations of classroom dynamics. In addition, I will build in other periodic exercises that draw attention to the operation of power in the classroom, especially the ways that conflicts are voiced and resolved and knowledges are constructed and validated. When a concern is brought to the table, I will ask all students what they think would be a good way to handle the issue rather than just address it directly myself. I hope that all learners will feel free to make suggestions as the class goes on and that they assume individual and collective responsibility for making appropriate changes to ensure, if not a "safe space," then a "safer space." In these ways, the classroom can become a dynamic space where students refuse shame, fear, and social death and claim their education.

Required Readings and Recommended Resources

Today we read the following activist-scholarship of Julia Sudbury (Oparah), Joy James, Stormy Ogden, Lisa Cacho, and Lena Palacios; in particular, their auto-ethnographic essays "grounded" in race-radical/critical race feminist activist scholarship:

- Julia Sudbury's (Oparah's) essay "Challenging Penal Democracy: Activist Scholars and the Anti-Prison Movement" (Sudbury 2009)
- Joy James' introductory chapter "Warrior Tropes" in her book *Shadowboxing: Representations of Black Feminist Politics* (James 1999)
- Stormy Ogden's auto-ethnographic essays "Pomo Woman, Ex-Prisoner, Speaks Out" and "The Prison-Industrial Complex in Indigenous California" (Ogden 2005; Ogden 2006)
- Lena Palacios's essay "'Something Else to Be': A Chicana Survivor's Journey from Vigilante Justice to Transformative Justice" and accompanying film (Palacios 2013; 2016)
- Lisa Cacho's "'You Just Don't Know How Much He Meant': Deviancy, Death, and Devaluation" (Cacho 2007)

To find out more about prison abolition; transformative justice; and community accountability goals, principles, and application, students will be encouraged to consult these movement-based resources:

Print

Chen, Ching-In, Jai Dulani, and Leah Lakshmi Piepzna-Samarasinha, eds. 2011. *The Revolution Starts at Home: Confronting Intimate Violence Within Activist Communities*. Brooklyn, NY: South End Press.

Community Accountability: Emerging Movements to Transform Violence, a special issue of *Social Justice: A Journal of Crime, Conflict & World Order* 37, no. 4 (2011–2012).

Palacios, Lena. 2016. "'Ain't No Justice . . . It's Just Us': Girls Organizing against Interpersonal and Institutional Violence." In *Girlhood Studies and the Politics of Place: Contemporary Paradigms for Research*, edited by Claudia Mitchell and Carrie A. Rentschler, 279–95. New York: Berghahn Books.

Online

Creative Interventions Toolkit (A Practical Guide to Stop Interpersonal Violence). http://www.creative-interventions.org/tools/toolkit/.

Hereth, Jane, and Chez Rumpf. 2014. "Community Accountability for Survivors of Sexual Violence Toolkit." https://carceralfeminism.files .wordpress.com/2014/04/cassv-reading-group-tlllkit.shifting-from -carceral-to-tj-feminisms_final.pdf.

INCITE! Women of Color Against Violence, and Communities Against Rape and Abuse (CARA). 2005. "Community Accountability within the People of Color Progressive Movement: Report from the INCITE! Women of Color Against Violence Ad-Hoc Community Accountability Working Group Meeting." http://incite-national.org/sites/default/files /incite_files/resource_docs/2406_cmty-acc-poc.pdf.

INCITE! and Critical Resistance: Statement on Gender Violence and the Prison Industrial Complex, http://www.incite-national.org/page /incite-critical-resistance-statement.

Russo, Ann, and Melissa Spatz. 2007. "Communities Engaged in Resist-ing Violence." Communities Engaged in Resisting Violence | Issue-Lab. Chicago: Women and Girls Collective Action Network, http://www.transformativeiustice.eu/wp-content/uploads/20i0/ii /communities_engaged.pdf.

Collectives and Organizations on the Web

African American Policy Forum	http://www.aapf.org/
Bay Area Transformative Justice Collective	https://batjc.wordpress.com/
CARA Communities Against Rape and Abuse	http://cara-seattle.blogspot.ca/
Chain Reaction: Alternatives to Calling the Police	http://alternativestopolicing.com/
Community United Against Violence	http://www.cuav.org/
CONNECT: Safe Families, Peaceful Communities	http://www.connectnyc.org/
Critical Resistance	http://criticalresistance.org/
Families of Sister in Spirit	http://familiesofsistersinspirit.tumblr.com/
FAR-OUT Friends Are Reaching Out	http://farout.org/
Generation FIVE	http://www.generationfive.org/
Generative Somatics: Somatic Transformation and Social Justice	http://www.generativesomatics.org/
INCITE!: Women of Color Against Violence	http://www.incite-national.org/
Justice NOW!	http://www.jnow.org/home.html
Native Youth Sexual Health Network	http://www.nativeyouthsexualhealth.com/
Philly Stands Up	https://phillystandsup.wordpress.com/about/
Philly Survivor Support Collect: Support for Survivors of Sexual Assault	https://phillysurvivorsupportcollective.wordpress.com/
Project NIA: Building Peaceful Communities	http://www.project-nia.org/
Safe OUTside the System: The SOS Collective	http://alp.org/community/sos
Support New York	http://supportny.org/
TGI Justice Project	http://www.tgijp.org/
Transformative Justice Law Project of Illinois	http://tjlp.org/
We Charge Genocide	http://wechargegenocide.org/
Young Women's Empowerment Project	https://ywepchicago.wordpress.com/

Assignment

This assignment is inspired by the activist-scholarship of Julia Sudbury (Oparah), Joy James, Stormy Ogden, and Lena Palacios: in particular, their auto-ethnographic essays "grounded" in race-radical/critical race feminist activist-scholarship. For good models, please refer to the required readings for today's lesson (see above).

You will produce a 5–7-minute video essay or digital story (accompanied by a five-page essay) that creatively and critically analyzes a memory, artifact, or lived experience that speaks to how you have been socialized within, touched/targeted/punished by, resistant to, and/or complicit with maintaining the prison regime. I encourage you to think through what it means—for yourself, your family, and your community—to be simultaneously privileged by, oppressed by, and complicit with systems of domination, control, and violence.

The initial step of this digital storytelling assignment is to free-write. In auto-ethnographic work, that means writing the "story" of a memory, artifact, or lived experience in simple terms, with no analysis. In essence, your "story" or narrative becomes the data from which your analysis can grow or be grounded. The second step is for you to produce the more polished, worked-through, edited, and analyzed paper: the one that has worked with the data, reflected upon it, and pulled in and grounded theoretical materials to help bolster your reading of it. Finally, you will produce a digital story in which you produce new and/or select pre-existing images, voice-overs, video clips, animation, music, etc. that effectively represent your auto-ethnographic memory work. In the beginning of the course, you will participate in digital storytelling workshops and iMovie and/or Adobe Premiere Pro media production software trainings.

When you reference academic works, use proper bibliographic citation and include a Works Cited at the end. Refer to at least two of the assigned readings and at least two additional resources from the list of resources and bibliography located at the end of the lesson plan. Ensure that this is a scholarly investigation and not just a nostalgic one: use readings, images, and found artifacts critically and reference accordingly.

Your essay should not exceed five typed, double-spaced pages.

Preview

In the following weeks, we will turn to another discussion of mortal urgency in which we analyze how Indigenous and race-radical women of color feminists have underscored how racialized, gendered, and sexualized violence intersect to build and sustain the carceral state. Indigenous and race-radical women of color feminists and PIC abolitionists have been at the forefront of analyzing how White supremacist settler state violence depends on heterosexism and heteronormativity and of the deep imbrication of race, gender, class, and sexuality within the capitalist, colonial world order.

We will also continue our debate exploring whether or not the institutionalization of race-radical, transnational feminist prison studies in universities, prisons, or other institutions would extend, perpetuate, maintain or challenge the carceral state.

....

Lena Palacios Gutekunst is an assistant professor in Communication Studies at the University of Minnesota. Her research and teaching focuses on prison abolitionism, Black, Indigenous, Latinx queer and trans feminisms, girls' studies, transformative justice and community accountability, media activism and media justice, health justice, as well as participatory action research. A career changer, she will be leaving academia and starting her studies at John Hopkins School of Nursing in order to become a Nurse Practitioner.

Note

Originally published in *Meridians* vol. 15, no. 1, 2016.

Works Cited

Cacho, Lisa Marie. 2007. '"You Just Don't Know How Much He Meant': Deviancy, Death, and Devaluation." *Latino Studies* 5, no. 2: 182. doi:10.1057/palgrave. lst.8600246.

Gilmore, Ruth Wilson. 2007a. *Golden Gulag: Prisons, Surplus, Crisis, and Opposition in Globalizing California.* Berkeley: University of California Press.

———. 2007b. "In the Shadow of the Shadow State." In *The Revolution Will Not Be Funded: Beyond the Non-Profit Industrial Complex,* edited by Incite! Women of Color Against Violence, 41–52. Cambridge, MA: South End Press.

Hartman, Saidiya V. 2007. *Lose Your Mother: A Journey along the Atlantic Slave Route.* New York: Farrar, Straus and Giroux.

INCITE! Women of Color Against Violence. 2005. "Gender Violence and the Prison Industrial Complex: Interpersonal and State Violence against Women of Color." In *Domestic Violence at the Margins: Readings on Race, Class, Gender, and Culture,* edited by Natalie J Sokoloff and Christina Pratt. New Brunswick, NJ: Rutgers University Press.

Jackson, Jessi Lee, and Erica R Meiners. 2010. "Feeling Like a Failure: Teaching/ Learning Abolition Through the Good the Bad and the Innocent." *Radical Teacher* 88, no. 1: 20–30.

James, Joy. 1999. *Shadowboxing: Representations of Black Feminist Politics.* New York: St. Martin's Press.

———. 2000. "Radicalizing Feminism." In *The Black Feminist Reader,* edited by T. Denean Sharpley-Whiting and Joy James, 239–58. Malden, MA: Blackwell Publishers.

———. 2002. *Shadowboxing: Representations of Black Feminist Politics.* New York: Palgrave Macmillan.

Million, Dian. 2011. "Intense Dreaming: Theories, Narratives, and Our Search for Home." *The American Indian Quarterly* 35, no. 3: 313–33.

Ogden, Stormy. 2005. "The Prison-Industrial Complex in Indigenous California." In *Global Lockdown: Race, Gender, and the Prison-Industrial Complex,* edited by Julia Chinyere Oparah, 57–71. New York: Routledge.

———. 2006. "Pomo Woman, Ex-Prisoner, Speaks Out." In *Color of Violence: The Incite! Anthology,* edited by INCITE! Women of Color Against Violence, 164–70. Cambridge, MA: South End Press.

Palacios, Lena. 2013. *Shadow Boxing: A Chicana's Journey from Vigilante Violence to Transformative Justice.* Ottawa, Ont.: SAW Video Media Arts Centre. http://www.youtube .com/watch?v=QV50FQ0UxZc&feature=youtube_gdata_player.

———. 2016. "'Something Else to Be': A Chicana Survivor's Journey from Vigilante Justice to Transformative Justice." *philoSOPHIA A Journal of Continental Feminism*, 6, no. 1 (Winter): 93–108.

Rojas, Paula X. 2007. "Are the Cops in Our Heads and Hearts?" In *The Revolution Will Not Be Funded: Beyond the Non-Profit Industrial Complex*, edited by INCITE! Women of Color Against Violence, 198–214. Cambridge, MA: South End Press.

Simpson, Leanne. 2011. *Dancing on Our Turtle's Back: Stories of Nishnaabeg Re-creation, Resurgence, and a New Emergence.* Winnipeg, MB: Arbetier Ring Publishing.

Sudbury, Julia. 2009. "Challenging Penal Democracy: Activist Scholars and the Anti-prison Movement." In *Activist Scholarship: Antiracism, Feminism, and Social Change*, edited by Margo Okazawa-Rey and Julia Sudbury, 17–35. Boulder, CO: Paradigm Publishers.

Karsonya Wise Whitehead

....

Rethinking Meridians
As a Critical Knowledge Project, a Pedagogical Offering, and a Black Feminist Quilted Narrative[1]

Abstract: Alice Walker in her book, *In Search of Our Mothers' Garden*, notes that when you write the book you want to read, you are both pointing and following your "direction of vision." As a writer and a Black feminist scholar, the author understood this to mean that she needed to craft the tools that would help her to do her work. *Rethinking Meridians* is the critical knowledge project, the tool, that she wanted to have in her hand when she was a classroom teacher. Consisting of articles and lesson plans, the special issue was designed as a disruption tool that would inspire teachers and students to transcend the notion of the classroom as a static, constrained, and unliberated space. By using the lens of *transdisciplinarity*, *Rethinking Meridians* examines Black feminist theory as a teaching tool and a pedagogical practice that challenges teachers to connect the work across disciplines and beyond them.

Education as a Form of Liberation

With the increasingly high stakes nature of teaching and the ongoing push to teach within the adopted Common Core, there appears to be very little room for teachers to incorporate the voices and experiences of anyone whose life is not already embedded within the curriculum. Given that there is an implied dominant circle of historical privilege—where the voices of those who are White, male, heterosexual, able-bodied, cis-gendered, middle class, educated, and Christian are assumed to be and taught as if they

MERIDIANS · feminism, race, transnationalism   Volume 19 Supplement 2020
DOI: 10.1215/15366936-8566418 © 2016 Smith College

were the norm—teachers must be provided with resources that are designed to decenter this "norm" and then center the voices of "the other." This is an ongoing challenge but, as scholars, we are committed to developing research agendas and writing and teaching resources that advance liberatory educational possibilities for non-dominant and marginalized communities. We center this work firmly within the Black feminist tradition, drawing heavily upon the historic and foundational work of Ida B. Wells, Anna Julia Cooper, Alice Dunbar-Nelson, Audre Lorde, and the Combahee River Collective and the current work of bell hooks, Kimberlé Crenshaw, Patricia Hill Collins, Paula Giddings, Barbara Ransby, Beverly Guy-Sheftall, Cheryl Wall, and Angela Davis (to name just a few). We do not have the option to resign in the face of difficulty or the luxury to hold our work hostage as we spend years pondering possible directions and solutions—because we create scholarship not simply for ourselves but for the unseen faces of people who depend on the unwavering commitment of scholars who take up justice work. We know that the ongoing work to rescue and reclaim the history and lives of Black women is important and that it is our duty—in the same vein as Alice Walker's early work to rescue Zora Neale Hurston—to collect and share their life and experiences "for the future of our children . . . if necessary, bone by bone." (Walker 1983, 92) This critical restoration work completed in the archives and then shared at the dinner tables, in book clubs, and more importantly, in classrooms, seeks to advance Paulo Freire's idea of "conscientization," opening it up and then expanding upon it. (hooks 1994, 14)

At the same time, we understand (and respect) that there is a necessary gulf that exits between the researcher and the teacher to ensure that every "good" research idea is not then tested on children, particularly those who exist precariously on the edge where the challenge of getting a good education is a daily struggle. So with these multiple streams of knowing in mind, we wrestled with how this new critical knowledge project of rethinking and re-centering *Meridians* as a text for teachers and students should be presented and positioned. Given that *Meridians* is available as both a print and an electronic source, we decided to challenge the contributors to think of this work in a two-dimensional way so that their text would be laden with hyperlinks where teachers could find additional resource materials to expand the lesson plan. This then became the focus of the effort to transform *Meridians* (even if just for a moment) into a pedagogical tool. It was quickly supported by teacher scholars across the country who were searching for materials that could be used to transform their classrooms into liberatory Black feminist think tanks where ideas are fostered, creativity is nurtured, all voices are welcomed, and all experiences are validated.

After some discussion about the #SayHerName project and the work that is being done to center and include the voices and stories of Black women and girls, Black feminist theory and #BlackGirlActivism were selected as the conceptual starting points for all of the lesson plans. Due to the variety of content area foci, and big ideas grounding the lesson plans, each lesson plan takes students on different learning paths but collectively the lessons represent multidimensional instructional opportunities for teaching about Black feminist theory. The tie that binds them together is that they each focus on the ways in which we understand and teach about Black feminist theory and the ways in which we conceptualize freedom, struggle, protest, and liberation. As a whole, the lessons demonstrate that rigorous and scholarly knowledge produced about and by Black women matters. The "absence" of Black women from mainstream U.S. history texts is not only disturbing, but also problematic in the twenty-first century classroom.[2] The erasure and omission of diverse views and perspectives in academic texts is a distortion that communicates an unspoken message to students that only certain groups of people (again, those within that pesky circle of privilege) matter in history. Organizing the development of lesson plan ideas for teaching Meridians challenges this deceptive practice and supplements this critical knowledge project, and we hope, empowers teachers to identify diverse and fruitful entry points to learning.

We recognize that the work collected here about Black feminist theory, about why we must #SayHerName, about nineteenth-century Black female activism, and about writing as a liberatory practice—unlike the multiple streams of research that currently exists about each of these areas—is just a small foray into the interdisciplinary work that needs to be done. It is organic and will continue to shift and grow and be corrected and disputed as new information is added and new conclusions are made. This is the work that comes with being a researcher, a scholar, and a teacher, the ongoing feelings of concern that the work is never finished and the research is never really complete. This is also some of the challenges that come with working to decenter the circle of privilege—it is excavation work (dirty and hard, sometimes with very little validation and reward). Even with this trepidation in mind, we decided to invite teachers and students into this conversation, fully aware that by having them participate in and add to this growing body of knowledge, they are starting the work of becoming an active agent in their own knowledge process.[3]

As we worked to complete this project, we struggled with how best to situate it: was it an interdisciplinary text or a multidisciplinary one? Was it a historical offering or did it fit within the parameters of women's and gender studies? Who were we ultimately trying to reach: teachers or scholars or students? Or could we organize a project that reached them all? Simple questions to be sure but ones we wrestled with in an effort to create a liberatory project that answered all of the questions that we had been grappling with within our own classrooms. With that in mind, we submit that this Black feminist theory critical knowledge project is best viewed through a transdisciplinary lens (one that we once used to rethink the pocket diaries of Emilie Frances Davis) and that teachers can work both across disciplines and beyond their own discipline to help students understand this work, to make sense of the work, and to ultimately find ways to embrace and own the work. Furthermore, this concept of Black feminist theory viewed through a lens of *transdisciplinarity* can thus be interpreted in two ways: 1) as a thread that runs through each of the lesson plans and essays, providing an opportunity for different disciplinary perspectives to be integrated to depict a meta-narrative of knowledge and teaching; and, 2) as a tool for pedagogical practice that challenges both the teacher and the students to transcend the notion of the classroom as a static place constrained by tests and assessments where what they learn and how they learn is in the hands of nameless and faceless bureaucrats; and, to instead recognize that they have agency over their own learning. The classroom is simply an extension of them and it is shaped every day by what they bring into the space, what they choose to discuss, and how they choose to engage with the material.

Finally, as the project began to take shape, we took seriously this idea of #BlackGirlMagic—as created and conceptualized by CaShawn Thompson—and we decided to simply reimagine the classroom as a liberated nonsexist *nonmisogynistic* anti-racist anti-classist space without any boundaries or borders. At the same time, we acknowledged that though we *are* magical, we are *not* magicians, and that the real work to transform the classroom is done by teachers who somehow find the strength to show up every day and work through the roadblocks of budget cuts, Common Core, and school administrators. It is with this information in mind that we offer this work to them as a critical knowledge project—tools to help them along the way; a pedagogical offering—lesson plans that can immediately be taught in the classroom; and, as a Black feminist quilted narrative—fully aware that all of our lives and experiences are tied and knitted together and that none of us could ever really be free, until all of us are free.

Section 1: #BlackGirlActivism: Reading the Personal as Political & Public

The essays and accompanying lessons plans are organized into three sections. The first section, #BlackGirlMagic, begins with an essay by Stephanie Troutman and Ileana Jiménez, "Lessons in Transgressions: #Black-GirlsMatter and the Feminist Classroom" which examines the ways in which teaching Black feminism in both high school and undergraduate contexts can inspire Black feminist activism in young Black women and girls. Drawing upon the work of bell hooks and the notion that "Feminism is for Everybody," the authors developed a pedagogical toolbox designed to teach hooks's texts for contemporary students. In "Black Feminism and Critical Media Literacy: Moving from Margin to Center," co-authors Ashley N. Patterson, Arianna Howard, and Valerie Kinloch examine and explore the interactions they had and the stories that were shared by an intergenerational group of Black women who termed their regular meetings "The Black Women's Gathering Place" (BWGP)—which eventually became a place where they engaged in practices of everyday activism (Collins 1990). Based upon this experience and upon their need to add their voices to the ongoing struggle to transform collaboratively spaces, they designed a lesson plan that represents the expansion of BWGP into a liberatory learning space.

In their essay, "Challenging Neoliberal Dreams of Girls of Color in a Digital Age," Kimberly A. Scott and Patricia Garcia use critical feminist theory to offer a critique of neoliberal approaches to technology education for girls of color while also providing a broad overview of the conceptual catalysts that shape the approach of COMPUGIRLS, a National Science Foundation-funded technology program. In the accompanying lesson plan, students are challenged to think deeply about identity and self and then design and create avatars that reflect how their identity is (and should be) constructed in virtual worlds. In the final essay in this section,

"A Transnational Black Feminist (TBF) Framework: Rooting in Feminist Scholarship, Framing Contemporary Black Activism," Kia M.Q. Hall explores the role of feminist scholar-activists in contemporary Black freedom movements such as Black Lives Matter. The lesson plan offers a closer look at TBF and how it can combine contemporary notions of activism with historic ideas of freedom to teach movement art.

Section 2: #BlackGirlFeminism: Existing, Teaching, and Learning on the Edges and Beyond

Building upon the work outlined in the first section, the lesson plans in #BlackGirlFeminism expand the lens of Black feminist thought to discuss issues as varied as the prison industrial complex and reproductive justice. In "From Slavery to Jane Crow to Say Her Name: An Intersectional Examination of Black Women and Punishment," Nishaun Battle explores the ongoing movement that has been happening around the country since 2012 exploring the question of whether anyone cares for the lives and experiences of Black women. The essay includes a collection of ideas and speeches from nineteenth-century Black women intellectual activists (Anna Julia Cooper, Fannie Barrier Williams, and Victoria Earle Matthews) that are used to bridge the gap between contemporary Black feminism and historic Black feminism. The lesson plan provides students with an opportunity to examine and explore the experiences of Black women in the criminal justice system. In similar fashion, Lena Palacios's essay, "Challenging Convictions: Indigenous and Black Race-Radical Feminists Theorizing the Carceral State and Abolitionist Praxis in the United States and Canada," examines what it means to be a race-radical woman of color feminist and how this understanding has helped the author to act strategically and tactically. This analysis is then critically applied as students (or participants) explore how Indigenous and Black race-radical feminists are currently at the forefront of antiviolence movement building in Canada and the United States. The lesson plan is designed for both the classroom and for community activists, and encourages participants ("students") to think about what it means—for themselves, their family, and their community— to be *simultaneously* privileged by, oppressed by, *and* complicit with carceral systems of domination, control, and violence.

In the essay "On Forbidden Wombs and Transnational Reproductive Justice," Jallicia Jolly takes a similar approach (of asking the participants to center themselves in the story) and proposes transnational reproductive justice as a useful approach to the liberation of multiple marginalized women. The accompanying lesson plan explores reproductive politics by unpacking the history; and, by investigating the praxis and possibilities of the creation and application of a transnational reproductive justice system. In "The Slow Poisoning of Black Bodies: A Lesson in Environmental Racism and Hidden Violence," Rita Turner explores environmental racism through the lens of the lead poisoning of Freddie Gray providing background and examples of how environmental degradation and exposure to toxins disproportionately affect people of color and the poor. In the lesson plan, students research current cases of environmental injustice and use creative and analytical writing to reflect on what they have learned.[4]

In the essay "#WhenIFellInLoveWithMyself: Disrupting the Gaze and Loving Our Black Womanist Self As An Act of Political Warfare," Jameta N. Barlow discusses the work of the Saving Our Sisters' (SOS) digital archive project to create and maintain a space where Black women can find healing, self-love, self-care and mental health, and well-being. In the lesson plan, Barlow provides teachers with an opportunity to engage deeply with the essay and to then decide and develop the best strategies for helping their students enter into and fully engage with the topic. In the final essay in this section, "Signifying, Narrativizing, & Repetition: Radical Approaches to Theorizing African-American Language," Bonnie J. Williams-Farrier explores how teaching language/dialect differences in majority White school settings may have highly negative effects on African-American Language speakers. Building upon this idea, the lesson plan invites students to think about how the English Language, as a field, is constantly evolving and changing in our diverse, ever-widening international community.

Section 3: #BlackGirlAgency: Saying Their Names Over & Over Again

In the final section of this journal, #BlackGirlAgency, we take a historic look at the roots of Black feminist activism starting with the work of Emilie Frances Davis, a freeborn nineteenth-century Black woman, whose daily practice of writing and recording her life was a conscious act of identity assertion. In "A Black Feminist Interpretation: Reading Life, Pedagogy, and Emilie," Conra D. Gist examines the ways in which Black feminism—as a concept, an applied theory, and a safety net—functions as a critical social theory designed to assist students in understanding the multiple ways that Black and brown women are marginalized through institution-alized structures and practices.[5] By exploring the ways in which Black feminism is a thread that runs through the Black woman's experiences, Gist effectively applies a Black feminist lens over Davis's work and the work that was done by Karsonya Wise Whitehead to interpret Davis's life and add her to the canon of Black women. In the lesson plan, students use Gist's essay and Davis's pocket diary entries to examine the ideas of Black feminism and actively apply it as a lens to interpret essays, articles, video clips, and music lyrics. Additionally, this article includes a second lesson plan designed by Whitehead that uses the writings of Emilie, Charlotte Forten, Ida B. Wells, and Alice Dunbar-Nelson to teach students how to become *forensic herstorical investigators*. Finally, this section includes a first-person essay from Regina N. Bradley, "Afterword: How I Use #BlackLivesMatter as an Entry Point & a Disruption Tool." In this unique offering (our final thoughts on teaching #BlackLivesMatter), the author uses their childhood (growing up in Albany, Georgia where whiteness was used a pedagogical tool) as a starting point and a tool to help craft and teach a #BlackLives-Matter course at a predominantly White institution in an effort to facilitate and curate impactful teaching moments.

#BlackGirlActivism: Exploring the Ways We Come Through the Storm

The same concepts—Black feminist theory, #SayHerName, and #BlackGirlActivism—and multiple ways that they can be explored, applied, and examined. This is what transdisciplinarity looks like when it is being liberally applied and used as an active tool and a lens to expand our knowledge base. Taken separately, teachers and researchers have essays, lesson plans, discussion questions, primary sources, cover art, poetry, and media links that can be used throughout the year to actively insert the life and experiences of Black women into every classroom and every discussion. Taken together, it is a powerful tool of disruption for the standard classroom and compels teachers and students to engage more fully with the material and with each other. In a broad sense, we envision that the included essays and lesson plans will be applied in the spirit of culturally responsive pedagogy, which Geneva Gay describes as validating, multidimensional, empowering, transformative, and emancipatory. (Gay 2010) Our commitment to this critical knowledge project compels us to rethink our work in the classroom and challenge teachers (from K-12 to the academy) to closely read the work with an eye attentive to the places where transformative and emancipatory learning possibilities are ripe.

We also encourage teachers and scholars to join us in the critical knowledge process by writing their own lesson plans and sharing them within the public spaces of engagement, where scholars co-create and co-design syllabi (we think in particular of the dynamic work that was done in the #SayHerName Syllabus, the #Charleston Syllabus, and the #Trump-Syllabus 2.0 to name just a few). The essays and lesson plan offered here are only initial offerings and are in no way representative of all that the field has to offer. We are excited to see how the work will continue to grow and be (re)interpreted across the spectrum. Finally, although we understand that this project is finished, the work to explore the impact of Black feminist theory and to think about the foundational work upon which the field is built upon is still just beginning. Our hope is that our work to interstitially knit stories together adds to the field and provides it with yet another space to grow and expand. We know that we stand taller because we stand on their shoulders and we benefit from their sacrifices and from their work to write us a new reality and to forge us a new gate through which we could enter into and find ways to contribute to the field.

Postscript

In October (2016), the Association for the Study of African American Life and History (ASALH) announced that the 2017 Black History Month theme will be "The Crises in Black Education," focusing on and highlighting the ongoing challenges faced by African American children attending inner city public schools. As a mother and a scholar, I was not surprised that the ASALH lens had shifted from celebrating our Hallowed Grounds (the 2016 theme) and our achievements At the Crossroads of Freedom & Equality (the 2015 theme) to raising the alarm about the places and spaces where we are losing ground. Beginning (most recently) with the release of Michele Alexander's ground-breaking book, The New Jim Crow, this country has been steeped in conversations about the prison industrial complex. I believe (with the latest facts and figures about the disparate state of Black education, in mind) that the Nation is finally starting to recognize and turn its attention to investigating the long-term detrimental effects of the inner city educational industrial complex. It is within this vein of crises and concern that I offer up this critical knowledge project to teachers and scholars as a tool of disruption to jumpstart the incredible energetic process of teaching and learning. Although this project was begun before ASALH's announcement, I believe that their 2017 BHM theme is only *further proof that the work that we do to liberate the classroom is both revolutionary and necessary.* —KWW

. . . .

Karsonya (Kaye) Wise Whitehead is associate professor of communication and African and African American studies at Loyola University, Maryland and the award-winning radio host of Today With Dr. Kaye. In 2019, she received the Exceptional Merit in Media Award from the National Women's Political Caucus. The *Baltimore Sun* named her as one of Baltimore's twenty-five "Women to Watch in 2019," and *Essence* magazine included her on the 2019 "Woke 100 List." Whitehead is the author of four books and a columnist for the *Afro-American Newspaper*.

Notes

Originally published in *Meridians* vol. 15, no. 1, 2016.

1   This essay draws heavily upon work that Conra Gist and I did to complete the *Rethinking Emilie* critical knowledge project. In that project, we actively applied the lens of transdisciplinarity and challenged our contributors to think deeply about writing as an act of identity politics, liberation, and assertion. The ideas from that introduction formed the basis of my work to think through this project and my desire to write this Introduction in the same vein in which I helped to write that one. I appreciate her generosity in allowing me to use that essay to form the basis of this Introduction. It is republished here with permission from the editor. (Whitehead and Gist 2014, 1–8); as the associate editor, Rita Turner worked with me to conceptualize the project, select and edit the essays and lesson plans. I appreciate the work that she did to complete the copyediting of the first drafts.

2   For more on the ways in which this absence impacts the classroom, see Schocker 2013, 23–31; and Collins 2010, 1–8.

3   For more on how knowledge streams change over time, see and compare the early research on the life of Malcolm X to Manning Marable (2011) or the mainstream work on Abraham Lincoln to Lerone Bennett, Jr. (2000).

4   Portions of "The Slow Poisoning of Black Bodies: A Lesson in Environmental Racism and Hidden Consequences" were originally published on *The Conversation* in 2015. They are republished here with the permission of the author.

5   Both "A Black Feminist Interpretation: Reading Life, Pedagogy, and Emilie" and the lesson plan were originally published in Whitehead and Gist 2014, 115–45. It is republished here with permission from the editor.

Works Cited

Bennett, Lerone, Jr. 2000. *Forced into Glory: Abraham Lincoln's White Dream.* Chicago: Johnson Publishing Company, Inc.

Collins, Patricia Hill. 1990. *Black Feminist Thought.* New York: Routledge, 1990.

Gay, Geneva. 2010. *Culturally Responsive Teaching: Theory, Research, & Practice*. New York: Teachers College Press.

hooks, bell. 1994. *Teaching to Transgress: Education as the Practice of Freedom*. New York: Routledge.

Marable, Manning. 2011. *Malcolm X: A Life of Reinvention*. New York: Penguin Books.

Schocker, Jessica B. 2013. "Representing African American Women in U.S. History Textbooks." *The Social Studies*, 104, no. 1.

Walker, Alice. 1983. "Zora Neale Hurston: A Cautionary Tale and A Partisan View." In *In Search of Our Mothers' Gardens: Womanist Prose*, 83–92. New York: Harcourt Press.

Whitehead, Karsonya Wise and Conra D. Gist. 2014. *Rethinking Emilie Frances Davis: Lesson Plans for Teaching Her Civil War Pocket Diaries*. Baltimore: Apprentice House.

Silenced Voices of Everyday Sheroes

. . . .

Samanta Tello, *Silenced Voices of Everyday Sheroes* (2016). Burnt wood, gold/ silver leaf, stains, and acrylic on wood panel, 36×36 in.

For far too long, women have been silenced by patriarchal societies in most, if not all, cultures. At times, this silencing has been done violently, yet sometimes it has been done in a gentle, subtle, even playful way. Women still speak, but often our voices are ignored, belittled, interrupted or shouted down.

With the interracial communication between female figures in my work, I seek to represent the power of unity of action that gives all women a unified voice—how one woman's voice can spark a chorus of women voices and create a cultural shift, how sharing their stories can make them feel supported and able to find the strength to advocate for themselves.

I think it is essential for us women to maintain our courage and persistence, continually claiming our time and our turn, and support each other while doing so. I believe one of the ways the male establishment keeps its power is by promoting female competition. In this work, I represent women interconnected as if they were part of a puzzle, with each piece, each woman, each culture, a proud part of a whole that would be incomplete if even one were left behind.

MERIDIANS · feminism, race, transnationalism   Volume 19 Supplement 2020
DOI: 10.1215/15366936-8759949 © 2020 Smith College

Keep up to date on new scholarship

Issue alerts are a great way to stay current on all the cutting-edge scholarship from your favorite Duke University Press journals. This free service delivers tables of contents directly to your inbox, informing you of the latest groundbreaking work as soon as it is published.

To sign up for issue alerts:

1. Visit **dukeu.press/register** and register for an account. You do not need to provide a customer number.

2. After registering, visit **dukeu.press/alerts**.

3. Go to "Latest Issue Alerts" and click on "Add Alerts."

4. Select as many publications as you would like from the pop-up window and click "Add Alerts."

read.dukeupress.edu/journals